Constitutional Public Reason

Constitutional Public Reason

WOJCIECH SADURSKI
University of Sydney,
University of Warsaw

OXFORD
UNIVERSITY PRESS

OXFORD
UNIVERSITY PRESS

Great Clarendon Street, Oxford, OX2 6DP,
United Kingdom

Oxford University Press is a department of the University of Oxford.
It furthers the University's objective of excellence in research, scholarship,
and education by publishing worldwide. Oxford is a registered trade mark of
Oxford University Press in the UK and in certain other countries

First Edition published in 2023

Published in the United States of America by Oxford University Press
198 Madison Avenue, New York, NY 10016, United States of America

British Library Cataloguing in Publication Data

Data available

Library of Congress Control Number: 2022941054

ISBN 978–0–19–286967–8

DOI: 10.1093/oso/9780192869678.001.0001

Printed and bound in the UK by
Clays Ltd, Elcograf S.p.A.

Preface

The legitimacy of democratically enacted laws is a key issue in contemporary constitutional theory—perhaps not *the* key issue, but certainly one of central dilemmas that various constitutional systems need to grapple with. It would appear that the question is particularly acute when a supreme or a constitutional court has the power to set aside statutes for their unconstitutionality, but the issue of legitimacy goes further than that. Whether or not judicial bodies have such an authority, a meaningful question that can always be asked is if a given law—be it sub-constitutional legislation or even a constitution itself—contains rules that are legitimate: that is, whether we all, subject to this law, have good moral reasons to respect and comply with it, regardless of whether or not we agree with the particular rule on merits. We, the concerned citizens, may as well adopt the hypothetical position of a constitutional judge, and model our thinking about the legitimacy of laws that apply to us on the reasoning typical of constitutional judges. Such a thought experiment naturally provides us with only one among many perspectives for evaluating laws—but not an insignificant one. After all, in a democratic society marked by deep moral and political pluralism, in which consensus on the merits of some controversial laws is unlikely, we need to have some standards for ascertaining whether a law is worth our respect—perhaps even our compliance—even if we happen to disagree with it. This is the function of the concept of the legitimacy of law.

A prevailing response to the question of legitimacy has focused on the *effects* of a given law: whether the consequences of the law are such that it does not impose unfair burdens upon anyone, however the unfairness is defined. This may be called (roughly, and not necessarily tracking the technical uses of this concept in the law and in scholarly literature) 'output legitimacy'. But there is another way that (subject to the same proviso) is called 'input legitimacy': what sort of considerations—including motives, intentions, and purported purposes or aims—warrant the law? It is with a variant of that approach that this book will be concerned. It will look at public reason (PR—an acronym that will be used throughout the book, despite its unfortunate connotations with that other PR).

PR is a concept frequently used in political philosophy but one that is less often seen in scholarship on constitutional law. As Mattias Kumm has noted as recently as in 2020: 'Surprisingly, notwithstanding the considerable literature on the idea of public reason among political philosophers, legal and constitutional scholars have engaged with the idea relatively little.'[1] It is not a modern idea,[2] but as a point of reference in this book I will only use a contemporary reinterpretation of the concept and further, only the most influential version of it, developed in John Rawls's idea of political liberalism. In Rawls's theory, PR is intimately tied up with the liberal principle of legitimacy which proclaims that only those laws that are based upon arguments and reasons to which no members of a society could have a rational reason to object can boast political legitimacy, and as such can be applied coercively even to those who actually disagree with them. Another way of expressing the same thought is the 'endorsability by all' thesis, which can be found in Jürgen Habermas's suggestion about how individual interests may appear in public deliberations: 'In practical discourses, only those interests "count" for the outcome that are presented as inter-subjectively recognized values and hence are *candidates* for inclusion in the semantic content of valid norms.' Habermas concludes: 'Only *generalizable* value-orientations, which all participants (and all those affected) can accept with good reasons as appropriate for regulating the subject matter at hand … pass this threshold.'[3] Perhaps the best recent articulation of PR (very much in line with Rawls's idea) was given by Charles Larmore who stated the fundamental directive of political liberalism by saying that 'basic political principles should be suitably acceptable to those whom they are to bind.'[4] The implication of this is clear: some arguments, if actually present in the minds of legislators or policymakers, are not qualified to figure in the public defence of a law. The law must be defensible in terms that belong to a forum of principle rather than an arena of political bargains, or power plays of naked interest, or competition between sectarian ideologies.

For all the problems, complications, and shortcomings of this idea (most of which will be confronted openly in Chapter 3), I will take it seriously and see how much mileage we can get from it when reflecting upon the legitimacy of law in a democracy. Part I will lay down the philosophical groundwork for the idea: I shall argue (in Chapter 1) that PR is a plausible interpretation of a broader concept of the common good, and that it is based on a justificatory constellation of certain ideas of respect for persons, equality, and freedom; I shall recalibrate

[1] Mattias Kumm '"We Hold These Truths to be Self-Evident": Constitutionalism, Public Reason, and Legitimate Authority', in Silje Langvatn, Mattias Kumm, and Wojciech Sadurski (eds.), *Public Reason and Courts* (Cambridge University Press 2020) 143, 143, footnote omitted.

[2] See Miguel Vatter, 'The Idea of Public Reason and the Reason of State: Schmitt and Rawls on the Political', (2008) 36 *Political Theory* 239.

[3] Jürgen Habermas, *The Inclusion of the Other: Studies in Political Theory* (MIT Press 1998) 81, both emphases in the original.

[4] Charles Larmore, *The Autonomy of Morality* (Cambridge University Press 2008) 146. For other well-known expressions of a similar idea, see Onora O'Neill, *Toward Justice and Virtue* (Cambridge University Press 1996) 54 ('Those whose actions and plans of action constantly assume the intelligent cooperation and interaction of many others, who differ in diverse ways, will also expect some at least of their reasoning to be *followable by these others*'), emphasis added; T.M. Scanlon, *What We Owe to Each Other* (Harvard University Press 1998) 189 (articulating a 'non-rejectability' requirement derived from contractualism).

the Rawlsian theory of PR to render it plausible and feasible for constitutional uses (Chapter 2); and I will defend it against the most representative challenges (Chapter 3). In Part II, I will provide an overview of the uses of the ideal of PR in some representative constitutional *national* systems,[5] and there is no escape from my sincere admission that by 'representative', I rather mean those with which I happen to be familiar: there is absolutely no pretence to the comprehensiveness of the overview which should be rather called a 'bird's eye view', the bird in question flying freely and arbitrarily over this or that country. I will introduce and discuss the idea of motive-based constitutional scrutiny (Chapter 4); I shall reflect upon some of the main problems that such a scrutiny raises, in particular regarding the evidentiary difficulties of reconstructing (or second-guessing) legislative motives, and also of 'harmonizing' motives and effects of legislation (Chapter 5); and then I will look at the uses of PR in the spheres of freedom of speech (Chapter 6), freedom of religion (Chapter 7), and anti-discrimination law (Chapter 8). In Part III of the book, I will posit the idea of a 'supranational public reason' and reflect upon the uses of this ideal in those (quasi-) constitutional systems that transcend national boundaries: I will suggest that public reason may be particularly suitable to the legitimacy of supranational regulations, which suffer from weak legitimacy based on democracy and consent (Chapter 9); and I will discuss, in some detail, one particular putative 'exemplar' of supranational PR, namely the European Court of Human Rights (Chapter 10).

[5] I should acknowledge a recent use of the concept 'Constitutional Public Reason' (which figures in the title of this book) in Ronald C. Den Otter, 'The Importance of Constitutional Public Reason', in Silje Langvatn, Mattias Kumm, and Wojciech Sadurski (eds.), *Public Reason and Courts* (Cambridge University Press 2020) 66, and earlier, in his *Judicial Review in an Age of Moral Pluralism* (Cambridge University Press 2009), Ch. 5.

Acknowledgements

Often, acknowledgements in academic books begin with a partly apologetic, partly self-deprecating (not necessarily sincere) confession that the book was too long in the making. This one is no exception, and my (sincere) excuse is that this work was interrupted by the felt need to write two other books, very quick in the making. But the duration of my work also explains why I incurred intellectual debts to such a large number of colleagues and research assistants (this latter category merging and overlapping with the former, so I will not draw a distinction here) in connection with this project:

Margot Brassil, Violeta Canaves, Adam Czarnota, Grainne de Burca, Ros Dixon, Kirsty Gan, Leszek Garlicki, Tom Ginsburg, Sam Goldsmith, Alon Harel, Sam Issacharoff, Nikila Kaushik, Pooja Khatri, Martin Krygier, Mattias Kumm, Silje Aambø Langvatn, Christopher McCrudden, Liam Murphy, Maria Paz Avila, Michael J. Perry, Niels Petersen, Philip Pettit, Rick Pildes, Robert Post, David Pozen, Dominik Rennert, Michel Rosenfeld, Michael Sevel, Sivan Shlomo-Agon, Alec Stone Sweet, Chantal Tanner, Alexander Tsesis, Jeremy Waldron, and Joseph Weiler. I was lucky, both as an academic and as a frequent traveller, to be able to share my ideas with colleagues at very many conferences and seminars, at Haifa Law School, Harvard Law School, Supreme Administrative Court (NSA) in Warsaw (a conference by 'Państwo i Prawo' journal), Loyola Law School in Chicago, University of Chicago Law School, University of Paris-Nanterre, University of Trento Faculty of Law, Tsinghua University in Beijing, National University of Singapore, Australian Society of Legal Philosophy (Sydney), University of Toronto Faculty of Law, National University of Singapore Faculty of Law, Thamassat University in Bangkok, Wissenschaftskolleg in Berlin, WZB Center for Global Constitutionalism in Berlin, Melbourne Law School, Academia Sinica in Taipei, Centro de Estudios Politicos y Constitucionales in Madrid, University of Amsterdam Faculty of Law, Harvard Law School, Kiyv-Mohyla Academy in Kiev, University of Western Ontario, Faculty of Law in London, Ontario.

My even greater gratitude is to those extraordinary academic institutions with which I have been associated. I am very grateful to NYU Law School, to Yale Law School, Cardozo Law School, Fordham Law School, and Rutgers University—five great universities with which I was associated as a visiting professor or research fellow over the years in which I worked on the book. I am grateful to the Centre for Europe at the University of Warsaw and, most of all, my home institution Sydney Law School, and of course, to my real home and my family in it.

Contents

Table of Cases

AUSTRALIA

CANADA

ECOWAS (THE ECONOMIC COMMUNITY OF WEST AFRICAN STATES) COURT

EUROPEAN COURT OF HUMAN RIGHTS

EUROPEAN COURT OF JUSTICE

GERMANY

INDIA

INTER-AMERICAN COURT OF HUMAN RIGHTS

ISRAEL

NEW ZEALAND

SOUTH AFRICA

UNITED STATES

List of Abbreviations

AB	Appellate Body of WTO
ACHR	American Convention on Human Rights
CoE	Council of Europe
CoM	Committee of Ministers
DSS	Dispute settlement system
ECHR	European Convention on Human Rights
ECOWAS	The Economic Community of West African States
ECtHR	European Court of Human Rights
EP	European Parliament
EU	European Union
GATT	General Agreement on Tariffs and Trade
HPAT	Homosexual Policy Assessment Team
IACtHR	Inter-American Court of Human Rights
ICANN	The Internet Corporation for Assigned Names and Numbers
ICJ	International Court of Justice
IMF	International Monetary Fund
ISO	International Standardization Organization
NGO	Non-governmental organization
OAS	Organization of American States
OECD	The Organisation for Economic Co-operation and Development
PISA	Programme for International Student Assessment
PR	Public reason
RCMP	Royal Canadian Mounted Police
RS	Reason of state
SRRP	Staff Relations Representation Program
TEU	Treaty on European Union
UDHR	Universal Declaration of Human Rights
UN	United Nations
WTO	World Trade Organization

PART I

PUBLIC REASON AND ITS DISCONTENTS

1
Justifying Public Reason

Public reason is an ideal which concretizes, in some special contexts (especially, in lawmaking) a broader value of a common good. But what is common good, and how exactly can we go about testing whether a legal system, and in particular constitutional law, embodies an acceptable idea of common good? After all, 'common good' is a notoriously complex and contested concept. In the first section of this chapter I will argue that a superficially attractive strategy of equating 'common good' with the common denominator of actually espoused individual preferences is chimerical and should be substituted by a strategy of identifying it with an outcome of pursuit of publicly admissible reasons, where 'public' is contrasted to self-interested individual preferences but rather derived from justification based on 'public reason'. But how to defend the idea of public reason itself? I will argue, in section 2, that it expresses the fundamental value of respect for persons. But respect per se is too vague and too thin a value to sustain a political ideal as weighty as that of public reason. Respect has to be seen as part of a constellation of values, of which freedom (section 3 of the chapter) and equality (section 4) are of particular importance. Each of these values enhances our political life in ways which can be explained in terms of another value; they are in a mutually supportive, interlocking, integrated scheme of political values, where each is understood and appreciated in the light of the other. The chapter defends an idea of 'respect for persons', in an active and relatively thin, recognition-based sense; of 'freedom', understood through a presumptive evil of coercion; and of 'political equality', in an outcome-oriented agency sense, as equality of political opportunity.

1. From Common Good to Public Reason

In a 2020 article, Samuel Freeman says: 'A convention of democracy is that government should promote the common good. Citizens' common good is based in their shared civil interests ... Citizens' civil interests ground what John Rawls calls "the political values of justice and public reason." '[1] This itinerary from the 'common good' to 'public reason' will be retraced, and explained, in this part of the chapter.

[1] Samuel Freeman, 'Democracy, Religion & Public Reason', (2020) 149(3) *Daedalus* 37, 37.

Constitutional Public Reason. Wojciech Sadurski, Oxford University Press. © Wojciech Sadurski 2023.
DOI: 10.1093/oso/9780192869678.003.0001

It is much easier to say what the common good *is not* rather than what it *is*. It is *not* an aggregate set of common actual first-order interests of all individuals in a given polity. To draw such an equivalence would be a false path, and I will first argue why it is false. After all, this would be a natural temptation in defining the common good: to identify those interests on which all individuals converge, or to find a common denominator for all private preferences. But even if such a set were to be ascertainable, it would necessarily be extremely narrow: much narrower than the intuitively persuasive notion of the 'common good' would demand.

In his monumental work on public reason, Gerald Gaus advanced a requirement that as members of the public we must not propose any rules which undermine someone else's good. Having conceded that we disagree about what is to the good of others, he nevertheless claimed that we may identify some unquestionable components of their (and our) good: 'we have . . . come to agree on some basic ingredients of a person's good, such as protection of her bodily integrity, basic liberties to make her decisions about most of the important aspects of her life, control over basic resources needed to live a life, and so on.'[2] But 'and so on' stands for an extremely short list of instances of other undisputable goods, and will not be helpful in a majority of controversies about 'common good' in real societies. The idea that no ideal put forward—no ideal of common good—may involve harm to some people's good (understood as their perceived interests) is clearly implausible because very rarely shall we be able to identify such rules and policies which satisfy the Pareto standard. Some policies may be perfectly justified—perfectly resonating with an intuitive notion of the 'common good' held by some of us—and yet will systematically undermine *some* person's interests, including what they see as legitimate rights (think affirmative action). And these are not merely cases of, as Gaus puts it, 'episodic sacrifices called for by the rules',[3] but rather systemic burdens imposed on some groups—and yet these are burdens which do not strike many of us as unfair and as detrimental to the 'common good'.

Consider this, seemingly attractive, instruction to legislators: 'The common good is served not by promoting the interests of some persons, in oblivion or at the expense of the interests of others, but by finding ways of serving the interests of all persons, or all concerned, fairly and equitably.'[4] But are we able to serve the actual interests of *all* persons? Surely it may turn out to be extremely difficult: some interests will have to give way, and we will need to strike trade-offs, or plainly disregard interests which do not register highly, or do not register at all, at some normative scales. For instance, '[i]n arguing that the common good

[2] Gerald Gaus, *The Order of Public Reason* (Cambridge University Press 2011) 303.

[3] Ibid. 302.

[4] B.J. Diggs, 'The Common Good as Reason for Political Action', (1973) 83 *Ethics* 283, 291.

requires the prohibition of child labor, the legislator claims that when the points of view of all are considered, and weighed in the balance, it is reasonable to outlaw employer benefits that demand the sacrifice of the children's vital interests—that to do so is to impose a reasonable restriction on employer interests, considering the fact that failure to do so leads to so large a sacrifice of the children's interests'.[5] But this only shows that a 'common good' resulting from such balancing of conflicting interests cannot be said to reflect a *convergence* of various interests. The conclusion (in this particular case, about the prohibition of child labour) is of course morally persuasive, but it is misleading to say that it marks a common denominator of different net interests and individual preferences: the appeals to common good are often made in the context of an appeal for individual persons to do something contrary to their net interests.[6]

Our expectations from the social world are vastly diverse as they are determined by myriad facts about which we differ: our psychological predispositions, or religious (or other philosophical) beliefs, our stations in life, the environments and situations into which we were born or into which we have been led by a combination of our choices, and the facts outside our control, etc. In the words of Philip Pettit,

> it is extremely unlikely that among the different sets of practices and policies available to a state, there is one that will be in the avowable interest of each ... The fact that people differ in their capacities and circumstances, their tastes and commitments, means that there is little or no chance that among feasible alternatives one and the same set of practices and policies will be in the avowable net interest of each.[7]

The words '*avowable* interests of each' are central here, and (even accepting arguendo that the common good *can* be equated with the avowable interests of all) we must be careful to see that 'avowable' means 'avowed' only if *thinly* controlled by generally accepted criteria of rationality and knowledge. The greater the control by generally accepted criteria of rationality, the less 'the avowable' will resemble 'the actually avowed', and the more paternalistic our criteria of the common good will become. Such a 'common good' will be unrecognizable to individuals as corresponding to their *actual* first-order interests; rather, it will be reflective of the views of an observer (under whatever the observer's criteria are) about what people *should* want were they truly rational. This is a strong and objectionable sort of paternalism which is broader than the one (admittedly, less offensive) aimed at offsetting the obvious defects in preference-formation. Rather,

5 Ibid. 291.
6 Brian Barry, *Political Argument* (Routledge & Kegan Paul 1965) 203, emphasis removed.
7 Philip Pettit, 'The Common Good' in Keith Dowding, Robert E. Goodin, and Carole Pateman (eds.), *Justice and Democracy: Essays for Brian Barry* (Cambridge University Press 2004) 150, 153–54.

this is the version of paternalism about which Isaiah Berlin wrote a long time ago, that 'it is an insult to my conception of myself as human being, determined to make my own life in accordance with my own (not necessarily rational or benevolent) purposes, and, above all, entitled to be recognized as such by others'.[8] So, for my further discussion I will assume that strong paternalism (going beyond correcting defects in knowledge, preference-formation, etc.) is a thoroughly *un*attractive conception for determining the limits of the state power over an individual citizen, and I will conclude that an idea of the common good as a set of common first-order individual interests is either disingenuous (if these interests are understood as 'avowable', in a paternalistic way) or impossible to ascertain (if those interests are understood as the interests actually espoused, corrected only by very thin standards of rationality).

There is a temptation, at this point, to embrace the idea of the common good as representing the set of individual first-order actual preferences *minus* those which would correspond to the attempts at free riding in the achievement of 'public goods' in the technical sense of the word, that is, in the sense which implies the requirements of coordinated production and indivisibility of consumption. My earlier mention of 'paternalism' in this context suggests that there may be a milder form of paternalism, which in fact is admittedly not paternalism in an objectionable sense of the word (and in addition, which does not collapse into correction of defects in preference-formation). It consists of the imposition of certain forms of behaviour for a person's own good (so in this superficial sense it *may* be initially seen as paternalistic) but in accordance with the person's *actual* preferences (hence not being paternalistic in an objectionable sense, if paternalism in a deeper moral sense, as depicted in the quote from Isaiah Berlin, consists in the displacement of a person's actual preferences). This happens in the familiar situation of the Prisoner's Dilemma, when certain restrictions (or duties) are in the interest of all members of a given class, but the immediate interests of a particular individual are even further maximized by violating the rule, provided that others adhere to it. In such cases, the coercive imposition of a proper mode of conduct upon an individual does not carry the moral defects of paternalism because it does not displace the actually espoused preferences in the name of preferences that, according to a legislator, the individual should espouse, but to the contrary, it gives effect to the actually expressed individual preferences.[9]

The identification of such a common good may be initially considered attractive: it would ascertain the actual individual preferences and, while arguing for an application of state coercion in the name of these interests, it would avoid the charge of objectionable paternalism because, as a solution to the Prisoner's

[8] Isaiah Berlin, *Four Essays on Liberty* (Oxford University Press 1969) 157.

[9] See Gerald Dworkin, 'Paternalism' in Ralf Sartorius, *Paternalism* (University of Minnesota Press 1983) 19, 23.

Dilemma, it would not be the case of displacing the actual preferences of individuals. Rather, the problem addressed by such a conception would be that the persons' *motivations* for action do not match their avowed *preferences*, and the distance between motivations and preferences needs to be bridged by the imposition of a rule with which everyone has to conform (and, crucially, a rule about which everyone knows that all others also must conform with).

But this attempt to identify the 'common good' with 'public goods' (in the technical sense of the word) is a non-starter because it encounters exactly the same problem as identification of the 'common good' with first-order private avowed interests, namely, the pluralism of views about what constitutes the public good in the first place, combined with an exceedingly narrow set of consensually agreed-upon public goods and their ranking. The assumption behind a non-paternalistic imposition of a rule as a solution to the Prisoner's Dilemma must be that all the 'coercees' have the same ranking of preferences, and that the achievement of a given public good figures on the top of their individual rankings. But in a real society, such an assumption is deeply problematic and unrealistic. For example, different people may calculate the relative costs and benefits of reduction of pollution differently (a clean environment being a typical case of a public good, with the associated conditions of concerted action to produce and non-exclusivity in consumption), and those who prefer to suffer an extra marginal amount of pollution rather than paying the extra marginal cost of pollution reduction have no reason to be persuaded by an argument that a particular restriction on pollution simply solves a collective action problem haunting the implementation of *their* actual preferences. As Russell Hardin has observed with regard to the collective-action argument: 'few instances of collective provision are likely to be uniquely preferred, so that we may wonder about the justice of coercing those whose preferences are overridden ... *Government may indeed overcome a collective-action problem, but it may overcome the wrong one for many of us.* Is it now justified in its coercion of those of us who lost?'[10]

This last question is not rhetorical but genuine, and occasionally there may be good reasons to give an affirmative answer: the government may be justified in applying such coercion provided that (for the sake of argument) it is a decision reached democratically, it had been preceded by a serious deliberation in which all stakeholders could equally participate, no fundamental or constitutional rights (and in particular the rights of minorities) are violated by the coercive action, etc. What the government (or its supporters) *cannot* say, though, is that the coercion follows the logic of a uniform solution to a collective-action problem and thus meets the actual avowed preferences of *all* those to whom the coercion is addressed. It admittedly meets the actual avowed preferences of *some* but not

[10] Russell Hardin, 'Public Choice Versus Democracy' in John W. Chapman and Alan Wertheimer (eds.), *Majorities and Minorities: Nomos XXXII* (New York University Press 1990) 184, 194, emphasis added.

others, and those others have no reason to identify the solution as a meeting their conception of 'common good' under the first-order preferences approach.

But this line of argument is not entirely a dead end for our purposes. Hardin's question, quoted above, implies that the quest for a common good may be directed towards matters which are more institutional and procedural than substantive. It may well be that the common good, in the context of inevitable plurality and incommensurability of diverse private interests, consists of having a fair, efficient, and reasonable *method* of aggregating these interests into a coherent whole, of adjudicating between conflicting ideals, and of finding compromises which are seen as honest and fair. That ideal of the common good is primarily an institutional one: it is the common good of having fair, impartial, honest institutions and procedures in the context of a stable pluralism of interests and disagreement as to ideals.

In itself, this is no small thing, and it may look like an attractive solution to our quest for the common good. But, come to think of it, it is deeply counter-intuitive. Suppose that you are making a plea for a particular action as warranted by the common good, as you understand it. Normally, the ideas that come to mind are actions that override the reasons derived from your private interests: you believe that there is a broader, non-private good at stake. This non-private good is not easily articulated in purely institutional or procedural terms: it is a *substantive* good, and also substantial enough to prevail over a set of legitimate private interests. A procedural-institutional ideal is not sufficiently weighty to withstand the competition from substantive private interests. It does not meet them on common ground, so to speak, so it is inadequate to match the imagery of the common good prevailing over private interests.

We have to search elsewhere. We must think a little harder about what is 'common' in the common good, which is substantively different from any amalgamation of private interests, and yet which is irreducible to purely procedural or institutional mechanisms. As a general compass, we should reclaim the most fundamental idea behind the 'publicness', namely that it is a common good defined *in contrast to private interests*. This way of contrasting 'common' and 'public'[11] might, however, falsely imply that the latter assumes an implausible idea of a public entity having its own existence separate from individuals, but this is not so: one may be a moral individualist, believing (plausibly) that any public interest derives its value exclusively from the effect it has on the lives and the good of individuals, and still draw a clear line between the realm of 'public' from the realm of commonality of private interests and preferences. Consider Robert Goodin's conception of the 'highest common concern', under which the public interest is an interest that people necessarily share (or something that they *want* to have in common, rather than what they just happen to have in common),

[11] For a classical distinction along these lines, see Barry, *Political Argument*, (n. 6) 190–202.

by virtue of their roles as members of the public, and which can be best promoted by concerted public action.[12] Such an understanding of the 'public interest', perfectly defensible under a moral individualistic conception of the society, is different from the 'common good', understood as the lowest common denominator of the actual preferences of individuals. Nevertheless, Goodin unnecessarily ties his conception to the idea of second-order preferences as a cornerstone of public interest. When he says: 'the fact that highest common concerns reflect an evaluative stance that people have taken toward their own preferences and values makes those higher-order value judgments, which are privileged for that very reason',[13] he reveals a non sequitur in his reasoning: even if people indeed have articulated their second-order preferences for each of their first-order preferences, it is not clear why second-order preferences (usually more vague and indeterminate) should override their first-order preferences (usually more precise and specific). No doubt these 'public interests' may be seen as nobler but are they still *theirs*, in a meaningful sense of the word? Further, there is nothing in the status of second-order preferences that makes them normatively superior to first-order preferences: some second-order preferences may be objectionable (think of 'a desire not to prefer to marry someone of another race, reflected in a miscegenation law'),[14] so it is a sleight of hand to automatically accord a higher normative status to higher order preferences merely because of their status as such.

When making a distinction between the asserted commonality of individual preferences and the common good, what we are drawn into is an essentially Rousseauian tradition, with 'Social Contract' being its locus classicus. Rousseau emphasized: 'There is often considerable difference between the will of all and the general will. The latter is concerned only with the common interest, the former with interests which are partial, being itself but the sum of individual wills.'[15] Under this interpretation, the will of all is an aggregation of individual preferences and suffers from the weakness of the first-order aggregate of preferences which we have noted earlier. In contrast, the 'common interest' is different—and must be addressed as something other than the aggregation of as many private preferences as possible; its *object* must have a different nature.

When adopting a 'common good' understood along these lines, we do not need to adopt other implications of Rousseau's theory of democracy, and in particular the dangerous idea that any given majority is the best exponent of the

[12] Robert E. Goodin, 'Institutionalizing the Public Interest: The Defense of Deadlock and Beyond', (1996) 90 *American Political Science Review* 331, 339.

[13] Ibid. 339.

[14] Cass R. Sunstein, 'Disrupting Voluntary Transactions' in J.W. Chapman and J.R. Pennock (eds.), *Markets and Justice: Nomos XXXI* (New York University Press 1989) 279, 286.

[15] Jean-Jacques Rousseau, 'The Social Contract' (trans. Gerard Hopkins) in *Social Contract: Essays by Locke, Hume and Rousseau*, with an Introduction by Sir Ernest Barker (Oxford University Press 1948) 274.

common good, with the fact of being outvoted indicating that members of the minority are simply mistaken as to the true substance of the public good on a given issue.[16] This idea, based in Rousseau upon the doctrine that each particular vote on day-to-day political issues is a sort of replication of the consensual general will which prefigures the formation of specific general wills, and a consequent idea that the majority is right in discerning the true general will (or, in our language, common good),[17] may be, I believe, safely separated from the idea of the possibility of incongruence between private and public interest, which can well be accommodated within a liberal-democratic theory. To anticipate an argument of his book a little, it is significant that John Rawls, when extolling the virtue of public reason in a democracy, and contrasting it with the conceptions of preference-based or comprehensive-conceptions-based democratic rule, drew a direct analogy between his idea of public reason (and the doctrine of civility on which it is based) and Rousseau's idea about voting; Rousseau, Rawls recalls approvingly, 'saw voting as ideally expressing our opinion as to which of the alternatives best advances the common good'.[18] Rousseau is enlisted by Rawls as an ally against 'common views of voting as a private or even personal matter',[19] and in my view some illiberal traits of his theory need not be an obstacle for using resources inherent in Rousseau's political ideas for the purposes of political liberalism. We may (as any reasonable person should) accept the general fact of incongruence between a sum aggregate of self-interests and the common good, without committing ourselves to any particular political mechanisms of ascertaining the common good, and of giving effect to its primacy over private interests in political decision-making. And if we accept the possibility, indeed the ubiquity of such incongruence, we may and should accept that, as citizens, we should be expressing our views about the best way of promoting (what we take to be) the common good rather than simply articulating our self-interest.[20]

[16] 'When a law is proposed in the assembly of the People, what they are asked is not whether they approve or reject the proposal in question, but whether it is or is not in conformity with the general will, which is *their* will. It is on this point that the citizen expresses his opinion when he records his vote, and from the counting of the votes proceeds the declaration of the general will. When, therefore, a view which is at odds with my own wins the day, it proves only that I was deceived, and that what I took to be the general will was no such thing. Had my own opinion won, I should have done something quite other than I wished to do, and in that case I should not have been free': 'The Social Contract' (n. 15) 390.

[17] According to Brian Barry, this idea of the author of the 'The Social Contract' has been 'badly misunderstood' by many of Rousseau's interpreters who fail to recognize that the congruence of political (legislative) majority with the correctness of identification of general will is, for Rousseau, a 'contingent' fact, dependent upon certain conditions, and means only that the majority is 'more likely than not to arrive at the correct answer', Barry, *Political Argument* (n. 6) 292–93. It seems to me that the text of Rousseau's work supports a stronger interpretation, but exegesis of Rousseau's writings is beyond the ambit of this chapter.

[18] John Rawls, *Political Liberalism* (Columbia University Press 1993) 219–20, footnote omitted.

[19] Ibid. 219.

[20] See Jeremy Waldron, 'Rights and Majorities: Rousseau Revisited' in John W. Chapman and Alan Wertheimer (eds.), *Majorities and Minorities: Nomos XXXII* (New York University Press 1990) 44.

While there may be legitimate fundamental disagreement among citizens about the decisions and the implementation of the common good and of the proper balance between different interests (in ways that Rousseau would not allow), this is a fundamentally *different* disagreement from the clash of individual interests.

Further, to accept the intelligibility of a distinction between the common good and private self-interest in our individual motivations does not call for any unrealistically demanding or altruistic approaches on the part of the citizen-voters. Rather, it corresponds to what Bruce Ackerman calls 'private citizenship'—a position he distinguishes from a 'perfect privatist' for whom the question 'What is good for the country?' boils down to 'What is good for me?'.[21] Readers of *We the People: Foundations* will remember that, apart from a 'private citizen' and a 'perfect privatist', there is yet a third character in Ackerman's cast, namely a 'public citizen', modelled on Ralph Nader, who 'combines an emphatic asceticism in personal life with a more-than-full-time commitment to the public good as he understands it'.[22] In contrast, a 'private citizen' (with an emphasis on *citizen*) is painfully aware that 'an ongoing commitment to informed citizenship may unduly deflect our energies from the struggles of everyday life'.[23] Still, and regardless of what actual course of action a person will undertake, she must at least acknowledge that '[a] sober consideration of the national interest may indicate that personal and local interests must be sacrificed to the general good'.[24]

The distinction is, of course, easy to assert in abstract but in practice it may well be blurred: we all know that we have remarkable capacities of representing (not just to others but also to ourselves) our self-interest as the public interest. The distinction is relatively easy to make when the interests in question are of a material or financial character: it is easy to draw a distinction in one's mind between, say, the tax system which is the best for the public interest (as I understand it, in the light of my conception of social justice, of economic theory etc.) and the tax system which would be the best for me, considering my individual financial situation. (Even here, however, the temptation is to identify one with the other so a degree of candour and a deliberate attempt at impartiality is required.) But when it comes to non-material interests and ideals, the distinction is much less easy to draw: if I believe that the death penalty is wrong (or right), or that abortion is morally wrong (or that it should be left for the woman to decide), it is difficult to see how the pursuit of this ideal can be represented as self-interest (how many people oppose the death penalty because they anticipate that they will commit the gravest crimes and wish to avoid the electric chair or gallows?).

[21] Bruce Ackerman, *We the People: Foundations* (Harvard University Press 1991) 232–33.
[22] Ibid. 232.
[23] Ibid. 234.
[24] Ibid. 234.

Writing about 'the pursuit of spiritual and associational ideals', Ackerman urged: 'as a private citizen, I must recognize that these great goods may be in conflict with the national interest: perhaps it is in the public interest that … my Church be denied tax revenues, or my income taxes to provide social security even for those Americans who look upon the pope as an anti-Christ.'[25] I am not sure that such a distinction between a 'sectarian' (for the lack of a better word)[26] non-material ideal and 'national interest' can be easily done, or even can be done at all, for all non-material ideals (death penalty and abortion spring to my mind as examples where I find it difficult to draw the line), but surely it can be done at least with respect to *some* non-material ideals, in particular when religious matters are at stake. It sounds plausible that, for the sake of argument, as an adherent to a particular church I can draw the line between my religious interest (which may consist in having this particular church established as a state church, my religion officially privileged in public life or in taxation, etc.) and on the other hand, the common good which calls for equal recognition of all other churches and religions which, in consequence, would call for a separation of state and *any* religion and non-recognition of *any* religious faith as a state orthodoxy. This calls for an aspiration of impartiality—perhaps modelled on Rawls's veil of ignorance as a theoretical experiment aimed at reducing the impact of our self-interest on our ideals of justice or Ackerman's 'neutral dialogue' or traditional 'impartial observer' perspective. In any event, we must presuppose that to draw such a distinction *is* possible: otherwise, the 'common good' as a category separate from individual self-interest is (from the perspective of an individual) untenable. I will accept, arguendo, that it *is* tenable, at least with respect to a large number of material and non-material interests and ideals.[27]

As my guide in the search for a plausible conception of such goods which citizens may acknowledge as being distinct from their own private or sectarian interests, I will take Philip Pettit. In his article about 'the common good', Pettit dismisses various ways of 'defining people's interests as citizens' (such as counting public interest as whatever members of the community collectively say is in the public interest, or what they would say under ideal circumstances of rational decision-making etc.)[28] The key, he says, 'lies in a fact about how the members may be expected to deliberate as they try to identify practices to implement and policies to pursue'.[29] What renders something a 'common interest' is the fact that 'according to publicly admissible criteria of argument, it is best

[25] Ibid. 298.

[26] For a similar use of 'sectarianism' (to denote a particularist conception of the common good), see Joshua Cohen, 'Deliberation and Democratic Legitimacy' in David Estlund (ed.), *Democracy* (Blackwell 2002) 87, 98; see also Michael J. Perry, *Human Rights in the Constitutional Law of the United States* (Cambridge University Press 2013) 125–26.

[27] For an argument that it is an eminently realistic picture of the voters' motivations, see Waldron, 'Rights and Majorities' (n. 20) 59 and 73–74 n. 28.

[28] Pettit, 'The Common Good' (n. 7) 159–61.

[29] Ibid. 162.

supported among feasible alternatives by publicly admissible considerations', or in other words, that 'it is best supported by the reasons that are publicly admissible within the group'.[30]

As one can see, this notion of the 'common good' is very demanding; it calls, first, for an identification of 'publicly admissible criteria of argument' and second, for an assessment that a given practice is *best* supported, out of the stock of all practices based on publicly admissible criteria of argument (which may be numerous), by the arguments which pass muster for public admissibility. Taken together, this is a very tall order. The first criterion, which we may call here the criterion of 'reasonableness', demands that a policy or practice (which is a candidate for the common good) be based on the sort of reasons which are acceptable under the criteria of public arguments in the given polity. The second, which may be called that of optimality, demands that the policy or practice meets those requirements to a higher degree than any other policy which would also be supported by those arguments.

For my part, I consider adding the criterion of optimality to the criterion of reasonableness to be *too* demanding. To use a parallel from constitutional adjudication (and in particular from the United States doctrine developed over the decades by the Supreme Court to scrutinize alleged legislative infringements on constitutional rights), it is like the move from a 'rational-basis' scrutiny to a 'strict' scrutiny of legislative measures. The former is satisfied when there is a rational relationship between a legislative measure and a legislative purpose that a lawmaker is constitutionally authorized to pursue; the latter is satisfied only when there is no other way of achieving a compelling (rather than *any*) constitutionally valid purpose. The latter is of course very difficult to demonstrate ("'strict" in theory and fatal in fact'),[31] with the onus of argument placed on the defenders of a given practice or law, and it expresses an institutional distrust in a given legislative measure as meeting constitutional requirements.

For the purposes of ascertaining the 'common good' no such distrust is warranted, and there may be a range of different (and sometimes mutually conflicting) measures which all meet the criteria of common good. This is all the more so since the 'common good' is a criterion to be assessed through generalized public discourse (politics, media, associations, universities, etc.) rather than in highly artificial and stylized judicial reasoning (which is a natural home of a formal scrutiny of legislative measures), and the chances of agreeing upon what meets the optimality criterion are low. Whether particular measures meet the publicly admissible criteria of argument to a higher degree than any other

30 Ibid. 163.

31 This is an oft-quoted characterization of the United States Supreme Court's use of 'strict scrutiny' in equal protection cases by constitutional scholar Gerald Gunther, 'The Supreme Court, 1971 Term—Foreword: In Search of Evolving Doctrine on a Changing Court: A Model for a Newer Equal Protection', (1978) 86 *Harvard Law Review* 1, 8.

measure will hinge upon deeply contested moral and political values. It seems that we may plausibly talk about something being a common good without it meeting the criterion of optimality. This does not strike me as counter-intuitive; to the contrary, when we describe something as being a common good, we do not imply that it is 'the best' but that it belongs to a range of good, or reasonable, solutions.

In sum, and borrowing from Pettit again, something constitutes a common good, or 'answers to the public interest of the members of the group', when 'it is supported … by the reasons publicly admissible amongst the members'.[32] For Pettit, examples of procedures for defining the common good from among the 'equally supported proposals'[33] include such devices (which are themselves endorsed by 'publicly admitted reasons') as 'a lottery, or the judgment of an impartial panel, or the judgment of a committee or court that is required to follow certain guidelines, or a majority vote among members or representatives'.[34] What is important, is that 'where the possibility of reasonable disagreement is acknowledged', the choice must be made 'on a basis that is itself endorsed by publicly admitted reasons'.[35] Of course, everything depends on *what* counts as publicly admissible reasons. Pettit gives some examples of what does *not* count as such reasons: 'Considerations that would not pass muster in group debate include self-seeking observations to the effect that such and such an initiative would give one member or subset of members an advantage over others, as well as expressions of what is required by an ideal or cause that is not shared by all.'[36]

As one can see, this sounds remarkably similar to the idea of 'public reason'. The common good, to simplify Pettit's formula, is a good attained as a result of employing public reason—a concept which has been most influentially restated in contemporary political philosophy by John Rawls. And while, in most of his writings, Rawls generally avoids the concept of 'common good', reserving the notion of the good to individual, comprehensive conceptions that rational individuals pursue in their own lives, this semantic convention need not prevent us from linking a plausible idea of the common good with a par excellence Rawlsian ideal of public justification and public reason. Indeed, the most Rawlsian of all Rawlsians, Samuel Freeman, summarizing Rawls' ideal of free and equal democratic citizens, wrote: 'They … have a higher-order interest in social and political conditions that enable them to freely pursue reasonable conceptions of the good. These fundamental interests of democratic citizens provide the ultimate basis for public reasoning about fundamental justice *and the common good*'.[37]

[32] Pettit, 'The Common Good' (n. 7) 164.
[33] Ibid. 163.
[34] Ibid. 164.
[35] Ibid. 163–64.
[36] Ibid. 162.
[37] Samuel Freeman, *Justice and the Social Contract* (Oxford University Press 2007) 223, emphasis added.

And Rawls himself, when describing, with admiration, Rousseau's idea of restrictions on what considerations are relevant for voting, as an idea parallel to Rawls's own understanding of public reason, stated: Rousseau 'saw voting as ideally expressing our opinion as to which of the alternatives best advances the common good'.[38] So there is a short and easy step from the 'common good' to 'public reason'.

But can that be all that needs to be said in support of the ideal of public reason? Unfortunately not. Suppose we accept that (1) the ideal of common good is, intuitively, hugely attractive, in the sense that it confers a strong value on any policy which can be shown to be consistent with the ideal, and (2) public reason follows from a particular, compelling, interpretation of the ideal of common good; from (1) and (2) it does not necessarily follow that (3) the ideal of public reason is compelling. It may be attractive but not compelling for if it rests exclusively on those same values which support the ideal of common good in the first place, then it must also share the vulnerabilities that the latter ideal displays. Even if we rest (as we should) the ideal of 'common good' on moral individualism, whereby all attractive ideals derive their worth from the role they have for individual members of the community, it does not sufficiently protect *individuals* against using community standards against them in ways which may be deemed intolerable. By defining the common good in ways which contrast it from purely private interests, we expose ourselves to the temptation of sacrificing some important individual values at the altar of the common good. Hence, we must provide 'public reason' with extra support from the values that better protect individuals in their dignity, and which cannot be traded off for the interests of others. This will be the purpose of the remaining sections of this chapter.

2. Respect for Persons as a Justification for Public Reason

'Fair cooperation on terms of mutual *respect for free and equal citizens* is the aim of political society in a liberal democratic state'.[39] This short sentence from an important recent book by Christie Hartley and Lori Watson encapsulates well the argument in the remainder of this chapter. It is interesting to note that Rawls himself spends remarkably little time *justifying* public reason [henceforth: PR] as a worthy ideal. In one of the very rare instances of trying to resurrect the *Theory of Justice*'s contractarian vocabulary and method in order to defend PR, Rawls says: 'when equally represented in the original position, no citizen's representative could grant to any other person, or association of persons, the political authority to [use the state's police power to decide constitutional essentials or basic

[38] Rawls, *Political Liberalism* (n. 18) 219–20, reference omitted.

[39] Christie Hartley and Lori Watson, *Equal Citizenship and Public Reason: A Feminist Political Liberalism* (Oxford University Press 2018) 48, emphasis added.

questions of justice as that person's, or that association's, comprehensive doctrine directs]. *Such authority is without grounds in public reason*.'[40] Rawls further adds that 'the guidelines and procedures of public reason are seen as selected in the original position',[41] and that they should be 'understood as proposed by the parties in the original position ... as fair terms of social cooperation in conducting public reason that we are ready to abide by provided others do',[42] and that they have the same grounds as principles of justice, that is, that they would be adopted by the parties in the original position;[43] in fact, principles of justice and the guidelines of PR 'are companion parts of one agreement'.[44] Whether this argument *adds* anything to the justification of, or merely reaffirms, the importance of PR, is a matter which would reopen the familiar controversies about the justificatory weight of Rawls's contractarian method, with its original position, the veil of ignorance, the maximin strategy, and reflective equilibrium.[45] I will not be rehearsing that discussion in this chapter[46] and will assume, as most of commentators on Rawls do, that PR is mainly justified by the ideal of respect for persons: the principle which requires that we not only give reasons to others in justifying coercive laws which will apply to them, but moreover that we give only such reasons that they can reasonably be expected to accept as justifications for such laws.[47] But this sounds more like an assertion than an argument, and it needs to be expanded.

The very idea of 'respect' has a number of meanings, but for our purposes two taxonomies are of particular importance. The first distinguished between what may be called 'evaluative' (or thick) and 'recognition' (or thin) respect. (In this, I largely follow a distinction by Stephen Darwall who distinguished between 'appraisal respect' and 'recognition respect'.)[48] The evaluative respect is 'thick' in the sense that it is essentially merit-based. We respect someone as a result of making a positive evaluation of something about that person: her achievements, virtue, character, effort, skills, talents, etc. It is of course a comparative concept: we respect *A* because she has achieved a higher rank on a particular scale than others; we may still respect those others, but less so. There must be also some who are ranked so low on that scale that we do not respect them at all. Respect, in the evaluative sense, is therefore a scarce good: to respect everyone equally would

[40] Ibid. 62, emphasis added.
[41] Ibid. 62.
[42] Ibid. 62 n. 17.
[43] Ibid. 225–26.
[44] Ibid. 226.
[45] For a critique, based on the original position, of Rawls's PR, see Christopher J. Eberle, *Religious Conviction in Liberal Politics* (Cambridge University Press 2013) 140–49.
[46] The literature on the derivation of principles of justice from the original position is enormous; for my part, I have discussed it in Wojciech Sadurski, *Giving Desert Its Due* (D. Reidel 1985) 57–76.
[47] See Charles Larmore, 'Public Reason' in Samuel Freeman (ed.), *The Cambridge Companion to Rawls* (Cambridge University Press 2003) 368, 374, and Charles Larmore, *The Autonomy of Morality* (Cambridge University Press 2008) 201.
[48] Stephen Darwall, 'Two Kinds of Respect', (1977) 88 *Ethics* 88, 36.

erode this sense of respect of any worth. 'People have much that is good and much that is bad about them, and we have reasons to respect them for whatever is good, and lack respect for them for whatever is bad'—this statement by Joseph Raz is as good an encapsulation of evaluative respect as they come.[49] Typical examples of manifesting respect in an evaluative sense are various practices of prize-giving, public honours, awards, praise, etc.

This notion of respect should be distinguished from what (following Darwall's terminology) may be called 'recognition respect'. It is a much thinner notion and attaches to a person simply by virtue of personhood and attributes which attach to the very fact of being human. There may be various religious grounds for respecting humans as being creatures of God, or philosophical-humanistic rationales for respecting humans for the reflective and emotional qualities which are part of the species to which they belong, for instance for the capacity of 'reflective self-evaluation that is manifested in the formation of second-order desires'.[50] An even thinner, and still persuasive, ground of recognition respect is in the concern for human beings in their common interests and vulnerabilities. Someone may object that this is to confuse the notion of respect with that of *concern* (and associated notions of care or empathy) but this is not so: the language of 'respect' is perfectly intelligible when employed in the context such as: 'We respect your privacy.' No evaluation of the use you make of your privacy is involved, but merely a recognition that a degree of privacy is in the interest of all human beings. When we choose not to *interfere* with your beliefs or actions regardless of our (for the sake of argument) mild disapproval of the substance of these beliefs or action (subject to the proviso just made about the threshold beyond which we do not owe you respect for your beliefs of which we strongly disapprove), then it is still a case of respecting someone's privacy, autonomy, sensitivity, freedom, etc.—in a moral and yet thinner sense than in the case of evaluative respect.

Of course, from the very fact that we owe persons respect, including a thin, evaluative kind of respect, it does not follow what specific respect-manifesting actions are required from us. This is only a first step leading to justifying a duty to provide justification in terms of public reason. But it is important to note that respect combines both requirements for actions and accompanying *sentiments*: an observable action itself is insufficient for ascertaining that respect (however minimal) has been paid. It is well explained by Leslie Green who looks at it from the perspective of a respect-receiver rather than respect-giver:

> People are sensitive not only to the way they are treated but also to the spirit in which that treatment is afforded. If one gives with the hand of treatment and takes away with the hand of attitude, they are likely to catch on, and that

[49] Joseph Raz, 'On Respect, Authority, and Neutrality: A Response', (2010) 120 *Ethics* 120, 279, 284.

[50] See Harry G. Frankfurt, 'Freedom of Will and the Concept of a Person', (1971) 68 *Journal of Philosophy* 5, 7, footnote omitted.

> will leave them without adequate assurance that they are being respected. A grudging bow is generally received in the spirit in which it is given.[51]

The fundamental distinction between evaluative and recognition respect should be kept separate from a second and simpler distinction applied to *manifestations* of respect, namely between active and passive respect. Active respect calls for doing something: for a positive action which manifests our appreciation of a person or her achievements. Negative respect requires failure to act: abstention from an action which would constitute lack of respect. The crossing of these two dichotomies is shown in Table 1.1.[52]

One may initially be tempted to think that evaluative respect is active while recognition respect is passive, and the examples given earlier fall into, respectively, cells 1 (evaluative and active) and 4 (recognition-based and passive) in the table. And indeed, these are perhaps the most typical examples of manifesting respect, either evaluative or recognition-based, in a society. The first consists of a number of practices of acknowledging, praising, and rewarding facts and features of individuals which we value highly: various practices of prize-giving, awards, public honours, etc. The latter may be summarily labelled as 'tolerance' by which I mean a moral attitude of not interfering with other people's conduct or beliefs, even though we are capable of prohibiting those conducts or beliefs, and even though we disapprove of them. Each element just mentioned is an important ingredient of 'tolerance', strictly speaking. First, it is a moral attitude: it is based on *moral* principles and not purely a matter of (to borrow Rawls's description in a similar context) modus vivendi. Second, we are *capable* of having a restrictive impact on those beliefs or conduct, if not by eliminating them altogether then at least by increasing the costs of holding/practicing them. (The impact may be as low as the voter's impact on the results of the election or a referendum—but it is still an impact.) In contrast, we cannot say that we 'tolerate' something if there is no way we can affect it anyway. Third, we *disapprove*

Table 1.1 Types of Respect

	Evaluative	Recognition
Active	1 Merit-based: award-giving, prizes, public honours etc.	3 Public reason
Passive	2 Deference	4 Tolerance

[51] Leslie Green, 'Two Worries about Respect for Persons', (2010) 120 *Ethics* 212, 219, footnote omitted.

[52] Note that the above manifestations of different types of respect provided in the Table 1.1 are not exhaustive of all the possibilities representative in each cell.

of this conduct or belief: there is no point in talking about 'tolerance' for actions or beliefs which we admire. But disapproval is mild: strong disapproval will mark the limits of our tolerance. And fourth, of course, we *abstain* from such interference. Each of these four characteristics would require additional refinement and qualifications, but this is not the point of this chapter; all that matters to us is that cell 4 contains familiar, passive manifestations of recognition respect.

But there may also be other, less typical but recognizable, combinations resulting from crossing these two taxonomies. There may be cases of respect which are both evaluative and passive, which I will call simply 'deference' (cell 2). We may abstain from an action towards a person (an action which we might otherwise be tempted to undertake) because of our high evaluation of that person's merit (knowledge, achievement, skills, etc.). We may for instance abstain from criticizing an eminent scholar out of a great evaluative respect for her work. Whether it is a wise attitude is beside the point: it is certainly recognizable in the real world, and it is both evaluation-based and passive. But there may also be reverse instances, namely of respect, which is based on thin, recognition grounds and yet which calls for a positive action, and public justification of coercive laws referring to PR belongs to this category (cell 3). It is active—because it requires a particular course of action: namely, in the process of arguing for coercive laws we should provide reasons which are endorsable by all those to whom these laws would apply. (One may, of course, characterize this duty in a negative way: as a duty to avoid arguments which are non-endorsable by all, but the point is, providing arguments of whatever character is a positive action, not omission.) And it is at the same time a thin, recognition-based respect because it is not conditioned by any comparative and high evaluation of something about our compatriots but only by concern for them as persons having certain recognizable, legitimate interests. It is related to the fact of reflective capacities of individuals which render them unique and thus deserving of recognition respect: since they are capable of reasoning about their behaviour and their preferences, our act of producing reasons for coercion engages individual capacities to reason about their preferences and choices even if they disagree with the specific substance of the coercive rules.

This way of putting things immediately indicates that respect, at least in the recognition-active sense, is not an autonomous value but should be seen as part of a broader constellation of values which incorporates moral worth into the value of respect. Respect, in this sense, derives its importance from the fact that it acknowledges certain basic interests which all individuals have, and which we all should recognize despite our disapproval for broader moral conceptions that those other persons espouse. What can these other values be? In the case of recognition respect, which triggers the duty to provide justification in terms of public reason, they can be described as the values of freedom, which dictates that all coercive restrictions of individual action are prima facie wrong and demand justification, and that of equality, which demands that an individual is not subjected to the law based on principles which she does not or cannot espouse, thus being reduced to a citizenship of secondary category. Both these values are prima facie only and are capable of being overridden by strong countervailing rationales that must be provided to an individual. They will be discussed, in turn, in the two remaining sections of this chapter.

3. Liberty and Public Reason

The principle of respect presupposes that not being subjected to coercion is prima facie good, and that consequently, the very objectionableness of using coercion towards an individual can be mitigated by supplying justification in terms of the ends which this person can share. Why would the fact of supplying a careful justification (in particular, in terms endorsable to the coercee) lessen the hurt of coercion? As Thomas Nagel has put it, 'when we force people to serve an end that they cannot share, and that we cannot justify to them in objective terms, it is a particularly serious violation of the Kantian requirement that we treat humanity not merely as a means, but also as an end. *The justification of coercion must meet especially stringent standards*.'[53] But what are the grounds of justification which are likely to mitigate the pain of coercion? It is useful here to recite Nagel's four-fold classification of the grounds of coercion in his book *Equality and Partiality*, which is based on different degrees of acceptance or acceptability of its grounds to a coercee:

> (1) grounds which the victim would acknowledge as valid; (2) grounds which the victim does not acknowledge, but which are nevertheless admissible because he is grossly unreasonable or irrational not to acknowledge them; (3) grounds which the victim does not acknowledge, without being irrational, but which are admissible under a higher-order principle which he does acknowledge, or would be unreasonable not to; and (4) grounds which the victim does not acknowledge—either reasonably or even somewhat unreasonably—and which are such that he cannot be required to accept a higher-order principle admitting them into political justification even if most others disagree with him.[54]

As one can immediately see, the grounds justifying coercion in this list decrease in force. The first is the easiest category: even though there is coercion,

[53] Thomas Nagel, 'Moral Conflict and Political Legitimacy', (1987) 16 *Philosophy & Public Affairs* 215, 238, emphasis added. See also, similarly, Thomas Nagel, *Equality and Partiality* (Oxford University Press 1991) 159.

[54] Nagel, *Equality and Partiality* (n. 53) 159–60.

it is consistent with the actual preferences of the coerced persons; a necessarily coercive resolution of the collective action problem (Prisoner's Dilemma) is an example. The use of force is necessary to actually implement the individuals' preferences about creation of public goods, so the point of the coercion may be seen as to enable a person to achieve her goals (congruent with public goods) rather than restrict her autonomy. An example of the second category is any reasonable criminal law prohibition: it is patently unreasonable for the offender to disagree with the grounds of the use of the coercion towards him. His liberty *is* restricted (the point to which I will return immediately below), but a justification for that is easy. The fundamental problem about punishment is not whether the criminal accepts the punishment, but whether it is justified anyway.[55] The third category is the most difficult problem for liberals (and the conception of PR is basically one possible answer to the problems triggered by the third category). Here a strong justification is required, and it will not always be effective, but once it is, it will largely reduce the oppressiveness of coercion. The fourth ground is the least acceptable from the point of view of reducing coerciveness: the enforcement of comprehensive moral or religious conceptions which a coerced person does not espouse belongs to the fourth category. This evokes a situation in which 'a person cannot reasonably be expected to agree to a system which authorizes the use of political power to enforce or promote values opposed to his own . . .'.[56] Here public reasons, or any other impartial, neutral justifications for coercion are not available, and so this type of restriction of freedom is the most palpable, and difficult to justify.

The connection assumed in the preceding paragraph, between (1) freedom, (2) coercion, and (3) justification in terms of reducing the oppressiveness of coercion (thus, improvement on freedom) may be seen by some as mistaken—not mistaken as an empirical proposition, because it is a fact that for most people coercion is actually seen as something presumptively bad, but wrong as a normative matter. One may deny that the actual and empirically observable aversion to coercion coincides with the normative prima facie wrongness of coercion—and one may operate with a value-laden notion of freedom where freedom to do things which are wrong has no moral worth at all; under such a conception, there is nothing morally wrong (even prima facie) in coercing a person not to do wrong things. One may, therefore, under such a value-laden conception of liberty, say that coercion which prevents murder or the coercively enforceable duty to pay taxes is not even prima facie wrong, and calls for no special justification, for instance because 'a collective decision to impose a duty not to kill and to threaten a serious sanction for any violation is not itself an insult to the dignity of subjects'.[57] But I disagree: such a moralized conception of freedom is unhelpful

[55] See Arthur Ripstein, *Equality, Responsibility, and the Law* (Cambridge University Press 1999) 8.
[56] Nagel, *Equality and Partiality* (n. 53) 161.
[57] Ronald Dworkin, *Justice for Hedgehogs* (Harvard University Press 2011) 367.

because it runs against powerful linguistic intuitions under which the 'freedom to do wrong' is not a contradiction in terms. Also, as a matter of a plausible normative theory, there is something prima facie good in not being coerced against one's will, as a result of which any coercion requires justification while letting a person act on her will calls for no equivalent need to *justify*.

The first point just made, namely the clash of this conception with widespread linguistic intuitions, has been well described by Bernard Williams. Williams begins with a plea to be faithful to actual common understandings in this context: 'We are constructing liberty as a political value, which means among other things that we can make sense of its role in political argument and political conflict, and generally of the experience of life under a political order.'[58] A restriction on liberty may be seen as rightful and yet as a cost in liberty. So even people who recognize that a particular coercive restriction applied to them (and to others) is justified may still consider it as a cost in terms of liberty infringement—even if it is a cost well worth paying. A moralized conception which is so divorced from linguistic usages such as this must be suspect.

Regarding the second point, which concerns normative moral theory, as H.L.A. Hart had noticed a long time ago, the need to justify coercion (a need which is intuitively plausible) suggests immediately that coercion is prima facie wrong:

> In asking [a question of justification] we are committed at least to the general critical principle that the use of legal coercion by any society calls for justification as something *prima facie* objectionable to be tolerated only for the sake of some countervailing good. For where there is no *prima facie* objection, wrong, or evil, men do not ask for or give *justifications* of social practices, though they may ask for and give *explanations* of these practices . . . [59]

To be sure, very often such justification will be quite obvious (as in most criminal-law prohibitions, at least in rational criminal legal systems), and therefore will not even register in our minds as something morally required, but one should not confuse self-evidence with the absence of duty to justify. Coercion, by definition, adversely affects our agency, and agency—understood as a capacity to do things congruent with our wishes and preferences—is prima facie good, though its good may be overridden by the quality of acts committed (or intended) by an actor. That is why, when we coerce people (or act in a way leading to coercion, for instance by advocating or voting for a party which proposes specific coercive laws, etc.) we owe the coercees a justification for the coercion, in terms of 'some countervailing good' (to use Hart's words) which can be recognized as such by

[58] Bernard Williams, *In the Beginning Was the Deed*, ed. Geoffrey Hawthorn (Princeton University Press 2005) 84.

[59] H.L.A. Hart, *Law, Liberty, and Morality* (Stanford University Press 1963) 20–21.

them. It is only in this way that the coercion may be endorsed by those to whom it is applied, and the distress produced by the coercion may be mitigated.[60] Furthermore, there is an intuitive and widespread sense that the burden of justification is proportionate to the gravity of coercion, in terms of its impact upon an individual's liberty: the more serious the impact of coercion on our liberty, the stronger the justification should be.[61] This may explain, for instance, why it is often thought that, everything else being equal, the burden of justification for a positive duty to act (or penalization of omissions), as in Good Samaritan duties, should be higher than the burden of justification for negative prohibitions (pardon the tautology) of actions; this makes sense insofar as it is plausible (as many people think) that positive duties restrict our liberty to a higher degree than prohibitions.[62] Everything else being equal (i.e., arguendo, the volume of harm resulting from an act/omission being the same), the higher a limitation on liberty, the stronger a duty to justify a coercive interference. If these intuitions are taken seriously then this is yet another indication that the duty of justification for coercive law is based upon a prior high value attached to individual freedom.

Some will deny, of course, that there is even a presumptive value in not being coerced and a presumptive wrongness in coercion as such, regardless of any subjective sense of distress triggered by coercion; they will say that coercion aimed at prohibiting wrong things does not involve weighing up and balancing the good in the prevention of wrong with the badness of coercion as such. Andrew Lister says: 'We do not weigh the benefit of being safe from murder and rape against the cost of losing one's freedom to murder and rape; we do not count frustrated desires to murder and rape as having any value.'[63] In his response, Gerald Gaus, who espouses (as I do) the view about a moral presumption against coercion, points at the harm of penalty—even though the harm may be justified overall, it is harm all the same, and the sense of sacrifice and regret does not vanish because of the final calculus that it is the right thing to do, on balance.[64]

What would we gain by adopting a terminological convention whereby there is no prima facie wrongness of coercion? The wrongness, under such a convention, would be fully parasitic on our evaluation of actions against which the coercion is addressed, so that the coercion not to do acts which are wrong would not have been even presumptively wrong. In terms of a duty to justify a coercive

[60] See, similarly, Eberle, *Religious Conviction in Liberal Politics* (n. 45) 97–102.

[61] See Ronald C. Den Otter, *Judicial Review in an Age of Moral Pluralism* (Cambridge University Press 2009) 53.

[62] See, e.g., P.J. Fitzgerald, 'Acting and Refraining', (1967) 27 *Analysis* 133, 138–39. As Fitzgerald suggests, 'to prohibit an act... leaves the subject free to do many alternative acts; to prohibit an omission (by requiring the act to be performed) leaves him free to do only *one* act, the act which he is forbidden to omit; and this is a more severe burden to place on the citizen than if he is merely forbidden to perform an act', ibid. 139.

[63] Andrew Lister, 'Public Justification and the Limits of State Action', (2010) 9 *Politics, Philosophy, and Economics* 151, 164.

[64] Gaus, *The Order of Public Reason* (n. 2) 482.

legislation (which is the only context that concerns us here), not much would be gained. We would be moving from a 'want-regarding principle' of freedom (because it is an uncontested fact that some people actually want to do things which others, rightly or wrongly, consider wrong and liable to social prohibition) to an 'ideal regarding principle' (to use Brian Barry's well-known distinction),[65] but our duty to justify our action would remain with equal force. The only difference would be that we would not have to justify our view about why the prohibited action is wrong. In such a case, we will not have a duty to show that this wrongness overrides the presumptive wrongness of coercion because we would not have adopted such a presumption in the first place. I fail to see in what way the duty to justify a coercive law is any different when the only thing we need to argue about is the wrongness of an action as contrasted to a wrongness of coercion. After all, we have already said that in many cases the presumption about wrongness of coercion will be very low (as in the case of murder or rape etc.). Hence, in terms of practical matters, namely the duty of justification for legislation, there is little (if any) practical difference between the value laden (ideal-regarding) and value neutral (want-regarding) conceptions of freedom. The only difference would be if someone, having adopted a value-laden, ideal-regarding conception of freedom, with no presumption against coercion whatsoever, argued that coercive laws require no justification to be produced to those against whom they are applied. But this seems starkly counter-intuitive in a democratic society.

4. Equality—Respect for Persons—Public Reason

The second value supportive of respect in our context is that of equal citizenship: it demands that we, as citizen-voters, are not put in the second category as far as the legislation is concerned. The relationship between second-class citizenship and disrespect is clear: think of the easy case of denying a particular category of citizens the vote. It is not merely a deprivation of a certain good such as an instrument of influencing the government, it also carries a symbolism of a lack of respect.[66] By analogy, it may be argued that founding a law on arguments which cannot be avowed by a given individual because of her identity is akin to excluding her from the political community on that given issue.[67] As Henrik Kugelberg says in a recent article: 'Citizens who are denied their status as civic equals by an exercise of state power do not have sufficient reason to accept that exercise of power.'[68]

[65] Barry, *Political Argument* (n. 6) 38–41.

[66] See Joseph Raz, *Value, Respect, and Attachment* (Cambridge University Press 2001) 172.

[67] See Charles B. Straut, 'Due Process Disestablishment: Why *Lawrence v. Texas* is a First Amendment Case', (2016) 91 *New York University Law Review* 1794, 1797.

[68] Henrik D. Kugelberg, 'Civic Equality as a Democratic Basis for Public Reason', (2021) *Critical Review of International Social and Political Philosophy*, https://doi.org/10.1080/13698230.2021.1905468, 3

But we need to be more precise about the nature of equality which is at stake in PR (and the associated value of respect), and only once we detect a conception of political equality which seems to be plausibly connected with PR do we need to reflect upon whether it is an attractive conception in the first place. For starters, we may distinguish between process- and effect-oriented political equality. The spectrum of process-related conceptions of equality ranges from very thin to very thick. As an example of a thin process-related political equality, consider what John Rawls called the principle of equal participation which he defined as the principle that 'all citizens are to have an equal right to take part in, and to determine the outcome of, the constitutional process that establishes the laws with which they are to comply'.[69] The problem with this ideal is that it is not ambitious enough: it is hard to see why anyone would, in a by-and-large liberal-democratic state, consider it as an ideal worth striving for. The ideal does not say anything about how equal the actual influence on the determination of outcomes will be: it only says than we all have an equal right to determine the outcome, and this ideal is met by a mere non-exclusion from the process. On the other end of the spectrum of procedure-oriented conceptions of equality, we have what Dworkin calls (without endorsing it) 'equality of influence', where a person's political influence is defined as 'the difference [a person] can make not just on his own but also by leading or inducing others to believe or vote or choose as he does'.[70] The ideal of equality of *this* type of influence is certainly ambitious; if anything, it is over-ambitious because (as Dworkin persuasively shows) to try to promote this type of equality we would need to compromise a number of important liberal-democratic values. At least some sources of departures from this type of political equality are perfectly legitimate: 'We regret some people's special influence because it is grounded in wealth, which we think should make no difference in politics. But we do not regret other people's special influence—Reverend King's, for instance—nor think this a defect in our democracy'.[71] Hence, equality of political influence does not qualify as an attractive conception of political equality either.

Is there a possibility that we may find a middle ground between a non-ambitious ideal of equal right to participate and the over-ambitious (and dangerous) ideal of equality of influence—a middle ground that would display none of the defects of both polar positions in political equality? I argued elsewhere that *the ideal of equality of political opportunity* may be just such a conception.[72] The concept itself is parasitic, of course, on a more generic concept of equality of opportunity, and if understood in a sufficiently robust way, as a 'genuine' rather than merely 'formal' equality of opportunity, when applied to a political sphere it seems to be more ambitious than equal right to participate and yet largely free

[69] John Rawls, *A Theory of Justice* (Harvard University Press 1971) 221.
[70] Ronald Dworkin, *Sovereign Virtue* (Harvard University Press 2000) 191.
[71] Dworkin, *Justice for Hedgehogs* (n. 57) 389.
[72] Wojciech Sadurski, *Equality and Legitimacy* (Oxford University Press 2009) 77–90.

of the dangers associated by Dworkin with equality of political influence. This is because equality of political opportunity does not commit us to eliminate all sources of differential political influence, including those which may be perfectly legitimate (the personal charisma of the speaker, their active commitment to public affairs, their high level of expertise, etc.). Echoing a broader conception of equality of opportunity *simpliciter* which demands that the influence of factors which are beyond a person's control should be eliminated from determining a person's situation, equality of *political* opportunity commits us to discriminate between legitimate and illegitimate sources of individual capacities to influence politics. For Dworkin, the lack of capacity to conduct exactly this sort of discrimination was (rightly) a major defect of the ideal of equality of political influence; for instance, such equality would 'prevent some people from tailoring their resources to fit the lives they wanted though leaving others, who had less interest in politics, free to do so'.[73] Now we certainly do not want *this* sort of equalization. Another strategy of equalizing political influence, Dworkin claims, would be by 'educat[ing] people not to attempt to influence others, with respect to political decisions, except in ways that do not rely on special advantages they might have, in experience or commitment or reputation . . . .'[74] Again, this would be a perverse ideal, and we certainly want to encourage rather than prevent people from influencing others based, among other things, on their superior experience or commitment or reputation. But the ideal of equality of political opportunity is immune to such objections; in fact, equality of opportunity is exactly tailored to identifying legitimate sources of unequal resources to achieve one's goals (mainly, in the choice-dependent factors), and to making these factors immune to equalization.

But how much mileage can we get from the principle of equality of political opportunity to support the value of respect associated with PR? Attractive though the ideal is, its connection with the rationale for PR is tenuous, at best. For we may well imagine ways of implementing this ideal without observing the principle of PR; in fact, equality of political opportunity is insensitive towards the *motives* for laws which citizens, legislators, or judges may have. *Why* supporters of a given law advocate it is not relevant to the equality of political opportunity of all others who will be affected by the law. And vice versa, we may imagine ways of respecting the principle of PR which will deny the principle of equality of political opportunity: a coercive law was enacted in accordance with a correct implementation of constraints on reasons, consistently with PR, but was passed while denying some citizens equal opportunity to affect its substance.

This may indicate that we need to again search for a conception of equality which will underwrite a respect–PR connection, and that we should abandon

[73] Dworkin, *Sovereign Virtue* (n. 70) 197, footnote omitted.
[74] Ibid. 197.

the search for a process-oriented conception and consider an alternative: an outcome-dependent conception of political equality. This seems intuitively plausible: process-oriented conceptions cannot do the work needed in this context because they are focused on an individual as a participant in the lawmaking process, and in the context of PR, inequality is not produced by how the law has come about, but rather how the law, in its outcome, can be presented and justified to an individual who may object to it *on its merits*. Actual equal participation of an individual in the process of lawmaking (under any of the conceptions of process-oriented political equality considered so far) is neither a necessary nor sufficient condition for respecting a person's equality viewed through the prism of PR. Offending against the principle of PR in lawmaking may not offend against a principle of process-based equality, under whatever preferred conception of such equality we adopt, if we design a process which will include the person on an equal basis with others, and vice versa, even if process-based inequality arises, it may be the case that the principle of PR has been observed in the discourse leading up to the adoption of the law. So we have to reflect upon an outcome-based conception of political equality which would sustain the PR–respect connection.

There may be two main conceptions of outcome-based political equality. First, we may look at an outcome-oriented political equality in a *distributive* sense;[75] and secondly, we may look at it through an *agency* angle. (This is not an exhaustive list but a partial taxonomy which serves to illuminate our current task.) A distributive conception connects political outcomes with our views of distributive equality: a political process lives up to political equality in this sense when it produces outcomes which match our ideas about a proper distribution of goods, controlled by law, to particular individuals. This is, for instance, the case of a recently influential conception of 'luck egalitarianism' which is committed to making sure that legal rules will help compensate only for those inequalities which are traceable to circumstances outside a person's control—a theory which I have discussed extensively elsewhere.[76] This is a characteristically distributive ideal of political equality because it is concerned with comparing a share of a given, legally relevant good held by one individual with those held by others. More specifically, distributive political equality concerns the relationship between particular properties (*P1*, *P2* ... etc.) of individuals and the amount of politically (including legally) controlled goods (*G1*, *G2* ... etc.) that these individuals possess. The practical point of a distributive approach to equality is to identify the properties which must *not* trigger unequal amounts of social goods. According to this approach, equality will be achieved, notwithstanding the fact that two individuals have an unequal amount of *P1* (for instance, inherited

[75] For the concept of 'distributional equality', see ibid. 11–12.
[76] Sadurski, *Equality and Legitimacy* (n. 72) chapter 5.

wealth or family status), whenever they have an equal amount of *G1* (for instance, salary). Political equality occurs whenever the political system maximizes such outcomes.

An agency-focused approach is different. It is not concerned with who-gets-what, and how it compares to other persons participating in the distributive scheme, but rather is concerned with the message that a given law sends to the society as a whole, and to those disadvantaged by a given law in particular, about the place that a group affected by a law occupies in the society. Rather than looking at particular distributions of valued goods, one citizen at a time, the agency approach is 'collective' in the sense that it looks at the overall structure of the society and attributes the property of political equality to the society as a whole. This second understanding is well captured by Ronald Dworkin when he says that 'Political equality is a matter not of political power but of political standing',[77] although in Dworkin's argument 'political standing' is connected with rights of equal participation, and hence with process-oriented values. But a broad notion of equal 'political standing' resonates well with the agency approach to political equality, as does the sentence which follows the just-quoted formula from Dworkin and which is so unmistakably Dworkinian: 'Democracy confirms in the most dramatic way the equal concern and respect that the community together, as the custodian of coercive power, has for each of its members.'[78] This may be rendered more specific in different ways: according to various popular formulae, such equality may require that there are no settled hierarchies, or relations of domination, or oppression, or exploitation. For such equality to be found it is insufficient to proceed, as we do in the case of distributional equality, by looking at what any two individuals receive as a function of this or that property held by (or attributed to) these two individuals.

A good example of a confrontation between agency-based and distributive approaches is provided in a well-known critique by Elizabeth Anderson of luck egalitarianism (and related theories), from a position which roughly corresponds to what I call here an agency approach. Against theorizing that is 'too narrowly focused on the distribution of divisible, privately appropriated goods, such as income and resources, or privately appropriated goods, such as welfare',[79] Anderson claims that 'the point' of equality is 'to abolish oppression—that is, forms of social relationship by which some people dominate, exploit, marginalize, demean, and inflict violence upon others', and positively, that equality expresses people's desires 'to live together in a democratic community, as opposed to an hierarchical one'.[80] Similarly, and also in a polemic with luck egalitarianism, Samuel Scheffler urges that the nature of our concern with equality as a value is

[77] Dworkin, *Justice for Hedgehogs* (n. 57) 390.
[78] Ibid. 390.
[79] Elizabeth Anderson, 'What Is the Point of Equality?', (1991) 109 *Ethics* 287, 288.
[80] Ibid. 313.

expressed in equal political citizenship: it is encapsulated in the reasons why 'it is important to us ... to live in a society in which citizens relate to one another as equals'.[81]

I do not want to suggest that Anderson and Scheffler are right and luck egalitarians are wrong; as a matter of fact, I have elsewhere defended luck egalitarianism against Anderson's and Scheffler's critiques.[82] Distributive and agency-based conceptions are two alternative approaches to political equality (of an outcome-oriented variety), and an endorsement of one need not result in the renunciation of another. In fact, it is puzzling why anyone should find the distributive and agency approaches antithetical.[83] Distributional equality is often a condition (necessary though certainly not sufficient) of agency equality, as is the case with equal distribution of a right to vote, and vice versa, agency equality provides a background for understanding the reasons behind the attractiveness of some ideals of distributional equality, such as luck egalitarianism: this is the ideal of people being held responsible for their actions but entitled to solidarity when brute bad luck strikes. However, from our point of view, that is, in the context of a search for a conception of equality that resonates with PR as a desideratum of respect for persons, it is clear that only an agency-oriented conception can do the work. To enact a law which is crucially justified on the basis of reasons that are alien to a person due to her membership in a particular religious or ideological group is to consign this person to second-class citizenship. The message of such a law to this person and fellow members of the group is: 'You are not of equal standing in our community. You certainly *are* a member of our community, insofar as we can enact a law which will apply to you, and which will bind you, but you are not an equal member, in a moral sense, because we need not try to find reasons for the law which will be endorsable by you.'

* * *

To summarize what has been said so far: we have seen how the general ideal of public reason expresses the fundamental value of respect for persons, but respect itself is too vague and too thin a value to sustain a political ideal as weighty as that of public reason. Respect has to be seen as part of a constellation of values, of which freedom and equality are of particular importance.[84] Each of these values enhances our political life in ways which can be explained in terms of another value; they are in a mutually supportive, interlocking, integrated scheme of political values, where each is understood and appreciated in the light of the

[81] Samuel Scheffler, 'Choice, Circumstance, and the Value of Equality', (2005) 4 *Politics, Philosophy and Economics* 5, 18.

[82] Sadurski, *Equality and Legitimacy* (n. 72) 148–61 and 200–07.

[83] I develop this argument further in ibid. 155–57.

[84] For a different, and much more succinct, exposition of public reason theory as based on interrelated values of respect, liberty, and equality, see Pavlos Eleftheriadis, *Legal Rights* (Oxford University Press 2008) 161–63.

other: respect, in an active and relatively thin, recognition-based sense; freedom, understood through a presumptive evil of coercion; and political equality, in an outcome-oriented agency sense. These three values interact and support each other in a configuration of moral ideals which render the principle of public reason attractive and, indeed, compelling. I have in mind an interrelationship of these values corresponding to what Ronald Dworkin eloquently (though in a different context) described as an 'integrated' scheme of values, contrasted to a 'detached' view: in the former, 'we suppose not only that an integrated value's existence depends on some contribution it makes to some other, independently specifiable, kind of value, ... but that the more precise characterization of a [sic] integrated value ... depends upon identifying that contribution'.[85]

But this is, of course, only one way of approaching the principle of respect in the circumstances of moral diversity. There is also an opposite view: one that sees in such avoidance to openly refer to one's comprehensive conception (even if none of its elements may be endorsed by our co-citizens) as the *failure* of respect to them, and demands that we sincerely disclose our full moral or religious conceptions, and engage openly with the ones with which we disagree. This alternative approach to the principle of respect, hostile to the ideal of public reason, has probably been best expressed by Michael Sandel:

> On a different conception of respect—call it the deliberative conception—we respect our fellow citizen's moral and religious convictions by engaging, or attending to them—sometimes by challenging and contesting them, sometimes by listening and learning from them—especially if those convictions bear on important political questions.... [T]he respect of deliberation and engagement affords a more spacious public reason than liberalism allows. It is also a more suitable ideal for a pluralist society.[86]

There is certainly some appeal in Sandel's conception: it calls for full candour, open disclosure of one's own ideals, and sincere 'engagement' with those we disagree with. It may well be that in general public discourse (unrelated directly to lawmaking) such an attitude better reflects an attitude of respect than the one constrained by requirements of public reason. But even then it is a contingent and controversial proposition. Often 'challenging and contesting' our fellow citizens' moral and religious (especially religious!) views may be received as arrogance and dismissal of their perspectives. When our fellow citizens espouse first principles which do not lend themselves to much interpersonal argument but

[85] Ronald Dworkin, 'Hart's Postscript and the Character of Political Philosophy' (2004) 34 *Oxford Journal of Legal Studies* 1, 16.

[86] Michael J. Sandel, Book Review (John Rawls, *Political Liberalism*), (1994) 107 *Harvard Law Review* 1765, 1794. For a similar link between the attitude of respect and the requirement of openness and full disclosure of one's real reasons, see William A. Galston, *Liberal Purposes* (Cambridge University Press 2002) 116.

are based on such non-rational grounds as intuition, illumination, or habit, the scope for convincing one another is very limited, and it is often more respectful to leave them as they are rather than to 'challenge and contest'. But the main point is, while Sandel's argument may be a reasonable account of interpersonal respect in general public discourse, it hardly applies to the lawmaking process and the discourse related directly to it. Public reason is about providing a rationale for a coercive law to be obeyed by citizens who do not necessarily think as we do about the common good. At this stage, the argument about 'contesting and challenging' other people's conceptions, as a way of showing them our respect, is pointless. At this stage, showing respect resonates better with 'the overarching civic importance of giving reasons to others that they can reasonably be expected to accept as justification for coercion on the part of the state',[87] than with Sandelian open contestation and challenge.

A final observation. The argument in this chapter assumes that the ideal of PR is based on robust moral values and not some form of moral agnosticism to value, for instance on moral relativism or scepticism. When it comes to moral relativism, adoption of such a metaethical stance would quite obviously undermine the axiological grounds of the ideal of PR itself: if all values depend, for their worth, on who is espousing them (or upon the circumstances in which they are contemplated, on any other factors of relativity of values) then PR loses its moorings in the values of respect, liberty, and equality, and urged in this chapter. However, moral scepticism has a different relationship with PR. It does not have to underlie PR, and I would venture it normally does not: the espousers of this idea are not torn by doubts and hesitations about its worth. But I am not sure that the adoption of a position of scepticism, in contrast to the adoption of relativism, necessarily undermines the epistemic possibility of PR. It may be that some people are inclined to espouse this ideal on the basis of their uncertainty about the right values, and I am not sure that there is necessarily a contradiction between being a moral sceptic and a supporter of the ideal of PR. A contradiction would only exist if moral scepticism committed a person to being uncertain about moral values *across the board*, whereas it is defensible that one may be *more* sceptical about first-order values (in particular about individual conceptions of the good) and less sceptical about second-order values, that is, the values which determine principles about reconciliation of moral diversity (about first-order values) in the society. Such a combination of epistemic certainty and uncertainty does not strike me as necessarily contradictory: the second-order values may be found by their endorsers to be more 'discoverable' and interpersonally justifiable than the first-order values. So it is precisely this uncertainty about the latter which may lead some people to adopt something like an idea of public reason,

[87] Den Otter, *Judicial Review in an Age of Moral Pluralism* (n. 61) 132–33.

placing special restraints upon the principles which may justify the use of legal coercion towards individuals.

In one of his energetic critiques of the idea of PR, David Enoch argued, not a long time ago, that 'it would be highly surprising if political liberalism had to presuppose a commitment to such highly controversial, clearly metaphysical (in Rawls's sense) theses like nihilism, skepticism, or relativism. It is no wonder, then, that Rawls and his followers go to great lengths to deny such commitments.'[88] Granted re nihilism or relativism: an attempt to erect the ideal of PR on either of these positions would indeed be 'highly surprising'. But this is not necessarily the case for moral scepticism. I adopt a weak view: that scepticism does not have to be adopted in order to justify PR, but not a strong view: that it must be rejected for this purpose. It is compatible with, though not necessary for, the ideal discussed throughout this book.

[88] David Enoch, 'Political Philosophy and Epistemology: The Case of Public Reason' in David Sobel, Peter Vallentyne, and Steven Wall (eds.), *Oxford Studies in Political Philosophy*, vol. 3 (Oxford University Press 2017), Oxford Scholarship Online, doi 10.1093/oso/9780198801221.001.0001, 5, reference omitted.

2
The Parameters of Public Reason

Public reason (PR) is narrower than the concept of public justification because only some reasons are allowable in the justification of a law. To be sure, some (typically, Kantian in their philosophical provenance) understandings of public justification are coextensive with PR. As Pavlos Eleftheriadis urges: 'Public, as opposed to private, justification means an argument that can be reasonably endorsed by others who disagree with us. It suggests an effort to find common ground on one issue, while respecting our mutual differences in others.'[1] As a normative theory, a directive that public justification should rely on reasons acceptable to others is unimpeachable; this is, in fact, the main idea adopted in this book. But as a definition of 'public justification', it is unhelpfully narrow: there may be views about public justification that do not endorse the ideal of PR, that are perhaps authoritarian, paternalistic, or moralistic in ways that do not boil down to a search for 'common ground' in justification, and yet are 'public' and 'justificatory' in the requisite senses. No conceptual clarity is achieved by narrowing down the concept of 'public justification' in this way.

But what sort of 'reason' or 'reasons' figure in the concept of 'public reason'? While the scholarly discussion about 'Public Reason' (including the discussion in the latter parts of this and in the following chapters) has focused mainly on questions related to the 'Public' aspect of it, the first two parts of this chapter addresses the *noun* in the concept 'public reason' rather than the adjective and, in doing so, will examine the ways in which 'public *reason*' (or public *reasons*, in plural and lowercase) can be said to resonate with *some* types of reasons—rather than others—as presented and defended in contemporary legal theory.

I will begin by identifying the concept of public reason by comparing it with Joseph Raz's celebrated concept of exclusionary reasons (section 1). I will then place the concept in a context of a discussion sparked by the distinction between 'internal' and 'external' reasons, which was made famous by Bernard Williams (section 2). I will then move from the noun to the adjective in 'public reason' and will adopt, as my main guideline, the helpful clarification by John Rawls that 'the idea of public reason is not a view about specific political institutions or policies' but, rather, 'it is a view about the kind of reasons on which citizens are to rest their political cases in making their political justifications to one another . . .'[2]

[1] Pavlos Eleftheriadis, *Legal Rights* (Oxford University Press 2008)57.

[2] John Rawls, 'The Idea of Public Reason Revisited' in *The Law of Peoples* (Harvard University Press 1999) 165–66.

Constitutional Public Reason. Wojciech Sadurski, Oxford University Press. © Wojciech Sadurski 2023.
DOI: 10.1093/oso/9780192869678.003.0002

This, I will show (in section 3) resonates with the attractive 'input model of democracy', and also with the idea, popular some two decades ago, of the 'state's neutrality' towards competing conceptions of the good. In an attempt to recalibrate Rawls's own conception of PR in order to be convincing in a constitutional context, I will suggest (in section 4) that the concept must be freed from two implausible limitations on its range urged by Rawls: about its scope of application (which Rawls wanted to limit to 'constitutional essentials') and about its agents (with the privileged position of judges in ascertaining public reasons for us). Section 5 is central in this chapter: it will explain the meaning of PR as a *legitimating* device in constitutional argument. Finally, section 6 will compare PR with a concept which may be seen to be contiguous to it: that of reason of state. I will show that, in some versions (what I will call a 'thin' meaning) reason of state is functionally equivalent to PR, but that it also has a problematic feature: it relies too heavily, well, on the *state*.

1. Public Reason and Exclusionary Reasons

A useful way of thinking about reason-constraining ideals, such as PR, is by using a category of 'exclusionary reasons': second-order reasons which dismiss those first-order reasons that do not *compete* with other, legitimate, reasons but which must be disqualified at the outset from serving as reasons for action even if, were they allowed to compete, they would have been pertinent to the decision in question and may have outweighed those other (eventually successful) reasons.[3] In a classical discussion by Joseph Raz, exclusionary reasons are 'second-order reason[s] to refrain from acting for some reason',[4] or, simply, 'reason[s] for disregarding other reasons for action'. I am not suggesting that all exclusionary reasons in Raz's sense are public reasons, but rather that public reasons, insofar as they are reasons for action (rather than simply reasons contemplated in a general discourse) belong to a category of exclusionary reasons because they exclude reasons for action which otherwise might be considered relevant and pertinent, all things considered. Non-public reasons that have to be set aside under the principle of PR remain valid; they do not evaporate or vanish but must nevertheless be disregarded whenever PR operates. One scholar who has helpfully employed Raz's concept of second-order reasons to discuss principles of justice in the context of the diversity of first-order reasons is Jeremy Waldron:

[3] I am grateful to Michael Sevel for discussion of this and related points.
[4] Joseph Raz, *Practical Reason and Norms* (2nd edn., Oxford University Press 1999) 39.

> one's views about justice are usually conclusions about the first-order reasons … for society's distributing rights and resources in certain ways. Once one becomes aware that those views are not shared by everyone in society, one acquires a second-order reason not to act peremptorily—at least not in the name of the whole society—on the basis of one's own estimate of those first-order reasons.[5]

Waldron, no friend to the idea of PR himself, has aptly characterized the move from first-order to second-order reasons triggered by the fact of moral diversity, and we may add that the concept of PR can be seen as one particular type of second-order reasons required by that move.

Incidentally, insofar as PR operates in the field of public *discourse*—the discourse about considering, advancing, defending, and rejecting proposals for binding laws—it may be seen as not strictly matching the Razian notion of exclusionary reasons, which are reasons for *action*, not for contemplation or discussion of certain actions. Criticizing one of his critics for an alleged misrepresentation of the concept, Raz points out that the critic, Stephen Darwall, focused much of his discussion of exclusionary reasons 'on the case for or against *considering* certain matters, which is irrelevant to the issue [of exclusionary reasons]'.[6] But, in the case of PR, a distinction between reasons for *considering* certain matters and reasons for *action* would be pedantic: the matters considered in the realm covered by PR are *actions* of a particular kind, namely, adopting coercive laws binding on citizens. Considerations of those legislative proposals are 'actions' in a meaningful sense of the word—they may be seen as certain stages of legislative process. Whether they can be distinguished (as a theory of PR should do) from a mere discussion, carried on without any legislative actions in mind, is something which will be considered separately (in Chapter 3, section 4).

Second-order exclusionary reasons may operate in a strong and in a weak sense: the former ones absolutely exclude acting on certain first-order reasons; the latter reasons remove some weight from those first-order reasons. At first blush, 'weak' exclusionary reasons may be seen as a misnomer because strictly speaking they do not 'exclude' anything, but rather reduce the weight of certain reasons in competition with others. Indeed, Raz himself seems to reject the very possibility of weak exclusionary reasons: 'The very point of exclusionary reasons is to bypass issues of weight by excluding consideration of the excluded reasons regardless of weight. If they have to compete in weight with the excluded reasons,

[5] Jeremy Waldron, *Law and Disagreement* (Oxford University Press 1999) 196.

[6] Joseph Raz, 'On Respect, Authority, and Neutrality: A Response', (2010) 120 *Ethics* 279, 299 n. 21. The article that is the subject of Raz's criticism in this case is Stephen Darwall, 'Authority and Reasons: Exclusionary and Second-Personal', (2010) 120 *Ethics* 257. Earlier, however, Raz had admitted that he may have contributed to the confusion (consisting in the mistaken thinking of exclusionary reasons as reasons 'to avoid thinking, considering, or attending to certain matters') in his early discussion of exclusionary reasons, *Practical Reason* (n. 4) 184.

they will only exclude reasons which they outweigh, and thus lose distinctiveness.'[7] This is unconvincing, although in practical terms, this weak sense may not have much significance because we usually establish the weakened weight of some first-order reasons *ex post*, on the basis that they eventually did not prevail, so the effect is the same as in the exclusion. (If, by contrast, they do prevail, what is the point of saying that their weight had been lowered by an exclusionary rule?) But it is only a practical point, not an analytical one, and 'usually' does not mean 'always'. Suppose you have a rule for a particular behaviour *R1* which constitutes an exclusionary reason for not considering any option inconsistent with *R1*, *unless they are particularly compelling* in the circumstances. An exclusionary reason functions then to deprive those excluded reasons of much of the weight that they would have in the absence of the exclusionary reason, but sometimes their initial weight may be of such stringency in the first place that even an exclusionary reason will be incapable of overriding them. (If no such occurrence could be envisaged it would mean that the excluded reason has no weight.) As an example, consider a proposition by Frederick Schauer that 'one who exceeds the speed limit in order to rush an injured person to the hospital has not rejected the [exclusionary] rule, and may very well follow it in cases of slighter but still present reasons to disregard it'.[8] We may then say that the person is not disregarding the exclusionary reason but only that the exclusionary reason is not strong enough to override particularly dramatic or urgent reasons not to follow it.

We might perhaps then be tempted to say that it is just a matter of competition among first-order reasons, and that introducing the concept of a second-order exclusionary reason does not add any explanatory value to the situation if such reason may be occasionally disregarded. But this temptation should be resisted, and the difference lies in the idea of what is 'normal' (as is the case of a routine competition of different first-order rules) and what is exceptional (as is the case of displacing the second-order exclusionary reasons). The language of the competition of first-order reasons would paint a poor picture of the nature of our decision-making under the circumstances of a speed limit which serves to most of us as an exclusionary reason: it would be inaccurate to say that we 'normally' consider it in competition with various reasons which may justify higher speed. Rather, the limit most of the time excludes those other reasons for action which, in the absence of the limit, would be perfectly appropriate to follow. However, in some special and extraordinary circumstances we may disregard the exclusionary reason because an unusual reason of great dramatic force has occurred. So in such cases, we may still talk of second-order exclusionary reasons but not of absolute strength: they do not prevail always and under all circumstances.

[7] Raz, *Practical Reason* (n. 4) 190.

[8] Frederick Schauer, *Playing by the Rules* (Oxford University Press 1991) 90.

An alternative account, which would save the idea of the absolute strength of exclusionary reasons, would be to say that they are narrower in *scope* than we initially thought, so that in the case of our example of the speed limit and rushing to bring the patient to the hospital what may seem to be a reason to override an exclusionary reason is in fact an exception to that reason. The speed limit rule (which provides an absolute reason) has an exception built into it (perhaps only tacitly), providing that it does not apply in the case of an emergency drive to the hospital. Such a solution could help reconcile the intuitive plausibility of the strength of the winning reason for action (in our example, rushing to the hospital) with the absolute strength of the exclusionary reason of the speed limit: the latter reason is still absolute but its scope of application is narrower than initially thought. However, this alternative account, of narrowing the scope of the reason in order to rescue the idea of absoluteness of second-order exclusionary reasons, seems to me inferior to the account that allows for exclusionary reasons to be occasionally overridable, because the latter seems to coincide better with the way we conventionally tend to think about such cases. The language of an override seems to be more faithful to our actual dilemmas in such situations than the language of exceptions.

The dimension of overridability is separate from the issue of the *specificity* of second-order exclusionary reasons. There are some rules that are highly specific—such as the particular rule of speed limits, which as we have just seen generates a reason which is overridable—and those which are equally specific but not overridable. Consider the age requirement for eligibility to be elected as President of the United States: it is unlikely that any reason provided for disregarding this exclusionary reason can ever prevail, however urgent the circumstances may seem. A minimum age rule provides a reason for the absolute disregard of any reasons for considering candidates who do not meet the age requirement. Dennis Thompson, when suggesting that public reason belongs to the category of 'precluded reasons' (which correspond to Raz's exclusionary reasons), provides the following examples of precluded reasons: '*overbroad* regulations, such as the . . . rule that forces pilots to retire at 60, the age requirement for voting in elections . . . ' etc.[9] These are indeed strict, unexceptionable, and non-overridable rules which preclude considering any reasons other than those specified in the rule for a particular decision: no argument, however weighty in the absence of the cited rule, can prevail over a strict rule in affecting the authoritative decision. But the fact that they are branded as 'overbroad' is not relevant to characterizing them as exclusionary: overbreadth is a matter of our judgement about an alleged discrepancy between a justificatory argument for a rule and the substance of the rule. In fact, every rule risks being over- or under-inclusive

[9] Dennis F. Thompson, 'Public Reason and Precluded Reasons', (2004) 72 *Fordham Law Review* 2073, 2075 n. 16, emphasis added.

because, by the very nature of rules, there is a discrepancy between the justification and the substance of a rule. Every rule generates second-order reasons for disregarding some reasons inconsistent with the rule, but overbreadth or under-inclusiveness are not features that generate exclusionary reasons.

I have just said that the dimension of specificity is separate from the question of absoluteness. But not every rule which generates an exclusionary reason is equally specific: the rules about excluding evidence obtained through unlawful means will be much less specific insofar as the unlawfulness of gathering the evidence may be a matter of judgement on which some reasonable people will *disagree*. There may be a mild correlation between the dimension of specificity and that of absoluteness in the sense that the absolute rules tend to be more specific while overridable (weak) rules will be more indeterminate. This may be because the 'cost' of having a rule (in terms of the inevitable disjunction between the justification for a rule and its substance) is mitigated by the specificity of a rule (at least there is no uncertainty about whether the rule should apply to a given case), while it is compounded in the case of more indeterminate rules. But there is nothing analytically necessary about it: we may have specific rules which generate either absolute or weak exclusionary reasons, and the same is the case with less specific rules. PR belongs to those exclusionary reasons which are no doubt less specific than, for instance, age or speed limits (there is certainly more room for reasonable disagreement as to whether a particular justification matches the criteria of PR than whether a particular person meets the requirement of age), but at the same time seems to be stronger and not overridable, in the sense that it does not allow for the consideration of certain first-order rules in the lawmaking process. I have deliberately said 'seems to be' because whether it should be so is a matter of substantive argument for the adoption of the principle of PR in the first place, and as such cannot be decreed by definitional considerations.

This is not to say that distinguishing between strong first-order reasons and second-order exclusionary reasons is always easy in practice: often what we take to be an exclusionary reason is on reflection better described as a strong first-order reason, or vice versa. This was well described by Joseph Raz who observed that a test case for the existence of exclusionary reasons (as opposed to strong first-order reasons) is 'a peculiar sense of unease, which will show itself when we wish to censure a person who acted on the balance of [first-order] reasons for disregarding the exclusionary reason and when we have to justify someone's acting on an exclusionary reason against claims that the person concerned should have acted on the balance of reasons'.[10] This 'sense of unease' provides a good explanation for the dilemmas occurring when PR is invoked (which, one should emphasize, is *not* Raz's context). Precisely because the introduction of the principle of PR into public discourse changes the outcome, it is often seen

[10] Raz, *Practical Reason* (n. 4) 41.

as disturbing the proper moral conclusion about a proposed legislation, and as being contrary to the principle that practical action should be based on the balance of all appropriate reasons relevant to the matter.[11] But at the end of the day, even when we observe the principle of PR as an exclusionary reason, the excluded (non-public) reasons *may* be conformed to, but only in an indirect way: they may be conformed to if they converge with other first-order non-excluded reasons; what *is* excluded is that they must not be a motivation (or a sufficient motivation) for legislative action.[12]

In one of his statements on exclusionary reasons, focusing on their pre-emptive character, Raz identified two ways in which authoritative directives 'are not beyond challenge'.[13] First, they may stop short of actually stating conclusively what should be done in certain circumstances but merely determine 'what ought to be done on the basis of certain considerations'[14] (for instance, determine what should be done based on economic considerations, without however displacing any non-economic considerations). This perhaps may be translated into a hypothetical norm: '*If* a decision is to be taken on economic grounds this is what should be done', but it is a big 'If' that in many actual circumstances may render the rest of the sentence irrelevant. Second, and more relevantly to our topic here, 'the authority may direct that the final decision must be based on economic considerations only, thus replacing all but the economic factors'.[15] The pre-emption here is addressed against a particular category of considerations (in this example, all non-economic considerations), rather than against specific types of reasons displaced by an exclusionary reason. It identifies a *type* of consideration which can trigger a decision and displaces whole *classes* of reasons for a decision which are consequently ruled out. This second example provided by Raz points to the way the ideal of PR may be thought of: it identifies the types of reasons that 'the final decision must be based on', or, in a negative formulation, the type of reasons that the governmental decision must not rest on. And it is of course important for our description that those reasons which are excluded by the ideal of PR are attractive and important in the first place: they are not excluded because they are insignificant. If the PR ideal excludes reasons for action which are sectarian in a religious or moral sense, it does not mean that they are excluded because of their low weight; the whole characteristic of an ideal of PR as an 'exclusionary' reason has bite only if the excluded reasons have a strong initial attractiveness towards individuals.

[11] See Jeremy Waldron, 'Public Reason and "Justification" in the Courtroom', (2007) 1 *Journal of Law, Philosophy and Culture* 107, 116–23.

[12] See Raz, *Practical Reason* (n. 4) 185: exclusionary reasons 'are not reasons for not conforming with the reasons. They are reasons for not being motivated in one's action by certain (valid) considerations.'

[13] Joseph Raz, *The Morality of Freedom* (Oxford University Press 1986) 46.

[14] Ibid. 46.

[15] Ibid. 46.

Incidentally, this characterization of PR in terms of second-order exclusionary reasons suggests that we must be careful about terminology: PR is sometimes used as a *principle* (which has a second-order, exclusionary character) and sometimes (usually, when the term 'public reasons' is used in plural) as an appropriate *reason for action*, allowed under a second-order principle of PR. When we ask: 'But do you have any truly public reasons for the proposed law?' we are using the concept of PR in the latter sense, of course, and then it concerns a first-order rule. The difference between these two usages is so obvious that in a given context it will be immediately evident which of these two senses is used, but for the sake of clarity this distinction should be made. Further, it should be announced at the outset that, unless the context clearly dictates otherwise, PR will be used in this book as a principle that has a second-order exclusionary status.

2. Internal and External Reasons

The discussion earlier in the chapter about the nature of reasons that figure in the conception of PR may indicate that there is some resonance between reasons-constraining theory (such as PR) and a well-known debate in philosophy about 'internal' versus 'external' reasons. The debate has been in recent decades spurred by a famous thesis by Bernard Williams, who suggested that basically all reasons for action are 'internal' in the sense that they crucially depend upon a person's own motivational set—upon her desires, projects, and beliefs. For something to be a reason for *A*'s action, *A* must have 'some motive which will be served or furthered by his' action.[16] To talk about purely *external* reasons—reasons which are not related in any way to '*A*'s existing motivations'[17]—the statement of which 'can be true independently of the agent's motivations'[18]—is, for Williams, a misnomer and incoherence. The way in which this debate connects with the idea of PR is that in justifying and legitimating authoritative rules, the idea of PR appeals to reasons (ideals, preferences, values etc.) which the individuals to whom the rules will apply already accept, or at least *which are acceptable to them*.

These last italicized words may suggest that the criterion of acceptance by the subject is highly suspicious and the whole appeal to the subject's values, disingenuous. As we will see, this has been one of the main strategies for those refuting the idea of PR. After all, if there is a gap between 'acceptance' and 'acceptability' (and there must be one, otherwise the latter term would be superfluous) then it must be bridged by the values of an external observer, who basically dictates what a subject *should* accept. I will return to this point at some length when discussing

[16] Bernard Williams, 'Internal and External Reasons', in *Moral Luck* (Cambridge University Press 1981) 101, 101.
[17] Ibid. 112.
[18] Ibid. 107.

the idea of reasonableness employed in the context of PR (Chapter 3, section 2), but for the time being it is sufficient to connect this point with Williams's 'internal reasons' thesis. The argument just referred to (that 'acceptability' has a suspicious link with the subject's actual acceptance) may be translated into the language of 'external reasons' in the following way: by attributing allegedly 'acceptable' reasons to a subject, the theory in fact collapses into 'external reasons' which, according to Williams, is an incoherent idea. We may say that an agent who lacks certain motivations 'is inconsiderate, or cruel, or selfish, or imprudent; or that things, and he, would be a lot nicer if he were so motivated',[19] but we cannot say that he has 'reasons' to do so.

But this is not the whole story. Two additional important points, made by Williams right after identifying 'internal reasons' as the only game in town when it comes to reasons, render the 'internal reasons' thesis less relativistic and subjectivist than it appears at the first sight. First, an agent's 'motivational set' must be understood broadly rather than narrowly; in addition to various first-order desires (often, but not necessarily, of egoistic character) we must include 'such things as dispositions of evaluation, patterns of emotional reaction, personal loyalties, and various projects ... embodying commitments of the agent'.[20] Adding these second-order preferences (although Williams does not use this term) significantly expands the set of reasons which we may legitimately ascribe to an actor, even if (as I have discussed at length elsewhere)[21] it also significantly broadens the scope for indeterminacy, malleability, and uncertainty in ascribing such preferences as the person's actual preferences. Second, Williams emphasizes that an agent's 'motivational set' need not be viewed as static: 'what we can correctly ascribe [to the agent] in a third-personal internal reason statement is also what he can ascribe to himself *as a result of deliberation* . . .'.[22] Further on, Williams added: 'As a result of such processes [of deliberation] an agent can come to see that he has reason to do something which he did not see he had reason to do at all. In this way, the deliberative process can add new actions for which there are internal reasons, just as it can also add new internal reasons for given actions.'[23] The condition is, as Williams frames it in a newer statement of the theory, that there must be 'a sound deliberative route from the motivations [the agent] already has'.[24] This seems to compound the problem of indeterminacy: the question of a 'sound deliberative route' does not allow for definite and determinate outcomes, but for Williams himself it was not a problem. Precisely to the contrary, it showed that the theory was faithful to the reality of moral problems: 'It is

[19] Ibid. 110.
[20] Ibid. 105.
[21] See Wojciech Sadurski, *Moral Pluralism and Legal Neutrality* (Kluwer 1990)111–19.
[22] Williams, 'Internal and External Reasons' (n. 16) at 103, emphasis added.
[23] Ibid. 104.
[24] Bernard Williams, 'Internal Reasons and the Obscurity of Blame' in *Making Sense of Humanity* (Cambridge University Press 1995) 35, 35.

sometimes held against the combination of the internalist view with this broad conception of deliberation that it leaves us with a vague concept of what an agent has a reason to do. But this is not a disadvantage of the position. It *is* often vague what one has a reason to do.'[25]

These two points identify the strategies available to advocates of the conception of PR to narrow the gap between 'actual acceptance' and acceptability. The first point indicates that, when inquiring about what values (ideals, preferences, reasons) people accept, it is not just a matter of ascertaining the explicitly declared first-order reasons for action, but also of looking into preferences about preferences, general inclinations, aspirations, ideals, etc., which may stand in an uneasy relationship to the first-order preferences but which may be equally, or more, symptomatic of an agent's *true* reasons. Consider a simple instance of second-order preferences: 'an alcoholic presumably has a strong first-order preference for drinking but may have a clear second-order preference for breaking his habit'[26]—which of these preferences comes closer to the real 'reason for action' of that person? At the very least, one may say that those reasons are not exhausted by first-order consumption preferences. Pre-commitments belong to a similar category as second-order preferences; in fact, they *are* second-order commitments, and the differences between them and other second-order preferences is that there is a clear temporal sequence between prior, second-order preferences, and posterior, first-order ones, so if we take a time-slice view and register a person's preferences (reasons for action) at a given point, the pre-commitments may be invisible. '[P]ersonal loyalties, and various projects . . . embodying commitments of the agent of an agent' (the terms used by Williams)[27] also significantly but very plausibly expand the range of a motivational set. This category captures, inter alia, what Robert Goodin has called 'reciprocal forbearances': they occur when each agrees to forgo his or her opportunities for gain at the other's expense, on condition that everyone else forgoes such opportunities.[28] Such mutual self-restraint may be less visible than an explicitly declared first-order value but surely should, under a plausible theory of rational action, displace the latter, because it has been undertaken by an agent precisely in anticipation of a subsequent occurrence of a first-order desire that the agent wants to override. There may be also reasons not explicitly espoused but only detectable through a person's conduct: those implicit preferences, discernible in human action rather than in declarations, may be closer to the 'true' moral position of an individual. A person may be strategic, or simply insincere, in his or her announcements; acts usually speak louder than words. To be sure, all these ingredients of a 'motivational set' are less determinate

[25] Ibid. 38, emphasis in original.

[26] John C. Harsanyi, 'On Preferences, Promises, and the Coordination Problem: Reply to Regan', (1985) 96 *Ethics* 68, 69.

[27] Williams, 'Internal and External Reasons' (n. 16) 105.

[28] Robert E. Goodin, 'Laundering Preferences' in Jon Elster and Aanund Hylland (eds.) *Foundations of Social Choice Theory* (Cambridge University Press 1986) 75, 82.

than the expressly declared first-order preferences but, as we have just seen, this need not be seen as a drawback of the concept.

Williams's second point suggests that the 'sound deliberative route' from values *X-1* to *X-2* may be quite long, and yet it is a route which must be travelled (by an agent), and monitored (by an observer), in order to see that the reasons 'acceptable' to a person are not too far removed from those that are actually accepted. In the process, some reasons will be added to the set *X-1* (e.g. like Monsieur Jourdain finding out about his prose, many agents may figure out that they really are secularists if they subject their actual values to the exercise of generalization, and then attempt to establish uniformity through the different ingredients of their overall moral position), and some will be discarded. An example provided by Bernard Williams is about this latter case, when we discard certain initial reasons for action after discovering an error of fact: a person thinks that she wants to drink a glass of (what he believes to be) gin but there is in fact petrol in the glass; she really does not want to drink it; what she wants is gin and not whatever-is-in-this-glass.[29] Correcting for errors of fact is rather uncontroversial: where a reason crucially depends upon the statements of facts, and this statement is clearly false (consider John Stuart Mill's example of a person who is ignorant of the fact that the bridge upon which she is about to step is unsafe),[30] then the reason is fatally tainted with invalidity. Another way of conceptualizing Williams's gin and Mill's bridge example is to distinguish, *pace* Donald Regan, between 'ultimate' and 'instrumental' preferences: Regan's example is of Jones who is willing to go to Chicago (an instrumental preference) in order to see his friend Brown (the ultimate preference).[31] If Brown is in fact in Los Angeles, then (assuming that Jones was sincere in declaring the reason for his intended trip) there is no moral problem in disregarding his instrumental preference of going to Chicago: it is the ultimate preference which corresponds with his *real* reason for action.

But the test of error is just one case among many ways of discarding wrongful reasons without being disingenuous; errors of reasoning are another. As Williams says, the 'claim that somebody can get to the conclusion' that he or she should do something 'by a sound deliberative route involves, in my view, *at least* correcting errors of fact and reasoning involved in the agent's view of the matter'.[32] Correcting errors of *reasoning* is a huge category. In a classical essay on legal moralism, Ronald Dworkin had identified a long catalogue of errors of reasoning which allow us to launder someone's views in order to reconstruct her moral position in a respectable sense of the word: those views need to be

[29] Williams, 'Internal and External Reasons' (n. 16) 102, Williams, 'Internal Reasons and the Obscurity of Blame' (n. 24) 36.

[30] John Stuart Mill, 'On Liberty' (1859) in John Stuart Mill, *On Liberty and Other Writings*, ed. Stefan Collini (Cambridge University Press 1989)96.

[31] Donald Regan, 'On Preferences and Promises: A Response to Harsanyi', (1985) 96 *Ethics* 56, 57.

[32] Williams, 'Internal Reasons and the Obscurity of Blame' (n. 24) 36, emphasis added.

controlled for absence of stereotyping (understood as unwarranted generalizations), parroting (i.e. merely referring to the reasons espoused by others) for consistency with the other views held by that person etc.[33]

There are limits to all this, of course, even if Williams spoke about 'at least' correcting errors of fact and reasoning (suggesting thereby that there may be more). Consequently, there are limits to PR's reasons for closing the gap between actual acceptance and acceptability. Just as, when crossing a certain line, 'internal reasons' subjected to too much laundering become indistinguishable from the dreaded (by Williams) 'external reasons'—that is, impositions of the moral views held by an external observer upon an agent, with no due regard for the latter's actual motivational set—so must PR not cross that line if it is not to become disingenuous in attributing certain views to a person. There will be some persons who will be found to be beyond the specific PR: there will be no 'motivational set' of theirs which may act as an anchor, as a starting point for a sound deliberative route leading to the values which may properly figure as the basis of that PR. To say that they really *have* these values because all reasonable people *should have* these values is disingenuous: a non sequitur expressed by such an inference symbolizes a disregard for people as they are. They are more (and less) than what they explicitly espouse as their first-order preferences right now; their motivational set is a much more complex aggregate than that. They are also more dynamic and capable of embarking upon a sound deliberative route, during which they will acquire some and discard other reasons for action. But they are not *anything* that an external observer—including an observer equipped with a PR filter of reasons for action—may want them to be. In this way, a theory of PR can learn a lot from Williams's 'internalist' theory of reasons: PR must engage with some of the actual values of the people over whom legitimacy of coercive political action is claimed.

3. Input Model of Democracy

In his essay on 'revisiting' the idea of public reason, Rawls explained that 'the idea of public reason is not a view about specific political institutions or policies' but, rather, 'it is a view about the kind of reasons on which citizens are to rest their political cases in making their political justifications to one another when they support laws and policies that invoke the coercive powers of government concerning fundamental political questions'.[34] This is a good characterization of the function of the concept. It is about 'the *kind* of reasons' provided for institutions and policies (rather than about the institutions and policies themselves). It is also about a category or a class of reasons, rather than a specification of the

[33] Ronald Dworkin, *Taking Rights Seriously* (Duckworth 1978)248–53.

[34] Rawls, 'The Idea of Public Reason Revisited', (n. 2) 165–66.

legitimate reasons themselves. One useful way of looking at PR is to view it as a specific self-discipline that the citizens of a liberal-democratic polity should exercise that compels them to screen off many of the motives and reasons they may otherwise be tempted to act upon.[35]

This focus on the nature of reasons provided for legislative and policy proposals resonates with what has been described as the 'input model of democracy': a model concerned less with 'who gets what, when, how',[36] but rather with the nature of arguments and claims pressed by different parties before the decision (typically, through a vote) is taken.[37] In his book on 'reflective democracy', Robert Goodin makes a strong plea for the input model of democracy by saying that:

> there must be more to a legitimate political process than can be captured in any mechanical aggregation process. What we should be doing in the political process is evaluating the competing claims of various parties on their merits. That must be a genuinely reflective process: internally contemplative in the first instance, interpersonally discursive in the second.[38]

He emphasizes that 'we need to be sensitive to inputs and the reasons people give for how they vote, if we are to address value-laden components of democratic discourse',[39] and that, while input democracy does not reject the final vote as an ultimate method of democratic decision-making, '[i]nput-democrats attach much more importance to what precedes the vote'.[40]

An inquiry into the nature of claims pressed by different parties is only one of a number of tests and requirements related to input democracy (others concern the question of expanding the franchise, creating conditions that equalize the weight of inputs of all people, improving the process of agenda-setting and interpersonal democratic deliberation that occurs before the vote)—but for our purposes it is the only aspect of direct relevance to the idea of PR. Goodin calls this aspect 'democratic deliberation within'—an extrapolation of deliberative democracy into the internally contemplative dimension; his suggestion is to 'ease the burdens of deliberative democracy in mass society by altering our focus from the "external-collective" to the "internal-reflective" mode, shifting much of the work of democratic deliberation back inside the head of each individual'.[41]

35 See Charles Larmore, *The Autonomy of Morality* (Cambridge University Press 2008) 213.

36 As in a classical formula by Harold Lasswell, *Politics: Who Gets What, When, How?* (P. Smith 1950).

37 Note that this distinction should not be confused with a distinction between input- and output-*legitimacy* of democratic systems, see, e.g., Fritz W. Scharpf, *Governing in Europe: Effective and Democratic?* (Oxford University Press 1999), chapter 1.

38 Robert E. Goodin, *Reflective Democracy* (Oxford University Press 2003) 152, footnote omitted.

39 Ibid. 148.

40 Ibid. 155.

41 Ibid. 170–71.

The emphasis on inputs—on the nature of the arguments and claims pressed in public discourse—may have its dangers, even if Goodin announces, wisely, that '[i]nternal-reflective deliberations are not a substitute for, but rather an input into, external collective decision procedures'.[42] We may be tempted to apply too rigorous conditions for the quality of inputs as a result of which we will disallow or 'launder' some inputs on the basis of their inadequately informed, unreasonable, or incoherent character. The analogy here is with an idea of 'laundering preferences' in the context of a discussion on paternalism:[43] the more we 'launder' them, the less they resemble the actual preferences that real people espouse, and the less credible is our assurance about being non-paternalistic in our approaches. Similarly, in the case of democracy, the more the 'inputs' are 'laundered', the more disingenuous our assurance about democratic legitimacy based on respect for individual inputs becomes. But being aware of this danger need not lead us to dismiss the very idea of focusing on the inputs—it should only protect us against abusing it for clearly non-democratic or paternalistic purposes.[44]

A useful way of thinking about the idea of PR as an input-based conception is to compare it to an idea, popular in the 1970s and 1980s, of state neutrality towards competing conceptions of the good as encapsulating the liberal theory of state legitimacy.[45] (The link between these two ideas was recently noted by Mattias Kumm, in his 2020 essay.[46]) It should be emphasized that I am not making the claim that PR is equivalent to the liberal ideal of neutrality—after all, there may be an approach to neutrality which requires the state to even-handedly accommodate various substantive conceptions of the good, each of which is non-endorsable to adherents of other conceptions, thus upsetting the ideal of PR. Rather, these two conceptions resonate with each other in the sense that they both attempt to capture an ideal liberal state in a simple formula.[47] When making arguments about the substance of liberal neutrality, a distinction is often made between neutrality with regards to the *effects* of a policy (a policy is neutral if, under one possible criterion, it equally contributes to the success of adherents to different conceptions of the good, or even, under a different formula, to the likelihood that different conceptions will be chosen in the society) and neutrality with regard to the *intentions* of a policymaker (under the broadest articulation,

[42] Ibid. 192.

[43] See Goodin, 'Laundering Preferences' (n. 28) 75.

[44] For a more canonical expression of the emphasis on reasons giving in deliberative democracy, see Joshua Cohen, 'Deliberation and Democratic Legitimacy' in David Estlund (ed.), *Democracy* (Blackwell 2002) 87.

[45] For my book-length discussion of this idea, see Sadurski, *Moral Pluralism* (n. 21)

[46] Mattias Kumm, '"We Hold These Truths to be Self-Evident": Constitutionalism, Public Reason, and Legitimate Authority' in Silje Langvatn, Mattias Kumm, and Wojciech Sadurski (eds.), *Public Reason and Courts* (Cambridge University Press 2020) 143, 151–52.

[47] The strong connection between the liberal ideal of 'impartiality' (a word used in a similar fashion to neutrality) and the ideal of 'public justification' (of which the ideal of PR is a part) is an important underlying feature of a classical article by Thomas Nagel, 'Moral Conflict and Political Legitimacy', (1987) 16 *Philosophy & Public Affairs* 215.

which I will make more complex in a moment, a policy is neutral if it is triggered by intentions which do not assume that one conception is superior to the alternative ones). The former branch of neutrality has been dubbed as output-oriented; the latter—about inputs.[48] For the time being, it is sufficient to say that a conventional (and convincing) way of thinking about these two types of neutrality is that neutrality of effects is impossible and undesirable.[49] *Mutatis mutandis*, PR is a conception about 'inputs', except insofar as the 'outputs' may serve as a reliable indicator of inputs often less easily discernible than outputs—a point which we will elaborate on, at some length, in the discussion of constitutional law's treatment of 'motive' and 'effects' (Chapter 5).

But the recent literature on liberal neutrality also further distinguishes (in a way helpful to theorizing about PR) between two types of input theory: intentions may be viewed through the prism of the *aims* of a policy or its *justification* (procedure).[50] To look at it from a negative angle, a policy may be non-neutral either because it aims at privileging a particular conception of the good over another or because in its justification it relies upon the superiority of a particular conception of the good over others. So we may have conceptions which are aim-neutral but not neutral in their justification (an example provided by Richard Arneson is about religious tolerance for all faiths because this is a principle of the only true religion, e.g. Quakerism) or, vice versa, non-neutral with regard to the aims but neutral with regard to justification (establishment of a dominant religion justified by an argument that it will strengthen civil peace).[51] If we now apply this distinction to the ideal of PR, it seems clear that, strictly speaking, it is about justification rather than about the sorts of aims which are admissible in the argument in favour of a particular law.

Having said that, however, I wish to observe that the distinction between 'justification' and the 'aim' of a law is highly contrived, and justifications for laws will usually refer to the *aims* to be promoted by the laws. True, one may think of admissible aims being argued on the basis of *in*admissible justifications, but one would hope that these are fairly non-typical cases. The very fact that Arneson (and also Alan Patten, who restates Arneson's argument) had to choose a highly non-typical case of a religion-based argument for religious tolerance to illustrate the combination of a neutral aim with non-neutral justification suggests that more often than not the two will be aligned with each other. And when there is a misalignment, it may be due to the fact that the 'aim' is seen through the prism of the law's *effects* rather than intentions, and that what we identify as a

[48] Alan Patten, 'Liberal Neutrality: A Reinterpretation and Defense', (2012) 20 *Journal of Political Philosophy* 249, 257.

[49] See, e.g., Jonathan Quong, *Liberalism without Perfection* (Oxford University Press 2011) 18; Samuel Freeman, 'Democracy, Religion & Public Reason', (2020) 149(3) *Daedalus* 37, 51–52

[50] Richard J Arneson, 'Neutrality and Utility', (1990) 20 *Canadian Journal of Philosophy* 215, 218–19; Patten, 'Liberal Neutrality' (n. 48) 255.

[51] Arneson, 'Neutrality and Utility' (n. 50) 218–19.

mismatch is between the aims and the effects (likely or actual) of the law. In the sequence of concepts—(1) justification, (2) aim, (3) effect—a mismatch between (2) and (3) is a more real and frequent possibility than a misalignment between (1) and (2).

This also anticipates the point underlying much of the discussion in Parts 2 and 3 of this book: that 'justification' (or motive, intention etc.) and 'purpose' (or the aim, purpose, objective, etc.) in constitutional law are coeval categories for the practical purpose of identifying whether a law meets the requirements of public reason. While, strictly speaking, the 'purpose' of an action may not be identical with the intention of an actor, nevertheless in the case of law such a distinction is really without difference. We attribute to lawmakers purposes either on the basis of their declared intentions about the aims they wish to attain, or on the basis of an 'objectified intention', as perceived in the most likely justification that can be supplied for a law having particular features and scope. There is a difference between these two approaches: the former attempts to actually identify the real intentions of legislators; the latter—the purposes most likely triggering a particular law enacted by a rational lawmaker. But it is a distinction between two ways of characterizing justifications for a law (actual versus 'objectified') and *not* a distinction between the intentions of the lawmaker and the aims of the law. (More on this, in Chapter 4, section 2).

4. The Scope of Public Reason

In a canonical formulation of PR by John Rawls, it is meant to apply to basic justice and constitutional essentials only. '[T]he limits imposed by public reason do not apply to all political questions but only to those involving what we may call "constitutional essentials" and questions of basic justice', says Rawls.[52] But this restrictive proviso, as a potential defence against some critics (for it allows for the rebuttal that what they argue about are specific authoritative decisions rather than constitutional essentials) seems unattractive. In fact, it is rather similar to the limitation on the scope of Rawls's theory of justice, which was meant to apply only to basic structure rather than to specific distributions. Right at the outset of *A Theory of Justice*, Rawls declared that '[t]he basic structure is the primary subject of justice because its effects are so profound and present from the start',[53] and he defined basic justice as 'the way in which the major social institutions distribute fundamental rights and duties and determine the division of advantages from social cooperation'.[54]

[52] John Rawls, *Political Liberalism* (Columbia University Press 1993) 214.
[53] John Rawls, *A Theory of Justice* (Oxford University Press 1971) 7.
[54] Ibid. 7.

Let us pursue this analogy. The confinement of the subject of justice to 'basic structure' served two markedly different purposes in the structure of Rawls's theory of justice: first, to emphasize that it was not a general theory of societal distribution applicable to any social sphere where a just distribution is called for, and hence, that it should not be applied to non-political realms of distribution or associations, such as churches or universities;[55] second, to warn that the two principles of justice as fairness should not serve as a test of any particular distributional result ('that the actual distribution conform at any given time ... to any observable pattern'),[56] but only to assess the basic structure which controls these distributions. It is this latter aspect of the confinement of the theory of justice to 'basic structure' which is of interest to us, as an analogy to the restriction on the scope of PR. In *A Theory of Justice*, Rawls had built, so to speak, a preventive defence into his theory against a charge of counter-intuitive outcomes by warning that: 'It is a mistake to focus attention on the varying relative positions of individuals and to require that every change, considered as a single transaction viewed in isolation, be in itself just. It is the arrangement of the basic structure which is to be judged, and judged from a general point of view.'[57] This restriction on the scope of principles of justice was subsequently emphasized by commentators who pinpointed that 'Rawls's principles apply to particular distributions only indirectly'[58] and that '[a] distribution cannot be judged in isolation from the system of which it is the outcome'.[59] Accordingly, they could dismiss those critics of Rawls who claimed that the two principles of justice may result in counter-intuitive or even perverse results: the critics, Rawls's defenders could say, mistakenly try to apply his theory of justice to specific distributional acts, contrary to Rawls's caveat about basic structure.

Not surprisingly, though, much of the debate about *A Theory of Justice* centred on specific distributions as much as around 'basic structure'; and moreover, the very distinction seemed untenable and unpersuasive. G.A. Cohen argued that the distinction is untenable if we only consider the 'basic structure' to be constituted not merely by legally coercive rules (which would render the scope of the theory of justice too narrow), but also by usage, customs and conventions. In the latter case, the choices that people make within a structure are constitutive of the basic structure itself, as the examples of family or market indicate: 'it is ... impossible to claim that the principles of justice which apply to family structure do not apply to day-to-day choices within it.'[60] Here is a good articulation of a

[55] Rawls, *Political Liberalism* (n. 52) 261.

[56] Ibid. 283.

[57] Rawls, *A Theory of Justice* (n. 53) 87–88.

[58] T.M. Scanlon, 'Rawls's Theory of Justice' in Norman Daniels (ed.), *Reading Rawls: Critical Studies of a Theory of Justice* (Basil Blackwell 1975) 169, 191.

[59] Chandran Kukathas and Philip Pettit, *Rawls: A Theory of Justice and its Critics* (Polity Press 1990) 67.

[60] G.A. Cohen, 'Where the Action Is: On the Site of Distributive Justice', (1997) 26 *Philosophy & Public Affairs* 3, 20.

dilemma regarding the range of theory of justice, as stated by Cohen, and worth quoting in full:

> [Rawls] must either admit application of the principles of justice to (legally optional) social practices, and, indeed, to patterns of personal choice that are not legally prescribed, *both* because they are the substance of those practices, *and* because they are similarly profound in effect, in which case the restriction of justice to [basic] structure, in any sense, collapses; or, if he restricts his concern to the coercive structure only, then he saddles himself with a purely arbitrary delineation of his subject matter.[61]

So it is not just that the borderline between basic structure and individual distribution choices is fuzzy; even if it were sharp, it would be untenable as a criterion for delimiting the range for the application of principles of justice. And one may wonder if, at times, Rawls himself has not ignored his own self-imposed limitation. When, for instance, he claimed that the difference principle gives effect to the principle of 'fraternity', the principle which asserts that we should not want 'to have greater advantages unless this is to the benefit of others who are less well off',[62] just like in a family its members 'commonly do not wish to gain unless they can do so in ways that further the interests of the rest',[63] it is clear that this is a requirement concerning individual motivations, occasioned by individual choices, rather than an element of basic structure, and so cannot be understood within the purely 'structural' approach. Similar observations may be, *mutatis mutandis*, extrapolated upon the limitation of the range of the application of the principle of PR. Rather than a sharp distinction, there is continuity between the essentials and specific decisions.

The burden of argument for confining the scope of PR to constitutional essentials and basic justice seems to fall on those who defend such a limitation; the question by Jonathan Quong: 'Why are all instances where citizens exercise political power over one another not subject to the idea of public reason?'[64] rings presumptively true. A proposal contained in the very title of a recent article by Spanish scholar Rubén Marciel Pariente 'Why not Extend Rawls' Public Reason Beyond Fundamental Issues?' sounds eminently plausible.[65] Rawls himself was vague about the criteria and reasons for the confinement of the scope of PR, saying that '[a] full account of public reason would take up' the question

[61] Ibid. 21–22.
[62] Rawls, *A Theory of Justice* (n. 53) 105.
[63] Ibid.
[64] Quong, *Liberalism without Perfection* (n. 49) 274. See, similarly, Thompson, 'Public Reason' (n. 9) 2085–86 (arguing for an extension of the reach of PR beyond 'basic justice' as understood by Rawls).
[65] Rubén Marciel Pariente 'Why not Extend Rawls' Public Reason Beyond Fundamental Issues?', (2020) 39 *Teorema* 105.

of how constitutional essentials differ from other political issues, 'and why the restrictions imposed by public reason may not apply to them; or if they do, not in the same way, or so strictly'.[66] Some Rawlsians undertook to provide such an account. T.M. Scanlon provided two arguments for restricting the use of PR to constitutional essentials and basic justice only, but neither is convincing. First: constitutional essentials require special justification because on these matters citizens have a lower practical influence than on matters which are subject to regular legislation.[67] But if citizens, in practice, have a greater chance of affecting public decisions on non-basic matters, then it would weigh in favour of a *higher* rather than lower urgency of equipping them with some criteria as to which reasons for (advocating) collective action are proper and which are not. If citizens are hardly ever able to participate in constitutional decision-making, the practical role of the idea of PR with respect to these matters is low. If, as Scanlon attests, 'in a just political order ... [citizens] do have a fair opportunity to make their opinions heard and affect the outcome through speaking and voting and through their representatives',[68] then it is imperative that they exercise this considerable power responsibly, with proper concern for their compatriots who will carry the burden of collective decisions taken through such means.

Second, Scanlon points out the 'feasibility' issue: on various matters of collective decisions which call for taxpayers' money, it is very hard to expect citizens to make their arguments (e.g. about the construction of a highway) in ways that do not reflect their 'competing reasons which ... reflect their comprehensive views'.[69] It may well be that on such distributive issues, where the only aspect of using coercion presents itself in a very thin and indirect way, through the power of taxation, all that matters for public decisions is that the decision corresponds to the distribution of preferences within the community. But still, *some* motives for decision will be excluded: imagine a person arguing that a new highway is necessary in order to serve only one, privileged ethnic group within the state, and that the poor or the unpopular groups do not need highways in their area. This would be a clear violation of the imperative of PR but would not apply to basic justice or constitutional essentials, and so flies under the radar of a theory of legitimacy based on PR restricted to basic structure and constitutional essentials. In defence of Rawls's conception, Scanlon explicitly connects the 'feasibility' reason for a restricted scope of PR with that of completeness of a political conception, and argues that if we expand the scope of PR, the resulting conception will be necessarily incomplete because it will fail to 'provide the basis for answering all questions that arise in the course of legislation'.[70] But as we shall see

[66] Rawls, *Political Liberalism* (n. 52) 214–15.

[67] T.M. Scanlon, 'Rawls on Justification' in Samuel Freeman (ed.), *The Cambridge Companion to Rawls* (Cambridge University Press 2003) 139, 163.

[68] Ibid.

[69] Ibid.

[70] Ibid.

later in this book (in Chapter 3, section 2), completeness does not require consensus on the balance of public reasons but only that nothing but *public* reasons are subject to weighing and balancing.

In addition, *what* constitutes part of the category of 'constitutional essentials' is eminently question-begging. Is it a matter of importance, or generality, or abstractness, of a particular rule or directive? Or should we perhaps follow some canonical constitutional texts in deciding what 'essentials' are truly 'constitutional'? For instance, one of the most resolutely self-avowed Rawlsians, Samuel Freeman, takes it as obvious that 'the abortion issue' is a 'constitutional dispute',[71] echoing Rawls himself who had used this issue as an instance to which PR may be applied.[72] Significantly, Rawls bracketed this characterization with the caveat: '*assuming* that this question is either a constitutional essential or a matter of basic justice . . .',[73] though he never attempted to justify this assumption. But why should it be so? Most constitutional documents do not resolve the matter in any determinate fashion. Is it because the Supreme Court of the United States defined access to abortion, under some conditions, as a matter of a constitutional (though implied) right to privacy? But if this criterion were to be taken seriously, then the category of constitutional essentials' would become counter-intuitively broad because a great number of very specific issues have been determined by the Supreme Court from time to time as falling under constitutional provisions. And why would the case law of one country, even as important as the United States, be a yardstick for what is a constitutional essential under a theory aimed at universality, if in a number of other democracies, the issues which are constitutionalized in the US are a matter for legislative decisions?

The point that I am making is not merely that the category of constitutional essentials is fuzzy at its borders but rather that we have no principled criteria at all to distinguish the essentials from non-essentials, and even if we had, there would be no good reason to reserve the requirement of PR to the former. If people are entitled to demand and receive public justification of a law which applies to them coercively, and if the availability of such public justification is a condition of the legitimacy of such coercive laws, then the distinction between basic justice/constitutional essentials on the one hand and statutory-based coercion on the other is arbitrary.[74] No wonder that for some commentators this is a matter of expediency rather than principle: according to one critic, 'Rawls's reason for limiting the scope of the public justification constraint seems to be that doing so gives the case for public justification its best chance of success, not because there is some

[71] Samuel Freeman, 'Public Reason and Political Justifications', (2004) 72 *Fordham Law Review* 2021, 2054.

[72] Rawls, *Political Liberalism* (n. 52) 243 n. 32.

[73] Ibid. 244 n. 32, emphasis added.

[74] See Lawrence B. Solum, 'Constructing an Ideal of Public Reason', (1993) 30 *San Diego Law Review* 729, 738.

deep or principled distinction between coercive laws and laws that bear on constitutional matters'.[75]

There *is* perhaps a method of rescuing Rawls's restriction of the scope of PR in a way which respects the principle that all acts of coercion by the state must be justified in a proper way. This is what Gerald Gaus calls a 'Radical Derivative Justification thesis' (which, it should be emphasized, Gaus discusses but does not endorse). Under this thesis, when a constitution is properly (i.e. by an appeal to PR) justified, and it regulates 'when and how all political power is to be exercised', all (non-constitutional) exercises of the power which are consistent with the constitution 'are themselves publicly justified'.[76] To paraphrase: the constitution prefigures, so to speak, all the acts done in accordance with it, and the constitution's legitimacy based on PR confers a similar legitimacy upon all the legislative (and other) acts. But it is sufficient to articulate this thesis to see what is wrong with it. An image of full substantive continuity between a constitution and all sub-constitutional acts is a fiction. While sub-constitutional acts (assuming that they are not unconstitutional) are indeed based on a constitution, this relationship does not necessarily take the form of simply making a general provision of the constitution more specific. By using very general, vague language, constitution-makers deliberately delegate to the lawmakers an authority to make decisions as they see fit: they are constrained, for sure, but the constraint is not expressly embedded in the text of the constitution in a way which would give support to the Radical Derivative Justification thesis.

Further, constitution-makers often use deliberate techniques to leave a broad sphere of legislative discretion to lawmakers. They often 'decide not to decide', not as a matter of a regrettable omission but rather as a conscious act of delegating certain constitutional questions to future lawmakers.[77] One such technique is for the constitution to announce that a certain matter will be determined 'by law', thus deferring a decision to future legislators (either authorizing or requiring a future legislature to decide about an issue). As Rosalind Dixon and Tom Ginsburg show, such a technique, quite widespread in contemporary constitutionalism, may have the advantage of reducing decision costs (at the stage of constitution-making) or even making the adoption of a constitution possible in the first place (when there is great deal of controversy on a particular issue between the parties engaged in constitution drafting), while at the same time identifying clearly who will be in charge of future decision-making on the matter (legislatures rather than courts).[78] But whatever technique is selected for

[75] Christopher J. Eberle, *Religious Conviction in Liberal Politics* (Cambridge University Press 2013) 352 n. 23.

[76] Gerald Gaus, *The Order of Public Reason* (Cambridge University Press 2011) 491, reference omitted.

[77] See Rosalind Dixon and Tom Ginsburg, 'Deciding Not to Decide: Deferral in Constitutional Design', (2011) 9 *International Journal of Constitutional Law* 636.

[78] Ibid. 655.

avoiding specific resolution of a matter in the constitutional text, whether it is by deliberate vagueness or by inserting the 'by law' clauses, in neither case can it be claimed that the substantive legitimacy (for instance, in terms of PR) of a law is in any way prefigured by the substantial legitimacy of a constitution on which the law is 'based'.

Rawls makes it clear that on non-essentials, political bodies are free to enforce their comprehensive doctrines: 'Citizens and legislators may properly vote their more comprehensive views when constitutional essentials and basic justice are not at stake; they need not justify by public reason why they vote as they do . . .'[79] But this is puzzling. Suppose the legislature votes on compulsory health insurance, and for the sake of argument, suppose that it does not implicate questions of constitutional essentials or basic justice. (If this assumption is implausible, think of another example of a coercive law without implications for basic justice and constitutional essentials, and if we cannot think of any non-trivial law *without* such implications, then it simply confirms that limiting PR to constitutional essentials and basic structure is meaningless because everything that is coercive and non-trivial has such implications, which is precisely the point I am making.) Shall we be happy to have legislators vote on the basis of their PR-*in*compatible comprehensive doctrines (for instance, refusing insurance to medical procedures which are condemned by their religion)? But *if* we can think of non-trivial coercive laws which have no constitutional (and basic justice) implications, then the moral-political importance of appealing directly to PR seems to be *higher* and not lower than in the case of laws with constitutional implications because, in the case of the latter laws, an appeal to the constitution indirectly does the job of ensuring compatibility with PR (on the assumption, which is necessary to adopt in a well-ordered constitutional state, that the constitution properly gives effect to PR, for instance in its bill of rights clauses). A constitution is, so to speak, a handmaiden of PR. But on non-constitutional issues, no such constitutional underwriting is available *ex hypothesi*, so the use of state coercion towards an individual should be supported by arguments from PR.

So far I have only been concerned with the subject-matter scope of PR, and now I will move to the agent-relative scope: to a question about *to whom* the PR imperative applies. When discussing the bearers of PR-related constitutional obligations, I will assume that they fall upon all actors involved in lawmaking: legislators and judges alike (as well as citizens-voters) must live up to the demands of PR. I will adopt a deliberately indiscriminate approach, assuming that PR (which may be seen as a quasi-constitutional principle), if normatively plausible, binds all actors of lawmaking in the same way. But of course it is an obvious simplification, and we know that different actors are differently affected *by other constraints* in their choices when engaged in lawmaking: the constraints are most stringent

[79] Rawls, *Political Liberalism* (n. 52) 235.

and canonical in the case of judges, more lenient in the case of legislatures, and even more lax in the case of citizens-voters. Judges are so constrained by a duty to provide reasons in terms of legitimate legal sources which should guide their decisions (their understanding of the text of a constitution, of the statute, the force of precedent, etc.) that it may seem that no room is left for contemplating the force of other constraints, such as PR: considerations of established sources of law *seem* to deplete any room for such moral-political constraints as that of PR.[80] I disagree with this view when it is stated in such a strong way, though a weaker articulation (that judges are less free to resort to PR than are legislators) is eminently plausible: judges must consider how established legal sources control a given matter, and only then fill the remaining space with considerations of PR (and other moral-political reason-restraining principles, if applicable). Viewed in this way, Rawls clearly has it wrong when he makes a sweeping statement that 'public reason is the sole reason the court exercises'.[81] And when he adds that '[b]eyond [applying public reason, the justices] are to go by what they think the constitutional cases, practices, and traditions, and constitutionally significant historical texts require',[82] he has it the other way round: PR is exercised in the spaces which are left undetermined by arguments from the text, precedent etc.

These remaining spaces need not be very slim, though.[83] When, for instance (and taking a deliberately extreme example) a constitutional court (a) considers the matter of constitutionality of a challenged statute *in abstracto*; (b) there is no, or very little, case law on this matter, or an established doctrine rejects the principle of *stare decisis* as applying to constitutional courts; (c) the constitution is relatively recent so there has been no, or very little, time to accumulate a constitutional custom of a binding interpretation of a given constitutional provision; and (d) a constitutional provision that controls a given matter is broad, vague, and open-ended, and it appeals to fundamental moral principles on which reasonable people may disagree—the force of constraints from established sources of law is relatively low, and the impact of *other* constraints (such as PR) upon judges is similar to its impact upon lawmakers (or even citizens-voters). Of course, an alteration in any of these four conditions may increase the distance between the role of judges and of legislators, and narrow the space for consideration of constraints other than those informed by established sources of law. But insofar as there is *some* space for such considerations (and it would take a wildly implausible theory of constitutional interpretation to claim that there is never

[80] This is the main point made by Waldron, 'Public Reason and "Justification"' (n. 11) especially at 127–30.

[81] Rawls, *Political Liberalism* (n. 52) 235.

[82] Ibid. 235–36.

[83] For a recent argument to the contrary, see Christopher F. Zurn, 'Constitutional Interpretation and Public Reason: Seductive Disanalogies', in Silje Langvatn, Mattias Kumm, and Wojciech Sadurski (eds.), *Public Reason and Courts* (Cambridge University Press 2020) 323. I believe that the four conditions listed in the present paragraph constitute a concise response to Zurn's argument.

such space, or that usually such space is minimal), my arguments below apply to judges, lawmakers, and citizens-voters indiscriminately, without considering the impact of institutional differences between these functions in the lawmaking process.

And, of course, there is not only a quantitative but also a qualitative difference between constraints acting upon judges and those acting upon legislatures: judges are not only expected to provide reasons in terms of legal sources, but those reasons must also be of a specific sort. This was well expressed in a dictum by Justice Frankfurter in *Lovett*, a case in which the United States Supreme Court struck down a particularly nasty device against 'subversives':

> Nothing would be easier than personal condemnation of the provision of the Urgent Deficiency Appropriation Act of 1943 here challenged ... But the judicial function exacts considerations very different from those which may determine a vote in Congress for or against a measure. And what may be decisive for a Presidential disapproval may not at all satisfy the established criteria which alone justify this Court's striking down an act of Congress.[84]

And he went on: 'It is not for us to find unconstitutionality in what Congress enacted although it may imply notions that are abhorrent to us as individuals or policies we deem harmful to the country's well-being'.[85] This is as good a statement of exceptionality of judicial reasoning as one can find: there are canons and conventions which control what counts as unconstitutional as opposed to 'harmful to the country's well-being', and while these canons and conventions are of course controversial and contested within any constitutional culture, they impose constraints upon judges which are more pressing than the constraints imposed upon legislators and public advocates of legal reform. A more subtle reflection on how the constraints of PR interact with other constraints that affect the roles of different lawmaking actors is something beyond the scope of this book, but I want to make it clear that, in contrast to some other writers commenting on the relationship between PR and constitutional law,[86] my aspiration is not to provide a justification for the exercise of judicial review of the constitutionality of statutes, or (more broadly) to argue about the special position of judges (vis-à-vis legislatures) in discerning and applying PR, but rather to show that the ideal of PR applies to (and is often respected by) judges, though not only and not necessarily primarily by judges. In this, I agree with Christopher Zurn

[84] *United States v. Lovett*, 328 US 303, 318–19 (1946) (Frankfurter J. concurring) (reference and footnote omitted).

[85] Ibid. 319.

[86] See Ronald C. Den Otter, *Judicial Review in an Age of Moral Pluralism* (Cambridge University Press 2009).

(a scholar otherwise much more sceptical of the use of PR by courts than I am) who, summarizing his findings about the (non-)use of PR by the US Supreme Court, observed that the issue of his analysis was not 'simply one about suitability of courts as forums of moral-political principle, but an issue of the comparative performance of various institutions and sites for the reasoned public discourse deliberative democrats hope to make the backbone of political practices'.[87] Even if constitutional and other courts fare worse in this 'comparative performance', both for institutional and doctrinal reasons, they certainly do not disappear from PR's radar.

The unfortunate court-centeredness of the Rawlsian theory of PR was thrown into sharp relief by Rawls's insistence that, as a test, we might inquire as to whether a particular argument for a new law belongs to the category of public reason by considering whether it could be used in a written opinion of the Supreme Court.[88] An idea of the Supreme Court as exemplar of PR, which was received by some authors with a degree of incredulity,[89] in order to maintain its plausibility should be read as referring to an *ideal* model of the court, rather than an account of the US Supreme Court as it actually functions. As Freeman explains, Rawls 'is not saying that the Supreme Court is an exemplar of public reason, but rather that it belongs to the office of a supreme court, as such, to be the exemplar of public reason'.[90] This may be a plausible construction of Rawls's 'exemplar' thesis, but it has the regrettable consequence of locating either an exclusive or predominant mission of being guided by PR in courts, and taking away responsibility for argument in terms of PR from other political institutions and from citizens. It also renders the concept of PR rather parochial, restricting it to those jurisdictions where top courts of appeal or constitutional courts conduct effective judicial review, and in addition where they provide elaborate, discursive reasoning justifying their verdicts. But there are legal systems to which the principle of PR may well be applied and yet which either lack constitutional adjudication or where decisions are accompanied by cursory and mostly formulaic reasons. We may well disconnect the general principle of PR from a US Supreme Court-centred reasoning.

87 Christopher F. Zurn, *Deliberative Democracy and the Institutions of Judicial Review* (Cambridge University Press 2007)219.

88 Rawls, *Political Liberalism* (n. 52) 254.

89 See Waldron, 'Public Reason and "Justification"' (n. 11) 133.

90 Freeman, 'Public Reason' (n. 71) 2066. In a recent reinterpretation of Rawls, Brian Kogelmann adopts an even stronger view about the role of the Supreme Court, describing it as 'the fountain of public reason', entrusted with the role of 'developing a set of considerations citizens may appeal to in order to adjudicate their disputes in the public sphere in a manner consistent with the demands of public reason': Brian Kogelmann, 'The Supreme Court as the Fountain of Public Reason', (2018) 24 *Legal Theory* 345, 355.

5. Public Reason and the Legitimacy of Law

PR plays a special role in the context of the issue of legitimacy of political power. In Rawls's theory, PR is intimately tied up with the 'liberal principle of legitimacy' which postulates that only those laws that are based upon arguments and reasons to which no members of the society have a rational reason to object can boast political legitimacy, and as such can be applied coercively even to those who actually disagree with them. In Rawls's words: 'Our exercise of political power is fully proper only when it is exercised in accordance with the constitution the essentials of which all citizens as free and equal may reasonably be expected to endorse in the light of principles and ideals acceptable to their common human reason'.[91] For a very similar statement, though without explicitly using the term PR and presenting it as a requirement of a good moral argument in deliberative democracy, consider the articulation of the principle by Amy Gutmann and Dennis Thompson:

> Citizens [should] try to offer reasons that other similarly motivated [by the rule of reciprocity] citizens can accept even though they recognize that they share only some of one another's values.... Reciprocity asks us to appeal to reasons that are shared or could come to be shared by our fellow citizens. [This form of moral reasoning] enables us ... mutually to respect one another as moral agents who share the goal of reaching deliberative agreement even when we disagree with one another's conclusions.[92]

This, while formulated in positive terms, is in fact based on a simple *negative* point: a law cannot claim any legitimacy towards me if it is based upon arguments and reasons that I have no reason to accept. For a good example of a negative formulation, consider Lawrence Solum's proposition:

> Reasonable citizens are under no obligation to regard themselves as legitimately bound by the authority of decisions that rest on deep premises that they cannot accept as reasonable. Given the fact of pluralism, many or most citizens will regard any legal decision that rests on deep and controversial premises of religious or moral doctrines as illegitimate in the sense that it lacks reasonable justification.[93]

The denial of legitimacy to such a law is based on the view that there must be *some* connection between the law and myself *qua* an addressee of the law—a

[91] Rawls, *Political Liberalism* (n. 52) 137.

[92] Amy Gutmann and Dennis Thompson, *Democracy and Disagreement* (Harvard University Press 1996) 14.

[93] Lawrence B. Solum, 'Public Legal Reason', (2006) 92 *Virginia Law Review* 1449, 1477.

connection that establishes some rational reasons to identify the good for myself in the law. The connection must be between the substance of the law and the preferences, desires, convictions, or interests of individuals subjected to it. If, under rational examination, no such connection can be detected, then I have no reason to accept the law as legitimate. As is clear, the category of PR serves to limit the range of rationales that can be invoked to justify (hence, legitimize) the proposed uses of coercion towards individuals. This requirement applies not only to politicians and legislators but also to all citizens because 'ideally citizens are to think of themselves *as if* they were legislators and ask themselves what statutes, supported by what reasons satisfying the criterion of reciprocity, they would think it most reasonable to enact'.[94]

The issue of legitimacy typically arises, from the individual citizen's perspective, when she asks herself why she should comply with a directive issued by an authority if she disagrees with the content of this directive. 'From the individual citizen's perspective' is an important proviso: in the PR/legitimacy link, a citizen's perspective on legitimacy ('why should I respect a given law?') is primary, and the authorities' perspective ('on what grounds can the authorities hold the citizens under a duty of respecting/obeying our laws?') is secondary and parasitic upon the former. This distinction is not unusual in theoretical reflection about legitimacy. In fact, the citizens' perspective is also clearly displayed in Joseph Raz's theory of legitimate authority, encapsulated in his 'service conception of authority', as viewed in particular in the 'normal justification thesis': legitimacy is ultimately derived from the citizens' interest in following the authorities' directives rather than from any facts about the authorities themselves.[95] To slightly paraphrase Raz's formula, if the law is successful in translating citizens' interests into authoritative directives, in such a way as to help citizens fulfil their genuine preferences, it is legitimate in their eyes.[96]

In contrast, we *may* have conceptions of legitimacy in which the authorities' perspective is primary and the citizens'—derivative. This perspective is perhaps seen in Philip Pettit's formula that '[t]he legitimacy question bears on the way in which [the set of rules that determine the claims that citizens have, relative to one another, within the state]—is *imposed on citizens*'.[97] Note that by contrasting the 'authority's perspective' and the 'citizens' perspective' I am not implying that the former is more 'authoritarian' while the latter, more democratic or freedom-sensitive. I am only making an analytical point about the structure of a theory, from which arises the question of what (the authority's right to rule, or the citizens' reasons to respect/comply with the law) is primary, and what is derivative.

[94] Rawls, 'The Idea of Public Reason' (n. 2) 135, footnote omitted.

[95] See Joseph Raz, *Ethics in the Public Domain* (Oxford University Press 1994)211–15.

[96] For such interpretation of Raz's conception, see Wojciech Sadurski, *Equality and Legitimacy* (Oxford University Press 2009) 3–12.

[97] Philip Pettit, *On the People's Terms* (Cambridge University Press 2012) 141, emphasis added.

But the authority perspective is not useful in elucidating the PR/legitimacy link because PR focuses on facts about the citizens to whom a particular type of justification for laws must be provided. More specifically, this question arises in the context of legitimacy when a person contemplates her *moral* duty to comply: if all that she wondered about was a *legal* duty, the question would be uninteresting because it would be tautological. Similarly, if she inquired only about practical reasons, in particular about the prudential reasons for compliance, the question would not reach the realm of legitimacy but rather would collapse into practical guidelines regarding avoidance of sanctions for non-compliance. The moral question is different from the legal and from the prudential one: it is a grand question (perhaps, *the* grand question) of political philosophy going back to Jean-Jacques Rousseau: how can we reconcile our individual freedom with our subjection to the 'general will' (however defined, as long as the 'general will' does not simply translate fully our individual preferences into the collective choice, as it never can)? So it is a question about the sources of public authority, and of its control over the individual; it is a question about the grounds of the duty of obedience to law by citizens. Liberals admit, of course, that this duty to obey is not unlimited—hence the acceptance of some room for civil disobedience—but they cannot go so far as to say that the duty to obey should be confined only to those authoritative directives with which we agree on merit. It would be an anarchistic position, and the very fact of the lawfulness of a given directive would not add any weight to the argument in favour of compliance.

From this point of view, the concept of 'legitimacy' serves as a marker to identify the point on a continuum between two extremes: the authoritarian position under which the very fact of authoritative enactment of a directive is a sufficient moral reason for compliance, and on the other side of the spectrum, an anarchistic position under which the fact of legal enactment does not add any weight to moral arguments for compliance, which is always conditional upon our substantive moral approval for the directive. Under a liberal approach, the fact of legal enactment is *an* argument for compliance (and in this, the approach is partly aligned with the authoritarian position), but it is not a *sufficient* reason and the duty of compliance is not absolute (and in this, it is partly aligned with an anarchistic position). The intermediate space that is occupied by a liberal position implies that there is a duty to comply with at least some authoritative rules which are not substantively accepted by a given person—and the task of this idea of legitimacy is to determine what are the criteria, grounds, and scope of a moral duty to comply with those rules.

As is well known, political philosophy has in store a large number of theories purporting to provide such criteria and grounds for the duty to comply with the rules we do not necessarily endorse substantively. Two among the most influential theories are by appeals to the idea of social contract and to deliberative democracy. The conception of public reason attempts to reconcile both these argumentative strategies. From the idea of social contract, it borrows the centrality of consensus which seems to be a foundation of authoritative social arrangements: we owe respect to authoritative decisions insofar as, and because, we can be seen to be their co-authors. This is only a hypothetical consensus, though, and a very thin one, based on the alleged common normative presuppositions implicit in political culture. But, while thin, it is not without moral significance: in fact, the use of contractual constructions in theorizing about justice and a good society has a fundamental significance which relates to the reciprocity of reasons to support (or not) political arrangements.[98] In turn, deliberative democracy informs the idea of PR by insisting that authoritative decisions, in order to be legitimate, must be justified (in both senses of the word: both actually justified and justifiable) to those who are bound by them. (Of course, not every 'deliberative democracy' conception converges with the theory of PR because not every such conception necessarily presupposes a similar idea of the *sorts of restraints* and limits upon public arguments: one of the leading theorists of deliberative democracy distances himself from 'public reason' by insisting, among other things, that he would allow 'argument, rhetoric, humour, emotion, testimony or storytelling, and gossip'[99] into public deliberation.)

To sum up: the reasonableness of political decisions, understood through the category of public reason, means a search for a consensus about those decisions by making sure that they are based on rationales which are justifiable to everyone, including to people who disagree with those decisions on merits. We will often disagree with a law without reaching the point of arguing over its unreasonableness, for instance because we believe that it is based on faulty empirical premises which are subject to good-faith contestation, or because we believe that it strikes the wrong balance between various values all of which are reasonable in themselves.[100] In such a case, a law may be seen as legitimate, while if it rests on deep premises that cannot be accepted by their addresses as reasonable, it may not be recognized as legitimate.

This sense of legitimacy resonates, I believe, though is not fully equivalent, with the approach to legitimacy sketched by Ronald Dworkin: legitimacy, he suggested, neither requires that only just governments are legitimate or that they are based on consent but rather on the recognition that the government treats citizens with equal respect:

> A plausible theory of legitimacy … must proceed on the … assumption that when citizens are born into a political community or join that community later, they just have obligations to that community, including the obligation to respect its laws … But they assume these political obligations only if and so long

[98] See Larmore, 'Autonomy' (n. 35) 199.
[99] John S. Dryzek, *Deliberative Democracy and Beyond* (Oxford University Press 2000) 1.
[100] See Solum, 'Public Legal Reason' (n. 93) 1477.

> as the community's government respects their human dignity. . . . I can have no obligation to a community that treats me as a second-class citizen . . .[101]

Note that Dworkin carefully associates legitimacy with a citizen's obligation 'to respect' the law, which is a milder obligation that that of 'obeying' or 'complying with' it. I think that this is a wise choice of words, and elsewhere I have argued at some length about why legitimacy gives rise to the duty of respect rather than compliance[102]—but for the present argument it is not relevant. What matters is that the individual duty triggered by political legitimacy connects with the threshold conditions for the substance of the laws that the government enacts. These threshold conditions are naturally lower than those of being 'just'—a citizen may still have a duty to respect the law with which she disagrees on merits, as long as the law, in Dworkin's formulation, does not confine the person to second-class citizenship; hence, expresses equal respect to her as to all other citizens. It is at this point that Dworkin's theory of legitimacy resonates with PR: PR is one way of giving effect to the requirement of respecting equal citizenship of all persons. PR's response to the requirement of equal citizenship (hence, to meeting the conditions for political legitimacy) is that all laws should be based only on such rationales that can be justified to, and are endorsable by, all those to whom they apply. Dworkin's specific criteria of equal citizenship are quite different (they incorporate a particular conception of human dignity based on the intrinsic value of each human life, and personal responsibility for a human life), and Dworkin specifically rejects the concept of PR[103]—but what matters is that the aspiration behind the PR-legitimacy link and Dworkin's conditions of political legitimacy are the same.

It is also important to reflect upon the legitimacy *of what* is at stake in the considerations related to PR. As the rationale of PR suggests, we are concerned about the legitimacy of *laws*, in terms of their content, rather than the legitimacy of the political authority, or of government. Why would that matter, and is it a meaningful distinction? One of the powerful critics of the idea of PR (without actually mentioning the term, but describing and criticizing a concept very much like PR), Joseph Raz, strongly rejected the aspiration of trying to find consensus within a stock of *reasonable* concepts only, as one possible theoretical approach to dealing with moral diversity, and argued that for the purpose of legitimacy the unreasonable views and people should also be taken into account. (I will return to the question of exclusion of unreasonable doctrines shortly in this part of the chapter.) As Raz says, referring explicitly to the ideas of Rawls and Nagel, 'every person counts' and '[t]he life and well-being of those with unreasonable views are just as likely to be affected by the actions of political authorities as the life and

[101] Ronald Dworkin, *Is Democracy Possible Here?* (Princeton University Press 2006)96–97.
[102] Sadurski, *Equality and Legitimacy* (n. 96) 12–17.
[103] Ronald Dworkin, *Justice in Robes* (Harvard University Press 2005) 251–54.

well-being of other people'.[104] '[T]heir life and well-being are of moral consequence', says Raz.[105] This is certainly true, but I claim that it is relevant only when we inquire into the political legitimacy *of the authorities* (or of the government), and the context of Raz's critique shows that it is exactly what he has in mind: he explicitly refers to the legitimacy of authority,[106] or legitimacy of government.[107] But when we speak about PR, and posit the idea of exclusion of unreasonable doctrines (the idea which Raz challenges), we have in mind the legitimacy of specific laws: of specific exercises of political authority, rather than of a political regime as such.

This is the only context in which PR is pertinent because the principle of PR is meant to serve as a yardstick for the evaluation of whether our support for a given coercive law is justified. And in the context of assessing the legitimacy of specific decisions or rules, it is not implausible to exclude manifestly unreasonable conceptions from the realm of views which enter into consideration as deserving proper respect. If the rationale for adopting PR as a legitimating device for decisions which exercise authority (thus, occasionally coercion) over others is articulated in terms of respect, liberty, and equality (as specified earlier in this book, in Chapter 1), then to incorporate in the reasons for decisions those concepts which are 'unreasonable' in the sense that they deny equal standing, liberty, and consequently, respect to other citizens, would contaminate the decision with illegitimacy.[108] Unreasonable citizens, so defined, are not excluded from the democratic constituency, are proper addressees of the attitude of toleration, and certainly can exercise their political rights (in particular, their rights of freedom of expression, association, and assembly) but are 'excluded from the constituency of public justification'[109] for the purpose of assessing a particular authoritative decision under a standard of liberal legitimacy.

To be sure, we *may* have a conception of legitimacy which, *by definition*, ties up legitimacy of the *government* (or regime as a whole) with that of specific laws, for instance by claiming that a government is legitimate when the laws it issues are, by and large, legitimate, or vice versa, that only (and all) those laws issued by a legitimate government are legitimate (with the criteria of legitimacy being content-independent). Under the former definitional convention, the legitimacy of the government is accumulated through the issuance of legitimate laws; under the latter, the legitimacy of the government confers legitimacy upon the laws it

[104] Joseph Raz, 'Disagreement in Politics' (1998) 43 *American Journal of Jurisprudence* 25, 33.
[105] Ibid. 33.
[106] Ibid. 34 ('the legitimacy of authority is conditional on the fact that people are rational self-directing agents . . .') and 37 ('So far I have argued against the unreasonableness-exclusion in tests for the legitimacy of political authority').
[107] Ibid. 37 ('it may turn out that only the unreasonable could reject the authority of their government. That authority may be illegitimate . . .)
[108] See, similarly, Samuel Freeman, *Justice and the Social Contract* (Oxford University Press 2007)238–39.
[109] Quong, *Liberalism without Perfection* (n. 49) 290.

enacts: the legitimacy of the government as such prefigures, so to speak, the legitimacy of its individual acts. But either connection is unhelpful as a definitional fiat. Legitimacy of the government is, intuitively, only indirectly tied up with the criteria of the content of laws that it issues: it has more to do with (what is usually called) 'input legitimacy' in terms of its electoral pedigree, of acting always in accordance with constitutional rules (only some of which are about the substance of the laws) etc. (At the extreme, we may have conceptions which apply the concept of legitimacy to the authorities only without assigning legitimacy as a meaningful attribute to individual norms. In Miguel Vatter's interpretation of Carl Schmitt, 'For Schmitt, only a political authority can be legitimate, not a legal norm. Legal norms can only be valid'.)[110] And intuitively, the relationship between the legitimacy of the government and the legitimacy of specific laws is tenuous at best. Neither is it true that all laws of an illegitimate government are necessarily illegitimate, except by virtue of a definitional fiat, nor is it the case that all laws of a legitimate authority are necessarily and always legitimate. There may be decisions taken by by-and-large legitimate authorities that breach the principles of legitimacy, for instance due to procedural defects or violation of rights which the regime otherwise respects. Coming back to the PR-legitimacy link: when we ask about the legitimacy of a specific law, we inevitably zero in on its substance, or at least we may say that it is the only focus that PR commands: PR provides a standard by which to judge the legitimate substance of a law or of a legislative proposal. So Raz's objection that unreasonable conceptions and people also should be counted, for the purposes of legitimacy, may be plausible but is not fatal to a conception of PR because it is about a different type of legitimacy than the legitimacy connected to PR and its associated set of conceptions, such as overlapping consensus and the exclusion of unreasonable comprehensive conceptions.

6. Public Reason and Reason of State

This part of the chapter can be read as a digression from the main sequence of argument; it is meant to elucidate the character of the notion of PR by confronting it with a contiguous concept, namely that of the reason of state (RS). There is a functional similarity, if not equivalence, between both concepts, at least under some understandings of RS, as will be clarified in a moment. They both resonate with the input model of democracy, as discussed above in section 3 of this chapter, with an emphasis on the nature of reasons and arguments pressed in the

[110] Miguel Vatter, 'The Idea of Public Reason and the Reason of State: Schmitt and Rawls on the Political', (2008) 36 *Political Theory* 239, 250.

public discourse, as opposed to output democracy, which is about the aggregation of reasons and claims, whatever they are.

Much of the problem with the concept of RS is that, at least in contemporary parlance, it seems to be used in at least three different senses: (1) as equivalent to the common good (which I will call a 'thin' sense of RS); (2) as a pretext or excuse for using unlawful, immoral, or otherwise improper means (which I will call a 'debunking' sense of RS); and (3) to denote those tragic choices when we may legitimately override our natural moral impulses in order to pursue public interest (which I will call a 'pre-emptive' sense of RS). As will become clear from the discussion that follows, the boundaries between the three senses are not precise and there are significant overlaps, but for the sake of simplicity, I will initially present these three senses as if they were distinct.

The first notion of RS (which can be termed Rousseauian, and which has been alluded to in Chapter 1, section 1 above) is an equivalent of the common good, public good, or public interest.[111] I am deliberately listing in one breath these three concepts which in the literature are not necessarily co-equivalent, in order to emphasize the 'thin' character of this concept. The state, as figuring in the notion 'reason of *state*', so understood, is merely a handmaiden for the common good, and not much necessarily hinges on the state-ness of this figure: it is simply that the 'constituency' of the common good in the world as we know it is usually taken to be correlated with the boundaries of the nation-state, and so the state figures in this concept as a level at which the common good is ascertained. The state is just a representative polity which is endowed with articulating, rightly or wrongly, common interests. To reiterate Pettit's formula discussed already in Chapter 1, section 1 of this book, the common good (or common interest) arises when 'according to publicly admissible criteria of argument, it is best supported among feasible alternatives by publicly admissible considerations', that is, 'that it is best supported by the reasons that are publicly admissible within the group'.[112] So while the common good is *that which arises from* such arguments and reasons, in order to test whether something constitutes the common good, we must crucially inquire into whether these considerations and reasons are 'publicly admissible' within a given group. This obviously raises the strong functional similarity between PR and RS.

The second concept of RS is a debunking (pejorative, ironical) notion because what I have in mind here are those usages of the concept which imply that it is a pretext, or a disingenuous way of defending an immoral or illegal or otherwise illegitimate action on the basis that it *allegedly* serves the interest of the state

[111] For an interpretation of Rousseau as identifying the 'reason of state' with the general will (which is a Rousseauian sense of the common good), see Luc Foisneau, 'Gouverner selon la volonté générale: la souveraineté selon Rousseau et les théories de la raison d'État', (2007) 3 *Les Études philosophiques* 463.

[112] Pettit, *On the People's Terms* (n. 97) 163.

understood as the privileged representation of the community. Of course, *what* defence of a state action is illegitimate, and therefore *which* usage of the concept of RS is properly called 'debunking', is in the eye of beholder. This is not devastating to my distinction. The only fact that matters is that we *can* recognize such usages, and indeed it seems to me that when RS is mentioned in English-language literature, it is more often than not used with condemnatory undertones.

Consider the eloquent passage from a letter by Hugh Trevor-Roper to an infamous British double agent Kim Philby, written (and eventually unsent) back in 1968: 'to serve unconditionally, to equate truth with *the reason of state* of any power, that to me is treason of the mind; and to make this surrender to a form of power that is cynical, inhuman, murderous, that to me is treason of the heart also'.[113] Or consider a lively discussion about the uses of torture in order to elicit vital information, which may be useful (as the proponents claim) in the 'War on Terror'. When, for instance, a critic of the state's actions says: 'Open government opposed *reason of state*, state secrecy and national security, often popularized as "big brother" and "faceless bureaucracy", with a system of public accountability based on principles of freedom of information tied to Article 19 of the Declaration of Human Rights.'[114] Or else consider this instance of the use of the concept: 'When taken to the extreme, sociological templates are used to portray potential adversaries of the political community. This happens when the reason of state (*raison d'ëtat*) clashes with the rule of law (*raison juridique*).'[115] In all these passages, clearly what the authors have in mind is a 'reason of state' which is a disingenuous or threatening argumentative device of the powerful. In this context, the concept of RS is usually referred to in a mocking or cynical manner; the English language has developed in a way that makes RS almost synonymous with state force thinly veiled by an appeal to the national interest. Presenting a liberal approach to the 'War on Terror', Dana Villa observes: 'liberalism developed precisely in opposition to this double threat: the deadly danger of religiously inspired violence and intolerance (on the one hand) and *cynical reason of state* (on the other).'[116] These days it is unlikely that the words 'reason of state' would be used by those who *defend* the use of such despicable methods; rather there is a focus on national security or safety, national self-defence etc. The notion 'reason of state' is more likely to be used by those who disapprove of such measures and who will attribute the 'reason of state' to the proponents of such uses of torture.

[113] Blair Worden, 'Two Letters on Treason' *The New York Review of Books*, 9 January 2014, 20, 21, emphasis added.

[114] Michael A. Peters, 'Information, Globalization and Democracy: The Utopian Moment?' *Global-e: A Global Studies Journal* (2 May 2008), https://www.21global.ucsb.edu/global-e/may-2008/information-globalization-and-democracy-utopian-moment accessed 26 July 2022, emphasis added.

[115] Matteo Tondini, 'Beyond the Law of the Enemy: Recovering from the Failures of the Global War on Terrorism Through Law', (2007) 3 *Jura Gentium: Rivista di filosofia del diritto internazionale e della politica globale*, 1.

[116] Dana Villa, 'Political Violence and Terror: Arendtian Reflections', (2008) 1 *Ethics & Global Politics* 97, 110, emphasis added.

There is something worryingly emotionless and authoritarian in appealing to RS as a way of justifying such horrendous violations of bodily integrity and human dignity.

Finally, the third concept is related to tragic choices, when in order to achieve a public interest (or, more usually, prevent a public harm) we need to do something that otherwise would be considered immoral or else illegitimate. This connection of RS to tragedy was vividly depicted by C.J. Friedrich who applied the notion of 'tragedy' to the 'profound shock which the human being suffers when he discovers that conflicts of values do exist, and do require a decision', and continued: 'The fundamental problem of politics is how to organize the community for the purpose of making such final decisions. The idea of the reason of state represents one possible answer.'[117] I will call this usage a 'pre-emptive' sense of RS, because RS here acts as a device to pre-empt an otherwise valid moral norm. The notion of 'pre-emption' is borrowed here from Raz; in a different context, Raz describes the pre-emptive nature of an authoritative directive as providing a reason for action 'which is not to be added to all other relevant reasons when assessing what to do, but [which] should replace some of them'.[118] He further explains that those 'other relevant reasons' appear at the level of justification of authoritative directives—as, *mutatis mutandis*, they also exist at the level of justification for RS in our *problématique*. As with Raz's authoritative directives, once they are formulated, they replace rather than add to those other moral reasons, so in the case of a pre-emptive notion of RS, once it is articulated, it supersedes any first-order considerations for political action. Used in this context, RS normally applies to the security (internal and external) and survival of state, based on an insight that, 'if the political order is assumed to be an essential condition of a free moral existence, the survival of this order becomes crucial'.[119]

It may help to illuminate this sense of RS by contrasting it with the former two senses: it has a partial analogy and partial disanalogy with the 'thin' and 'debunking' senses of RS. It is analogical to the 'thin' sense in that it is an *approving* sense of RS: if an RS is properly ascertained, then it is right to pursue it, even if it clashes with a legitimate private interest (as in the thin sense) or with an otherwise valid moral norm (as in the pre-emptive sense). The difference is in the tragic dimension: the pre-emptive sense indicates a violation of a norm which otherwise is moral, and which would be peremptory, save for the clash with RS. But this tragic dimension is absent from the 'thin' sense: there is nothing morally peremptory about something being in my private interest. I do not have even a prima facie moral obligation (much less, an all-things-considered moral duty) to pursue my private self-interest. It may be legitimate for me to pursue it (when it does not clash with any moral obligation), but it is not my duty. So RS in

[117] C.J. Friedrich, *Constitutional Reason of State* (Brown University Press 1957) 127.
[118] Raz, *Ethics in the Public Domain* (n. 95) 214.
[119] Friedrich, *Constitutional Reason of State* (n. 117) 6.

the thin sense does not operate as to 'pre-empt' the validity of an otherwise moral rule—the job it does, by definition, in the pre-emptive usage of RS.

So far as the confrontation between a pre-emptive and a debunking sense is concerned, the analogy is that in both cases we have a clash between prima facie moral duties, and in both cases RS prevails over the competing moral duties. The contrast lies in the moral vector of this clash: in the debunking sense, we use RS to denote an *illegitimate* privileging of a norm allegedly serving RS over an otherwise valid moral norm (such as an absolute prohibition of torture). We use RS to condemn it: we believe that the pre-emption is unjustified. However, in the pre-emptive usage our valuation is opposite: we may deplore and greatly regret the overriding of a valid moral norm but, all things considered, we believe that it is justified under the circumstances. Remember that at a deeper level of justification, those other valid norms (first-order norms) have been already amalgamated into the second-order norm of RS (for instance, when considering the use of torture to extract information from suspected terrorists, we had already—for the sake of argument—absorbed the values of individual dignity, prohibition of infliction of bodily harm etc., alongside the importance of national security, into the second-order norms of RS). But at the level of application, the rule of RS pre-empts the first-order moral rules: the fact that they nevertheless maintain their high moral validity in our eyes colours the situation as truly tragic.

This last comparison, that between the pre-emptive and debunking uses of RS, shows why none of these two concepts is really useful as a *working* concept of RS. I understand the 'working' concept of RS (just as is the working concept of PR) to be something that people of diverse viewpoints and ideologies may agree upon. We should aspire to a working concept of RS which is not entirely dependent upon which side of the substantive disagreement you are on. And if so, the only workable conception seems to be offered by what I have dubbed here as the 'thin' use of RS: RS as an equivalent of the common good (common interest, public interest), as ascertained and articulated by the state.

The discussion so far indicates a strong functional similarity between RS and PR. PR is about the 'inputs'—about the nature and quality of arguments which may be legitimately pressed in the process of demanding a particular authoritative policy or law. The same applies to the case of RS: as interpreted here, the most plausible understanding of RS is as an idea of common good which is about the reasons and arguments admissible in a given group. But there is a difference, and it revolves, of course, around the word 'state'. So far I have been writing about the 'reason of state' but focused on the 'reason' only, thus discerning the functional equivalence with 'public reason'. But now is the time to turn to the other component of the term. The 'state' (in RS) is not necessarily equivalent to 'public' (in PR). RS is, naturally, inherently, and almost trivially, state centred. As Gianfranco Poggi noted in his path-breaking book, 'Not for nothing is the great European debate about *ratio status* (*raison d'état*) largely coeval with the diffusion of the term of "state" itself and its equivalent in various European languages'.[120] This linguistic development parallels the development of modern European nation-states. As Poggi continues:

> the upshot of that debate was too limited in scope: it consisted, essentially, in the negative conclusion that a ruler might have to disregard the dictates of religion and morality in pursuing the realm's greatness and security; positively, it saw too exclusively the ruler's personal qualities of leadership (his *virtú*, in Machiavellan vocabulary) as the source of the rationality to be applied to that pursuit.[121]

As the vitality of modern nation-states reaches its limits, with the states' monopoly on rationality being increasingly challenged both at civil society and transnational levels, and as Poggi's two 'upshots' reveal their negative consequences, the notion of RS becomes increasingly divergent from that of PR. There are at least two differences. One is about who is the interpreter and enforcer of a given 'reason'; another is about the scope of 'constituency' within which a given 'reason is ascertained'. The first is the *who* question, the latter is the *where* question. These two matters will be now discussed in turn.

Regarding the question of who the authoritative interpreter of a 'reason' is (whether 'public' or 'of state'), a liberal conception, which is a philosophical ecosystem for the theory of PR, operates with a thesis that there is continuity—in terms of moral entitlement, authority, and responsibility—between individual citizens and public officials. In fact, a citizen-voter *is* a public official, and the role she performs (and which goes well beyond the one-off act of voting, but also includes other forms of disciplining the representatives and participating in public discourse) is qualitatively the same as the role performed by public officials. Within the perspective of the continuity thesis, there is no room for a qualitative distinction between citizens and the state: the state is a dependent rather than an autonomous entity, and as such is of no special interest to a normative political theory (other than, of course, that citizens have an interest in the good functioning of their political institutions insofar as they are efficient articulators of their collective preferences). As an articulator and enforcer of PR, the state is fully parasitic, so to speak, on the reasons pressed by citizens who act in an 'official' capacity when they participate in public discourse aimed at making or repealing the laws. At a normative level, it is the opposite of what Gianfranco Poggi describes as a 'state-centred understanding of the state' which sees 'the state—a set of institutions specifically concerned with accumulating and exercising political power—as itself constituting a distinctive social force, vested with interests

[120] Gianfranco Poggi, *The State: Its Nature, Development and Prospects* (Stanford University Press 1990) 185.

[121] Ibid. 185–86.

of its own, which affect autonomously, and sometimes decisively, the state's own arrangements and policies'.[122] What may be a convincing descriptive account to a sociologist (as Poggi is), is anathema to a normative political philosophy of liberal democracy.

But this normative irrelevance of state is not exclusive to the *liberal* theory; in fact, my idea of the irrelevance of state is similar to that which was articulated by perhaps one of the most famous illiberal contemporary legal and political philosophers, John Finnis, in the context of a theory of distributive justice. Addressing the issue of state coercion in enforcing schemes of distributive justice (in the context of criticizing Robert Nozick's theory of property), Finnis wrote that:

> the State need be doing no more than crystallize and enforce duties that the property-holder already had. Coercion, then, comes into play only in the event of recalcitrance that is wrongful not only in law but also in justice. Distributive justice is here, as in most contexts, a relation between citizens, or groups and associations within the community, and is the responsibility of those citizens and groups.[123]

Finnis's idea was offered with respect to the theory of justice, but *mutatis mutandis* it well illustrates the normative irrelevance of the state in the area of political authority and obligation. Thus, the notion of 'reason of *state*', as compared to public reason, may imply that the state is an independent actor, which may have its own 'reasons', and which are not simply continuous with the reasons of its individual citizens, properly aggregated. It also may imply that it may be a final and authoritative interpreter and enforcer of its reasons, inconsistently with the continuity thesis. This is an unfortunate implication, with potentially illiberal and authoritarian connotations. Of course, these are just implications of a rhetorical rather than conceptual nature, and one may use the concept of RS with appropriate provisos attached to it which will preclude any such implications and link it with the continuity thesis. But in such a case, there is no reason to use RS rather than PR, which comes with no such implications.

There is a second difference between RS and PR, as mentioned earlier, and it concerns the range of the 'reason constituency' (by analogy to 'justice constituency'),[124] by which I mean a group within which the reason is ascertained. Different ranges of people may yield different 'public reasons' which apply to laws or policies within this group. But even if there is no incongruence between

[122] Ibid. 98.

[123] John Finnis, *Natural Law and Natural Rights* (Oxford University Press 1980) 187–88.

[124] For the notion of 'justice constituency', see Julius Stone, *Social Dimensions of Law and Justice* (Maitland 1966) 117 (where he defines it as a 'transcending community, among whose members justice is to be done by allotting among them the gains and losses of social action').

different rules yielded by different reasons at different levels of membership, we usually consider one group as dominant in our concerns: we usually attach our commitments, concerns, sense of responsibility, and the range of togetherness, to one particular group, at least predominantly, with others being at a lower rank of these concerns and commitments.

The concept of RS *may imply* that such a group is coextensive with a state. While it *may* be (and indeed, for most of us, *is*) the scope of our dominant group, in the sense just mentioned, it need not be always so, and in any event, whether it is, should come as a result of a substantive argument rather than by force of the concept used. We may adopt a cosmopolitan perspective which denies the state an independent moral role in identifying the group within which our dominant loyalties and concerns are located. With John Finnis we may say that:

> [w]e must not take the pretensions of the modern state at face value. Its legal claims are founded ... on its self-interpretation as a complete and self-sufficient community. But there are relationships between men, which transcend the boundaries of all *poleis*, realms, or states.... If it now appears that the good of individuals can only be fully secured and realized in the context of international community, we must conclude that the claim of the national state to be a complete community is unwarranted and the postulate of the national legal order, that it is supreme and comprehensive and an exclusive source of legal obligation, is increasingly what lawyers would call a 'legal fiction'.[125]

This is as good a statement as any of a cosmopolitan position, a position which, in the words of an author coming from a completely different ideological background than Finnis, describes as a 'call[ing] into question [of] one of the most powerful convictions concerning society and politics, which finds expression in the claim that "modern society" and "modern politics" can only be organized in the form of national states'.[126] If we call this conviction into question, and if we refuse to accord the nation-state an automatically privileged role in crystallizing a political community (if, in the already quoted words of Finnis, we do not 'take the pretensions of the modern state at face value'), we must then conclude that RS is an unwarranted reading of PR insofar as it forecloses an argument about the proper range (scope) of the constituency within which our public reasons are to be articulated. After all, we may well adopt a view that our 'reason constituency' is multi-layered, with strong and important commitments oriented towards different ranges of constituencies, or we may identify our dominant constituency

[125] Finnis, *Natural Law and Natural Rights* (n. 123) 149–50.
[126] Ulrich Beck, *Cosmopolitan Vision* (trans. Ciaran Cronin) (Polity Press 2006) 24.

at a different level that the nation-state (think about the growing sense of loyalty and commitment to the European Union (EU) by citizens of EU Member States, with various linkages, party structures, and (Non-governmental organizations) NGOs set up at EU level). Again, we may attach a cosmopolitan proviso to our notions of RS, but it will be awkward and possibly confusing. Better to stick to 'public reason'.

3
Defending Public Reason

The very idea of public reason (PR) is relatively simple, when spelled out in its most basic version: laws are only legitimate when supported by reasons which are endorsable by all those who will be bound by them. But its simplicity is deceptive, and its refinement is best achieved by considering its most powerful critiques.

In this chapter I will begin by consideration of the 'non-feasibility objection': an argument that, in a deeply polarized society (precisely the sort of society which triggers the need for the PR principle in the first place), it is impossible to identify a sufficient consensus that may provide a stock of arguments which constitute sufficiently public reasons, endorsable by all (section 1). I will then move on to discuss two aspects of what may be called a core case against PR: that, depending on the interpretation of the ideal, it is either 'too thin' or 'too thick'. The former objection claims that PR is a toothless ideal which would eliminate nearly nothing from public discourse; the latter, its mirror image, is that the adoption of this ideal would lead to a drastic erosion of public discourse. As to the former argument, advanced by Ronald Dworkin, I will show (in section 2) that this objection is tenable only if we adopt an implausibly subjectivist conception of *reasonableness* used in tandem with the ideal of PR. As to the latter argument, that adoption of the ideal of PR would lead to a drastic erosion of public discourse, I argue (in section 3) that this disregards the distinction between generalized public discourse and the advocacy of laws that are to actually become legislation, broadly speaking. Next, in section 4, I will discuss the fundamental argument (propounded by Jeremy Waldron) that the adoption of PR as a reason-constraining device necessarily distorts and weakens the process of public justification because it excludes, *ex ante*, some reasons which may be relevant and pertinent to the issue at hand, and if they are not relevant and not pertinent, those reasons will be defeated anyway, without the need for a highly artificial device such as PR. I will demonstrate that the requirement of public reason rests on the same type of restrictions on public arguments which we adopt as legitimate in many spheres of argument and justification anyway. Finally, in section 5 of the chapter I will consider, and rebut, the argument that the ideal of PR is detrimental to the principle of candour in public, and that it provides participants of the discourse with incentives for deception and insincerity. I will argue, in particular, that one should not confuse 'strategic' choice of argument, triggered

Constitutional Public Reason. Wojciech Sadurski, Oxford University Press. © Wojciech Sadurski 2023.
DOI: 10.1093/oso/9780192869678.003.0003

by the concern for efficiency of persuasion or by the principle of respect to the audience, with deception and insincerity.

The main point of this chapter is less polemical than clarificatory: in the process of rebutting some main objections to the ideal of PR, I hope to elucidate and finetune it so as to render it both attractive and feasible in constitutional reasoning.

1. The Feasibility of Public Reason

I will first consider what is perhaps the most important and the most perplexing question, namely whether the very idea of PR is *feasible*, that is, whether, in actual society, we can identify a sufficiently thick and broad class of reasons that may count as '*public* reasons'—providing determinate and PR-compatible answers to questions, as they *de facto* arise in a society, about coercive rules governing human behaviour. Obviously, if no such thick and broad set is discernible, the stability of a liberal society is fundamentally undermined: this necessarily happens if there is no sufficient support for the 'overlapping consensus' within public reasons so as to outweigh the contrary views and positions to which citizens are also attracted. But I will assume that we *can* identify such a set of actually shared reasons. In fact, I will assume (as a number of other commentators on Rawls do)[1] that PR is actually 'overdetermined' because, under Rawls's theory, there may be a number of reasonable answers to any given issue (PR serving basically as a device to eliminate patently *un*reasonable answers), and that is why it is unlikely that PR will ever be incomplete. On the contrary, we may expect that in a given society, we will be able to identify a PR-compatible stock of opinions and beliefs that are sufficiently broad and thick to sustain the legitimacy of laws. Note, incidentally, that 'broad' and 'thick' are two distinct descriptors. In order to be feasible, a stock of views must be sufficiently broad, so that its range is roughly equivalent to the coverage of the most important legal regulations, and sufficiently thick, so that those views can be stated with a degree of precision and not merely as platitudes so vague as to be meaningless.

The question of the existence of such a stock of opinions and beliefs brings together complex normative and empirical issues, for instance of the degree of commonality of certain views in the community. After all, 'Public reason presupposes a kind of political community that is unified by shared beliefs and ideas'.[2] I will put these empirical issues to one side. Does this defeat the point of this book? Not really. I do not think that the project of PR is properly viewed as

[1] See Samuel Freeman, 'Public Reason and Political Justifications', (2004) 72 *Fordham Law Review* 2021, 2055–56.

[2] Samuel Freeman, 'Introduction: John Rawls—An Overview', in Samuel Freeman (ed.), *The Cambridge Companion to Rawls* (Cambridge University Press 2003) 1, 39.

relying upon a social or political account of the degree of moral consensus in society, but rather that it is better viewed as a directive or imperative, addressed to an individual in her capacity as a citizen, about the sort of motives which are and which are not suitable to act upon when engaging in advocacy for a coercive law. In that interpretation of PR, I take my cues from Rawls's reformulation of his initial idea of PR, and from his important statement that 'the idea of public reason is not a view about specific political institutions and policies' but rather 'it is a view about the kind of reasons on which citizens are to rest their political cases in making their political justifications to one another when they support laws and policies that invoke the coercive powers of government concerning fundamental political questions'.[3]

Under one interpretation, PR is even ascertained not in terms of any existing set of views and beliefs accepted in real society, but rather 'as a task, an ideal, an imperative'.[4] While it is an intriguing idea, it is not Rawls's own understanding of PR: Rawls states expressly that justifications regarding basic justice and constitutional essentials 'are to appeal only to presently accepted general beliefs and forms of reasoning found in common sense'.[5] In any event, so understood, PR would not compel us to inquire into the feasibility issue at all, unless at a purely psychological level.

Will this approach—aspirational and focused on an individual reasoner—help avoid problems related to a (putative) lack of consensus on PR in society? It is important to realize that what we are dealing with under the label of 'feasibility' is a matter of completeness, and that PR may be viewed as incomplete in two ways: either due to its 'inconclusiveness', which is when there is no sufficient overlapping consensus among individuals converging upon PR-compatible justifications for law, or due to its 'indeterminacy', which occurs when an individual citizen does not have sufficient PR-compatible justifications that would provide an answer to a question about law.[6] We need to keep these two questions separate. The first, namely that of putative inconclusiveness, is best articulated as 'whether all reasonable citizens affirming reasonable comprehensive doctrines can accept the political resolution provided by public reason on the basis of their comprehensive doctrines'.[7] The second, that of 'indeterminacy', is whether public reason, in the mind of an individual, can always dictate the political resolution of an issue which is on the public agenda and demands a legal determination.

Suppose we put aside the question of inconclusiveness—suppose that we assume that in a contemporary, pluralistic democracy we normally have an

[3] John Rawls, 'The Idea of Public Reason Revisited', in *The Law of Peoples* (Harvard University Press 1999) 165–66.

[4] Michael Baur, 'On Actualizing Public Reason', (2003–2004) 72 *Fordham Law Review* 2153, 2174.

[5] John Rawls, *Political Liberalism* (Columbia University Press 1993) 224.

[6] In this discussion I follow the taxonomy used by Micah Schwartzman, 'The Completeness of Public Reason', (2004) 3 *Politics, Philosophy & Economics* 191.

[7] Freeman, 'Public Reason' (n. 1) 2054–55.

over-supply rather than a deficit of PR-compatible arguments in public culture of these societies, and that this over-determinacy is not embarrassing for the principle of PR. What matters is that the principle of PR will preclude some reasons from being acted upon, and not that it should identify a unique reason, much less a unique *balance of public reasons*, to be accepted uniformly by all. After all, different reasonable people may end up with a different resolution to the weighing and balancing of the various public reasons which may apply to a given situation, as shown by Rawls's own example of public reasons applicable to the abortion issue.[8] Rawls indicates (without much argument) that the issue is controlled by public reasons as due respect for human life, freedom, and equality of women, and society's interests in the family and the ordered reproduction of society. Rawls's own weighing and balancing leads him to a resolution which happens to coincide with the current legal status quo in the United States (a right to abortion during the first trimester), but there is nothing self-evident about it, and reasonable people will (and do) disagree. This disagreement is not devastating for the principle of PR; all that matters is that the reasons which are weighed and balanced against each other (with different outcomes for different people) are all of a properly 'public' character.

But what about 'indeterminacy' in the mind of an individual citizen? There may be four different categories of putative indeterminacy of this type: (1) a person (*A*) has no (moral) views about a given issue at all, (2) a person has strong moral views but they belong to a non-public category, and holds no (or very weak) PR-compatible views on that matter, (3) a person espouses both non-public and public reasons about a given issue, and they are of similar strengths but mutually incompatible, (4) a person has various conflicting PR-compatible views on a given issue.

Suppose an issue of legislation on doctor-assisted suicide enters into the agenda of public discourse, and citizens are asked to pronounce on it. Now in case (1) on our list in the previous paragraph, there is 'indeterminacy' of a non-problematic kind. It is commonplace that in a democracy not everyone is required to have a view about everything that is the subject of public debate (and lawmaking), and it is a generally recognized democratic right to abstain from a debate (and eventually from voting) on a given issue. As some political scientists such as Henry Mayo have maintained, a case may sometimes be made for individual abstention, even by persons with an interest in politics, in addition to the fact that not everyone is actively interested in politics.[9] By not having a view, a non-active voter simply (and non-objectionably) agrees to abide by the outcome of normal democratic decision-making without participating in it on this given issue, just as a decision to abstain from voting on a particular issue signifies a

[8] Rawls, *Political Liberalism* (n. 5) 243 n. 32.

[9] See Henry B. Mayo, *An Introduction to Democratic Theory* (Oxford University Press 1960) 122–23.

blanket acceptance of the majority verdict (if that is the voting procedure in a given assembly). It is by no means a renunciation of democratic values.

To be sure, there is a dimension of disanalogy between non-voting and not having a view in a public discourse leading up to generating PR, but it is a disanalogy which *strengthens* the case for abstention in public discourse as compared to an act of voting. One may argue, and it has been an argument actually made in democratic theory, that even if one is indifferent with regard to a party choice in the elections, one should vote nevertheless because everyone should support the maintenance of electoral democracy.[10] This is all the more so since there is a clear danger of free-rider considerations in the voting context: in a society of rational maximizers no one would vote unless they thought that nobody else would, with devastating results for the system of electoral democracy.[11] But no such reasoning is applicable to public reasons leading up to generation of a PR: if someone genuinely is indifferent as to the matter, or is undecided about the best outcome, then her abstention from discourse does not undermine the integrity of public discourse. To the contrary, the system would be distorted if everyone thought that they were obliged (politically and morally) to have a view on any given matter placed by someone else on the agenda. In any event, this is not a problem specific to PR, but to moral indecision, ignorance, apathy, etc. in general, and it cannot serve as an argument to demonstrate the indeterminacy of PR.

I will relegate case (2) to a discussion below. In case (3) there is no indeterminacy of the sort which would pose a problem for PR at all: if the very principle of PR is justified (which I accept here *arguendo*), *A* is under a duty to set aside his or her non-public opinions and act only (including, advocating for laws) based on his or her PR-compatible views.

Case (4) is a replication of interpersonal inconclusiveness, but in the mind of an individual. It is a rare case, however, that various reasons of the requisite kind (i.e. of the PR-compatible kind) fully cancel each other in our minds. Suppose *A* holds two major PR-compatible opinions about doctor-assisted suicide, and they point in opposite directions: that each should be allowed, regardless of one's philosophy, to make an autonomous decision about one's end of life (thus supporting doctor-assisted suicide), and also that the availability of assistance in suicide creates perverse and dangerous opportunities for people to put pressure on a terminally sick and greatly suffering person to terminate his life (thus countering a proposed law regarding such assistance). It is unlikely that a rational person will persist with such a total stand-off between two opposing views about one and the same thing forever—but if she does, and if various tie-breaking strategies that help to make individual decisions in hard cases (postponement, delegation,

[10] See Frank Cunningham, *Theories of Democracy* (Routledge 2002) 106.

[11] See ibid. 106, referring to Anthony Downs, *An Economic Theory of Democracy* (Harper and Row 1957)267–72.

deference to authority, random choice, etc.) are not successful, we may then conclude that the person is better characterized as belonging to category (1)—and simply opts out from public discourse. Having two mutually self-cancelling opinions on a given issue at the same time amounts to not having a conclusive opinion on that issue at all.

So it is only category (2) which is truly embarrassing for the conception of PR. Consider the following scenarios: (a) *A* feels very strongly for religious reasons (sacredness of life, life belongs to the Divine Creator) that doctor-assisted suicide should be prohibited and does not espouse any PR-compatible opinions about it one way or another, or (b) *A* espouses such opinions but with lower intensity than holding her religious opinions. We need to disaggregate this category into two sub-categories: 2(a) in which there are no PR-compatible views about a given matter in a person's mind, and 2(b) in which there *are* such views, but they count for less than non-public justifications. In category 2(b) much depends on the distance between non-public and public views on a given matter in one's mind: if the distance is great, then for all practical purposes the case falls into category 2(a) (there are some PR-compatible genuine justifications, but they are so weak in the person's mind that they really do not register in her reasoning—then what's the point of mentioning them?) But if the distance is not all that great, and (to make the argument sharper) we say that in a person's mind, a PR-compatible argument is only marginally weaker than a non-public argument, then if (as we assume *arguendo*) the principle of PR is attractive, *A* has a duty to disregard those slightly stronger non-public arguments and rely only on PR-compatible ones. (Whether adopting such a position violates the principle of sincerity and candour in public life is something that I will consider in the last section of this chapter.) But category 2(a) is a big problem for the concept of PR. Suppose *A* feels really strongly about doctor-assisted suicide and cannot think of any non-trivial public reasons about the matter which she can sincerely and publicly espouse. To tell *A* that she is (morally) banned from advocating for, and voting on, the law when she can make it only on non-public grounds is to effectively silence her and relegate her to a second-class category on this given issue. But on the other hand, to tell her that (morally speaking) that she is entitled to act on this justification is to contaminate public discourse, and the process of lawmaking, with arguments which are not endorsable by all, with all the moral consequences of such contamination.

This is a truly tragic choice, and the one on which the concept of PR cannot pronounce: it cannot pronounce upon its own limits. All that can be expressed is a hope that such cases do not occur all that often, and that the reality of modern democratic societies in which there is a conspicuous absence of non-public arguments in public discourse, and in particular in law-related discourse on issues such as doctor-assisted suicide (where, privately, many people think about it largely in terms of their non-public reasons) suggests that the proportion of cases belonging to category 2(a) will be rather negligible. This is of course only conjecture, and in real life it may or may not be empirically supported. The stability of a liberal society depends crucially on how narrow category 2(a) is. It also depends on how 'contaminating' the category will be, that is, whether people who hold 2(a) on any given issue (such as our example of doctor-assisted suicide) will, on this basis, reject the principle of PR as such, or rather tend to confine their inability to be governed by PR to individual, discrete issues. For dilemmas belonging to category 2(a) are always about a specific issue rather than about employing the principle of PR in general, and there is nothing to suggest that people who are unable to accept the resolution of a particular issue by PR must be led to reject the principle of PR in all other cases which demand a legal resolution.

2. 'Too Thin': The Issue of Reasonableness

As Ronald Dworkin observed, Rawls operates with two understandings of public reason which are not necessarily equivalent. The first is revealed in the 'equal endorsability by all' criterion, and seems to Dworkin to be too weak; the second is discerned in Rawls's distinction between political and comprehensive conceptions, with the proviso that public reason must place itself within the former in order to fit the 'overlapping consensus'—and this version of PR seems to be too strong.

As to the first understanding, Dworkin has expressed doubts as to whether PR so understood (in Dworkin's interpretation it is characterized as the 'doctrine of reciprocity') excludes anything at all. As Dworkin argues: 'If I believe that a particular controversial moral position is plainly right ... then how can I not believe that other people in my community can reasonably accept the same view, whether or not it is likely that they will accept it?'[12] The second interpretation of public reason by Rawls is even more problematic, although for opposite reasons. This is the requirement of locating public reason within arguments that can be properly considered 'political' (hence, positioned within an overlapping consensus) as opposed to comprehensive. This, in turn, seems to be a much too rigorous requirement, compared to intuitively acceptable common practices: to consistently purge public debate of all political proposals made on (controversial) moral or religious grounds would lead to an undue erosion and impoverishment of public discourse, and would carry obvious discriminatory dangers.

So we have a dilemma: we can identify two alternative readings of PR, but the first reading ('reciprocity') is much too lenient, certifying almost all views as complying with PR, while the second reading ('overlapping consensus') is much too

[12] Ronald Dworkin, *Justice in Robes* (Harvard University Press 2005) 252.

demanding, compared to our common sense understandings of reasonableness in public discourse. Does it fully disqualify the very idea of PR as playing a role in a test for the legitimacy of law? I do not think so. In this part of the chapter I will only discuss the first horn of the dilemma—that PR is a much too lenient test, not capable of disqualifying almost any regulations. But the very fact that someone sincerely considers his or her publicly provided rationale as reasonable does not necessarily mean that this view is justified from a more objectified or interpersonal point of view. Consider again Rawls's formula of reciprocity: 'we must give [the other citizens] reasons they can not only understand ... but reasons we might reasonably expect that they, *as free and equal citizens*, might reasonably also accept.'[13] The italicized proviso indicates an objectified ingredient to the condition of reciprocity: it is not good enough that proponents are subjectively convinced of the eminent reasonableness of their postulates, but these postulates, when implemented, must satisfy the conditions of free and equal citizenship for all. The reasonableness condition in the quoted formula ('reasons we might reasonably expect ... ') supports an *objectified* reading of reciprocity, and 'we' in the quoted phrase should not be understood, I would suggest, as 'we the citizens involved actually in mutual reasons-giving', but rather 'we as impartial observers' (or, which comes to the same, 'we, the reasonable citizens', with reasonableness determined in an inter-subjective fashion). So it is not the case that citizens meet the reciprocity requirement merely when they sincerely believe that they express political values that others might be expected to endorse: such a belief should be, in addition, 'objectively' reasonable.

'Reasonable' beliefs, in Rawls's perspective, are those which are espoused by reasonable citizens (indeed, 'reasonable citizens' are defined by their affirmation of reasonable beliefs),[14] and they are not all those who *consider themselves* reasonable (as Dworkin assumes for the purpose of his *reductio ad absurdum*), but those who are willing to cooperate with others *on fair terms*, as free and equal, who recognize the consequences of the 'burdens of judgement', who have a sense of justice, etc.[15]Indeed, one may say that 'reasonableness' does not pertain to the characteristics of individuals as such but rather to an objectified, interpersonal judgement about fairness in interactions among individuals; 'the reasonable person' needs to be understood as the embodiment of an idea of fair terms of social cooperation.[16] This is precisely the Rawlsian concept of

[13] Rawls, 'The Idea of Public Reason' (n. 3) 138, emphasis added.

[14] This, as Rawls says, is an 'assumption': Rawls, *Political Liberalism* (n. 5) 59. For an extended defence of the thesis along these lines, see Jonathan Quong, *Liberalism without Perfection* (Oxford University Press 2011).

[15] Rawls, *Political Liberalism* (n. 5) 81. Those criteria are also scattered throughout the book, see, e.g., ibid. 49–50.

[16] See Arthur Ripstein, *Equality, Responsibility, and the Law* (Cambridge University Press 1999) 7, reference omitted.

'reasonableness': reasonable citizens, Rawls succinctly says, 'desire for its own sake a social world in which they, as free and equal, can cooperate with others on terms all can accept'.[17]

He occasionally goes even further, by suggesting that citizens should 'count[] certain primary goods, such as the equal basic rights and liberties, the fair value of the political liberties and fair equality of opportunity, as social bases of self-respect',[18] they 'endorse some form of liberty of conscience and freedom of thought',[19] 'a form of toleration',[20] etc. But even without those extraordinarily thick requirements of reasonableness, there is a good deal of 'critical morality' as opposed to 'positive morality' (to use an old-fashioned distinction)[21] at work here, and clearly unreasonable conceptions of the good—intolerance, for instance, or racism—will be excluded from an overlapping consensus.[22] This is perfectly plausible. To use an analogy with the doctrine of liberal neutrality (already referred to in Chapter 2, section 3), one may see why liberal neutrality, based as it is on some substantive moral principles (such as equal moral agency or self-determination of individuals), must lead to the exclusion of *some* doctrines from the domain of neutrality. Extending neutral treatment to conceptions of the good that are antagonistic to the liberty of others would not leave those others with a fair opportunity to lead a fulfilled life.[23] Someone who would espouse a conception which denies equality and liberty to proponents of other conceptions would forfeit a claim to have his conception recognized for the purpose of assessing 'reasonableness' because he would be saying both that the law must recognize respectfully his conception as reasonable and that it must show such respect by enacting laws which deny the same respect to others.[24]

Further, Rawls talks approvingly of 'deliberative democracy' as the concept that 'limits the reasons citizens may give in supporting their political opinions to reasons consistent with their seeing other citizens as equals'.[25] Some putative rationales for legal regulations may be viewed as not universalizable by their very nature: not lending themselves to figuring in the justifications of legal coercive rules, regardless of the subjective convictions of espousers of those rationales.

[17] Rawls, *Political Liberalism* (n. 5) 50.

[18] Ibid. 82, footnote omitted.

[19] Ibid. 61.

[20] Ibid. 62

[21] See H.L.A. Hart, *Law, Liberty, and Morality* (Stanford University Press 1962) 17–18.

[22] See Samuel Freeman, 'Political Liberalism and the Possibility of a Just Democratic Constitution', (1994) 69 *Chicago-Kent Law Review* 619, 643.

[23] See Alan Patten, 'Liberal Neutrality: A Reinterpretation and Defense', (2012) 20 *Journal of Political Philosophy* 249, 253.

[24] This last phrase deliberately paraphrases Alan Patten who writes about a person holding a conception which denies others a right to self-determination: 'He would be in the position of saying *both* that the state is wrong not to respect his fair opportunity to be self-determining *and* that it show such respect by adopting policies that deny that very same opportunity to others', ibid. 254, footnote omitted.

[25] Rawls, 'The Idea of Public Reason' (n. 3) 139 n. 21.

Perhaps all religious justifications are by their very nature 'non-endorsable by all' because those who are not adherents to a given faith have no reason whatsoever to endorse a rationale which is crucially based on that faith. (A non-believer may accept the conclusions of the argument based on religious rationales but not the rationales themselves.) It may well be the case that every believer is confident that his beliefs are truly reasonable, and that they are so self-evidently reasonable that every reasonable person must accept them. But this is not necessarily the only conviction accompanying religious beliefs. If, for example, someone believes in revelation as a source of religious faith then naturally she cannot maintain that every reasonable person has good reason to accept views based on that faith. So these religious beliefs cannot become part of PR—and so the very conception of PR is not as toothless as the first limb of the dilemma articulated by Dworkin would imply.

In fact, Dworkin himself concedes that moral positions based on religious convictions are such that not everybody has a reason to embrace them, and yet he maintains that 'Rawls offers no reason to think that the test of reciprocity excludes any reasonable convictions *beyond religious convictions*'.[26] Now *this* would, in itself, be a significant use of public reason (and a significant demonstration that a public reason requirement *does* exclude many moral positions), but surely there is more to it—namely those positions that, under an impartial observer's test, deny some groups and categories equal moral standing at the outset. And of course, as even the just-quoted sentence by Dworkin confirms, Rawls would exclude *non*-reasonable conceptions from the stock of comprehensive conceptions eligible for ascertaining PR: there is not even a presumption that racists, religious fundamentalists, neo-Nazis, and others who deny free and equal status of all citizens 'would be amenable to public reason',[27] irrespective of their subjective views about how 'reasonable' they are. So Dworkin's claim that PR has no critical edge is unfounded.

These remarks about an 'objectified' notion of reasonableness point to a dilemma. If we define reasonableness too thickly, for the purpose of discerning the stock of doctrines that will yield PR, the whole device of PR becomes redundant because all the work of justifying the law is done by reasonableness itself. A very thick definition of reasonableness basically substitutes the substantial conceptions of the reasoner for the conceptions of other people who also are the constituency of PR, so to speak. This was well observed by Bernard Williams, though not in the context of Rawls's conception of legitimacy or the idea of PR, but which applies well to the highly artificial notion of 'reasonableness' adopted by Rawls and his followers for the purposes of PR: one 'may invoke absolute or universal conditions of legitimacy, which any 'reasonable' person should accept;

[26] Dworkin, *Justice* (n. 12) 253, emphasis added.
[27] Freeman, 'Introduction' (n. 2) 40.

but in doing this, he speaks to an audience in a given situation, *who share these conceptions of reasonableness*, or whom the theorist hopes to persuade . . . to accept them'.[28] This is precisely the case with the 'reasonableness' adopted for the purposes of PR: when all reasonable people are expected to accept certain ideas figuring in public reasons, this is because they already share the specific liberal conception of reasonableness. And it would be excessively authoritarian, with a consequence of placing such a requirement in conflict with the value of liberty which—as noted in Chapter 1—is one of the underlying ideals behind the concept of PR. Such a consequence was eloquently depicted by David Enoch in one of his relentless philippics against PR:

> If . . . the main rationale for some public-justification requirement is that people should not be subjected to rules they reject, then idealizing in a way that restricts the requirement to just the reasonable, or just those reasoning nicely, or whatever, seems inconsistent with the underlying rationale.[29]

On the other hand, if we define reasonableness very thinly, then there is a risk that some repugnant views will make it into the stock of doctrines considered for the purpose of ascertaining PR, and can contaminate the law with racism, sexism, or some other illegitimate motives. Recently, it was conceptualized by Kevin Vallier, a leading PR scholar, as a matter of 'idealization' in public reason: coercion, Vallier claims in an important 2020 article, must be justified to an idealized (as opposed to real) community, but the standards of idealization must be moderate, that is, they cannot be used to attribute reasons to individuals that stray too far from their actual commitments.[30] Vallier is on a right track—but how far is too far? I am only stating this dilemma without trying to solve it, because any solution must be context-dependent and rely on common sense. It is on a case-by-case basis that we must ascertain whether the requirement of PR that we articulate is thin enough to allow the views with which we disagree on merit but consider reasonable, and thick enough to disqualify conceptions which manifestly deny equality and freedom to other citizens. A particular application of the doctrine of PR should not be biased towards 'our' views and at the same time should not be toothless. No abstract solution for finding such a middle road can be articulated but, for functional reasons, that is, for the reasons of the *functions* that reasonableness plays in the construction, it is probably fair to say that one should err on the side of thin rather than thick criteria of reasonableness, so that the PR device does not become superfluous. Reasonableness should aim at eliminating some clearly unreasonable doctrines but leaving in

[28] Bernard Williams, *In the Beginning Was the Deed*, ed. Geoffrey Hawthorn (Princeton University Press 2005) 136, emphasis added, brackets removed.

[29] David Enoch, 'The Disorder of Public Reason', (2013) 124 *Ethics* 141, 165, footnote omitted.

[30] Kevin Vallier, 'In Defense of Idealization in Public Reason', (2020) 85 *Erkenntnis* 1109.

the space of overlapping consensus a number of comprehensive reasonable doctrines (in which case PR serves the useful function of an effective constraint on reasons in lawmaking), rather than becoming such a tough filtering device that only one (or very few) comprehensive doctrines will pass muster, in which case PR is redundant, as all the scrutiny has been already done by applying the reasonableness test.

What is important to keep in mind in this context is that there is no continuity between good reasons that all reasonable people may adopt for having certain beliefs *in their own lives*—to guide their individual course of life with the assurance that it is based on valid and wise reasons—and good reasons to publicly press, advance, and adopt as guiding coercive political action among individuals living in the society.[31] This discontinuity is not seen as a puzzle, much less an aberration in one's overall moral physiognomy, but rather as a necessary implication of a liberal approach to the exercise of coercive powers which must be justified by special types of considerations, not applicable in individual moral reasoning about one's own moral good. Rather than asking oneself, as one does regarding one's own conception of moral good, what the true, or otherwise valid, moral rules in the political sphere are, one must necessarily take into account the existence and concerns *of the others*, who may not share one's own conception for reasons which are not lamentable or discrediting. Hence, person *X* may well adopt a certain justifiable reason for action with the confidence that it is a valid one, and at the same time accept that *Y*'s reasons for action, different from *X*'s, are also reasonable and valid ones: there is no incoherence in the healthy diversity of reasons which may properly guide individual courses of action. So if *X* decides that, as rules of justice go (governing interactions between *X* and *Y* and many other agents) she must adopt a different rule from the one she would have adopted only for herself, then in one sense it may be seen as a 'second best' (because the rule will diverge from the one already confirmed as morally right), but 'it is the absolute best in another sense, because it takes into account the morally relevant fact of pluralism and the need for some effective decision in political society'.[32]

One way of explaining this fact of divergence between moral reasons adopted for oneself and moral reasons which should govern our relationships with others in the circumstances of pluralism is through Rawls's notion of 'burdens of judgement'. As Rawls explains, rational and reasonable people, in the circumstances of liberty, will come up with different judgements because (1) the evidence bearing on a case is complex and often hard to evaluate; (2) there may be a reasonable disagreement about the weight which should be accorded to particular considerations; (3) our moral concepts are often vague and indeterminate, so we may

[31] See Thomas Nagel, 'Moral Conflict and Political Legitimacy', (1987) 16 *Philosophy & Public Affairs* 215, 221.

[32] Pavlos Eleftheriadis, *Legal Rights* (Oxford University Press 2008) 58.

differ about the interpretation of these concepts; (4) the way we assess evidence is often due to our life experiences, which are of course different; (5) there may be often different kinds of considerations on both sides of an issue and reasonable people may find it hard to decide how to assess them; and (6) social institutions often restrict admissible values, so we often face difficulties in setting priorities among values.[33] None of these sources of differences in our judgements (and the list is not exhaustive) can be traced to any irrationality: none has to do with bias, ignorance, selfishness, etc. which can be 'laundered' through a thorough reasonableness scrutiny. As one can see, the list is rather untidy: it contains sources of disagreement having different status and significance (for instance, one may justifiably claim that category (6) is less of an *explanation* than a *critique* of social institutions, if their design is such that they distort or screen off the relevant arguments which can be admitted), so the catalogue of 'burdens of judgements' should not be considered as set in stone—but they identify some of the types of sources of reasonable disagreement about the good.

To be sure, there may also be reasonable disagreement about principles of political action[34] because public reason under-determines the right course of action—there may be several courses of action which all meet the requirement of PR, but this will be a *different* disagreement than reasonable disagreement about comprehensive conceptions of moral good. This is because reasons for *political* action are discontinuous with these individual sets of conceptions for individual lives. They must appeal to what Nagel calls aptly 'a common ground of justification',[35] and more specifically, under the ideal of PR, pass the test of endorsability by others who are affected by the action—a test which obviously would be absurd if applied to one's individual conception of the good. In fact, it would be equivalent to saying that one has no, or no determinate, conception regarding one's own life.

The discontinuity thesis (*sans le mot*, but very much along the lines of disputing a proposition that we may have different sets of reasons to guide our own life and political action, and that the latter are independent of the former) was criticized by Joseph Raz who had found the line drawn by Rawls and Nagel between the two spheres puzzling and incoherent.[36] Raz articulated his critique

[33] Rawls, *Political Liberalism* (n. 5) 56–57.

[34] This is the point made forcefully by Jeremy Waldron who endorses the idea of burdens of judgment and then extends it upon the field of political disagreement (or disagreement about justice), see Jeremy Waldron, *Law and Disagreement* (Oxford University Press 1999)112–13 and 151–53. Waldron is correct to argue that there may be reasonable disagreement about justice (or more generally, political action) but incorrect, in my view, when he says that sources of disagreement are the same regarding conceptions of the good and conceptions of justice.

[35] Nagel, 'Moral Conflict' (n. 31) 232.

[36] Joseph Raz, 'Facing Diversity: The Case of Epistemic Abstinence', (1990) 19 *Philosophy & Public Affairs* 3. Note that Raz's article had been published before Rawls's *Political Liberalism* appeared and addresses mainly, as far as Rawls is concerned, the two articles which had foreshadowed the book: John Rawls, 'Justice as Fairness: Political not Metaphysical', (1985) 14 *Philosophy & Public Affairs* 225 and John Rawls, 'The Idea of an Overlapping Consensus', (1987) 7 *Oxford Journal of Legal Studies* 1.

in the language of 'autonomy' of political theory, the strong (and objectionable) version of which he attributed to Rawls. Under a weak version (and I am paraphrasing Raz here), political conceptions are just species of broader moral conceptions: they are valid moral conceptions simply applicable to a sphere of political issues, such as distributive justice. There is no room for a 'discontinuity thesis' (to use the language I have just employed) on such a weakly autonomous notion of political theory. However, continues Raz, Rawls adopts a vision of the autonomy of politics in a strong sense, where the validity of political moral conceptions does not depend on the validity of other (assumedly, personal) moral views. Nevertheless, Raz asserts, such a strongly autonomous conception is implausible for two reasons. First, justification of political values depends on their proper integration into 'a comprehensive view of human well-being';[37] second, the practical implications of any political value depends on how conflicts with other, non-political values will be resolved, and so their validity cannot be abstracted from those other, non-political values.

None of the 'two decisive objections'[38] by Raz is convincing. The first, about the allegedly immanent links between political values and specific (and admittedly, controversial) conceptions of human well-being, is an assertion in search of argument. Much will depend here on how one understands the interdependence between political values and 'comprehensive views of human well-being'. Suppose you espouse, as your strictly 'political' value, a robust protection of freedom of speech. In what sense is it *necessarily* connected with an idea of human well-being? Trivially, it does not make sense for you to endorse freedom of speech unless you think that, down the line, it will be *good* for the individuals who are within the range of its benefits. But the *way* in which it may benefit them makes all the difference. If your endorsement of freedom of speech is based on the idea that it is a necessary means of implementing a particular ideal of human perfection, and this is the only way in which you connect freedom of speech with human well-being, then Raz is right. But if you believe that freedom of speech is connected with other *political* values, which have only an indirect connection with human well-being, then the discontinuity thesis becomes much more plausible. So if, for example, your endorsement of freedom of speech is based on your view that it is a necessary condition of democratic self-government, or of tolerance to people whose ideas you despise—then the connection of this political value (freedom of speech) with a specific ideal of human well-being is tenuous at best. To be sure, eventually you must adopt *some* conception of the good to confer a value on freedom of speech—such as that people's well-being is dependent upon political democracy, or upon tolerance—but such a thin connection cannot support the strong proposition asserted by Raz about the

[37] Raz, 'Facing Diversity' (n. 36) 23, reference omitted.
[38] Ibid.

embeddedness of political values within specific conceptions of human well-being. It is obvious, but trivial. Freedom of speech can be equally endorsed by people who have diametrically different views about the conditions of human well-being, but all can converge on the values of democracy or tolerance, and in this sense freedom of speech remains autonomous towards, or discontinuous with, ideas about conditions for human well-being. While the value of freedom of speech *in abstracto* is underwritten by an idea that respecting freedom of speech is, all things considered, good for individuals, the specific contours, limits, and justifications of freedom of speech are independent of any particular conceptions of human flourishing. You can specify them without taking a stand in controversies about what is the best moral vision for a fulfilled individual life.

The second point made by Raz is stronger, and his rejection of the autonomy of political theory seems to hinge on this second point. This is fundamentally a matter of priority of political values vis-à-vis non-political ones, which Rawls asserts and Raz denies. In Raz's words, 'the practical implications of any value depend on whether it conflicts with other values, and if so, which of the conflicting values prevails . . .'. Since, Raz continues, 'a strongly autonomous political theory prevents us from considering its political values in the comprehensive context of a complete moral theory, it cannot yield practical conclusions. It can neither assure us that conflicts do not arise nor adjudicate when they do arise'.[39] Now there are two ways, for the purpose of this particular argument, in which political values may conflict with other values. They may conflict with other *political* values. This, of course, cannot be embarrassing to the autonomy of political theory: the conflict remains within the political sphere, and there must be internal, political resources for adjudicating among those conflicts. But this cannot be the main point of Raz's objection. What he depicts, as an exhibit for his thesis about non-autonomy of political theory (in a strict sense), is a conflict between a political value and a *non-political* value. So suppose we have, on the one hand, a political value (e.g. freedom of political speech) and on the other hand, a non-political value being a part of a comprehensive conception of someone's moral good (say, a sense of pride of belonging to a particular community, which confers a highly valued sense of identity upon this individual). A political value, in a particular circumstance, conflicts with a non-political value: an exercise of freedom of speech threatens someone's pride of belonging to a community that a speaker vilifies. This, I think, is a paradigmatic example of the conflict which Raz has in mind.

This is a matter of the *primacy* of one value over another. In one sense, Raz is correct: a strictly political theory cannot, in itself, provide us with a reason to prefer a political value (here, freedom of speech) over a non-political value (here, the pride of belonging which is threatened by vilification of one's group).

[39] Ibid.

Neither is the converse true: a vilified person's comprehensive theory cannot give us reasons to prefer *her* value over the value of freedom of speech. Whichever is our pre-theoretical intuition about priority, we must find some second-order standpoint which will allow us to adjudicate between these two values. The situation is no different from any conflict of values, or claims, or rights. It is true, the political value of freedom of speech (as is our example here) per se cannot dictate its priority vis-à-vis other values. But neither can a personal, comprehensive conception of the good do so: in itself, it cannot proclaim its own priority over other values (including political ones), which may from time to time conflict with it. Priority is a second-order issue with regard to values which conflict with each other. At the end of the day, each moral reasoner, individually, prioritizes political values which she considers valid, compared to her own comprehensive conception of the good.[40]

But the priority issue cannot be embarrassing to the autonomy of political theory in the way Raz claims it is. To say that, in itself, the theory cannot dictate and justify its own priority vis-à-vis other moral conceptions does not imply that political conceptions, per se, are incomprehensible, or inconsistent, or incomplete in any way, in isolation from those other, non-political values. To return to our example, from saying that freedom of speech (a political conception par excellence) in itself does not tell us when and why it has priority over other values (some of which are patently non-political), it does not follow that freedom of speech is chimerical, or incomprehensible, or incomplete, without considering a 'comprehensive context of a complete moral theory',[41] to use Raz's words. Raz is correct in suggesting that 'practical conclusions' must incorporate both political and non-political values, but the fact that, when asking ourselves 'what is to be done?' we need to take on board the whole set of considerations, and consider everything, cannot be an argument against 'autonomy', in the strong sense of the word, of particular subsets of our comprehensive moral landscape.

To illustrate to what fantastic lengths Raz goes in rejecting the discontinuity between public/political morality and personal/individual morality, and consequently claiming no autonomy of the former, it is useful to refer to his argument about a similar version of the discontinuity thesis in Nagel's conception of liberalism. When discussing Nagel's examples of cases in which, even if someone holds a true belief nevertheless one should not be (according to Nagel) pressing this belief as a basis for political action, Raz evokes the issues of, inter alia, nuclear deterrence and capital punishment. The views of Nagel that such public issues are to be treated in a way different from individual morality Raz dismisses as 'especially weak arguments', and he continues:

[40] See Quong, *Liberalism without Perfection* (n. 14) 232–33.
[41] Raz, 'Facing Diversity' (n. 36) 23.

> while the morality of state-wielded nuclear deterrence or capital punishment is inevitably a matter on which the state must take a view, the state's relation to nuclear weapons owned by private individuals or to capital punishment meted out by them is on par with its relation to private abortions. Is it reasonable to hold that considerations which determine the morality of nuclear threats and of the death penalty should determine public policy regarding their use by the state, but should be excluded from affecting public policy regarding their use by individuals?[42]

In his search for establishing continuity between true beliefs in one's own personal morality and reasonable beliefs guiding public coercive action, Raz constructs highly convoluted examples of a nuclear threat by a private individual or capital punishment inflicted privately. The former is extremely unlikely in the world as we know it, and the latter is incoherent; it is part of the very concept of 'capital punishment' that it is state-inflicted, and 'capital punishment' by a private individual is a bizarre synonym for a murder. If anything, the improbability of Raz's examples used in his polemic with Nagel demonstrates rather than undermines the idea of discontinuity, and of the autonomy of morality governing the public sphere.

3. 'Too Thick': Drawing the Line between Discussion and Decision-Making

It is now time to consider the second horn of the dilemma articulated by Dworkin: the claim that PR is much too rigorous a test because it would disqualify many more justifications than our intuitions or common sense would dictate. This second reading of PR is based on hostility towards admitting 'comprehensive', philosophical-religious arguments into the domain of public discourse, in order to be able to construct 'overlapping consensus'. A critic of PR in this second sense may say (and a legion of critics *have* said)[43] that it is intuitively plausible that participants in public discourse about law should be able—indeed, even encouraged—to cite, and appeal to, their deep philosophical conceptions, including religious or religion-equivalent ones, based on certain views of the universe, society, and individuals.

This suggests that the concept of 'overlapping consensus', if it is to inform a plausible model of PR, must undergo some modifications and refinements in order to make it compatible with widespread liberal-democratic intuitions. One (rather obvious) preliminary thing to note is this: PR (and the overlapping

[42] Ibid. 42 n. 85.

[43] See, inter alia, references to Jeremy Waldron, Mark Tushnet, and John Dryzek in this section of the chapter.

consensus) does not compel us to admit only reasons which are not part of comprehensive conceptions: it requires us only to dismiss these political reasons which are part of some comprehensive conceptions but not others. The very fact of citing or appealing to (or being supported by) a deep philosophical rationale cannot disqualify a given argument from figuring in PR. What matters is that when we refer to our 'comprehensive' doctrines, we must appeal only to those which are 'reasonable' (in the sense discussed in the previous part of this chapter), and therefore to those which lend themselves to producing 'public political values' (the values that all citizens may accept, such as due respect for human life, the ordered reproduction of society over time, or equality of men and women)[44] which may properly figure in PR. Those values may belong to different 'comprehensive' doctrines, but this fact is not fatal to political liberalism because '[t]he only comprehensive doctrines that run afoul of public reason are those that cannot support a reasonable balance of political values'.[45] Of course the crux of the matter is *what* balance of political values will be deemed 'reasonable'—but here we revert to the substantive ('objective') criteria of free and equal citizenship etc. And these criteria may well allow for a relatively broad spectrum of 'reasonable' political solutions to any given issue (thus mitigating the objection to excessive rigour of PR): 'It is true that the balance of political values a citizen holds must be reasonable, and one that can be seen to be reasonable by other citizens; but *not all reasonable balances are the same*.'[46]

It must be emphasized that what matters in the conception of PR is that we put forward only such proposals *for a coercive law* which may be accepted even by people who do not share our deep philosophical views—which in practice means that these proposals must be capable of being defended *also* on some other grounds. In fact, this is what Rawls himself acknowledged in his reformulation of PR by explaining that we may 'introduce into political discussion at any time our comprehensive doctrine, religious or nonreligious, provided that, in due course, we give properly public reasons to support the principles and policies our comprehensive doctrine is said to support'.[47] Rawls acknowledges the role of *other* forms of discourse, which do not have the character of 'public reasoning' (the title reserved for proposals leading to officially adopted laws and policies), such as the 'declaration' which occurs when 'we each declare our own comprehensive doctrine, religious or nonreligious',[48] with no requirement of public reason applicable here. This is important because occasionally the requirement of 'public reason' has been interpreted as if it applied to public debate in general—a requirement which would of course lead to a radical erosion of public discourse. In

[44] These three 'public political values' are provided by Rawls as implicated by the question of abortion, *Political Liberalism* (n. 5) 243 n. 32.
[45] Ibid. 243, footnote omitted.
[46] Ibid. 243, emphasis added.
[47] Rawls, 'The Idea of Public Reason' (n. 3) 144.
[48] Ibid. 155.

fact, however, even such a 'declaration' is for Rawls instrumental to the purposes of public reason: 'The aim of doing this is to declare to others who affirm different comprehensive doctrines that we also each endorse a reasonable political conception belonging to the family of reasonable such conceptions.'[49]

This point is further amplified by Rawls's explanation that 'the introduction into public political culture of religious or secular doctrines, provided the proviso [of subsequently producing proper public reasons] is met, does not change the nature and content of justification in public reason itself'.[50] Indeed, Rawls at times suggests not only permissibility but even the importance of introducing those comprehensive doctrines into the public sphere, for instance: 'We may think of the reasonable comprehensive doctrines that support society's reasonable political conceptions as those conceptions' vital social basis, giving them enduring strength and vigor',[51] and mentions the 'benefits of the mutual knowledge of citizens' recognizing one another's reasonable comprehensive doctrines'.[52]

But Rawls himself never explicated in any depth or clearly enough the distinction between open general debate (what he sometimes calls 'background culture') and discourse leading to authoritative decisions—a point noted by Charles Larmore who reminds us of the distinction between '*open discussion*, where people argue with one another in the light of the whole truth as they see it, and *decision-making* where they deliberate as participants in some organ of government about which option should be made legally binding'.[53] Some critics of public reason disregard the distinction between the general discussion (governed, as it should be, by the principle of freedom of expression) and the arguments effectively triggering legislative, coercive proposals. For one, John Dryzek attributes to Rawls's public reason 'a set of commitments that individuals must adopt if they are to be *admitted to the public arena*',[54] and even an idea that 'deliberators' must be committed to certain process values (impartiality, civility, reciprocity) 'before they can be admitted to the forum'.[55] A sharp statement by Mark Tushnet: 'It would be crazy to suggest that voters have to restrain from invoking religious reasons *when they discuss politics*'[56] may well apply to an 'open discussion' but not to public discourse where citizen-voters act in their 'official' capacity, so to speak, and where the point is to argue for a particular coercive law or policy. One way of conceptualizing the distinction between the two types of discourse is by remembering that PR is intrinsically related to the idea of

[49] Ibid. 155.
[50] Ibid. 153.
[51] Ibid. 153.
[52] Ibid. 154.
[53] Charles Larmore, The *Autonomy of Morality* (Cambridge University Press 2008) 210.
[54] John S. Dryzek, *Deliberative Democracy and Beyond* (Oxford University Press 2000) 169, emphasis added.
[55] Ibid. 169, italics removed.
[56] Mark Tushnet, *Taking the Constitution Away from the Courts* (Princeton University Press 1999) 91, emphasis added.

legitimacy; legitimacy, in turn, is part and parcel of law-related discourse, with the coercive implications of making a successful argument for legal change, but not of an open debate unrelated to law proposals.[57]

The distinction between the two types of discourse, one belonging to the sphere of activism, another to 'mere' discussion, seems intuitively plausible. Admittedly, the distinction is less clear when applied to public discourse led by citizens rather than by public officials: what is eventually meant to lead to an authoritative solution (and therefore becomes advocacy rather than a mere 'declaration', to use Rawls's term) is not always articulated at the outset when we engage with each other (including via mass media) in a political discussion.

Sometimes the *special settings* and circumstances of an argument make it clear that we are on the side of 'advocacy' rather than 'declaration'. Consider the special case of legal scholarship and, more specifically, of a normative (rather than a purely descriptive) legal theory concerned with arguing about the desirability of this or that legal regulation. It seems clear that, in making the case for a particular legal rule or judicial decision, scholars in a way prefigure the positions of legal authorities and should try to articulate only public reasons in defence of their position. A view of Lawrence Solum who argued to the contrary, and claimed that '[t]he ideal of public legal reason that applies to legal practice should not apply directly to legal scholars when they debate and discuss legal policies or normative legal theories',[58] is therefore questionable, even though Solum weakens the force of this assertion by adding immediately that such restraint of public reason should bind normative legal scholarship 'indirectly': 'When normative legal theorists take up this particular task, advising judges about what they should do and what reasons they should give for doing it, they necessarily assume those restraints for political morality that constrain those whom they advise.'[59] Perhaps it is pedantic on my part but I fail to see what is 'indirect' (as opposed to 'direct') about this restraint, and I believe that this function of normative legal scholarship is so universal and ubiquitous that we may conclude that the principle of PR *should* constrain the arguments provided by legal scholars for the use of legal coercion. Still the uncertainty reflected by Solum's reluctance to characterize this imperative as 'direct' only confirms that the borderline between 'advocacy' and a mere 'declaration' is often fuzzy, though not meaningless. Fuzziness is a property of a great many distinctions which are nevertheless meaningful and intelligible to reasonable persons.

But perhaps some will claim that the line between general discussion and advocacy is not merely fuzzy but impossible to draw at all? Justice Holmes's famous dictum 'every idea is an incitement'[60] can be easily paraphrased as 'every idea

[57] See Charles Larmore, 'Public Reason' in Samuel Freeman (ed.), *The Cambridge Companion to Rawls* (Cambridge University Press 2003) 368, 383.
[58] Lawrence B. Solum, 'Public Legal Reason', (2006) 92 *Virginia Law Review* 1449, 1479.
[59] Ibid. 1480.
[60] *Gitlow v. NY*, 268 U.S. 652, 673 (1925) (Holmes, J. dissenting).

is advocacy', without any loss of plausibility. In fact, an expression of an idea in public and about a public matter, without the slightest intention of advocating a particular public solution or policy, may seem pointless. Consider the immediately following sentences in Holmes' dissent: '[An idea] offers itself for belief, and, if believed, it is acted on unless some other belief outweighs it or some failure of energy stifles the movement at its birth. The only difference between the expression of an opinion and an incitement in the narrower sense is the speaker's enthusiasm for the result.'[61] This may well also capture the (alleged) difference between expression of an opinion and advocacy of a policy—and if so, undermine the line that separates advocacy for law from general public debate. But such an undermining is deeply counter-intuitive. It would commit us to a view that whenever we express an opinion on matters of public interest, we are engaged in activism aimed at bringing about a change in this direction. It is clearly inconsistent with the experience of actual communicative actions in our social life. It would also impose upon us an almost unbearable burden of the recognition that whatever we say in public is an act of advocacy: we would all be constant activists. However, we often express views and opinions where the only practical intention we may have is to convince our hearers to them (and sometimes, not even that) but not to bring about a change in the world in a direction consistent with our opinion. It is neither useless nor absurd to engage in an explanation of our views about social issues without any advocacy motive. We may want others to better understand 'where we come from', to use a colloquial formula, but not necessarily to convince them to any particular action specified by our conception. In fact, rather than a sharp antinomy, there is a *continuum* of communicative acts, with a mere 'declaration' in Rawls's sense at one pole of the spectrum, and advocacy forming part of the decision-making on the other. The requirement of appealing to public reasons intensifies as we move from the former to the latter extreme on the spectrum and relaxes as we move towards the 'declaration' end of the continuum.

Take the example of the conscientious objector who benefits from a legal protection for such exemptions as, for example, from military service. One may still believe that he has a moral duty to explain his position to other members of society, but this explanation does not aim at changing the law (assume, for the sake of argument, that law properly protects such objections) nor to convince others to adopt a similar philosophical position: the objector wants to be released from some general duties in order to protect his moral integrity but does not want to generalize this exemption upon all; he is no proselytizer. Such a duty of explanation is plausible and detachable from any persuasive purposes. I believe this is the idea that Jeremy Waldron had in mind when he wrote:

[61] Ibid. 673.

> People have a right and perhaps a duty to explain themselves to their fellow citizens—to do the best they can to put into words a sense of why they feel so strongly about a given policy or proposal. They may do this not in any way that is intended to be persuasive but simply to convey to their fellow citizens, in case they are interested, the sort of view that they hold.[62]

Such exposition of our views to others resonates well with Rawls's (already quoted) appreciation of the 'benefits of the mutual knowledge of citizens' recognizing one another's reasonable comprehensive doctrines'.[63] These benefits may be diverse, and do not necessarily encompass the actual process of decision-making: such practice may be useful in other ways than leading to a change in valid legal rules.[64] By presenting our views to others the best we can, we may affect the ways in which others understand, respect, evaluate us, etc. and consequently treat us. Still it is not advocacy—not by a long shot. So if a workable distinction between 'declaration' and advocacy is a prerequisite of plausibility of the very idea of PR, the prerequisite can be convincingly established.

What is important is that, when the context is one of public deliberation leading (in the aspirations of speakers, or the understanding of the audience) to state-adopted coercive laws or policies, the requirement of public reason does not apply only to officials but to citizens as well. Indeed, when citizens speak in that way, publicly advocating this or that coercive law, they play the role of officials. For this purpose we might adopt a 'continuity thesis': a thesis that there is continuity in terms of moral entitlement, authority, and responsibility, between individual citizens and public officials. In fact, a citizen-voter *is* a public official, and the role she performs (and which goes well beyond the one-off act of voting, but also includes other forms of disciplining the representatives and participating in public discourse) is qualitatively the same as the role performed by public officials. (As I have suggested elsewhere, this continuity applies to the 'motivations, intentions, preferences' etc. of individual voters and of their representatives in parliament).[65] It is not merely a description but also a normative ideal; citizens should feel and behave *as if* they were individual lawmakers, even though the result is authoritative only after all votes are counted (just as is the case in the representative assembly or, for that matter, in any collective authoritative body). As Rawls has said:

> When firm and widespread, the disposition of citizens to view themselves as ideal legislators, and to repudiate government officials and candidates for

[62] Jeremy Waldron, 'Isolating Public Reasons' in Thom Brooks and Martha C. Nussbaum (eds.), *Rawls's Political Liberalism* (Columbia University Press 2015) 113, 132.
[63] Rawls, 'The Idea of Public Reason' (n. 3) 154.
[64] See Waldron, 'Isolating' (n. 62) 132.
[65] Wojciech Sadurski, *Equality and Legitimacy* (Oxford University Press 2008) 24–27.

> public office who violate public reason, is one of the political and social roots of democracy, and is vital to its enduring strength and vigor. Thus citizens fulfil their duty of civility and support the idea of public reason by doing what they can to hold government officials to it.[66]

And earlier, in *Political Liberalism*, he connected this point explicitly with a theory of PR by saying: 'in a democratic society public reason is the reason of equal citizens who, as a collective body, *exercise final political and coercive power over one another* in enacting laws and in amending their constitution.'[67]

4. Distorting the Process of Justification?

Before I move to the central argument made by Jeremy Waldron in an impassioned philippic against the Rawlsian conception of PR,[68] let me deal with his related though more marginal objection, namely what can be called an argument arising from the exaggeration of heuristic difficulties. PR, we are told, when understood as a matter of reciprocity and civility, 'underestimates people's ability to grapple with unfamiliar views that start out with no foothold in their own mentality or motivational set'.[69] But Waldron is able to make this puzzling observation only because he conceptualizes PR (viewed through the prism of civility and reciprocity) as based on the principle that '[a]nything I offer as a contribution in public debate I must offer as something for others to grasp, consider, and engage with', and goes on to attribute to PR adherents an idea that 'since I know that we have different comprehensive conceptions, offering something which draws deeply on my comprehensive conception is not offering something which all others can grasp, consider, and engage with'.[70]

As a terminological aside, on which nothing substantive hinges but which may be useful in order to prevent any confusion, it is worth mentioning that the use of 'civility', quite frequent in the context of discussions of PR, might be seen as misleading because it may suggest a duty of politeness, etiquette, courtesy, and good manners in public discourse, and a stricture that such discourse should not be excessively confrontational or sharp. While these qualities may be seen as of importance (or not), they are unrelated to PR. Rawls defines 'civility' in terms of PR only (the duty of civility requires us 'to be able to explain to one

[66] Rawls, 'The Idea of Public Reason' (n. 3) 135–36, footnote omitted.

[67] *Political Liberalism* (n. 5) 214, emphasis added, see also ibid. 217–18.

[68] As Waldron admits, having articulated this critique: 'this is not my main argument in the present paper', Jeremy Waldron, 'Public Reason and "Justification" in the Courtroom', (2007) 1 *Journal of Law, Philosophy and Culture* 107, 113. His main argument will be considered later in this section of the chapter.

[69] Ibid. 112, footnote omitted.

[70] Ibid. 112.

another . . . how the principles and policies they advocate and vote for can be supported by the political values of public reason';[71] indeed, the connection between Rawls's 'civility' and PR may be seen as tautological.

Waldron's argument just summarized assumes an excessively weak version of PR, and PR in a thicker understanding requires not merely that we offer conceptions which others can 'grasp, consider, and engage with' (to use Waldron's own terms) but also that others can *share*, at least under some circumstances. Rawls, it should be remembered, demands explicitly that we must give other citizens reasons they cannot only understand, but reasons that they 'may reasonably be expected to *endorse* in the light of principles and ideals *acceptable* to them . . .'[72] To 'grasp, consider and engage with' is relatively easy, and of course one does not need anything like PR to achieve it. It is not unthinkable for religious persons to *understand* ('grasp, consider, and engage with') an atheist's mindset, and vice-versa, even though Waldron asserts, implausibly, that the 'Rawlsian line of argument ... radically exaggerates the unfamiliarity of religious arguments to nonbelievers . . .'[73] An anti-utilitarian may have a better grasp of utilitarianism than an adherent to a utilitarian philosophy etc.

But it is one thing to say that a particular comprehensive conception is graspable, and another that it is endorsable by me.[74] Waldron's objection to PR rests on an implausibly exaggerated ignorance of other people's views and replaces the normative problem with an epistemic one, thus distorting the character of PR in its canonical version. Indeed, some twenty years before the criticism just mentioned, Waldron himself had articulated something very much like PR: 'If there is some individual to whom a justification cannot be given, then so far as *he* is concerned, the social order had better be replaced by other arrangements, for the status quo has made out no claim to *his* allegiance.'[75] While it is formulated through a negative rather a positive angle, and the words about 'giving a justification' must be read restrictively in a broader context of Waldron's argument referring as it does to the idea of social contract and government by consent—this is a strikingly elegant articulation of the main intuition behind the idea of PR.

Let me move now to the key argument by Waldron, namely his criticism of the idea of PR as distorting the rationality and justness of justification. Summing up his discussion of the very idea of justification and reason-giving, Waldron says:

[71] Rawls, *Political Liberalism* (n. 5) 217.

[72] Ibid., emphases added.

[73] Waldron, 'Public Reason' (n. 68) 112 n. 27.

[74] See Kent Greenawalt, *Private Consciences and Public Reasons* (Oxford University Press 1995) 145.

[75] Jeremy Waldron, *Liberal Rights* (Cambridge University Press 1993) 44, emphases in the original. The article reprinted in this volume from which this passage is excerpted was originally published in 1987.

> Official or civic deliberation is serious, momentous even, in its consequences, and surely we ought to pay attention to the most serious reasons, whatever their character, when the stakes are this high.... We need to get it right. But how can we be sure we are getting it right if we restrict the range of reasons we are interested in?[76]

The first thing to note about this critique of Waldron's is that it is not addressed against PR only but against *any* constraints on the range of reasons which can be provided in justification of public policy (or any other decision for that matter). Indeed, from the very concept of 'justification' (as a practice of providing reasons for action) Waldron infers a principle that it must be 'open and inclusive',[77] and that it 'involves no restriction on the range of reasons that it is appropriate to mention'.[78] Of course, reasons based on false statements of fact, or which are irrelevant to a given choice, or which do not have a certain normative significance that it is claimed they have, will have to be excluded from the process of justification, though people will frequently disagree about whether any of these conditions are present in a given case.[79] But, as Waldron claims, these are *the only grounds* on which the very idea of justification excludes the invocation of statements of reasons.

While this last proposition sounds analytical and descriptive, in the context of Waldron's argument it is openly normative. Exclusion of whatever reasons that may have a bearing upon a particular decision inevitably detracts from the rationality (and often, the justness) of the decision. Having reviewed examples of such a detrimental effect of exclusion of reasons upon the decisions reached (a point to which I will return in a moment), Waldron states a more general directive: 'to the extent that a given context *is* supposed to involve the unalloyed practice of justification, there should be no restrictions on the reasons it is appropriate to cite and no holding back in the search for reasons that might possibly pertain to the merits of the decision under scrutiny.'[80]

This, remember, is made in the context of criticizing the very idea of PR as a particular device for the exclusion of reasons in the process of public justification of coercive laws. Can the 'no restrictions on reasons' imperative be applied to this realm? At first blush, it seems counter-intuitive: in public matters, especially when leading to a coercive decision or act, we use (often impliedly and tacitly) all sort of rules about excluded reasons. Some of these exclusions are not of absolute strength but nevertheless are important and intuitively plausible. For instance, Jon Elster seems to capture an important and uncontroversial truth about

[76] Waldron, 'Public Reason' (n. 68) 123.
[77] Ibid. 117.
[78] Ibid. 116, footnote omitted.
[79] Ibid. 116–17.
[80] Ibid. 122, footnote omitted.

public discourse when he says that '[i]n a political debate it is pragmatically impossible to argue that a given solution should be chosen just because it is good for oneself. By the very act of engaging in a public debate—by arguing rather than bargaining—one has ruled out the possibility of invoking such reasons'.[81] It is not an analytical truth, but it is nevertheless a law of public debate that any appeals to self-interest are usually ineffective and frowned upon.

Consider some examples of certain justifiably excluded reasons in realms *other* than public debate (after all, Waldron offers his view as a rejection of any reasons-exclusion from any area of justification). When a police officer stops me for speeding, my justification for my action (and against his issuing of a speeding ticket) that 'God told me to do so' will not count at all, not even at the outset as a prima facie reason to be subsequently compared to and possibly defeated by other reasons: it will not compete against the considerations of public safety. (In contrast, my explanation that I was speeding in order to get to the hospital in an emergency *may* be considered, although whether it will prevail is another matter.) A 'reason' for awarding victory to a marathon runner who did not come first but claims (accurately, for the sake argument) that on the day before he had a nervous breakdown which should be considered as an impediment relevant to the award, will not count as a justification for decision: it will not even be put on balance against arguments of fairness to other runners. Of course, Waldron might retort that these examples belong to a category of reasons which are irrelevant or the normative significance of which is different from what is claimed by an agent (which are among the three categories which he explicitly excludes from justification). But this is precisely the point: some *categories* of reasons are considered, *in limine*, inadmissible, and to say that they are irrelevant or that their normative significance has been mistaken by whoever makes the claim, does not add anything to the judgement that they should not be considered as part of justification. To say that a given putative reason is 'irrelevant' is merely to say that, for whatever reasons, it has been excluded from figuring in the justification for a particular decision. We deal with the concept of excluded reasons all the time in social life, and often they are taken as perfectly plausible. And here a distinction between different realms of public discourse is crucial: while in an open discussion it would be acceptable (even if bizarre) for someone to *propose* an idea that God's order should exculpate speeding drivers ('acceptable' though unlikely to convince, I hasten to add), or that in decisions about marathon awards, a runner's state of mental health should be taken into account, in the real-life justifications leading up to authoritative decisions or rules such reasons will be disqualified at the outset. They are pre-empted. They vanish from the process of justification before they have attempted to register in the calculus of reasons.

[81] Jon Elster, 'The Market and the Forum: Three Varieties of Political Theory', in Jon Elster and Aanund Hylland (eds.), *Foundations of Social Choice Theory* (Cambridge University Press 1986) 103, 112–13, footnote omitted.

Here is a possible criticism of the relevance of my two examples (speeding, marathon) along the following lines. The true reason why the cited 'excluded reasons' are excluded in cases such as these is simply because they are contrary to the established and publicly announced institutional rules: respectively, of traffic law or of sport. They are 'excluded' in a purely formal sense, that is, they are not permitted by the existing law on the matter, and not because there is something wrong (in the sense of substantive irrelevance or mistaken normative significance) in citing them in a public deliberation leading up to the change of law. These 'reasons' for dismissing them, the argument may go, do not belong to a category of moral reasons which are properly part of a justification, but they are institutional rules controlling a particular set of authoritative decisions. I do not think that such a rebuttal of the force of these examples would be effective. To see why not, consider a hypothesis hypothetical in which the traffic police officer from our example has a wide discretion in deciding when speeding is justified and hence not culpable (e.g. traffic police may exculpate a driver for speeding when 'it was justified under the circumstances'), and that marathon umpires from our second example have a broad discretion to decide who should be awarded the prize (for instance by disqualifying the actual winner on various vague grounds of cheating, or unnerving other runners). Still, the hypothetical 'reasons' (respectively, from the command of God or from illness) would be likely disqualified at the outset. Further, if someone participating in the public discourse about the *change* of the relevant law suggested those grounds for decisions, it would probably be considered absurd, and rejected without much discussion.

But rather than mere hypotheticals, we can now provide some real-life legal examples of excluded reasons, enjoying widespread intuitive approval. Consider various rules of evidence which provide for the exclusion of evidence derived from unlawful searches and interrogations (the 'poisoned fruit' doctrine), or inadmissibility of testimony if someone is subject to a privilege (spousal, or lawyer's, or priest's), etc.[82] No doubt, at least some of the evidence obtained in these ways could be seen as capable of providing relevant reasons for a decision, and at the same time their exclusion is widely considered to be perfectly appropriate. This shows that, in practice, we do not accept a categorical ban on *any* exclusion of reasons in public justification, at least in some areas. And remember, Waldron's objection to PR, discussed just now, was an objection to *any* reasons-exclusion in public justification, and it is on the strength of this general hostility to exclusions per se that he argues against the idea of PR as a special case of reasons exclusion. Interestingly, Waldron himself briefly considers the

[82] This example had been used by Rawls in his first extended statement of PR, see Rawls, *Political Liberalism* (n. 5) 218–19.

example of exclusionary rules in trial proceedings, and here is how he articulates their rationale:

> they bear witness to the fact that justification and the pursuit of truth are not the only aims of the criminal justice system: we also aim to sustain the dignity of the accused, the purely procedural aspects of the fairness of the process, and the public policy goals implicated in privilege and other exclusionary rules.[83]

This is a remarkable admission because precisely those same rationales can be provided for many other practices of rules exclusion in public discourse leading up to the adoption of or change in coercive law. This seems to fit PR quite well: the dignity of citizens (in particular those who philosophically may disagree with the adopted law), and public policy goals having to do with, say, civility and compliance with law, may well be the legitimate aims justifying exclusion of non-public reasons.

Incidentally, there is one puzzling point in the just-quoted passage when Waldron says that '*justification* and the pursuit of truth are not the only aims of the criminal justice system'.[84] With regard to the 'pursuit of truth', this is obviously correct: criminal trial exclusionary rules may actually minimize our chances of detecting the truth about the offender and crime. But why would they show that 'justification' is compromised in criminal trial, to the benefit of other purposes? After all, those additional aims served by exclusionary rules, such as 'the dignity of the accused, procedural fairness in the process, and public policy goals', can be seen as being built into the overall justification of a judicial decision rather than being external to the justification of the decision. It may sound fastidious on my part, but this language helps Waldron convey a message of any exclusion of rules as being detrimental to a justification of a decision—the position which I am questioning here.

The general and abstract point about *any* rule exclusion being anathema to the very idea of justification is further supported by Waldron in a series of examples scattered throughout his article which amount to what may be called an 'intuitive-inductive' argument. The structure of the argument is to show that in a number of specific cases arguing in favour of or against a particular legal rule, an intuitively correct position would be only (or best) supported by arguments normally inadmissible under the principle of PR. The upshot is that, if we want to reach those conclusions about law (and we do), we need to disregard the constraints of PR. One example is about an absolute prohibition on torture: a position for which Waldron himself is deservedly famous. His positive example is that of Mr Cocks, a UK delegate to the conference preparing the European

[83] Waldron, 'Public Reason' (n. 68) 123–24.
[84] Ibid. 123, emphasis added.

Convention on Human Rights in 1949, who used openly and unquestionably religious language in order to propose a total ban on torture; the negative example is that of Alan Dershowitz who uses simple cost-benefit analysis to justify the use of non-lethal tortures under some circumstances.[85] Waldron's conclusion about this confrontation: 'Without the religious reasons, the case against torturing the terrorist—the case that must be opposed in our reasoning to the saving of hundreds or thousands of lives—consists in some limp rhetoric about personhood and the terrorist's "dignity".'[86] Another example is that of slavery and the infamous *Dred Scott*[87] case: Waldron cites a noble dissent by Justice McLean who used religious language *par excellence* to show why the plaintiff slave should not be regarded as a chattel.[88] Waldron's observation: 'McLean violated Rawls's constraints [of PR] and he did so in the very institutional setting that is supposed to be an exemplar of their operation.'[89] The third example is about a hypothetical decision 'to abolish all welfare assistance to the poor'; referring to St. Matthew's Gospel, Waldron derives 'a staggeringly important reason in favour of a duty to help the poor' from an evangelical imperative of not turning one's back on the Son of God, and yet, a reason which under PR 'is not supposed to be publicly cognizable'.[90]

There are several problems with the 'intuitive-inductive' method, the first being that an intuition which supports the strength of an entire argument may be itself controversial and not shared by everybody, including by some people who are reasonable and who have thought through the matter. This may well be the case with the example of the torture of a terrorist. While I, for one, fully share Waldron's (and Mr Cocks's) position on the matter, I can acknowledge that Alan Dershowitz may have a point, and that a better way of sorting out binding legal conclusions should be to let one and the other side carry out the discourse within the constraints of PR so that they do not talk in a language which is either incomprehensible or unacceptable to another side in the controversy.

More importantly, however (and in case someone thinks that the last suggestion discriminates against the anti-torture view by depriving it of its best arguments), for the intuitive-inductive argument to be persuasive, we would have to be convinced that in these three cases (or any other cases which may be provided in this context) no reasonable, compelling, and powerful PR-compatible arguments can be supplied for the 'correct' side of the controversy. The point is not about what type of arguments (religious or otherwise) have been effectively provided, but whether equally powerful arguments for these intuitively correct positions *can be provided* using the language of PR rather than in sectarian language.

[85] Ibid. 119–20.
[86] Ibid. 120.
[87] *Dred Scott v. Sanford*, 60 U.S. 393 (1856).
[88] Waldron, 'Public Reason' (n. 68) 121–22.
[89] Ibid. 122.
[90] Ibid. 119.

Viewed in this light, Waldron's observations are one-sided and unconvincing. Can there be no secular (and PR compatible) arguments for universal assistance to the poor of equal moral force as the imperative taken from St Matthew's Gospel,[91] and which for non-believers may be equally compelling and deep as for Waldron is the warning that 'neglecting to help the poor is a way of turning one's back on the Son of God'?[92] Is the view that each human being 'bears the impress of his Maker, . . . and . . . is destined to an endless existence'[93] unparalleled in a repertoire of good secular arguments which we can find against slavery? And finally, in a discussion about torture, if we disregard religious arguments and still want to make a sustained anti-torture argument, are we condemned only to some 'limp rhetoric about personhood and the terrorist's "dignity"', as Waldron suggests?[94]

Let us focus on this last example. The way Waldron draws an alternative is: either you stick to PR and then you end up with something like a Dershowitz position (because, as Waldron sarcastically asks: 'How could anyone reasonably object to the use of torture to save thousands of lives in a case like this [namely, the terrorist attacks of September 11, 2001]?'[95] and refers in this context to Dershowitz's usage of a 'simple cost-benefit analysis' which leads him to support non-lethal torture in some cases),[96] *or* you openly resort to religious arguments and then you have at your disposal the best available reasons to support an absolute ban on torture. Both horns of this alternative are highly questionable. On one hand, it is unclear why Dershowitz's cost-benefit analysis ('it is surely better to inflict nonlethal pain on one guilty terrorist who is illegally withholding information needed to prevent an act of terrorism than to permit a large number of innocent victims to die')[97] should be seen as an exemplar of a PR-compatible argument. Rather, it sounds like a vulgar use of traditional act-utilitarianism which, under Rawls's language, should be seen as an instance of a 'comprehensive conception', and therefore be inadmissible under PR.

Be that it may, and even if Dershowitz's utility calculus is cognizable under PR, the second horn of Waldron's alternative is strikingly unpersuasive. Why would he say that, shorn of religious arguments, opponents of torture would be confined to some 'limp rhetoric about personhood and the terrorist's "dignity"'?[98] What is inescapably 'limp' about arguments based on a conception of

[91] '[I]f what St. Matthew's Gospel says is true, then there is a staggeringly important reason in favour of a duty to help the poor', ibid. 119.

[92] Ibid. 118, footnote omitted.

[93] *Dred Scott* 60 U.S. 393, 550 (McLean, J. dissenting), quoted by Waldron, 'Public Reason' (n. 68) 121.

[94] Waldron, 'Public Reason' (n. 68) 120.

[95] Ibid. at 119.

[96] Ibid. 119 n. 57.

[97] Alan M. Dershowitz, *Why Terrorism Works* (Yale University Press 2002) 144, quoted in Waldron, 'Public Reason' (n. 68) 119 n. 57.

[98] Waldron, 'Public Reason' (n. 68) 120.

personhood and equal dignity? Sure, in the philosophy libraries we can find many shallow arguments on dignity—but then we can also find many examples of limp and shallow *theological* arguments. Indeed, the very sentence from Mr Cocks's 1949 speech used by Waldron as an instance of a powerful religious argument against torture: 'I say that to take the straight beautiful bodies of men and women and to maim and mutilate them by torture is a crime against high heaven and the holy spirit of man. I say that it is a sin against the Holy Ghost...'[99] etc.—may strike many today as singularly ineffective and even eccentric. It is arguable that the phrase may have sounded more natural and appropriate as an argument to be made in public in the late 1940s, when it was actually made. But this is not embarrassing to the principle of PR: its content is mutable and context- and time-sensitive.[100] As Rawls said, 'Political liberalism ... does not try to fix public reason once and for all in the form of one favoured political conception of justice ... [N]ew variations may be proposed from time to time and older ones may cease to be represented'.[101] But Waldron refers to these statements approvingly in 2008. Strangely, in an article published three years earlier, Waldron had referred to those very words by Mr Cocks in a quite different light: 'It is all very well to talk about "sins against the Holy Ghost" and "offences against heaven and humanity", but these are not exactly legal ideas, *and it is unlikely that they resonate even with my good-hearted readers ...*'.[102] So it is very hard to agree with Waldron that 'if [religious arguments against torture] are excluded, the considerations that are stacked up in favor of torture ... seem easily capable of justifying it'.[103]

The scepticism about the weight of secular (PR-compatible) arguments in favour of an absolute ban on torture, and about the allegedly 'limp' nature of anti-torture arguments in terms of dignity and personhood, is surprising—and Exhibit No. 1 against Waldron's scepticism is Waldron himself. In his own influential writings[104] Waldron has unfolded an impressive range of sustained and powerful arguments supporting an absolute ban on torture—and at least in some of his articles,[105] he resorted to *secular* arguments *par excellence*, most of which would be perfectly PR-compatible. In a deservedly famous article appearing in the *Columbia Law Review*, there is an eloquent philippic against any toleration of torture by law, but in its seventy pages there is not a single religious

[99] Quoted ibid. 119.

[100] See Chad Flanders, 'The Mutability of Public Reason', (2012) 25 *Ratio Juris* 180.

[101] Rawls, 'The Idea of Public Reason' (n. 3) 142, footnote omitted.

[102] Jeremy Waldron, 'Torture and Positive Law: Jurisprudence for the White House', (2005) 105 *Columbia Law Review* 1681, 1710–11, footnote omitted, emphasis added.

[103] Waldron, 'Public Reason' (n. 68) 119–20.

[104] Waldron's writings on torture have been collected in Jeremy Waldron, *Torture, Terror, and Trade-offs: Philosophy for the White House* (Oxford University Press 2010).

[105] Elsewhere he has also developed a religious-based argument against torture, see Jeremy Waldron, 'What Can Christian Teaching Add to the Debate about Torture?', (2006) 63 *Theology Today* 330. I will refer to this article below.

or theological argument which I could identify. Waldron resorts, among other things, to a 'pragmatic case'[106] for an absolute prohibition (the power to use torture occasionally is very likely to be abused, intelligence officers are likely to lie about what is at stake, etc.),[107] and more importantly to an argument that torture is repugnant to the very spirit of 'our law'[108] which consists of the ideas that law is not brutal in its operation, is not savage, and does not rule through abject fear and terror.[109] In making these irrefutable propositions, Waldron appeals to the values of the 'dignity and agency'[110] of those who are subject to the law, and these appeals to human dignity are anything but 'limp'. As a matter of fact, a section of his article devoted to the absolute character of prohibition on torture opens with a question: '[C]an we make sense—*without resorting to religious ideas*—of the idea of a noncontingent prohibition [of torture], a prohibition so deeply embedded that it cannot be modified or truncated . . . ?'[111]—and the answer he gives is resoundingly affirmative. Another article by Waldron, written for a theology journal, is significantly entitled 'What Can Christian Teaching *Add* to the Debate about Torture?' (emphasis added), containing references to 'the sacredness of the human individual',[112] 'what God requires of us',[113] and to 'a gateway for the demonic to enter human affairs'.[114] Such references are naturally missing from Waldron's 'secular' writings, as he urges and expects that 'the Christian position will *coincide and lend support* to the absolute legal prohibition [on torture]'.[115] This is a far cry from an implausible proposition that, shorn of theological justifications, our arguments for an absolute prohibition of torture are weak, unpersuasive, ineffectual, or 'limp'.

The idea of constraints-free public justification is therefore deeply implausible, and the quality of public justification of laws does not depend upon there being no constraints on reasons which can be provided for the proposed laws. Constitutional rights serve as constraints upon what can be effectively proposed for legal change (though of course they do not have the same effectiveness at constraining what can be proposed for constitutional amendment): '[I]f one has anything like a robust concept of rights then one also has a robust concept of excluded reasons.'[116] Similarly, a constitutional separation of powers serves as a set of constraints upon what can be proposed for a procedural arrangement or

106 Waldron, 'Torture and Positive Law' (n. 102) 1717.
107 Ibid. 1716.
108 Ibid. 1717.
109 Ibid. 1726.
110 Ibid.1726, see also ibid. 1734.
111 Ibid. 1711, emphasis added.
112 Waldron, 'Christian Teaching' (n. 105) 336.
113 Ibid 337.
114 Ibid 341.
115 Ibid 336, emphasis added.
116 William A. Galston, 'Symposium Response', (2007) 1 *Journal of Law, Philosophy and Culture* 191, 194. In this passage, I follow Galston's taxonomy of purposive, moral, and constitutional exclusions.

assignment of powers between particular institutions. There may be also 'purposive constraints': purposes served by particular institutions inform the sets of reasons which can be provided in the context of those institutions.[117] And of course there may be moral exclusions of reasons: the reasons for violating a person's or a group's dignity will be excluded from the justification of a law on intrinsically moral grounds. Reasons excluded by such constitutional or purposive or moral grounds are not excluded in a different way than PR excludes non-public reasons under political liberalism: this is not exclusion from the general debate (much less exclusion under the sanctions of law) but exclusion from constituting effective reasons for a proposed law.

5. Public Reason and the Principle of Candour

A call to use public reasons in public discourse (being part of advocacy for a legal change), even if in the minds of proponents of a given legal rule they are part of broader, more comprehensive conceptions, indicates that there are potential problems with the distinction between *motivations* and *arguments*: there is a risk that someone may use PR only as an *ex-post* rationalization—as a disguise for a different set of real justifications which have the 'prohibited' non-public (sectarian) character.

For instance, one's real motivation for arguing for a prohibition of blasphemy may be the religious injunctions of one's church, though one's publicly stated rationale will cite public order or respect to all individuals, no matter what their beliefs are. At first blush, it should not be such a big problem: as long as some public reasons are *sufficient* to sustain the proposal, we should not worry about the *actual* motivations. But is it a satisfactory solution? Isn't it a recipe for hypocrisy and deception? As Elisabeth Wolgast observed: 'The representative who recasts his objections [to a bill to which he in fact objects on religious grounds] to conform to public reason not only argues with less than maximum force, but also speaks disingenuously', and she adds:

> One's reasons for holding a position are integral to the position itself. They are not chosen after the position is arrived at, except disingenuously ... [I]n dealing with our peers, it is dishonest to misrepresent our reasons for a view, and speaking so would justify criticism as much as would a legislator's argument that masks his interest in being rewarded.[118]

[117] See ibid.

[118] Elizabeth H. Wolgast, 'The Demands of Public Reason', (1994) 94 *Columbia Law Review* 1936, 1943–44.

There is a temptation, for a political liberal, to respond that actual motivations are irrelevant in Rawlsian liberalism: '[P]olitical liberalism does not require actual motivation.... Provided citizens are reasonable, political liberalism does not ask how they relate public political values to their comprehensive views'.[119] Indeed, the whole logic of the overlapping consensus is such that people come with different justifications (Kantian, utilitarian, Christian, etc.), but all that matters is whether there is a common denominator at a much shallower level, cognizable under PR. But this is too quick a response. If the values of sincerity and candour are important to the integrity of public discourse (and they obviously are), we have to be able to test the degree of congruency between a comprehensive conception actually affirmed by a person and, on the other hand, a public policy proposal as supported by a publicly affirmable reason. It is true that for the purpose of judging the legitimacy of a certain legal proposal, all that is needed is the weight of public reasons which support it, but in order to gauge the sincerity of affirming those public reasons, we must be able to ascertain the more comprehensive conceptions, which do not disappear but stay in the background, so to speak. Not only do we want solely public reasons to be present in the discourse leading to legal regulations, but we also want candour, transparency, and openness.

So the argument against PR from the basis of insincerity has to be taken seriously. But I do not think that this objection is devastating to the idea of PR. For one thing, the directive of using PR in one's advocacy or constitutional scrutiny of laws may have a powerful therapeutic and self-reflexive role. Take the example, already mentioned, of blasphemy laws. Suppose that for me a publicly cited reason (public order) is not strong enough, and in itself would not move me to advocate a ban on blasphemy; the real work of motivating me against tolerance for blasphemy is done by my religious views. Now perhaps these two sets of expectations—PR as a sole ground of legitimate laws on the one hand, and sincerity on the other—are in conflict with each other; perhaps the requirement of PR necessarily creates powerful perverse incentives for making strategic representations in public discourse that will naturally erode sincerity? But I would not be so pessimistic about it. After all, it is usually the case that for any given legal or policy proposal we may have a number of different motivations and reasons: in our example (blasphemy) I may be moved both by my religious and non-religious motives, including (among the latter set) those which qualify as PR. All may be *genuine* motivations, even if some may weigh more heavily on my mind than others. When participating in public discourse, we are not mechanical articulators of a specific set of motives we actually possess, but we also make certain selections and choices.

119 Micah Schwartzman, 'The Sincerity of Public Reason', (2011) 19 *Journal of Political Philosophy* 375, 390.

These selections may be 'strategic' but not necessarily in a manipulative and negative sense of the word: they may be strategic because we may anticipate that some arguments will have different effects upon our audience than others, and we adjust our presentation to this anticipation. The notion of an audience indicates that 'public reasons' are 'public' in at least two senses: that they are sufficiently widely shared (which we may call a substantive notion of publicness), and that they are actually presented in public settings (which, for a want of the better word, can be called a procedural sense of publicness). Note, incidentally, that these two notions are independent from each other, and that we can conceive the substantive notion of 'publicness' without the procedural one. This scenario is recognized by Philip Pettit, who suggests that the notion of publicly admissible reasons can be applied also to non-democratic societies.[120] But this book is concerned with democratic societies only, and it recognizes the importance of both substantive and procedural senses of publicness.

So far I have focused almost exclusively upon the former meaning of publicness, but the procedural aspect is equally important. It suggests that in articulating our reasons for laws we must take into account the fact of their public presentation and the possible responses, feedback, critiques, rejections, etc.). PR can therefore be taken as a rhetorical device, in the sense of rhetoric as public argumentation meant to persuade the audience ('[w]herever there is a process of public argumentation, there is rhetoric').[121] Of course, 'the audience' need not be defined narrowly as a particular judge, jury, courtroom, town hall meeting, likely readers of a particular newspaper, etc.; the audience may be generalized into a 'universal audience', and we may accept, with Neil MacCormick, the 'new rhetoric's' position that 'whatever argument would convince the audience of all intelligent and concerned persons, evaluating issues in a disinterested way, is a sound one'.[122] But even such a broad generalization has its limits: it is informed by the context of a society which we know, in which we live, within which our arguments will have a higher or lower persuasive value, and the further we move into the 'universal audience' pole on the spectrum ranging from the particular to the universal, the lower the significance of actual people's responses to the arguments which we articulate in public.[123] The anticipation of the audience's responses, and their actual occurrences, will inevitably affect our selection of the arguments—and it is a good thing too.

[120] Philip Pettit, 'The Common Good', in Keith Dowding, Robert E. Goodin, and Carole Pateman (eds.), *Justice and Democracy: Essays for Brian Barry* (Cambridge University Press 2004) 150, 164–65.

[121] Neil MacCormick, *Rhetoric and the Rule of Law* (Oxford University Press 2010) 17.

[122] Ibid. 19, referring approvingly to the work of Chaim Perelman on 'new rhetoric'.

[123] This is the case, in my view, of George Christie's theory in George C. Christie, *The Notion of an Ideal Audience in Legal Argument* (Kluwer 2000). In fact, I do not think that the notion of *audience* plays any operative role in Christie's argument—but this is not the place to conduct a sustained critique of this thoughtful book.

Some of these selections may be guided by prudential considerations related to efficiency: we anticipate that some kinds of arguments may be more persuasive than others. If you care about convincing another person then you may be advised to appeal to premises that this other person accepts or is likely to accept, and this consideration will inform the use of reasons as justification for your position.[124] However, some of the reasons for preselection of arguments may be more dignified, informed as they are by our sense of respect to others. We may know that if we appeal, in our anti-blasphemy advocacy (to continue the use of this example) to *our* religious beliefs, this may show a lack of sufficient respect to those in the wider audience who do not share our religion. If, however, we select our arguments in a way which is meant to show proper respect to all members of the audience, we will be likely to emphasize PR arguments and screen off sectarian ones. After all, as argued in Chapter 1, the very idea of PR is informed by the overriding principle of respect to others, Hence, in choosing *which* of the arguments, from within a variety of motivations we actually espouse, we should represent in public discourse, we should properly be influenced by this overriding principle of respect.

While psychologically it may be occasionally difficult to distinguish the best reasons which we morally justify to ourselves and moral reasons which should govern our interactions with others (and thus which are the only reasons which we should use in advocacy for law), this distinction is essential in public justifications about what law we should adopt, as I have already argued in section 4 of this chapter at some length. The very fact that we are engaged in advocacy about law means that we adopt a role of a citizen, hence an 'official' (this role is of course more obvious, and without quotation marks, when we *are* officials in a common sense of the word). Our moral perspective is then special, one may say 'artificial' (without any pejorative connotation of the word), because it is divorced from the moral perspective which we adopt as an individual reflecting upon moral principles to govern our own life. This artificiality may be presented as a form of self-discipline related to performing a role of an official.[125]

It may well be that this process of self-discipline will have a self-educational effect on an advocate of a given position, and that in the process of prioritizing PR for the purposes of public representations she will learn to prioritize them in the set of her inner motivations too; after all, there is a reflexive feedback process between what we believe and what we say. We are not passive receptacles of sets of political views and proposals but rather we have a self-reflective attitude to them: we keep modifying them, updating, bringing coherence, etc., and much of this reflexivity occurs even as we articulate them in public. An account of a mechanical, one-way relationship between holding a belief and articulating

[124] See Ronald C. Den Otter, *Judicial Review in an Age of Moral Pluralism* (Cambridge University Press 2009) 142.

[125] See Eleftheriadis (n. 32) 58–59.

it, according to which an articulation is a simple reflection of antecedently held views, is unconvincing: in the process of articulation (and, in particular, in the process of public presentation) we refine, modify, sometimes even repudiate what we had held in the beginning. I believe that basic introspective evidence of anyone involved in writing and public speaking, including teaching, would confirm the proposition about this complex, reflexive, and two-way relationship between a belief (as a fact about the state of mind) and its articulation. (Think of a manner of speaking of the type: 'Let us see where this argument will lead us . . .'. We construct an argument as we go on articulating it.) This observation weakens the charge of insincerity, if sincerity is understood as correspondence between our actual beliefs and their articulation because, to put it crudely, our beliefs are to some degree *affected* by their articulation.

When trying to live up to the ideal of PR we often have to ask ourselves a counter-factual question: if (for example) I am initially motivated religiously to defend a particular political view (in particular, a view about the shape of a coercive law), would I still defend my view if I were not motivated by purely religious (or other sectarian) convictions? The task facing a person who is moved to support a particular political position for 'comprehensive' reasons but wishes to comply with the PR requirements is not easy but, ultimately, is recognizable to everyday psychology. She must ask herself two questions: (a) can she think of public reasons which are *sufficient* to justify a given position?; and (b) would she, on reflection, endorse those reasons? So these are, respectively, requirements of (a) sufficiency and (b) sincerity, and they have to be jointly met in order for a PR-compatible argument to be properly stated. Sufficiency (adequacy) is obvious: a public reason provided publicly must be capable of upholding the weight of justification of a given policy: it must not be disproportionate or plainly inadequate. The requirement of sincerity is based upon a counter-factual just mentioned: would you still defend a policy if all you had at your disposal in your argumentative repertoire were the arguments complying with PR? This is a counter-factual which is not too convoluted or excessively complex, and a test to employ is perhaps asking oneself whether this particular position might be reasonably supported by those who do *not* share my religious (or deep philosophical) convictions. Such counter-factual test is not really an independent motivational test,[126] but it is rather a way of checking the sincerity of a person's belief that public reason may be supplied for a given position, and that it is sufficient to support it. 'If a person cannot imagine being motivated by a public reason, or cannot imagine others who hold different comprehensive views being motivated by it, then that reason does not suffice to justify that person's political position.'[127] Note that 'imagining being motivated' is not the same as 'having been actually

[126] See Schwartzman, 'The Sincerity of Public Reason' (n. 119) 395.
[127] Ibid.

motivated' but, under a self-reflexive approach to participation in public discourse, it does not necessarily offend the requirement of sincerity.

This may be put in a different way. Within a given set of political preferences, just like within a set of individual consumption preferences, we may have first-order and second-order preferences. This is a well-known and well-described fact. We have certain expectations regarding the political and legal system, but we also have certain ideas about how to manage, revise, order, prioritize, and publicly articulate those expectations and claims. (And this applies not only to an individual reasoner but also to public discourse: we may discuss fundamental political issues, but we may also discuss the terms of debate about political issues—as we often do.) There is nothing necessarily hypocritical or insincere when we downplay some and upgrade others genuine preferences in public presentation. Everything depends on the *reasons* for those second-order ideals about how to manage our first-order political preferences, and if those reasons are noble, then the strategic management of political preferences should not be derided as a sign of insincerity or hypocrisy. For example, it sounds psychologically plausible to hold the following combination of views: (1) I believe that abortion is wrong on religious grounds (my initial and principal motive for anti-abortion conviction), and also because it diminishes respect for human life in general (which I articulate in PR-compatible terms), and also (2) I believe that only the arguments which are PR-compatible should be made in the public discourse about the law. The second-order view (2) allows me to decide about which of my first-order views of type (1) I will publicly articulate when advocating for a legal regulation. And the charge of insincerity or hypocrisy would be effective only if I sincerely thought that the PR-compatible reasons within set (1) were insufficient to support the desired law but I would use them (and only them) anyway in order to maximize the chances of giving legal effect to my religious-based reasons.

To use yet another example of the vocabulary made popular not long ago, the requirement of PR will act as a set of gag rules. There is nothing bad about this *per se*; as we know from Stephen Holmes, 'gag rules' often perform positive and constructive functions: 'Communities, like individuals, can silence themselves about selected issues for what they see as their own good.'[128] PR is a species of a broader class of 'strategic self-censorship'.[129] But where at least some of Holmes' most prominent 'gag rules' are based on a desire to avoid political divisiveness,[130] PR has a different aim: it provides laws with legitimation based on the principle of respect, supported by equal liberty of all individuals. Its main concern is not

[128] Stephen Holmes, 'Gag Rules or the Politics of Omission', in Jon Elster and Rune Slagstad (eds.), *Constitutionalism and Democracy* (Cambridge University Press 1988) 19, 57. Rawls's public reason (*sans le nom*) is cited by Holmes in his preliminary set of examples of gag rules, ibid, 20–21.

[129] The concept is Holmes's, see ibid. 19.

[130] Ibid. 43–50.

about a smooth functioning of political institutions in a stable and cohesive community, as many of Holmes's gag rules are (especially those related to the Establishment Clause of the US First Amendment), though in their effects they will often overlap. More generally, the point of PR is not to keep certain *issues* off the political agenda, as many gag rules require, but rather disallowing certain *arguments* for collective decisions: it is not about agenda-narrowing but about the range of available justifications.

The imperative of PR may, therefore, have salutary side-effects upon you and me: individual reasoners are compelled to reflect upon our own reasons for advocating certain views in the public domain, to apply some filtering devices to them, and to disentangle religious (or other comprehensive) views from publicly cognizable reasons. It is a form of self-discipline. It may be beneficial for our self-awareness, in the context of public presentation of our ideals. While it may be difficult, it is not impossible; after all, much of the public debate in liberal democracies is conducted today in non-religious terms (consider how unusual the rhetoric of Mr Cocks, cited by Waldron and referred to above,[131] about theological reasons for opposing torture, would sound today). After all, it is not that those liberal-democratic societies have undergone such massive secularization that religious views have no salience among people—far from it. Religious beliefs have a very firm stronghold in the United States, and in many other Western societies. And yet scholars writing about the use of openly religious arguments in support of major legislative proposals, for instance in the United States, find very few examples to identify such practices. For instance, Kent Greenawalt in his *Private Consciences and Public Reasons* distinguished between certain ritualistic or symbolic references to religion in political practice and religion actually cited as the main motive for a legislative proposal in the United States. Consider, for example, this brief characterization of the approach taken by Ronald Reagan: '[He] said at a prayer breakfast at the 1984 Republican convention, "[T]he truth is that politics and morality are inseparable. And as morality's foundation is religion, religion and politics are necessarily related". He did not, however, often make explicit religious arguments for particular political positions.'[132]

If appeals to purely religious reasons in debates about the law in contemporary liberal-democratic societies are few and far between (and when they do occur, they are usually ineffective and disregarded: consider the rarity of purely religious arguments in debates about abortion, euthanasia, blasphemy, etc.), it suggests that, in reality, participants of public discourse do not have any great trouble disentangling religious from publicly admissible reasons. And in the process, we may actually come to believe that public reasons, initially adopted on strategic grounds, are as plausible as our original motives: in this way, the

[131] See section 5 of this chapter.

[132] Greenawalt, *Private Consciences* (n. 74) 153, footnote omitted, emphasis added.

idea of PR may have strong transformative potential. Pressure to conform to the idea of PR may even have a positive educative and reformatory effect upon some 'problematic' participants of public discourse. People holding views whose only justification is publicly non-admissible, for instance because it is sectarian in an invidious way (racist, bigoted), who are then told in discussions on legal proposals that they may resort only to PR-compatible arguments, may, over time, internalize those arguments, even if initially they had presented them publicly with a dose of insincerity.[133] By forcing, or inducing, public speakers to hide their base motives, the principle of PR may create for them incentives to actually internalize the stated ones. (Consider Elster's argument, attributed by him to Pascal, that one will eventually end up having the preferences that one initially was faking.)[134]

But, when all is said and done, it may well be the case that in a particular instance PR will be used in a disingenuous way, insincerely, and to disguise some real motives which cannot be substituted by the language of PR, except with great difficulty and no small measure of hypocrisy. For instance: imagine that the only argument I have in my mind in support of anti-blasphemy law is an intense desire to protect my religion against criticisms; no other argument is of the slightest importance to me. In such cases, the use of PR is vulnerable to the criticism of insincerity. If PR is governed by the overriding rule of respect for persons (see Chapter 1), then this respect for persons must also prevent us from representing our reasons for proposed laws in a deceptive, manipulative way. If the *only* (or a predominant) reason which actually moves us to advocate certain proposals are sectarian (religious, or self-interested, or comprehensive moral conceptions which are deeply contested, etc.),[135] and we cannot plausibly imagine accepting as sufficient the public reasons that people who do not share our actual reasons can endorse, then the motives for using PR (respect for others) in the first place should also prevent us from deceptive presentations of PR masquerading for *de facto* 'banned' motivations. In any event, the hope is that for the reasons provided in the preceding paragraphs, the situations which will lead to PR becoming disingenuous and insincere will not happen too often.

Some would go a step further and, building upon the idea of the 'civilizing force of hypocrisy', say that it really does not matter whether public arguments are sincere or not: all that matters is that they are presented in a way that conforms to public reasons. In public discourse, we are asked to behave *as if* we were moved by publicly admissible reasons, even if in fact we are acting for self-interested

[133] See Schwartzman 'The Sincerity of Public Reason' (n. 119) 397. This is akin to Jon Elster's thesis about the 'civilizing force of hypocrisy', Jon Elster, 'Deliberation and Constitution Making', in Jon Elster (ed.), *Deliberative Democracy* (Cambridge University Press 1998) 97, 111, italics removed.

[134] Elster, 'The Market and the Forum' (n. 81) 113.

[135] For a similar definition of 'sectarian' non-religious moral conceptions, see Michael J. Perry, *Human Rights in the Constitutional Law of the United States* (Cambridge University Press 2013)125–26.

motives. As Jürgen Neyer observes, 'Actors who in truth seek to maximise their own interests or those of their clients, and who care not for the common good, nevertheless often use the mode of [public] justification in political discourse.'[136] But from this empirical observation, it does not follow that it does not matter whether the actors in public discourse believe in the reasons they provide or not. If those reasons are clearly inconsistent with their true reasons, the ideal of respect for their compatriots is undermined. Neyer concludes, from the observation just quoted: 'Simply put, discourses of justification do not require that participants have altruistic attitudes or that they want to promote the common good.'[137]

But the alternative: *either* the pursuit of factional interest regardless of the interests of others *or* the adoption of altruistic attitudes and being moved by common good—does not exhaust the list of available possibilities. Persons may pursue their interests based on arguments which can be accepted by others who do not necessarily identify with those specific interests and yet cannot reject the rationales on which they are based. There is nothing odd about such a combination of attitudes. I may wish to have my preference implemented by public policy, but only if I can sincerely find a justification which connects it with the common good. *This* is the space occupied by public reason (neither blatant pursuit of self-interest nor pure altruism), supported as it is by respect to others, and that is why a total disconnect between one's reasons and the reasons publicly affirmed is damaging to the concept.

[136] Jürgen Neyer, 'Justice and the Right to Justification: Conceptual Reflections' in Dimitry Kochenov, Gráinne de Búrca and Andrew Williams (eds.), *Europe's Justice Deficit?* (Hart 2015) 211, 219.

[137] Ibid. 219.

PART II

CONSTITUTIONAL PUBLIC REASON IN MUNICIPAL LAW

4
Motive-based Judicial Review: Introduction

At the end of the previous chapter, I used blasphemy as an example of arguing for the same legal rule either from the perspective of public reason (PR) or from perspectives antithetical to PR. I used the case of blasphemy as a purely hypothetical example—something that can stand for any other moral issue the legal enforcement of which can be defended from different perspectives. This example was useful for rhetorical reasons: since blasphemy is a relatively insignificant matter these days, it can serve as an instance where disagreement is relatively mild, and so is unlikely to elicit strong reactions from a reader.

It is now time to move on from a thought experiment to real life. What I depicted as a choice between religious and PR-based ways of arguing about blasphemy has been actually paralleled by how anti-blasphemy laws (or their equivalents) evolved in several democratic-liberal countries. In England and Wales, blasphemy had been construed in the past as a wrong against God,[1] and an old dictionary defined 'blasphemy' as 'offering some indignity to God, any person of the Trinity, any messengers from God, his holy writ, or the doctrines of revelation'.[2] The law protected the religious beliefs and feelings of Christians; in a standard formulation, 'Every publication is said to be blasphemous which contains any contemptuous, reviling, scurrilous or ludicrous matter relating to God, Jesus Christ, or the Bible or the formularies of the Church of England ...'.[3] Christian values rested on the asserted truth of certain theological propositions, and blasphemy law banned challenges to those propositions.[4] Since the mid-nineteenth century, however, the concept of blasphemy has been undergoing change, with the emphasis placed decreasingly on substance and increasingly on style and on causing offence to the religious audience.[5] The offence was abolished

[1] See Helen Pringle, 'Regulating Offence to the Godly: Blasphemy and the Future of Religious Vilification Laws', (2011) 34 *UNSW Law Journal* 316, 316. As Robert Post summarizes, 'The particular province of blasphemy was to prevent disrespect toward God ... ', Robert C. Post, 'Cultural Heterogeneity and Law: Pornography, Blasphemy, and the First Amendment', (1988) 76 *California Law Review* 297, 305.

[2] James Barclay, *A Complete and Universal English Dictionary* (London, 1782), quoted in *Joseph Burstyn, Inc. v Wilson*, 343 U.S. 495, 525 (1952) (Frankfurter, J. concurring in the judgment).

[3] Lewis Frederick Sturge, *Stephen's Digest of the Criminal Law* (Sweet & Maxwell, 9th edn. 1950) 163.

[4] See Post, 'Cultural Heterogeneity and Law (n. 1) 307.

[5] For a brief account of this evolution, see Post, 'Cultural Heterogeneity and Law (n. 1) 307–10.

Constitutional Public Reason. Wojciech Sadurski, Oxford University Press. © Wojciech Sadurski 2023.
DOI: 10.1093/oso/9780192869678.003.0004

in 2008, and for all practical purposes it was replaced by religious vilification laws, which prohibit actions that are threatening and intend to stir up religious hatred, hence which appear to be PR-compatible.[6]

In Australia, where blasphemy laws have not been explicitly abolished across the nation,[7] but are considered in desuetude, and where the last successful prosecution of blasphemy was in 1871,[8] blasphemy has been absorbed into the (non-religion specific) category of obscenity or offensiveness.[9] Anti-vilification laws list religion, ethnicity, nationality, gender, etc. as grounds for restraining perpetuation of hatred or vilification.[10] Three states (Queensland, Tasmania, and Victoria) introduced laws which expressly outlaw religious vilification; a typical provision reads: 'A person must not, on the ground of the religious belief or activity of another person or class of persons, engage in conduct that incites hatred against, serious contempt for, or revulsion or severe ridicule of, that other person or class of persons.'[11] This is a far cry from the old-fashioned blasphemy laws: the new prohibition seems to be fundamentally oriented towards the goals of public order and the dignity of persons rather than the protection of a sectarian set of beliefs. In fact, some of these laws were enacted with public justifications which sound very much like PR: for instance, the Victorian statute (note the name: *Racial and Religious Tolerance Act*) contains a statement of objectives such as the promotion of 'the full and equal participation of every person in a society that values freedom of expression and is an open and multicultural democracy', and which maintains 'the right of all [citizens] to engage in robust discussion of any matter of public interest'.[12] What proponent of PR could object to *that*?

In the United States, the last relevant decision of the Supreme Court was *Joseph Burstyn, Inc. v. Wilson*,[13] in which a state law that prohibited the showing of a film which was 'sacrilegious' was struck down. As the Court said, 'the censor is set adrift upon a boundless sea amid a myriad of conflicting currents of religious views . . .'.[14] In an eloquent concurring opinion, Justice Frankfurter noted the close link between the 'blasphemous' and the established church,[15]

[6] In 2006, the Racial and Religious Hatred Act 2006 (UK) c 1 inserted the following provision into the Public Order Act 1986 (UK) c 64: 'A person who uses threatening words or behaviour, or displays any written material which is threatening, is guilty of an offence if he intends thereby to stir up religious hatred.'

[7] Statutory provisions against blasphemy remain in Tasmania, and common law provisions continue in New South Wales, Victoria, and South Australia, see Pringle, 'Regulating Offence to the Godly' (n. 1) 320.

[8] Ibid. 319.

[9] Ibid. 321.

[10] See ibid. 321, referring to the federal Broadcasting Act.

[11] Racial and Religious Tolerance Act 2001 (Vic) s. 8(1).

[12] Racial and Religious Tolerance Act 2001 (Vic) s. 4(1).

[13] 343 U.S. 495 (1952).

[14] Ibid. 504.

[15] Ibid. 528 (Frankfurter J. concurring in the judgment).

and also observed (changing the Court's metaphor) that '[b]lasphemy was a chameleon phrase which meant the criticism of whatever the ruling authority of the moment established as orthodox religious doctrine'.[16] While some scholars note that the Supreme Court has never explicitly stated that criminalization of blasphemy is unconstitutional,[17] *Burstyn* and an earlier decision in which the Court had held (among other things) that charges of breaching the peace against a person for playing a record that attacked the religion could not stand because there was 'no assault or threatening of bodily harm, no truculent bearing, no intentional discourtesy, no personal abuse',[18] suggest that a prohibition of blasphemous expressions would not pass constitutional muster in the United States.

There are, of course, countries and legal systems where various provisions protect religious feelings and sensitivities in ways closer to the anti-blasphemy paradigm than the religious vilification paradigm adopted by the United Kingdom and Australia, and which do not resemble the US rejection of anti-sacrilegious laws. But then it is not my proposition that PR has an unquestioned foothold all over the world and in all spheres. All I am suggesting is that in some of the jurisdictions that have adopted regulations that are most attractive to a liberal-democratic taste, the influence of the idea of PR has been palpable in this sphere. This chapter commences by tracing the ways in which PR—usually, *sans le nom*—has made it into constitutional interpretation around the world. In section 1, I will show that the 'unconstitutional motives' doctrine, which is of course a useful vehicle for PR, often ostensibly targets 'purposes' of lawmakers rather than their motives, and that in actual judicial decisions in systems as different as the US, Canada, Germany, Australia, or South Africa, these terms are used interchangeably. I will then acknowledge the recognition of a theory akin to public reason in US constitutional doctrine, as exemplified by a theory developed by Richard Pildes (section 2). The central argument of this chapter is in section 3: it will show how heightening the levels or standards of scrutiny of a given legislation may correspond, in different legal systems, to a judicial attempt to discern true motives by legislators, and in particular, to screen out non-public reasons from legislation. By reference to a theory developed by Laurence Tribe, the last section of the chapter will consider the clash between judicial and legislative functions occasioned by motive scrutiny—a clash which may put the very legitimacy of judicial review on the line.

[16] Ibid. 529 (Frankfurter J. concurring in the judgment), reference omitted.

[17] Arnold H. Loewy, 'Morals Legislation and the Establishment Clause', (2003) 55 *Alabama Law Review* 159, 163 n. 27. But note that at least one state appellate court declared (in 1970) that the Maryland blasphemy statute was unconstitutional, on the basis of conflict with the First Amendment's religion clauses, *State v. West*, 263 A.2d 602, 604–05 (Md. Ct. Spec. App. 1970).

[18] *Cantwell v. Connecticut*, 310 U.S. 296, 310 (1940).

1. Unconstitutional Motives or Purposes?

Prohibition of blasphemy or of religious vilification, from which I began this chapter, is just one example among many of the employment of the principle of PR in constitutional argument—an issue which will now be discussed more generally. As the survey contained in this and the following chapters of the book will indicate, it is not unusual to identify arguments made in the process of constitutional scrutiny of laws in terms of 'public reasons', even if this philosophically sounding concept is not used. At the most general level, the idea has been articulated well by the Constitutional Court of South Africa as a requirement of the very principle of 'legality', which provides the minimum threshold for the exercise of public power and which is meant 'to promote the need for governmental action to relate to a defensible vision of the public good'.[19] A 'defensible vision of the public good' is another way of talking about the *reasons* for the law, which must be properly 'public' and properly 'defensible'. The defensibility of reasons which must be sufficiently 'public' identifies the conditions of legitimacy of coercive state rules. As Aharon Barak puts it, the legitimacy component of laws in a democracy 'is made up of the proper purpose and the means to achieve that purpose, which limit the constitutional right in a proper manner'.[20] This is perhaps the best definition which encapsulates the principal point behind the proportionality analysis (though, as will be shown below, a PR-focused scrutiny has a role not only when the proportionality analysis in its canonical version is conducted). Of course the words 'in a proper manner' identifies the main space upon which the proportionality analysis acquires its critical edge, especially at the stage of scrutinizing the 'necessity' of restrictions and the 'balancing sensu stricto'. But an identification of purposes (which corresponds, as I claim, to the idea of public reasons) is an irreducible starting point for the entire analysis.

This brings us to the issue of the critical function of constitutional doctrines in scrutinizing the legitimacy of statutory rules, and especially those that prima facie restrict constitutional rights. I have in mind a family of doctrines which refer to 'unconstitutional motives' as tainting the legislation as unconstitutional. The main precept behind this approach is the idea that at least some prohibitions on government refer most naturally to intentions.[21] While appeals to religious justifications will be perhaps the most obvious case of a violation of the principle of PR ('The legitimacy of secular legislation depends ... on whether the State can advance some justification for its law beyond its conformity to religious doctrine'),[22] the requirement of PR is broader than that and yields prohibitions upon

[19] *Prinsloo v. Van der Linde & Another* 1997 (3) SA 1012 (CC) para. 25.

[20] Aharon Barak, *Proportionality: Constitutional Rights and their Limitations* (Cambridge University Press 2012) 245.

[21] See Charles Fried, 'Types', (1997) 14 *Constitutional Commentary* 55, 64.

[22] *Bowers v. Hardwick*, 478 U.S. 186, 211 (1986) (Blackmun, J. dissenting).

all motivations which are not reasonably universalizable, just as religious arguments are not.

But is motive-focused scrutiny pertinent in all major systems of constitutional scrutiny of statutes? According to some scholars of comparative constitutional law, the US constitutional model is typically 'intent-based', as opposed to the European ('continental') model which is said to be more 'impact-based'.[23] The impact orientation (and I will be using 'impact' and 'effect' here as equivalents) is said to be concerned with the *effects* of legislative action or inaction; it is found largely in the German-style 'proportionality analysis', and in particular in its last, most demanding prong (often called proportionality or balancing *sensu stricto*), which consists of comparing the costs of interfering with a constitutional right with the benefit of achieving a constitutionally legitimate purpose or maximizing another right. The law is constitutional if the benefits of interference prevail over the costs of restriction. Further, the impact orientation is said to reflect a low level of suspicion towards the government, where there is 'less need to look for illicit or hidden intentions lying behind its actions'.[24]

In contrast, the US model of constitutional review (and in particular the review of constitutionality of restrictions on rights) is said to be mainly concerned with the intentions behind legislative actions, to be reflected basically in this aspect of 'balancing' which consists in finding out whether the legislator used the least restrictive means to achieve a constitutionally important purpose (the 'necessity' test), and reveals a high degree of distrust in legislative intentions or motives. American-style constitutional balancing is said to be an important 'tool to smoke-out hidden illicit government motives'.[25] This proposition, with regard to the United States at least (whether the characterization of European continental systems as primarily impact-oriented is correct is an issue to which I will return in a moment),[26] is well supported by the case law of courts (including the Supreme Court) which often inquire into potentially impermissible motives, not only in such obvious areas as freedom of expression (to discern, for instance, whether a restriction has been motivated by intolerance towards a disfavoured opinion or protecting the authorities against criticism), freedom of religion (to see whether the regulation has been enacted out of favouritism or hostility to a religion), or anti-discrimination law (to discern racial or gender prejudice as a possible motive for the law), three areas which will be discussed at some length later in this part of the book, but also with regard to the less usual suspects, for instance under the Dormant Commerce Clause (to strike down laws motivated

[23] Moshe Cohen-Eliya and Iddo Porat, *Proportionality and Constitutional Culture* (Cambridge University Press 2013) 64–81.

[24] Ibid. 65, footnote omitted.

[25] Ibid. 68, footnote omitted.

[26] But see Niels Petersen, 'Legislative Inconsistency and the 'Smoking Out' of Illicit Motives', (2016) 64 *American Journal of Comparative Law* 121, 122–23, who challenges the contrast drawn by Cohen-Eliya and Porat, Proportionality and Constitutional Culture (n. 23).

by economic protectionism), the prohibition on bills of attainder (to see whether the laws, notwithstanding their formally non-penal character, have been triggered by punitive motives), or even the constitutional right to travel (to discern statutes enacted to serve the purpose of discouraging interstate migration).[27] However, it needs to be emphasized that, while this conscious emphasis on the illicit motives is characteristic of the US legal system, this is not to say that courts there disregard constitutionally questionable *effects*, or that they refuse to consider them unless accompanied by a strong suspicion of improper motives. In the equal protection jurisprudence in the United States, it has been well established that if a law has 'a significantly discriminatory impact' then, no matter what motives are likely, it fails to meet the requirements of non-discrimination.[28] (This will be further discussed in Chapter 8.)

While in US constitutional jurisprudence the 'flushing out' of impermissible motives for legislation through scrutiny of the means-ends relationship is often done explicitly, in other legal systems, including those following European or Canadian-style proportionality analysis, it is sometimes only implicit but not non-existent, as will be shown in the examples taken from those jurisdictions further in this and the following chapters. For starters, consider these two examples from Germany—arguably the most important home for European-style proportionality analysis. In a 2016 decision, the German Federal Constitutional Court considered the constitutionality of the federal states' (*Länder*) monopoly on sports betting and lotteries.[29] The official purpose for such monopoly was to combat the dangers of gambling addiction—a plausible (if not absolutely non-controversial, considering its possibly paternalistic character) *ratio legis*; indeed, the Court explicitly stated that the aim of combatting gambling addiction 'is a particularly important goal related to the public interest'.[30] Using what it called (following the European Court of Justice, as it then was called) the 'hypocrisy test',[31] the German Court asked itself whether the asserted purpose of combatting the dangers of gambling addiction was truly at the heart of the monopoly, or whether the state was actually after the revenue from offering lotteries and sports betting (which was considerable). The main argument to corroborate this hypothesis was the way in which the state of Bavaria (the defendant in the case) advertised gambling. These advertisements seemed aimed at garnering new

[27] See Caleb Nelson, 'Judicial Review of Legislative Purpose', (2008) 83 *New York University Law Review* 1784, 1855–56, and cases cited ibid. nn. 291–93. For a non-exhaustive catalogue of constitutional clauses under which motive-based inquiries have been conducted, see also Louis S. Raveson, 'Unmasking the Motives of Government Decisionmakers: A Subpoena for Your Thoughts?', (1985) 63 *North Carolina Law Review* 879, 883 n. 17–25.

[28] See, e.g., *Connecticut v. Teal*, 457 U.S. 440, 446 (1982).

[29] BVerfG v. 28.03.2006, 1 BvR 1054/01—*Sportwettenmonopol* [FCC of 28 March 2006, 1 BvR 1054/01—*Monopoly on Sports Betting*] BVerfGE 115, 276.

[30] Para. 98.

[31] ECJ Case C-46/08 *Carmen Media Group Ltd. v. Land Schleswig-Holstein and Others* [2010] ECR I-8149.

customers and thus could be regarded as actually exacerbating and spreading, instead of limiting, gambling addiction in the population. The design of the monopoly thus seemed to belie its purpose. But one might ask what is wrong with maximizing state revenue, as a plausible candidate for a public reason? And the Court's answer was that the impropriety of such purpose involved the unconstitutional exclusion of private businesses from competition in this industry, and worse, that it created incentives for the state to actually *promote* betting and gambling, with all the negative consequences in terms of addiction. As the Court commonsensically observed, the adoption of the earnings purpose 'can lead (seductively) to a situation where the state ultimately undertakes the admission of betting and the supply of opportunities to bet in the sense of cultivating a passion for betting, wherein betting is marketed like a recreational activity that is in principle unobjectionable'.[32] In this way, the Court effectively 'flushed out' impermissible legislative motives through a proportionality analysis—without explicitly saying so.

It was not the first time in its history that the German Constitutional Court discerned an improper pursuit of power or funds by state governments which attempted to use—eventually, without success—legitimate-sounding purposes to protect their interests amounting to a cynical grab of power. In one of the earliest instances of invalidating a law for lack of legitimate aim,[33] the Court struck down the so-called 'Collection Law' (*Sammlungsgesetz*) in 1966, a law which had awkwardly persisted in the German legal order from 1934.[34] The law required every person and every organization that wanted to raise money for charity to get prior permission, and the decision of whether to grant the permission or not was at the complete discretion of public authorities. It could be revoked at any point, and the authorities could confiscate the raised funds and use them in whatever way they deemed fit. Originally, the law was unashamedly protective of Nazi interests: only NSDAP was exempted from the regulation. However, three state governments chose to defend the law (which they were still applying at the time, long after the fall of the Third Reich) on the grounds that it no longer had a National-Socialist character, but instead served to protect people from unwanted solicitation.[35] But the Court (acting in an abstract review procedure, after the complaint was brought by the Bundestag) would not accept an argument about such a fundamental change to the underlying purpose of the law. The unlimited discretion

[32] Para. 123.

[33] The first time the FCC invalidated a law on the basis of lacking a legitimate purpose was on 14 December 1965 when three judgments on church taxes were handed down, 1 BvR 412/60, 1 BvL 31/62 and 1 BvL 2/60. In the first judgment, the Court struck down state laws which extended the duty to pay church taxes to certain corporations, and in the second and third judgments, the laws which extended the duty to pay church taxes to spouses of church members even if the spouses themselves did not belong to the church.

[34] FCC judgment of 5 August 1966, 1 BvF 1/61; BVerfGE 20, 150.

[35] Para. 7.

of the authorities served 'to protect the NSDAP and served the fight against independent charities and churches',[36] and the original regulations could not 'match ... the intentions of a democratic legislator respectful of a liberal democratic order'.[37] While *some* regulations of collections may serve legitimate aims, such as 'to protect the public from fraud, unfair competition and other offences', these 'public safety' concerns would also 'dictate the limits of state supervision' and thus 'less intensive controls'.[38] In this way, an analysis of the design of the law was used to flush out illegitimate purposes.

Before going any further I wish to make an important terminological caveat. The concepts of 'motives' and 'purposes' are used often interchangeably in this context, although of course their strict vocabulary meanings are not the same: a motive may be seen as a subjective reason for a particular action while purpose denotes *what* a person (or an institution) wants to achieve, not *why*. Every motive I have may, tautologically, figure as my purpose, but not every purpose which I have actually motivates me to action in order to achieve this purpose. This distinction corresponds, roughly, to two types of reasons for action that philosophers distinguish: motivating reasons and explanatory reasons. (These two types of reasons should be distinguished from *normative* reasons: those that figure as good reasons for actions, in the eyes whoever pronounces that judgement). While *motivating* reasons are those that actually motivate an agent—they refer to the desires and/or beliefs necessary to explain the agent's behaviour and in light of which she actually acts; *explanatory* reasons, by contrast, are those that, *from the perspective of an agent*, favour her action.[39] In a legal context, however, the distinction is pedantic. Some American legal scholars note that when the US Supreme Court refers to legislative goals which are adequately known, it refers to 'purposes', but when they have not been adequately known, and in particular when the Court refuses to rely on them, they will be labelled 'motivation'.[40] But this usage (described but not endorsed by Clark) seems to put the cart before the horse because whether the Court *should* rely on legislative motives (or purposes) is precisely what is at stake in the discussion, and 'motives' should be ascertained independently of whether the Court decides to rely on them.

Alexander Bickel attached high importance to the distinction between motives and purposes, understanding the former as a subjective will or reason to act and

[36] Para. 30.

[37] Para. 31.

[38] Para. 33.

[39] See Maria Alvarez, 'Reasons for Action: Justification, Motivation, Explanation' in Edward N. Zalta (ed.), *The Stanford Encyclopedia of Philosophy* (Winter 2017 edition), https://plato.stanford.edu/entries/reasons-just-vs-expl/ (last accessed 2 August 2022).

[40] See, e.g., J. Morris Clark, 'Legislative Motivation and Fundamental Rights in Constitutional Law', (1978) 15 *San Diego Law Review* 953, 956.

the latter as a more objectified foreseeable effect of an action.[41] As Bickel suggested, some of the difficulty about appealing to legislative motives 'is due to confusion between, on the one hand, a finding of motive properly speaking . . . and, on the other, a determination of the 'purpose' which . . . is either the name given to the Court's objective assessment of the effect of a statute or a conclusory term denoting the Court's independent judgment of the constitutionally allowable end that the legislature could have had in mind'.[42] But even apart from the fact that (as will be evidenced in a moment) the courts themselves are often oblivious to this distinction and use the concepts interchangeably, this difference cannot be of constitutional consequence because it is more about the types of *evidence* that a court is allowed to use in order to determine the motive rather than about the legitimacy of the motive inquiry in the first place. It is perfectly intelligible to say that we care about legislative motives but look for their symptoms in the objectified purposes (in the eyes of an impartial observer, for instance), but it would not make sense to claim that all we are interested in are objectified purposes and we do not care at all whether they were prefigured in any way in the legislators' motives. Perhaps the most compelling formula was offered by Justice Stevens (in a dissent): 'Our precedent provides that we evaluate purpose based upon what the objective indicia of intent would reveal to a reasonable observer'.[43] So the distinction just mentioned pertains to evidentiary matters rather than to the appropriateness of the motive/purpose inquiry.

A true difference is perhaps that, in contrast to motives, we may attribute purposes not only to persons but also to things, objects, rules, and states of affairs: one cannot substitute 'motives' for 'purposes' in questions such as 'what is the purpose of the university?' or 'what is the purpose of the NAFTA agreement?'. But this difference is of no interest to us because, in the context of scrutinizing legislative motives or purposes, what matters are the objectives (to bring in yet another synonymous word) which can be attributed to human beings: for instance, as the makers, creators, or perpetrators of a certain state of affairs or objects. It is true that sometimes we use the concept of a purpose of a thing or a state of affairs in a way in which we deliberately abstract from the motivations of the makers, and attempt to construct a purpose independent of motives, for instance the purpose which most rationally may be attributed to such a state of affairs by an impartial observer, or by us. But this is precisely the sort of substantive discussion about various theories of motives/purposes which proposes different standards for ascertaining them, and no clarity is gained, or argumentative value added, by a definitional fiat whereby motives would be 'subjective' and purposes 'objective' in that way. As judges themselves often use 'motives' and 'purposes' in one breath, as equivalent concepts, especially when both are contrasted

[41] Alexander M. Bickel, *The Least Dangerous Branch* (Bobbs-Merrill 1962) 208–21.
[42] Ibid. 209.
[43] *Salazar v. Buono*, 559 U.S. 700, 755 (2010) (Stevens J. dissenting).

to the *effects*-based scrutiny,[44] our discussion here will track this judicial usage.[45]

An indirect confirmation of the equivalence of 'purposes' and 'motives' may be found in the judicial usages of the 'purposes' (or 'objectives') of the law when judges refuse to assign to old laws *changed* (legitimate) purposes but discern them at the point of their enactment, and see them as frozen in time, so to speak. (An eloquent articulation of this approach was offered a long time ago by Justice Holmes: '[I]t would be a new doctrine in constitutional law that the original invalidity could be cured by an administration which defeated their intent.')[46] Such an approach would make no sense if the 'objectives' (or 'purposes') were significantly different from motives: it would then be perfectly plausible to say that, while motives remain frozen in time (because they are just a historical fact), the purposes keep changing with the changed circumstances. And yet, judges often refuse to adopt this dynamic approach to purposes of the legislation when reviewing its constitutionality under the objectives prong of scrutiny. Consider one of the landmark constitutional cases in the Canadian Supreme Court's case law, the *Big M* case (which will be discussed in more detail in Chapter 9). The case concerned the legitimacy of Sunday-closing laws, under the Canadian Charter's freedom of religion clause. Chief Justice Dickson rejected the submission made in support of the constitutionality of the Lord's Day Act that 'the purpose of legislation may shift, or be transformed over time by changing social conditions'.[47] This principle continues to apply in Charter jurisprudence. Thus, while Chief Justice Dickson accepted that the *effect* of the Lord's Day Act at the time of judgement 'may be more secular ... than it was in 1677 or 1906, such a finding cannot justify a conclusion that its purpose has similarly changed',[48] the religious character of the law's purpose remained. Such an understanding of the

[44] See, e.g., White J. delivering the opinion of the Court in *Washington v. Davis*, 426 U.S. 229 (1976) and referring to *Palmer v. Thompson*, 403 U.S. 217 (1971): 'The opinion [in *Palmer*] warned against grounding decisions on legislative *purpose or motivation*, thereby lending support for the proposition that the operative *effect* of the law rather than its *purpose* is the paramount factor,' 426 U.S. at 243, emphases added. See also the Court's reference to *Davis* in *Village of Arlington Heights v. Metropolitan Housing Development Corp.*, 429 U.S. 252 (1977): 'Davis does not require a plaintiff to prove that the challenged action rested solely on racially discriminatory *purposes*. Rarely can it be said that a legislature or administrative body operating under a broad mandate made a decision *motivated* solely by a single concern ... When there is proof that a discriminatory *purpose* has been a *motivating* factor in the decision, this judicial deference is no longer justified,' 429 U.S. 265–66, emphases added. There are also examples from outside the United States. In a decision on freedom of speech by the German Federal Constitutional Court (to which we will turn in Chapter 6), the Court established the standards of 'generality' of laws which limit constitutional freedom of speech, under Article 5 of Basic Law, and observed: 'For encroachments on Article 5.1. of the Basic Law it follows that their *purpose* may not aim to ensure that protective measures are taken towards impacts of specific expressions of opinion that remain purely intellectual. The *intention* of preventing statements with content that is damaging or dangerous in their conceptual consequence rescinds the principle of freedom of opinion itself and is illegitimate ... ,' BVerfG v. 4.11.2009, 1 BvR 2150/08—*Wunsiedel* [FCC of 4 November 2009, 1 BvR 2150/08—*Wunsiedel*], BVerfGE 124, 300, para. 49, emphases added.

[45] For a similar point, see Nelson, 'Judicial Review of Legislative Purpose' (n. 27) 1787 n. 5.

[46] *Giles v. Harris*, 189 U.S. 475, 487 (1903).

[47] *R v. Big M Drug Mart Ltd.* [1985] 1 SCR 295, 334.

[48] Ibid. 336.

law's 'purpose'—as stable and determined by the objectives that the lawmakers felt worth pursuing at the time of the original enactment—confirms that, for practical purposes, 'objectives' and 'purposes' in the context of constitutionality of legislation are indistinguishable from the motives or intentions.

While the motive-based scrutiny of unconstitutionality in the United States and also in a number of other jurisdictions is pervasive, the courts would often deny that this is what they were doing. Back in 1810, Chief Justice John Marshall evoked a scenario 'that impure motives should contribute to the passage of a law', and while he acknowledged that these 'are circumstances most deeply to be deplored', at the same time he insisted that '[i]t may well be doubted how far the validity of a law depends upon the motives of its framers'.[49] (It should be noted, however, that the rejection of motive-based inquiry in this judgment is narrower than the sentence, taken out of context, would suggest. The challenge to the law by the legislature of Georgia, which permitted the state to sell huge tracts of public land to four private companies, was that the enacting legislators had been bribed. So what Justice Marshall refused to do was not so much to inquire into what purposes the legislature sought to achieve, but rather whether the vote had been triggered by corrupt motivations.)[50] Over a century later, another great judge, Justice Benjamin N. Cardozo, observed in a dissent: 'There is a wise and ancient doctrine that a Court will not inquire into the motives of a legislative body or assume them to be wrongful';[51] he refused to accept the majority's approach which he characterized as resting 'upon the ruling that another purpose, not professed, may be read beneath the surface, and by the purpose so imputed the statute is destroyed'.[52] A few years later, in a decision which reads today as an embarrassing case of the judicial endorsement of misogyny, in upholding a state ban on employment of female bartenders (except for wives or daughters of male owners of bars) Justice Frankfurter stated, as a self-evident fact: 'We cannot cross-examine either actually or argumentatively the mind of Michigan legislators *nor question their motives*.'[53]

These are the statements by three of among the greatest lawyers in the history of the US Supreme Court. So what is puzzling, perhaps even striking, is the combination of the ubiquity of motive-based constitutional inquiry, usually presented as an inquiry into the 'purposes' or 'objectives' pursued by the legislator, with the frequent denials by courts that they engage in such an inquiry, and/or that it is an appropriate way to proceed. For instance, in a concurrence in a 1968 decision, Justice Black announced that 'this Court has consistently held that it is not for us to invalidate a statute because of our views that the 'motives' behind its passage were improper ... ';[54] and three years later, with respect to

[49] *Fletcher v. Peck*, 10 U.S. 87, 130 (1810).
[50] See Nelson, 'Judicial Review of Legislative Purpose' (n. 27) 1796–99.
[51] *United States v. Constantine*, 296 U.S. 287, 299 (1935) (Cardozo, J. dissenting), references omitted.
[52] Ibid. 298–99.
[53] *Goesaert v. Cleary*, 335 U.S. 464, 466–67 (1948), emphasis added.
[54] *Epperson v. Arkansas*, 393 U.S. 97, 113 (1968) (Black, J. concurring).

equal protection clause jurisprudence, the Supreme Court declared, in *Palmer v. Thompson*, that 'no case in this Court has held that a legislative act may violate equal protection solely because of the motivation of the men who voted for it'[55]—a quote which John Hart Ely accompanies with a terse remark: 'surely that historical claim was wrong'.[56]

Similar denials can be found in the jurisprudence of high courts outside the United States. For example, in Australia, in *Bank of NSW v. Commonwealth*, Chief Justice Latham explained that 'the motives of Parliament, and, as a general rule, the objects which a Parliament seeks to achieve, are not relevant to questions of constitutional validity'.[57] The High Court has framed this abstention in political terms—it is not for the judiciary to 'determine political necessities',[58] and it should not undertake any inquiry into whether a given law is 'politically, economically, or socially desirable or undesirable'.[59] Examples of this type of language abound in the early years of the High Court of Australia. In *Huddart Parker Ltd. v. Commonwealth*, Justice Rich confirmed his view that there is a relevant distinction between the motive of a legislative enactment on the one hand, and its 'purpose or operation' on the other. 'The object of an Act is to be gathered from its necessary effect, and not from some purpose or motive which the legislature may be supposed to have had.'[60] In the same case, Justice Dixon also separated legislative motive from the inquiry, explaining that once it is established that the legislature has the power to enact a given law, 'it becomes irrelevant how, or upon what grounds, or for what motives it is exercised'.[61] The same Justice Dixon offered similar comments in *Melbourne Corporation v. Commonwealth*, in which he confirmed that in order to conclude that a federal law is within power, it is enough that it 'has an actual and immediate operation within a field assigned to the Commonwealth as a subject of legislative power', and the fact that the law 'discloses another purpose and that the purpose lies outside the area of federal power are considerations which will not in such a case suffice to invalidate the law'.[62] And yet, as we will see, in more recent case law, and in particular where the law infringes on constitutional rights, the Australian courts applied the proportionality analysis precisely to do that which Justice Dixon had denounced—namely, to discern the true purposes underlying the legislation.

Yet another example of a court denying an interest in motives—as opposed to purposes—is provided by the South African Constitutional Court in the *UDM* case concerning legislative amendments allowing for 'floor crossing'

[55] *Palmer v. Thompson*, 403 U.S. 217, 224 (1971), quoted in John Hart Ely, *Democracy and Distrust* (Harvard University Press 1980)136–37.
[56] Ely, *Democracy and Distrust* (n. 55) 136.
[57] *Bank of NSW v. Commonwealth* (1948) 76 CLR 1, 186.
[58] *Amalgamated Society of Engineers v. Adelaide Steamship Co. Ltd.* (1920) 28 CLR 129, 151.
[59] *Australian National Airways Pty Ltd. v. Commonwealth* (1945) 71 CLR 29, 70 per Rich J.
[60] *Huddart Parker Ltd. V. Commonwealth* (1931) 44 CLR 492, 500–01 per Rich J.
[61] Ibid. 515 per Dixon J.
[62] *Melbourne Corporation v. Commonwealth* (1947) 74 CLR 31, 79 Per Dixon J.

in the Parliament. The amendments were necessitated by a split in an opposition party, and the applicants challenged the constitutionality of the legislation, claiming among other things that 'the legislation is intended and has been designed to serve the purpose of the ruling party', and allowing it to take advantage of the breaking up of the opposition party.[63] The Court reacted sternly by saying that the appellants' argument 'equates purpose with motive', and that courts 'are not ... concerned with the motives of the members of the legislature who vote in favour of particular legislation ... unless it infringes rights protected by the Constitution ... '.[64] It then found that the subject matter of the legislation, which it defined as the retention and loss of membership, was within the Parliament's power to legislate, and that 'the purpose of the disputed legislation was to make provision for members of the legislatures to change their party allegiances without losing their seats'.[65] But this contrast between a 'motive' and a 'purpose' is not credible: one may say that the majority's motive was to make such provision; whether the provision for a politically safe floor-crossing is triggered by a 'motive' or a 'purpose' seems like a pedantic distinction. The contrast is not so much between a motive and a purpose but between two different motives (or purposes, if you like): one, attributed to the majority by the appellants (protection of the interests of the majority party) and one found by the Court (making it possible for the opposition party members to cross the floor without losing the seat). And the assertion that the distinction motive/intent and purpose is merely pedantic may be confirmed by the fact that some writers, credibly, use the two concepts interchangeably or in one breadth, as for instance in a recent article by a US legal scholar reporting that 'the Supreme Court has held official action to a very different standard when unconstitutional *intent or purpose* is invoked'[66] or that '*purpose or intent* is the overarching concept used in the Equal Protection Clause cases ... '.[67]

2. Exclusionary Reasons in Constitutional Law

An appeal to legislative motives or purposes in US constitutional law is often implicit only, but this does not make it any less powerful—except that to discern it, one has to engage in an interpretation of judicial decisions going behind a mere reading of their texts. An excellent example of such an interpretation is provided by an important article by Richard Pildes in 1994, in which he provides

[63] *United Democratic Movement v. President of the Republic of South Africa and Others(No. 2)* 2003 (1) SA 495 (CC) paras. 15–17.
[64] Ibid. para. 56.
[65] Ibid. para .57.
[66] Brandon L. Garrett, 'Unconstitutionally Illegitimate Discrimination', (2018) 104 *Virginia Law Review* 1741, 1474, see also 1479, 1501, emphasis added.
[67] Ibid. 1500, emphasis added.

an account of constitutional adjudication in contrast to a balancing-of-rights account.[68] Rather than the Court engaging in balancing of competing rights, Pildes claims, it can be better seen as engaging in a two-step inquiry: defining boundaries between different spheres of authority, and then articulating the appropriate principles that legitimate state action in a particular sphere under scrutiny. In the latter tier of reasoning, what is crucial for the Court is to see what principles—what purposes for state action—are appropriate to a given sphere, and which constitute excluded reasons: purposes which, considering the proper common understanding of a given sphere, must not figure in justification of state action. The latter principles act very much as Raz's exclusionary reasons: reasons not to act on certain reasons which are pre-empted by acceptable meanings of a given sphere of state authority, and this makes them analogous to public reason (as described earlier in this book in Chapter 2, section 1 as congruent with Raz's exclusionary rule).

This is a rough paraphrase of Pildes's theory. Interestingly, the first dimension of the analysis reads rather as applying the celebrated idea of Michael Walzer regarding distinct 'spheres of justice' which are tightly demarcated from each other, to be controlled by distinct principles applicable as they are to one sphere but not necessarily to another, and informed by collective understandings of a particular public good subject to social distribution in a given sphere.[69] Even strikingly similar language is used, about 'carv[ing] up social and political place into distinct spheres'.[70] But from the point of view of our subject matter here, it is the second dimension of Pildes's theory that is more relevant, namely identifying 'excluded reasons' in particular spheres of authority scrutinized by the Court: 'recognizing that certain reasons are simply excluded from being acceptable bases for action',[71] and certifying certain reasons as appropriate to a given state action. This is often only *implicit* in the Court's reasoning but no less significant for that.

Consider one particular case study provided by Pildes: that of voting rights. Pildes compared two of the central cases in this area which at first blush may seem inconsistent in method and in substance: *Lassiter v. Northampton County Board of Elections*[72] and *Harper v. Virginia Board of Elections*.[73] In *Lassiter*, the Court had upheld a literacy test as a condition of the franchise; in *Harper*, seven years later, the Court struck down a requirement to pay state poll taxes as conditioning an exercise of the right to vote. Pildes explains the difference by reference to the proper understanding of a social practice in a given sphere, and the resulting implications for excluded (or approved) reasons: 'Literacy tests and

[68] Richard H. Pildes, 'Avoiding Balancing: The Role of Exclusionary Reasons in Constitutional Law', (1994) 45 *Hastings Law Journal* 711.
[69] Michael Walzer, *Spheres of Justice* (Basil Blackwell 1983)6–10.
[70] Pildes, 'Avoiding Balancing' (n. 68) 723.
[71] Ibid. 714.
[72] 360 U.S. 45 (1959).
[73] 383 U.S. 663 (1966).

poll taxes differ, in Court's view, precisely because they rest on different justifications and reflect different theories about the nature of voting.'[74] In *Lassiter*, Pildes claims, '[t]he justification for literacy tests is that they help define a political community with the relevant competence for political participation';[75] in *Harper*, however, 'the very justification for poll taxes is in itself the obstacle to their constitutionality'.[76] The same conception of the nature of voting, and of the political community, may support both decisions because in one case, the justification is found as continuous with the broader theory of voting, and in the second case, it is contrary to it.

Naturally, one may object to the outcome in *Lassiter*: there may be all sorts of severe problems with the literacy test, one point of view being what conception of political community it sustains when viewed as a legitimate reason for restricting a right to vote. Significantly, and today somewhat distressingly, some judges believed that literacy tests and poll tests are actually based on the *same* or very similar justifications, and are thought to be equally related to the task of 'promot[ion of] civic responsibility'.[77] In his dissent to *Harper v. Virginia State Board of Education*, Justice Black (whom Justice Stewart joined) connected the poll tax requirement with a broader political philosophy of voting, suggesting that

> it was probably accepted as sound political theory by a large percentage of Americans through most of our history, that people with some property have a deeper stake in community affairs, and are consequently more responsible, more educated, more knowledgeable, more worthy of confidence, than those without means . . .[78]

And soon after he referred to *Lassiter* claiming that literacy tests 'find justification on very similar grounds'.[79] This may suggest that, under some philosophical understandings of the voting in a democratic state, literacy and property tests stand or fall together—differently than under Pildes's interpretation. (While they stand together in Justice Black's dissent in *Harper*, they fell together under the Voting Rights Act of 1965, the successive amendments of which gradually led to a permanent ban on literacy tests throughout the United States by 1975.)[80] But this is largely beside the point; we will always disagree about the substance of a particular reason and its relevance to the broader nature of a

[74] Pildes, 'Avoiding Balancing' (n. 68) 743.
[75] Ibid. 743
[76] Ibid. 744.
[77] *Harper v. Virginia State Board of Education*, 383 U.S. 663, 685 (1966) (Black, J. dissenting).
[78] Ibid. 685 (1966) (Black, J. dissenting).
[79] Ibid. 685 (1966) (Black, J. dissenting).
[80] For a brief history of this legislation, see Samuel Issacharoff, Pamela S. Karlan, and Richard H. Pildes, *The Law of Democracy: Legal Structure of the Political Process* (4th edn., Foundation Press 2012) 56–57.

particular constitutional practice, while agreeing that *some* connection between such a motivating reason and the outcome is crucial to the finding of (un) constitutionality—which is the main point being pressed in this book.

3. The Level of Judicial Scrutiny and Detection of Illicit Legislative Motives

There is a clear connection between standards of review of laws and the call for public justification in terms of appropriate reasons. In principle, though, the very idea that motives *matter* for a judgment of constitutionality does not necessarily imply any particular judicial role in scrutinizing those motives; from an adoption of the general idea that motives/purposes are relevant to the validity of the law, no particular degree on the scale of activism-deference follows. We may well accept the wisdom of a motive-based principle and at the same time be willing to adopt a strong presumption of constitutionality of legislative motives. If the US Supreme Court's decisions do indicate a general tendency to grant high deference to Congress and to state legislature so far as the inquiry into purpose is concerned,[81] then it does not follow that motives are irrelevant for the Court, but only that the Court will largely accept the legislature's motives as proper, and will only question them in exceptional cases.

A leading law review summarized it recently: 'When evaluating a claim that an action arose from an unconstitutional motive, courts often take two steps: they examine evidence of bad motive and determine accordingly the nature of judicial review. Evidence of bad motive triggers higher scrutiny; otherwise, the default is rational basis review.'[82] But in practice, a heightened scrutiny of laws may be seen as a vigorous enquiry into the reasons behind the law, stemming from an uncertainty, scepticism, or suspicion as to the nature of the real reasons behind the law—or at least frustration that no such reasons have been provided by the legislature.[83] The way in which balancing, US-style, is used to flush out unconstitutional (but hidden) motives is normally illustrated by the use of 'strict scrutiny' of legislative intrusions of rights: both its tiers, namely regarding the means-ends relationship and regarding the significance of the ends of legislation, may be properly seen as aimed at discerning (and, if found unconstitutional, disqualifying) the true legislative motives. Higher-than-usual scrutiny is normally justified by a suspicion that improper motives are at work and requires a close connection between the asserted aim and the legislative means adopted. In

[81] Laurence H. Tribe, *American Constitutional Law* (2nd edn., Foundation Press 1988) 817.

[82] Note, 'The Supreme Court—Leading Cases', (2018) 132 *Harvard Law Review* 132, 332, footnotes omitted.

[83] See Ronald C. Den Otter, *Judicial Review in an Age of Moral Pluralism* (Cambridge University Press 2009)54, footnote omitted.

a classic account provided by John Hart Ely, the flushing out of motives through the use of a stricter-than-usual scrutiny operates in the following way:

> The 'special scrutiny' that is afforded suspect classifications ... insists that the classification in issue fit the goal invoked in its defense more closely than any alternative classification would. There is only one goal the classification is likely to fit *that* closely, however, and that is the goal the legislators actually had in mind. If that goal cannot be invoked because it is unconstitutional, the classification will fail. Thus, functionally, special scrutiny, in particular its demand for an essentially perfect fit, turns out to be a way of 'flushing out' unconstitutional motivation ...[84]

Traces of such an approach may be found also in the Canadian Supreme Court. In *R v. Advance Cutting and Coring Ltd.*,[85] writing for the dissenting judges, Justice Bastarache had 'difficulty accepting' submissions regarding whether the purported objectives of the impugned laws were the 'true objectives'. The provisions under review comprised an industrial relations regime governing the Quebec construction industry. Employers could only hire individuals who held competency certificates. In effect, this rule required workers to join one of five unions that enjoyed a statutory monopoly over the issuing of those certificates. The judge rejected the asserted objectives of providing a system of 'structured collective bargaining and to provide for competency requirements', finding 'no logical relationship' with the impugned provisions themselves.[86] However, Justice Bastarache did not discuss exactly what the true objectives might have been. To Sujit Choudhry, a 'plausible way' of interpreting the judgment is that the judge believed the true purpose of the regime was to provide the unions concerned with that monopoly, restricting the supply of construction workers in return for 'labour peace'—in more damning terms, 'a form of illegitimate special-interest legislation which protected the interests of five construction unions from economic competition for no offsetting public interest'.[87] That purpose clearly could not figure in an official justification for the law.

The same reasoning, this time not in the dissent but in the judgment, may be found in another Canadian case. In *Figueroa v. Canada (Attorney General)*,[88] the Supreme Court found that a fifty-candidate minimum for registration as a political party under the Canada Elections Act infringed section 3 of the Canadian

84 Ely, *Democracy and Distrust* (n. 55) 146, footnote omitted. Note that in this excerpt Ely refers to heightened scrutiny of legislative classifications, that is to alleged discrimination, but it is easily applicable to all cases of strict scrutiny of legislative interferences with constitutional rights. See also Cass R. Sunstein, *The Partial Constitution* (Harvard University Press 1994) 30.

85 [2001] 3 SCR 209.

86 Ibid. 257–58.

87 Sujit Choudhry, 'So What is the Real Legacy of *Oakes*? Two Decades of Proportionality Analysis under the Canadian *Charter*'s Section 1', (2006) 34 *Supreme Court Law Review* 501, 510.

88 [2003] 1 SCR 912.

Charter of Rights. Turning to the justification analysis, the Attorney General offered three separate possible objectives for the rule: 'to improve the effectiveness of the electoral process, to protect the integrity of the electoral financing regime, and to ensure that the process is able to deliver a viable outcome for our form of responsible government'.[89] The Court found no clear connection between the measures under review and the asserted objectives. Choudhry argues that this too 'suggests that the true objective may have been rather different—to protect larger political parties from *electoral* competition to the detriment of the public interest.'[90]

In Australia, a form of proportionality analysis (often, *sans le nom*) is similarly used to discern the actual purposes of legislation, and check whether they pass constitutional muster. There are some constitutional instances in which the proportionality principle is expressly applied; namely, when the characterization of an impugned law turns on the nature of its purpose. The clearest examples of such cases are constitutional challenges to laws enacted in purported exercise of heads of federal legislative power defined by the High Court in purposive terms, as opposed to definitions by reference to subject matter (which, quantitatively, is a rule). Among these are the defence power (section 51(vi)) and the external affairs power (section 51(xxix)) when used to support the domestic implementation of international treaties.[91] In order for a law to fall within the scope of such a power, it must be shown that the law can be regarded as 'reasonably appropriate and adapted' to the relevant constitutional purpose—a canonical formula for proportionality, Australian-style. In this characterization context, leading constitutional scholar Leslie Zines observed general acceptance of the view that 'a law that uses means that are disproportionate to a legitimate end within power may indicate that the object of the law is not that which would bring it within power'.[92] (By contrast, in order for a law to fall within the scope of a 'subject matter' power, it must be found to have a 'sufficient connection' to the relevant power.)

This test has been adopted, in particular, where legislation is alleged to infringe constitutional freedoms or guarantees, both implied and express. In the Australian context, this applies in particular to the implied freedom of political communication, or to the freedom of interstate trade, commerce, and intercourse under section 92 of the federal Constitution. The court will then consider the proportionality of any such infringement to the achievement of a legitimate end in pursuit of which the impugned law is enacted, in order to determine whether that infringement is 'appropriate and adapted' to the achievement of a legitimate

[89] Ibid. 950.
[90] Choudhry, 'So What is the Real Legacy of Oakes? (n. 87) 510.
[91] See, e.g., *Commonwealth v. Tasmania (Tasmanian Dam Case)* (1983) 158 CLR 1, particularly per Deane J. at 260.
[92] James Stellios, *Zines's The High Court and the Constitution* (The Federation Press 2015)58.

objective. The High Court established, in a foundational decision on the implied constitutional right of freedom of political communication (*ACTV*),[93] a doctrine of varying degrees of scrutiny required for different types of legislative restrictions on rights, not unlike (though using different language) the US Supreme Court's hierarchy of levels of scrutiny. In particular, the High Court of Australia established that laws that restrict 'ideas or information' (as contrasted to laws 'merely' restricting the 'activity or mode of communication'), will require a 'compelling justification' based in some significant competing public interest.[94] Those laws must also be minimally restrictive, or no more restrictive than is reasonably necessary to achieve the protection of that competing public interest.[95] More recently, these terms were invoked in *Hogan v. Hinch*[96] where the High Court acknowledged the distinction between 'incidental' and 'direct' burdens on communication, and cited *ACTV* regarding the stricter standard of justification analysis to be applied in the case of the former; those laws that directly prohibit or restrict political communication 'will be much more difficult to justify'.[97]

This hierarchy of levels of scrutiny clearly focuses the Court's attention on the legitimacy of the objective in pursuit of which the law was enacted. In the judgment by Chief Justice Mason in *ACTV*, the lack of proportionality between the measure and the alleged aim is a sign that a different, more invidious aim was at work: where the impairment of free communication is 'disproportionate to the attainment of the competing public interest',[98] that disproportionality will suggest that 'the purpose and effect of the restriction is in fact to impair freedom of communication'.[99] In this particular case, constitutionality of bans on political advertising during election periods was under scrutiny. The government argued that the underlying objective of the impugned legislation was to 'safeguard the integrity of the political system'.[100] A ban on political advertising would vastly reduce the campaign funds that parties and candidates required to contest the election. Nevertheless, the majority of judges found the restriction disproportionate, and unfairly privileging the established parties by limiting media access for new or independent candidates. As such, the impugned law 'plainly fail[ed] to preserve or enhance fair access to the mode of communication which [was] the subject of the restriction'.[101]

In some systems of constitutional review, the idea of a hierarchy of standards of scrutiny (with the implication, as just observed, that heightened level of scrutiny serves to ferret out illicit motivations) is rejected, at least as a matter of an

93 *Australian Capital Television Pty Ltd. & NSW v. The Commonwealth* (1992) 177 CLR 106.
94 Ibid. 143.
95 Ibid. 143.
96 (2011) 243 CLR 506, 555.
97 (1992) 177 CLR 106, 169.
98 Ibid. 143.
99 Ibid. 144.
100 Ibid. 129.
101 Ibid. 146.

official doctrine. The South African Constitutional Court, for example, has explicitly rejected invitations to interpret the constitutional template of proportionality (s 36(1)) as a requirement that different degrees of scrutiny be applied for different rights. In the course of the justification in *Christian Education South Africa v. Minister of Education*,[102] a case concerned with the alleged infringement of religious freedoms, Justice Sachs for a unanimous Court briefly explained the 'highly controversial' strict scrutiny test adopted in the United States.[103] The matter concerned a challenge to a schools act which prohibited corporal punishment; the challenge was based on the grounds that such punishment is an integral part of the Christian ethos, and that the blanket prohibition of its use in schools violates individual, parental, and community rights to practice freely their religion. In the course of rejecting the submissions by the appellant education association in that case as to the correct interpretation of section 36, Justice Sachs made it clear that the terms of that provision did not import a strict scrutiny approach. The particular problems attendant upon the limitation of certain rights and freedoms—here, the freedom of religion—do not affect the standard that must be applied in the limitations analysis. Rather, what section 36 requires of the Court 'is an overall assessment that will vary from case to case'.[104] The provision permits those limitations that are 'reasonable and justifiable in an open and democratic society based on human dignity, equality and freedom, taking into account all relevant factors'.[105] Thus, Justice Sachs concluded that a standard the Court must adopt is 'the nuanced and contextual one required by section 36, and not the rigid one of strict scrutiny'.[106] (In this case, the Court accepted the legislature's purpose of the outlawing of the physical punishment in the school, as related to the promotion of 'respect for dignity and emotional integrity of all children'.)[107]

But it is one thing to say that the Court will consider case-by-case reasons which would trigger a higher scrutiny (in comparison with a certain default, deferential position) and another to say that no differing standards of review can be discerned at all. The latter is certainly not true. Two South African constitutional scholars, referring to the contextual, case-by-case view of Justice Sachs doubt 'whether this approach is dramatically different from one based on different levels of scrutiny'.[108] Their view is that, in practice, there is a hierarchy of rights, in terms of the strength or justification required to save any law impairing those rights from constitutional invalidity. To Stu Woolman and Henk Botha, the

[102] *Christian Education South Africa v. Minister of Education* 2000 (4) SA 757 (CC) [29]–[31].
[103] Ibid. [29].
[104] Ibid. [31].
[105] Ibid. [36].
[106] Ibid. [31].
[107] Ibid. [50].
[108] S. Woolman and H. Botha, 'Limitations', in Stu Woolman and Michael Bishop (eds.), *Constitutional Law of South Africa* (2nd edn, Juta 2014) 34–71.

rights to life and human dignity appear to rank highest,[109] and one may add the right to equality to this catalogue.[110] It is also significant that section 36 of the Constitution lists, among the factors which need to be taken into account in assessing limitations of rights, 'the nature of the right' and 'the importance of the purpose of the limitation'.[111] This suggests that there is a constitutionally embedded variable standard of scrutiny which depends not only on the hierarchy of rights but also on the nature of justification for its limitation (in terms of the purpose). A canonical US doctrine, with its highly stylized three-level scrutiny framework, is only one (and not necessarily the best) way to express the idea that the heightening of the level of scrutiny may be seen as an exercise in flushing out illicit motivations.

The flushing out of true motives, when initial suspicion is warranted, is also helped by the second aspect of the heightening of the scrutiny, in addition to the 'necessity' or 'least restrictive alternative', namely by a requirement of high importance of the aim asserted. Again to quote from John Hart Ely: '[E]ven a perfect fit between the classification in issue and the goal the state is arguing shouldn't be enough to allay your initial suspicion if that goal is so unimportant that you have to suspect it's a pretext that didn't actually generate the choice.'[112] The triviality of the goal (even if admissible in low-suspicion cases) is a reason to believe that it is merely a pretext for an action de facto motivated by reasons which are not publicly citeable.

In fact, the second aspect of strict scrutiny in the US version, namely a requirement of the special importance of purposes asserted when a suspicion of illicit motives is justified, suggests immediately that the difference between American-style balancing and the European-style proportionality *sensu stricto* is largely overdrawn. Proportionality *sensu stricto*, it may be reminded, requires the weighing and balancing of costs and benefits resulting from a legislative action: costs in terms of infringement of a right and benefits in terms of maximizing a constitutionally valid purpose (including another right at stake). It may be thought that this tier of the European proportionality analysis makes it significantly different from balancing US-style: while the first two tiers of proportionality can be well discerned in the balancing analysis (namely, suitability and necessity, the former being labelled a relationship of means to the end, the latter, the least restrictive alternative), the third tier of European proportionality,

[109] See, e.g., *Ex parte Minister of Safety and Security & Others: In re: S v. Walters & Another* 2002 (4) SA 613 (CC) [28]: 'The right to life, to human dignity and to bodily integrity are individually essential and collectively foundational to the value system prescribed by the Constitution. Compromise them and the society to which we aspire becomes illusory. It therefore follows that any significant limitation of these rights, would for its justification demand a very compelling countervailing public interest'.

[110] See Aharon Barak, 'Proportionality and Principled Balancing', (2010) 4 *Law & Ethics of Human Rights* 1, 9–10.

[111] Section 36.1.(a) and (b).

[112] Ely, *Democracy and Distrust* (n. 55) 147–48.

namely the comparison of costs and benefits *may be thought* to be absent from the balancing conducted through the US strict scrutiny test. But it is not so: the exclusion of 'trivial' (even if constitutionally permitted) purposes under the strict scrutiny presupposes calculus and trade-offs between the purpose and the intrusion on a right. Whether the purpose can be properly deemed 'trivial' transpires as a *result* of comparing it with a legislative restriction; 'triviality' is an outcome rather than an ingredient of the comparison. If, when suspicion of wrongful motives is justified, we determine that a purpose is too trivial (thus, serves as a pretext) to justify an interference with a right, it is because we have tacitly conducted a calculus of these two values: the values of the maximization of an aim asserted by the legislator, and the value of the cost of harm to a right. It is exactly the same comparison and calculus that is conducted in the balancing analysis *sensu stricto*, European style. And it is only once, under a strict scrutiny test, we have established the relative 'triviality' of the goal, that we may suspect that a goal as trivial as *that* must be a cover-up for something else, namely for an unconstitutional motive. It is based on an assumption of basic rationality of lawmakers who would not make extremely poor trade-offs.[113] In this way, a motive analysis (the flushing out of illicit motives) under a strict scrutiny test is functionally dependent upon weighing and balancing of the sort which is substantially the same as in proportionality *sensu stricto*. If this last test requires that, in order to prevail over protection of an individual right, the public aims of the law must be of sufficient weight, then the court will have to require not just *any* legitimate aim, but an aim of special importance, to be cited in defence of the law—otherwise it will fail to do the job in the balancing analysis.

In his book on proportionality, Aharon Barak objects to such merging of the assessment of the importance of the aim with the balancing of the right infringed versus the legitimate aim purported. These are two separate steps of the analysis, Barak insists, and should be kept apart. 'The lack of proportionality does not turn the purpose into an "improper" one; the conflict with the constitutional provision is not a matter of purpose but rather of the means chosen to achieve that purpose, means that limit the constitutional right in a disproportionate manner.'[114] As a matter of elegance in judicial argument, such separation of the purpose scrutiny and the balancing scrutiny is to be applauded. However, when a dimension of 'importance' (or urgency) of the aim pursued is introduced, so that the aim scrutiny is not binary (legitimate/illegitimate) but allows for a dimension of degrees of importance, it is rather unrealistic to imagine that a judge may make such a judgement about the purpose in full isolation from the judgement about the importance of the right infringed. To take Barak's own example in this context, that of 'a law limiting freedom of expression in order to protect

[113] See Cohen-Eliya, *Proportionality and Constitutional Culture* (n. 23) 70.
[114] Barak, *Proportionality* (n. 20) 248.

national security':[115] an evaluation of the importance of the benefit of increased national security *in the particular context of the case* cannot be viewed entirely in isolation from how significant the decrease of enjoyment of freedom of expression by the citizens is. These two factors are not considered *in abstracto* but rather contextually, and so rather than keeping them apart and confining them to separate stages of judicial scrutiny, their *comparison* seems to be natural.

Occasionally, the importance of the aim is explicitly emphasized in the constitutional text, as is the case of the Constitution of South Africa which lists 'the importance of the purpose of the limitation [on a right]' among the factors to be taken into account in judging the legitimacy of the limitation.[116] In *Magajane v. Chairperson, North West Gambling Board*, Justice Van der Westhuizen offered the following reading of that requirement:

> [T]he importance of the purpose of the limitation, is crucial to the analysis, as it is clear that the Constitution does not regard the limitation of a constitutional right as justified unless there is a substantial state interest requiring the limitation ... The court must carefully review the public interest served by the statutory provision and determine the weight that this purpose should carry in the proportionality review.[117]

More frequently, however, the requirement of special urgency of purpose is a product of case law. This requirement is clearly present in the Canadian jurisprudence under the Charter of Rights. Following a determination that a given law infringes the Charter (which is a preliminary step, not determinative of the outcome), the inquiry proceeds to a justification analysis—it must be determined whether the limitation on the relevant right is a legitimate one. That analysis involves scrutiny both of the purpose for which the right is limited (or effects of the infringement, or both) and the means by which it seeks to achieve that purpose; the latter is the domain of proportionality analysis. As far as the character of purposes is concerned, the test was formulated by Chief Justice Dickson with the unanimous support of the Supreme Court in *R v. Oakes*.[118] The judgment of Chief Justice has 'taken on some of the character of holy writ',[119] and remains the operative framework for the analysis today. In order to justify a law found to infringe the Charter, the objective of the law must be of 'sufficient importance to warrant overriding a constitutionally protected right or freedom'.[120] That standard is met when the objective relates to 'concerns which are pressing and substantial in a free and democratic society'.[121] By these terms, section 1 of the

115 Ibid. 248.
116 Section 36.1 (b).
117 *Magajane v. Chairperson, North West Gambling Board* 2006 (5) SA 250 (CC) [65].
118 [1986] 1 SCR 103.
119 Peter Hogg, *Constitutional Law of Canada* (Thomson/Carswell 2014) para. 38-17.
120 [1986] 1 SCR 103, 138, citing *R v. Big M Drug Mart Ltd.* [1985] 1 SCR 295, 352.
121 [1986] 1 SCR 103, 138–39.

Charter provides that the exclusive purposes for which the legislature may impose limitations on rights or freedoms are consistent with those values which (broadly, but not all-inclusively) underlie Charter rights themselves.[122] In *Oakes*, Chief Justice Dickson provided what has become a famous litany of the values of a 'free and democratic society' in furtherance of which a rights violation might be justified. These included 'respect for the inherent dignity of the human person, commitment to social justice and equality, accommodation of a wide variety of beliefs, respect for cultural and group identity, and faith in social and political institutions which enhance the participation of individuals and groups in society'.[123]

While in theory the requirement of special urgency of purposes is well matched to the task of flushing out improper motivations, in practice the test has been rarely treated as particularly demanding, thus weakening the test's capacity to ascertain true motives. To remain within the space of the Canadian example, legal scholars recognize that in practice, this first stage of the section 1 justification analysis is rarely the hurdle at which laws will fall. To be sure, the judgment of Chief Justice Dickson in *Oakes* and the terms of section 1 itself frame the inquiry in a way that compels the Court to undertake a strict and exacting assessment of the underlying motive of the law. In a leading case focusing on the illicit character of legislative purposes, *R v. Big M Drug Mart Ltd.*,[124] it was argued by the state that the legislation in issue was a reasonable limit on the Charter on the basis of the secular justification that a day of rest is inherently beneficial, and that it 'may as well be the day traditionally observed in our society'.[125] Chief Justice Dickson forcefully rejected this argument. The law had been found to offend the Charter on the basis of its religious purpose of compelling the observance of the Sabbath. The fact that it achieved a secular goal that had 'never been found by [the Supreme Court] to be the motivation for the legislation' would not then save it. If a law is found to offend the Charter by its purpose, it is not justified under section 1 simply because it simultaneously achieves a goal that is consistent with the Charter. But apart from this exceptional case, it has generally been relatively easy for the state to convince the Canadian courts that legislative acts which limit rights and freedoms do so in accordance with these requirements,[126] and the actual role of the proper purpose is not central.[127] Indeed, one study indicated that in the first ten years after the adoption of the *Oakes* test as the canonical framework for section 1 justification analyses (1986–1997), the requirement that the

[122] Choudhry, 'So What is the Real Legacy of Oakes? (n. 87) 505.
[123] *R v. Oakes* [1986] 1 SCR 103, 136.
[124] *R v. Big M Drug Mart Ltd* [1985] 1 SCR 295. Note that *Big M* was decided prior to *Oakes*, but the judgment is unambiguous on this issue—the legislative objective was the constitutional flaw in the Lord's Day Act.
[125] Ibid. 353.
[126] Hogg, *Constitutional Law of Canada* (n. 119) para. 38-23.
[127] Barak, *Proportionality* (n 20) 283, footnote omitted.

objective behind a Charter infringement be 'sufficiently important' in the *Oakes* sense was met in 97 per cent of all cases (eighty-four of eighty-seven).[128]

Nevertheless, there *have* been occasional cases in which the Canadian Supreme Court took the task of scrutinizing the urgency of the purposes seriously, even if it ended up with an affirmative answer regarding constitutionality. In *Irwin Toy*,[129] the Court found that certain provisions of the *Consumer Protection Act* infringed freedom of expression under the Charter (s 2(b)) by imposing restrictions on commercial advertising that targeted children under the age of 13. In the discussion of whether the infringement was justified under section 1, the majority considered the role of evidence in the course of an inquiry into legislative objectives. Having earlier concluded that the purpose of the legislation was to restrict both the content and forms of expression for the goal of child protection, the discussion was concerned not with whether the alleged purpose was the true purpose of the legislation, but whether that purpose was itself a pressing and substantial one. This question turned in part on the extent to which children needed protecting. The laws were found to be aimed at the 'protection of a group which is particularly vulnerable to the technique of seduction and manipulation abundant in advertising'.[130] As evidence for the fact of this vulnerability, the Attorney General relied on a US Federal Trade Commission report on children's advertising, which contained a thorough review of related scientific studies.[131] The majority accepted that the legislature's decision to limit advertising to children was motivated by the goal of protecting a group particularly susceptible to commercial manipulation.[132] Thus, the Attorney General satisfied the first stage of the *Oakes* test—the objective *was* pressing and substantial.

In his comparative analysis of the German and Canadian proportionality tests, Dieter Grimm considered it 'quite instructive' that 'almost no Canadian law fails because of an insufficient purpose'.[133] In Germany, the purpose of a law reviewed under the purpose-oriented stage of scrutiny need only qualify as 'legitimate'—it must simply be a purpose that is not prohibited under the Constitution. However, to Grimm, the distinction with the Canadian approach 'seems to disappear in practice' where 'any lawful purpose' will be regarded as sufficient. The main function of this analysis, then, is to 'eliminate the small number of runaway cases'.[134] The majority of Canadian section 1 justification analyses have been decided on the basis of the minimum impairment requirement—to Hogg, the 'heart and soul of section 1 justification'.[135] And this fact was not

[128] Leon E. Trakman, William Cole-Hamilton, and Sean Gatien, 'R v Oakes 1986–1977: Back to the Drawing Board', (1998) 36 *Osgoode Hall Law Journal* 83, 95.

[129] *Irwin Toy Ltd v. Quebec (Attorney General)* [1989] 1 SCR 927.

[130] Ibid. 987.

[131] Ibid. 988.

[132] Ibid. 990.

[133] Dieter Grimm, 'Proportionality in Canadian and German Constitutional Jurisprudence', (2007) 57 *University of Toronto Law Review* 383, 388.

[134] Ibid. 388–89.

[135] Hogg, *Constitutional Law of Canada* (n. 119) para. 38-26.

lost on Canadian judges themselves. In *Alberta v. Hutterian Brethren of Wilson Colony*,[136] Justice LeBel described the generally limited role of the inquiry into legislative objective in the context of the section 1 justification analysis. He noted that courts 'only rarely' scrutinize the purpose behind a legislative enactment, that the 'threshold of justification remains quite low', and that laws 'almost never' fail this stage of the justification test. Indeed, Justice LeBel considered it proper that the inquiry into purpose should be so stunted—to him, courts should 'avoid too close questioning of the policy reasons underlying a law', this task being better suited to 'the political and parliamentary process'. Justice LeBel argued that courts should also be slow to engage in close scrutiny of legislative objective, and refrain from 'treating the purpose with undue emphasis on its sanctity'. His position is based on the imprecision involved in defining legislative objective, which is not always expressed with clarity in the instrument under review—for that reason, according to Justice LeBel, its identification will 'often amount to a judicial construct based on such evidence as is available'.[137]

It was already mentioned, following Dieter Grimm, that in Germany the scrutiny of legislative purposes rarely, if ever, calls for a special urgency of the aim to justify an infringement of a right; usually what is needed is that the purpose is allowed by the Constitution. But it does not follow that judges are always deferential towards the purposes cited by the legislator, as the example of the *Monopoly of Sports Betting* case has already shown. Nor does it mean that constitutional judges will always be satisfied with manufacturing legitimate purposes from the terms of legislation itself. Consider a remarkable dissenting opinion by Justice Hassemer in the *Prohibition of Incest* decision of the Federal Constitutional Court in 2008,[138] in which the Court upheld the prohibition based on the combination of purposes to protect 'the family order', to protect the 'subordinate partner' of an incestuous relationship, and to prevent genetic diseases of children born in these relationships.[139] Importantly, the Court, in its powerful concluding argument, combined these various purposes which it dubbed *nachvollziehbarer* (roughly translatable as 'rationally intelligible') and as corresponding to *Rechtsgüter* (rights-based interests) with the societal condemnation, or more precisely, powerful societal conviction about the need to punish (*Strafwürdigkeit*) incest—explaining that the legislator may legitimately mirror in criminal law a socially based *Unrechtsbewusstsein* (awareness of a wrong).[140] In his dissent, Justice Hassemer methodically debunks each of the three *Rechtsgüuter*-based purposes (showing that there is no rational connection between the criminal prohibition, as crafted in the

[136] *Alberta v. Hutterian Brethren of Wilson Colony* [2009] 2 SCR 567.
[137] Ibid. 643.
[138] BVerfG v. 25.02.2008, 2 BvR 392/07, BverfGE 120, 224.
[139] Paras. 41–50.
[140] Para. 51.

code, and any of these purposes) but his special irk is reserved for the paragraph just described, about the law mirroring conventional morality about the need to punish certain acts: 'Maintaining a societal consensus concerning value judgments ... cannot ... serve as a justification for a criminal norm ... Strengthening of morality can only function as an indirect aim and result of a just, clear, rational and coherent criminal justice system.'[141] This reads like a German equivalent of the US-style rejection of the role of law in reproducing social prejudice. On an even more general level, however, Justice Hassemer's dissent warns against concocting purposes to assist the legislator:

> The legislator ... was unable to decide in a clear and consistent manner which aims the provision was supposed to pursue, and neither did the legislator make sure that these purposes are in line with the scope of the provision.... It cannot be reliably ascertained what the legislator actually wanted to protect, and therefore whether the norm achieves this purpose.[142]

Of course, the crucial step for the motive analysis is to determine *when* scrutiny of legislation should be heightened, that is, *when* the initial suspicion that illicit motives are at work is justified. We do not have any direct access to legislative motivations, and we must be able to draw the principled distinction between suspicious cases where flushing out is needed, and those cases triggering only a lenient scrutiny. 'Suspicion' itself is much too blunt an instrument to perform the work of distinguishing between cases requiring different levels of scrutiny, especially if these distinctions are so consequential, because of course the higher the level of scrutiny, the more likely the determination of unconstitutionality resulting from the scrutiny. And, in order to avoid the danger of circularity, 'suspicion' must be based on some more 'objective' characteristics than a mere feeling that the legislator acted for illicit motives. In other words, the wrongness of motives must be a *conclusion* rather than the starting point of the scrutiny. So what can be the triggers for a higher-than-usual scrutiny?

Each context will of course yield different sets of indicia which may justify a heightened level of scrutiny, and thus a higher suspicion that wrong motives triggered a legislative action. They will be different in the cases of intrusions on freedom of speech, on freedom of religion, or on the right to equal protection, the right to association and assembly, etc. Scrutiny of the first three freedoms will be discussed, in more detail, later in this book (Chapters 7, 8, and 9), with the aim of detecting PR at work.

[141] Para. 100.
[142] Para. 99.

4. Motive Scrutiny and the Legitimacy of the Judicial Role

The general reticence towards inquiring vigorously into legislative motives may be explained by the concerns for the limits of judicial legitimacy, and the likelihood of a dramatic clash with legislative authority. This is one of the main points made in a seminal article by Laurence Tribe, which I will now discuss in some detail.

In his article, Tribe proposed a bifurcated use of motive-based scrutiny: judicial inquiry into possibly illicit motivations may be justifiable with regard to 'legislative actions distributing benefits or opportunities' (such as setting criteria for voting, employment, housing, etc.), but not to 'legislative actions laying down general rules of conduct, or creating governmental institutions or practices',[143] or at least there should be a strong presumption against such generalized use of motive-based scrutiny.[144] Tribe asserts that he 'cannot think of' any input-based principles[145] that should require the 'invalidation of otherwise constitutional rules of behavior or institutional arrangements that a government body has put in place for *reasons* that violate those principles'.[146]

But there are two problems with the bifurcated approach postulated by Tribe. First, the distinction between these two types of cases is extremely difficult to draw: basically every (or almost every) case of a 'rule of behaviour'/'institutional arrangement' may be presented as a distribution of opportunities, or vice versa. For instance, was the subject matter of a regulation scrutinized in *Palmer v. Thompson*[147] (discussed at length in the next chapter) a case involving the creation of a governmental practice (which could have been defined, in that case, as a rule that if the running of public facilities cannot be guaranteed for safety or cannot be done economically, the government was permitted to close them, unless fundamental rights were at stake) or was it a distribution of benefits (characterized as the principle that the government has a duty to provide public recreational facilities because it compensates the poorest for lack of access to privately owned facilities of this kind, and it will be forbidden to withdraw the already existing benefits if the withdrawal has racially disparate impact)? The indeterminate character of the distinction seems to be almost irremediable, and more importantly, whether one decides to characterize a case as belonging to the first or the second category will largely depend on where one stands on the merits of

[143] Laurence H. Tribe, 'The Mystery of Motive, Private and Public: Some Thoughts Inspired by the Problems of Hate Crime and Animal Sacrifice', (1994) *Supreme Court Review* 1, 22.

[144] The case for such a scrutiny with regard to these categories, Tribe says, 'seems quite weak', ibid. 22, footnote omitted.

[145] He defines input-based principles, in distinction to output-based principles, in a manner roughly corresponding to a distinction between motive- and effect-based scrutiny adopted here, see ibid. 19.

[146] Ibid. 23–24.

[147] 403 U.S. 217 (1971).

the issue: it is therefore non-neutral towards the outcome of the case, and thus totally unhelpful as a threshold principle.

Second, even if we *can* draw the distinction meaningfully, it is unclear why the second (and arguably, more important) category of cases should be immunized from a motive scrutiny. Generally, Tribe suggests that:

> [i]f a government-enacted rule of conduct is constitutionally inoffensive both on its face and as applied ... the fact that the rule would not have been promulgated ... but for the enacting body's desire to achieve a constitutionally forbidden result tells us nothing more than that the government body engaged in an *unsuccessful attempt* to violate the Constitution.[148]

But it seems entirely question-begging, for whether an 'attempt' was indeed 'inoffensive' hinges upon a prior, unargued and highly controversial proposition, that laws enacted for wrongful reasons do not violate the Constitution (including, anyone's individual rights), which is precisely the matter under discussion.

This can be further tested in a puzzling theoretical exercise offered by Tribe. He develops his argument by drawing an analogy with exclusionary rules in criminal evidence law, which may *seem* to be similarly justified as the judicial motive-based scrutiny, but then he suggests two differences which, he claims, are fatal to the principle of motive scrutiny in law. First, exclusionary rules may be seen as useful prophylactic measures towards law-enforcement bodies, in particular in the context of police misconduct, but '[r]espect for the Congress as a coordinate branch, and for the sovereign state legislatures, is difficult to reconcile with such a strong prophylactic use of judicial review'.[149] It is therefore an argument from the separation of powers, judicial deference, and proper respect for the legislature; the perception is that interbranch tensions increase when judges examine decision-makers' motives.[150] The argument has some force, and occasionally motive-based scrutiny is being criticized precisely on that ground, including by some judges. For example, in a dissent in *De La Cruz v. Tormey*,[151] a case considering an allegation that that the lack of campus child care facilities is indirectly discriminatory against women, Judge Wallace asserted: '[W]henever the federal judiciary begins to probe the motives of state officials or members of the coordinate branches of the federal government, serious questions arise about whether the constitutionally prescribed limits of the judicial branch have been exceeded'.[152] But this criticism goes only so far: *if* someone already accepts an

[148] Tribe, 'The Mystery of Motive' (n. 143) 23, footnote omitted.
[149] Ibid. 25.
[150] See Theodore Eisenberg 'Reflections on a Unified Theory of Motive', (1978) 15 *San Diego Law Review* 1147, 1148.
[151] 582 F.2d 45 (1978).
[152] Ibid. 72 (Wallace J., dissenting), reference omitted. Judge Wallace characterized it as the 'most substantial' of his objections against a motive-oriented judicial scrutiny, ibid. 71–72.

overall system of judicial review of democratically enacted legislation (and such acceptance hinges of course on arguments unrelated to the motive/effects issue), then it is hard to imagine a better candidate for judicial scrutiny and criticism than the illicit motives, or unconstitutional purposes, that the legislature may wish to pursue. And it is unclear why motive-scrutiny would be more intrusive into the legislature's position or more disrespectful of the lawmakers than scrutiny regarding effects.

Or is it? One *may* suggest that an inquiry into effects may, at worst, detect a mere legislative *error*, while an inquiry into the legislative motivations may lead to questioning of the legislator's honesty or integrity: 'a finding of illicit motivation is tantamount to an accusation that the decision-maker violated his constitutional oath of office.'[153] But this unnecessarily over-dramatizes the distinction: there may be minor faults in motivations and major errors in effects; the effect/motivation distinction does not correlate neatly with the degree of gravity of unconstitutionality. Secondly, as we shall see in Chapter 6, effects and motives are often so 'harmonized' with each other, effects being an indicator of motives and (more rarely) vice versa, that a distinction between a mere error and grave dishonesty simply does not make sense. Third, if inquiries into motives often result in identifying something disingenuous or dishonest about the legislator, so be it: as citizens we must bite the bullet and admit that such things happen, and we need to have institutional means of remedying and preventing legislative dishonesty. When we think about the laws which strike us intuitively as motivated by particularly improper motives, 'against the grounds for nonintervention [we] must set the interests favoring judicial invalidation on an illicitly motivated legislative act—the injury and insult felt by those at whom it is aimed . . . .'[154] This is the most important point of the present argument: illicit motivations should be seen as a sufficient ground for invalidation because, without more, they taint the legislation as reprehensible, expressing lack of respect for certain groups of people who cannot endorse, or cannot seem to be equally included by, the legislation in question.[155] The very fact that a law originates from some improper motives may be harmful per se to some groups, regardless of whether any other harms occur or not. So while there may be various ways of 'harmonizing' motive- and effect-oriented inquiry, with the latter usually serving as a reliable indicator of the former, the detection of illicit motives, with or without an appeal to effects, should be seen as a sufficient ground for invalidation.

Tribe's second aspect of an alleged disanalogy between exclusionary rules and judicial inquiry into legislative motives/purposes is that, in the case of the former, there are also good non-deterrent reasons for observing the rule, such as that to

[153] Paul Brest: 'Palmer v. Thompson: An Approach to the Problem of Unconstitutional Legislative Motive', (1971) *Supreme Court Review* 95, 129, footnote omitted.
[154] Ibid. 130.
[155] See Aziz Z. Huq, 'What is Discriminatory Intent?', (2018) 103 *Cornell Law Review* 1211, 1251.

allow illegally obtained evidence may aggravate the original violation by making the victim suffer the additional deprivations 'as a consequence of basing a conviction on the fruits of the unconstitutional search or seizure',[156] while in the case of judicial inquiry no similar aggravation occurs: 'The refusal to strike down a law on the basis of illicit motivation does not itself constitute a further violation of anyone's individual rights.'[157] But there are two problems with this argument. First, it merely assumes something that needs to be demonstrated, namely that issuing the laws based on improper motives does not violate anyone's rights. If the argument of the first chapter of this book is correct, that non-public reasons, when triggering a coercive law, show a fundamental lack of respect to those to whom it applies, then the persistence of an improperly motivated law constitutes an ongoing violation of rights of its subjects. It is a per se violation, even without considering any further effects upon the victims.[158] Second, the breach of a defendant's *legitimate* interests is only aggravated by a conviction based on illegally obtained evidence if the conviction is unjust: no-one has a right not to be convicted if one has actually committed a crime, no matter how the evidence was gathered. The exclusionary rules seem therefore to be based only on 'deterrent' grounds rather than on the questionable point that a conviction may add extra hardship to the defendant.

[156] Tribe, 'The Mystery of Motive' (n. 143) 25.
[157] Ibid. 26.
[158] This point is made emphatically by Garrett, 'Unconstitutionally Illegitimate Discrimination' (n. 66).

5

Problems with Motive-based Scrutiny—and Some Judicial Solutions

The point of the argument in the previous chapter was not to claim the priority of motive-oriented scrutiny over a form of scrutiny which focuses on effects as a vehicle of bringing public reason (PR) to constitutional review. Rather, it was to reclaim a theory, often unpopular in contemporary constitutional theory and practice, that illicit reasons for legislation are an important criterion of its illegitimacy, and hence, unconstitutionality. But how can we second-guess the true motives of legislators and screen off those which are not properly 'public'?

This chapter opens with a 1971 judgment of the US Supreme Court that illustrates the controversy regarding allegedly insurmountable obstacles facing a judge when attempting to ascertain the true motives, or purposes, of a law under scrutiny (section 1). Although no evidence of motives in the form of public statements by lawmakers was produced in *Palmer v. Thompson*,[1] common sense dictates that the most likely motive behind the discriminatory regulation and 'the evidentiary inquiry' is 'relatively easy', as Justice Powell said (delivering the opinion of the Court) in another judgment, *Village of Arlington*,[2] affirming that impermissible motives behind official action are a necessary element of a finding of discrimination. On occasions, a court may even have direct insight into legislators' motives as revealed through their own statements and affirmations (section 2); in the just-quoted *Village of Arlington*, Justice Powell listed such circumstances 'especially where there are contemporary statements by members of the decision-making body, minutes of its meetings, or reports. In some extraordinary instances the members might be called to the stand at trial to testify concerning the purpose of the official action … '.[3] Often the evidence is only indirect but still very convincing, along the lines of '*res ipsa loquitur*' (section 3, where Canadian jurisprudence to illustrate this point will be discussed). And often the argument about motives is based on a reasoning about the effects of the regulation under scrutiny: the two strands of reasoning (about motives and effects) should not be seen as mutually antithetical (section 4). Often effects are seen as a threshold, or a prerequisite of a subsequent inquiry into motives, which completes the argument about unconstitutionality; while another way of

[1] 403 U.S. 217 (1971).
[2] *Village of Arlington Heights v. Metro. Hous. Develop. Corp.*, 429 U.S. 252, 266 (1977).
[3] Ibid. 268.

Constitutional Public Reason. Wojciech Sadurski, Oxford University Press. © Wojciech Sadurski 2023.
DOI: 10.1093/oso/9780192869678.003.0005

harmonizing motives and effects may be by seeing effects as indicators of most likely motives (section 5). The complex interaction between the two strands of reasoning is also illustrated by the phenomenon of changed predicted effects and changed purposes attributed to old laws (section 6). Finally, it is clear that judicial scrutiny of legislative purposes/motives is greatly facilitated—indeed, mandated—in those constitutional systems which openly embrace proportionality analysis as a canonical model for constitutional scrutiny, as illustrated in this chapter by top courts in South Africa and Israel (section 7). A general point that the conception of public reason naturally triggers a motive-based scrutiny is well captured by this statement in a recent piece by Micah Schwartzman: '[H]olding that motivations can be relevant to whether acts are permissible seems like a fairly natural extension of a commitment to treating others on the basis of reasons that they can reasonably accept.'[4]

1. The Story of *Palmer v. Thompson*: Evidentiary Difficulties?

'Almost everyone in Jackson, Mississippi, knew that the city closed its swimming pools solely to avoid integration.'[5] This majestic phrase, resembling a great novel's opener, is the first sentence of a long article by Paul Brest about *Palmer v. Thompson*. The US Supreme Court's judgment concerned a decision by the city of Jackson which, after having its racially segregated swimming pools and other public attractions declared unconstitutional as a violation of the Fourteenth Amendment, decided to desegregate some spaces but otherwise to close all of its public pools, claiming that it was neither safe to operate the pools on an integrated basis, nor was it economically feasible to do so. Justice Black, in the opinion for the Court, provided two justifications for refusing to conduct a motive-based inquiry, neither of which were convincing. The first was about the alleged evidential difficulties in ascertaining legislative motivation, and the second was about 'futility'. I will consider them in reverse order.

The futility argument can be quickly dispensed with. As Justice Black asserts: 'If the law is struck down for this reason [of bad legislative motive], rather than because of its facial content or effect, it would presumably be valid as soon as the legislature or relevant governing body repassed it for different reasons.'[6] In *Palmer*, the argument of 'futility' based on the possibility of reenactment was

[4] Micah Schwartzman, 'Must Laws Be Motivated by Public Reason?' in Silje Langvatn, Mattias Kumm, and Wojciech Sadurski (eds.), *Public Reason and Courts* (Cambridge University Press 2020) 45, 59.

[5] Paul Brest: 'Palmer v. Thompson: An Approach to the Problem of Unconstitutional Legislative Motive', (1971) *Supreme Court Review* 95.

[6] 403 U.S. 225.

prefigured by a similar argument made by Chief Justice Warren in *O'Brien* three years earlier:

> What motivates one legislator to make a speech about a statute is not necessarily what motivates scores of others to enact it, and the stakes are sufficiently high for us to eschew guesswork. We decline to void essentially on the ground that it is unwise legislation which Congress had the undoubted power to enact *and which could be reenacted* in its exact form if the same or another legislator made a 'wiser' speech about it.[7]

But it is sufficient to articulate the 'futility' argument to see that it is entirely question-begging: 'repassing' the law, now enacted for the right reasons, does not sound absurd, at least not any more absurd than when an appellate court reverses a trial court's judgment for giving effect to inadmissible evidence, and then the initial judgment is confirmed on its merits upon remand, but now for the right reasons.[8] And of course one may imagine that a change of reasons will affect a change of its 'facial content', especially if the possibility of applying strict scrutiny by a court is expected (and perhaps even feared) by the legislature. If the act is re-enacted by a lawmaker, now for the right reasons, what can be wrong about it?

The other argument by Justice Black in *Palmer* was about the evidential difficulties of ascertaining the motivation[9]—something which, in the case at hand, does not sound credible: the matter was about the closure of racially integrated pools, and as the dissent showed,

> [t]he circumstances surrounding this action and the absence of other credible reasons for the closings leave little doubt that shutting down the pools was nothing more or less than a most effective expression of official policy that Negroes and whites must not be permitted to mingle together when using the services provided by the city.[10]

To be fair, Justice Black acknowledged *both* arguments suggesting illicit motivations, as cited by petitioners ('that the … pools were closed because of ideological opposition to racial integration in swimming pools'),[11] *and* also the possibility of acceptable motivations ('the pools were closed because the city council felt they could not be operated safely and economically on an integrated

[7] *United States v. O'Brien*, 391 U.S. 367, 384 (1968), emphasis added.
[8] See, similarly, Brest, 'Palmer v. Thompson' (n. 5) 125.
[9] 403 U.S. 224–25.
[10] Ibid. 241 (White J. dissenting).
[11] Ibid. 224–25.

basis').[12] Nevertheless, evidentiary difficulties figured prominently in Justice Black's judgment.

There is a powerful dissent in *Palmer* by Justice White (with whom two other justices joined)[13] addressing Justice Black's refutation of motive-oriented inquiry. As he said,

> I am quite unpersuaded by the majority's assertion that it is impermissible to impeach the otherwise valid act of closing municipal swimming pools by resort to evidence of invidious purpose or motive. Congress has long provided civil and criminal remedies for a variety of official and private conduct. In various situations these statutes and our interpretations of them provide that such conduct falls within the federal proscription only upon proof of forbidden racial motive or animus.[14]

He then went on to provide the authorities for adopting a motive-conscious inquiry into *private* conduct (racially motivated refusal to contract for the sale of real estate, racially motivated refusal to serve a customer in a restaurant, racial animus triggering a conspiracy to assault African-Americans),[15] and held that:

> Official conduct is no more immune to characterization based on its motivation than is private conduct, and we have so held many times. The police are vulnerable ... if they subject a person to false arrest for vagrancy for the purpose of harassing and punishing [him] for attempting to eat with black people, ... or if they intentionally tolerate violence or threats of violence directed toward those who violated the practice of segregating the races at restaurants.[16]

To be sure, none of these cases of official conduct belonged to a category of legislative action. However, Justice White next went on to consider precisely that. He referred to *Whitcomb v. Chavis*,[17] a case of the Court handed down only a week before *Palmer*, concerning changes in voting districts in the state of Indiana. While the Supreme Court reversed the lower court's ruling that the plan under challenge operated to minimize or dilute the voting strength of African-Americans, it nevertheless cautioned that 'the courts have been vigilant in scrutinizing schemes allegedly conceived or operated as purposeful devices to further racial discrimination',[18] and the redeeming feature for the plan under challenge was that 'there is no suggestion here that Marion County's ... multi-member

[12] Ibid. 225.
[13] Brennan and Marshall JJ.
[14] 403 U.S. 241 (White J. dissenting).
[15] Ibid. 241–42.
[16] Ibid. 242, references omitted, internal quotation marks removed.
[17] 403 U.S. 124 (1971).
[18] 403 U.S. 242 (White J. dissenting) quoting *Whitcomb* at 149.

district, or similar districts throughout the State, were conceived or operated as *purposeful devices to further racial or* economic *discrimination*'.[19] Justice White concluded that in *Palmer*, African-American 'plaintiffs should have every right to prove that the action of the city officials was motivated by nothing but racial considerations'.[20] This was followed by a careful and very detailed examination of the context of the closure of municipal pools in the city of Jackson. The evidence cited included, inter alia, an indication that '[t]he conclusion of city officials that integrated pools would not be "economical" was no more than "pure speculation" ';[21] that the desegregation of other city facilities did not cause any 'disorder or violence',[22] and generally, that there was no evidence that 'the pools could not be operated safely and economically on an integrated basis'.[23]

Based on the totality of evidence, Justice White concluded that 'by closing the pools solely because of the order to desegregate, the city is expressing its official view that Negroes are so inferior that they are unfit to share with whites this particular type of public facility',[24] and that '[c]losing the pools without a colourable non-discriminatory reason was every bit as much an official endorsement of the notion that Negroes are not equal to whites as was the use of state National Guard troops in 1975 to bar the entry of nine Negro students in to Little Rock's Central High School . . . '.[25] And while Justice White places an important accent on the disparate *impact* of the city's decision,[26] it is clear that the burden of argument is on the official unlawful motivations and reasons behind the city which 'has only opposition to desegregation to offer as justification for closing the pools'.[27]

The dissent by Justice White asserts what seems to be obvious: it is not beyond the capacity of judges to ascertain, in a particular case and knowing a particular context, which of these motives are more plausible. Consider an analogy from gerrymandering: an obvious scenario is that of a redistricting plan, undertaken during a period when the legislature is under no obligation to do it, and which results in a significant dilution of the voting strength of a particular racial group, especially one that has been discriminated against in the past in its access to the vote. This was exactly what occurred in *League of United Latin American Citizens v. Perry*,[28] a 2006 decision in which the US Supreme Court reviewed such a redistricting plan in Texas, implemented after Republicans gained control of the state legislature, and which resulted in significant changes to a Latino-majority district. As Justice Stevens declared in his dissent, 'the narrow question

[19] Ibid. 242–43, emphasis in original, quoting *Whitcomb* at 149.
[20] Ibid. 243.
[21] Ibid. 258.
[22] Ibid. 259.
[23] Ibid. 259.
[24] Ibid. 266.
[25] Ibid. 266–67.
[26] See ibid. 269.
[27] Ibid. 271.
[28] 548 U.S. 399 (2006).

presented by the statewide challenge in this litigation [was] whether the State's decision to draw the map in the first place, when it was under no legal obligation to do so, was permissible',[29] and immediately suggested: 'It is undeniable that *identifying the motive* for making that basic decision is a readily manageable task'.[30] He also relied on an observation by Justice Breyer in *Vieth*,[31] an earlier gerrymandering case (in dissent) that 'the presence of midcycle redistricting, for any reason, raises a fair inference that partisan machinations played a major role in the map-drawing process'.[32] Justice Stevens further added: 'The conclusion that courts can easily identify the motive for redistricting ... is reinforced by the record in this very case. the District Court unambiguously identified the sole purpose behind the decision to promulgate [the new plan]: a desire to maximize partisan advantage.'[33]

Another interesting voting rights case in which the Supreme Court expressly engaged in motive-oriented scrutiny and found no trouble detecting unconstitutional motives was *Hunter v. Underwood*,[34] a decision which unanimously struck down an Alabama rule which restricted voting for individuals 'with questionable moral turpitude' as revealed in having committed some specifically enumerated crimes. It was clear that the crimes enumerated were more frequently committed by African-Americans but, interestingly for our purposes here, rather than going only along the path of indirect discrimination and disparate racial impact, the Court engaged in an 'impermissible racial motivation' type of argument. Justice Rehnquist acknowledged, somewhat perfunctorily, that '[p]roving the motivation behind official action is often a problematic undertaking',[35] and referred in this context to the usual authorities for this proposition, including *United States v. O'Brien* with its famous passage containing a recital of reasons about the difficulties of second-guessing legislative motives,[36] but quickly suggested that 'the sort of difficulties of which the Court spoke in *O'Brien* do not obtain in this case'.[37] He then engaged in a short but powerful historical analysis of the Alabama Constitution Convention of 1901 (from which the provision under challenge originated), and had no trouble in showing that the intent of disenfranchising blacks was a powerful 'motivating factor'[38] for this provision, stating that the moral turpitude clause 'certainly would not have been adopted by the convention or ratified by the electorate in the absence of the racially

[29] Ibid. 457 (Stevens J. concurring in part and dissenting in part).
[30] Ibid. 457, emphasis added, reference omitted.
[31] *Vieth v. Jubelirer*, 541 U.S. 267 (2004).
[32] 541 U.S. 367 (Breyer J. dissenting), quoted in 548 U.S. 458 (Stevens J. concurring in part and dissenting in part), reference omitted.
[33] 548 U.S. 458 (Stevens J. concurring in part and dissenting in part).
[34] 471 U.S. 222 (1985).
[35] Ibid. 228.
[36] 391 U.S. 367, 383–94 (1968), quoted in 471 U.S. 228.
[37] 471 U.S. 228.
[38] Ibid. 231.

discriminatory motivation'.[39] Justice Rehnquist then referred to an argument put forward by counsel for the state who claimed that, even conceding that racial motivation had been the original ground for the 1901 provision, the succeeding eighty years somehow 'legitimated'[40] the provision, including by the fact that some of the crimes with most discriminatory impact which had been indicators of moral turpitude for the purpose of the law were later struck down by the courts, and therefore those that remained were 'acceptable bases for denying the franchise'.[41] But Justice Rehnquist firmly maintained that the original motivation for the provision irreversibly tainted the provision: regardless of whether the provision 'would be valid if enacted today without any impermissible motivation, we simply observe that its original enactment was motivated by a desire to discriminate against blacks on account of race . . . .'[42]

The *Hunter* analysis was subsequently applied in a number of discrimination cases, including the disenfranchisement of felons when racial animus behind such regulations was claimed. In a typical federal decision belonging to the latter category, the court 'first examine[s] whether racial discrimination was a substantial or motivating factor in the state's decision to deny the right to vote to felons', and if there *is* evidence of such motivating factor, the court then asks 'whether the state can show that the provision would have been enacted in the absence of any racially discriminatory motive'.[43] In the particular case from which these words are taken, the majority of the Court of Appeals was satisfied that a discriminatory motive was absent when Florida legislators decided in 1968 to re-enact, with changes, the original felon disenfranchisement law dating back to 1868.[44] A dissenting judge disagreed, stating that the 're-enactment' must not be considered 'in a vacuum',[45] and that '[w]here the state has not demonstrated any race-neutral basis for the re-enactment, there can be no "break" in the chain of invidious intent'.[46] He went into the records of deliberations by the sub-committee that deliberated on this provision, in the Constitutional Revision Committee and in the Florida legislature,[47] concluding that there was no evidence that the legislators had 'an independent, legitimate motivation' which would have 'cleansed the taint of racial animus'.[48] But note that neither Judge Kravitch writing for the majority nor Judge Barkett in dissent argued about the impossibility or even great difficulty in discerning the legislative intentions: they just disagreed about *what* these intentions really were.

[39] Ibid. 231.
[40] Ibid. 233.
[41] Ibid. 233.
[42] Ibid. 233.
[43] *Johnson v. Governor of the State of Florida*, 405 F.3d 1214 1223 (11th Cir. Fla. 2005).
[44] Ibid. 1223–27.
[45] Ibid. 1244 (Barkett J. dissenting).
[46] Ibid. 1245, reference omitted.
[47] Ibid. 1245–46.
[48] Ibid. 1246.

All this suggests that the level of difficulty in ascertaining motives is a contingent matter and will vary from case to case, and in some cases, there will not be any alternative reasonable explanations for legislative actions other than illicit motives.

An important line of US Supreme Court cases that may constitute an exhibit for a thesis that legislative motives often play an important role in the Court's judgments, and that the Court finds no basic evidentiary problems in identifying illicit motives, is what has been dubbed 'the Court's animus canon':[49] a series of judgments related to rulings authored by Justice Kennedy, primarily concerning gays and lesbians. (One should note, however, that 'animus' is not coextensive with 'purpose' or intent';[50] the law may be based on a non-public reason compatible basis and yet not be triggered by any animus but, for example, by greed or corruption. The reverse is not true, however: it is plausible to believe that an animus-triggered law will normally have an illicit purpose. One may therefore say that animus is a sufficient but not a necessary condition of a law based on illicit intentions.) The series of rulings began with *Romer v. Evans*,[51] a judgment which invalidated a Colorado ballot initiative which would amend the state constitution to nullify all non-discrimination protections of LGBT persons. *Romer* is worth a closer look, for our purposes. The decision stands, inter alia, for the principle that animus towards unpopular groups cannot be the basis for a legal measure, and here, more specifically, it was reflected in the determination that moral disapproval of homosexuality by the people of Colorado, without more, cannot trigger the state's prohibition on private discrimination against this group of people. As Justice Kennedy explained in the opinion for the Court, 'the sheer breadth' of Amendment 2 'is so discontinuous with the reasons offered for it that the amendment seems inexplicable by anything but animus towards the class it affects'.[52] He made the purpose-oriented scrutiny clear, and announced: 'By requiring that the classification bear a rational relationship to an independent and legitimate legislative end, we ensure that classifications are not drawn *for the purpose* of disadvantaging the group burdened by the law'.[53] And he drew the conclusion that the proposed law was 'born of animosity toward the class of persons affected',[54] because there is no relationship between the breadth of the Amendment and the rationales offered for it (which, presumably, would be legitimate) such as respect for the liberties of landlords and employers who have

[49] Joseph Landau, 'Process Scrutiny: Motivational Inquiry and Constitutional Rights', (2019) 119 *Columbia Law Review* 2147, 2199, footnote omitted.

[50] See, similarly, Kelsey Curtis, 'The Partiality of Neutrality', (2018) 41 *Harvard Journal of Law & Public Policy* 935, 963–64.

[51] 517 U.S. 620 (1996).

[52] Ibid. 632.

[53] Ibid. 633, emphasis added.

[54] Ibid. 634.

personal and religious objections to homosexuality, or the need of the state to conserve resources to fight discrimination against other groups.[55]

In response, Justice Scalia offered a proposition that people are '*entitled* to be hostile toward homosexual conduct'.[56] The statement exploits the ambiguity of the subject matter of this 'entitlement'. Under freedom of speech, people are of course entitled to criticize homosexual conduct, and under freedom of association people are entitled to set up organizations which are hostile to homosexuals, etc.[57] But the entitlement does not translate into a right to enact laws which give expression to this hostility, even if such laws would enjoy majority support, and would trample upon the rights of its target group. No-one has a right to have such hostility transformed into law—this would be antithetical to the idea of PR—unless, of course, such hostility would be based on a plausible determination of interpersonal harm. After all, 'hostility' towards thieves or blackmailers can be legitimately translated into law precisely because it can be justified on a plausible PR-compatible argument. In fact, in his dissent, Justice Scalia draws an explicit analogy between 'animus toward homosexual conduct' and hostility towards murder or toward cruelty to animals[58]—the cases of legally enforced 'hostility' that are perfectly compatible with PR. Somewhat perversely, the use of such analogy may be indirect evidence of adoption by Scalia of the idea of PR, notwithstanding his bizarre declaration about a 'right to hostility'. In fact, much of Scalia's argument defending the Amendment is in terms which sound conducible to PR language, such as 'the perceived social harm of homosexuality',[59] or 'Colorado's reasonable effort to preserve traditional American moral values',[60] thus suggesting a degree of national consensus around the condemnation of homosexuality, and an explanation that abolition of criminal sanctions for homosexual acts does not signify abandonment of the view that homosexuality is 'socially harmful', but only that enforcement of such laws would implicate intolerable intrusions into the intimate lives of citizens.[61]

This line of judgments continued into *Lawrence v. Texas*,[62] which invalidated a Texas anti-sodomy statute on 'animus' grounds and culminated in *United States v. Windsor*[63] (which invalidated a law defining marriage as restricted to being between a man and a woman), and *Obergefell v. Hodges*[64] (which recognized the freedom of same-sex couples to marry). Indeed, 'animus' must be the

55 Ibid. 635.
56 Ibid. 644 (Scalia, J. dissenting), emphasis in original.
57 See Ronald C. Den Otter, *Judicial Review in an Age of Moral Pluralism* (Cambridge University Press 2009)71.
58 517 U.S. 644 (Scalia J. dissenting).
59 Ibid. 651 (Scalia J. dissenting).
60 Ibid. 651 (Scalia J. dissenting).
61 Ibid. 644 (Scalia J., dissenting).
62 539 U.S. 558 (2003).
63 570 U.S. 744 (2013).
64 576 U.S. 644 (2015).

archetype of improper motivation.[65] And it is worth noting that even in *Trump v. Hawaii*—a decision which failed to invalidate presidential actions despite their demonstrable religious animus, Justice Kennedy (concurring with the majority) found it useful to cite his own judgment in *Romer* and acknowledge that 'in some instances, governmental action may be subject to judicial review to determine whether or not it is "inexplicable by anything but animus" '.[66]

The fact that various courts 'have rested judgments on findings of improper motivations—on records supporting those findings beyond serious dispute',[67] in itself perhaps may not be a conclusive argument (perhaps all these courts erred?) but should place a very serious burden on whoever would argue about the impossibility of such an inquiry. This is of course not to say that it is uncontroversial, either empirically or legally, to determine what sources of evidence about allegedly illicit motives are reliable and permissible for judges to appeal to. And within the history of US constitutional review of legislative motives, there have been different stages in this respect: there were times when the burden of proof of impermissible motivations was very demanding and virtually the only source that was allowed to shed light on such questions was the text of the challenged statute itself,[68] yet, more recently, there have been periods when courts in the United States were willing to examine legislative history and even to hear testimony about the internal legislative process in order to determine the reasons for which a statute was enacted.[69] A 2008 seminal article by Caleb Nelson provided a comprehensive account of these changes,[70] and what transpires from this account is that one should be careful not to extrapolate from disagreements as to the *sources* of knowledge about purposes upon the very principle that wrong purposes taint legislation as unconstitutional.

The difficulties of discerning true (or most likely) motives are often wildly exaggerated. In a recent article, Aziz Huq provides a useful taxonomy of various evidentiary strategies which may plausibly maximize the discovery of true motives, and while his analysis mainly concerns discrimination, the argument may be transposed, *mutatis mutandis*, to other areas of law. The first on Huq's list is 'the semantic content of laws and regulations'[71]—situations in which the very text of the law suggests some improper motives (one example provided by Huq is that of the *Lukumi Babalu*[72]—to be discussed in more detail in Chapter 7, section

[65] See Landau, 'Process Scrutiny' (n. 49) 2201; Note, 'Developments in the Law—Chapter Four: Animus and Sexual Regulation', (2014) 127 *Harvard Law Review* 1767.
[66] *Trump v. Hawaii*, 138 S. Ct. 2392, 2423 (2018) (Kennedy, J. concurring), quoting *Romer v. Evans*, 517 U.S. 620, 632 (1996).
[67] Brest, 'Palmer v. Thompson' (n. 5) 120, footnote omitted.
[68] See, e.g., judicial approaches described by Caleb Nelson, 'Judicial Review of Legislative Purpose', (2008) 83 *New York University Law Review* 1784, 1795–811.
[69] See, e.g., ibid. 1850–58.
[70] Ibid. passim.
[71] Aziz Z. Huq, 'What is Discriminatory Intent?', (2018) 103 *Cornell Law Review* 1211, 1267.
[72] *Lukumi Babalu Ay, Inc., v. the City of Hialeah*, 508 U.S. 520 (1993).

1—in which the Court invalidated a local ordinance banning ritual slaughter, and one of the grounds for invalidation was the use in the law of religiously coloured words such as 'sacrifice' or 'ritual').[73] The second category of evidentiary measures are official statements,[74] and here one can refer, for example, to the statements by President Trump accompanying his anti-immigration measures as discussed in the next part of this chapter, or, as provided by Huq, references in the House Committee Report regarding the Defense of Marriage Act, which referred to 'Judeo-Christian morality', considered by the Supreme Court in *Windsor*[75] when ascertaining the purpose of the Act.[76] Huq notes the unwillingness of courts to use evidentiary measures often, but observes that 'it is hard to conceive of reasons to ignore [official] statements—already made and available as proof—when their content provides prima facie evidence of improper intent'.[77] The third, and somewhat more complex, set of evidentiary strategies are those appealing to 'history and consequences'.[78] This may not be the best label for the category, but the strategy which it is meant to describe is clearly recognizable: 'a mismatch between expected consequences and legitimate policy justifications'[79] may lead to a conclusion that a given measure was adopted for different reasons than its officially announced justification proclaims. This is a common method of argument where either under a 'strict scrutiny' approach or 'proportionality analysis', a court questions the motives of the legislator and implies (or says explicitly) that the official statements of goals, purposes, or intent are pretextual or insincere. (Examples of such an approach abound in this book.) The fourth approach on Huq's list is that of 'civil discovery', including 'interrogatories, depositions, and document production'[80] meant to provide evidence of a real motive. Huq notes, with disapproval, that (at least with regard to anti-discrimination case law), 'federal courts have been preternaturally cautious about civil discovery against the government'.[81] The last on his list is statistical evidence (of discrimination, in particular), and while, again, Huq notes that judicial attitudes to statistical evidence have been inconsistent,[82] scepticism of such evidence is 'unwarranted and unwise': while statistics per se do not *prove* anything, it plausibly shows the *likelihood* of bias as a motivating factor of the law.

As I said, the list provided by Huq can be extrapolated from discrimination-focused reasoning to constitutional reasoning on improper motives more generally, and many of these strategies are present, in different configurations, in the

[73] Huq, 'What is Discriminatory Intent?' (n. 71) 1268.
[74] Ibid. 1270–74.
[75] 570 U.S. 744 (2013).
[76] Huq, 'What is Discriminatory Intent' (n. 71) 1270.
[77] Ibid. 1273.
[78] Ibid. 1274–77.
[79] Ibid. 1274.
[80] Ibid. 1277.
[81] Ibid. 1278.
[82] Ibid. 1282.

cases (both in the United States and in other legal systems) discussed later in this and the following chapters.

2. Direct Insights into Motives

The second category in the just-summarized catalogue of evidentiary sources for ascertaining true motives, compiled by Huq, are the official statements of lawmakers who occasionally may openly admit to their animus against a burdened group, as in President Trump's immigration-related executive actions prohibiting entry into the United States of individuals from a range of Muslim-majority countries.[83] The President was as careless—or candid, if you prefer—as to precede and accompany the ban by Twitter posts saying, among other things, 'I think Islam hates us' and 'We're having problems with Muslims coming into the country'.[84] But in *Trump v. Hawaii*,[85] the importance of those explicit motives was played down by the conservative majority, and in his dissent, Justice Breyer admitted that '[m]embers of the Court principally disagree about ... whether or the extent to which religious animus played a significant role in the Proclamation's promulgation or content ...'.[86] So the problem identified by the majority was not so much the legal standard for discriminatory intent, but the factual record relied upon.[87] Perhaps the most realistic explanation for the outcome of *Trump v. Hawaii* is that, since Trump's statements had been constitutionally (and one may add, morally) indefensible, the majority opted for an easy path: a doctrine of deference to the executive branch on issues of national security and immigration, thus evading the need for substantive scrutiny of the top executive's motives.[88]

This shows that we may occasionally have direct insight into legislative motives, without the intermediary of effects which may or may not be a useful evidentiary tool. And the sources of this direct insight may include statements by members of the legislature themselves, and in particular legislators themselves testifying before the courts.[89] To be sure, in *Village of Arlington*, Justice Powell emphasized that such testimonies may occur only in extraordinary circumstances, that they may be subject to limitations imposed by privilege,[90] and that '[p]lacing a decisionmaker on the stand' usually should be avoided.[91] However,

83 Executive Order No. 13769, 82 Fed. Reg. 8977 (27 January 2017).

84 Quoted in Landau, 'Process Scrutiny' (n. 49) 2173 n. 151.

85 *Trump v. Hawaii*, 138 S. Ct. 2392 (2018).

86 138 S. Ct. 2427 (Breyer, J. dissenting).

87 See Brandon L. Garrett, 'Unconstitutionally Illegitimate Discrimination', (2018) 104 *Virginia Law Review* 1741, 1496.

88 This is the view (paraphrased for the purposes of this account) of Sotomayor J., 138 S. Ct. 2433 (Sotomayor, J., dissenting).

89 Ibid. 268.

90 Ibid. 268.

91 Ibid. 268 n. 18.

even though in many instances decision-makers may be privileged to refuse to testify or submit to discovery, if a decision-maker's claim of privilege is overruled, she must testify.[92] Since it is rightly thought that the threat to legislative and administrative independence is subordinate to the courts' obligation to review the decision, evidence which is essential to that review (including, about the motives for the decision) should not be barred by the interests of decision-makers.[93]

Motive-oriented inquiry may be also exercised through studying testimonies by supporting administrative staff in legislatures; for instance, in *Miller v. Johnson*,[94] a case of racially discriminatory gerrymandering, the Court referred to the testimony of Linda Meggers, an operator of a state 'reapportionment computer', to support the claim that race was a predominant factor in the redrawing of the electoral districts under scrutiny in that case.[95] US courts have been also considering statements and testimonies by other decision-makers whose views may illustrate the motivations of those who enforce the law. For example, in *Mieth v. Dothard*,[96] a district court in Alabama concluded that the minimum height requirement for state troopers was purposefully discriminatory against women, based in part on testimony by Colonel E.C. Dothard, the Director of the Department of Public Safety who testified 'that he feels that women should not be State Troopers'.[97] In *Armstrong v. O'Connell*,[98] a district court in Wisconsin considered that 'the most probative direct evidence of the intent with which the myriad decisions for the operation of the [Milwaukee Public School] system were made over the years remains the testimony relied upon by the court in the original decision in this case',[99] which 'supports the finding that the defendants did act with a purpose or intent to cause invidious racial discrimination'.[100] This was preceded by Judge John W. Reynolds' observation that these statements indicate 'a generally low regard for the customs and traditions of members of the Negro race as perceived by those officials'.[101] Finally, courts may gauge the legislative intentions by referring to various minutes, reports, and proceedings of legislatures: as the Supreme Court said, 'The legislative or administrative history may be highly relevant, especially where there are contemporary

92 See Louis S. Raveson, 'Unmasking the Motives of Government Decisionmakers: A Subpoena for Your Thoughts?', (1985) 63 *North Carolina Law Review* 879, 972.

93 See ibid. 992.

94 515 U.S. 900 (1995).

95 Ibid. 918.

96 418 F. Supp. 1169 (M.D. Ala. 1976).

97 Ibid. 1180. But note that the judgment about discriminatory intent was based on this testimony and on the *effects* of the requirement: 'Considering these statements of Colonel Dothard, *together with the statistics* that show that almost all women are excluded by the 5 feet 9 inch, 160 pound physical qualifications, the Court finds that the challenged employment requirements were intended to be discriminatory', ibid. 1180, emphasis added.

98 451 F. Supp. 817 (E.D. Wis. 1978).

99 Ibid. 826–27.

100 Ibid. 827.

101 Ibid. 826.

statements by members of the decisionmaking body, minutes of its meetings, or reports'.[102] A US legal scholar summarized the trend: 'modern-day judges are perfectly willing to go beyond the objective indicia of legislative purpose when investigating whether facially neutral laws were actually motivated by illicit racial considerations.'[103]

However, it is rare that US courts would rest their judgment solely on the motive inquiry in any constitutional case, regardless of its effects.[104] Such exceptional cases concern the situations when the purpose scrutiny belongs to an *explicit* legal test of constitutionality, as in the purpose tier of the First Amendment's Establishment Clause. A good example is *Stone v. Graham*,[105] which found that Kentucky's requirement of posting a copy of Ten Commandments in every public classroom lacked any secular purpose (but even then, the Court based this purpose-oriented conclusion partly on its reading of the statute's effects),[106] or in *McCreary County v. ACLU of Kentucky*,[107] where the posting of the Ten Commandments in a courthouse was found to have an entirely religious purpose. (This will be discussed further in Chapter 9 of this book.) In his article of 1985, Louis Raveson offered two cases to illustrate the proposition that 'The [Supreme] Court has held that in some instances a finding of illicit purpose itself is sufficient to invalidate the challenged statute or administrative action':[108] *Rogers v. Lodge*[109] and *Epperson v. Arkansas*.[110] But a close reading of *Rogers*, a decision which invalidated an 'at large' voting system on the basis of the racially discriminatory purpose of the system, suggests that much of the argument of the majority opinion written by Justice White rested upon racially disparate *effects*.[111] In turn *Epperson* was really decided on a mixed test of purpose and effect: Arkansas's prohibition of teaching of evolution in schools was struck down on the basis of the test established in *Abington School District v. Schempp*,[112] of 'the purpose and primary effect of the enactment',[113] and Justice Fortas, in delivering the opinion of the Court, never explicitly referred to the Arkansas authorities' purpose in enacting the law as a sufficient cause for invalidation. Perhaps such reference exclusively to the purpose may be found at the very end

[102] 429 U.S. 268. See also *Hunter v. Underwood*, 471 U.S. 222 (1985) where evidence about proceedings surrounding the Alabama Constitutional Convention of 1901 was used to demonstrate that facially neutral provisions of the state constitution were motivated by a desire to discriminate against African-Americans.

[103] Nelson, 'Judicial Review of Legislative Purpose' (n. 68) 1851, footnote omitted.

[104] See ibid. 1856, footnote omitted.

[105] 449 U.S. 39 (1980).

[106] Ibid. 42.

[107] 545 U.S. 844 (2005).

[108] Raveson, 'Unmasking the Motives of Government Decisionmakers' (n. 92) 883, footnote omitted.

[109] 458 U.S. 613 (1982).

[110] 393 U.S. 97 (1968).

[111] 458 U.S. 623–27.

[112] 374 U.S. 203 (1963).

[113] Ibid. 222, cited in 393 U.S. 107.

of the Court's opinion: 'The law's effort was confined to an attempt to blot out a particular theory because of its supposed conflict with the Biblical account, literally read.'[114]

In a 1997 case of an alleged retroactivity in criminal law, the Supreme Court addressed an argument that a purpose of the legislation was to increase the quantum of punishment, and said: 'Whether such a purpose alone would be a sufficient basis for concluding that a law violated the *Ex Post Facto* Clause when it actually had no such effect is a question the Court has never addressed.'[115] The Court occasionally even said explicitly that it would not invalidate an otherwise legitimate action simply because an illicit motive was present,[116] though it is doubtful whether this assurance can be taken seriously because the requirement of motive for disparate impact cases does precisely that.[117]

Therefore, insofar as the theory of public reason postulates that wrongful (because non-public) motives are sufficient to taint a law as illegitimate, this is not fully mirrored in current US law, which is tentative about this point, and in which the wrongness of motives usually enters into the picture in conjunction with invidiousness of effects. This unwillingness to consider wrongful motives alone, as a sufficient ground for unconstitutionality, was echoed in the past by some influential academic pronouncements, such as that 'it is altogether possible for a law which is the expression of a forbidden motive to be a good law'.[118] Immediately after the quoted sentence, the authors of the seminal article on equal protection ask: 'What is to be done with a law which, passed with the most questionable of motives, still makes a positive contribution to the public good?.'[119] One answer is that the scenario is most unlikely. This is, however, only conjecture. Another better answer may be that the scenario painted in the question is a contradiction in terms because questionable motives themselves necessarily produce negative effects (such as, in the case of non-public reasons, the effects in terms of lack of respect and creation of a second-class citizenship). A third answer is that the *re*enactment of such law with good motives may be the best solution. A fourth

[114] 393 U.S. 109.

[115] *Lynce v. Mathis*, 519 U.S. 433, 444 (1997). Similarly, in 2005, the Court of Appeals for First Circuit, in a decision under the dormant Commerce Clause, observed: 'there is some reason to question whether a showing of discriminatory purpose alone will invariably suffice to support a finding of constitutional invalidity under the dormant Commerce Clause', *Alliance of Auto. Mfrs. v. Gwadosky*, 430 F.3d 30, 36 n. 3 (1st Cir. 2005). Bruce Marshall Selya J. then went on to quote from a popular constitutional law treatise stating that there would be an analytical difficulty arising when 'a law motivated wholly by protectionist intent might fail to produce significant discriminatory effects', ibid. 36 n. 3, citing Kathleen M. Sullivan and Gerald Gunther, *Constitutional Law* (15th edn., Foundation Press 2004) 275.

[116] See, e.g., *United States v. O'Brien*, 391 U.S. 367, 382–83 (1968); *City of Erie v. Pap's A.M.*, 529 U.S. 277, 292 (2000).

[117] See, similarly, Calvin Massey, 'The Role of Governmental Purpose in Constitutional Judicial Review', (2007) 59 *South Carolina Law Review* 1, 35–36.

[118] Joseph Tussman and Jacobus tenBroek, 'The Equal Protection of the Laws', (1949) 37 *California Law Review* 341, 360.

[119] Ibid.

response is that if the calculus of benefits (in terms of good effects) and harms (resulting from wrongful motives) yields a net benefit, the law may stay as it is—to the regret of a PR theorist. In any event, the point of the argument here is to show that we *may* have a motive inquiry in a 'pure' form, which does not resort to effects as evidence for wrongful motives.

However, if we understand the motive inquiry through the lens of a detection of *the most likely purpose* which the legislators attempted to pursue, it is not unusual (even if, admittedly, rare) for constitutional courts around the world to disqualify the laws on the basis of an illicit purpose. The famous Canadian decision in *R v. Big M Drug Mart Ltd.*[120] is a case in point. The legislation at issue was the federal Lord's Day Act, which imposed a general prohibition on the performance of various forms of commercial activity on Sundays. The Court held that the Act, by its purpose, infringed upon the Charter-protected freedom of religion in section 2(a). Chief Justice Dickson conducted a detailed examination of the legislative history behind the Act, to conclude that its object was to compel observance of the Christian Sabbath. A finding of invalid purpose is determinative of this stage of the Charter analysis, without any need for consideration of the law's effects—the Court was clear on this point, stating that 'effects can never be relied upon to save legislation with an invalid purpose'.[121] In the course of the judgment, Chief Justice Dickson noted the value of a purpose-based analysis in ensuring that adequate consideration is given to the protection of rights: 'The assessment by the courts of legislative purpose focuses scrutiny upon the aims and objectives of the legislature and ensures they are consonant with the guarantees enshrined in the Charter.'[122] While legislation can infringe the Charter by either its purpose or effects, Chief Justice Dickson established the principle that an illegitimate purpose negates the need for any inquiry into the actual effects of the legislation—an enactment with an illegitimate purpose will be unconstitutional on that ground, and cannot be saved by its actual effects.[123]

This statement of principle was significant. The impugned provision did not compel observance of the Sabbath by imposing any positive obligation upon Canadian residents to attend church, engage in any spiritual reflection, or to pick up a Bible. Nor did it actually require them to rest. The appellant and supporting interveners made submissions to this effect, arguing that the Lord's Day Act contained no compulsion of religion. They asserted that merely requiring abstention from work on a Sunday 'does not, in itself, have any religious significance. Its effect is, therefore, merely secular.'[124] However, in light of the principle above, there was no need to consider this secular effect in any detail.

[120] [1985] 1 SCR 295.
[121] Ibid. 334.
[122] Ibid. 331–32.
[123] Ibid. 334.
[124] Ibid. 349.

Significantly, Chief Justice Dickson would even reject an argument that the law in question was reasonably thought to be *also* serving a secular aim. The appellants submitted that if the Act did violate the right of religious freedom under the Charter, the Act's provisions constituted a 'reasonable limit, demonstrably justifiable in a free and democratic society on that right', and therefore could be saved by section 1 of the Charter. The limit, it was argued, could be reasonable on the basis of the secular justification that a universal day of rest is inherently beneficial, and that it may as well be the day traditionally observed. However, Chief Justice was able to dispose of this argument briefly. The achievement of a secular goal by a law that offends the Charter for its religious purpose in compelling observance of the Sabbath will not save the law. (This case will be considered in more detail in Chapter 7, section 4).

The decision in *Big M Drug Mart Ltd.* became an important guiding post for other constitutional courts, in particular for the South African Court, for which it served, among other things, as a basis for a doctrine of unconstitutional purposes. In a joint minority opinion in *S v. Jordan* (a case which will be described in the next part of this chapter), Justices Sachs and O'Regan cite *Big M Drug Mart* in the context of an observation that '[t]here may be times when a statute is manifestly in breach of constitutional rights, where the purpose of the statute is to foster a constitutionally invalid purpose'.[125] They interpret the judgment of their Canadian counterpart to mean that even secular effects (in this case, of providing a common day of rest for all citizens) cannot rescue a statute which 'had a clearly unconstitutional purpose' (in this case, of providing special state recognition for 'the Christian Sabbath'); in such a situation, 'the statute could not avoid constitutional invalidity'.[126] Both Canadian and South African top courts provide examples of invalidating statutes based on their illicit purposes only.

3. '*Res Ipsa* (often) *Loquitur*'

As the last examples from Canada and South Africa show, outside US constitutionalism, inquiring into the actual motives for legislative action has often been found to be relatively unhindered by evidentiary difficulties. Niels Petersen may be right to observe that, in general, '[d]enying the legitimacy of the purpose requires courts to second-guess legislative policy goals'[127]—nevertheless, in some cases such 'second-guessing' is well-founded and eminently plausible. Consider the case of *Mounted Police Association of Ontario v. Canada (Attorney General)*,[128] which is one of very few cases in which the Supreme Court has

[125] *S v. Jordan & Others (Sex Workers Education and Advocacy Task Force & Others as Amici Curiae)* 2002 (6) SA 642 (CC) [106].

[126] Ibid. [106].

[127] Niels Petersen, *Proportionality and Judicial Activism* (Cambridge University Press 2017) 117.

[128] [2015] SCC 1.

found the purpose of an impugned Act to contravene the Charter. At issue was the Public Service Labour Relations Act, which regulated public servants' participation in employee associations. By virtue of the narrowed definition of 'employee' for the purposes of that Act, members of the Royal Canadian Mounted Police (RCMP) were prohibited from collective bargaining and confined to a non-unionized labour relations regime.

The applicants submitted that the imposition of such a regime infringed the Charter-guaranteed freedom of association under section 2(d). Delivering the judgment for the majority, Chief Justice McLachlin and Justice LeBel noted first that the section 2(d) jurisprudence of the Supreme Court had gradually 'evolved to affirm a generous approach' to the guarantee of freedom of association in the field of labour relations.[129] The purpose of the so-called Staff Relations Representative Program (SRRP) within the Mounted Police, which was supposed to be a substitute for fully fledged unionization, was found to infringe section 2(d). Chief Justice McLachlin and Justice LeBel examined the history of labour relations within the RCMP, which revealed sustained hostility on the part of the Canadian government and RCMP management towards unionization by members of the force. Legislation in the early twentieth century had prohibited unionization by any member of the mounted police, just as a trend emerged amongst Canadian municipal police forces towards unionization. Associational activities of any form were prohibited from 1918 until 1974, with those who contravened this prohibition subject to instant dismissal.[130] These elements of the historical relationship pointed to a clear purpose in the government's imposition of the SRRP—'to prevent the formation of independent RCMP members' associations for the purposes of collective bargaining'. The legislation was, for that reason, directly contrary to section 2(d) of the Charter.[131]

A further element of the regime was found to infringe the Charter on the basis of Its purpose—the exclusion of RCMP members from the application of the Act by virtue of the definition of 'employee' for the purposes of that Act. The definition provision expressly excluded any person who was a 'member or special constable of the RCMP' or who was otherwise employed by the force on terms comparable to one of its members. These instruments had the purpose of denying RCMP members their right of freedom of association and excluding them from a labour relations regime that otherwise introduced collective bargaining to the federal public service. That purpose was clearly improper, and breached section 2(d) of the Charter. No insurmountable evidentiary problems were encountered by the judges in their purpose analysis.

This is not to say that the ascertainment of purpose or motive will always be easy, and that the '*res ipsa loquitur*' standard will always point to a single,

129 Ibid. [46].
130 Ibid. [17].
131 Ibid. [107]–[110].

determinate purpose. An easy assumption that a statute somehow itself reveals its objective in a determinate way may be deceptive.[132] Consider the Canadian Supreme Court's decision in *Sauvé v. Canada (Chief Electoral Officer)*[133] concerning the denial of a right to vote to certain categories of prisoners and whether it violated section 3 of the Canadian Charter. Taking issue with the government's attempt to frame its objectives in broad and symbolic terms, Chief Justice McLachlin for the majority noted emphatically that 'Parliament cannot use lofty objectives to shield legislation from Charter scrutiny'.[134] The government offered two general objectives for the introduction of section 51(e) and the denial of the right to vote to prisoners: '(1) to enhance civic responsibility and respect for the rule of law; and (2) to provide additional punishment, or "enhanc[e] the general purposes of the criminal sanction"'.[135] Chief Justice McLachlin expressed significant doubts regarding the extent to which these objectives truly lay behind the enactment, observing that 'the Parliamentary debates offer more fulmination than illumination'. Nonetheless, on the basis of no more than 'some glimmer of light', as the trial judge put it, Chief Justice McLachlin was prepared to accept these objectives.[136] The discussion then turned to whether these objectives were constitutionally valid and sufficiently important to justify the violation of the Charter. Chief Justice suggested that the answer to these questions was almost guaranteed to be positive, as a result of the vague and symbolic character of the purported aims. The issue that she took with these objectives was that 'the broader and more abstract the objective, the more susceptible it is to different meanings in different contexts, and hence to distortion and manipulation'.[137] She stated outright that the 'rhetorical nature' of the legislative objectives offered by the government rendered them 'suspect'—they did not identify the particular problem the government sought to address, nor show why it was so pressing as to justify the limitation of a Charter right.[138] Despite this reiteration of the importance of a vigorous analysis of legislative objectives, Chief Justice McLachlin 'grudgingly accepted' them,[139] and proceeded to the proportionality analysis in the name of prudence. The law failed all three elements of the proportionality test.

Chief Justice McLachlin's views in *Sauvé* relate to a strand of the *Oakes* legacy that Sujit Choudhry considers critical—the role of evidence in supporting arguments at each stage of the justification analysis, and the 'reality of policy making

[132] Peter Hogg, *Constitutional Law of Canada* (Thomson/Carswell 2014) para. 38-19.
[133] [2002] 3 SCR 519.
[134] Ibid. 538.
[135] Ibid. 540.
[136] Ibid. 540.
[137] Ibid. 540–41.
[138] Ibid. 541–42.
[139] G. Grant Amyot, '"A Matter of Philosophical Preference?" Political Philosophy and Judicial Reasoning in the *Sauvé* case' (2011) 29 *National Journal of Constitutional Law* 1, 6.

under conditions of factual uncertainty'.[140] This also includes the stage of reasoning which concerns the governmental purposes pursued by the legislation in question. Canonical sets of the sources of evidence about the purposes of lawmakers include in Canada 'the title and text of the act, the legislative debates preceding its enactment, and ... report[s] of the ... Law Reform Commission that informed the drafting of its provisions'.[141] Often extensive use is made of the history, including declarations of lawmakers or advocates of the law at its inception, and to whether they have been affected by subsequent developments. In *Zylberberg v. Sudbury Board of Education*,[142] the Ontario Court of Appeal considered a regulation under which public schools were required to conduct Christian religious learning exercises such as scripture reading and the recitation of the Lord's Prayer at the start or close of each school day. The Court found that the law 'imposed Christian observances upon non-Christian pupils and religious observances on non-believers', and infringed section 2(a) on that basis.[143] The Court had no doubt that the exercises had a religious purpose when they were first made mandatory in the late nineteenth century. They referred to a report of the founder of the Ontario public school system in which he stated that 'Christianity is the basis of our whole system of elementary education'.[144] The last amendments to the impugned regulation had occurred in 1978 and were informed by a report of the Committee on Religious Education in the Public Schools of the Province of Ontario. This report reinforced the religious character of the exercises, recommending their continued presence in the school day, and arguing that their absence would indicate that 'religion was not an integral part of life'.[145] The evidence did not support the government argument that the objectives of the regulation were in fact secular.

4. Interconnections between Motive and Effect Inquiries

There is an interesting disagreement in *Palmer v. Thompson*[146] (discussed at length in section 1) between Justice White and the majority opinion in interpreting one of the Court's earlier decisions, *Griffin v. County School Board of Prince Edward County*.[147] *Griffin* was about school desegregation, and contained a somewhat similar scenario to that of *Palmer*, whereby all public schools were closed in a county in Virginia and so-called 'private schools' were set up in

[140] Sujit Choudhry, 'So What is the Real Legacy of *Oakes*? Two Decades of Proportionality Analysis Under the Canadian *Charter*'s Section 1' (2006) 34 *Supreme Court Law Review* 501, 503.
[141] See *R. v. Edwards Books and Art Ltd.* [1986] 2 SCR 713, 744–45.
[142] (1988) 65 O.R. (2d) 641.
[143] Ibid. 654.
[144] Ibid. 661.
[145] Ibid. 661.
[146] 403 U.S. 217 (1971).
[147] 377 U.S. 218 (1964).

order to avoid desegregation orders. According to the majority in *Palmer*, *Griffin* displayed 'a focus . . . on the actual effect of the enactments, not upon the motivation which led the States to behave as they did'.[148] In response, Justice White quoted a passage from *Griffin*, which asserted that the closure of public schools and the operation of private schools was done 'for one reason, and one reason only',[149] namely to ensure the existence of a segregated school system, and then observed: 'if effect was all that the Court considered relevant in Griffin, there was no need to mention underlying purpose . . .'.[150] This disagreement helpfully sets the stage for a discussion on the motive/effect contrast in the case law in the United States, and in other jurisdictions, which will be discussed later in this chapter.

In actual judicial practice, motive- and effect-based inquiries need not be seen as antithetical, as is evidenced by US judicial review. Soon after *Palmer* (which announced, as we have seen, very controversially, that *any* inquiries into legislative motives are inappropriate) came *Washington v. Davis*,[151] which made legislative motives the cornerstone of a discrimination analysis. *Davis* generally stands for the proposition (reinforced only a few months later by the *Village of Arlington* case)[152] that disparate impact, absent the decision-makers' discriminatory intentions, is insufficient for a finding of discrimination. However, Justice White, delivering the opinion for the Court, admitted that '*[n]ecessarily*, an invidious discriminatory purpose may often be inferred from the totality of the relevant facts, including the fact, if it is true, that the law bears more heavily on one race than another'[153]—thus drawing a rather tight, even if only contingent, link between impact and motive analysis, whereby the latter is evidenced by the former. Justice White, as we have seen in the previous chapter, had authored a powerful dissent in *Palmer*, so it is not surprising that in *Davis*—a decision which apparently reversed *Palmer* as far as the relevance of motives is concerned—he had undertaken to distinguish both cases from each other, and in the process to redeem *Palmer* as good law, one would imagine largely *malgré lui*. 'The opinion [in *Palmer*] warned against grounding decision on legislative purpose or motivation, thereby lending support for the proposition that the operative effect of the law rather than its purpose is the paramount factor'[154]—admits Justice White. And here is how he explains a difference between that message of *Palmer* and the current decision, in *Davis*:

148 403 U.S. 225.
149 377 U.S. 231, quoted in 403 U.S. 264 (White J. dissenting).
150 403 U.S. 265 (White J. dissenting)
151 426 U.S. 229 (1976).
152 429 U.S. 252 (1977).
153 426 U.S. 242, emphasis added.
154 Ibid. 243.

> [T]he holding of the case [*Palmer*] was that the legitimate purposes of the ordinance—to preserve peace and avoid deficits—were not open to impeachment by evidence that the councilmen were actually motivated by racial considerations.... [T]he decision did not involve, much less invalidate, a statute or ordinance having neutral purposes but disproportionate racial consequences.[155]

But this is more ingenious than convincing. If anything, *Palmer did* involve a statute for which neutral or legitimate purposes were claimed by the authorities and accepted at face value by the majority of the Court, and the fact that it was not invalidated was precisely the problem depicted and decried in White's powerful dissent in *Palmer*. So the enhanced emphasis on motives in *Davis* may be seen as bringing a new and significant element to *Palmer*, to the point at which it may be seen as overruling it on the issue of motives, rather than affirming it. *Davis* has been subsequently understood by the Court as establishing the principle that, in disparate impact cases a motive inquiry is necessary in order to establish discrimination—even though the justices disagreed about whether such an inquiry is relevant when there is an explicit racial classification, for instance in affirmative action decisions.

It is interesting to note that the motive-oriented scrutiny changes its political function depending on the type of equal protection matter at issue. In disparate impact cases, the requirement of discriminatory motives as a factor in finding discrimination has been generally disfavoured by liberal (left, progressive) scholars and judges on the basis that it renders a determination of discrimination more difficult and raises an extra hurdle for the actions of progressive reformers. However, in affirmative action cases the opposite is true: conservatives argue for a disregard of motives as a factor in determining the level of scrutiny (which, as we know, is usually determinative of the outcome), and claim that the very fact of race-conscious classification should trigger strict scrutiny. In contrast, progressives believe that in affirmative action cases, the character of the purpose *is* relevant: if the purpose is benign (such as to compensate for persisting historical disadvantages), the standard of scrutiny should be more lenient than in invidious discrimination cases, because no suspicion of wrongful motives is warranted. Consider two iconic cases at different historical stages of the US affirmative action saga: *Bakke* and *Gratz*. In *Regents of University of California v. Bakke*,[156] Justice Powell (delivering the judgment for the Court) refused to lower the standard of scrutiny due to the purportedly remedial nature of the programme,[157] while liberal judges demanded that 'racial classifications

[155] Ibid. 243.
[156] 438 U.S. 265 (1978).
[157] Ibid. 300–05.

designed to further remedial purposes' should be subjected to intermediate scrutiny.[158] Twenty-five years later in *Gratz v. Bollinger*,[159] Chief Justice Rehnquist (delivering the judgment of the Court), echoing Powell's argument in *Bakke*, maintained that all racial classifications must be strictly scrutinized regardless of who benefits from such a classification,[160] while Justice Ginsburg (following in the footsteps of the Brennan Four in *Bakke*) said that when a classification is used for the purpose of inclusion and overall equality, a general proscription on race-conscious classifications does not apply.[161] There is a logic in this reversal of roles and it mirrors the changed functions of 'colour blindness' (which may be seen, for our purposes, as the direct opposite of a motive scrutiny): for invidious discrimination cases, colour blindness plays a progressive role,[162] but in affirmative action cases, it supports, and is used by, conservative critics of such programmes.

In a different case, a federal judge, dissenting from a Court of Appeals for the Ninth District decision of 1978 (regarding an allegation of gender discrimination by a college which opposed the establishment of childcare facilities) suggested a way of 'harmonizing' *Davis* and *Palmer*, or respectively, motive- and effect-scrutiny, in the following way:

> From *Palmer* we learn that if no discriminatory effects have been shown, discriminatory intent cannot affect the constitutional validity of the decisions of local officials. *Davis*, in turn, teaches that once discriminatory effects are present, intent becomes very important. The synthesis, of course, is that it is only *after* discriminatory effects are shown that intent becomes relevant to the validity of a legislative or administrative act.[163]

And Judge Wallace continued:

> In cases such as *Davis*, where the existence of a certain legislative motive has been declared to be a necessary element of a prima facie case, the courts must, of course, inquire whether that intent exists. As I have said, however, that inquiry need not be made until a threshold showing or, in the case of judgment on the pleadings, an allegation of discriminatory effect has been made.[164]

This seems to be a reasonable solution for judicial practice; indeed, in those judicial pronouncements, either in majority or dissenting opinions, which affirm the

[158] Ibid. 359 (Brennan, White, Marshall, Blackmun JJ. concurring in the judgment in part and dissenting in part).
[159] 539 U.S. 244 (2003).
[160] Ibid. 270.
[161] Ibid. 301–02 (Ginsburg J. dissenting).
[162] See *Plessy v. Ferguson*, 163 U.S. 537, 559 (1986) (Harlan J. dissenting).
[163] *De La Cruz v. Tormey*, 582 F.2d 45, 71 (1978) (Wallace J. dissenting), reference omitted.
[164] Ibid. 72 (Wallace J. dissenting).

importance of motive inquiry, it is usually accompanied by a finding of wrongful effects, for instance of a discriminatorily disparate impact upon different categories of citizens. But this is not embarrassing to a theory of public reason as an explanation of these cases or these arguments. There may be different ways of 'harmonizing' these two strands of inquiry.

5. Effect as a Threshold and as an Indicator of Motives

One such method of harmonization may be, as Judge Wallace suggested in the just-quoted dissent in *De La Cruz*, that effects are seen as a *threshold*, or a prerequisite of a subsequent inquiry into motives, which completes the argument about unconstitutionality (as the case may be). Another means of 'harmonization' may be by seeing effects as being indicators of most likely motives: in this case, effects stand as a measure of a motive, the latter being the true cornerstone of unconstitutionality. Consider the following suggestion by Justice Stewart, in his opinion for the Court, albeit hidden in a footnote: 'Proof of discriminatory intent must *necessarily* usually rely on objective factors ... The inquiry is practical. What a legislature or any official entity is "up to" may be plain from the results its actions achieve, or the results they avoid.'[165] Earlier, Justice Stevens in his concurrence in *Washington v. Davis* had expressed the same idea somewhat more cautiously: '*Frequently* the most probative evidence of intent will be objective evidence of what actually happened rather than evidence describing the subjective state of mind of the actor. For normally the actor is presumed to have intended the natural consequences of his deeds.'[166]

Such an inference from effect to the motive is based on general empirical knowledge of the world: we know that some effects are usually triggered by some types of motives, and the probability that the effect *E* (for instance, a widely irregular border of a voting district) was *not* brought about by a motive *M* (an attempt to reduce voting power of a particular social group) is minimal.[167] In addition, the substance of an act, combined with the anticipation of its likely effects, will usually constitute an important aid in discerning the motives when we are uncertain as to the most likely motive within a range of motives, of varying importance and validity, to have affected the adoption of a statute. As Justice Kennedy noted in *League of United Latin American Citizens*, delivering the opinion of the Court: 'We should be skeptical ... of a claim that seeks to invalidate

[165] *Personnel Administrator v. Feeney*, 442 U.S. 256, 279 n. 24 (1979), citation omitted, emphasis added.

[166] 426 U.S. 253 (Stevens, J. concurring), emphasis added.

[167] See Brest, 'Palmer v. Thompson' (n. 5) 121, and the example he provides of *Gomillion v. Lightfoot*, 364 U.S. 339 (1960), where the Supreme Court set aside a change in the shape of a city from a square to an 'uncouth twenty-eight-sided figure', *Gomillion* 340, in order to remove almost all black voters (but not a single white voter) from the city limits.

a statute based on a legislature's unlawful motive but does so without reference to the content of the legislation enacted.'[168] But occasionally, there may be a reverse connection: the awareness of the purpose behind a legislative measure may help judges ascertain its effects. It was observed that '[p]urpose can be quite useful in helping courts to take account of the full range of effects which flow from a given piece of legislation. . . . Consideration of purpose will not answer whether the effects of an act are constitutional. But purpose may help a court to determine what those effects will be'.[169] In such cases, the effects-based doctrine uses motive only as evidence of effects.[170] In particular, this may be useful when common empirical knowledge indicates that an attempt to pursue certain purposes will lead to particular effects, and it is better to strike the law down before those effects, often with irreparable harms, occur.[171]

In actual judicial arguments, the line between these different patterns of harmonization may be blurred—but this does not upset the argument that, at least at times, judges implement (*sans le nom*) a public reason-based theory whereby illicit motives (accompanied by troublesome effects) taint a regulation as unconstitutional. And I am making this proposition deliberately weak ('at times') because I do not suggest that judicial scrutiny into motives or purposes will always be appropriate; in fact, often the effect-based inquiry is all that matters because, judging from the effects, there is not even a prima facie suspicion that illicit motives may have been at work (a point to which I will return below). Or, vice versa, there may be situations in which all that matters is the effect inquiry precisely because effects are so obviously unconstitutional that no further inquiry into motives is needed, and as a matter of argumentative economy, a judge may end at that. In *Vriend v. Alberta*,[172] the Canadian Supreme Court considered a challenge by a former laboratory coordinator at a Christian school, following the termination of his employment in accordance with a school policy against hiring homosexuals. Mr Vriend initially sought redress before the Alberta Human Rights Commission. However, the Commission declined to take any action on the basis that the Alberta Individual's Rights Protection Act did not include sexual orientation as a prohibited ground of discrimination. The legislation was challenged as inconsistent with section 15 of the Canadian Charter (equality before the law and prohibition of discrimination), and ultimately came before the Supreme Court. The Court declined to examine the question of whether the Alberta government had a discriminatory purpose in its omission of sexual orientation as a ground of discrimination against which its human rights

[168] *League of United Latin American Citizens v. Perry*, 548 U.S. 399, 418 (2006).

[169] Note, 'Legislative Purpose and Federal Constitutional Adjudication', (1970) 83 *Harvard Law Review* 1887, 1893.

[170] See Lawrence A. Alexander, 'Introduction: Motivation and Constitutionality', (1978) 15 *San Diego Law Review* 925, 931.

[171] For an example, see Note, 'Legislative Purpose' (n. 169) 1893–94.

[172] [1998] 1 SCR 493.

legislation provided protection. The majority judgment on this issue noted that it was 'unnecessary to decide' whether the legislature had such a purpose, given that 'a finding of discrimination does not depend on an invidious, discriminatory intent'. That is, the discriminatory effects of the legislation were sufficient to invalidate it in themselves.[173]

But one must not protest too much. When legal scholar Calvin Massey claims: 'Because it is the real world effects of government action that harm or help people, the default criterion for assessing constitutional validity should be the effects of the challenged government action'[174]—for a proponent of the idea of public reason, a red alert light flashes: wrongful motives, when triggering legislation, *also* 'harm people'. We *may* adopt a default rule, as suggested by Massey, in the sense that it is usually easier to proceed via the effects path, and if we reach a verdict of unconstitutionality, it is the end of the story. But it is not the end of the story if we encounter suspicion of wrongful motives on the way, regardless of whether we like the effects or not.

There is a big difference between using effects as a reasonable indicator of a motive, with wrong motives being the true target of inquiry because these are the motives which taint the legislation as wrong, and on the other hand, using effects as an independent and sufficient source of the wrongness of legislation. There are all sorts of problems and difficulties with the latter theory, some of them well depicted years ago by Lawrence Alexander in his Introduction to a *San Diego Law Review* symposium on motive-oriented constitutional theory. Often there is no consensus, Alexander observed, about which specific effects are relevant, and often two or more mutually inconsistent effects may be permitted, and sometimes all that is mandated is a proper procedure to be followed with no consequences attached to the effects produced by these procedures etc.[175] These points are undoubtedly well-taken but I do not rely on any inherent weaknesses of the effect theory *per se* in my argument. Rather, I assume that often, in morally loaded cases, it is clearly inadequate to provide an explanation about what is really wrong about the legislation: often the wrongness resides primarily in the wrong reasons for the legislation, and everything else follows from this original sin, so to speak. And even if 'everything else' (in terms of effects) does *not* follow, the wrongness of motives in itself is a grave cause for concern, for a plethora of reasons articulated earlier in this book, and in particular having to do with a failure of respect when public reason does not motivate a piece of legislation.

But nothing in this book should suggest that I consider illicit motives or reasons for legislation to be a *necessary* condition of unconstitutionality: there

173 [1998] 1 SCR 546–47.

174 Massey, 'The Role of Governmental Purpose' (n. 117) 3. In fairness to Massey, it should be added that his 'default criterion' is relatively weak; he acknowledges immediately that '[t]here are . . . a number of exceptions to the general rule that effects should matter most', ibid. 4.

175 Alexander, 'Introduction' (n. 170) 927–30.

may be all sorts of different categories of unconstitutionality, including fundamental legislative error when a legislator enacts an irrational measure which cannot lead to the asserted purpose. Consider a case of death penalty introduced (or maintained) sincerely for reasons exclusively (or predominantly) of deterrence, while empirical studies challenge its effective deterrent effect. Scott Bice was right to note that the justification process serves, inter alia, to identify instances in which the negative *effects* of governmental action are a sufficient basis for invalidation under 'racial' equal protection, even though that action was not caused by racial prejudice.[176] This is obvious: the fact that illicit motivations contaminate a particular piece of legislation with a special type of defect does not mean that it cannot be defective for any other reason. Removing prejudice (or, for that matter, sectarianism, irrationality, and other motivations that do not pass the test of PR) is an important—but not the only—task of constitutional review. There are many occasions on which constitutional doctrine is quite naturally and adequately stated in terms of effects, with an accompanying balancing test not raising any special concerns, as in the cases of the prohibition against unreasonable searches and seizure.[177] Moreover, in some cases an exclusive emphasis on motives may have perverse consequences: as already noted earlier in this chapter, many commentators committed to the case of racial equality in the United States deplored *Washington v. Davis* and its progeny, because making discriminatory motives a necessary factor in a successful claim for discrimination reduced the chances of overturning policies with clear disparate racial impact.[178] This is not a criticism of motive-oriented scrutiny, but only of the *exclusivity* of such scrutiny, which is not a wise approach to take. And, to repeat, there will be cases when the impact is all that is needed to invalidate a law; in addition, it should be stressed that under some constitutional provisions, impact-based scrutiny will be *more* natural than a motive-based scrutiny: 'some provisions are not understood to impose any purpose-based restrictions on legislative power.'[179]

6. Dynamic Purposes and Effects

Of course, often it will be difficult to actually distinguish effect- and motive-based inquiry. One reason for this is that inquiry into effects can be addressed either to actual effects, as they have already occurred at the time of constitutional *challenge* (which may include unintended effects and side-effects of the law) or

[176] Scott H. Bice, 'Motivational Analysis as a Complete Explanation of the Justification Process', (1978) 15 *San Diego Law Review* 1131, 1133, emphasis added.

[177] See Charles Fried, 'Types', (1997) 14 *Constitutional Commentary* 55, 59.

[178] The literature is voluminous; among the early critical comments on *Washington v. Davis* along these lines, see Kenneth L. Karst, 'The Costs of Motive-Centered Inquiry', (1978) 15 *San Diego Law Review* 1163.

[179] Nelson, 'Judicial Review of Legislative Purpose' (n. 68) 1786.

into foreseen effects, at the time of the *enactment* of a rule. The actual effects of a rule at the time of challenge may be different from their effects at the time of enactment or even at an early stage of the rule being in force; the effect may be influenced by changed circumstances in the world which impacts the rule.

However, it is generally thought that changing an initially proper rule which becomes constitutionally improper due to changed circumstances is typically a role for a legislator rather than the judiciary. It would seem to go too far in extending judicial review into the function of monitoring the changing constitutionality of a rule over time if the rule has already been correctly found to be constitutional at an early stage of its operation. For instance, if at a time *T-1* a judge finds an affirmative-action programme constitutional because (for the sake of argument) it significantly contributes to a more 'diverse student body' at a university, will it be proper for a judge at a time *T-2* to assert that precisely the same type of programme has outlived its rationale (for instance, because a sufficiently 'diverse student body' has been already achieved in a given university) with the consequence that the programme, in its actual effects, has become unconstitutional? Such a change to constitutional qualification will come as a result of a complex empirical inquiry which is normally seen to be outside judicial competence and expertise. But if the effects are measured as predictions at the time of enactment, regardless of the actual effects at the time of constitutional challenge, then they are virtually indistinguishable from legislative intentions and purposes. It would be pedantic in the extreme to claim that the effects anticipated, expected, and hoped for by the legislator are separate from legislative motives, intentions, and purposes. In fact, they are one and the same.

Just as there may be a change in the *effects* of a law between the moment of enactment and the time of constitutional scrutiny, so there may be a changed ascertainment of the *purposes* which motivate the law: there may be a transition from purpose *P-1* at the time of the enactment to purpose *P-2* which reasonably justifies maintenance of the old law, even if it was enacted for wrong motives originally. This of course makes sense only if we understand the motives for a law in an objectified sense rather than as a set of subjective intentions of a particular group of lawmakers at the time of the enactment.[180] Consider the judgment of the South African Constitutional Court in *S v. Jordan*,[181] in which the Court upheld the penalization of prostitution against the objection that it was indirectly discriminatory against women. The majority of the Court found no discrimination, direct or indirect, because it found that the law was gender-neutral, and that prohibition of commercial sex by way of punishing both a customer and a prostitute was a proper way of 'pursu[ing] an important and legitimate

[180] See, similarly, Julian Rivers, 'Proportionality and Variable Intensity of Review', (2006) 65 *Cambridge Law Journal* 174, 196.

[181] *S v. Jordan & Others (Sex Workers Education and Advocacy Task Force & Others as Amici Curiae)* 2002 (6) SA 642 (CC).

constitutional purpose, namely, to outlaw commercial sex'.[182] What is of interest for us is a minority joint judgment authored by Justices Sachs and O'Regan who insisted that the law was discriminatory because it relied upon the reinforcement of a pattern of sexual stereotyping 'which is itself in conflict with the principle of gender equality'.[183] Importantly, the two judges also dealt with a broader question of whether the prohibition on prostitution constituted an impermissible imposition of morality by the state, by which they meant an imposition of morality which cannot be squared with 'the text and spirit of the Constitution itself'.[184]

It is at this point that Justices Sachs and O'Regan inquired into the purposes of the act, past and current. They accepted, for the sake of argument, that the act in question was drafted with the purpose of imposing a particular morality on the population—one that condemned sex outside of marriage.[185] 'The question then arises whether the legislation must be regarded as having been saddled once and for all with this illegitimate purpose, or whether it can be regarded as having assumed a new purpose that would be legitimate and justifiable in an open and democratic society.'[186] The justices considered (what they called) the 'shifting purpose doctrine' as it operates in Canada and the United States.[187] But ultimately they found that similarly to the United States and Canada, where social transformation has at different times rendered obsolete the motivation underlying existing legislation, South Africa was undergoing a metamorphosis. For this reason, the law 'retain[s] from the past only what is defensible and represents a radical and decisive break from that part of the past which is unacceptable'.[188] Justices O'Regan and Sachs noted that if they were to take into account the motives and intentions of the Parliament at the time when they enacted all the pre-1994 statutes that are still on the books today, they would be forced to invalidate almost all of them. But the 'mere fact that the original legislative purpose of the statute might have been incompatible with current constitutional standards, does not deprive it of the capacity to serve a legitimate governmental purpose today, unless its express language and intent is ... manifestly inconsistent with constitutional values.[189]

The two justices therefore ultimately found that the legislation was capable of interpretation consistent with current constitutional principles, even though from the wording of the Act one may presume that it was intended to impose a particular outdated view of morality and if such views were imposed now, they would conflict with the values of the Constitution.[190] As two South African

[182] Ibid. [15].
[183] Ibid. [59].
[184] Ibid. [104].
[185] Ibid. [107].
[186] Ibid. [108].
[187] Ibid. [109–10].
[188] Ibid. [111].
[189] Ibid. [112].
[190] Ibid. [113–14].

commentators argued, this avoids the 'trap of assuming that the legislative purpose is something fixed and static, nor conflating the purpose of a law with the subjective intent of those who enacted it'.[191] They warn, however, that there are problems with the 'shifting purpose' doctrine. '[I]t may be used to justify measures that are so tainted by the discriminatory or the authoritarian underpinnings of the original enactment that they may continue to entrench harmful stereotypes.' However, they observe that the Court is 'alive to these dangers and has rejected attempts to justify overly racist or sexist provisions in terms of a less offensive objective'.[192] In this way, real historical legislative motivations do not necessarily translate into contemporary purposes of the law; these purposes are not set in stone but are capable of reinterpretation as the most plausible reasons for keeping the law on the books.

Let me finally note that at times it will not be absolutely clear at what level of generality to pitch the identification of an intention or a purpose of the law under challenge: in other words, there will be an important question 'The purpose of *what*?' which will need to be addressed as a preliminary matter. The cases just reviewed do not lend themselves to such an ambiguity, but it may not always be the case, especially if the defender of a law (typically, a state) attempts to elevate the level of generality (to render a critical scrutiny less effective) or bundle together a number of purposes, so as to water down the illicit nature of one particular purpose or motive at work. An example from the Canadian constitutional jurisprudence helps make this point. It is generally accepted that attempts to define legislative purpose in a section 1 analysis (i.e. the analysis as to whether a given restriction on a Charter right can be justified in a free and democratic society) should be guided by the principle that the only reason for embarking on the search for the legislative objective is aimed at determination as to whether there is a sufficient justification for an infringement of the Charter.[193] Thus, the terms in which the objective is expressed should relate directly to the infringement itself—it should provide a reason for the breach. As Justice McLachlin clarified in the majority judgment in *RJR MacDonald v. Canada (Attorney General)*,[194] the relevant objective is that of the '*infringing measure* ... The objective of the impugned measures ... is somewhat narrower than the objectives of the wider legislative and policy scheme in which it is found'.[195] If an objective is expressed in terms that are too broad, the concern is that its importance will be overstated, which risks compromising the subsequent proportionality components of the justification analysis. The subjects of the Charter challenge in that case were provisions of the Tobacco Products Control Act banning the advertising

[191] Stu Woolman and Henk Botha, 'Limitations' in Stu Woolman and Michael Bishop (eds), *Constitutional Law of South Africa* (2nd edn., Juta 2008) 34.8.
[192] Ibid.
[193] See Hogg, *Constitutional Law of Canada* (n. 132) para. 38-20.
[194] [1995] 3 SCR 199.
[195] Ibid. 335.

of tobacco products. The Attorney General conceded these provisions infringed the Charter-protected freedom of expression. For the purposes of the section 1 justification argument, Justice McLachlin explained that the provisions in question could not be said to have as their object the general protection of Canadians from the health risks posed by tobacco use. Rather, their specific purpose was to 'prevent people in Canada from being persuaded by advertising and promotion to use tobacco products'.[196] That was found to be a legitimate, sufficiently important objective to warrant an infringement of freedom of expression.

7. Proportionality and Purpose-oriented Scrutiny

An example of a constitutional court which has relatively frequently referred to wrongful purposes, or to the deficit of proper purposes invoked by the government in defence of its law, is provided by the South African Constitutional Court. I will return to some of the interesting cases of the Court in subsequent chapters but here it will suffice to mention three cases on the limitation of important constitutional rights where the invalidation resulted fundamentally or exclusively from the purpose inquiry. In *Richter*,[197] the Constitutional Court confirmed the constitutional invalidity of a regulation of the Electoral Act, which limited the right to vote of certain categories of South African citizens who were registered as voters if they were absent from the country on polling day. Justice O'Regan held that the provision constituted an unjustifiable limitation on section 19 of the Constitution, stating that the government 'has not sought to point to any legitimate government purpose served by restricting the categories of registered voters who qualify for a special vote, and I can think of none'.[198] In *Centre for Child Law*[199] the Court held that certain criminal law provisions which imposed minimum sentences for certain serious criminal offences applicable to 16 and 17 year olds, were constitutionally invalid, as contrary to children's rights under section 28 of the Constitution. Regarding the purpose of the legislation, an affidavit submitted on behalf of the Minister recorded views expressed in the legislature in 1997 about the impugned laws. That purpose, the majority surmised, was 'to elicit the social benefits that a legislative bulwark' against certain serious crimes committed by 16 and 17 year olds would deliver.[200] However, this was found unsatisfactory because 'even the clear articulation of... policy objectives [was] lacking'.[201] Finally, in the *NICRO*

[196] Ibid. 335.

[197] In *Richter v. Minister for Home Affairs & Others (with the Democratic Alliance & Others Intervening, and with Afriforum & Another as Amici Curiae)* 2009 (3) SA 615 (CC).

[198] Ibid. [78].

[199] *Centre for Child Law v. Minister for Justice and Constitutional Development & Others* 2009 (2) SACR 477 (CC).

[200] Ibid. [51]–[52].

[201] Ibid. [53].

case,[202] the Court declared the constitutional invalidity of certain provisions of the Electoral Act that deprived 'convicted prisoners serving a sentence of imprisonment without the option of a fine of the right to participate in elections' for the duration of their imprisonment.[203] As Chief Justice Chaskalson for the majority explained in the judgment, the limitation of the right to vote is taken very seriously in South Africa, in light of the nation's recent history, 'where denial of the right to vote was used to entrench white supremacy and to marginalise the great majority of people' of the country.[204] Thus, the majority explained, if the government seeks to limit that right, and the purpose of the measure it enacts in the course of so doing is not self-evident, it is critical that the government provide the Court with sufficient material to understand that purpose—which was not the case here. In particular, the Court reviewed two purposes cited by the government, namely that making arrangements for these prisoners to vote would put a significant strain on the resources of the Electoral Commission, and that if the current law were to be changed, it would give the impression that the government was soft on crime. The Court rejected both arguments, having regard to the significance of the right impaired and the fact that arrangements had been made to enable some other categories of prisoners to vote. In the absence of any legitimate purpose for the limitation, the impugned law was found invalid.

Generally speaking, inquiry into the purpose of a law under scrutiny is facilitated in South Africa by an explicit constitutional mandate: section 36(1) of the South African Constitution provides a canonical list of the considerations to be taken into account when scrutinizing legislative limitations on rights, with 'the importance of the purpose of the limitation' being the second of those considerations. As the commentators on the Court encapsulated the Court's doctrine, at a minimum the Court must ensure that 'the purpose is not inconsistent with the values of an open and democratic society based on human dignity, equality and freedom'.[205] Stu Woolman and Henk Botha identify objectives the Court has found to be at odds with these values: retribution;[206] re-inscribing historical patterns of prejudice and disadvantage among racial groups;[207] the enforcement of laws animated by bigotry or intolerance dressed up as morality;[208] and the absence of sufficient guidance in a legislative provision as to how an official ought to exercise the discretion granted to her.[209] In turn, examples of objectives that

[202] *Minister of Home Affairs v. National Institute for Crime Prevention and the Re-integration of Offenders (NICRO) & Others*, 2005 (3) SA 280 (CC).

[203] Ibid. [2].

[204] Ibid. [47].

[205] Woolman and Botha, 'Limitations' (n. 191) 34.8.

[206] *S v. Williams & Others* 1995 (3) SA 632 (CC) [86].

[207] *Bhe & Others v. Khayelitsha Magistrate & Others* 2005 (1) SA 580 (CC) [72].

[208] *National Coalition for Gay and Lesbian Equality & Another v. Minister of Justice & Others* 1999 (1) SA 6 (CC) [37].

[209] *Dawood & Another v. Minister of Home Affairs & Others; Shalabi & Another v. Minister of Home Affairs & Others; Thomas & Another v. Minister of Home Affairs & Others* 2000 (3) SA 934 (CC).

have passed constitutional muster include: the promotion of equality, dignity, and national unity;[210] the protection of children from the degradation and indignity brought about by corporal punishment and child pornography;[211] the fortification of the judicial process;[212] and the insistence that members of the defence force do not prejudice or further the interests of a political party.[213]

It is not surprising that the South African constitutional jurisprudence gives rise to reflections which are strikingly similar to the theory of public reason, both as an attempt at generalizing constitutional case law, and/or as a normative template for scrutinizing legislation under section 36. Denise Meyerson is, deservedly, credited by several academics as the originator of this position.[214] The key to her argument in her book written and published right at the outset of South African post-apartheid constitutionalism, is the idea of 'neutral harms'—as those 'in whose prevention all reasonable people have at least some interest'[215] in contrast to a 'non-neutral harm' (that the government is not authorized to suppress) which is 'harm dependent for its occurrence on an intractably disputed though personally reasonable belief'.[216] That way, as a commentator on Meyerson observes, in accordance with the Rawlsian conception of public reasons, 'legitimate reasons for limiting rights will ... be "public reasons"... as opposed to *sectarian* ones'.[217]

Justice Sachs referred to Meyerson's work with approval in the already mentioned *Christian Education* case in the course of acknowledging the difficulties of proportionality analysis in cases in which the state seeks to justify a limitation on religious rights. In that case, the appellant religious association argued that a total ban on corporal punishment in religious schools violated their religious freedom under section 15 of the Constitution, and their right to practise their religion under section 31. The Court assumed that the impugned law did limit the religious rights of the association's members and proceeded to the justification analysis. In that analysis, the 'most complex problem' Justice Sachs perceived was that 'the competing interests to be balanced' in the course of the limitations analysis once a rights infringement is found 'belong to completely different conceptual and existential

[210] See *Islamic Unity Convention v. Independent Broadcasting Authority & Others* 2002 (4) SA 294 (CC) [45]–[46].

[211] *Christian Education South Africa v. Minister of Education* 2000 (4) SA 757 [39]–[50] and *De Reuck v. Director of Public Prosecutions (Witwatersrand Local Division) & Others* 2004 (1) SA 406 (CC) [61]–[67].

[212] See, e.g., *Beinash & Another v. Young & Others* 1999 (2) SA 116 (CC) [17]; *S v. Steyn* 2001 (1) SA 1146 (CC) [31]; *LS v. AT & Another* 2001 (2) BCLR 152 (CC) [30]–[31].

[213] *South African National Defence Union v. Minister of Defence & Another* 1999 (4) SA 469 (CC) [11], [28], and [32].

[214] Stephen Gardbaum, 'Limiting Constitutional Rights', (2007) 54 *UCLA Law Review* 789, 842 n. 196.

[215] Denise Meyerson, *Rights Limited: Freedom of Expression, Religion and the South African Constitution* (Juta 1997) 22.

[216] Ibid. 23.

[217] Nicholas Smith, 'Freedom of Religion in the Constitutional Court', (2001) 118 *South African Law Journal* 1, 8, emphasis in original.

orders'—that is, religious conviction and associated practices on the one hand, which are based in faith, and the countervailing public or private interests that are not, and are 'evaluated mainly according to their reasonableness'.[218] Justice Sachs quoted the terms Meyerson uses to frame this disjunction when she observes that religious matters are 'neither confirmable nor disconfirmable by public evidence',[219] and '[t]he use of common standards of reason cannot help reasonable people to converge on the truth in the area of religion'.[220] In that realm in particular, governments will have to justify limitations on constitutional rights by providing 'a justification for its measure to which all reasonable people would, if asked, accord some degree of force'.[221] Justice Sachs quotes Meyerson as she continues: 'the state is obliged . . . to justify limitations on constitutional rights from a point of view from which all citizens can reason', and not by reference to reasons 'whose normative force depends on an intractably disputed point of view'.[222]

As already noted, an open constitutional inquiry into legislative motives/purpose has been greatly facilitated in South Africa by an express constitutional provision in which purposes figure as part of the scrutiny of constitutionality of legislative restrictions of rights. The same is the case with, inter alia, Israel where section 8 of the Basic Law: Human Dignity and Liberty, lists a 'proper purpose' of a law as the third of four criteria of constitutionality (the other three being enactment by a law, conformity with the values of the State of Israel, and restriction of a right to an extent no greater than what is required). It is, therefore, a step prior to proportionality review—a review firmly adopted in Israel since the 1990s and conducted under the Basic Laws which confer upon the Supreme Court authority to review primary Knesset legislation. The Basic Laws set out a limitations clause that restricts the infringement of rights 'to an extent no greater than is required'.[223] Influenced by German and Canadian jurisprudence, the Supreme Court interpreted this clause as setting a requirement of proportionality. If a law infringes on constitutional rights without a proportional and worthy purpose, it is deemed to be unconstitutional and in violation of the Basic Laws.[224] In its case law, the Supreme Court—occasionally supporting its doctrines by reference to the landmark Canadian case in *R v. Oakes*—added that the purpose of legislation, in order to justify an infringement, must be 'important and essential',[225] or,

[218] *Christian Education South Africa v. Minister of Education* 2000 (4) SA 757 (CC) [33].

[219] Meyerson, *Rights Limited* (n. 215) 17 cited by Sachs J. at *Christian Education South Africa v. Minister of Education* 2000 (4) SA 757 (CC) [33], n. 35.

[220] Meyerson, *Rights Limited* (n. 215) 18.

[221] Ibid. 12.

[222] Ibid. 17, cited by Sachs J. in *Christian Education South Africa v. Minister of Education* 2000 (4) SA 757 (CC) [33] n. 35.

[223] *Basic Law: Human Dignity and Liberty* (5752—1992) s. 8.

[224] Assaf Meydani, *The Anatomy of Human Rights in Israel* (Cambridge University Press 2014) 33.

[225] *United Mizrahi Bank Ltd. v. Migdal Cooperative Village, CA 6821/93* [1995] IsrLR 1, p. 128 [81] President Meir Shamgar. In this paragraph, President Shamgar cites *R. v. Oakes* [1986] 1 SCR 103 [114].

in a different articulation, must 'serve an important social objective regarding human rights'.[226] This formulation has been repeated throughout Israeli case law. The Court affirms Court President Barak's statement that a violation of a constitutional right is permitted insofar as it is intended to serve an important social purpose.[227] Yet another formula has been that '[a] purpose is deemed proper if it constitutes a social goal in a society sensitive to human rights'.[228] 'Sensitivity to human rights', as a defining criterion of a proper purpose, has been interpreted broadly, so as to also encompass public goals such as national security: according to the Court, a law that seeks to protect national security interests is a law that is sensitive to human rights. This is because at its core, it is a law whose purpose is the protection of a person's right to life. This is sufficiently sensitive enough to human rights principles to be determined as a proper purpose.[229]

When determining the purpose of offending legislation, the Israeli Supreme Court looks at a number of different sources to form an opinion on legislative intention: explanatory notes and speeches accompanying the first reading in the Knesset[230] (though occasionally the Court would consult explanatory notes and find that they do not contain any details regarding the intended purpose);[231] the wording of a piece of legislation;[232] the background to the enactment of the law (in one of the landmark cases, the Court observed that the 'background to the enactment of the law' was '[a]n armed struggle . . . between Israel and the Palestinian entity in which the Palestinian public is playing an active role' (thus inferring that the law's purpose was protecting security of the residents of Israel));[233] or even occasionally evidence from how other legal systems perceive the purposes of a law enacted in similar circumstances.[234]

All in all, whenever the Supreme Court of Israel has engaged in purpose scrutiny, it has hardly ever expressed perplexity caused by possible evidentiary problems. This is partly because it has facilitated its role by oscillating between what its President, Professor Barak called a 'subjective purpose' and an 'objective' one. In the *Adalah* case Justice Barak said:

[226] *United Mizrahi Bank Ltd. v. Migdal Cooperative Village* CA 6821/93 [1995] IsrLR 1, p. 240 [91] President Aharon Barak.

[227] See *Adalah Legal Center for Arab Minority Rights in Israel v. Minister of Interior*, HCJ 7052/03 [12] Eliezer Rivlin J.

[228] *Szenes v. Matar*, HCJ 6126/94 (1999) [21] President A. Barak.

[229] *Gal-On v. Attorney General*, HCJ 466/07 (2012) [11] E. Levy J.

[230] *Commitment to Peace and Social Justice Society v. Minister of Finance*, HCJ 366/03 [5] E. Levy J.

[231] *United Mizraci Bank* (n. 225) 150 [82] President (Ret) Meir Shamgar.

[232] *A v. State of Israel* CrimA 6659/06 [20] President Dorit Beinisch.

[233] *Adalah Legal Center for Arab Minority Rights in Israel v. Minister of Interior*, HCJ 7052/03 [24] Vice-President Emeritus M. Cheshin.

[234] Ibid. [33] President Aharon Barak.

> The question is whether the purpose of a piece of legislation is only its subjective purpose, which focuses on the motive that underlies the legislation; or perhaps the 'purpose' of the legislation is only the objective purpose, which focuses on the purpose at the time of deciding the question of constitutionality; or perhaps the 'purpose' is determined— as it is with regard to the interpretation of legislation– in accordance with both its objective and subjective purpose together.[235]

While no express answer to this dilemma is provided by Justice Barak in this case, in his book on proportionality Aharon Barak articulates and defends 'a combined test', whereby 'the purpose of the limiting legislation would be considered proper only if it satisfies both the subjective and the objective tests'.[236] Nevertheless, the ambiguity of 'objective/subjective' purpose in the Court's case law, and a flagged option of choosing a hybrid conception, clearly allowed the Court to avoid the usual evidentiary problems regarding the reconstruction of actual legislative motives. In his book, the sense that evidentiary difficulties are unimportant when it comes to the detection of a motive, or intent, or 'subjective purpose' was articulated by Barak when he opines that '[t]here are several ways by which the intention of a multi-member body [such as legislature] can be identified',[237] and pointed at the US Supreme Court's strict scrutiny case law as a method of identifying intent. Further, the ex-President of the Israeli top court urges that 'one can learn from the pre-legislative history, the legislative history, and the post-legislative history on the intent that was envisioned by the legislative body at the time the law was enacted'.[238]

The Israeli Supreme Court's case law provides examples where the Court infers the likely motives of the legislators based on the substance of the law, in combination with the background factual circumstances; the '*res ipsa loquitur*' principle seems to be at work. Consider the case of *Member of Knesset Oron v. Chairman of Knesset*[239] which concerned the regulation of radio stations in Israel. The Israeli Knesset enacted an amendment to the law governing the operation of radio stations in Israel; the amendment permitted radio stations that had been operating continuously for five years without a permit to be legalized. The context to this amendment was that previously there were only two radio stations that were operating with permits (legally) in Israel, and alongside them a number of illegal radio stations that had been operating without permits. A motion was filed in the Supreme Court against this amendment by a left-wing member of the Knesset, Minister of Knesset Oron, who argued that the Knesset's agenda in passing this

235 Ibid. [60] President Aharon Barak.
236 Aharon Barak, *Proportionality* (Cambridge University Press 2012) 298, footnote omitted.
237 Ibid. 301–02, footnote omitted.
238 Ibid. 302.
239 1030/99 (2002).

legislative amendment was intended to legalize a specific, radical right-wing radio station (Channel 7) that had previously been operating unlawfully. The Court agreed with the arguments presented by Oron and unanimously declared the amendment unconstitutional.

The judgment of Justice Theodore Or is of particular interest here because he examined what the intention of the authors of the amendment was. The appellant argued that the amendment's purpose was improper because the intention of the legislator was to enact a standard that was specifically designed to fit the circumstances of one particular radio station. The amendment was intended to legalize Channel 7, a private radio station that is well-recognized as a right-wing station.[240] The defendants (the Knesset) admitted that one part of the purpose of this amendment was to allow for the legalization of Channel 7. However, they also argued that the broader purpose of the amendment was the promotion of pluralism in freedom of expression.[241]

In ascertaining the intentions of the legislator, Justice Or examined the debates and second reading speeches. He observed that the members of Knesset who were in opposition to the amendment believed that the purpose of legislating the amendment was to legalize the operations of Channel 7, whilst the members of Knesset who supported the amendment, who believed that it was intended to create pluralistic media representation, did not deny that this objective was *also* intended to include the authorization of the transmission of Channel 7. The members of Knesset were forthright in stating that they had initiated the amendment with this being an element of their agenda for introducing it.[242] In light of the language of the amendment and the way it was presented by Knesset, Justice Or came to the opinion that the amendment incorporated two purposes at different levels of abstraction. He found that there was no doubt that the lower-level purpose of the amendment was specifically to allow for the authorization of Channel 7. However, to err on the side of caution, Justice Or said that he was also willing to accept that a higher level of purpose existed in the amendment and that was the promotion of pluralist representation in communication. Justice Or determined that the lower-level purpose, authorizing the transmission of Channel 7, was certainly improper while the higher-level purpose was proper.[243] He then, however, refused to determine the situation of clash between an improper specific purpose and a proper general purpose, on the basis that it was not necessary in the present case because the amendment would otherwise fail the proportionality test, based on the employment of disproportionate means to achieve either of these purposes. What matters to the argument here is that the combination of the background facts, the speeches in the legislature, and the text

240 Ibid. [32] Justice Theodor Or.
241 Ibid. [32].
242 Ibid. [33]–[34].
243 Ibid. [34].

of the law yielded a plausible second-guessing of true legislative motives. And even though, so far, the Israeli Supreme Court has not invalidated any law based on a declaration of improper legislative purpose (preferring to use other tiers of proportionality as the grounds of invalidation), the discussion above shows that it does not shy away from construing, based on different sources, the most plausible purposes pursued by the legislators.

6
Freedom of Speech, Viewpoint Regulation, and Wrongful Legislative Motives

The salience of motive-oriented scrutiny is clearly visible in the field of freedom of speech. Some time ago, it was observed that:

> for free speech problems regarding the exchange of ideas, the challenging party establishes a first amendment violation by showing that the decisionmaker's action was *motivated* solely by ideological considerations likely to compromise the rights to acquire information or ideas, or subtly to influence the party's beliefs . . .[1]

More recently, the author of these words, Elena Kagan, argued generally in her wide-ranging article that the 'First Amendment law, as developed by the Supreme Court over the past several decades, has as its primary though unstated object the discovery of *improper governmental motives*. The doctrine comprises a series of tools to flush out illicit motives and to invalidate actions infected with it'.[2] This chapter will trace the connections between some persuasive doctrines of freedom of expression and attempt to specify and make more explicit the 'improper governmental motives', hinted at by Professor Kagan (as she then was), which contaminate a speech regulation. It will be shown, in particular, that the requirement that regulations be viewpoint neutral resonates with the fundamental principles of public reason (PR). In section 1, I will describe the relationship between the harm of speech and the viewpoint represented by the speech under regulation; in section 2, I will finetune a distinction between regulations based on subject matter and those based on viewpoint, and in section 3, I will explain why this distinction is relevant to detecting and distinguishing between different putatively improper motivations of speech regulations, such as paternalism and intolerance.

[1] John Donovan, 'Unconstitutional Motivation Analysis and the First Amendment: The Further Demise of a 'Wise and Ancient Doctrine'', (1983) 33 *Case Western Reserve Law Review* 271, 291–92, emphasis added.

[2] Elena Kagan, 'Private Speech, Public Purpose: The Role of Governmental Motive in First Amendment Doctrine', (1996) 63 *University of Chicago Law Review* 413, 414, emphasis added.

Constitutional Public Reason. Wojciech Sadurski, Oxford University Press. © Wojciech Sadurski 2023.
DOI: 10.1093/oso/9780192869678.003.0006

1. Speech, Harm, and Viewpoint

Speech may harm people—and speech regulation oriented towards eliminating or reducing harm is compatible with the demands of PR. But regulation of speech may also be based on hostility towards ideas expressed or the willingness to screen out some information or opinions from the public domain regardless of its harmfulness. These motives for suppression are illegitimate; they are incompatible with PR because they are not endorsable by the holders of those opinions or information. Much of the American debate about—and the difficulty raised by—the proper role of government in regulating speech centres around a distinction between harm-based and hostility-based restrictions of speech. The line between both types of motivation can be fine,[3] but in principle, this distinction (corresponding, as it does, to PR-compatible and PR-incompatible motives) explains much about US First Amendment speech jurisprudence. This line marks the difference between 'government censorship' and 'legitimate, reasonable, neutral justifications' (based on prohibiting 'special harms')[4] for speech regulation.

This is where the motive for restrictions acquires crucial importance. The general principle governing US First Amendment jurisprudence (and also, as will be shown, outside the United States) may be formulated as follows: restrictions that express a viewpoint that is preferred (or, conversely, disliked) by the government should be subjected to very strong scrutiny, with the implication that it will likely be invalidated. In contrast, restrictions that are viewpoint-neutral, and which do not discriminate among different viewpoints, may be subject to more lenient scrutiny because there is little reason to suspect that they result from improper governmental motives. The latter restrictions are sometimes presented as content-based rather than viewpoint-based, which is imprecise. I will return to this point below.

But first I wish to consider the relationship between harm-based restrictions of speech (which, presumptively, are perfectly unimpeachable from the point of view of PR) and content-based restrictions based upon hostility to a point of view, which do not pass muster with PR. Is it a distinction with a difference? Consider the example of a restriction which would command quasi-universal endorsement even by the most radical libertarians: that of child pornography. A proponent of a viewpoint-based theory (a theory which presumptively prohibits viewpoint restrictions) may say: this restriction is perfectly compatible with my theory because it is targeted at a very special kind of harm rather than a viewpoint. It is not the 'viewpoint' which is the target of the restriction, but the real harm done to children. A proponent of a viewpoint-based theory may cite Geoffrey Stone's formula that 'the government may not restrict expression *simply*

[3] Ibid. 422 n. 27.

[4] For this distinction, framed in these words, see *R.A.V. v. City of St. Paul*, 505 U.S. 377, 434 (1992) (Stevens, J. concurring).

because it disagrees with the speaker's views'[5] and maintain that in the case of child pornography, the restriction is imposed not *simply* because of its disagreement with a pornographer's perspective, but that it just so happens that pursuing the aim of preventing great harm coincides with the restriction of viewpoints which are supportive of the harm. The primary aim, the argument *may* go, is to avoid harm, and '[t]hat aim might dwarf, or *even be unaccompanied by*, any bias toward the point of view expressed'.[6]

The italicized words in the quote from Steven Shiffrin indicate a theoretical problem: can we really envisage a harm-oriented regulation of speech that is completely 'unaccompanied by' any dislike of the point of view expressed? At a minimum, there will be always a 'point of view' that the harm claimed by the lawmaker is insignificant or is not harm at all. But this articulation of the harm-viewpoint connection renders it trivial: we can always concoct a 'point of view' parallel to the task of harm-reduction. When, for instance, a regulator wants to minimize an obvious harm arising from false or misleading advertisements by lawyers without necessarily at the same time targeting all other advertisements (an obvious content-based regulation),[7] we can always attribute it to a 'viewpoint' that the harms of false advertisement by this professional group are of a special character. But this attribution is not interesting, because this 'viewpoint' description does not add anything to the harm language.

What is more interesting and important, for our purposes, is an *opposite* situation: can we imagine viewpoint-oriented restrictions *unaccompanied* by the targeting of harm? Some believe that we cannot. Laurence Tribe, for instance, suggested that '*All* viewpoint-based regulations are targeted at some supposed harm, whether it be linked to an unsettling ideology like Communism or Nazism or to socially shunned practices like adultery'.[8] And if any putative viewpoint-based restriction in fact collapses into harm reduction, the idea that viewpoint-based restrictions reveal illicit motivations is in trouble.

However, the very fact that we can identify content-based speech regulations which are fundamentally harm-oriented, containing only a minor viewpoint-dislike ingredient, *is* significant for the application of PR in constitutional law: such laws will not, normally, lend themselves to the search for illicit motives. Whether we encounter an opposite scenario—a viewpoint-oriented restriction which is harm-insensitive—may therefore be of lower importance for

[5] Geoffrey R. Stone, 'Content Regulation and the First Amendment', (1983) 15 *William & Mary Law Review* 189, 227, emphasis added, footnote omitted.

[6] Steven H. Shiffrin, *The First Amendment, Democracy, and Romance* (Princeton University Press 1990) 18, footnote omitted, emphasis added.

[7] See *Bates v. State Bar of Arizona*, 433 U.S. 350 (1977) . In this decision, the Supreme Court invalidated a law which would ban truthful advertisements by lawyers. At the same time, Blackmun J., who delivered the opinion of the Court, suggested that a law targeting *false* advertisements by lawyers may be constitutional, ibid. 383.

[8] Laurence H. Tribe, *American Constitutional Law* (2nd edn., The Foundation Press 1988), 925, emphasis in original.

PR theory. Even if we answer the question in the negative, there will still be room for PR, at least in certifying the PR-compatibility of harm-oriented speech regulations. Perhaps we can say this: viewpoint-based restrictions which look harm-insensitive occur when there is significant disagreement as to whether a given speech is indeed harmful, and even if there is consensus about its harmfulness, where there is disagreement about the gravity of harm and whether it prevails over the harms of restrictions. When, however, there is a high degree of consensus about the harmfulness of speech and about its gravity, which would be likely to easily prevail over the harmfulness of the cost of restrictions (as in the case of the prohibition of child pornography), we do not need to come to the viewpoint-related argument. It is redundant; it does not add anything to the argument that the gravity of the harm of speech prevails over the harm of regulation. This is particularly visible in the example of so-called 'fighting words', defined as 'those [words] which by their very utterance inflict injury or tend to incite an immediate breach of the peace'.[9] The articulation of a 'viewpoint' targeted by a legislator does not add anything to our firm and widely shared views about the harm arising from verbal assaults captured by this concept. When, however, there is a degree of disagreement and uncertainty about the harm of speech weighed and balanced with harm of regulation (as in regulating the defamation of public officials, of hate speech, or of milder forms of pornography), viewpoint-oriented analysis acquires real bite. Viewpoint-characterization of a regulation may be therefore parasitic on the fact that the assessment of harm in question is controversial.

So far, the argument has proceeded as if the concept of 'harm' applies to freedom of speech in the same way as to any other legally protected individual freedom, namely, that the identification of net harm (harm of speech prevailing over the harm of regulation) is all that is required to justify restriction. But this perspective disregards the fact that the principle of freedom of speech is a *special* freedom protected under the harm to others principle, and that its special character means that the government must produce weightier justifications for restricting freedom of speech than for restricting many other freedoms. As a result, harm which would justify the restriction of non-communicative action must be tolerated under the principle of freedom of speech, which is not simply reducible to freedom *simpliciter*. There are many arguments that can be provided for such an understanding of freedom of speech, and many justifications can be given for the special immunity of this freedom to a simple harm-benefit calculus.[10] What matters for our discussion here is that some of the arguments for immunizing

[9] *Chaplinsky v. New Hampshire*, 315 U.S. 568, 572 (1942).

[10] Wojciech Sadurski, *Freedom of Speech and Its Limits* (Kluwer 1999), chapter 1. For a discussion of the principle of freedom of speech as a special, independent principle, not reducible to the general principle of freedom and to a simple harm calculus, see Frederick Schauer, *Free Speech: A Philosophical Enquiry* (Cambridge University Press 1982) 5–10.

freedom of speech from normal restrictions on freedom *simpliciter*—that is, from the ordinary harm calculus—are that harm following from speech may be often mitigated by counter-speech ('more speech' as a remedy to bad speech), or that people by and large are unlikely to be persuaded by much of the reprehensible speech, or that the government may have special incentives to underestimate the benefits and overestimate the harms of putatively bad speech, etc. These are the factors which, under many convincing theories of freedom of speech, occur in the case of speech, but not necessarily in many other exercises of human liberty, and which supports a greater reticence in regulating speech compared to regulating various other individual freedoms. (Of course, there may be other special kinds of freedom which also demand exemption from the usual harm calculus: from the fact that freedom of speech is *special*, it does not follow that it is *the only* special freedom in a liberal-democratic society, in this sense.)[11]

Note, however, that some exercises of speech lend themselves better to this analysis than others. Generally, various mitigating circumstances such as mentioned in the previous paragraph consist in the fact that for speech to become harmful, it must be heard (or read), understood, and interpreted by other people; in other words, that it must be mediated by other people's minds. The harm occurs when other people (normally, *many* people) become convinced of the speaker's message: for instance, when they are convinced by his racist hatefulness, or misleading advertising, or degrading opinions about someone. These cases coincide with content regulation, because the harm arises out of the content imparted to the public space. And so when we talk about content regulation, we have in mind the regulation of speech the harmfulness of which occurs only, or primarily, through the intermediation of the hearers' (or readers', or viewers', etc.) minds, and when we may hope that the just-mentioned mitigating factors may occur. That is when content regulation discourse is relevant.

But there are situations which do not fit this scenario—for example, when the harm is produced without, or only with very insignificant, mental intermediation by the members of the audience, and when we can scarcely count on the audience offering up the aforementioned mitigating factors as 'counter-speech'. 'Fighting words' is a paradigmatic category of speech where the mental intermediation of the audience plays almost no role in producing the harm. The harm occurs in the moment, and by the very fact of uttering certain words in a certain fashion, and the fact that the persuasion of hearers is not instrumental to the production of harm implies the inappositeness of describing the situation in terms of the 'viewpoint' or 'content' of the speech. Another paradigmatic example is child pornography, insofar as the harm consists fundamentally in a crime committed against children and recorded for the production of such films or pictures. The same harm occurs when national secrets are passed through

[11] See Schauer, *Free Speech* (n. 10) 9.

communicative action to an enemy, or in insider trading, also through passing of information. The fact that such actions do not usually register in our minds as 'speech', for the purposes of the protection of freedom of speech, may largely be due to the fact that the usual effects connected with speech, which render it deserving of presumptive protection and having to do with the effects of persuasion, do not occur here. There is no act of persuading anyone of anything in order to produce instantaneous harm; there is no 'perlocutionary'[12] effect of the speech which is required for production of harm. In such cases we do not need any content- or viewpoint-based account, because it does not add anything to an account in terms of harm.

Of course, there will be also cases in which it may be difficult to assign a given expression to one or another of the categories just described, and there will be expressions which have mixed consequences: both harm in terms of persuading others as well as instant damage to the target (defamation may be an example of a mixed case, where the wrong consists both in immediately infringing the dignity of the defamed person, and in lowering her reputation in the eyes of others). There will be also cases where, although the wrong requires mental intermediation, the likelihood of the usual mitigating factors in effectively countering the effect of bad speech is small (e.g. consider the case of misleading advertisements, where we normally have limited capacity to verify the truthfulness of ads before we have harmed ourselves by relying on them). But for our purposes here, a highly stylized distinction between the two categories of harm-producing speech is sufficient. In the first category, when the harm is produced by the 'mental intermediation' of the audience, the language of viewpoint or content is perfectly apposite because the causation of harm is necessarily dependent upon the content or viewpoint being absorbed mentally by the audience. In the second category, the factor of harm-producing intermediate processes of understanding, interpreting, and absorbing the message is insignificant. We can therefore talk about harm directly, in isolation from content or viewpoint, because the latter concepts do not add anything to what we already know: that certain kinds of speech produce harm.

There is one other theory which figures highly in arguments supporting the 'special' character of speech and its exemption from the ordinary harm calculus: namely, that the government has greater incentives to overestimate the harms of speech compared with the costs of non-speech.[13] From this perspective, it is not so much that speech per se is special but rather that governmental *responses* to speech are particularly troubling because of the patterns of incentives affecting governmental actions. The incentive-based theory stems from the commonsensical observation that lawmakers tend to be self-interested and, for

[12] On 'perlocutions', see John Searle, *Speech Acts* (Cambridge University Press 1969) 45–47.
[13] See Schauer, *Free Speech* (n. 10) 80–85.

that reason, have fundamentally distorted perceptions of what constitutes the harm to be averted by legislative action. They will, understandably enough, be likely to view strong criticisms of their actions with antipathy and suspicion, and they will perceive them as harmful to the public good. In reasoning about the legal restrictions that they contemplate, they will tend to neglect the incidences of overinclusion in a proposed legal restriction. Overinclusion in laws regulating freedom of speech means that a statute 'comprehends a substantial range of applications to activity protected by the First Amendment, in addition to the unprotected activities it legitimately prohibits'.[14] At the same time, the argument goes, legislators will tend to be excessively receptive to arguments for underinclusion, that is, the arguments which point to a need to expand a given restriction based upon allegedly similar cases. The argument is that legislators will tend to overestimate harm that affects their electoral chances and will underestimate possible harm produced by their own political activities. In order to compensate for this distortion produced by self-interest, it is necessary to enhance the importance of free speech, and consequently insulate it from the ordinary operation of the harm calculus.

This argument provides an additional reason to distinguish between different cases of harm-production by speech, along the lines just sketched: these incentives normally occur in the case of *political* speech, where the government may wish to protect itself against public scrutiny of its actions. This is, of course, a typically content- or viewpoint-oriented regulation, and we have very strong grounds to suspect the government of illicit motivations. But, in contrast, in those cases where harm is produced instantly, as in 'fighting words' or child pornography, we do not have any special reasons to suspect the government of a self-serving miscalculation of harms and benefits, and so no special presumption against regulation is justified. That is why, also under this theory, a distinction between content-based and harm-based restrictions is warranted, and corresponds to a distinction between, respectively, restrictions which trigger high levels of suspicion of illicit motives, and those which are compatible with PR.

2. Content, Subject Matter, and Viewpoint

So far in this chapter I have been treating content-based regulations in an undifferentiated manner, but now is the time to move on by making a distinction between content-based (as a broader notion) and viewpoint-based (as a narrower notion) restrictions. These two notions are sometimes used interchangeably, and the very idea of a viewpoint-based approach is sometimes captured by the concept of 'content-based' restrictions. In one of the most oft-quoted phrases

[14] *Turchick v. United States*, 561 F.2d 719, 721 (8th Cir. 1977), footnote omitted.

in the First Amendment canon, Justice Marshall said: 'above all else, the First Amendment means that the government has no power to restrict expression because of its message, its ideas, its subject matter, or its content.'[15] And to reinforce the impression that he really *meant* it, he added: 'Any restriction on expressive activity because of its content would completely undercut the "profound national commitment to the principle that debate on public issues should be uninhibited, robust, and wide open".'[16] But this is an obvious overstatement, which cannot be taken seriously either as an account of the First Amendment law or as a normative proposition. Regarding the first point (descriptive), if Marshall's statement were to be taken at face value, it would, for instance, completely undermine the legally established (and perfectly reasonable) idea of a hierarchy of categories of speech which call for varying degrees of legal protection under the US First Amendment. Think, for instance, of standards of protection for political speech,[17] and for commercial speech,[18] not to mention maliciously defamatory speech of non-public figures,[19] or obscene speech.[20] In addition, Marshall's proposition is formulated in a categorical mode ('*no* power', '*any* restriction', '*completely* undercut') while, under the First Amendment authoritative doctrine, the prohibition on content restrictions is only presumptive, and can be overridden under a sufficiently high standard of scrutiny. What Marshall presents as an absolute prohibition is merely a manner of describing the very exacting scrutiny of governmental regulations of speech. Second, Marshall's statement is not attractive as a normative proposition: a law which would attach equal importance (and provide equal protection) to a graphic depiction of sexual intercourse as to a political speech in an election campaign would be morally unappealing.

To be sure, one can appreciate the reasons for the position according to which *any* differentiation of restriction based on substance of speech is objectionable. The principle that 'a court should not attempt to differentiate or allow the state to differentiate the value of particular messages'[21] can, at first blush, claim support from powerful libertarian arguments. The risk of entrusting an authoritative body with the power of assigning a different value to different categories of speech, even before they consider the harm of specific speech, is manifest. But demanding a uniform standard is unrealistic and normatively unattractive. Even in the United States, which may be seen as the paragon of a strongly libertarian approach to protection of speech, 'it is clear that some speech may be regulated not merely because it is harmful but also because the government need not, for

15 *Police Department of Chicago v. Mosley*, 408 U.S. 92, 95 (1972).
16 Ibid. 96, quoting *New York Times v. Sullivan*, 376 U.S. 254, 270 (1964).
17 See, e.g., *Whitney v. California*, 274 U.S. 357 (1927).
18 See, e.g., 44 *Liquormart Inc. v. Rhode Island*, 517 U.S. 484 (1996).
19 See, e.g., *Gertz v. Robert Welch Inc.*, 418 U.S. 323 (1974).
20 See, e.g., *Miller v. California*, 413 U.S. 15 (1973).
21 Archibald Cox, 'The Supreme Court, 1979 Term—Foreword: Freedom of Expression in Burger Court' (1980) 94 *Harvard Law Review* 1, 28.

that category of expression, meet the ordinary, highly protective standards for regulating speech'.[22] Most importantly, uniformity of levels of scrutiny could be, ironically, damaging to the general system of protection of speech. Dispensing with the hierarchy of categories of speech which call for varying degrees of legal protection would, more likely than not, result in a lowering of speech protection across the board. As an illustration of this effect, consider a *Harvard Law Review* note about the Supreme Court's 1990 decision on child pornography *Osborne v. Ohio*.[23] The majority applied an 'intermediate scrutiny' approach, but failed to expressly classify the speech in question as of 'low value'. This failure, according to the (anonymous) authors of the Review Note, could 'erode the protection of 'core' speech as well'.[24] As the Note further suggested: '[b]ecause *Osborne* did not openly endorse the "low-value" approach, lower courts might conclude that child pornography is core speech and that *Osborne* is an example of a relaxed strict scrutiny analysis.'[25] As a result, '[c]ourts could view *Osborne* as generally relaxing the strict scrutiny requirements that the government have a compelling interest in order to regulate protected speech . . .'[26]

So Marshall's statement that 'the government has no power to restrict expression because of its message, its ideas, its subject matter, or its content' is not only not reflective of the authoritative understanding of the First Amendment, but also may have, ironically, non-libertarian consequences for the overall system of freedom of expression. From our point of view in this chapter, Marshall's dictum is additionally misleading because it unhelpfully merges subject matter-based and viewpoint-based approaches (for the sake of clarity, and consistently with vocabulary meaning, I will now be using these two different notions which belong to a broader class of 'content-based' restrictions and contrast them with 'content-neutral' ones). It has been widely accepted that the latter restrictions (viewpoint-based) are more pernicious, and should be regarded with more suspicion, than the former ones (subject matter-based). As Justice Stevens observed in his concurrence in the famous cross-burning case: 'As we have long recognized, subject-matter regulations generally do not raise the same concerns of government censorship and the distortion of public discourse presented by viewpoint regulations. Thus, in upholding subject matter regulations, we have carefully noted that viewpoint-based discrimination was not implicated.'[27] The question is, how can this difference be explained?

Before attempting to answer this question, it is worth noting that something like the idea of 'viewpoint neutrality' is present in the ways other legal systems protect freedom of speech, even if different terminologies are used. In Germany,

[22] Cass R. Sunstein, *Democracy and the Problem of Free Speech* (Free Press 1993) 124.
[23] 495 U.S. 103 (1990).
[24] Note, 'The Supreme Court, Leading Cases', (1990) 104 *Harvard Law Review* 129, 245.
[25] Ibid, footnote omitted.
[26] Ibid.
[27] 505 U.S. 434 (Stevens J. concurring).

for instance, an idea very similar to the rule of viewpoint neutrality was articulated by the Federal Constitutional Court when interpreting the constitutional requirement that any legal limitation to (inter alia) constitutional freedom of speech (Art 5.1.1. of the Basic Law) must be contained in the 'provisions of general laws' (Art. 5.2). In a 2009 decision of the Court which encapsulates its evolving jurisprudence on freedom of speech,[28] it has been observed as meaning that 'the legal interest in question [which justifies the restriction] must be protected per se, without regard to a specific opinion … and that links to content must therefore be neutral with regard to the various political currents and ideologies'.[29] Elsewhere in the same judgment, the Court held that the 'generality' of laws meant that 'they prove to be consistent and abstractly thought in terms of the legal interest and are designed *regardless of views* which are found to be held in specific instances'.[30]

What is perhaps ironic is that the German Court undertook to elaborate its understanding of viewpoint neutrality in a decision which *upheld* the constitutionality of a law that is definitely *not* viewpoint-neutral: a 2005 amendment to the Criminal Code which makes it a punishable crime to approve of, glorify, or justify the National Socialist rule of arbitrary force. But the Court made it clear that its approval for this law is a clear exception to the 'generality' requirement, or 'an exception to the ban on the special legislation for opinion-related laws'.[31] The exception, the Court stressed, is justified on the basis of 'the unique nature of the crimes committed under the historical National Socialist rule of arbitrary force and the resultant responsibility for the Federal Republic of Germany'.[32] Exception aside, the Court's understanding of 'generality' bears a strong resemblance to US-style viewpoint neutrality. Further, and importantly for our purposes here, the Court explicitly links the issue of generality (viewpoint neutrality) with legislative purposes/intentions: for the law to be general, in a requisite sense,

> their *purpose* may not aim to ensure that protective measures are taken towards impacts of specific expressions of opinion that remain purely intellectual. The *intention* of preventing statements with content that is damaging or dangerous in their conceptual consequence rescinds the principle of freedom of opinion itself and is illegitimate …[33]

Another legal system in which an idea similar to 'viewpoint neutrality' can be seen is New Zealand. In a comment on the High Court's decision about a

[28] BVerfG v. 4.11.2009, 1 BvR 2150/08—*Wunsiedel*, BVerfGE 124, 300.
[29] Ibid, para. 33.
[30] Ibid, para. 35, emphasis added.
[31] Ibid, para. 41.
[32] Ibid, para. 45.
[33] Ibid, para. 49, emphases added.

swastika display on a residential house,[34] Bede Harris, a legal scholar, used terms identical to the 'viewpoint neutrality' discourse in criticizing the judgment. While agreeing with the outcome (the Court upheld a ban on swastikas), Harris claimed that a similar conclusion could have been reached 'on considerations of time and place', and without any regard to the content or the viewpoint of the expression. 'The issue of viewpoint neutrality is central to freedom of expression, yet was not addressed in the judgment', Harris deplored, and added: '[t]he result was a decision which, by restricting the ambit of permissible expression to what conforms to prevailing notions of ideological acceptability, quietly legitimated viewpoint censorship.'[35] Regardless of the merits of this argument with regard to that particular court judgment, it is clear that by using the harsh notion of 'viewpoint censorship', the author endorsed a position of strong distaste towards regulating the speech based on the viewpoint it expresses.

The distinction between viewpoint neutrality and subject-matter neutrality makes good sense if we adopt the template of a motive-oriented approach to freedom of speech jurisprudence. It is not the case that subject-matter regulations do not implicate motive scrutiny, or even that they necessarily implicate motive scrutiny to a lesser degree than viewpoint regulations. But in real life, viewpoint regulations evoke improper motivations more urgently and obviously than subject-matter motivations. Geoffrey Stone captured this difference well when saying that 'the probability that an improper motivation has tainted a decision to restrict expression is far greater when the restriction is directed at a particular idea, viewpoint, ... than when it is content-neutral'[36] (note, incidentally, the unfortunate tendency to contrast the viewpoint approach to *content* neutrality as if these two options exhaust the possibilities, thus leaving subject-matter restrictions outside the dichotomy). The main point I am making here is that, within a subset of content regulations, viewpoint regulations implicate and reveal *different* motivations than subject-matter regulations do, and that this more invidious character of the motivations triggering viewpoint regulations explains our higher degree of hostility towards viewpoint than towards subject-matter regulations.

A hint about the nature of the difference may be suggested by an already quoted phrase in Justice Stevens' concurrence in *R.A.V.*: 'subject-matter regulations generally do not raise the same concerns of government censorship and the distortion of public discourse presented by viewpoint regulations.'[37] These two defects of viewpoint regulations (governmental censorship and discourse distortion) are allegedly missing from subject-matter regulations. But if so,

[34] *Zdrahal v. Wellington City Council* [1995] 1 NZLR 700 (HC).

[35] Bede Harris, 'Viewpoint Neutrality and Freedom of Expression in New Zealand', (1996) 8 *Otago Law Review* 515, 537–38.

[36] Stone, 'Content Regulation' (n. 5) 230.

[37] 505 U.S. 434 (Stevens J. concurring).

then *what* is the concern about subject-matter regulation that triggers a higher scrutiny than content neutral regulations (i.e. regulations of time, place, and manner—which, after all, may greatly reduce the circulation of ideas and information), though admittedly lower than for viewpoint regulations? There must be something about subject-matter regulations that makes them symptomatic of *some* wrongful governmental motives, but not *that* wrongful as is for restrictions based on viewpoint.

Before suggesting an underlying distinction in the defects of both types of regulations, let me go back to Justice Marshall's opinion in *Mosley*. Soon after making his extravagant claim about the absolute impermissibility of any content-based regulations, Marshall went on to say: 'Necessarily ... government may not grant the use of a forum to people whose views it finds acceptable, but deny use to those wishing *to express less favored* or more controversial views. And it may not select *which issues are worth discussing or debating* in public facilities.'[38] This statement clearly belongs to the vexed and excessively complicated 'public forum' doctrine, which it will be prudent to stay away from in this chapter, but for our purposes we may treat it as a helpful characterization of a difference between viewpoint-based restrictions (in the first sentence of the quoted passage) and subject-matter restrictions (in the second sentence). For Marshall, both are equally reprehensible from a constitutional point of view, but we do not need to endorse this implication. It is not particularly hard to reconstruct a possible defect in governmental motivation for the first type of restriction: it is an official dislike (or its opposite, official preference) for a particular viewpoint, ideology, or opinion. As Geoffrey Stone put it, referring to a famous formula by Alexander Meiklejohn, 'by effectively excising a specific message from public debate, [a viewpoint discriminatory law] mutilates "the thinking process of the community"'.[39] So the main deplorable result of such laws is that they skew public debate, rather than that they limit or impoverish public discourse.

To be sure, the 'skewing of public debate' may also occur as a result of arguably content-neutral regulations.[40] But when a restriction limits public expression in a content-neutral manner, the pattern of distortion is largely erratic and unpredictable. It may just be an unfortunate case that viewpoint A is hit harder than viewpoint B. But if such a disproportionate impact is by and large random, and if it could not be anticipated, much less intended, then it is perhaps deplorable but not unfair. There are, however, circumstances in which the legislators and judges *do* have a way of anticipating which viewpoints will be disadvantaged and which will be favoured. If they then tailor a visibly content-neutral restriction to

[38] 408 U.S. 92, 96, emphases added.

[39] Stone, 'Content Regulation' (n. 5) 198, quoting Alexander Meiklejohn, Political Freedom (Harper 1960) 27.

[40] See Martin Redish, 'The Content Distinction in First Amendment Analysis', (1981) 34 *Stanford Law Review* 113, 131.

fit this anticipation in order to achieve a specific result which favours one side of the controversy, then that will be an example of indirect viewpoint discrimination. Consider a restriction on leafletting, supported officially by arguments about reducing litter. It may look like a content-neutral restriction (all leaflets are prohibited, regardless of content), but may operate as indirect viewpoint discrimination because one party to a particular controversy may lack the resources to propagate their cause by other means, and this financial disadvantage may well correlate with a particular ideology. So when we contemplate cases of viewpoint discrimination, it is proper to also include indirect discrimination in this category. As with the concept of discrimination *simpliciter*, the recognition of indirect discrimination does not undermine the distinction between discriminatory and neutral regulations.

Just as it is important to insist that a clear line be drawn between viewpoint-based and content-neutral restrictions, so it is important to draw a principled line, within the category of content-based regulations, between those which are subject matter-based and those which are viewpoint-based. This was the main question raised by *Rosenberger v. Rector & Visitors of the University of Virginia*,[41] and the different answers given to the question of whether a university's denial of funding for a religious student newspaper was a subject-matter regulation or a viewpoint-based regulation were determinative of the outcome. The majority believed the latter, and largely on this ground, decided that the denial of funds was a violation of the First Amendment. In the opinion for the Court, Justice Kennedy tends to blur the distinction between both types of regulation ('the distinction is not a precise one'),[42] but in the end concludes that 'viewpoint discrimination is the proper way to interpret the University's objection to [the student newspaper]' because the University did not 'exclude religion as a subject matter' but rather 'select[ed] for disfavored treatment those student journalistic efforts with religious editorial viewpoints'.[43] This sounds like an ad hoc rationalization. Without inquiring into the likely *motives* for the denial of funds, Kennedy does not tell us why he interpreted the restriction as based on a religious viewpoint as contrasted to a restriction based on religion as the subject matter of the newspaper. Consider, for a moment, an analogy between restrictions on religious expression (as was the case in *Rosenberger*) with restrictions on *political* expression. When a restriction does not specify any particular political view to be affected by a regulation, a restriction on political speech, per se, seems to be better characterized as subject matter-based rather than viewpoint-based. And, incidentally, *this* is how the US Supreme Court characterized the exclusion of political speech from various fora as consistent with the First Amendment. For example, the Court upheld a municipal public transport ban on political advertising on trains,

[41] 515 U.S. 819 (1995).
[42] Ibid. 831.
[43] Ibid. 831.

upheld a ban on the entry of political speakers into a military base, and upheld the exclusion of political speech from a charity drive in a federal workplace.[44] In all these cases, the outcome was due to the characterization of political speech as subject matter, not viewpoint. Why would 'religion' then describe a viewpoint? As the result of such characterization, political speech receives lower protection compared with religious speech.

The point I want to make is not that the distinction is unstable, but rather that it can only be intelligibly drawn if we compare the evil captured by the 'subject-matter regulation' category with that described by 'viewpoint regulation', and that this will inevitably lead us to an enquiry into legislative motives. And this is the burden of Justice Souter's argument in the section of his dissent in *Rosenberger* that addresses the free speech clause of the First Amendment. He emphasizes that the relevant inquiry is 'not merely whether the University bases its funding decisions on subject-matter of student speech', but rather whether the University is 'impermissibly distinguishing among competing viewpoints'.[45] These are, for him (as for the argument pressed in the present chapter) two distinctive questions. Further, he states (echoing an earlier judgment of the Court) that in distinguishing between the two types of regulation, 'the government's purpose is the controlling consideration'.[46] This resonates with the argument that the two types of regulations correspond to distinctive governmental motives, or purposes, both of which are prima facie objectionable, but differently so.

As far as the motive behind viewpoint-based restrictions is concerned, it can be discerned from the evil that such restrictions produce: we infer here, as we do so often in the law, from effects to motives/purposes. As Justice Souter says in his dissent, 'the prohibition on viewpoint discrimination serves that important purpose of the Free Speech Clause, which is to bar the government from skewing public debate'.[47] As we have already seen, the 'skewing of public debate' by the authorities is an evil which can be properly targeted by the legal principles of the protection of speech. Souter helpfully states the obvious: 'It is precisely this element of taking sides in a public debate that identifies viewpoint discrimination and makes it the most pernicious of all distinctions based on content.'[48] Governmental partisanship is thus the main sin targeted by the principle of viewpoint neutrality. Partisanship (favouritism) and intolerance (official dislike) are two sides of the same coin.

[44] See *Lehman v. City of Shaker Heights*, 418 U.S. 298 (1974) (public transport); *Greer v. Spock*, 424 U.S. 828 (1976) (military base); *Cornelius v. NAACP Legal Defense & Ed. Fund*, 473 U.S. 788 (1985) (charity drive).

[45] 515 U.S. 893 (Souter J. dissenting).

[46] Ibid. 894 (quoting *Ward v. Rock Against Racism*, 491 U.S. 781, 791 (1989)).

[47] Ibid. 894.

[48] Ibid. 895.

3. Intolerance and Paternalism in Regulations of Speech

If intolerance is the proper word to describe the attitude behind viewpoint-based regulation, what is the likely and at the same time reprehensible motivation for a second defect, namely the government's selection of issues worth discussing and debating, and by implication, issues not worth discussing in public? Let me anticipate my conclusions before I develop my argument: the likely motive behind such preference or reprobation for an entire subject matter is one of paternalism, and the sort of paternalism implicated in subject-matter restrictions is likely to be *less* objectionable than the sort of intolerance for a point of view discernible through viewpoint regulation. This explains the lesser antipathy to subject matter-based restrictions compared to viewpoint regulations.

In terms of *effects*, the distinction between the two types of governmental intervention is clear but is normatively non-conclusive: subject-matter interventions impoverish public debate by removing a particular issue from the agenda, while viewpoint regulations skew the debate in a particular direction, favoured by the government. Both of these effects may be deplored as a case of governmental 'censorship', but they work differently, and it is plausible that the effects of agenda-narrowing are more tolerable than the effects of privileging a particular viewpoint. Suppose public university *A* refuses to fund any student media activities (a student newspaper, for instance) having as their object a discussion of religious issues, from whatever perspective, and then under a different scenario, university *B* refuses funding only to pro-religious (or only atheistic) groups.[49] The latter effect *may be* seen to be more reprehensible because the debate has been biased in a direction expected by the rulemaker, university *B*. But is it a convincing interpretation? After all, the impoverishment of the debate in terms of subject-removal by university *A* may also have devastating effects on public discourse. And there may be something instantly paradoxical about accepting the legitimate power of the public body to *entirely* remove a particular subject from the forum, but not to prohibit only some viewpoints while leaving others intact: doesn't the greater power include the lesser? So we really need to reconstruct the most likely *motives* of official action in both cases to appreciate the different status of both types of restrictions.

Continuing our example of a public university refusing any funding to a student group which intends to discuss religious issues (university *A*): a condition of the grant is that religion will not be on the agenda. What reasons for such a regulation applying to the entire subject matter might the university have? To make our thinking sharper, we must exclude, for the sake of argument, indirect viewpoint discrimination: we must assume that we have controlled for a

[49] This example roughly corresponds to the facts of *Rosenberger v. The University of Virginia*, 515 U.S. 819 (1995).

situation where the subject is a proxy for a viewpoint. And we need to bracket purely legal (institutional) arguments, to the effect that a constitutional provision in a given legal system, as authoritatively interpreted by courts, permits subject matter but not viewpoint-based regulations of speech. We need to find the likely moral or political arguments, because what we search for is not a purely formal characterization of official action but the best, or the most likely, *justification* of such action.

In my view, the most likely justification for subject-matter regulation in our imaginary university *A* would be the view that discussing religion is, at least under some circumstances and in some settings (those which are relevant to the university funding) not good *for the discussants themselves*, for instance because it is divisive, brings or amplifies antagonisms within the student body, diverts their attention from more pressing issues or from their studies, etc. Now, each of these rationales may sound silly (and they probably *are* silly, to some extent), but they are not outright absurd, and they are not inconceivable as rationales for such a refusal. In fact, they seem to me to be the most likely and plausible explanations for such an action. And this is, of course, a paternalistic argument par excellence: intervention in an action for the benefit of willing, adult participants, against their avowed preferences.

As we know, no regulation is based on a single rationale, and we can think of some other, non-paternalistic motivations for the prohibition in our example: for instance, the university may fear public disorder on campus arising out of religious antagonisms. More generally, issue suppression may be often seen as a condition of orderly and constructive debate. 'Gag rules', a phenomenon defined and analysed by Stephen Holmes, already mentioned in Chapter 3, are often a way of making a debate orderly, and indeed, of making it possible. As Holmes puts it, 'strategic self-censorship seems to be an almost universally employed technique of self-management and self-rule'.[50] So what matters for the characterization of a regulation as paternalistic (and for the normative implications of such characterization) is which of the rationales is dominant. The public order rationales seem to me to be clearly secondary, pretextual, and largely disingenuous, because these effects are relatively easy to control and cabin without interfering with speech. In contrast, paternalistic concerns are not as easily addressed without minimizing the likelihood of discussions about religion at the campus, and to refuse funding seems like a reasonable means to that end. But under different scenarios, subject-matter restrictions are more congruent with non-paternalistic rationales. In its decisions belonging to the public forum doctrine, the US Supreme Court has long established that in a so-called 'non-public forum', access may be 'based on subject matter and speaker identity so long as the distinctions drawn

[50] Stephen Holmes, 'Gag Rules or the Politics of Omission', in Jon Elster and Rune Slagstad (eds.), *Constitutionalism and Democracy* (Cambridge University Press 1988) 57.

are reasonable in light of the purpose served by the forum and are viewpoint neutral'.[51] Earlier, the Court had similarly determined that in a public property which is not technically a traditional public forum, in addition to content-neutral restrictions, 'the State may reserve the forum for its intended purposes, communicative or otherwise, as long as the regulation on speech is reasonable and not an effort to suppress expression merely because public officials oppose the speaker's view'.[52] So here we have a clear distinction between the dreaded viewpoint regulations and subject-matter regulations, which may be perfectly reasonable because they are consistent with the purposes of the forum (in the case of *Perry*, it was about access to the interschool mail system). In such cases, the rationale for the different normative status of viewpoint- and subject-matter regulations is clear: the latter may have a good PR-compatible rationale. After all, as already mentioned when invoking 'gag rules', topic suppression may be aimed at having an orderly discussion (think about agenda-free public meetings).[53]

To see that paternalistic motivations are the likely, though not the only, triggers of many subject-matter restrictions, consider the landmark decision in 1992 in which the High Court of Australia struck down, as contrary to an implicit constitutional right of the freedom of political communication, a legislative provision which would prohibit the broadcast of paid political advertisements during the election campaign, and instead impose upon broadcasters a duty to provide free time to political parties, according to a complex formula.[54] One of the two dissenting judges, Justice Brennan, reconstructed (approvingly) the legislative aims behind the regulation, primarily as the 'minimising of the risk of corruption of the Parliament and the reduction of an untoward advantage of wealth in the formation of political opinion'.[55] Unlike the majority, Justice Brennan found the restrictions in question to be 'comfortably proportionate' to those important objects, the achievement of which would 'go far to ensuring an open and equal democracy'.[56] He then expressed the application of the proportionality principle in this context as follows: '[A] law may validly restrict a freedom of communication about political or economic matters' where it serves 'some other legitimate interest and it must be proportionate to the interest to be served.'[57]

Justice Brennan characterized the regulation in question clearly in terms of subject-matter restrictions—though he did not use these words. This is, admittedly, only one of many ways of characterizing the restriction at stake; another would be to say, using US constitutional language, that it is a 'time, place, and

[51] *Lamb's Chapel v. Center Moriches Union Free School District*, 508 U.S. 384, 392–93 (1993).
[52] *Perry Education Association v. Perry Local Educators' Association*, 46 U.S. 37, 46 (1983).
[53] See Stephen Holmes, 'Precommitment and the Paradox of Democracy' in Jon Elster and Rune Slagstad (eds.), *Constitutionalism and Democracy* (Cambridge University Press 1988) 195, 232–35.
[54] *Australian Capital Television Pty Ltd & NSW v. The Commonwealth* (1992) 177 CLR 106.
[55] Ibid.156.
[56] Ibid. 161.
[57] Ibid. 150.

manner' type of restriction. It applied only to paid advertisements in broadcast media: other equally 'political' contents were beyond the regulation's scope. As Justice Brennan observed, 'All news, current affairs and talk-back programmes are unaffected by the restrictions. The print media are unaffected. The other methods of disseminating political views such as public meetings, door knocks and the distribution of handbills are unaffected'.[58] This is all true. However, it is equally true that within the content-neutral category of 'paid advertisements on broadcast media', the regulation used a subject-matter distinction between political and all other advertisements. So, for our purposes it is clearly a subject-matter regulation.

In the course of his argument, Justice Brennan explains why such a restriction does not raise serious problems: 'Television advertising is brief, its brevity tends to trivialise the subject; it cannot deal in any depth with the complex issues of government. Its appeal is therefore directed more to the emotions than to the intellect.'[59] He then goes on to summarize some empirical studies and parliamentary reports, both in Australia and in the United States, which show the distorting and generally negative impact of political advertising. While he acknowledges that 'the formation of political judgment is not solely an intellectual exercise', he nevertheless would grant the Parliament authority 'to make a low assessment of the contribution made by electronic advertising to the formation of political judgment'.[60]

Now this opinion clearly smacks of paternalism. While not stated explicitly, one way of understanding Justice Brennan's message is that it is actually bad for citizens to form their political judgements based on TV advertisements. They risk having their rationality distorted, and of having their 'prejudices, fears and uncertainties' reinforced, as a result of 'the repetition of catchwords until they attain truth by familiarity'.[61] Admittedly, this is not the only reading of Justice Brennan's argument (another may be through the collective harm to democracy), and not the only argument in defence of the provisions under scrutiny (the main one is to reduce the chief impediment in political participation).[62] But it is *a* plausible argument: people who want to form their electoral choices in a rational and responsible manner are actually harmed (the argument goes) when exposed to political advertising. They may also be harmed by exposure to any *other* advertising, of course, but this other harm does not register with the purposes of the argument in which a right is defined as freedom of *political* communication (with no right of free communication per se asserted, as is the case in the Australian constitutional system). It therefore shows, as my broader

[58] Ibid. 160.
[59] Ibid. 160.
[60] Ibid. 161.
[61] Ibid. 161.
[62] Ibid. 155.

argument in this context suggests, that a paternalistic motivation is a likely ingredient of many subject-matter restrictions on speech.

But what difference does it make whether a regulation is based on intolerance (as is the case of viewpoint-based restrictions) or on paternalism (as is the case of subject matter-based regulations)? Put bluntly, why is paternalism *less bad* than intolerance, so that the difference can properly explain the different degrees of scrutiny of viewpoint-based and subject matter-based regulations, and their associated motivations? The best explanation must show that paternalism—at least of the sort likely to underlie subject-matter regulations—is a less objectionable moral position than the official intolerance of a particular opinion, as discernible in viewpoint-based regulations. And this will be the burden of the argument below.

First, however, it is important to realize that both positions, paternalism and intolerance, are significantly *different* from each other. Paternalism is not intolerance: it would be a misnomer to characterize the act of removing a particular subject matter from public debate as 'intolerance' towards a particular *topic*. Indeed, it is hard to understand how a rational person may 'dislike' an issue (as opposed to disliking a particular 'take' on an issue). One may of course dislike the very fact that a particular issue is debated, but this is just the *effect* of a motive which still needs to be established: it is merely an announcement rather than a rationale for one's desire to remove a subject. One may, for instance, dislike the fact of discussing electoral politics in the workplace or in an army barracks, but it must be an attitude based on some further reasons which are not captured by the concept of intolerance or dislike.

Also, and vice versa, intolerance is not paternalism: when we are objecting to a particular viewpoint, and believe that it should be suppressed, rarely do we articulate such an objection because of the concerns for those who share and express that viewpoint. Suppose that someone advances the principle that the majority's dislike of an opinion is a sufficient ground to warrant the prohibition of that opinion. There is nothing paternalistic about such a principle because paternalism occurs when someone's liberty is restricted on the basis of an argument about *that person's* good. However, protecting the majority against offence restricts the speaker's liberty for the alleged benefit of the hearer—*another person* who, it is urged, wants to be protected against the unpleasant sensation of being offended.

We may generalize about the last point. It is not plausible to believe that viewpoint-based restrictions can be based on paternalistic motives, that is, upon a genuine concern for the speakers rather than the hearers. If expressing a view is seen as harmful to the speaker (a condition of paternalistic intervention) then it may be for one of the following reasons: (1) because the lawmakers believe that acting upon a given view will be harmful to the speakers; or (2) because they believe that the view is so immoral that the very act of expressing it causes a self-inflicted moral harm; or (3) in order to protect the speaker against a violent reaction by a hostile audience. As far as (1) is concerned, such a motivation seems irrational: we may well protect persons from self-inflicted harms by prohibiting an action (for instance, driving without a safety belt), but not by prohibiting the *expression of support* for an action. Restrictions on expressions of a particular view in order to prevent harm resulting from acting upon that view may be rational only insofar as we want to protect the *hearers* (who, as we fear, may be persuaded to take a harmful course), but not the speakers. It is therefore not paternalistic. As far as (2) is concerned, the motivation is not genuinely paternalistic but moralistic. To say that we may prevent self-inflicted 'moral harm' is a manner of speaking that an expression which is considered immoral can be prohibited. This is because the only sense that can be made of the notion of self-inflicted 'moral harm' is that the person failed to meet what we consider to be proper moral standards.[63] Only (3) is a genuine paternalistic motive. This, however, seems to apply to exceptional and rare circumstances only: we may think of a great number of viewpoint-based restrictions where the motive of protecting the speakers against violent response is highly unlikely. And while paternalistic arguments *may* support restrictions on unpopular expressions, it is a widely accepted principle, in particular in the United States, that a hostile audience per se should not motivate a restriction on speech, the argument being that such a restriction would amount to a 'heckler's veto' to an unpopular view. So it is probable that the most likely (even if exceptional) paternalistic support for viewpoint restrictions lacks sufficient legal traction: it is rejected not because it is paternalistic, but because its adoption endangers the system of the protection of unpopular speech.

So far, I have argued that, typically, viewpoint restrictions are based on legislative motivations which may be characterized as intolerance, while subject-matter restrictions are based on paternalism. It is time now to address the following question: what does it matter? Since viewpoint restrictions are normally (and properly) viewed as more problematic than subject-matter restrictions, and the former should trigger a more searching scrutiny than the latter, the argument must be made that paternalism is a less reprehensible attitude for the legislators to take than intolerance.

I am not claiming of course that paternalism is a non-objectionable—much less that it is a benign—moral position. There may be some paternalistic restrictions which are intolerable, and on the other hand, there may be intolerance-based restrictions which are so mild as to be justifiable. So in abstract terms, it is difficult to argue that paternalism, as such, is less objectionable than intolerance.[64] And one can see why, in abstract terms, paternalism in the sphere of

[63] See Joel Feinberg, *The Moral Limits of the Criminal Law, Harm to Others*, vol. 1 (Oxford University Press 1984), 65–70.

[64] See Frederick Schauer, 'Categories and the First Amendment: A Play in Three Acts', (1981) 34 *Vanderbilt Law Review* 265, 285.

speech can be seen as anathema to free society. The central values which underlie freedom of speech: individual autonomy and self-fulfillment ('people will perceive their own best interests if only they are well enough informed')[65] as well as democratic self-government ('the people in our democracy are entrusted with the responsibility for judging and evaluating the relative merits of conflicting arguments'),[66] are the very values which are endangered by paternalistic intervention, which assumes that, at times, people are not the best judges of their interests. Restraining people for their own good is incompatible with the values of autonomy, self-fulfillment, and self-government which support a robust system of protection of freedom of speech.

But in the context of speech restrictions on a particular subject matter, some instances of paternalism may be compatible with (and under a stronger argument, even mandated by) the values of respect for individuals. This is for the reasons which were pressed in H.L.A. Hart's restatement of Mill's harm principle: the anti-paternalistic zeal of Mill was based on his belief in individual rationality and knowledge which is unpersuasive today. 'Mill carried his protests against paternalism to lengths that may now appear fantastic',[67] Hart famously asserted. There is no denying that paternalism in the area of freedom of speech may often be deeply offensive: for instance, to argue that some information should be limited because it will merely upset the hearers is incompatible with the fundamental dignity of the hearers as mature individuals who can make their own judgement about the speech they are exposed to. But paternalism endorsed as a solution to collective action problems, or to dilemmas resulting from imperfect knowledge or defective preference formation, need not be always offensive to the dignity of individuals. This is, more generally, the case when the removal of subject matter is considered good for the audience members *for reasons other than their alleged incapacity to evaluate information.*

Consider again the already used example of religious debates in a university. Whatever the reasons may be for the university's refusal to fund a religious discussion (university *A* in our example at the beginning of section 3 of this chapter), distrust of the audience based on suspicion that they will not be able to properly evaluate the information is unlikely to figure among them. This would be a truly reprehensible rationale, but the imaginary university's decision to deny funding would be very unlikely to stem from *that* paternalistic motive. Rather, the more likely argument would be that it will create greater divisiveness which is not good for participants.[68] To be sure, it is still a paternalistic intervention, but it is not as objectionable as if it were based on distrust of their good judgement.

[65] *Virginia Pharmacy Board v. Virginia Consumer Council*, 425 U.S. 748, 770 (1976).

[66] *First National Bank of Boston v. Bellotti*, 435 U.S. 765, 791 (1978) (footnote omitted).

[67] H.L.A. Hart, *Law, Liberty, and Morality* (Stanford University Press 1963) 32.

[68] In fact, the fear of divisiveness had been occasionally cited by the US Supreme Court as a major rationale for the Establishment Clause of the First Amendment, see *Lemon v. Kurtzman*, 403 U.S. 602, 622 (1971).

It is paternalistic in the broad sense of the word (because it is an unwanted intervention based on the perceived good of the person), but it is not paternalistic in the *offensive* meaning of the word, where individuals' actual preferences are displaced by the regulator. In the religion-on-campus example, the good of avoiding divisiveness may be recognized by the individuals themselves, even if they do not have the sufficient motivation to pursue it, not knowing how others will behave.

An act which imposes constraints upon a person's liberty for her own good, but which can be recognized by that person as necessary in order to achieve the goal espoused by that person, is not 'paternalistic' in a stronger, more objectionable sense. Rather it is the sort of paternalism which imposes constraints upon individual action in order to produce a collective good or to avoid a collective harm. Or, to put it somewhat differently, it consists of the foreclosure of certain individual actions that, if taken by many, would make everybody or nearly everybody worse off, and which people have an incentive to take unless assured that others will also abstain from an action producing sub-optimal collective results.

This variety of paternalism, resulting from an attempt to solve the Prisoner's Dilemma just described, has been recognized as not exactly fitting the usual premonitions against forcing people for their own good.[69] (I have already discussed this non-objectionable version of 'paternalism' in Chapter 1, section 1 of this book). In a genuine Prisoner's Dilemma, foreclosure of one avenue of action is a condition for the attainment of the optimal solution for every participant. In the absence of such a foreclosure (in our example, a restriction on a subject matter), a suboptimal result will be attained. It is therefore very likely that most of those whose freedom is restricted by a regulation would recognize that they are better off by virtue of universal compliance with the rule. So while the constraint is paternalistic in the broad sense of the word (because it restricts the choices open to individuals based on their own good), its motivation is not paternalistic because it does not depend on the argument that those people cannot recognize what is really good for them. Instead, it gives effect to their actual choices which can be implemented only when there is mutual compliance enforced by a legal constraint.

What criterions may be used to distinguish between an objectionable and a tolerable paternalism? The yardstick should surely be whether a limitation of freedom (here, freedom of speech) for the sake of the agent herself gives effect to a fundamental disrespect for her own sincerely held values. As Isaiah Berlin had suggested a long time ago, what is wrong about paternalism is that it is 'an insult to my conception of myself as a human being, determined to make my own life in accordance with my own (not necessarily rational or benevolent) purposes'.[70] But not every version of paternalism *sensu largo* (which occurs

[69] See, e.g., Cass R. Sunstein, 'Legal Interference with Private Preferences', (1986) 53 *University of Chicago Law Review* 1129, 1140–45.

[70] Isaiah Berlin, *Four Essays on Liberty* (Oxford University Press 1967) 157.

whenever a person's liberty is restricted for her own benefit) is at the same time such an objectionable paternalism *sensu stricto*, which expresses the sort of insult that Berlin was writing about. If a paternalistic (*sensu largo*) suppression of the subject matter from a particular forum correctly follows a calculus about the costs of an unrestricted forum to the participants in the forum themselves, there is no necessary objectionable paternalistic defect in it. Hence no actual values espoused by the participants are being overridden; it is not the case of Big Brother telling them, 'You may like to discuss this matter but we will not allow you because it is not good for you'. Instead, we are forced to behave in accordance with the values which we actually espouse, but which we tend to disregard sometimes in our conduct.

* * *

In this chapter, I have tried to establish that viewpoint-restrictions and subject-matter restrictions (two subcategories of a broader genus of content-based restrictions of freedom of speech) correspond to two perceived wrongful motivations in regulating speech: respectively, intolerance and paternalism. The fact that these two types of regulation are (plausibly) viewed as triggering unequal levels of scrutiny can be best explained by the fact that these two moral defects of motivations are of unequal moral weight: paternalism (at least in the forms likely to inform subject-matter regulation) is less objectionable than intolerance. This provides a normative explanation for the broader idea that the law of freedom of speech is often aimed at ferreting out improper motivations for regulation.

At times, however, we focus entirely on the effect of harm rather than improper motives. When the harm is produced instantly by the very fact of uttering certain words, and where the mental intermediation of the audience is insignificant in harm production, the language of wrongful motives is redundant: harm prevention is a sufficient justification for restriction of speech. But it is not embarrassing to a motive-based theory because these are 'easy cases' in which the distinctiveness of speech compared to non-speech disappears, and they often do not even register in our thinking as restrictions on freedom of speech.

7

Illicit Legislative Intentions in the Separation of State and Religion

In an important 2016 article, leading American constitutional scholar and Harvard Law School professor Richard H. Fallon forcefully defended the general proposition that courts (and most importantly, the United States Supreme Court) should abstain from relying exclusively on illicit legislative intent as the basis for invalidating a statute.[1] The Court should instead rely on 'substantive tests of invalidity' which, to Fallon, primarily meant the text and effects of the legislation under scrutiny. Intention is not totally irrelevant, but its function should be limited to determining the level of scrutiny: 'courts should normally subject a challenged statute to elevated judicial scrutiny whenever a challenger can demonstrate that an actual majority of the enacting legislature probably voted for it *with constitutionally forbidden intentions*'.[2] Considering that the fact of subjecting a law to 'elevated judicial scrutiny' is often determinative of the outcome of scrutiny (the higher the standard, the more likely the law is invalidated), in practice Fallon's proposition may be seen to resonate largely with unconstitutional motives theory, and its variant, namely public reason (PR).

In this chapter, I will show that the strong normative warning against using illicit legislative purposes as the exclusive basis for the invalidation of statutes is *not* respected in the field of separation of state and religion in several democratic constitutional systems. I will show that in the top courts in countries as different as the United States (sections 1 and 2), Australia (section 3), Canada (section 4), South Africa (section 5), Germany (section 6), and Israel (section 7), legislative motives serve as the crucial factor for judicial decisions: either for upholding the law when wrongful motives are absent (e.g. in Australia) or for invalidating the law when prohibited purposes are detected. In all the landmark judgments discussed below, the religious motives for the legislation were either viewed as exclusive grounds for the judgment or otherwise dominated the effects of legislation as factors for the determination of a judicial outcome.

[1] Richard H. Fallon, Jr., 'Constitutionally Forbidden Legislative Intent', (2016) 130 *Harvard Law Review* 523, 589.

[2] Ibid. 530, emphasis added.

Constitutional Public Reason. Wojciech Sadurski, Oxford University Press. © Wojciech Sadurski 2023.
DOI: 10.1093/oso/9780192869678.003.0007

1. The United States and Secular Legislative Purposes

There is no denying that the constitutional jurisprudence of the United States exerts a powerful gravitational pull upon other democratic constitutional systems. Therefore, a general introductory observation on the role of constitutionally forbidden legislative intent in the United States is in order. As a general proposition, it is true that American courts would only rarely—if ever—rest their judgment solely on the motive inquiry when deciding a constitutional case. In Chapter 6, I cited an important article by Caleb Nelson, who noted that 'courts rarely have to decide whether a statute can be held unconstitutional solely because of its purpose if the statute does not actually have the effects that the legislature intended'.[3] But there are some exceptional cases where purpose scrutiny belongs to an *explicit* legal test of constitutionality, as in the purpose tier of the First Amendment's Establishment Clause (which is also the case, as we shall see later in this chapter, with the Australian Constitution). In Establishment Clause of the First Amendment cases, and especially under the test articulated in *Lemon v. Kurtzman*, the Supreme Court has sometimes held statutes invalid if they have the primary, forbidden purpose of promoting or inhibiting religion.

Lemon v. Kurtzman and its progeny are useful to us as they show how the purpose, or motive, of a legislative action is objectified; it is not an actual subjective set of legislative intentions or motives. This was expanded over thirty years after *Lemon* by the Supreme Court in an important Establishment Clause case, in a sentence which contains a good (if non-exhaustive) litany of the objective indicia of purpose: 'The eyes that look to purpose belong to an objective observer, one who takes account of the traditional external signs that show up in the text, legislative history, and implementation of the statute, or comparable official act'.[3] In this way, it is illustrative of Rawls's 'Proviso', which allowed for the presence of 'comprehensive' doctrines in arguments about the law as long as proper public reasons *can* be provided for the law.[4] One of the main doctrines in US Supreme Court jurisprudence on the separation of state and religion is precisely the so-called '*Lemon* test'. In *Lemon v. Kurtzman*,[5] the Court established a three-part test for determining if a state had violated the non-establishment of religion requirement of the First Amendment: where state law and policy (1) must have a

[3] *McCreary County v. ACLU of Kentucky*, 545 U.S. 844, 862 (2005), internal quotation marks omitted.

[4] Rawls defines it as the 'requirement' which 'allows us to introduce into political discussion at any time our comprehensive doctrine, religious or nonreligious, provided that, in due course, we give properly public reasons to support the principles and policies our comprehensive doctrine is said to support': John Rawls, 'The Idea of Public Reason Revisited' in *The Law of Peoples* (Harvard University Press 1999) 144.

[5] 403 U.S. 602 (1971). The case concerned the constitutionality of state grants to religious schools; the Court held that aid to parochial schools violates the non-establishment clause of the First Amendment.

secular purpose; (2) its principal effect must not advance nor inhibit religion; and (3) it must not foster an excessive governmental entanglement with religion.

It is beyond the scope of this chapter to consider the Court's inconsistencies in the manner in which the *Lemon* test was subsequently applied, and it is irrelevant to this discussion that critics have questioned whether the *Lemon* test is useful in the first place.[6] What matters here is the first prong of the test: the secular purpose requirement which served, inter alia, to invalidate mandating classroom display of the Ten Commandments,[7] permitting prayer before public school athletic events,[8] or mandating display of the Ten Commandments in courthouses.[9] But notwithstanding the categorical phrasing of the secular purpose requirement, the existence of a purpose to aid religion will not itself doom a law so long as a legitimate non-religious, public purpose can be invoked to support it.[10] All the Supreme Court requires is that there is a secular justification *available* for governmental actions, even if the legislators did not actually have that justification in mind.[11]

What matters, therefore, is not so much *the actual motive* that legislators had, but the theoretical availability of a secular purpose for a given proposal. This arguably sounds weak and perhaps creates scope for uncertainty and malleability. Consider this famous example of a judicial disagreement about the existence or otherwise of a secular purpose. In *Edwards v. Aguillard*,[12] the US Supreme Court scrutinized the constitutionality of a state law, called the 'Balanced Treatment for Creation-Science and Evolution-Science Act', which forbade the teaching of evolution unless accompanied by instruction in so-called creation science. The majority concluded that the Act did not match the requirement of a secular purpose because, in the words of Justice Brennan, '[the] legislative history documents that the Act's primary purpose was to change the science curriculum of public schools in order to provide persuasive advantage to a particular religious doctrine ... [and that] embodies the religious belief that a supernatural creator was responsible for the creation of humankind'.[13] Preceding this conclusion was Justice Brennan's general statement that '[while] the Court is normally deferential to a State's articulation of a secular purpose, it is required that the statement of such purpose be sincere and not a sham'.[14] In a strongly worded dissent, Justice Scalia thought the invocations of secular purpose were perfectly sincere: 'The

[6] For a critique, see, e.g., Martha C. Nussbaum, *Liberty of Conscience* (Basic Books 2008) 287–91.

[7] *Stone v. Graham*, 449 U.S. 39 (1980).

[8] *Santa Fe Indep. School Dist. v. Doe*, 530 U.S. 290 (2000).

[9] *McCreary Cty. V. ACLU of Kentucky*, 545 U.S. 844 (2005).

[10] See Jerome A. Barron and C. Thomas Dienes, *First Amendment Law in a Nutshell* (West Publishing 1993) 411.

[11] See Mark Tushnet, *Taking the Constitution Away from the Courts* (Princeton University Press 1999) 77.

[12] 482 U.S. 578 (1987).

[13] Ibid. 592.

[14] Ibid. 587.

people of Louisiana, including those who are Christian fundamentalists, are quite entitled, *as a secular matter,* to have whatever scientific evidence there may be against evolution presented in their schools . . . .'[15]

This is an interesting and difficult case because it shows how malleable and indeterminate the detection of true motivations, as opposed to reasonable arguments, may be in practice. Brennan's judgment represents a non-deferential approach that refuses to manufacture reasonable arguments which *can be* provided for a given law and enquires into the most likely motivation that the lawmaker actually had for passing the law. Justice Scalia's approach is deferential to the lawmaker, and is oriented less towards discerning (through, say, legislative history, *travaux préparatoires*, the context for the adoption of a law, public debates accompanying it, etc.) any of the actual reasons that weighed on lawmakers' minds (he explicitly urged his colleagues to abandon any attempt at 'discerning the subjective motivation of those enacting the statute')[16] and more towards a rational inquiry into whether the act, as whole, may have a secular purpose. And he concludes that, 'as a secular matter', religious people are entitled to have religion-inspired theories taught in public schools. An immediate objection to Scalia's formulation may be: if *that* is a secular matter, what would count as a religious one? But that objection would be too hasty: the question of secular purpose becomes a second-order matter; the purpose of representing a variety of theories, including religiously inspired ones, is in itself secular. It is purpose which may be, reasonably and without duplicity, articulated in purely secular terms: in terms of diversity, academic freedom, the exposure of school students to a variety of perspectives which they will encounter in their society anyway, etc.

On this general methodological issue about how to discern the secular purpose, I think that Scalia was right and Brennan wrong, even though I am persuaded by Brennan that the actual motivations of those particular lawmakers (and the motivations of the electorates that supported and pressed for them) *were* religious. What matters is whether *we can* attribute to a given legislation a likely secular rationale and establish whether there is a reasonable link between the rationale and the legislation, so that the rationale is not so clearly insignificant, or so indirectly and remotely connected with the legislation, that it is clearly pretextual or disingenuous. (This is a function that a proportionality analysis is best equipped to perform, and so it is no wonder that the author of a fundamental monograph on proportionality finds strong links between proportionality and reasonableness, the former being a more structured and transparent form of the latter.)[17]

Aguillard was not the last decision of the US Supreme Court with direct relevance to our argument. In *McCreary County v. ACLU*,[18] the 'Ten Commandments

15 482 U.S. 633 (Scalia J. dissenting), emphasis added.
16 Ibid. 636.
17 Aharon Barak, *Proportionality* (Cambridge University Press 2012), chapter 13.
18 545 U.S. 844 (2005).

in the Courthouse' case, the Court established, under the *Lemon's* 'secular purpose test', that the analysis of the purpose must proceed from the perspective of a 'reasonable observer'. In the present case, such an observer 'could only think that the Counties [which had posted large copies of Ten Commandments in their courthouses] meant to emphasize and celebrate the Commandments' religious message'.[19] The figure of the 'reasonable observer'[20] plays an important role in the judgment of the Court, which also uses it to emphasize a context-based inquiry into the purpose: 'reasonable observers have reasonable memories, and our precedents sensibly forbid an observer "to turn a blind eye to the context in which [the] policy arose"'.[21] So while there is an element of objectivity to the purpose-based inquiry (objectivity indicated by the very characterization of a '*reasonable* observer'), the use of legislative history and other publicly available materials about the statute's pedigree is not only permitted but also required, as part of the context. The Court, as it declares, does not presuppose 'an absentminded objective observer' but rather posits one who is 'familiar with the history of the government's actions and competent to learn what history has to show'.[22] In this way Justice Souter, who delivered the opinion of the Court, replicates Justice Brennan's position from *Aguillard* that objectivizing the purpose inquiry must have its limits, and that a degree of knowledge about context, that is, the actual motives of the legislature, is needed. And in this iteration of the ongoing dispute over the meaning of the purpose-based inquiry, Justice Scalia once again urged his colleagues to focus on purpose as discernible from the actual effect of the law. Ridiculing the Court's use of the figure of the 'reasonable observer' in its opinion, Justice Scalia noted that, under the Court's interpretation, 'the legitimacy of a government action with a wholly secular effect would turn on the *misperception* of an imaginary observer that the government officials behind the action had the intent to advance religion'.[23] To be sure, in this dissent, as before, Justice Scalia explicitly advocated for the abandonment of *Lemon*'s purpose prong,[24] but in the absence of such a move, his approach may be read as a directive to abandon any inquiry into actual motives and to infer purpose from the effect only.

More recently, in the 2010 decision of *Salazar v. Buono*, the figure of the 'objective observer' or 'reasonable observer' (two concepts used now interchangeably) has reappeared—again in the context of the Establishment Clause, and again in the specific context of detecting illicit legislative motivations.[25] In order to avoid implications related to the Establishment Clause, the government used a

[19] Ibid. 869.

[20] The figure was earlier introduced by O'Connor J. in her concurrence in another establishment clause case, *see Capitol Square Review and Advisory Board v. Pinette*, 515 U.S. 753, 780 (1995) (O'Connor, J. concurring in part and concurring in judgment).

[21] 545 U.S. 866, quoting 530 U.S. 315, footnote omitted.

[22] Ibid. 866, reference omitted.

[23] Ibid. 901 (Scalia J. dissenting), emphasis in original.

[24] Ibid. 902.

[25] *Salazar v. Buono*, 559 U.S. 700 (2010).

Congressional statute (the Department of Defense Appropriation Act of 2004) to transfer a piece of land with a large, clearly visible cross erected in 1934 to commemorate soldiers who died in World War I to a private party in exchange for other land in the nearby national preserve. A district court dismissed Congress' motives as illicit, basically aimed at retaining the cross, contrary to an earlier injunction. But the Supreme Court, by a 5:4 majority, disagreed, and in the process the plurality opinion again recruited the so-called 'objective observer'. While doubting whether the test applies to religious symbols on private property, Justice Kennedy, who authored the judgment of the Court, in an opinion joined by two other justices, recalled that the test of a reasonable observer 'requires the hypothetical construct of an objective observer who knows all of the pertinent facts and circumstances surrounding the symbol and its placement'.[26] In his dissent, Justice Stevens made it clear that the test of a reasonable/objective observer is focused upon the likely *motives* of the legislator: 'Our precedent provides that we evaluate purpose based upon what the objective indicia of intent would reveal to a reasonable observer ... The plurality nowhere engages with how a reasonable observer would view Congress' "policy of accommodation" for this cross,'[27] From this extract, we can see how this case reiterates the basic disagreement already prefigured in *Aguillard*: depending on the level of knowledge of the actual context surrounding the adoption of the legislation is attributed to a 'reasonable observer', she may either be more suspicious of a legislator's actual purposes or more willing to credit the legislation with publicly attributable purposes. An objective (or reasonable, or impartial) observer is a highly versatile character and can act as a useful *porte-parole* for judges on either side of the divide prefigured in *Aguillard*.

When writing about the separation of church and state, Robert Audi formulated 'the principle of secular rationale', articulated as follows: '[O]ne should not advocate or support any law or public policy that restricts human conduct unless one has, and is willing to offer, adequate secular reason for this advocacy or support.'[28] But Audi immediately adds that this principle is 'normative, not genetic',[29] which means that it *would* allow for advocacy that is actually religiously inspired, and that it *would* allow one to be more impressed by religious arguments than by secular arguments. Further articulating the 'principle of secular rationale', Audi claims that 'whatever other considerations one brings to the relevant contexts of advocacy or support, one [should] put forward such advocacy or support only if one *also* has and is willing to offer adequate secular reason for the view in question'.[30] Borrowing Audi's terminology, I would take

[26] Ibid. 721, reference omitted.
[27] Ibid. 755–56, (Stevens J. dissenting), references omitted.
[28] Robert Audi, 'The Separation of Church and State and the Obligations of Citizenship', (1989) 18 *Philosophy & Public Affairs* 259, 279.
[29] Ibid.
[30] Ibid. 280, emphasis in original.

the PR requirement as having a 'normative, not genetic' character: the question is not whether a particular proposal for a public policy is actually motivated by someone's comprehensive philosophical doctrine, but only whether it *can be* rationally supported by reasons which are self-standing, that is, separate from such comprehensive doctrines. It is probably fair to say that most of our publicly stated demands regarding the law are actually motivated by our 'comprehensive' conceptions and are not anathema to a theory of PR. All we need to see is whether those comprehensive conceptions may support such publicly admissible reasons as being sufficient to justify a given law.[31]

It should be also mentioned that even in those cases in which religious purpose is the basis for *invalidation*, the US Supreme Court has occasionally observed that a religious purpose may not be a *sufficient* ground for invalidation. In the already mentioned *McCreary County* (the 'Ten Commandments in the Courthouse' case), while the Court maintained in the main text of the judgment that the presence of an 'ostensible and predominant' legislative purpose to promote religion violates the Establishment Clause of the First Amendment, the Court found it appropriate to include in a footnote that '[i]n special instances we have found good reason to hold governmental action legitimate even where its manifest purpose was presumably religious'.[32] To support this caveat, the Court cited *Marsh v. Chambers*,[33] a case which upheld a state legislature's retention of a chaplain on the basis of traditional practice. In some other religion-related cases, the US Supreme Court has explicitly combined motive (understood as equivalent to 'purpose') with effect, producing an objectified version of purpose. In a leading Sunday-closure decision in 1961 (and Sunday-closure laws will figure prominently in the rest of this chapter, when discussing other jurisdictions), the Court upheld a set of statutes that prohibited many retail establishments from opening on Sundays. There, the Court said that while such laws may have originally had the purpose of promoting religion in general or Christianity in particular, they acquired 'a present purpose and effect' that stood 'wholly apart from their original purposes or connotations', and that the current purpose of the laws is to provide a uniform day of rest for all citizens.[34]

Similarly, some monuments originally established for religious reasons have with time transformed their symbolic meanings, acquiring non-denominational or even secular significance. In a recent US Supreme Court decision, a cross established in 1925 as a tribute to soldiers who gave their lives in the World War I, was deemed part of the 'common cultural heritage' disconnected from the

[31] Micah Schwartzman puts it more elegantly: 'Public reasons presented as *pro tanto* justifications in the political domain may be supported by nonpublic values that give a person moral or ethical motivation,' Micah Schwartzman, 'The Sincerity of Public Reason', (2011) 19 *Journal of Political Philosophy* 375, 389.

[32] 545 U.S. 589 n. 10.

[33] 463 U.S. 783 (1983).

[34] *McGowan v. Maryland*, 366 U.S. 420, 445 (1961).

religious significance of the cross.[35] Interestingly, Justice Alito who delivered the opinion for the Court draws an analogy with the Notre Dame Cathedral which (especially after the tragic fire) 'remains a symbol of national importance to the religious and nonreligious alike'.[36] Regarding the Blandensburg Cross in Maryland, which was the subject of the controversy in *American Legion*, the Court found that 'the symbol took on an added secular meaning',[37] and in addition that removing I would 'strike many as aggressively hostile to religion'.[38] And in his concurrence, Justice Gorsuch amplified this point, severing this argument from the 'passage of time', 'because what matters when it comes to assessing a monument, symbol, or practice isn't its age but its compliance with ageless principles'[39]—thus suggesting that the non-religious symbolic significance of objects such as the cross may have contained strong (indeed, dominant) secular ingredients from the very beginning.

So while motive accompanied by impact is often encountered in First Amendment Religion Clause judgments, it is difficult to say whether a *compelling* judgment of the US Supreme Court can be found which strikes down a law merely for its improper impact on free exercise, explicitly renouncing any reference to a likely intention, motive, animus, or purpose. *Lukumi Babalu Ay, Inc., v. the City of Hialeah*[40] is often viewed as a leading authority for the proposition that courts should look to the effects of a statute when determining whether or not it is neutral in the free exercise scrutiny.[41] And indeed, in *Lukumi* there is a strong statement: 'The First Amendment does not refer to the purposes for which legislators enact laws, but to the effects of the laws enacted.'[42] What is significant, however, is that this is a maxim by Justice Scalia made in his *concurrence*; in contrast, the main opinion for the Court, penned by Justice Kennedy, makes it clear that the finding of unconstitutionality of a prohibition on 'ritual slaughter' (practised by Santeria believers) by a local authority in Hialeah was triggered by a serious suspicion that the ban was improperly *motivated*. It is interesting to trace Justice Kennedy's argument, based on a two-track approach to free exercise scrutiny. If the law is neutral and of general application, then the Court adopts a strong presumption of constitutionality; if, however, the law is not neutral or not of general applicability, it must be justified by a 'compelling governmental interest', which in practice means that it is likely to be invalidated. As to the question of neutrality, Kennedy said that a law is not neutral 'if *the object* of a law is to infringe upon or restrict practices because of their religious motivation'.[43] This

[35] *American Legion v. American Humanist Association*, 139 S. Ct. 2067, 2083 (2019).
[36] Ibid. 2084.
[37] Ibid. 2089.
[38] Ibid. 2085.
[39] Ibid. 2102 (Gorsuch J., concurring in the judgment).
[40] 508 U.S. 520 (1993).
[41] See Kelsey Curtis, 'The Partiality of Neutrality', (2018) 41 *Harvard Journal of Law & Public Policy* 935, 966.
[42] 508 U.S. 558 (Scalia J. concurring in part and concurring in judgment).
[43] Ibid. 533, emphasis added.

happened, Kennedy continues, when the law discriminates 'on its face', that is when it 'refers to a religious practice' without any 'secular meaning' discernible from the language or the context of the law.[44] But these are easy cases: a law may also be non-neutral even if it is not facially discriminatory (when 'religion' is not mentioned explicitly in the text): 'The Free Exercise Clause protects against *governmental hostility* which is masked as well as overt.'[45]

It is here that things get difficult: cases of overt hostility to religion are rare, but when it comes to covert hostility, how can it be discerned? In looking at the prohibition of Santeria religion in a small city in Florida, Justice Kennedy puts together a number of pieces of evidence to support the conclusion that suppression of the central element of the Santeria worship was the real purpose of the ordinances.[46] For instance, he claims that the use of the words 'sacrifice' and 'ritual', while not conclusive, indicates 'the improper *attempt* to target Santeria' by the council.[47] Second, Justice Kennedy referred to the city resolutions accompanying the ordinances, in which religious concerns were explicitly voiced.[48] Third, 'the effect of a law in its real operation is strong evidence of *its object*',[49] and here the effect was that 'almost the only conduct subjected to [the city ordinances] ... is the religious exercise of Santeria church members'.[50] To be sure, Justice Kennedy does acknowledge that the laws were also triggered by 'multiple concerns unrelated to religious animosity', such as the prevention of the suffering and mistreatment of animals. Nevertheless, the conclusion he drew from the overall effects of the laws was that they reveal 'an *impermissible attempt* to target petitioners and their religious practices'.[51]

Further, Justice Kennedy explicitly connects the 'neutrality' analysis with that of equality, stating that various 'objective factors', such as those established to show the non-neutrality of city ordinances, at the same time 'bear on the question of *discriminatory object*'[52] of the laws. To be precise, Justice Kennedy is not saying that non-neutrality is equivalent to discrimination, but rather that in trying to discern non-neutrality, one may 'find guidance in ... equal protection cases'.[53] Combining non-neutrality (in Free Exercise jurisprudence) with equal protection case law in this way, Kennedy finds 'evidence [of] significant *hostility* exhibited by residents, members of the city council, and other city officials toward the Santeria religion and its practice of animal sacrifice'.[54] This part of his

44 Ibid. 533.
45 Ibid. 534, emphasis added.
46 Ibid. 534
47 Ibid. 534, emphasis added.
48 Ibid. 534–535.
49 Ibid. 535, emphasis added.
50 Ibid. 535.
51 Ibid. 535, emphasis added.
52 Ibid. 540, emphasis added.
53 Ibid. 540.
54 Ibid. 541, emphasis added.

opinion—incidentally the only one in which the majority of the Court refused to join—is strongly permeated with a motive-based analysis under which the purpose (defined here as an 'object' of the law) is seen as crucial to identify its non-neutrality (or discriminatory) character. It is here that Justice Kennedy quotes various statements by members of the city council which are explicitly addressed against Santeria and concludes: 'This history discloses *the object* of the ordinances to target animal sacrifice by Santeria worshippers because of its religious motivation.'[55]

What general lessons can be drawn from *Lukumi Babalu* for our purposes in this part of the chapter? Not every law that burdens a religion—that imposes disproportionate burdens of followers of a particular religion, or on religious compared to non-religious people—is suspicious, as violative of religious equality. Some laws which impose general standards on all may, as an incidental effect, burden a religion, but as long as they are suitable to achieve some important social goals (that a lawmaker is constitutionally mandated or permitted to pursue), or if they plausibly target an important evil to eliminate, they are defensible.[56] The main question is, are these laws sufficiently neutral? And the standards of neutrality have to do mainly (though not exclusively) with the 'object' of the law—the 'object' understood here (as the context of Kennedy's opinion suggests) as an objective, purpose, or motivation of the lawmakers. The object of a neutral law must be such that it is not animated by hostility towards religion (or towards a particular religion), nor targeting particular religious conduct. If non-neutrality can be found on the face of the law (i.e. if the law explicitly targets a religion), the analysis may end there, and nothing can save the law. But even if the law is facially neutral, it may be covertly non-neutral, and in order to discern its non-neutral character, we must look into the context in order to see whether the law can be seen to be aimed at targeting a religion. This context contains a lot of different things: the terms of the law, the debates accompanying its enactment, and even its effects, insofar as the effects are often good indicators of the 'object'. If, having put together all this evidence, we conclude that the law burdening a religion has as its *object* the targeting of a religion, it is non-neutral. It discriminates against this religion, in a deeply objectionable way.

Let us also note that this emphasis on discriminatory intent has triggered some strong criticisms. Stephen Carter noted that, under the same circumstances, the city council of Hialeah 'would be within its rights if it suppressed Santeria by accident instead of on purpose . . .'[57] This may be right but much hinges upon what

[55] Ibid. 542, emphasis added.

[56] This was the main point of an important decision handed down by the US Supreme Court three years before *Lukumi Bubalu*, namely *Employment Division, Department of Human Resources v Smith*, 494 U.S. 872 (1990), which established that the free exercise clause does not create a blanket 'religious exemption' from general, religiously neutral laws even if they have the effect of restricting a religious practice (peyote smoking, in that case).

[57] Stephen L. Carter, 'The Resurrection of Religious Freedom?', (1993) 107 *Harvard Law Review* 118, 129.

it means to produce an effect 'by accident': Carter contrasts it to a purposeful suppression, but there is another way of understanding it: as an incidental side-effect of an otherwise reasonable regulation. Under the latter meaning, the city council's steps appear much more respectable. Carter continues that a purpose-based theory 'provides a disincentive for the city to determine whether a proposed action will harm a religion'. But this is a non-sequitur: the true disincentive may be to the city frankly disclosing its legislative intentions, thus opening itself up to a purpose-based analysis.[58] One may therefore argue that if we adopt a purpose-based scrutiny, it would be a disincentive for candour in lawmaking. But as long as the 'object' is culled from many *other* sources (as in Kennedy's opinion), and not just from legislative deliberations, explanations of the vote, or *travaux préparatoires*, this regrettable consequence may not occur.

To conclude this section: I am not claiming that in the context of the First Amendment religion cases, the existence of improper motivations—such as hostility to religion as such, to specific religion, or to non-religion—is necessary, but I claim that often it appears in the absence of any analysis of effects, or as accompanying and tainting those effects as unconstitutional.

2. On the Uses and Misuses of Religion in Judicial Opinions and Amicus Curiae Briefs

Direct references to explicitly non-public reasons, such as religious grounds in a judicial decision, are exceedingly rare, which may be seen as a tribute to the ideal of public reason, even if *sans le mot*. An American legal scholar spoke, with a marked degree of disapproval, about the phenomenon of 'the concealment of religious values in judicial decision-making', observing that, these days, 'the explicit and meaningful use of religion in the judicial process—especially ... the reliance on precepts associated with the[] traditionally dominant religious denominations—is regarded by many as inappropriate on a number of fronts'.[59] This, he claims, is despite the fact that—in all likelihood—judges' religious beliefs do influence their reasoning.[60] Kent Greenawalt, in an important 2005 book, observed that it is very rare to find a religious principle aimed at supporting a legal conclusion: 'A judge may refer to Christian tenets to help put a legal problem or doctrine, or social attitudes, in a historical perspective, but she is not likely to say that an otherwise debatable legal conclusion is

[58] See Shannon L. Doheny, 'Free Exercise Does Not Protect Animal Sacrifice: The Misconception of *Church of Lukumi Babalu Aye v. City of Hialeah* and Constitutional Solutions for Stopping Animal Sacrifice', (2006) 2 *Journal of Animal Law* 121, 137.

[59] Scott C. Idleman, 'The Concealment of Religious Values in Judicial Decisionmaking', (2005) 91 *Virginia Law Review* 515, 534.

[60] Ibid. 520–23.

correct because it conforms to Christianity or some other supposedly true religious understanding.'[61]

Greenawalt provides one example of a rare exception—so rare as to merit the status of an exception which confirms the rule—being the case of a separate opinion delivered by Justice Henderson sitting on the Supreme Court of South Dakota who, when opposing visitation rights for a lesbian mother, wrote back in 1992: 'Until ... she can establish ... that she is no longer a lesbian living a life of abomination (see Leviticus 18:22), she should be totally estopped from contaminating these children.'[62] Further on in his separate opinion (and beyond what Greenawalt quoted in his book), the judge of South Dakota ruminated: 'It appears that homosexuals ... are committing felonies, by their acts against nature and God. Actus naturae, actus Deus. This is an old legal phrase, which became a legal maxim. Literally it means an act against nature is an act against God.'[63] And then: 'There appears to be a transitory phenomenon on the American scene that homosexuality is okay. Not so. The Bible decries it. Even the pagan "Egyptian Book of the Dead" bespoke against it,'[64] etc. etc. It may also be added that four years earlier, the same Justice Frank E. Henderson had said, when dissenting in a case involving the termination of parental rights based on the physical abuse of children, that

> A family is the core unit of society, not the State, and it is the most powerful institution in society.... Birth is a mystery of God's creation. Fostered by human love, children are entrusted to parents as a part of God's great plan. In perpetuating the human race, God set parents over children, and the Law should be ever so cautious in interfering with that edict.[65]

And in a footnote, before citing several biblical sources, he explained: 'This author appreciates that we are not an ecclesiastical Court. However, we draw upon scripture for strength and guidance. This is because our Nation is founded upon, basically, a Judeo-Christian ethic.'[66]

One may find some other occasional direct references to religious reasons in US court decisions in recent decades—though very rarely by the US Supreme Court.[67] In a 1973 case concerning the use of a criminal defendant's silence

[61] Kent Greenawalt, *Private Consciences and Public Reasons* (Oxford University Press 1995) 142.

[62] *Chicoine v. Chicoine*, 479 N.W.2d 891, 896 (S.D. 1992), (Henderson J. concurring in part and dissenting in part), footnote omitted, quoted in Greenawalt, *Private Consciences and Public Reasons* (n. 61) 142 n. 2.

[63] 479 479 N.W.2d 896 (S.D. 1992 (Henderson J, concurring in part and dissenting in part), footnote omitted.

[64] Ibid. 897, reference omitted.

[65] *In re S.L. and L.L.*, 419 N.W.2d 689, 697 (S.D. 1988) (Henderson J. dissenting), footnote omitted.

[66] Ibid. 691 n. 2 (Henderson J. dissenting).

[67] For such a rare example, see Burger C.J.'s concurrence in *Bowers v. Hardwick*, where he asserted that the condemnation of sodomy is 'firmly rooted in Judaeo-Christian moral and ethical standards', 478 U.S. 186, 196–97 (Burger, C.J. concurring). It should be observed that, on the face of it, this looks more like an appeal to religious values in order to construct the community standards controlling a

against him, the Supreme Court of Michigan quoted with approval a 1923 opinion of a judge of the Supreme Court of Missouri: 'This humane rule has higher sanction than mere judicial precedent. At the trial of Jesus before the Sanhedrin, we read . . .'[68] and then followed a lengthy quotation from Matthew's Gospel, without any further comment, and as conclusive to the resolution of the case at hand. Further, in 1973, the Missouri Court of Appeals identified sexual intercourse as an inherent right of marriage and asserted, among other sources for this proposition, that '[t]his right is sanctioned by the Judeo-Christian ethic', by quoting *Genesis* and *Mark*.[69] A dissenting justice in a sexual abuse case heard in the Supreme Court of New York referred to the Bible (with a direct quote from Matthew) to substantiate the universal condemnation of crimes against the young.[70] Some of these quotes come from concurring or dissenting opinions—which in itself is significant enough because it shows that those few judges who refer to religious sources do it usually when they are freer to say what they are actually thinking, and when they are less bound by the dominant conventions of public reason.[71]

Of course, there may be references to religious sources in contexts which do *not* take the form of using religious faith to support a particular doctrinal determination. For example, such references may be evident when judges need to ascertain—in a descriptive rather than normative matter—what the particular moral belief of a particular religious community is, for instance in order to decide whether it is indeed 'religion' in a constitutional (or statutory) sense when the law attaches consequences to the religious character of a particular position, institution, or organization. They will need to make such findings in cases involving discrimination based on religion or by an allegedly religious institution, and on tax and other exemptions based on the religious status of an entity, etc. Similarly, judges may have to inquire into the meaning and validity (the validity from an internal point of view of a religious order, that is) of religious precepts when it is necessary to make legally correct decisions, for instance in cases of disputes within or between religious entities, and in child custody cases where the parents' religious beliefs bear on the issue of custody or adoption,[72] etc. Regarding the latter issue, courts have established that religion may

legal status rather than a direct appeal to religion. None of the sources referred to by Burger to substantiate his assertion are purely religious documents.

[68] *People v. Bobo*, 390 Mich. 355, 362, 212 N.W.2d 190, 194 (Mich. 1973)

[69] *Cox v. Cox*, 493 S.W.2d 371, 373 (Mo. Ct. App. 1973), footnote omitted. Clemens J. also observed, as another source for this proposition, that this right 'probably has its roots in the ancient concept that a wife was a husband's chattel', ibid. 373.

[70] *People v. Jagnjic*, 85 A.D.2d 135, 143 (N.Y. App. Div. 1st Dep't 1982) (Lupiano, J. dissenting).

[71] See Scott C. Idleman, 'The Role of Religious Values in Judicial Decision Making', (1993) 68 *Indiana Law Journal* 433, 477 n. 157.

[72] See Donald L. Beshle, 'God Bless the Child? The Use of Religion as a Factor in Child Custody and Adoption Proceedings', (1989) 58 *Fordham Law Review* 383.

be a significant (though not the only) factor in custody determinations.[73] In particular, courts have found that if a particular religion is already part of a child's identity, then the relative ability of parents to tend to the religious needs of a child may be a proper consideration.[74] Some courts suggested that a child's exposure to different 'religious models' should be considered beneficial,[75] while other courts found that religious differences are confusing and harmful to children.[76] Either way, religion figures in judicial findings on the best interests of the child—but not because a judge endorses a particular religion, but rather takes note of the very fact of a religious upbringing as a factor of the child's needs, if already established in a child. (By the same token, courts found that denying an adoption on the grounds of the applicants' atheism would be unconstitutional.)[77]

But such references do not contradict the principle of PR because they are not used, per se, in support of a particular legal decision. It is not their persuasiveness as sources of moral appropriateness, or of right and wrong, but rather the fact that they are, descriptively, of a religious character that figures in the judge's argument. The argument is not religious per se: religion figures in them contingently, as a factor of a broader secular good (such as the best interests of a child)—just as in the famous Amish community case, where the preservation of a religious community in accordance with its wishes could be seen as part of the best interests of that community as a whole.[78]

One particular use of religion which may be more problematic, but could be appropriate in some cases, is when the law refers to community standards as a legal test, and where some of those standards may have, partly at least, a religious character. Those religious precepts attain the status of sources (though not *the* sources) of community standards, and they may need to be recognized in the process of the judicial reconstruction of those standards. There is a rather fine line between the legitimate ascertainment of religious values as part of the reconstruction of community standards for the purpose of legal decision on the one hand, and the direct appeal to religious values to support the validity of a

[73] See *Frank v. Frank*, 26 Ill. App. 2d 16, 20, 167 N.E.2d 577, 580 (1960). Interestingly, the dissenting judge seems to have viewed the religious customs of the child's new home as decisive for the issue of custody: 'He was baptized a Catholic and goes to church every Sunday. He lives in an average working-class neighborhood. The defendant proposes to bring up the boy as a Catholic in the same home where she and her present husband are practicing the Protestant religion, and their daughter will be brought up as a Protestant', 167 N.E.2d 581 (Burman, J. dissenting).

[74] See *Bonjour v. Bonjour*, 592 P.2d 1233, 1239–40 (Alaska 1979).

[75] See *Felton v. Felton*, 383 Mass 232, 418 N.E.2d 606 (1981) ('a diversity of religious experience is itself a sound stimulant for a child', ibid. 235).

[76] See *Morris v. Morris*, 271 Pa. Super. 19, 412 A.2d 139 (1979) ('it is beyond dispute that a young [5] child reared into two inconsistent religious traditions will quite probably experience some deleterious physical or mental effects', ibid. 25).

[77] *In re Adoption of 'E'*, 59 N.J. 36, 279 A.2d 785 (1971) ('We, as judges, regardless of our own personal beliefs and religious affiliations, cannot take the position that children may be placed only in the homes of believers until they are able to choose for themselves which course to pursue. Under the First Amendment we are incompetent to do so', ibid. 54).

[78] *Wisconsin v. Yoder*, 406 U.S. 205 (1972).

legal decision on the other—but it is precisely that line which separates legitimate reasons from illegitimate reasons for law and legal decisions, and it can be done only in specific contexts.

It is also clear that occasionally decisions really belonging to the latter category are disguised as cases falling under the former category. For example, how should one particular New York city court's reasoning in 1989 be classified? In that case, when reviewing a statutory prohibition on public nudity, the court appealed directly to the Bible, from which long excerpts were included in the decision, to identify the status of nudity in 'public perceptions and decency'.[79] Judge Regan preceded his appeals to the Bible, which read more like a sermon than a judicial opinion, with a statement:

> There is no question that—historically at least—the United States is a society which accepts Judeo-Christian teachings. While we are pluralistic in composition, the great majority of our people observe Judeo-Christian moral standards. If law-makers refer to those standards for guidance in enacting laws to achieve public morality, therefore, they will, more likely than not, accomplish their purpose.[80]

But if we remove the obvious hyperbole about society 'accepting' Judeo-Christian teachings, including the suggestion of contemporary consensus on these religious grounds, there is no doubt that religious sources have affected community standards to a large degree, and it is perhaps in *this* capacity (rather than a direct test for legal validity) that those sources may be taken into account by a judge.

One unintended but inevitable consequence of the legitimate use of religion in this sense is the privileging of the dominant religion(s) over other religions, because it is clear that only they have a significant impact upon, and participate in, setting community standards. That is why Scott Idleman's directive of 'impartiality' ('because American society and its judicial system are heavily Judeo-Christian in background, especially Protestant Christian, impartiality may only be possible when a judge does survey the landscape of religious thought and, when making her decision, takes account of this survey'),[81] while no doubt well-intentioned, is inappropriate in the context of discerning community standards, because some religious beliefs will have an insignificant or in fact no impact upon the formation of such standards. In advancing this idea, Idleman seeks to tell judges what they should do whenever they advert 'to religious values for the purpose of reaching a well-informed, impartial decision';[82] more specifically,

[79] *People v. David*, 146 Misc. 2d 115, 120 (N.Y. City Ct 1989).
[80] Ibid. 120.
[81] Idleman, 'The Role of Religious Values in Judicial Decision Making' (n. 71) 483 n. 177.
[82] Ibid. 483.

when defining 'secular purpose' under the Establishment Clause of the First Amendment (the *Lemon* test). But it is clear that compared to the first, legitimate, use of religious sources (appealing to religion in order to identify community standards as a test of legal validity of a decision), Idleman's 'ecumenical' use of religious sources involves the second use of religion (directly appealing to religion as a test of the legal validity of a decision), as in the former usage, 'impartiality' has no special place. After all, 'if judges were attempting to use religious tenets to discover what really is right, they would have no reason to favour the religions that happen to be dominant in a given country.[83]

Finally, a note about amicus curiae briefs in the United States. While there is a real scarcity of direct references to religious sources in judicial opinions and judgments, one *would* expect that such references will be ubiquitous in amicus curiae briefs filed by religious organizations: after all, this is the sort of argument that their constituencies and probably the general public would expect them to advance, especially in 'moral cases' where, by their very nature, religious institutions would have strong and settled views. A study on amicus curiae briefs filed by religious organizations in the period between 1954 (starting with *Brown v Board of Education*)[84] through to 2006, on cases involving morally controversial issues such as homosexuality, abortion, and euthanasia (the three topics which attracted by far the most amicus curiae briefs), as well as segregation and affirmative action, etc. is quite telling in this regard.[85] Of the forty-five briefs filed in this period by religious organizations, one-fourth of the briefs did not refer to religion at all. In particular, the two most politically conservative religious organizations avoided almost all religious references.[86] But in the remaining three-quarters of the briefs examined in that study, most of those religious references which Andrew Mansfield quotes sound really quite 'secular': for instance, (in the context of affirmative action) that '[t]he Jewish tradition has always been sensitive to the plight of the stranger',[87] or (in the context of doctor-assisted suicide), that '[i]t is a basic principle of Jewish law and ethics that "man does not possess absolute title to his life or body"';[88] or (in the context of the death penalty), that 'God's power to forgive is greater than humanity's power to do evil'.[89] These references, while obviously religious, do not take the form of insisting that the law should absolutely track the religious teaching of an organization filing an amicus

[83] See Greenawalt, *Private Consciences and Public Reasons* (n. 61) 148.
[84] 348 U.S. 886 (1954).
[85] Andrew S. Mansfield, 'Religious Arguments and the United States Supreme Court: A Review of Amicus Curiae Briefs Filed by Religious Organizations' (2008), available at http://works.bepress.com/andrew_mansfield/5 (last accessed 1 June 2020).
[86] Ibid. 18.
[87] The American Jewish Committee's brief in *Grutter v. Bollinger*, 539 U.S. 306 (2003), quoted in Mansfield, 'Religious Arguments and the United States Supreme Court' (n. 85) 18.
[88] Agudath Israel's brief in *Cruzan v. Director, Missouri Dept. of Health*, 497 U.S. 261 (1990), quoted in Mansfield, 'Religious Arguments and the United States Supreme Court' (n. 85) 19.
[89] The Evangelical Lutheran Church of America's brief in *Roper v. Simmons*, 543 U.S. 551 (2005), quoted in Mansfield, 'Religious Arguments and the United States Supreme Court' (n. 85) 20.

curiae brief, but rather of showing that a particular religious view coincides with a universal morality and, as such, should inform the Court's decision.

3. Non-establishment of Religion in Australia

In Australia, purpose is explicitly written into the constitutional protection of freedom of religion: section 116 of the (federal) Constitution is formulated in a way which makes the validity of law turn on the banned purposes. The section contains four specific guarantees under the heading that the Commonwealth is 'not to legislate in respect of religion'. Its separate components preclude the Commonwealth from making any law '*for* establishing any religion', '*for* imposing any religious observance', or '*for* prohibiting the free exercise of any religion' (all emphases added) and prohibit the imposition of a religious test 'as a qualification for any office or public trust under the Commonwealth'. The non-establishment and the free exercise clauses (corresponding to the two religion clauses in the United States First Amendment) are of course the most important and have indeed been interpreted by the highest court of Australia in a way that underlines the centrality of purpose. Under the textual-formalistic approach dominant in Australian constitutional review, this was made easy by the wording of section 116 ('*for* establishing any religion', etc.).

As an example of a purpose-focused construction of the non-establishment clause in Australia, consider *Attorney-General (Vic); Ex rel Black v. Commonwealth*.[90] The impugned laws comprised a scheme by which the federal government provided funding to church schools. It was argued by the plaintiffs that the provision of funding in this manner amounted to an 'establishment' of religion, and thereby infringed section 116. Justice Murphy, in the lonely dissent, would have found the law invalid, arguing that the constitutional provision should be interpreted broadly, such that a law was 'for' establishing any religion if it simply was 'relevant to' or 'with respect to' establishing any religion.[91] But the majority rejected this approach. As Chief Justice Barwick noted, the use of the word 'for' in the Australian constitutional provision requires that the establishment of religion be 'the object of the making of the law'—that objective must be its 'express' and, in his opinion, 'single purpose'.[92] Section 116 prohibits the making of any law 'intended and designed' to establish or 'set up' a particular religion 'as an institution of the Commonwealth'.[93] The Constitution, he argued, prohibits legislation that 'intends and seeks' to establish a religion, and is in that sense purposive.

[90] (1981) 146 CLR 559.
[91] Ibid. 622.
[92] Ibid. 579.
[93] Ibid. 583.

Nothing in the terms of the impugned legislation expressly authorized the use of Commonwealth funds for the purpose of the establishment of a religion.

Turning now to the second clause, an important Australian case touching on the issue of purpose in the free exercise clause is *Kruger v Commonwealth* (known as the 'Stolen Generations case').[94] The Northern Territory legislation at issue had authorized the forced removal of Australian Aboriginal and Torres Strait Islander children from their families. The plaintiffs in this case included Indigenous Australians who were removed from their families as children under the impugned legislation and a mother whose child was forcibly removed from her custody. They challenged the constitutionality of the Aboriginals Ordinance 1918 (NT), its subsequent amendments, and the federal Acts under which they were enacted, seeking a declaration of invalidity on several grounds. The claim was unsuccessful, but several arguments touched on issues of freedom of religion in a way relevant to our discussion in this chapter. As mentioned above, section 116 of the federal Constitution prohibits, inter alia, the making of any law '*for* prohibiting the free exercise of any religion' (emphasis added). The plaintiffs alleged that by authorizing the removal of Aboriginal children from the environment in which they could engage with their native tribal culture, the Ordinance was a law 'for prohibiting the free exercise of any religion' and was invalid to that extent. This attempt to invoke Australian constitutional freedom of religion was ultimately unsuccessful but was the subject of interesting judicial discussion.

Of all the High Court judges, Justice Gaudron was most receptive to the submission. She accepted the argument in principle, acknowledging that a final decision would depend on questions of fact that were not argued before the Court. She took the view that the use of the word 'for' in the constitutional provision rendered purpose the sole criterion for invalidity under section 116.[95] Justice Gaudron acknowledged that laws will often have multiple purposes, and that one particular purpose 'may be subsumed in a larger or more general purpose'.[96] The latter point was illustrated in this case. The Commonwealth pleaded that the true purpose of the Ordinance was 'the protection and preservation of persons of the Aboriginal race'.[97] To Justice Gaudron, one clear purpose of the Ordinance was to 'remove Aboriginal and half-caste people' and keep 'them in Aboriginal reserves and institutions'.[98] That purpose was not inconsistent with the broader purpose asserted by the government. However, taking the argument one step further, nor was it necessarily inconsistent with the purpose of removing Aboriginal children from their families and communities, with the effect of stopping them from participating in community cultural and religious practices. This argument

[94] (1997) 190 CLR 1.
[95] Ibid. 132.
[96] Ibid. 133.
[97] Ibid. 133.
[98] Ibid. 133.

could be taken another step further again, to the form taken by the plaintiffs' submission: that among the purposes of the Ordinance was not only the removal of Indigenous children from their communities, but that by doing so, the government sought to prevent those children from participating in community religious practices.[99]

Another judge engaging with the purpose-related argument, Justice Toohey, rejected the argument that such purpose can be attributed to the Ordinance. He reinforced the point that the object of the law was critical—the use of the word 'for' in section 116 indicated that legislative purpose may be taken into account in determining whether a given law infringes the Constitution. He also acknowledged that a given law may bear more than one purpose. He recognized the possibility that the purpose of the impugned Ordinance could have been to 'impair, even prohibit the spiritual beliefs and practices of the Aboriginal people in the Northern Territory'. However, he found that the language of the law itself did not reveal any such purpose and had received no further evidence on this question.[100] Similarly, Justice Gummow explained the significance of the use of the word 'for' in section 116, which requires the Court to take account of the legislative purpose behind the impugned law. However, he adopted a narrow view of the constitutional protection. The Ordinance contained no requirement as to the religion with which children should be raised or educated, nor any proscription or regulation of religious conduct of any form. Thus, while the effect of the law may have been to deny the plaintiffs any involvement in or exposure to the religion of their communities, Justice Gummow (Justice Dawson agreeing) saw no evidence that it was made for that purpose.[101] Chief Justice Brennan also flatly rejected the proposition, finding that none of the laws in question could be considered to infringe section 116, because none of them bore the purpose of achieving any object that that section prohibited.[102] As this summary indicates, purpose played a crucial role in the judges' arguments though they thought that the true purposes of the law did not taint it as unconstitutional under the free exercise clause of section 116.

4. Secular Legislative Aims in Canada

Both Australian cases discussed in the previous section show how a purpose-oriented analysis resulted in the challenged laws being *upheld*: no impermissible purpose was found. Other jurisdictions, which will be discussed now, will provide examples of a purpose-oriented analysis of religion clauses which resulted

[99] Ibid. 133.
[100] Ibid. 86.
[101] Ibid. 160–61.
[102] Ibid. 40.

in *invalidations*. All these cases are governed expressly by what Laurence Tribe calls 'input' principles (as already discussed in Chapter 4, section 4), namely principles which 'turn on what considerations went into the government's action, and not merely what impact that action has on the world'.[103] They are useful for us here because, when doubt about the very legitimacy of appealing to motives is removed (because such an inquiry is expressly mandated by the law), we may observe how motives can be discerned, especially when they are understood in an 'objectified' manner, equivalent to the most likely purpose pursued by a legislator.

The famous Canadian decision of *R v. Big M Drug Mart Ltd.*[104] is a case in point. The legislation at issue was the Lord's Day Act, which imposed a general prohibition on the performance of various forms of commercial activity on Sundays. The Court held that the Act, by its purpose, infringed upon the Charter-protected freedom of religion in section 2(a). Justice Dickson conducted a detailed examination of the legislative history behind the Act to conclude that its object was to compel observance of the Christian Sabbath. A finding of invalid purpose is determinative of this stage of the Charter analysis, without any need for consideration of the law's effects—the Court was clear on this point, stating that 'effects can never be relied upon to save legislation with an invalid purpose'.[105] In the course of the judgment, Justice Dickson noted the value of a purpose-based analysis in ensuring adequate consideration is given to the protection of rights: 'The assessment by the courts of legislative purpose focuses scrutiny upon the aims and objectives of the legislature and ensures they are consonant with the guarantees enshrined in the Charter.'[106] While legislation can infringe the Charter by either its purpose or effects, Justice Dickson established the principle that an illegitimate purpose negates the need for any inquiry into the actual effects of the legislation—an enactment with an illegitimate purpose will be unconstitutional on that ground and cannot be saved by its actual effects.[107] This statement of principle was significant. The impugned provision did not compel observance of the Sabbath by imposing any positive obligation upon Canadian residents to attend church, engage in any spiritual reflection, or pick up a Bible. Nor did it actually require them to rest. The appellant and supporting interveners made submissions to this effect, arguing that the Lord's Day Act contained no compulsion of religion. They asserted that merely requiring abstention from work on a Sunday 'does not, in itself, have any religious significance. Its effect is, therefore, merely secular.'[108] However, in light of the principle above, there was no need to consider this secular effect in any detail.

[103] Laurence H. Tribe, 'The Mystery of Motive, Private and Public: Some Thoughts Inspired by the Problems of Hate Crime and Animal Sacrifice', (1994) *Supreme Court Review* 1, 19.
[104] [1985] 1 SCR 295.
[105] *R v Big M Drug Mart Ltd.* [1985] 1 SCR 295, 334.
[106] Ibid. 331–32.
[107] Ibid. 334.
[108] Ibid. 349.

Significantly, Justice Dickson would even reject an argument that the law in question was reasonably thought to be also serving a secular aim, in addition to a religious one. The appellants submitted that if the Act did violate the right of religious freedom under the Charter, the Act's provisions constituted a 'reasonable limit, demonstrably justifiable in a free and democratic society on that right', and therefore could be saved by section 1 of the Charter. The limit, it was argued, could be reasonable on the basis of the secular justification that a day of rest is inherently beneficial—'everyone accepts the need and value of a universal day of rest from all work, business and labour and it may as well be the day traditionally observed in our society'. However, Justice Dickson was able to dispose of this argument briefly. The achievement of a secular goal by a law that offends the Charter for its religious purpose in compelling observance of the Sabbath will not save the law.

Let us consider this judgment in more detail as it is probably Exhibit No. 1 in the argument about the salience of motive-oriented scrutiny. As already explained, the Canadian Supreme Court in *Big M Drug Mart* found that the Lord's Day Act infringed freedom of religion under the Charter of Rights by its purpose. Justice Dickson identified two possible characterizations of the purpose of Sunday-closing legislation. First, through a religious lens, Lord's Day legislation could be seen as 'securing public observance of the Christian institution of the Sabbath'. Alternatively, in a secular light, these Acts provided 'a uniform day of rest from labour'. Both religious and secular elements may be present within a single piece of Sunday observance legislation—'indeed, it is almost inevitable that they will be', where the prohibition is on employment for one day of the week, and that particular day is the Christian Sabbath.[109]

The Court examined the legislative history underpinning Lord's Day legislation, and was left in 'little doubt that it was religious purpose which underlay' its enactment in England.[110] Citing various pieces of early legislation with titles such as the Sunday Fair Act, and the Act for the Keeping of Holy Days and Fasting-Days, the Court noted direct references to the direct injury and offence caused to God by engagement in 'bodily labour' and 'religious non-observance' on Sundays.[111] Justice Dickson then traced the evolution of these Acts into modern times, with the English Sunday Observance Act of 1677 identified as the 'model for Canadian pre-Confederation legislation'. This Act was largely re-enacted with 'only minor alterations' in Upper Canada in 1845. The federal Lord's Day Act followed in 1906 and 'embodied the basic framework and much of the language of the ... Sunday Observance Act. After four consolidations, it still exhibit[ed] these same essential characteristics' in its modern form.[112] Justice Dickson then

[109] Ibid. 316.
[110] Ibid. 317.
[111] Ibid. 318.
[112] Ibid. 319.

conducted a detailed survey of the Canadian and American case law for the purpose of determining whether the Act fell within provincial or federal legislative competence.[113] The authorities simply did not permit any finding of a secular purpose. The courts had treated it as an Act intended to compel sabbatical observance throughout its history—a purpose 'long-established and consistently maintained' by Canadian courts.[114] 'If I am a Jew or a Sabbatarian or a Muslim, the practice of my religion at least implies my right to work on a Sunday if I wish. It seems to me that any law *purely religious in purpose*, which denies me that right, must surely infringe my religious freedom.'[115]

It is clear, throughout the judgment, that what Justice Dickson had in mind was sort of an 'objectified' motive: the purpose that can be rationally ascribed to a law, rather than the actual state of mind of lawmakers. On his reading of the Charter, any legislative imposition of a day of rest on Sundays must be secular: 'The diversity of belief and non-belief, the diverse socio-cultural backgrounds of Canadians make it constitutionally incompetent for the federal Parliament to provide legislative preference for any one religion at the expense of those of another religious persuasion.' Justice Dickson acknowledged that earlier, prior to the introduction of the Charter, there may have been a time 'when people believed in the collective responsibility of the community toward some deity', during which state-mandated religious observance could have been a legitimate government objective. Since the Charter, however, such an object could not be considered legitimate:

> With the Charter, it has become the right of every Canadian to work out for himself or herself what his or her religious obligations, if any, should be and it is not for the state to dictate otherwise. The state shall not use the criminal sanctions at its disposal to achieve a religious purpose, namely, the uniform observance of the day chosen by the Christian religion as its day of rest.[116]

Thus, the 'true purpose' of the Act—to 'compel the observance of the Christian Sabbath'—infringed the freedom of conscience and religion under section 2(a) of the Charter.

The 'objectified' motive analysis adopted by the Canadian Supreme Court can be confirmed by a case in which the Court reached an opposite decision but as a result of employing a similar methodology to that in *Big M*. In *R v. Edwards Books and Art Ltd.*,[117] the Court upheld a Sunday closing law—there was sufficient evidence that its enactment was not driven by any religious purpose, but

[113] Ibid. 319–31.
[114] Ibid. 331.
[115] Ibid. 338, emphasis added.
[116] Ibid. 351.
[117] *R v Edwards Books and Art Ltd.* [1986] 2 SCR 713.

rather intended to provide 'uniform holidays to retail workers'.[118] The conclusion as to the purpose was reached by reference to the title and text of the Act, the legislative debates preceding its enactment, and a report of the Ontario Law Reform Commission that informed the drafting of its provisions.[119] Each of these sources indicated that secular, and not religious values or motivations, lay at the foundation of the legislation. The Act included various other holidays such as Canada and Labor Day—clearly secular holidays. It provided exemptions for recreational businesses, small businesses, and tourism, all of which are incompatible with the types of activities traditionally permissible on the Sabbath. Legislative debates contained direct acknowledgement that a secular course was appropriate on the recommendation of the Law Reform Commission. Among the reasons the Commission gave for its recommendation that the Ontario legislature adopt a 'uniform weekly pause day' were to facilitate the holding of community events and to enable people to spend time off with 'family, friends, or even among crowds', as is the 'expressed preference of most people'. The Commission's selection of Sunday rather than any other day was based on secular, not religious reasons, with specific acknowledgement that the religious significance of the day in Ontario was decreasing and it was becoming increasingly characterized by 'a high degree of social interaction and leisure activities among family and friends'.[120] Thus, Chief Justice Dickson was satisfied that the law was not a 'surreptitious attempt to encourage religious worship'.[121]

The application of the proportionality analysis has greatly assisted the Supreme Court of Canada to ferret out unconstitutional motives in freedom of religion (as in many other) cases. More recently, the Court reiterated that 'the legislative objective cannot be to impose or favour, or to express or profess, one belief to the exclusion of all others'.[122] In *Mouvement laïque québécois v. Saguenay (City)*, the 8:1 majority explained that a law with a religious purpose is inconsistent with this principle, and is therefore inconsistent with the freedom of religion provision of the Quebec Charter of Rights.[123] At issue in this case was a by-law governing the recitation of a prayer at the opening of council meetings, challenged for its infringement of the freedom of conscience and religion. The city argued that this practice was not, in fact, religious in character. In rejecting this assertion, the Court examined, inter alia, the preamble of the by-law. While it stated that the purpose of the law was to 'ensure decorum and highlight the importance of the work of the councillors', this goal was secondary to the religious

[118] Ibid. 744.
[119] Ibid. 744–45.
[120] Ibid. 744–45.
[121] Ibid. 744.
[122] [2015] SCC 16 [81].
[123] Although this case was brought under s. 3 of the Quebec Charter governing freedom of religion, the Court noted that 'it is well established that s. 3 should be interpreted in light of the principles that have been developed in relation to the application of the Canadian Charter', ibid. [68].

purpose: there were many measures besides prayer that the City of Saguenay could have adopted in order to ensure decorum.[124] The Court considered that the preamble emphasized 'above all' the goal of continuing the practice of prayer recital in line with the desire of the members 'to pursue it on the basis of their individual rights and freedoms, in particular their rights to freedom of expression, conscience and religion'. Thus, the Court concluded, the prayer was 'intended as support by the City for the religion professed by individual councillors'.[125] This clearly amounted to an impermissible, religious purpose.

5. Religious Freedom in South Africa

The Canadian *Big M Drug Mart* case has played a prominent role in South African case law concerning selling alcohol in contravention of the provisions of the Liquor Act that prohibit the sale of alcohol on a Sunday (the other 'closed days' being Good Friday and Christmas Day). The President of the Constitutional Court, Arthur Chaskalson, writing for the majority, made extensive reference to *Big M Drug Mart* and endorsed the position, in that case, that a law which compelled sabbatical observance of the Christian Sabbath *would* offend the religious freedom of those who do not adhere to Christian beliefs.[126] In this case, however, the Court found that a law that prohibited certain activities on Sundays for purposes that were 'not purely religious and which [did] not constrain the practice of other religions' would not be rendered unlawful by the mere fact the Christian Sabbath fell on that day.[127] Whereas the Canadian Act bore a 'purely religious purpose and was designed to compel adherence to the Christian Sabbath', Chaskalson P. had 'difficulty in seeing how [the South African provisions could] be said to compel sabbatical observance or to promote any particular religion'.[128] It seemed to Chaskalson P. that the purpose of the closed day provisions was 'to curtail the selling of liquor to the general public on such days', and was not rooted in any religious objective.[129]

However, there is an interesting and eloquent dissent by Justice O'Regan who, having reviewed the text of the Act (the 'closed days' all had religious significance for Christians)[130] and the legislative history (which suggested to her that the purpose and effect of the Act, both at the time of its enactment and now, was 'to give special recognition to the holy days of one religion and not others')[131] concluded

124 Ibid. [127].
125 Ibid. [100].
126 *S v Lawrence; S v Negal; S v Solberg* 1997 4 SA 1176 (CC) [89].
127 Ibid. [89].
128 Ibid. [90].
129 Ibid. [90].
130 Ibid. [125].
131 Ibid. [126].

that the selection of the 'closed days' constituted an 'endorsement of Christianity in conflict with the Constitution'.[132] In contrast, the secular purposes cited in defence of the law (such as to restrict the consumption of alcohol on the days when there are many road users) were not sufficient, in her view, to justify such an infringement of religious freedom. Interestingly, there is also a separate opinion of Justice Sachs attached to the same judgment: according to him, while the provisions indeed serve illegitimate, religious purpose,[133] nevertheless the law is defensible by reference to secular objectives, such as that of 'reducing alcohol intake on these particularly high-risk days'.[134] As one can see, for Justice Sachs the existence of illegitimate objectives does not conclusively taint the law as unconstitutional as long as proper and important secular objectives can be ascertained.

6. German Secular Rationales

Just as in Canada and in South Africa, the issue of compulsory closing on Sundays has been the subject of constitutional litigation in Germany, and just as in Canada, the Federal Constitutional Court has engaged in a complex purpose- and motive-bound analysis, trying to disentangle religious from secular rationales.[135] The difference between the two countries is that the German Court was unwilling to directly hinge its decision upon the 'freedom of religion' of non-believers or non-Christians, and much less on the freedom of religion of Christian churches (who initiated the complaint against relaxation of Sunday closing laws). Rather, the German Court relied on its finding of a 'positive dimension' to the constitutional freedom of religion, that is, 'a positive obligation of the state to protect the interest in question'[136]—the interest here being that of Catholic and Protestant churches.

After constitutional reform in 2005 in which Sunday closing laws became a state rather than federal competence, some states (*Länder*) attempted to ease strict prohibitions dating back to the Weimar Constitution, and that had been subsequently incorporated into the Basic Law. After Berlin authorities passed a law in 2006 allowing shopping on ten Sundays a year as well as lifting the ban on all four Sundays in Advent, the Churches sued Berlin before the Federal Constitutional Court.[137] The Court considered, as the legal basis for its review, a subtle combination of the provision of the Weimar constitutional act still in force

132 Ibid. [132].
133 Ibid. [159].
134 Ibid. [176].
135 I am grateful to Dr Dominik Rennert for his research on German law, and for his translations of German decisions.
136 Para. 134 of the *Sunday Closing Law* case, cited below.
137 BVerfG v. 1.12.2009, 1 BvR 2857/07, 1BvR 2858/07—*Sonntagsschutz* [BVerfG of 1 December 2009, 1 BvR 2857/07, 1BvR 2858/07—*Sunday closing laws*]; BVerfGE 125, 39. No official English translations were provided by the Court.

(Art 139, providing for compulsory Sunday closing) and Article 4 of Basic Law (freedom of religion). But what is of relevance to us is the Court's analysis of a mix of religious and secular purposes for compulsory Sunday closing. Throughout its long judgment, the Court repeatedly referred to a combination of 'secular-social purpose, [and] also a religious-Christian purpose' (para. 139), 'the connection between religious and social aspects in the protection of Sundays and Holidays' (para. 140), and the fact that the Sunday-closing provisions have both a religious element and a secular-social element. The way the Court's rhetoric plays both of these elements against each other, so to speak, is interesting and indicates the Court's desire to carefully hedge its bets, neither falling foul of the constitutional doctrine of neutrality, nor letting down the churches' reliance on a constitutional promise. Whenever it considers religious aspects (for instance, by showing that the Sunday closing provision is located in the 'religion and religious societies' section of the Weimar Constitution,[138] or by referring to the parliamentary rapporteur who appealed directly to religious rationales during the debates on the Weimar Constitution),[139] the Court immediately brings in secular aspects related to 'recreational activities' and 'social interaction'.[140] The Court never tries to systematically separate one ingredient from the other, nor does it attempt to show that secular purposes are *sufficient* to uphold Sunday closing regulations. If anything, it is more concerned with the opposite claim, namely showing that Sunday closing properly implements the 'positive obligation' of the state towards the interests of the churches. In a passage that reveals Germany's constitutional idiosyncrasy on the matter, it says: 'The duty of the state to remain ideologically [*weltanschaulich*] and religiously neutral does not conflict with a concretization of the obligation to protect Art. 4 [of Basic Law] ... and Art. 139 [of the Weimar Constitution].'[141] So in contrast to both of the main Canadian decisions on the same topic that identify the dominance of a religious rationale over the secular (in *Big M*), or vice versa (in *Edwards Books*) as discussed earlier in section 4, the German Sunday closing law decision involved the intermingling of both types of rationales, such that one feels that virtually any specific outcome could have been mandated. In the end, the fact that the provision had a *constitutional* status was decisive.

The purpose/motive orientation is even more evident in those German constitutional decisions which deal with religious symbols, especially in a school

[138] Ibid. para. 141.

[139] Ibid. para. 139.

[140] Ibid. para. 139.

[141] Ibid. para. 148. The word *weltanschaulich* is an adverb corresponding to the noun *Weltanschauung*, a word that is not easily translatable and is often used in English texts without translation. It perhaps best translates to worldview and tries to capture secular equivalents of religion. The use of the words 'ideologically' in the passage in the main text is perhaps the least awkward, but the reader should keep in mind the original German usage. It should be noted that whenever the German Court refers to 'neutrality' in this context, it always uses the standard phrase *religiös-weltanschauliche Neutralität*.

context, such as the presence of crosses (crucifixes) in classrooms and the wearing of headscarves by teachers. By way of general background, it should be explained that under the authoritative doctrine of the Constitutional Court, relationships between state and religion are governed by the meta-principle of neutrality, which is seen to have three main aspects: (1) non-identification of the state with religion, (2) non-discrimination among different religions, and (3) non-evaluation by the state of religious contents.[142] While the third dimension has a rather marginal and auxiliary character, the former two are central and highly controversial, and both are engaged by all three religious symbols cases described below. It should, however, be mentioned at the outset that the general principle of 'neutrality' towards religions and worldviews [*religiös-weltanschauliche Neutralität*] is not construed by the German Court in a 'strict' way (which would correspond to the 'wall of separation', or *laicité*-like interpretation), but rather as a 'supportive' or 'open' neutrality, which lends itself to the state's cooperation with various religions, as long as they are not endorsed and the non-discrimination principle is respected.[143] What this cryptic formula really means in practice can be ascertained only by an analysis of the landmark cases in the area.

The *Crucifix* decision of 1995 was one of the most controversial decisions of the Federal Constitutional Court.[144] The Court found the Bavarian practice of placing crosses in classrooms of public schools was an infringement of the 'negative' freedom of religion of non-Christian students. The judgment lends itself to two different (though mutually compatible) readings, either in terms of effects or in terms of motives/purposes. While the effects-oriented reading (emphasizing the impact that crosses in the classrooms have upon non-Christian students, and/or their parents) is perfectly plausible, as is the reading of legislative motives, which directly aligns itself with the main argument of this chapter.

The Court began by characterizing the motives of the state legislators who stressed the non-religious purposes of the crucifix in the classroom in the following way. The government of Bavaria had emphasized how German culture was informed by Christianity; 'the cross [is] not an expression of a certain confession or faith, but an essential part of the common Christian-occidental [*christlich-abendländisch*] tradition of our culture'.[145] As the Bavarian government put it, it is also the task of public schools to teach 'those values and norms that, crucially informed by Christianity, have become in large parts the common heritage of occidental culture'. Hence, the purpose of the regulation is to make sure that 'primary public schools convey exactly these values without embracing

[142] See *Headscarf I* decision, BVerfG v. 24.9.2003, 2 BvR 1436/02—*Kopftuch I* [FCC of 24 September 2003, 2 BvR 1436/02, BVerfGE 108, 282, paras. 42–43.

[143] *Headscarf I* para. 43.

[144] BVerfG v. 16.5.1995, 1 BvR 1087/91—Kruzifix [FCC of 16 May 1995, 1 BvR 1087/91—Crucifix]; BverfGE 93, 1. There is no official English translation provided by the Court.

[145] Ibid 5.

theological positions that would be in contradiction to the principle of religious-ideological neutrality of the state'.78 But the Federal Constitutional Court took issue with this characterization of the purposes behind the law, one reason being that such a perspective of the meaning of the Cross erodes it of its actual religious value. As the Court said:

> [t]he cross is still one of the religious symbols specific to Christianity. In fact, it is its main religious symbol.... It would be a profanation of the cross and contrary to the self-understanding of Christianity and the Christian churches if one considered it... as a mere expression of occidental tradition or as a cult-like symbol without any religious content.[146]

Note the delicious irony of the argument. In defence of the religious neutrality of the state, the Federal Court adopts a position *internal* to the religion and defends the main religious symbol against a possible trivialization by its widespread usage in a secular setting. In contrast, in order to defend the wide presence of the religious symbol, the state legislator underplays its essentially religious meanings and characterizes it in general, rather anodyne, socio-cultural terms. But this is, of course, just a matter of two opposing rhetorical strategies. As a matter of substance, the Court held that the introduction of 'Christian elements in a public primary school' should be kept to a minimum and finds that having crosses in a classroom crosses the line between the acceptable and illegitimate uses of religious symbols. And, the Court adds, again taking an 'internal' religious perspective: the Cross 'symbolizes the essential core of the Christian faith which may have formed the western world in multiple ways, but which is in no way shared by all members of society, but rather rejected by many in their exercise of their right from Art. 4.1 of Basic Law [freedom of religion]'.[147] In terms of the illegitimate motive analysis, the argument is clear: the shape of the Bavarian law reveals an intention to impose some specific religious symbolism upon all, including those who do not espouse this religion—and *this* legislative purpose violates the principle of neutrality.

Two 'headscarf cases' decided in 2003 and 2015 constitute a pair of famous and controversial decisions by the Federal Constitutional Court. While the background of both cases is constant—the situation of the Muslim minority in Germany—the starkly divergent outcomes may be attributed to the changed and more consolidated position of that minority than to the evolving jurisprudence of the Court. In the first decision, the Court permitted state legislatures to ban teachers from wearing headscarves. In the second, the Court revised its earlier position and declared such a ban unconstitutional.

[146] Ibid. 19–20.
[147] Ibid. 23–24.

In *Headscarf I*,[148] the Court begins by considering three possible justifications for the ban—and finds each of them unsatisfactory—essentially undertaking a classical proportionality analysis conducted by reference to the stated purposes of the act. The three purposes, as ascertained by the Court, are: (1) to educate students in conformity with the principle of neutrality, (2) to safeguard parents' freedom to determine their children's education, and (3) to protect (negative) religious freedom of the child.[149] None of these purposes are actually served by the ban, the Court asserts, because expert findings on the influence that headscarves have on schoolchildren are inconclusive.[150] Up to this point, one might expect that everything points to an invalidation of the ban. Not so, the Court says, and adopts a rather awkward middle ground: the ban is not unconstitutional per se but is unconstitutional in this specific case only because there was no state law explicitly allowing a ban. Instead, the school officials had relied on their own general powers as the teachers' supervisors to prohibit the wearing of the headscarf.[151] The Court seemed to be sceptical about such situations (because 'increasing religious diversity could also be welcomed in the school and used as a medium to exercise mutual tolerance, thereby contributing to integration'),[152] but ultimately considered that the state legislator could use the option, within its legitimate range of discretion, of adopting such bans. But what was important was that the state legislator, rather than the school executives, could only issue such bans.

This solution came under attack in the *Headscarf II* case,[153] where the Court effectively overruled its earlier judgment.[154] Resting a headscarf ban merely on the abstract risk of conflicts, the Court said, cannot justify the considerable infringement upon the religious freedom of the teachers. Only when conflicts within a specific school actually arise could a ban limited to the teacher in question be justified, when all other means of mediation have been exhausted, such as transferring the teacher to a different class. The main rationale for the second *Headscarf* case, however, was the discriminatory character of the ban in the first place. There, the Court found that it constituted an unconstitutional discrimination against members of religions other than Christianity or Judaism.[155] This reveals—though the Court did not say it in so many words—a religious animus

[148] BverfG v. 24.9.2003, 2 BvR 1436/02—*Kopftuch I* [FCC of 24 September 2003, 2 BvR 1436/02—*Headscarf I*], BverfGE 108, 282.

[149] Ibid para. 49.

[150] Ibid para. 56.

[151] Ibid paras. 62–71.

[152] Ibid para. 65.

[153] BVerfG v. 27.1.2015, 1 BvR 471/10, 1 BvR 1181/10—*Kopftuch II* [FCC of 27 January 2015, 1 BvR 471/10, 1 BvR 1181/10—*Headscarf II*]. No official English translation was available at the time of writing this paper.

[154] The judgment in 2015 was handed down by a different section (*Senat*) of the Court than the one in 2003.

[155] *Headscarf II* para. 124.

against the Muslim religion and prejudice regarding its specific precepts, for example about gender inequality. The Court said:

> [t]here are no valid justifications for discriminating against religious demonstrations that are not rooted in Christian and occidental culture and tradition … Especially the general assumption that wearing a Muslim headscarf … is a sign … of a comprehensive … inequality between man and woman and thereby affects the wearer's suitability for teaching positions is unacceptable.[156]

At this point the Court makes an explicit appeal to legislative motives. As a general proposition, actual motives must be recognized and cannot be replaced by new, more acceptable ones in the process of defending the statute: 'Respect for the democratically legitimated legislator makes it impossible to give, by way of interpretation, a new meaning to a law that is clear *in its purpose* and wording or to fundamentally change the normative content of a provision …'[157] And the motive of the legislator, the Court observes, *was* discriminatory. Citing parliamentary records, the Court says: 'Both the draft initiators and in the remaining process, the *motive* predominated not to pass a provision that would prohibit the wearing of monk's habits or the Jewish kippa.'[158] In this way, the legislature's motives for adopting the ban, and the corresponding purposes, taint it as unconstitutionally discriminatory.

An interesting case at the intersection of religious freedom and individual freedom in general, specifically concerning freedom in marriage, came up in one of the first decisions of the German Federal Constitutional Court in which the proportionality analysis hinged partly on an argument alleging the lack of a legitimate legislative purpose. In the second of a series of three 'church tax cases', the Court had to consider whether the duty to pay church taxes also extended to the spouses of church members who did not belong to the tax-paying church of the other spouse. Note, incidentally, that none of the constitutional cases before the FCC concerned the constitutionality of church taxes as such, but only considered controversies about from *whom* the tax could be levied. In the first case, the Court struck down state laws that extended the duty to pay church taxes to certain corporations,[159] while in the second case, the issue was whether spouses who were not members of a church still had to pay church tax, in addition to their income tax, if their spouse was a member.[160] (The third case concerned a factual situation which was a variant of the second case.)[161] The Court summarized the

[156] Ibid. para. 129.
[157] Ibid. para. 132, emphasis added.
[158] Ibid. para. 135, emphasis added.
[159] Judgment of 14 December 1965, 1 BvR 412/60, BVerfGE 19, 206.
[160] Ibid. 226.
[161] Ibid. 242.

legislative purpose behind the provision challenged in the second case as 'the argument that the tax obligation of a spouse that is not a member of the taxing church or the religious community is justified by the nature of marriage as a permanent union between partners that comprises all areas of life' (para. 37)—and resoundingly dismissed it. It pointed out that in 'inter-faith marriages', what is missing is precisely the joint acceptance of certain religious beliefs and obligations, and to accept that such a divergence violates the nature of the marriage 'would contradict the liberal order of the Basic Law' (para. 38). As the Court said, under that order both spouses are free to pursue 'their own paths in religious matters', and this does not constitute a fault in marital obligations (para. 38). The Court celebrated the tolerance that spouses in inter-faith marriages owe each other, and argued that consequently, one spouse's tax obligations towards his/her church cannot bind the other (para. 38). On this basis, the Court had no problem in showing that the law had no legitimate purpose and was therefore unconstitutional. This is a secular, liberal vision of a marriage, and it rejects the possibility of imposing the sectarian religious views of the nature of the marriage upon one of the spouses.

7. Freedom of Religion in the 'Jewish and Democratic State' of Israel

The legal systems considered so far in this chapter—the United States, Australia, Canada, South Africa, and Germany—share a general underlying commitment to the ideal of a secular state, and even if the parameters of secularism are differently calibrated in these constitutional systems, they all exemplify the idea of the separation of state and religion. Hence, the detection of *par excellence* religious purposes of a law is a strong prima facie reason for deeming it unconstitutional. The situation is more difficult in the states where general constitutional commitments depart from the ideal of secularism, even broadly understood. The detection of the religious purpose of a law does not per se disqualify such laws. And yet, even in such states, the application of the proportionality analysis helps to identify religious purposes that are not properly pursued by the legal means adopted by a legislator.

A good example of such a legal system is Israel, a state defined by its major constitutional act as 'a Jewish and democratic state'.[162] This description, as we will see in a moment, has yielded decisions in which religious purpose is present in ways that most probably would be deemed unconstitutional in the other legal systems considered so far. And yet, despite the constitutional characterization

[162] *Basic Law: Human Dignity and Liberty* (5722—1992). I am grateful to Ms Chantal Tanner for her research on Israeli law.

of the State of Israel, Judaism is not proclaimed as the official religion, and the foundational document of the state—its Declaration of Independence—declares 'complete equality of social and political rights to all its inhabitants irrespective of religion ...' as well as 'freedom of religion' and safeguards for 'the Holy Places of all religions'.[163] As a result, Israeli legal scholars have struggled with the conceptualization of the constitutional status of religions in the Israeli state, and have usually come up with labels such as 'hybrid'. For Professor Shimon Shetreet of the Hebrew University in Jerusalem, hybrid means 'between non-intervention in religious affairs, on the one hand, and the inter-involvement of religion and government in several forms on the other ...'[164]

The 'inter-involvement' of which Shetreet speaks is well illustrated by the cases in which the Supreme Court of Israel recognized that the aim of safeguarding religious feelings and observant religious lifestyle constitutes a proper purpose under Israeli law, while the Court at the same time policed the boundaries of state action to achieve these purposes. The leading case in this line of jurisprudence is *Horev v Minister of Transportation*,[165] where at stake was a direct clash between the rights and freedoms of the religious Jewish community to express their religious practices and the rights of the secular communities to practice their secular lifestyle. Under scrutiny was an order by the Minister of Transportation to close Bar-Ilan Street in Jerusalem to motor traffic on Sabbaths and Jewish holidays. The decision was challenged by secular residents of the secular population in Jerusalem, who argued that the road closures infringed upon their right to freedom of movement.

The Court commenced its analysis of the purpose of the order by establishing that the values of the State of Israel, as 'Jewish and democratic', were relevant to the question of purpose. Thus, the Court found that it was 'beyond dispute that consideration of religious sensibilities is commensurate with the values of the State of Israel as a Jewish state. Indeed, a Jewish state is sensitive to the religious feelings of every one of its citizens.'[166] In this case, the proper purpose test needed to examine the objective of the restriction on freedom of movement caused by the legitimate purpose of protecting religious sensitivities.[167]

In the judgment, President of the Court Aharon Barak cited a number of prior judgments in which religious factors have been interpreted as a relevant consideration.[168] For example, in the exercise of discretionary powers instituting daylight savings time, religious needs are permitted to be taken into account.[169]

[163] Israeli Declaration of Independence, 14 May 1948.
[164] Shimon Shetreet, 'Freedom of Religion in Israel' (Speech delivered at the World Conference Against Racism, Durban, 20 August 2001) http://mfa.gov.il/MFA/MFAArchive/2001/Pages/Freedom%20of%20Religion%20in%20Israel.aspx (last accessed 9 June 2020).
[165] *Horev v. Minister of Transportation*, HCJ 5016/9.
[166] Ibid. [55] President Aharon Barak.
[167] Ibid. [65] President Aharon Barak.
[168] Ibid. [48] President Aharon Barak.
[169] *Segel v. Minister of the Interior*, HCJ 217/8, 439 [7].

Similarly, the interests of the religious and secular populations are permitted to be considered when establishing industrial and agricultural standards. Likewise, religious sensibilities may be considered in exercising the discretion to prohibit the performance of a play that may offend the audience's religious sensibilities.[170] In the end, however, having established 'injury to religious sensibilities' as a valid consideration, the Court found that the Minister of Transportation had not adequately considered the interests of secular residents, and as such, the ministerial order was struck down.

Although President Barak found the purpose of the Minister's decision to be proper and in accordance with the values of freedom of religion, he determined that the closure of the road on the Sabbaths must not be restrictive beyond what is strictly necessary. He declared an absolute closure of Bar-Ilan Street throughout the entire Sabbath day to be excessive. It is incumbent upon authorities to apply the least restrictive measures possible. Thus, President Barak concluded that:

> [f]or our purposes, the least restrictive means would be a partial closure, during prayer times, at which time religious feelings are most offended, rather than imposing an absolute closure. This is undoubtedly the case from the perspective of the secular residents, who would be unable to reach their homes throughout the Sabbath, were an absolute closure to be imposed.[171]

While this conclusion (leading to an invalidation of the ministerial order) sounds much like an effects-based finding of discrimination, the correlation of effects and motives in the Court's reasoning is clear. The Minister, the Court said, had not considered the interests of secular inhabitants seriously enough; an implication is that their interests were not regarded with sufficient respect by the executive. This ingenious use of proportionality analysis allowed the Court to strike down the order as discriminatory based on lack of respect for the 'victims' of the order, while at the same time paying lip service to the protection of religious sensibilities as a legitimate governmental goal in a state which is 'Jewish and democratic'.

[170] *Keinan v. Film and Play Review Board for Films*, HCJ 351/72, 814 [8] Landau J.
[171] *Horev v. Minister of Transportation*, HCJ 5016/9, [83] President Aharon Barak.

8

Standards of Scrutiny, Equal Protection, and Illicit Motives for Discrimination

In Chapter 4, section 3, I have shown how the uses of heightened levels of scrutiny of legislative acts may be best explained by reference to the judicial attempts to flush out the real motives of the legislator. Let me recall here the most succinct and compelling description of this connection, by John Hart Ely:

> The goal the classification in issue is likely to fit most closely, obviously, is the goal the legislators actually had in mind.... The 'special scrutiny' ... insists that the classification in issue fit the goal invoked in its defense more closely than any alternative classification would. There is only one goal the classification is likely to fit *that* closely, however, and that is the goal the legislators actually had in mind.[1]

The language of levels of scrutiny is applicable to a number of areas in which the scrutiny of putative legislative intrusions into constitutional rights is involved, but perhaps nowhere else is this connection between levels of scrutiny and the motive-based analysis as clear as in the field of equal protection, or non-discrimination.

Of all forms of discrimination, that based on race is perhaps the most invidious, and (alongside gender-based discrimination) may serve as a paradigmatic way of denying equal protection to a group. Of course, the salience of race differs from country to country, and context must be taken into account if one wishes to make any generalizations. No doubt, race discrimination is particularly salient in the United States, and it is important to realize the significance of detecting discriminatory motives or purposes as a way of ascertaining the denial of public reason in law: of course, non-discriminatory motives do not guarantee that the law implements public reason, but discriminatory motives deny it unquestionably (a non-discriminatory purpose is a necessary but not sufficient condition of public reason). One of the landmark judgments of the US Supreme Court proclaimed famously that '[t]he basic equal protection principle [is] that the invidious quality of a law claimed to be racially discriminatory must ultimately be traced to a racially discriminatory *purpose*'.[2]

1 J.H. Ely, *Democracy and Distrust* (Harvard University Press 1980) 145–46, endnotes omitted.
2 *Washington v. Davis*, 426 U.S. 229, 240 (1976), emphasis added.

Constitutional Public Reason. Wojciech Sadurski, Oxford University Press. © Wojciech Sadurski 2023.
DOI: 10.1093/oso/9780192869678.003.0008

This will be an assumption vindicated in this chapter, though its aspirations are not limited to *racially* discriminatory laws, and not only to US law. In section 1, I will take a concept of 'suspect classifications' seriously and will look into the most likely features that may render a classification 'suspect', which inevitably—as I shall argue—leads us to the question of legislative motivations behind a legal classification. In section 2, I will offer a theory which may help us operationalize the idea of 'prejudice' by looking at external 'indicia' of such prejudice, hence, of suspect classifications. Illustrations will be taken from the United States and South Africa. In section 3, using examples from India and Canada, I shall offer some instances of how judges actually figure out the presence of impermissible motives behind a legal classification. (I should perhaps add that the chapter is rather cursory because I have already developed a similar account of motives-based theory of legal discrimination at some length in one of my recent books.)[3]

1. Suspect Classifications and Prejudice

As a starting point, we may take the concept of '*suspect* classifications' seriously as a term of art developed in US Fourteenth Amendment jurisprudence.[4] We normally use the language of 'suspicion' when we have doubts about something, while not being absolutely sure. *If* we had no initial doubts or qualms about a piece of legislation, we would settle for a simple, lenient scrutiny; on the other hand, if we *knew* legislation to be discriminatory, no further scrutiny would be needed, and we might as well reach directly for our conclusion. So the language of 'suspicion' captures the circumstances in which we place certain argumentative burdens on whoever defends a given legislative measure .

But we need more than a mere *suspicion*; we need at least some rough contours of what makes the suspicion justified. In turn, this can be spelled out only if we have some general theory about what constitutes 'discrimination'; we cannot describe our grounds of suspicion unless we have at least some preliminary, even pre-theoretical, ideas about what constitutes discrimination in the first place, and one way of doing it is to characterize some illicit legislative motivations as discriminatory. After all, there are also classifications that may be irrational, but which are not triggered by any wrongful motive, and where the language of discrimination may strike us as exaggerated. These can be seen as

[3] Wojciech Sadurski, *Equality and Legitimacy* (Oxford University Press 2008) Ch. 3.

[4] On racial classifications viewed as suspect, see e.g. *Korematsu v. United States*, 323 U.S. 214, 216 (1944), *McLaughlin v. Florida*, 379 U.S. 184 (1964), *Fullilove v. Klutznick*, 448 U.S. 448, 508 (1980) (Powell, J. concurring). Other criteria have also occasionally been viewed as constituting suspect classification, including alienage (*Graham v. Richardson*, 403 U.S. 365, 372 (1971)), national origin (*Hirabayashi v. United States*, 320 U.S. 81, 100 (1943)), and gender (*Craig v. Boren*, 429 U.S. 190 (1976)), though in the latter case, it triggered an intermediate rather than a strict scrutiny. For an early scholarly treatment, see Joseph Tussman and Jacobus tenBroek, 'The Equal Protection of the Laws', (1949) 37 *California Law Review* 341, 356.

errors of judgement on the part of the legislator, and can be detected even by rational-basis scrutiny, without any need for suspicion-based strict scrutiny. For instance, to set the level of eligibility for a driver's licence at the age of forty would most probably be considered irrational, producing excessive under-inclusion intolerable even under a very lenient scrutiny, and yet very few people would 'suspect' worse attitudes on the part of the legislator than mere silliness. But when we reflect upon paradigmatically invidious discriminations in the past and at the present time, we do not usually come up with examples such as *this*. Rather, we think immediately about racist, sexist, homophobic, or religious discriminations that cannot simply be characterized as an error in legislative judgement: they are evils, not mistakes. To discriminate against a group of people, for instance on the basis of its racial or gender characteristics, 'has a significance which is not adequately captured by saying that it involves not treating them in accordance with relevant criteria';[5] there is an added moral value of reprobation beyond (and sometimes, beside) a charge of mere irrationality. And the most intuitive ground for such a heightened moral reprobation of paradigmatic discriminations is that we consider them to be wrong because they stem from evil motives, not from merely mistaken judgements about a classification's rationality; we believe that they are triggered by prejudice, hostility, dislike, bias, self-imposed ignorance, unfair stereotyping, etc.

Tom Campbell has captured this well in asserting that 'discrimination is the perpetration of unjustifiable inequality in consequence of bigotry'.[6] 'Bigotry', just as 'prejudice', is of course a vague and capacious category, and Campbell explained that the discrimination-inducing motives normally comprise 'dogmatically held beliefs involving stereotyped images of groups ... and negative emotional responses to these stereotypes, ranging from expressed hostility to habituated indifference'.[7] This definition may be further refined. For example, in a recent article, Aziz Huq has helpfully distinguished cases of 'animus' (understood as a 'taste' or 'desire' basically not to have contact with a disliked group), from beliefs based on stereotypes which are in turn based on negative generalizations, and from the intent to promote one's own status by denigrating others.[8] But as a starting point, Campbell's is probably as good a characterization of discrimination as one can find, and its advantage is that it connects the description with an appeal to the *sources* of special moral wrongness of discrimination, compared to a neutral term, 'classification'. These sources are linked to the wrongful motives for a particular legal classification. Consider, for example, the following argument in favour of a deferential scrutiny of legislative classification:

[5] Tom Campbell, 'Unlawful Discrimination', in Wojciech Sadurski, (ed.), *Ethical Dimensions of Legal Theory* (Rodopi 1991) 153, 156.

[6] Ibid. 163. See also Ronald Dworkin, *A Matter of Principle* (Harvard University Press, 1985) 302, 314.

[7] Campbell, 'Unlawful Discrimination' (n. 5) 153.

[8] Aziz Z. Huq, 'What Is Discriminatory Intent?', (2018) 103 *Cornell Law Review* 1211, 1242–59.

> The distinctive legislative response ... to the plight of those who are mentally retarded demonstrates that ... the lawmakers have been addressing their difficulties in a manner that *belies a continuing antipathy or prejudice* and corresponding need for more intrusive oversight by the judiciary.[9]

By implication, when suspicion of 'antipathy or prejudice' *is* warranted, a more 'intrusive' scrutiny of legislation is justified.

This approach also resonates with Dworkin's 'banned sources' theory of discrimination, articulated as it was in contrast to a 'banned categories' theory that attaches the discriminatory character of classification to the nature of criteria which serve as the basis of classification.[10] 'Banned sources' theory, in Dworkin's conceptualization, 'insists that preferences that are rooted in some form of prejudice against one group can never count in favour of a policy that includes the disadvantage of that group'.[11] In contrast, the 'banned categories' theories demand merely that 'certain properties or categories, including race, ethnic background, and perhaps gender, not be used to distinguish groups of citizens for different treatment ...'.[12] It is easy to note that the latter set of theories are, more often than not, attached to the fact of the 'immutability' of certain individual properties (expressed sometimes in the 'colour-blindness' theory),[13] and one place where immutability was expressly invoked as part of a defence of colour-blindness was a dissent by Justice Stewart in *Fullilove v. Klutznick*,[14] a US Supreme Court decision upholding certain state preferences for minority business enterprises. As Justice Stewart said, 'The color of a person's skin and the country of his origin are immutable facts that bear no relation to ability, disadvantage, moral culpability, or any other characteristics of constitutionally permissible interest to government'.[15]

But the proposition that immutability in itself may confer discriminatory character upon a classification is highly implausible.[16] It is perhaps enough to state the most natural and principled rationale for immutability-based theory, such as that people should not be treated differently by virtue of properties beyond their control,[17] to see how weak and vulnerable this theory is, in addition to being inconsistent with a large number of actual social and legal practices which intuitively seem unobjectionable (think about the distribution of educational

[9] *Cleburne v. Cleburne Living Center*, 473 U.S. 432, 443 (1985), emphasis added.

[10] Ronald Dworkin, *Law's Empire* (Fontana 1986) 384–87.

[11] Ibid. 384.

[12] Ibid. 384.

[13] In its judicial life, the theory can be traced to a famous dissent by Harlan J. in *Plessy v. Ferguson*, 163 U.S. 537, 559 (1896) (Harlan J. dissenting). Its contemporary uses are displayed by opponents of race-conscious affirmative action, see, e.g., *Grutter v. Bollinger*, 539 U.S. 306 353, 368, 371 (2003) (Thomas J. dissenting).

[14] 448 U.S. 448 (1980).

[15] Ibid. 525 (Stewart J. dissenting).

[16] See Sadurski, *Equality and Legitimacy* (n. 3) 111–24.

[17] See Dworkin, *Law's Empire* (n. 10) 394.

and professional opportunities which, to a large degree, rest on individual properties over which persons have no control).[18] Both as a general theory, and also based on our empirical knowledge of the world, the idea that a criterion of classification may, per se, render a classification discriminatory does not make much sense. To start with, as a general theory it is difficult to find a compelling moral justification for a *generalized* hostility towards classifications based on immutable characteristics. One possible trope may be the argument that immutable characteristics (race, gender) are more closely linked to one's identity than the alterable properties which are more defining of a person's changeable roles in a society. But this is a non-starter: there may be immutable characteristics which are hardly connected with the important identity of a person (the shape of one's nose, assuming that it is not alterable through cosmetic surgery) and on the other hand, there may be alterable 'roles' which may be highly central to one's identity (trade-union membership, for instance). Further, one would need a good reason to be produced for hostility against drawing classifications based on identity-related traits. No such argument (other than a vague concern about 'identity politics')[19] comes to my mind.

There may be a second, perhaps more promising, strategy for defending antipathy towards classifications based on immutable characteristics: it may be thought that it is unfair to impose legal burdens upon individuals based on the criteria that prevent them from liberating themselves from these burdens by escaping a burdened group. This concern can be heard in Justice Brennan's opinion (partly concurring, partly dissenting) in *Bakke*.[20] Brennan argued in favour of applying an 'intermediate' level of scrutiny to classifications based on race, gender, and illegitimacy, and as the reason for heightening the standard of scrutiny (though not all the way up to a strict level), he offered the fact that each of these criteria 'is an immutable characteristic which its possessors are powerless to escape or set aside'.[21] But this is a puzzling argument; it suggests that a classification would be non-discriminatory if a person singled out by it would be capable of 'escaping' it. Why would protection against discrimination be contingent upon the (in-)escapability of a protected category? Isn't it analogous to saying that there is nothing wrong with homophobic insults as long as their victims may escape the insult by changing their sexual orientation?

As our knowledge of the world tells us, there is hardly *any* characteristic which, necessarily and per se, renders a classification discriminatory by its very presence: classifications based on race, religion, gender etc. may or may not be discriminatory, and they may not be perceived as such by a group picked up by

[18] See ibid. 394–95.

[19] As sketched for instance in Claus Offe, '"Homogeneity" and Constitutional Democracy: Coping with Identity Conflicts through Group Rights', (1988) 6 *Journal of Political Philosophy* 113.

[20] *University of California Regents v. Bakke*, 438 U.S. 265 (1978).

[21] Ibid. 360 (Brennan, White, Marshall, and Blackmun JJ. concurring in part and dissenting in part).

those classifications. And not all citizens feel humiliated when a racial or religious classification is deployed towards them; some may feel great pride.[22] There is nothing self-evidently wrong about resting a classification on immutable characteristics,[23] and vice versa there is nothing inherently innocuous about a classification being based on individual properties which are alterable through a human action. In addition, the wrongness of a classification must not depend on whether we have a theory that a particular human property is alterable or not, especially when people seriously disagree about such alterability. Think of sexual orientation or religious affiliation: are these 'alterable' properties? and why should it matter for a theory of discrimination anyway? Religion, in some important ways *is* involuntary, in the sense that often people do not freely 'choose' their faith (and in addition, they see this unchosen character as an important element of strength of their religious commitment, as evidenced by conceptions of predestination or revelation), but also in an important sense *is* alterable, because we know that people occasionally do change their religious affiliations or abandon faith altogether. But why would the discriminatory character of religious classification be dependent upon whether a person 'chose' her religion or was born into it, or was chosen by God, for that matter? Will religious classifications become less problematic by virtue of the general adoption of a sociological conception of religion which emphasizes free religious choice? Religious classifications are unjust (when they *are* unjust) not because people normally do not choose their religion but when that classification expresses prejudice.

Ironically, a hint about the connection between racial classification and wrongful motives can be found in Justice Clarence Thomas dissent in *Grutter*[24]—a judgment in which the US Supreme Court upheld the University of Michigan Law School's affirmative admission programme. It is 'ironic' because Justice Thomas himself strongly rejects affirmative action—an area which is particularly hospitable to the argument that the absence of wrongful motives renders a classification innocuous. Justice Thomas states: 'The Constitution abhors classifications based on race, not only because those classifications can harm favored races *or are based on illegitimate motives* . . .'[25] So we have a gesture towards an illegitimate motives theory of discrimination—though a gesture only, without a follow-up. It is worth citing the remaining part of the sentence: '. . . but also because every time the government places citizens on racial registers and makes relevant to the provision of burdens and benefits, it demeans us all.'[26] This is pure rhetoric, amplified by the question-begging assertion that 'racial classifications are *per se* harmful'[27]—but the mention of 'illegitimate motives' is worth retaining

22 See Huq, What is Discriminatory Intent?' (n. 8) 1254.
23 See Campbell, 'Unlawful Discrimination' (n. 5) 158.
24 *Grutter v. Bollinger*, 539 U.S. 306 (2003).
25 Ibid. 353 (Thomas J. dissenting), emphasis added.
26 Ibid. 353.
27 Ibid. 371.

because it squares with the general argument here, namely that strict scrutiny (expressing, as it does, a suspicion of wrongful motives) is a reasonable device for smoking out illicit motivations.

Such an argument has been made expressly in another important decision of the US Supreme Court, handed down in the same year that *Grutter* was decided. In *Lawrence v. Texas*,[28] the Court struck down a penal provision prohibiting private homosexual conduct. Justice O'Connor, in her concurrence, described the factors determining the level of scrutiny under the Fourteenth Amendment in the following way:

> Laws such as economic or tax legislation that are scrutinized under rational basis review normally pass constitutional muster, since 'the Constitution presumes that even improvident decisions will eventually be rectified by the democratic processes'. We have consistently held, however, that some objectives, such as a 'bare desire to harm a politically unpopular group', are not legitimate state interests. When a law exhibits such a *desire to harm a politically unpopular group*, we have applied a more searching form of rational basis review to strike down such laws under the Equal Protection Clause.[29]

As one can see, in this passage Justice O'Connor combines a political theory of democracy which, normally, is capable of self-correction, with a motive-oriented scrutiny of classifications singling out 'politically unpopular groups' which have the effect that they require stronger judicial protection. The first sentence in the above-quoted passage is the default position, *à la* Footnote Four and *à la* John Hart Ely, embracing a deferential review of usual, routine classifications on the basis that the possibility of a legislative revision of such classifications is a norm. The last two sentences are about an exception to the norm, when a politically unpopular group is likely to encounter obstacles in rectifying disadvantageous laws. An added value in O'Connor's passage is her express mention of wrongful 'objectives', such as a 'desire to harm'.

There will be easy cases and there will be hard cases, the latter leading to a strongly warranted 'suspicion', in the sense suggested at the opening of this chapter. It would fly in the face of common sense, for example, to say that in the case of racial segregation on public transport, we are fundamentally incapable of determining whether a regulation was triggered by racist animus, hostility, and prejudice, or by some more benign motive, such as (to give a deliberately nonsensical example) the aesthetic value of having people of different races sit together in different sections of the train.[30] However, not all cases are so clear-cut. Truly hard

[28] 539 U.S. 558 (2003).

[29] Ibid. 579–80, citations omitted (O'Connor J. concurring in the judgment), quoting 473 U.S. 440 (1980) and *US Dept of Agriculture v. Moreno* 413 U.S. 677, 686 (1973), emphasis added.

[30] As Richard Fallon observed, 'In light of history and familiar psychology ... some types of action—as identified either by their contents or their effects—can be seen in the aggregate as

cases (for instance, race-conscious preferential admission or protective labour legislation for women) will call for the use, in our decisions about the level of scrutiny of the classification, of a *working* theory of discrimination. To say merely that strict scrutiny is justified whenever any such classification appears to be based on prejudice, hostility, or other invidious motives would leave us with a standard almost impossible to apply in particular cases, other than the most obvious ones. We need some more objective indicia of wrongful motives in order to avoid the need to second-guess the true motives inclining legislators to enact a particular regulation. To put it differently, we need criteria that are reasonably well correlated with prejudice but which themselves are more verifiable than prejudice itself. These criteria are not about motives for classification but rather about the structural characteristics of a classification which are proxies for wrongful motives. They may cohere into a 'motive-neutral definition of unlawful discrimination'[31] which is, nevertheless, embedded in a moral and political analysis connected with the identification of sources of discrimination as invidious motives.

2. Indicia of Illicit Motives

This has been a long-winded way of explaining the method by which we should think about triggers of strict scrutiny. Since we cannot have direct and reliable access to legislative motivations, and the theory of discrimination relies crucially upon the identification of illicit motives, I wish to offer three indicia of wrongful motivations which justify a suspicion that a classification was informed by wrong motives. These indicia are not taken from thin air but are rather formulated on an inductive basis: on the basis of our awareness that various invidious discriminations, historically and today, about which intuitively we have no doubts as to their basis in wrongful motivations, have usually displayed these indicia, so that even if we cannot reach those motivations directly in a classification under scrutiny, we can infer their role through the presence of these indicia.

This, as one can see, is a 'reflective equilibrium'-based methodology, which is a special case of a coherence-oriented theory of moral reasoning. Reflective equilibrium, in Rawls's interpretation, consists of achieving a rough coherence between, on one hand, our 'considered convictions of justice', understood as specific moral responses to issues which demand evaluations in terms of justice, and, on the other hand, our general 'principles of justice', understood as abstract moral maxims.[32] The underlying assumption is that we all hold certain moral

likely to reflect forbidden purposes', Richard H. Fallon Jr., 'The Supreme Court, 1996 Term—Foreword: Implementing the Constitution', (1997) 111 *Harvard Law Review* 54, 95, footnote omitted.

[31] Campbell, 'Unlawful Discrimination' (n. 5) 155.

[32] John Rawls, *A Theory of Justice* (Oxford University Press 1972) 19–20.

beliefs of different level of abstractness, and also we hold them with different degrees of conviction. The 'reflective equilibrium' methodology consists of using those judgements which we hold with the greatest force of conviction (which may be located at any level of abstractness) as our 'provisional fixed points' against which we will evaluate other moral views for their coherence with those 'fixed points'. Fixed points, though, need not be set in stone, but are also subject to change, on reflection—hence the ever-dynamic character of the methodology.

This method seems well-suited for our purposes when discussing indicia of discrimination because, as will be remembered, what we need is to identify those circumstances in which our initial 'suspicions' about wrongful motives at play are compelling, and which in turn should trigger a stronger than usual scrutiny of the classification. This means that, usually, we will be dealing with hard cases, when we are of two minds about whether a given classification is truly and invidiously discriminatory; if we were certain about it, we would not be speaking of a 'suspicion'. Reflective equilibrium is designed precisely to test those cases 'where our present judgments are in doubt and given with hesitation'[33] by appealing to whatever are our 'fixed points', that is, those 'judgments ... which we now make intuitively and in which we have the greatest confidence'.[34] So, for example, in the area of anti-discrimination law and policies we may be 'in doubt' as to whether affirmative action in the fields of employment or higher education is discriminatory or not, just as we may be in doubt whether the exclusion of women from active military duties, or religious exemptions from otherwise generally binding obligations, or the disenfranchisement of certain classes of convicted prisoners, is discriminatory or not. But, these days, very few people would hold serious moral doubts (and if they do, very few of us would wish to treat them with respect) about whether the disenfranchisement of women or racial minorities, or racial segregation in public transport and education, or curfew requirements imposed on an ethnic group, are discriminatory. Furthermore, on these latter examples, most of us believe that discrimination in these cases is blatant and morally reprehensible; in other words, that it is not merely a case of a classification based irrationally on an irrelevant property, but a practice which is demeaning and insulting to its victims. And while often the making of such descriptive arguments with the use of the 'we' or the 'most of us' as a subject of a phrase may seem arbitrary and question-begging, in *these* particular cases a broad moral consensus in contemporary democratic societies warrants making such statements. To summarize, the point is to elaborate the test of prejudice (or other similar wrongful motives) using the unquestionably discriminatory classifications as a starting point so as to be able to apply it to those moral

[33] Ibid. 19.
[34] Ibid. 19.

disagreements on which we may have doubts and need clear-headed answers in today's actual controversies.

Here are the three indicia meant to perform that role.

First, it is intuitively plausible to say that, historically, invidious discrimination has usually been a product of political or legislative action by a politically powerful group against those unrepresented (or underrepresented) in the political and legislative process. Hence, the burdens imposed by a majority (in a democratic system) or by political elite upon a minority or upon an underrepresented group, raise immediate suspicion of activation by invidious motives. In contrast, this suspicion is not warranted when a legislator grants *benefits* to a group which is beyond, or at the margin of, the political process, while burdens of the new regulation are to be borne by the majority whom the legislator represents. As Judge J. Skelly Wright famously said, 'when a decision maker chooses to disadvantage members *of his own* racial or ethnic group, it may hardly be supposed that he is acting out of prejudice, ignorance, or hostility.... When the majority group acts to disadvantage itself for the benefit of the minority, there should be a strong presumption of legality'.[35] The same point was nicely made, using the familiar language of 'suspicion', by John Hart Ely: 'When the group that controls the decision making process classifies so as to advantage a minority and disadvantage itself, the reasons for being unusually suspicious, and, consequently, employing a stringent brand of review, are lacking.'[36]

There is no suggestion here that testing specific cases under this first indicium will always be easy and bring about self-evident answers. A paradigm case would be a situation in which a particular burden is imposed upon a minority which is totally disenfranchised and which has had no impact upon the legislative process whatsoever, but such cases are relatively rare (perhaps legislation adversely affecting non-nationals clearly belongs to this category). In each case, we shall need to first identify a group who are affected adversely by a given classification and then determine whether they have had a 'proper' impact upon the legislative and political process which produced this classification. A sheer numerical argument will not be enough: a numerical minority may have a disproportionately high impact, and a numerical majority may have had a low impact, upon the legislation. A complex empirical argument is needed to fill this indicium with a real meaning in specific cases. But even if such an argument will be occasionally contested, this should not be a major problem for the overall argumentative strategy: remember, this indicium is only a part of a larger set of indicia, and further, its significance is not to result in a conclusive judgement of discrimination

[35] J. Skelly Wright, 'Color-Blind Theories and Color Conscious Remedies', (1980) 47 *University of Chicago Law Review* 213, 234–35, footnotes omitted.

[36] John Hart Ely, 'The Constitutionality of Reverse Racial Discrimination', (1974) 41 *University of Chicago Law Review* 723, 725.

but only to determine when a higher 'suspicion' (hence, a tougher test of a relationship between the classification and its aim) is warranted.

The second ground for suspecting that a classification is motivated by hostility or prejudice is that it has the effect of perpetrating, strengthening, or freezing an existing pattern of disadvantage. One feature of discriminatory regulations has usually been that they add insult to injury, so to speak, in petrifying the existing structure of social burdens and disadvantages. Frank Michelman suggests that one of the characteristics of invidious discrimination is 'a high degree of adaptation to uses which are oppressive in the sense of *systematic and unfair devaluation, through majority rule*, of the claims of certain persons to nondiscriminatory sharing in the benefits and burdens of social existence'.[37] The same insight is expressed In Justice Ginsburg's dissent in *Gratz*,[38] where she mentions '[a]ctions designed to burden groups *long denied full citizenship stature*'[39] as requiring especially careful judicial scrutiny. In cases where the burden of a particular regulation falls unevenly on different groups, burdens borne by a group which is generally disadvantaged and traditionally worse-off raise a much higher suspicion of prejudice than burdens suffered by the traditionally privileged. In contrast, such suspicion may be allayed if a group burdened by a regulation matches the description in *San Antonio Independent School Dist. v. Rodriguez*: 'the class is not saddled with such disabilities, or subjected to such a history of purposeful unequal treatment, *or relegated to such a position of political powerlessness* as to command extraordinary protection from the majoritarian political process.'[40] Similarly, the South African Constitutional Court declared that 'the position of the complainants in society and whether they have suffered in the past from patterns of disadvantage . . .' constitutes one of the factors to be considered in finding whether the discrimination is unfair.[41] In this judgment, the Court confirmed the declaration of the constitutional invalidity of treating homosexual acts as an offence in various pieces of legislation.

In the US equal protection doctrine, a similar idea is reflected in the concept of 'discrete and insular minorities', spelled out in the famous Footnote Four to *Carolene Products*.[42] The full statement is worth recalling: 'prejudice against discrete and insular minorities may be a special condition, which tends seriously to curtail the operation of those political processes ordinarily to be relied upon to protect minorities, and which may call for a correspondingly more searching judicial inquiry.'[43] There is an important lesson to be learnt from the use of the

[37] Frank I. Michelman, 'The Supreme Court, 1968 Term—Foreword: On Protecting the Poor Through the Fourteenth Amendment', (1969) 83 *Harvard Law Review* 7, 20, emphasis added.

[38] *Gratz v. Bollinger*, 539 U.S. 244 (2003).

[39] Ibid. 301 (Ginsburg J. dissenting), emphasis added.

[40] 411 U.S. 1, 28 (1973), emphasis added.

[41] *National Coalition for Gay and Lesbian Equality & Another v. Minister of Justice & Others* 1999 (1) SA 6 (CC) para. 19.

[42] *United States v. Carolene Products Co.*, 304 U.S. 144, 152 n. 4 (1938).

[43] Ibid.

'discrete and insular' characterization in Stone's formula, but to discover it we need to go behind the two adjectives and reflect upon the rationales for using them. After all, as Bruce Ackerman has shown, neither discreteness nor insularity are particularly helpful today in identifying the groups which require special protection from legislative process because the process itself does not serve them as well as others: some groups which are anonymous rather than discrete (e.g. sexual minorities) or some groups which are dispersed rather than insular (women?) may well deserve more protection.[44] But the use of these words becomes convincing when we see them as proxies for special vulnerabilities *in society*, not just in the legislative or political process. Legal disadvantages which have to be specially scrutinized by courts, Justice Stone tells us in the footnote, petrify, strengthen, and freeze, but do not create, the existing structures of disadvantage and discrimination. The group's reduced access to lawmaking is not simply a tautological matter of being outvoted but, more generally, of coming to the legislative process from an already disadvantaged social position. And whether Justice Stone had precisely this theory in mind or not, it is clearly consistent with the rationale of the third paragraph of his footnote four. For it is only when we see the minoritarian status of a group in the general social context of the overall pattern of disadvantage that we may begin to appreciate the conditions which 'tend[] seriously to curtail the operation of those political processes ordinarily to be relied upon to protect minorities'.[45]

A group which is locked into a pattern of systemic disadvantage, or a group which is the object of widespread social stereotypes that induce others to perceive the members of that group as incapable of performing particular jobs or public functions, cannot expect proper protection from the legislative process even if only because the group is unlikely to enter into coalitions with others, which is a condition of success in a pluralist democracy. This is the fundamental message of footnote four: the law must more stringently protect those groups which, due to social factors of their disadvantage, cannot protect themselves politically in a democratic state. 'Discreteness' and 'insularity' may or may not describe the objective social factors which are indicative of a group's disadvantage well, but what matters is the rationale for having such factors. A sociological theory that would claim that groups which are insular and discrete have greater difficulties in forming successful coalitions by virtue of their insularity and discreteness may be wrong, but a theory behind a search for some such factors is certainly correct. It is the theory which affirms that, to some groups, the path of revising problematic legislation through routine political process is not available (or is less readily available than to other groups), for instance because they are too weak economically to effectively enter the political game, or so

[44] B.A. Ackerman, 'Beyond *Carolene Products*', (1985) 98 *Harvard Law Review* 713, 722–31.
[45] 304 U.S. 152 n. 4 (1938).

unpopular among the majority electorate that supporting their cause is a liability for other politicians, or because widespread stereotyping renders other groups unwilling to enter into coalitions with them. So contrary to Justice (as he then was) Rehnquist's belief, discrete and insular minorities (in the *Carolene Products* sense) are not to be easily found 'at every turn in the road',[46] and contrary to Justice Powell's view, in order to activate the footnote four rationale it is not sufficient to note 'that one group is disadvantaged by a particular piece of legislation, or action of government . . .'.[47] Rather, such groups are disadvantaged by the fact that their access to lawmaking is particularly difficult and limited due to social disadvantages suffered by members of these groups.

The third indicium of suspicion is linked to the stigmatizing effect of the discrimination. One of the most powerful effects of unquestionably invidious discrimination is that, in addition to imposing disadvantage upon an already disadvantaged group, it also fosters a sense of the group's inferiority vis-à-vis the rest of the community. It is part of a broader system which stigmatizes the group and treats its members as inferiors.[48] Stigmatization may (and usually does) work in both ways: reinforcing a sense of inferiority on the part of victims and confirming grounds for contempt towards victims in the eyes of perpetrators. This often operates through what Robert Merton called a 'sociological euphemism': the kind of conceptual apparatus that helps us ignore 'social structures which are so organized as to systematically inflict pain, humiliation, suffering, and deep frustration upon particular groups and strata'[49] while we, non-members of such groups and strata, tend to assign such publicly caused suffering to individual paranoia or excessive sensibility. The landmark decision of *Brown v. Board of Education* invalidated school segregation on the ground that it 'generates a feeling of inferiority as to [African-Americans'] status in the community that may affect their hearts and minds in a way unlikely ever to be undone'.[50] Racial stigma was movingly characterized by Justice Brennan in *Bakke*, who compared it to the effect that affirmative action may have upon a non-member of otherwise disadvantaged minority, such as Mr Bakke: '[Bakke was not] stamped as inferior by the Medical School's rejection of him . . . Unlike discrimination against racial minorities, the use of racial preferences for remedial purposes does not inflict a pervasive injury upon individual whites in the sense that wherever they go or whatever they do there is a significant likelihood that they will be treated as a second-class citizens because of their color.'[51] Discrimination is, after all, the end result of a

[46] *Sugarman v. Dougall* 413 U.S. 634, 657 (1973) (Rehnquist J. dissenting).

[47] Lewis F. Powell, Jr., '*Carolene Products* Revisited', (1982) 82 *Columbia Law Review* 1087, 1091.

[48] See Judith A. Baer, *Equality Under the Constitution* (Cornell University Press 1983) 139.

[49] R.K. Merton, 'Insiders and Outsiders: A Chapter in the Sociology of Knowledge', (1972) 78 *American Journal of Sociology* 9, 38.

[50] 347 U.S. 483, 494 (1954).

[51] 438 U.S. 375 (1978) (Brennan, White, Marshall, Blackmun, JJ. concurring in part and dissenting in part).

process whereby external differences (in race, class, religion, gender) are transformed into differences of value, or worth, of particular groups. It insults particular group members identified through their group membership.[52]

Perhaps discrimination's most invidious effect is in reflecting and strengthening stereotypes and prejudices against a group as a whole, so that it becomes a legal weapon in the service of an irrational hatred. The International Convention on the Elimination of All Forms of Racial Discrimination links, in its Preamble, racial discrimination to the 'doctrine[s] of superiority based on racial differentiation', which it depicts as 'scientifically false, morally condemnable, socially unjust and dangerous'.[53] Similarly, in a case referred to earlier in this chapter, the Constitutional Court of South Africa observed that the 'discriminatory prohibitions on sex between men reinforces already existing societal prejudices and severely increases the negative effects of such prejudices on their lives'.[54] Openly referring to the *purpose* of the anti-sodomy legislation, the Court said: 'The nature of the power and its purpose is to criminalise private conduct of consenting adults which causes no harm to anyone else. It has no other purpose than to criminalise conduct which fails to conform with the moral or religious views of a section of society.'[55] This, the Court concluded, cannot qualify as a legitimate purpose for a criminal prohibition.[56] In a similar case, the same Court struck down, as discriminatory, the Marriage Act's definition of marriage as being a union between one man and one woman, observing inter alia: 'It might well be that negative presuppositions about homosexuality are still widely entertained in certain sectors of our society. The ubiquity of prejudice cannot support its legitimacy.'[57]

Considering its pedigree, it should not come as a surprise that the South African Constitutional Court has been willing to discern stigmatizing messages in various discriminatory laws, beyond cases involving sexual orientation. In *Bhe*, it considered whether the legal framework governing the law of intestate succession was constitutional, and one issue (apart from the clearly discriminatory distinction between succession rules for whites and for 'Africans') was whether the customary law of succession, codified in the statute under scrutiny and giving effect to the system of primogeniture, whereby women do not participate in the intestate succession of deceased estates, violated the Constitution. The Court answered in the affirmative, saying that it 'implies that women are not fit or competent to own and administer property'[58]—a clearly stigmatizing

[52] See Campbell, 'Unlawful Discrimination' (n. 5) 164.

[53] International Convention on the Elimination of All Forms of Racial Discrimination (1965), Preamble.

[54] *National Coalition for Gay and Lesbian Equality & Another v. Minister of Justice & Others* 1999 (1) SA 6 (CC) para. 23.

[55] Ibid. para. 26.

[56] Ibid. para. 38.

[57] *Minister of Home Affairs & Another v. Fourie & Another* 2006 (1) SA 524 (CC) para. 113.

[58] *Bhe & Others v. Khayelitsha Magistrate & Others* 2005 (1) SA 580 (CC) para. 92.

implication. The Court's judgment was courageous, but also 'awkward', to use a characterization by Theunis Roux, because the case 'pitched the constitutional value of equality squarely against the cultural traditions and underlying social values of the majority of South Africa's population'.[59] In *Union of Refugee Women*, the Court upheld a law which provided that only South African citizens or permanent residents could work in the security industry, but in a powerful dissent, Justices Mokgoro and O'Regan found the implicit premise that foreign nationals are inherently less trustworthy than South Africans is 'not supported by any evidence placed before the Court and [which] would amount to unfair and damaging stereotyping of foreign nationals'.[60] In *Khosa*, the Court found the social assistance law which reserved pensions and child grants for South African citizens only and not permanent residents unconstitutional: the Court agreed that the applicants were part of a vulnerable group in society and that this was 'intentional, statutorily sanctioned unequal treatment of part of the South African community' which 'has a strong stigmatizing effect'.[61] The distinction 'almost inevitably creates the impression that permanent residents are in some way inferior to citizens and less worthy of social assistance'.[62] Finally, in *Hoffmann* the Court considered the employment practice of South African Airways of automatically refusing applications for flight attendant positions by HIV positive applicants. The Court found that HIV positive people are vulnerable and suffer great prejudice. 'Any discrimination against them can . . . be interpreted as a fresh instance of stigmatisation . . .'.[63]

So we have three tentative indicia to justify 'suspicion' that a classification is motivated by wrongful reasons, such as hostility or prejudice: (1) the fact that the regulation burdens a politically powerless group (or at least, a group under-represented in the lawmaking process), (2) the fact that a regulation contributes to, or freezes, the existing pattern of social disadvantage, and (3) that the burdens inflicted upon a target group by a regulation in question have a stigmatizing effect. Arguably, these do not amount to a fully 'objective' test, and reasonable people may still disagree whether a given regulation matches any of these three conditions. Nonetheless, these indicia taken together are certainly much less subjective, vague, and indeterminate than a criterion of prejudice or hostility, without more. Therefore, they lend themselves better to a *working* theory of discrimination which can be adopted by people who otherwise disagree about their fundamental values, such as justice or the moral good.

[59] Theunis Roux, *The Politics of Principle: The First South African Constitutional Court, 1995-2005* (Cambridge University Press 2013) 249.

[60] *Union of Refugee Women & Others v. Director, Private Security Industry Regulatory Authority & Others* 2007 (4) SA 395 (CC) para. 121.

[61] *Khosa & Others v. Minister of Social Development and Others, Mahlaule & Another v. Minister of Social Development* 2004 (6) SA 505 (CC) para. 73.

[62] Ibid. para. 74.

[63] *Hoffmann v. South African Airways* 2001 (1) SA 1 (CC) para. 28.

Precisely because each of these three indicia allow for judgements of degree (which is why reasonable disagreements may occur, concerning whether a particular regulation matches any one of them), it is unnecessary to decide, in abstract terms, whether they should *all* be present, or whether one is enough, to trigger a heightened scrutiny. If there is a very high correlation between a given regulation and only one indicium, this would probably be sufficient to warrant stricter than usual scrutiny. But the presence of two, or all three, in a given regulation, certainly strengthens the case for strict scrutiny. And it is clear that the three indicia are interrelated.

It is also important to remember that, even if all three are present, it will not be the end of the story; this only comprises a reason to subject a regulation displaying these characteristics to strict scrutiny, but not to determine immediately that invidious discrimination has taken place. Occasionally, a discriminatory classification *may* pass this test, and US jurisprudence provides some (admittedly, extremely rare) examples of a classification surviving strict scrutiny. The first such case was the now thoroughly discredited *Korematsu v. United States*,[64] in which the Supreme Court for the first time established such a test for racial and ethnic classifications, upholding the exclusion of American citizens of Japanese extraction on the West Coast from their homes during a period of perceived danger of Japanese invasion. Arguments about suspect classification surviving a strict test have been made occasionally in the context of affirmative action cases. For instance, in *Fullilove v. Klutznick*,[65] the plurality opinion written by Chief Justice Burger asserts, obiter, that the classification under challenge (i.e. special set aside contracts for minority business enterprises) 'would survive judicial review under either 'test' articulated in the several *Bakke* opinions',[66] that is, also the strict test. One of the 'tests' articulated in *Bakke* to which Burger refers says: 'Racial and ethnic distinctions of any sort are inherently suspect and thus call for the most exacting judicial examination',[67] and in a somewhat different articulation: racial and ethnic classification must be 'precisely tailored to serve a compelling governmental interest'.[68] These are certainly 'strict' tests. A more recent example is provided by the already mentioned case of *Grutter v. Bollinger*,[69] although there may be some disagreement about whether the judgment really used strict scrutiny, or something a little less stringent. While Justice O'Connor, delivering the opinion of the Court, announced that strict scrutiny is required whenever racial classification (as in the case at hand) is reviewed,[70] nevertheless at times she appears to mitigate the strictness of the test actually applied, for

64 232 U.S. 214 (1944).
65 448 U.S. 448 (1980).
66 Ibid. 492.
67 438 U.S. 291 (1978).
68 Ibid. 299.
69 359 U.S. 306 (2003).
70 Ibid. 326.

instance by saying that '[n]arrow tailoring does not require exhaustion of every conceivable race-neutral alternative',[71] thus sensibly weakening the 'necessity' tier of the scrutiny. Nevertheless, the cases of strict scrutiny resulting in an upholding of a measure are all exceptions rather than the rule, and the survival of a strict test by a legislative classification is, by its very nature, a rare and extraordinary occurrence.

3. Judicial Uses of the Wrongful-motives Conception

So far, in this chapter, the motive- or purpose-based conception of discrimination has been discussed using illustrations taken from the United States and South Africa. However, such a conception can be indirectly supported by those jurisdictions in which the constitutionality of distinctions, under equal protection rules, explicitly depends upon the purpose for which the distinction has been adopted, in particular in the context of laws aimed at the preferential treatment of traditionally disadvantaged groups. In India, where Article 14 of the Constitution (the general equality provision) is silent about the purpose scrutiny, the case law established that if the legislation prima facie breaches equality by classifying a particular class as different, the classification must first be based upon 'intelligible differentia' and second, the state must prove a rational relation between 'intelligible differentia' and the purpose sought to be achieved by the legislation.[72] If these two points cannot be established, the law is invalid. Legal scholar Chintan Chandrachud has argued that the test clearly incorporates a purpose-based inquiry where it requires a classification based on 'intelligible differentia'. This is because, logically, to operate with the rational means-end analysis, the intelligible differentia can only be 'judged with reference to the purpose of the law rather than in the abstract'.[73]

How an appeal to legislative purpose—and, more specifically, an express attempt by a court to discern the actual purpose through the use of proportionality scrutiny—may crucially affect the outcome is well illustrated by contrasting the judgments of the Indian Supreme Court and the High Court of Delhi in cases concerning classification based on sexual orientation. In *Suresh Kumar Koushal*

[71] Ibid. 339.

[72] *Budhan Choudhry v. State of Bihar* 1955 SCR (1)1045 at 1049; see also *State of West Bengal v. Anwar All Sarkarhabib* (1952) SCR 284; *Ram Krishna Dalmia v. Justice Tendolkar* (1959) SCR 279.

[73] Chintan Chandrachud (2016), 'Proportionality, Judicial Reasoning, and the Supreme Court', University of Cambridge Legal Studies Research Paper No. 12/2016, available on SSRN: https://papers.ssrn.com/sol3/papers.cfm?abstract_id=2720080. To be sure, occasionally the Supreme Court used what it called the 'non-arbitrariness test' under Art. 14, from which legislative purpose was absent. This stream in the Indian non-discrimination jurisprudence has been criticized by Indian legal scholars, see Tarunabh Khaitan 'Legislative Review Under Article 14', in Sujit Choudry, Madhav Khosla, and Pratap Bhanu Mahta (eds.), *The Oxford Handbook of the Indian Constitution* (Oxford University Press 2016) 699, 712.

v. Naz Foundation,[74] the Supreme Court of India considered a challenge (brought by an NGO which assists HIV/AIDS patients) against an Indian Penal Code prohibition on 'carnal intercourse against the order of nature'. In its judgment upholding the provision, the Court observed that: '[T]hose who indulge in carnal intercourse in the ordinary course and those who indulge in carnal intercourse against the order of nature constitute different classes and the people falling in the latter category cannot claim that Section 377 suffers from the vice of arbitrariness and irrational classification.'[75] In conducting the Article 14 analysis, the Court did not identify whether there were intelligible differences for the law's classification, or if there was a rational nexus between the differentia and the legislature's object for making the law. While there was an opportunity to apply the 'legislative purpose' element of the classification doctrine, the Court failed to apply it in this case. As a critic of the judgment observed,

> Applying proportionality, if the Court were to find that the law was enacted for the regulation of private morals, it would need to justify why this was a legitimate basis for limiting fundamental rights. On the other hand, if the Court chose to adopt the petitioners' argument that section 377 had the public health rationale of preventing HIV/AIDS, it would also need to establish why less restrictive measures (such as educational initiatives) could not be deployed to achieve the same objective.[76]

Another Indian legal scholar, criticizing this judgment, observes that the Court 'wastes no ink trying to identify the state objective being pursued, or asking whether the measure has any nexus with that objective'.[77]

In contrast, when the High Court of Delhi had considered a challenge to the same provision in *Naz Foundation v. Government of NCT of Delhi*,[78] it struck down (in a decision subsequently overturned by the Supreme Court of India in *Koushal*) the provision under proportionality analysis which included express detection of the legislative purpose. As the Court said, the anti-sodomy provision targets the homosexual community as a class and is motivated by an animus towards this vulnerable class of people. The Court rejected the government's counterargument that the state interest is overriding, holding that the state interest 'must be legitimate and relevant' for the legislation to be non-arbitrary and must be proportionate towards achieving the state interest. If the objective is irrational, unjust, and unfair, necessarily classification will have to be held as unreasonable. In this case, the Court held, the provision 'has no other purpose

74 (2014) 1 SCC 1.

75 Ibid. [42].

76 Chandrachud, 'Proportionality, Judicial Reasoning, and the Supreme Court' (n. 73).

77 Tarunabh Khaitan, '*Koushal* v *Naz*: Judges Vote to Recriminalise Homosexuality', (2015) 78 *Modern Law Review* 672, 677.

78 (2010) Cri LJ 94.

than to criminalise conduct which fails to conform with the moral or religious views of a section of society'.[79] As an Indian commentator noted, one of the innovations that this judgment introduced to the anti-discrimination case law in India is the requirement of strict judicial scrutiny of any laws infringing constitutional equality.[80]

The Canadian Charter, and the case law based on it, provides another good example of the equality doctrine incorporating scrutiny of purposes. Section 15 of the Charter protects citizens against discrimination. It provides for equality before and under the law, and equal protection in the following terms: while subsection (1) announces a general anti-discrimination principle, subsection (2) provides that this principle 'does not preclude any law, program or activity that has as its object the amelioration of conditions of disadvantaged individuals or groups including those that are disadvantaged because of race, national or ethnic origin, colour, religion, sex, age or mental or physical disability'. Not surprisingly, subsection 2 gave rise to a significant purpose-based analysis in cases in which governments seek to save legislation shown to distinguish between persons on a prohibited ground. Legislation is thus saved on the basis of its ameliorative objectives. Clearly, the reference in subsection 2 to the 'object' of the programme ameliorating disadvantage indicates that the 'legislative goal rather than actual effect' will be the 'paramount consideration' in assessing whether a given measure falls within its scope.[81] The Court confirmed its role in scrutinizing the alleged object of a given programme or legislative instrument, by noting that the application of this test does not mean that the Court 'must slavishly accept the government's characterisation of its purpose'. Rather, a court hearing a challenge under section 15 'could well examine legislation to ensure that the declared purpose is genuine'.[82]

In the landmark case of *R v. Kapp*, the Court considered a licensing system for fishing activity that was only available to members of three particular 'aboriginal bands', and found that the programme indeed had a legitimate ameliorative goal: to address the social and economic disadvantage suffered by aboriginal Canadians.[83] In that case, Chief Justice McLachlin and Justice Abella, when delivering judgment for the majority, made reference to the judgment of Justice Simonsen in *Manitoba Rice Farmers Association v. Human Rights Commission (Man.)*,[84] in which he had acknowledged that a 'bald declaration by a government' that its legislative programme has the object of ameliorating a relevant

79 Ibid. [92].

80 Tarunabh Khaitan, 'Reading *Swaraj* into Article 15: A New Deal for All Minorities', (2009) 2 *NUJS Law Review* 419, 426–27. Note that the New Delhi Court scrutinized the law under Art. 15 of the Constitution of India which, in contrast to a generally worded Art. 14, specifies particular banned grounds of discrimination and spheres of life to which it applies.

81 *R v. Kapp* [2008] 2 SCR 483, 513.

82 Ibid. 514.

83 Ibid. 518–20.

84 (1987) 50 Man. R (2d) 92 (QB).

disadvantage does not of itself fulfil the requirements under section 15(2)—'the government cannot employ such a naked declaration as a shield to protect an activity or program which is unnecessarily discriminatory'.[85] On the other hand, the Supreme Court acknowledged the need to take care to avoid unduly inhibiting legislative action that seeks sincerely to promote equality. For this reason, 'the government should be given leeway' in its adoption of programmes that have an ameliorative purpose.[86]

While the Canadian Court has not been using the US-style framework of different standards of scrutiny, it is clear that the detection of an 'ameliorative purpose' served the Court to lower the usual, rigorous standard of scrutiny into racial or ethnic classifications. The Court explicitly framed the inquiry into an asserted ameliorative purpose in terms of whether it was 'rational for the state to conclude that the means chosen to reach its ameliorative goal would contribute to that purpose'. A rational distinction will reveal a 'correlation between the program and the disadvantage suffered by the target group'.[87] Section 15(2) of the Charter would then protect from further review any distinctions on prohibited grounds that 'serve and are necessary to the ameliorative purpose'.[88] The advantage of this approach is clear—it 'permits significant deference to the legislature' in its pursuit of innovative ameliorative schemes, but ensures this deference is underpinned by robust judicial review in those instances 'where a program nominally seeks to serve the disadvantaged but in practice serves other non-remedial objectives'.[89] This approach is well aligned with the general proposition that benign (for instance, remedial, restorative, or 'ameliorative') purposes release the scrutinizer from the highest degree of suspicion of wrongful motives which would otherwise trigger the most rigorous scrutiny of the relationship between classification and its purposes.

This, let us note, resonates well with the view by Tom Campbell, which I invoked earlier in the chapter, that the moral and political aim of the discrimination analysis is to pick up, through legal scrutiny, cases of 'prejudiced disfavouring'. If no objectionable motive such as prejudice is involved in an 'ameliorative' programme, then even if it involves classifications based on racial or gender grounds, no suspicion of wrongful motives is warranted. This, according to Campbell, 'ensures the lawfulness of affirmative action programmes for it permits benefits to be distributed on, for instance, racial grounds to groups which are subject to prejudiced disfavouring, even if it worsens the position of members of other racial groups which are not targets for adverse social prejudice in that society'.[90]

[85] Ibid. para. 51.
[86] *R v. Kapp* [2008] 2 SCR 483, 514–15.
[87] Ibid. 514–16.
[88] Ibid. 516.
[89] Ibid. 516.
[90] Campbell, 'Unlawful Discrimination' (n. 5) 155.

PART III
SUPRANATIONAL PUBLIC REASON

9

Constitutional Legitimacy beyond the State

The new 'post-Westphalian' constitutional architecture of the world is one in which some authoritative rules, standards, norms, and policies are derived from sites of governance beyond the state and not embedded directly in states. It is, in other words, a world marked by the growing denationalization of authority, and has produced a major challenge to constitutional theory. This new architecture has usually been described as the expansion of constitutionalism beyond the scope of nation-states.[1]

While I will examine some (quasi-) supranational adjudicative bodies (and in particular, the European Court of Human Rights (ECtHR), discussed in the next chapter), in this chapter I examine all sorts of supranational norm-producing authorities, which admittedly would need to be distinguished from each other by a more nuanced discussion. There are a plethora of bodies and organizations of various kinds in the supranational sphere. Some are adjudicatory and others are regulatory. Some are regional and others are universal. Some are 'public' and others are non-state (such as the Internet Corporation for Assigned Names and Numbers (ICANN) or the International Organization for Standardization). Some enact peremptory rules and others only issue soft law, such as the Council of Europe's Venice Commission (the European Commission for Democracy through Law) or the OECD's PISA (Programme for International Student Assessment). They may be territorial or functional, autonomous or embedded in other international organizations, etc. They all wield various types of authority and elicit various degrees of compliance from communities across national borders. They all create standards meant to control the conduct of states—and also of individuals, firms, associations, and other entities. Even though they are not mere extensions of states, their decision-making is largely independent of states, and they cannot rely on authority based on state-specific canons of accountability and democracy. They often establish standards which, formally speaking, may be seen as non-binding, but in fact can become effectively authoritative in ways which are not different from national decision-making.[2] Gráinne de Búrca

[1] See, e.g., Antje Wiener et al., 'Global Constitutionalism: Human Rights, Democracy and the Rule of Law', (2012) 1 *Global Constitutionalism* 1.

[2] Gráinne de Búrca, 'Developing Democracy Beyond the State', (2008) 46 *Columbia Journal of Transnational Law* 221, 235.

Constitutional Public Reason. Wojciech Sadurski, Oxford University Press. © Wojciech Sadurski 2023.
DOI: 10.1093/oso/9780192869678.003.0009

provides, inter alia, an example of the guidelines and norms issued by the Basil Committee on Banking Supervision, which was originally established with the aim of improving the quality of international banking. These highly influential standards were subsequently adopted by many states. As a consequence, the International Monetary Fund (IMF) and the World Bank made compliance with the standards compulsory for indebted countries dependent on them. This serves to show how 'the fragmented but complexly interwoven transnational governance domain can render decisions authoritative, even when they are originally non-binding'.[3]

More recently, Liam Murphy has objected to the characterization of various decisions and standards as 'law', such as those of 'the purely private International Standardization Organization (ISO)', by suggesting that 'though they can have pervasive impact both on domestic law and decisions by treaty-based international organizations, surely [they] do not have legal force'.[4] But in my view, a discussion of whether to characterize such decisions in the way described by de Búrca or referred to by Murphy as 'law' or something else is not particularly interesting. Replace 'legal force' with 'authoritative effect' in Murphy's just quoted phrase and the proposition seems much less obvious than he would suggest. Murphy continues: 'It is true that ISO standards are incorporated into legal regulations, for example through the WTO . . . but that fact does not make the standards themselves legally binding—no more so than regulation of banks and other financial institutions that refers to and incorporates the decisions of private ratings agencies makes Moody's a lawmaker'.[5] Again, replace 'legally binding' with 'authoritative', and the idea of the ISO (as an example of a supranational authority) issuing authoritative standards becomes much more plausible, insofar as (1) the standards are issued with the intention of guiding the behaviour of various state or non-state entities, (2) the standards are received as such by the intended addressees, and (3) the negative consequences of disregarding those standards by those whom they are intended to control mean that non-compliance becomes an excessively costly option. The broader notion of 'authority' is better suited to transnational normative phenomena than the narrower notion of 'law', because it frees us of intuitive assumptions about law being a comprehensive and final normative order, which are inapposite in situations involving interdimensional conflicts, competition, and overlap between normative orders in the supranational sphere.[6]

In sum, supranational bodies and organizations often issue binding norms or directives despite not having traditional, hierarchically structured means of

[3] Ibid. 235.
[4] Liam Murphy, *What Makes Law* (Cambridge University Press 2014) 165.
[5] Ibid.166.
[6] See, similarly, Michael Giudice, 'Global Legal Pluralism: What's Law Got to Do with It?' (Book review of Paul Shiff Berman, *Global Legal Pluralism* (Cambridge University Press 2012)), (2014) 34 *Oxford Journal of Legal Studies* 589, 604–05.

enforcement. Further, these bodies can rarely appeal to explicit state consent, typical of classical international law, to support the authoritative character of their norms—and yet they question the claims by states' of the exclusive authority to govern all aspects of public life in their territories. In addition, there is the phenomenon of 'the proliferation of institutions and the blurring of issue area boundaries' at the 'horizontal' level,[7] in that different decision-makers and norm-producers address similar issues in different supranational fora. The traditional division of authority along functional lines has disappeared. Significantly, there is not only a striking 'multiplication of norm-producing institutions in the global legal sphere, but also ... the fact that the entities in question can no longer be comprehended by a single institutional model, least of all one based on classical interstate agreement'.[8] This, among other things, greatly increases the possibility of clashes between different norms, all coming from the supranational sphere, and increases uncertainty, ambiguity, inconsistencies, gaps, and instability (while also creating incentives for forum shopping by state and non-state actors)[9] of the global normative order. Neil Walker nicely dubbed it 'the new disorder of orders': a situation in which '[s]tates are now joined by a plethora of other autonomous or semiautonomous units of legal order within the global configuration, and each of these units must negotiate their boundary relations *inter se* as well as with the states themselves'.[10]

The challenge for constitutional scholarship in the face of the multiplicity of normative constitutional orders, in the face of 'a variegated and increasingly dense tapestry of global governance',[11] consists of an urgent need to rethink and refashion a number of key concepts which we still use and are likely to continue to use. These concepts, however, were born in the Westphalian world, a world marked by the exclusivity or, at least, the clear dominance of the nation-state in the constitutional game: constitutionalism, *pouvoir constituant/constitué*, sovereignty, citizenship, democracy, legitimacy ... In this chapter, I focus on the last concept—legitimacy—because it is directly related to the general theme of this book: namely, public reason as a constitutional legitimacy-conferring device. As I will attempt to show, legitimacy is not as closely tied up with the nation-state as democracy or (in its traditional understanding) constitutionalism are. It therefore lends itself well to an analysis of supranational authority, at least

[7] Laurence R. Helfer, 'Constitutional Analogies in the International Legal System', (2003) 37 *Loyola of Los Angeles Law Review* 193, 211.

[8] Turkuler Isiksel, 'Global Legal Pluralism as Fact and Norm', (2013) 2 *Global Constitutionalism* 160, 168.

[9] See Helfer, 'Constitutional Analogies in the International Legal System' (n 7) 212; see also Isiksel, Global Legal Pluralism as Fact and Norm' (n. 8) 188.

[10] Neil Walker, 'Beyond Boundary Disputes and Basic Grids: Mapping the Global Disorder of Normative Orders', (2008) 6 *International Journal of Constitutional Law* 373, 385.

[11] Joel P. Trachtman, 'Constitutional Economics of the World Trade Organization', in Jeffrey L. Dunoff and Joel P. Trachtman (eds.), *Ruling the World? Constitutionalism, International Law, and Global Governance* (Cambridge University Press 2009) 206, 208.

as a pivotal concept, by reference to which the other may be refashioned. For there is a growing sense that global constitutionalism undermines familiar roots of legitimacy[12]—and these roots, one may add, are primarily of a democratic character. The dilemma was very well articulated in a recent article by Christopher Zurn:

> With no clear democratic constitutional legislators at the transnational and international levels, but with insistent pressures for legal structures within which to carry out conflict resolution and regulation, courts above the nation-state have simultaneously become active developers of law and foci of concern about their very authority to take on such development.[13]

In the triangle of concepts—legitimacy, democracy, national statehood—the usual reaction to the dilemma raised by the absence of democracy at the international level, where strong supernational authorities have emerged, has been an attempt to uncouple the strict link between national statehood and democracy, and in the process, to confer a degree of legitimacy on supranational authorities. In section 1 of this chapter, I will argue that such an uncoupling is unconvincing, and I will suggest that, within the same triangle, the uncoupling of legitimacy and democracy is a more promising strategy (section 2). As explained in section 3, the legitimacy of supranational authority is grounded on the type of arguments provided by supranational entities, and in particular, their appeal to 'public reason'—which is a legitimacy-conferring device well-suited to supranational authorities. I will then describe, in section 4, the difference between my account of supranational public reason and Rawls's own account of public reason operating in the sphere of, as he calls it, the Society of Peoples (this long digression takes a partly exegetical form and may be skipped by a reader without much damage to following the main line of my argument). As case studies, I go on to consider two regional courts of human rights, the Inter-American and West African (section 5), and separately the World Trade Organization (WTO) (section 6). (The case of the European Court of Human Rights will be discussed in the next chapter, as it deserves special attention). In section 7, I will argue that we should not see the relationship between statehood legitimacy (optimally based on electoral democracy) and supranational legitimacy (based on public reason) as mutually antagonistic and engaged in a zero-sum competition, but rather as allowing scope for synergy. In section 8, I will reflect upon the relationship between constitutional and international law, viewed in light of the emergence of a legitimate authority beyond the state.

[12] See Wiener et al., 'Global Constitutionalism' (n. 1) 6.

[13] Christopher F. Zurn, 'Constitutional Interpretation and Public Reason: Seductive Disanalogies', in Silje Langvatn, Mattias Kumm, and Wojciech Sadurski (eds.), *Public Reason and Courts* (Cambridge University Press 2020) 323, 345, footnote omitted.

1. Uncoupling Democracy from Statehood

We all know how the traditional argument goes: the only, or at least the *main*, standard of political legitimacy is democratic in nature (whether we construe democracy as direct, or representative, or deliberative, or a combination of these different conceptions), and democracy can only flourish within the nation-state. Hence, there is either no possibility or no need to democratize transnational governance. These days, this argument is mainly honoured in its rejection: critics of the traditional democracy/statehood nexus attack this 'methodological nationalism' by decoupling democracy and the nation-state. They either identify (in the empirical version of the counter-argument) or postulate (in the normative version) democracy in the supranational sphere. But this approach has not been very successful thus far and indeed, it lacks promise.

Exhibit No. 1 in the empirical version of the counter-argument is usually the European Union (EU). There are, however, two problems with the EU *qua* an exemplar of supranational democracy.[14] First, the EU is not typical of supranational polities. If anything, it is very *non*-typical ('*sui generis*') among contemporary sites of supranational authorities, and this may explain the visible EU-orientedness (some would say, fixation) among scholars of post-national constitutionalism. In many respects, the EU does not even remotely resemble a traditional 'state'. It has none of the paradigmatic instruments or competences of statehood such as the power to levy taxes, to coerce its citizens to comply with criminal law, or to defend its population against outside aggression, and it is ultimately based on international law-type treaties rather than a constitution. On the other hand, the EU has long departed from the space occupied by classical supranational organizations—to a much higher degree than any other supranational entity in the modern world. For example, it has much broader and more pervasive competences compared with 'regular' international organizations, its decision-making is now based on majority vote and not consensus, it can affect the legal status of individuals in member states directly, it possesses a common currency (in much of its territory) and common citizenship, and its member states have surrendered the right to conclude international treaties in areas belonging to the exclusive competence of the EU. Even if there are other supranational organizations that possess *some* of these characteristics, the sheer cumulative effect is such that the EU has far transcended the paradigmatic international organizations as we know them elsewhere.

[14] For an example extrapolating from an argument regarding the EU to 'global basic structure', see Andreas Follesdal, 'When Common Interests Are Not Common: Why the Global Basic Structure Should be Democratic', (2009) 16 *Indiana Journal of Global Legal Studies* 585; see also Michael Zürn, 'Democratic Governance Beyond the Nation-State: The EU and Other International Institutions', (2000) 6 *European Journal of International Relations* 183.

The second problem with the EU as an alleged exemplar of supranational democracy is that democratic procedures within the EU institutions are at best embryonic: at the EU level, democracy is more a matter of aspiration than reality. The new Article 10 of the Treaty on the European Union (TEU), which proclaims that 'the functioning of the Union shall be founded on representative democracy', is only a promise: the words 'shall be' literally have to be read in the future tense, rather than in the imperative meaning. To be sure, the assurance by the Lisbon Treaty is impressive and eloquent; the language of institutional structure *à la* statehood-based democracy is unmistakeable.[15] But the Treaty's rhetoric is deceiving, and the EU is far from the ideal of a fully developed representative democracy. The only truly representative body (the European Parliament [EP]) is relatively weak, and holds an ancillary role in legislation, as it is even incapable of initiating legislation. Rather, lawmaking is awkwardly divided between technocratic (Commission), intergovernmental (Council), and parliamentary (EP) bodies in a way that barely resembles any established principles of separation of powers. Key decisions (in the Council) are taken as a result of behind-the-scenes political negotiations and horse-trading with very little transparency and accountability. Further, the outcomes of direct elections (to the EP) have only had an indirect effect upon the composition of the main executive body (the Commission), etc.

It may well be that the EU's various democratic deficits will be progressively eliminated in the future. I, for one, am in favour of democracy-promoting ideas such as the 'parliamentarization' of the EU (so that the composition of the Commission reflects the results of EP elections), founding the EU's institutional structure upon the tripartite principle of the separation of powers, incentives for the establishment of European political parties, and the enhancement of the European Citizens' Initiative.[16] These are all matters for the future and, for the time being, democratic deficit within the EU remains pervasive, no matter how some scholars would like to define it out of existence.[17] Indeed, for many observers, the fact that the main source of the EU's democratic character is indirect and lies in the democratic legitimacy of the Member States that participate in EU policy-making (either through the participation of democratic governments in the Council,[18] or the participation of democratic parliaments' in Union-wide

[15] As a French scholar of the EU has observed caustically: '*Tout est là pour convaincre qu'il y a bien, au cœur du quartier européen de Bruxelles, un système politique* complet, *premier example au monde d'une démocratie supranationale accomplie*' ['Everything is in place to convince us that, in the heart of Brussels' European quarter, there is indeed a complete political system, the world's first example of a fully implemented supranational democracy'], Antoine Vauchez, *Démocratiser l'Europe* (Seuil 2014) 14.

[16] For an outline, and endorsement, of possible EU reforms along these lines, see Wojciech Sadurski, 'Democratic Legitimacy of the European Union: A Diagnosis and Some Modest Proposals', (2012) 32 *Polish Yearbook of International Law* 9, especially 33–42.

[17] Perhaps the most influential exponent of this tendency is Giandomenico Majone, 'Europe's "Democratic Deficit": The Question of Standards', (1998) 14 *European Law Journal* 5.

[18] This was the main point of a famous judgment handed down by the German Constitutional Court on 30 June 2009, on the ratification of the Lisbon Treaty, BVerfG, 2BvE/08.

lawmaking)[19] *weakens* rather than supports the case for the EU as a site of *supranational* democracy. Whether the EU's institutions are moving towards greater democratic functioning, independent of being parasitic on the democratic character of its member states, is a matter of conjecture, or hope.

The second version of the counter-argument against the democracy/statehood nexus is normative. It is based on the observation that simply extending or extrapolating democratic schemes from the nation-state to global constitutionalism is not possible and is anyway not necessary. Rather, in the process, the very meaning and nature of democracy must be fundamentally transformed. But the nature of this transformation has never been convincingly explicated. The claim is that when conceptualizing supranational democracy, we should try to craft conceptions of democracy that are *not* based on the template of municipal democracy and to accept that international or supranational democracy will look quite different from the way it operates at the national level. This is what may be called a 'transformative' conception, which is what theorists of cosmopolitan democracy invite us to adopt. These theorists usually draw a picture of a multilayered scheme of governance reliant on a thorough dispersion of decision-making powers.[20] Quite apart from the vague, indeterminate, and possibly utopian character of such visions, a question arises as to whether such a dispersed pattern of authority, which largely relies on the contestatory functions performed by various civil society actors, and on 'unconstrained and uncoerced communication' within the realm of 'transnational civil society',[21] would be still 'democratic' in the meaningful sense of the word. As James Bohman observes, commenting upon John Dryzek's vision of transnational governance based on informal networks, communication, and contestation: 'why should we call such governance "democratic" even in some minimal sense? Does it provide for the basic possibility of democratization, so that those who suffer injustice in the current democratic system have a real basis on which they may effectively make claims to justice?'[22] Though he does not put it in so many words, Bohman's rhetorical question indicates that supranational democratic governance along cosmopolitan lines may actually be *retrogressive* when compared with state democracies, in terms of some important democratic values such as minority protection or even the representativeness of its decision-makers.

[19] Following on from earlier declarations and protocols to EU treaties, in Protocols no. 1 and 2 (respectively, on the role of national parliaments, and on the application of the principles of subsidiarity and proportionality), the Treaty of Lisbon established mechanisms to involve national parliaments in providing oversight of the principle of subsidiarity in EU lawmaking.

[20] See, e.g., Erik O. Eriksen, *The Unfinished Democratization of Europe* (Oxford University Press 2009); Joshua Cohen and Charles F. Sabel, 'Global Democracy?', (2004–05) 37 *NYU Journal of International Law & Politics* 763.

[21] John Dryzek, *Deliberative Democracy and Beyond: Liberals, Critics, Contestations* (Oxford University Press 2002) 131.

[22] James Bohman, 'From *Demos* to *Demoi*: Democracy across Borders', (2005) 18 *Ratio Juris* 293, 305.

A simple extrapolation of national statehood up onto the global level sounds even more utopian, urging us to think of a system of world government that replicates schemes of democratic government at a global scale.[23] Such an extrapolation begins with a question: 'If democracy is so appropriate in the nation-state setting, why should not democratic procedures and institutions be extended to the global setting?'[24] It is, at first blush, a good question. However, a plea by a representative advocate of such a world government for a 'far-reaching global stateness—able effectively to employ sufficient coercive power'[25] immediately reveals the unrealistic and perhaps perilous character of the vision. Unrealistic—because we live in a world of multiple states, and a world state is unlikely to emerge in the foreseeable future. Perilous—because in a world 'where trust is often in short supply across cultural divides',[26] the emergence of sufficient levels of trust and emotional commitment at a worldwide level as is necessary for efficient political action is much less likely than in smaller polities. In any event, we have precious few examples of democratic action at the supranational level. Rather, national statehood and sub-national governments remain the main sites of democracy in the modern world.

This is not to say that striving for more democracy in transnational settings should be neglected and abandoned at the outset. Just as the EU's attempts to democratize its institutions by bringing them closer to the model of parliamentary representation, to the principle of the separation of powers, and to aspects of direct democracy is an eminently worthwhile task, so it is in the various domains of transnational governance, where any space for injecting it with democratic representation and accountability should be seized. This was the main point of an important 2008 article by Gráinne de Búrca who makes a plea for a 'democratic-striving approach' to governance beyond the state, an approach which 'acknowledges the difficulty and complexity of democratizing transnational governance yet insists on its necessity, and identifies the act of continuous striving itself as the source of legitimation and accountability'.[27] The two parts of the just-quoted sentence, separated by the conjunction 'yet', identify the difference between aspiration and actual practice. The aspiration is noble, but the 'difficulty and complexity' of bringing it about seems enormous, other than in some narrowly confined spaces of transnational governance. While de

[23] See e.g. William E. Scheuerman, 'Cosmopolitanism and the World State', (2014) 40 *Review of International Studies* 419. For the most influential account of such projects in modern literature, see David Held, *Democracy and the Global Order* (Stanford University Press 1995), especially 273–74. For a good account of similar conceptions in the German-language literature, see Armin von Bogdandy, 'Globalization and Europe: How to Square Democracy, Globalization, and International Law', (2000) 15 *European Journal of International Law* 885, 899–900.

[24] Richard Falk and Andrew Strauss, 'On the Creation of a Global Peoples Assembly: Legitimacy and the Power of Popular Sovereignty', (2000) 36 *Stanford Journal of International Law* 191, 191.

[25] Scheuerman, 'Cosmopolitanism' (n. 23) 439.

[26] Philip Pettit, *Just Freedom* (Norton 2014) 158.

[27] De Búrca, 'Developing Democracy Beyond the State' (n. 2) 237.

Búrca provides convincing examples of such specific sites that lend themselves to increased democratic practices, albeit in rather embryonic forms—such as the anti-poverty policies of international financial institutions (the World Bank and the IMF)—she wisely stops short of making a claim that they may provide a blueprint for a generalized participatory-representative transnational democracy.[28] Philip Pettit argues that 'international rules and agencies' do not raise any major problems for *democracy*, at least in theory, because 'the states that set them up ought to be capable of controlling such agencies'.[29] But it is enough to cite the evidence provided by Pettit for this proposition—'The appointed officials in international agencies and institutions are subject to the constant threat of being called to book, whether as a result of hostile media publicity, hostile NGO criticism, or internal whistleblowers'[30]—to see how thin these aspects of the democratic control of international bodies are in comparison with their national counterparts.

Of course, one should be careful to avoid comparing the *actual* supranational sphere, marked as it is by fundamental democratic deficits wherever we look, with an *ideal* of nation-state democracy (as constitutional lawyers are sometimes tempted to do, mistaking textual constitutional rules for political reality), but rather we should compare it to real-life democratic practices. We should avoid idealizing domestic political institutions; we know that in most countries, the actual functioning of democracies is increasingly characterized by declining parliamentary power (not only under pressure from globalization), the concentration of power in party leaderships, deep rifts along the lines of class, race, religion, etc., declining participation in elections, and the growth of various largely unaccountable bodies, such as constitutional courts or central banks. But even by a comparison against these imperfect and often defective democratic practices, the supranational sphere, as it is presently constituted, is glaringly non-democratic.

One way of reconciling state-based democratic legitimacy with the authority of supranational norms is to show that a particular norm enjoys authority in a given state by virtue of the conduct of democratically legitimated state actors. This is what Paul Schiff Berman had in mind when he pointed out that 'there is nothing inherently illegitimate ... about a state-sanctioned court's considering norms articulated in an international forum'.[31] Indeed, in such cases, the court may not be seen as acting against the will of the polity within which its acts, but rather as giving effect to this will, which may well encompass the will to align itself with supranational norms. Elsewhere in his important book, and in a similar

[28] As she says, 'The concept of a democratic system of transnational governance is ... one which is incomplete by design ...', ibid. 251. See also ibid. 276 (emphasizing the 'modesty' of the proposal for a democratic-striving approach).

[29] Pettit, *Just Freedom* (n. 26) 170.

[30] Ibid. 169–70.

[31] Paul Schiff Berman, *Global Legal Pluralism* (Cambridge University Press 2012) 304.

spirit, Berman observes that 'at least when foreign, international, or nonstate norms are formally incorporated in domestic law, such incorporation usually occurs through domestic political actors . . .'[32] In these cases, the democratic legitimacy of such incorporation is, of course, a function of the democratic legitimacy of domestic actors, whether they are executives, legislatures, or courts. We are not concerned here with cases which fit this pattern of incorporation but rather those cases where the role of municipal/national actors is more passive, and when it is difficult to identify a positive act amounting to an 'incorporation' that opens the door to supranational rule. And the wording of Berman's proviso, '*at least* when . . . ',[33] indicates that this is only part of the story of the authority of supranational law within states.

2. Uncoupling Legitimacy from Democracy

The upshot of the foregoing is that uncoupling democracy from the nation-state is a non-starter, at least for the time being. My proposed strategy is different. Within the triangle of nation-state, democracy, and legitimacy, I suggest that rather than uncoupling democracy from statehood, we should uncouple legitimacy from democracy. To be clear, I do not want to dilute the normative standards by which we evaluate supranational sites of authority, but rather to revise them, by adjusting those standards to the new constitutional architecture, one that is no longer exclusively state-centered. As Anne Peters observes, the language of global constitutionalism may help emphasize the disconnection of legitimacy from the nation-state: 'the constitutionalist reading [of international law] should clarify that the legitimacy of norms and of political rule does not depend on the structures of government or governance being exactly state-like'.[34] In fact, if we model our thinking about supranational authority in terms of legitimacy rather than democracy, this process may ratchet up standards for the protection of human rights, or the environment, or labour etc. to a level that reliance on democracy may not satisfy.

We may also come to the eminently plausible conclusion that tying up legitimacy with democracy (the latter being strongly connected to national statehood) is improper, because decisions made by states do not pay due regard to the concerns of all of stakeholders. The effects of state decisions often transcend the boundaries of a particular state (think of environmental pollution, overfishing of the seas, or compelled migration), yet statehood-bound democracy is not responsive to those externalities. If the level at which a decision is made, or where

[32] Ibid. 94.
[33] Ibid. 94, emphasis added.
[34] Anne Peters, 'The Merits of Global Constitutionalism', (2009) 16 *Indiana Journal of Global Legal Studies* 397, 410.

a norm is generated, does not correspond adequately to the scope of its effects, the legitimacy of the norm or decision is fundamentally flawed. This is so even if democratic mechanisms are fully respected at the state level, because the constituency of the democracy does not correspond to the range of those who are adversely affected by the norm or decision, and to them such norms or decisions are undemocratic.[35] Correspondingly, if there is a *failure* to grapple with a problem of transnational or global scope, the fact that decisions are made (or norms generated) on a national level—even if in full respect for democratic procedures—is part of the problem, rather than a solution to the system's lack of legitimacy. Mattias Kumm observes: 'the *inactivity* of international actors and the underdevelopment of institutional capacities on the international level come into view as serious legitimacy concerns'.[36] Indeed, one of the founding rationales for the General Agreement on Tariffs and Trade (GATT) system, which paved the way for the WTO, was the perception that (protectionist) policies made in one country may have negative effects upon people in a different country, the latter being denied a forum for influencing those decisions. Hence, the WTO's main function is 'to neutralise the domestic power of protectionist interests' and to 'overcome domestic process deficiencies'.[37] This understanding was expressly articulated by the WTO Appellate Body which proclaimed that when a decision taken in one state affects economic interests in other WTO member states, their interests should be taken into account, either through negotiations between concerned states or through an attempt to mimic multilateral solutions ('simulated multilateralism') in the domestic legislative process.[38]

The point of disentangling democracy and legitimacy is not to disparage or downplay democracy, or to claim that it is greatly overrated, but rather to put it in its proper place. In a world of plural sites of constitutionalism, we need to be careful not to insist on democratic conditions of legitimacy everywhere. We should try not to overburden constitutionalism with democracy, so to speak. Democracy is a noble and magnificent ideal, but legitimacy does not absorb everything that is noble and magnificent. There are authorities and systems of decision-making the legitimacy of which does not rely upon democratic participation or representation: consider, for example, courts, administrative agencies, public banks, or military organizations. (To be sure, one *can* make an

[35] See Andreas L. Paulus, 'The International Legal System as a Constitution', in Jeffrey L. Dunoff and Joel P. Trachtman (eds.), *Ruling the World? Constitutionalism, International Law, and Global Governance* (Cambridge University Press 2009) 69, 96.

[36] Mattias Kumm, 'An Integrative Theory of Global Public Law: Cosmopolitan, Pluralist, Public Reason Oriented' (unpublished draft, no date) 42, emphasis in original. I am grateful to Professor Kumm for his kind permission to refer to and quote this unpublished paper. See also Mattias Kumm, 'The Cosmopolitan Turn in Constitutionalism: An Integrated Conception of Public Law', (2013) 20 *Indiana Journal of Global Legal Studies* 605.

[37] Anne Peters, 'The Constitutionalisation of International Organisations', in Neil Walker, Jo Shaw, and Stephen Tierney (eds.), *Europe's Constitutional Mosaic* (Hart 2011) 253, 262, reference omitted.

[38] See Thomas Kleinlein, 'Judicial Lawmaking by Judicial Restraint? The Potential of Balancing in International Economic Law', (2011) 12 *German Law Journal* 1141, 1171–72.

argument that such entities, at a municipal level, operate within a greater democratic context and that they derive their legitimacy, indirectly, from the democratic institutions which appoint, supervise, monitor them etc.[39] But '*in*directly' is a key word: sometimes the remoteness of a given entity from a democratically legitimated institution is so great that the argument ceases to be convincing.) Hence, we need to unbundle supranational authorities, and put democracy in its proper place.

But what *is* the proper place of democracy? As a first approximation, we may perhaps say that democracy is a crucial factor of legitimacy only in decisions and norms which are 'choice-sensitive'; that is, where it is important for decisions to reflect the actual distribution of preferences and views in the society, no matter what the modes of formation and quality of these views are. In this area, the right authoritative decisions (norms, standards, etc.) are those that mirror, as accurately as possible, the actual distribution of preferences—that is, the choices that people actually made.[40] If we look at the proper scope of democracy in this way, we will likely find that the range of decisions for which 'choice sensitivity' is the proper standard is, in reality, rather narrow. The textbook examples of choice-sensitive decisions (e.g. whether available public funds should be used to build a new stadium or a new road system) indicate that stark alternatives, where prima facie either choice is equally reasonable and the tiebreaker is about the degree of social support, are rare. In most cases, what matters for the legitimacy of decisions, democratic or otherwise, is the *sorts of reasons* that were or could have been provided for them. And often the mere fact of a particular distribution of preferences is insufficient (or even irrelevant) for the legitimacy of decisions that mirror this distribution, unless we deal with decisions which are very simple or very trivial—something that rarely occurs in politics. There is, after all, nothing intrinsically good about satisfying preferences—or acting upon people's choices—whatever they are, and *that* would have to be a tacit assumption underlying the choice-sensitivity conception of good collective decisions.[41]

An immediate response to this is that we need a second-order theory about how to demarcate the choice-sensitive from choice-insensitive realms. Dworkin's observation that 'the second-order question whether any particular first-order question is choice-sensitive or -insensitive is itself choice-insensitive'[42] is correct but not particularly helpful: we need a way of drawing a line between the two spheres that does not offend against intuitive principles of legitimacy. An infinite regression looms large here: can we draw such line other than by an appeal to democracy? The usual argument is to point out that we do not have non-arbitrary ways of judging the legitimacy of collective decisions, even in

39 For such argument, see de Búrca, 'Developing Democracy Beyond the State' (n. 2) 230–32.
40 See Ronald Dworkin, *Sovereign Virtue* (Harvard University Press 2000) 204.
41 See Andrei Marmor, 'Authority, Equality and Democracy', (2005) 18 *Ratio Juris* 315, 340–41.
42 Dworkin, *Sovereign Virtue* (n. 40) 204–05.

non-choice-sensitive cases, other than by reference to democracy. In this perspective, democracy becomes a sort of default mechanism because we do not have anything better (as in Churchill's oft-quoted maxim about democracy). Indeed, it may well be that of all authoritative solutions, democratic decision-making is the least arbitrary. But why should it be the most *legitimate*? Even if democratic decision-making is the default procedure for a second-order line drawing between choice-sensitive and choice-insensitive realms, in this case democracy is just a contingent procedure for mapping the scope of democracy itself, rather than a legitimacy-conferring device in its own right.

As I have argued at length in Chapters 1–3, the legitimacy of political decisions crucially depends upon the sorts of *reasons* provided for these decisions—and not only 'provided', but also demonstrable, as the most likely purposes pursued by a decision-maker. This is what the 'public reason' conception of legitimacy is about. So far in this book, I have tacitly assumed that the natural home for 'public reason' is a bounded polity, typically confined to the boundaries of the nation-state. Now, I wish to consider its applicability to supranational authorities.

One of the implications of the concept of legitimacy adopted earlier in the book is largely influenced by Joseph Raz's 'service conception of authority', where the standard of legitimacy is located in the citizens' perception that authoritative directives are useful for them in pursuing their prior goals.[43] That is, legitimacy is something that must be perceived as such *by* someone, and more particularly, by the addressees of norms, decisions, or rules; it is in the eyes of the beholder, so to speak. When combined with perceptions of other people, legitimacy is *conferred* by subjects to authorities, rather than announced by authorities. Authorities may aspire to or claim legitimacy, but it exists only when it is recognized by those whom the putatively legitimate directives are addressed to.[44] This feature has a special importance in the supranational sphere, where the variety of circumstances, interests, traditions, and cultures is wider than on a national scale, and where these differences may trigger more widely divergent perceptions of the legitimacy of authoritative norms.

Recently, there has been a lively scholarly discussion among EU scholars about applying the idea, articulated and made famous by Rainer Forst, of a 'right to justification' as a meta-right, 'a right [of every human being] to be recognized as an agent who can demand acceptable reasons for any action that claims to be morally justified and for any social or political structure or law that claims to be binding upon him or her', to the EU's legitimacy discourse.[45] Using this concept, Jürgen Neyer suggested that the right to justification *rather than democracy*

[43] Joseph Raz, *Ethics in the Public Domain* (Oxford University Press 2001) 214.

[44] See John Tasioulas, 'The Legitimacy of International Law', in Samantha Besson and John Tasioulas (eds.), *The Philosophy of International Law* (Oxford University Press 2010) 97, 103.

[45] Rainer Forst, 'The Justification of Human Rights and the Basic Right to Justification: A Reflexive Approach' (2010) 120 *Ethics* 711, 719.

may provide the best grounding for the legitimacy of that supranational polity. Building upon his earlier article,[46] Neyer has more recently reasserted that, while applying democratic standards to the EU is futile ('a category mistake'),[47] the EU's legitimacy can be best defended on the basis of 'justice as justification', understood as the 'outcome of a well-ordered discourse among political institutions, courts and individuals'.[48] Forst protests against the use of his conception in this way, and (to paraphrase) urges that importantly, democracy is already built into the right to justification, because the latter is 'not just the right to be *provided* with justifications but also the right to be an *agent* of justification: discursively producing, contesting, rejecting and constructing justifications with others'. He adds: 'the rule-making authority must be constituted by those subjected to its norms, and the norms must express the justified judgment of those subjects, arrived at under fair conditions of a basic structure of justification.'[49]

As an account that connects reason-giving with democratic procedures, this is all eminently reasonable. Yet it does not address *our* problem, the existence of forms of legitimating discourses at the supranational level that do not approximate, as a model, the democratic institutional forms as we know them from the statehood experience—in other words, without adopting the procedural and institutional methods of involving 'those subjected to [the] norms' in norm-making. As Neil Walker correctly observed, commenting on the Forst-Neyer exchange, 'the right to justification operates at too high a level of abstraction to provide, on its own, a compelling answer to the questions of justice in the EU'. He added: 'If we think back to the motivational, normative and structural problems that attend the problem of supranational democracy, none of these disappear just because democracy is now blended with considerations of justice.'[50] One may paraphrase Walker: none of these problems disappear just because we have blended democracy with considerations of a 'right to justification'. Hence, in accordance with the conventional thinking on democracy deficits at various levels of supranational authority, I use 'democracy' principally in an institutional sense. I keep it conceptually separate from the principle of public reason, because we know that the latter may or may not operate within institutional democratic settings.

[46] Jürgen Neyer, 'Justice, Not Democracy: Legitimacy in the European Union', (2010) 48 *Journal of Common Market Studies* 903.

[47] Jürgen Neyer, 'Justice and the Right to Justification: Conceptual Reflections', in Dimitry Kochenov, Gráinne de Búrca, and Andrew Williams (eds.), *Europe's Justice Deficit?* (Hart 2015) 211, 212.

[48] Ibid. 213.

[49] Rainer Forst, 'Justice, Democracy and the Right for Justification: Reflections on Jürgen Neyer's Normative Theory of the European Union', in Dimitry Kochenov, Gráinne de Búrca, and Andrew Williams (eds.), *Europe's Justice Deficit?* (Hart 2015) 227, 229.

[50] Neil Walker, 'Justice in and of the European Union', in Dimitry Kochenov, Gráinne de Búrca, and Andrew Williams (eds.), *Europe's Justice Deficit?* (Hart 2015) 247, 255.

Finally, a caveat is needed. I am not making a claim that the use of public reason is *the only*, or even necessarily the most important factor in legitimating supranational authorities. There are a great number of other factors that will depend upon the sort of institution we consider. In the case of supranational adjudicatory bodies, a large set of institutional factors (regarding, for instance, the selection and tenure of adjudicators, guarantees of their personal qualities, independence, and impartiality), and procedural variables (such as guarantees of fairness, transparency, publicness, and/or confidentiality, equal treatment of parties concerned, allowing third-party intervention, efficiency of secretariats or/and registrars, possibilities of appeal from decisions) are also in play. The pattern of reasoning used by decision-makers, including the pervasiveness of arguments matching the requirements of public reason, is one among the many factors which contribute to the overall legitimacy of supranational authorities. An evaluation of the relative force of this factor vis-à-vis those other factors is beyond the ambit of this chapter and cannot be undertaken *in abstracto* anyway.[51]

3. Public Reason in the Supranational Sphere

How much mileage can we get from the idea of public reason as a legitimating device in new post-national or supranational constitutional structures? Quite a lot. Supranationalism is a space where there is a degree of synchronization between national and international actors in pursuit of the legitimacy of political authority, which are based on standards that justify authoritative directives by appealing to public reasons (i.e. reasons which it is unreasonable for the parties concerned to reject). Scrutiny of such exercises of authority conducted in accordance with the public reason ideal may be seen by those parties as legitimate by virtue of its reasonableness, residing in the patterns and substance of justification. If those parties and, in particular, individual citizens (but also associations, business entities, NGOs, etc.), can contest decisions taken at the national level and demand scrutiny of claims that improper or insufficient reasons have been provided by the state and its institutions at the supranational level, supranational legitimacy may be produced without concern for the democratic (or otherwise) pedigree of those supranational scrutineers.

This general account may strike a reader as irritatingly Panglossian, so before trying to substantiate it, I need to make two caveats. It does not apply of course to the *entire* supranational sphere (I am not making an absurd claim that every

[51] For a good catalogue of procedural and institutional factors contributing to the legitimacy of international adjudicatory institutions, see Nienke Grossman 'Legitimacy and International Adjudicative Bodies', (2009) 41 *The George Washington International Law Review* 107; see also, generally, Armin von Bogdandy and Ingo Venzke, 'On the Democratic Legitimation of International Judicial Lawmaking', (2011) 12 *German Law Journal* 1341, 1356–68.

supranational authority, as we know them, follows the pattern of public reason), nor does it apply to *any* exercise of authority by those supranational institutions that I intend to use as exemplars of supranational public reason. Rather, it is a certain ideal model of what happens when they are at their best. The point of my account is to show that some supranational authorities open up space for legitimating their non-state-based authority by appealing to public reason, thus effectively filling the gap created by the absence of democratic legitimacy. Of course, much more would have to be added to this account—it is deliberately tentative, and also relies on other specifications of public reason in general. Some of the requirements of public reason are not specific to the supranational sphere, though at a supranational level they acquire a special urgency due to the absence of democratic decision-making as a default legitimating factor. A feature of supranational adjudication by courts and tribunals is the absence of the normal, institutional surroundings of a court acting at a national level, placed within the tripartite separation of powers that establishes its canonical function and restricts its argumentative devices by the principles of judicial restraint, deference to the legislature, and the binding role of the developed body of constitutional and statutory texts, etc. These phenomena do not exist at a supranational level, or exist to a much lower degree, thus placing more of a burden upon the quality and nature of the supranational court's arguments.

Allen Buchanan has developed a convincing theory of international human rights, based on the epistemic requirements of having a credible public justification: '[t]he legitimacy of an international order grounded in the commitment to human rights depends in part upon whether there is a credible public justification for human-rights norms' and decisions by international human rights institutions.[52] Supranational lawmaking and adjudication must meet the general requirements of epistemological value that apply to all authorities, such as the accuracy of statements of facts when they are crucial for a judgment, openness to diverse points of view in order to search for good reasons for decisions, deliberate screening off of prejudice, hostility, and self-interest, in providing public justification for authoritative decisions and norms, etc. These requirements amount to an overall threshold quality for legal decisions, and to the significance of justifying legal decisions in a satisfactory way. Others are more specific to *supranational* authorities: epistemic access to broad comparative material and to an enlarged sample of views, and the capacity to harmonize and coordinate norms and actions on a large scale, etc.[53] More detail, supplementing these necessarily

[52] Allen Buchanan, 'Human Rights and the Legitimacy of the International Order', (2008) 14 *Legal Theory* 39, 63. For an epistemic approach to the practice of the WTO, employed to launch a critique of its practices from the point of view of its (non-)reliance on credible economic knowledge, see C.A. Thomas, 'Of Facts and Phantoms: Economics, Epistemic Legitimacy, and WTO Dispute Settlement', (2011) 14 *Journal of International Economic Law* 295.

[53] For an emphasis of universality as a value to be pursued by international adjudication, see Andreas Paulus, 'International Adjudication', in Besson and Tasioulas (n. 44) 207, 219.

vague requirements, will hopefully become apparent in the discussion of the case studies below.

In the remainder of this book, I will provide four examples to show 'public reason' at work as a provider of legitimacy (without relying on democracy, at least of an electoral kind) in the supranational sphere, in four quasi-constitutional supranational systems of adjudication: the ECtHR (the discussion of which is postponed to the next chapter), two other regional human-rights courts, and the Appellate Body of the WTO. These four different instances of 'deliberative, supranational constitutionalism' do not necessarily claim legitimacy based on the *consent* of the states concerned, and certainly not based on a participatory/electoral democracy, but rather on their commitment to shared principles that are today taken to be fundamental. All three characterizations within the label 'supranational, deliberative constitutionalism' are important. That is, the adjudicatory institutions in this category are: (1) *supranational*, in that they operate in the international sphere but pierce the veil of the state, rather than dealing with states as unitary entities; (2) *deliberative*, because the force of their determinations relies crucially upon the strength of the arguments provided; and (3) *constitutional*, in that they may censure (though not necessarily immediately invalidate) certain national laws and regulations, duly adopted, as incompatible with higher supranational norms.

In this context, I would like to use the concept usefully coined by Jürgen Neyer of 'justificatory discipline'.[54] It has, for our purposes, two main interrelated aspects. The first is that individuals or collective entities (when they act as associations of or agents for their members) have a right to demand and receive justification whenever their liberty is constrained. Supranationalism operates by exercising supra-state control over the sorts of reasons states provide to their citizens. Second, while compliance of states with supranational determinations is by-and-large voluntary (in the sense that, as a rule, supranational adjudicatory bodies do not have enforcement mechanisms similar to their national counterparts), it is otherwise disciplined, based largely on deliberation and the strength of reasons provided. When diverse state and non-state actors need to solve specific problems of a global dimension, it is the force of reasons, and persuasiveness of reason-giving, that may provide grounds for the legitimacy of supranational standards and decisions. A condition is that the nature of the reasons provided for such standards and decisions is such that 'others can be expected to acknowledge, even as they disagree about how variety of relevant reasons add up'.[55]

These different kinds of transnational legitimate authorities are supported by different kinds of transnational networks that constitute quasi-communities; no legitimate authority can exist transnationally without such supporting networks.

[54] Neyer, 'Justice, Not Democracy' (n. 46) 913.
[55] Cohen and Sabel, 'Global Democracy?' (n. 20) 780.

The *expertise* which they possess—or claim to possess—may be a source of legitimacy to some transnational authorities: various standard-setting bodies that regulate transnational industries, cross-border trade and finance, transnational professions, sports authorities, etc. Standard-setting authorities are rarely created and maintained democratically but rely on an acknowledgment by the addressees of regulations, often on the basis of recognized technical expertise, or at least of their capacity for efficient *coordination* and in finding solutions to collective-action problems.[56]

The legitimacy of supranational quasi-constitutional entities is complexly related to the authority of states. The legitimacy of state institutions, largely based on democratic grounds, may support or weaken legitimacy in the supranational sphere. In any event, the legitimacy of international entities is not a simple extension of the political authority of states founded on their consent as international actors. (I will return to this point below in section 8). One reason for this is that those supranational adjudicatory or regulatory bodies do not engage with the states as single unitary entities. Rather, they pierce the veil of the state, and interact with particular actors within the state or on a sub-state level.[57] Various actors within states may have diverse and sometimes mutually conflicting interests and incentives for engaging with supranational authorities. Hence, there is the possibility of synergy between supranational and national sites of authority even though the symbiosis is always fragile and tentative, resting as it does on an alliance between supranational authority with only *some* state institutions and actors. Precisely for this reason, there is always scope for tensions, conflicts, and frictions between different sites of authority that are not easily captured by the traditional notion of 'sovereignty'.

It will not be surprising that the best examples of supranational public reason in action are provided by *judicial* or quasi-judicial bodies.[58] Ultimately, the authority of judicial bodies rests upon the force of their argument. Even if the states within their jurisdiction commit themselves to respect and abide by their rulings, there is usually no system of enforcement other than of a symbolic 'naming and shaming' character. Only rarely—as is the case in EU law—is the implementation of decisions of the top court (the Court of Justice of the European Union, or CJEU) entrusted to national courts. This produces a strong 'embeddedness',

[56] See Samantha Besson, 'The Authority of International Law—Lifting the State Veil', (2009) 31 *Sydney Law Review* 343. For a note of scepticism whether the coordinating function is sufficient for legitimacy of institutions of global governance, see Allen Buchanan and Robert O. Keohane, 'The Legitimacy of Global Governance Institutions', (2006) 20 *Ethics & International Affairs* 405, 408–09.

[57] For a discussion of this aspect of supranational adjudication, see Laurence R. Helfer and Anne-Marie Slaughter, 'Towards a Theory of Effective Supranational Adjudication', (1997) 107 *Yale Law Journal* 273, 287.

[58] See Alec Stone Sweet, 'A Cosmopolitan Legal Order: Constitutional Pluralism and Rights Adjudication in Europe', (2012) 1 *Global Constitutionalism* 53, 54–55.

meaning that supranational decisions 'can be implemented without governments having to take actions to do so'.[59]

4. Supranational Public Reason and Rawls's 'Public Reason of the Society of Peoples'

Some observations about the difference between 'Supranational Public Reason' as used here, and the concept of 'public reason of the Society of Peoples' used in John Rawls's *The Law of Peoples*,[60] are in order. This is because the concept of public reason, debated in contemporary political philosophy and used in the present book, is based on Rawls's theory, especially as expounded in *Political Liberalism* and his essay 'The Idea of Public Reason Revisited'. (Incidentally, the latter essay was published in the same volume as *The Law of Peoples*, which suggests at least a degree of affinity with the concept of 'public reason of the Society of Peoples'.) One would therefore think that when Rawls himself extrapolated his initial 'public reason' concept (constructed, as it was, for a bounded liberal society) into the international sphere (in addition, announcing that 'the role of public reason among free and equal peoples is analogous to its role in a constitutional democratic regime among free and equal citizens'),[61] then it would seem natural to adopt a Rawlsian understanding of public reason in the 'Society of Peoples' (his phrase for the international sphere governed by the idea of the Law of Peoples).

And yet, 'supranational public reason' as used for the purpose of my discussion here is fundamentally different from Rawls's 'public reason of the Society of Peoples'. The main difference is that Rawls's international public reason (or, to use Rawls's terminology, the public reason in the 'Society of Peoples'), concerns a *horizontal* realm, that is, the relationship between the states, or the peoples (I will discuss this distinction in a moment). In contrast, supranational public reason, as used in this chapter, is primarily about vertical relations, that is, between supranational authorities (courts, regulatory agencies, executive bodies, etc.) and, on the other hand, states and other entities. That Rawls's concept applies only to horizontal relations is obvious: as he says, it concerns 'the ideals and principles of the *foreign policy*',[62] the 'mutual relations' of liberal peoples 'as peoples',[63] 'a foreign policy and affairs of state that involve other societies',[64] and 'the political relations among peoples'.[65] As one can see, the locus of Rawlsian

[59] Robert O. Keohane, Andrew Moravcsik, and Anne-Marie Slaughter, 'Legalized Dispute Resolution: Interstate and Transnational', (2000) 54 *International Organization* 457, 458.
[60] John Rawls, *The Law of Peoples* (Harvard University Press 1999).
[61] Ibid. 55.
[62] Ibid. 55, emphasis added.
[63] Ibid. 55.
[64] Ibid. 56.
[65] Ibid. 57.

international public reason is international law and international relations, traditionally conceived, and about the relations between states (called here, the peoples). The 'horizontality' of Rawls's conception is bolstered by the whole idea of the Law of Peoples (as a conception, not just the title of the book). This is the proper space for Rawlsian international public reason, as it concerns the relationships traditionally controlled by international law and international relations between sovereign states. In the very first sentence of *The Law of Peoples*, Rawls declares that by Law of Peoples, he understands 'a particular political conception of right and justice that applies to the principles and norms of international law and practice'.[66] This understanding is also reinforced by the methodology adopted by Rawls in the book. While maintaining, with some revisions, his signature method of the social contract when designing the Law of Peoples, Rawls assumes that 'peoples' is to be understood as unitary corporate bodies, rather than individuals who are represented in the original position (I will return to this point below).

Some may say that the intergovernmentality of Rawls's Law of Peoples (and consequently, his concept of international public reason) is toned down by the fact that the entities that are the actors and addressees of public reason are 'peoples' rather than states. Assume for a moment that this is the case. The Law of Peoples in its application to relationships between various peoples in the planet would still be purely horizontal, and would say nothing about supranational public reason, as understood here. But in any event, in Rawls's book, this is a distinction without difference. 'Peoples' are understood by Rawls not as 'united by a common language and shared historical memories', but rather as sharing a 'basic structure' which affects the life of all members.[67] This basic structure consists of institutions, rules, and procedures that control the rights and duties of individual members. In particular, the conduct of 'liberal peoples' is 'organized and expressed in their elections and votes, and the laws and policies of their government'.[68] The consequence is that his 'peoples' are largely identical to societies bounded by state frontiers. It is significant that in Rawls we do not find any strong support for the idea that stateless 'peoples' are the equal partners of all other 'peoples' in the international community of 'peoples'.[69] On the contrary, we do find several hints that only 'peoples' that are territorially defined and represented by a government, register in Rawls's conception. At the beginning of his book, we are told that 'an important role of government, however arbitrary a society's boundaries may appear from a historical point of view, is to be the

[66] Ibid. 3.

[67] Ibid. 25. For a discussion, see J. Donald Moon, 'Rawls and Habermas on Public Reason: Human Rights and Global Justice', (2003) 6 *Annual Review of Political Science* 257, 264–66.

[68] Rawls, *The Law of Peoples* (n. 60) 25.

[69] See, similarly, Allen Buchanan, 'Rawls's Law of Peoples: Rules for a Vanished Westphalian World', (2000) 110 *Ethics* 697, 699.

effective agent of a people as they take responsibility for their territory and the size of their population . . .'[70]

Of course, the 'horizontality' of Rawls's Law of Peoples is not merely an incidental feature of the theory, but it is adopted *for some reasons*. An investigation into these deeper reasons is necessary in order to sharpen the difference between the two conceptions of public reason in the international sphere—his, and the conception advocated in this book. In order to explain this distinction, I will proceed in the following way. I will first describe two 'puzzles' that arise from Rawls's theory: the status of illiberal (though 'decent') peoples in *The Law of Peoples*, and the special characteristics of the social contract employed to set out the principles making up *The Law of Peoples*. I will then suggest that the underlying moral value, adopted by Rawls in *The Law of Peoples*, is toleration, as understood in a very particular and controversial way. Finally, I will explain why the meaning of toleration adopted by Rawls for the purposes of *The Law of Peoples* is deficient, and therefore why his understanding of international public reason (underwritten, as it is, by his conception of toleration) is unacceptable.

The first, and perhaps most striking, puzzle in Rawls's theory is the status of 'illiberal decent peoples' in his theory. The distinction between liberal peoples and the other category of 'well-ordered' societies which are also 'worthy of membership in a Society of Peoples' is of central importance to Rawls's book and its reception. To be characterized as *liberal*, a state must meet certain relatively stringent requirements for liberal-democratic institutions, including those described in Part III of *Political Liberalism*. The problem begins with the characterization of those societies that are *not* liberal, and yet deserve to be recognized as 'equal participating members in good standing of the Society of Peoples'.[71] The main aim of such 'recognition' is the ascertainment of 'how far liberal peoples are to *tolerate* nonliberal peoples'.[72] 'Toleration', in this context, goes far beyond simple non-intervention: it includes, on the part of the liberal peoples, 'a duty of civility requiring that they offer other peoples public reasons appropriate to the Society of Peoples for their actions'.[73] In this way, illiberal and yet decent peoples enter the community where public reason governs mutual relationships.

There are three main ways in which illiberal/decent peoples, in Rawls's terminology, depart from the standards of liberal peoples. First, they incorporate certain 'basic inequalities among their members'.[74] Second, there is *some* liberty of conscience but not '*equal* liberty of conscience',[75] and this may include, for instance, an established state religion, as long as other religions are not persecuted.[76] Lastly, these peoples lack what we would consider normal political,

[70] Rawls, *The Law of Peoples* (n. 60) 8.
[71] Ibid. 59.
[72] Ibid. 59, emphasis added.
[73] Ibid. 59.
[74] Ibid. 70.
[75] Ibid. 70, emphasis added.
[76] Ibid. 76.

representative democratic institutions, but instead have a 'decent consultation hierarchy'.[77] For a liberal, embracing societies tainted by such important defects into the community of peoples raises serious dilemmas.[78] If we refuse, in our own societies, to respect those moral-political conceptions that would postulate redesigning our societies along these illiberal lines, why should we respect such societies abroad? A liberal who accepts the position of normative individualism assesses the value of social institutions, rules, and practices through the prism of their effect upon the legitimate interests of the individuals affected, and, in particular, those interests linked to their liberty and equality.

After describing an imaginary illiberal but decent state, 'Kazanistan' (no separation of church and state; establishment of a favoured religion with all top positions filled by followers of this religion; no democratic institutions but only a 'decent consultation' system; only a very thin toleration of dissent, etc), Rawls observes: 'I think enlightenment about the limits of liberalism recommends trying to conceive a reasonably just Law of Peoples that liberal and nonliberal people could together endorse.'[79] This is effectively a declaration concerning the outer 'limits of liberalism' and a look at the world 'outside' those limits. Can we really accept this declaration without having regard to the inexcusable damage done to the value-laden presuppositions that warranted our endorsement of the liberal principles in the first place? For example, consider the damage done to the presupposition articulated simply but effectively by Brian Barry in his impassioned book, that '[n]obody, anywhere in the world, should be denied liberal protections against injustice and oppression'?[80]

Posing this question is all the more important since the conception of the Law of Peoples should not be seen as aimed at formulating a set of policy guidelines for liberal-democratic governments about how to deal with various non-liberal states and governments in the world. It does this too, but only indirectly and secondarily. It would be an error to read it as merely a theoretically elaborated statement of *Realpolitik* with a set of prescriptions for how liberal governments should treat different categories of states in their foreign policy.[81] A theory such as Rawls's in *The Law of Peoples* should be seen as critical and normative rather than pragmatic and prudential. It concerns certain *ideals* with respect to an international system rather than a set of *Realpolitik* prescriptions and should be judged itself under these standards. Now one trope that *might* help clarify Rawls's reasons for embracing non-liberal peoples in this way is by considering his own self-characterization of his theory as a 'realistic utopia'—his favourite and frequently repeated formula of the conception of the Law of Peoples. The

[77] Ibid. 71.

[78] See Gerald Gaus, *The Order of Public Reason* (Cambridge University Press 2011) 432.

[79] Rawls, *The Law of Peoples* (n. 60) 78.

[80] Brian Barry, *Culture and Equality* (Polity Press 2001) 138.

[81] See, similarly, Martha Nussbaum, *Frontiers of Justice* (Harvard University Press 2006) 230; Euan MacDonald, *International Law and Ethics After the Critical Change* (Martinus Nijhoff 2011) 249.

first extended introduction of the notion of 'realistic utopia' indicates the nature of the problem: 'political philosophy is realistically utopian when it extends what are ordinarily thought to be the limits of practicable political possibility and, in so doing, reconciles us to our political and social condition.'[82] There is an inevitable tension between the aspiration of 'extending the limits of political possibility' and 'reconciling us to our conditions', or between 'the realistic' and 'the utopian' in the 'realistic utopia'.

In *The Law of Peoples*, this tension is clear when we consider the moral *status* of the inclusion of non-liberal (though 'decent') peoples into the Society of Peoples. On the one hand, there are some hints in Rawls's book that suggest that the presence of those societies is not something morally positive *per se*, but rather that they are embraced grudgingly, as a concession to political reality, in the manner of non-ideal theory, and that they need not be seen as something stable and persistent in the Society of Peoples.[83] A message of liberal universalism is evident in the suggestion that one of the functions of liberal tolerance towards non-liberal decent peoples may be its positive impact upon those societies in terms of encouraging their development towards liberalization and democratization.[84] Alas, there is much in the book that supports the opposite interpretation of the status of the inclusion of various 'Kazanistans' into the Law of Peoples. This opposing interpretation supports the idea that the presence of liberal *and* non-liberal peoples is morally significant, stable, accepted in a non-grudging fashion, and need not be overcome. At the very end of the book, Rawls observes: 'not all peoples can reasonably be required to be liberal',[85] and there is no sense of regret in this statement and in its context. The strongest indication that the inclusion of non-liberal decent societies is itself of moral significance is provided by the (already noted) recognition of the existence of liberal and non-liberal peoples alike in the Society of Peoples *as part of the ideal theory* of international justice. However, the moral reasons for this significance are unclear—particularly if one considers Rawls's various observations concerning the moral defects of hierarchical societies, which imply that liberal-democratic norms constitute a yardstick for the moral evaluation of hierarchical, decent societies.[86] The only solution to this puzzle is in the specific notion of toleration adopted by Rawls—a point to which I will return below.

Before that, however, we need to look at the second great puzzle about the Law of People, namely, its redesign of the concept of 'social contract', compared to Rawls's prior account in *A Theory of Justice*. In moving from *A Theory of Justice* to

[82] Rawls, *The Law of Peoples* (n. 60) 11.
[83] See ibid. 83.
[84] Ibid. 122.
[85] Ibid. 122.
[86] See Seyla Benhabib, 'Is There a Human Right to Democracy? Beyond Interventionism and Indifference', in Claudio Corradetti (ed.), *Philosophical Dimensions of Human Rights* (Springer 2012) 191, 192–95.

The Law of Peoples, Rawls effected some very significant changes in the description of the conditions of social contract, and these changes are responsible for the startling thinness of the Law of Peoples as a *critical* theory of international justice. The main change was in the composition of the 'participants' in the deliberative process in the original position: those operating in *A Theory of Justice* as spokespersons for the *individuals* who are representative of different social groups and strata are replaced in *The Law of Peoples* by '*peoples*' as the relevant parties to the social contract.

It is important to recognize the implications of this move. If *individuals* were to be represented in the original social contract, the confining of the rules of international justice to the eight principles that Rawls articulates would be indefensible.[87] Under the method of social contract behind the veil of ignorance, principles of international justice would have to consist of the rules plausibly agreed to by the representative individuals, *each unaware of the specific society to which they belong*. This type of ignorance would correspond best to *A Theory of Justice*-style veil of ignorance, that is, the ignorance as to (among other things) one's place in a real society in which one finds oneself once the social contract has been concluded. And if the parties *qua* individuals, unaware as to their geographical location in the world, were to write the rules of international justice, they would surely go for something much thicker than the minimalist conception described in *The Law of Peoples*. The risk of harm that would be incurred upon finding oneself in a deeply inegalitarian and undemocratic society (even though still 'decent' by *The Law of Peoples* standards) would be too catastrophic for the parties to agree to the principles of *The Law of Peoples*. They would surely opt for much more rigorous and demanding requirements as to the internal social institutions of the various 'peoples' making up the world population, and for much stronger rules for international economic redistribution. If, in contrast, it is the 'peoples' who are represented in the original position, understood as unitary corporate bodies, the Law of Peoples as a fair system of international justice becomes much more convincing.

Consequently, a major change effected in the transition from *A Theory of Justice* to *The Law of Peoples* in the design of the conditions of the social contract is found in the selectiveness of the composition of the parties in the latter. In *A Theory of Justice*, no representative position in a society, however defined, was *a priori* excluded from playing a role in formulating the hypothetical social contract. By contrast, in *The Law of Peoples*, only some peoples are included in the contract-making: namely the 'well-ordered' peoples (the category that, in Rawls's taxonomy, occupies the two highest positions in the classifications of peoples on

[87] The eight principles of the Law of Peoples are: (1) freedom and independence of peoples; (2) duty to observe treaties; (3) equality of the peoples; (4) duty of non-intervention; (5) the right of self-defence as the only reason to instigate war; (6) honouring of human rights; (7) restrictions in the conduct of war; and (8) a duty to assist other peoples, Rawls, *The Law of Peoples* (n. 60) 37.

the planet: the liberal and non-liberal but 'decent' peoples). All the remaining peoples (which Rawls divides into 'outlaw states', 'societies burdened by unfavorable conditions' and 'benevolent absolutisms')[88] remain beyond the pale, and do not participate in the contract. This, of course, is a consequence of the 'peoples-based' rather than the 'individuals-based' contract: if the rules of international justice were to be contracted by representatives of individuals, surely the unfortunate inhabitants of the last three categories of states would be in greatest need of the benefits deriving from the critical potential of international justice.

As a model representing moral reasoning about the principles of justice, the social contract takes a very pale form in *The Law of Peoples*.[89] To begin with, the concept of reflective equilibrium—which played such an important role in shaping the conditions of the original position in *A Theory of Justice*—barely exists in *The Law of Peoples*.[90] In *A Theory of Justice*, reflective equilibrium was an effective and helpful device precisely because it suggested a procedure for bringing our general moral principles (about which we feel reasonably confident but still are prepared to modify, within limits) and our more specific judgements of justice (again, considered as *provisional* fixed points of our moral argument) into line with each other; we are ready to 'work from both ends' up to the point at which the principles will match the convictions. But in *The Law of Peoples*, where 'reflective equilibrium' only exists in a declaratory and pale fashion, with no implications similar to those in *A Theory of Justice* drawn from it, the subsequent process of reasoning is left in a moral vacuum. No wonder that this process was merely given a cursory account in *The Law of Peoples*. Indeed, it is basically reduced to the following statement: 'the representatives of well-ordered peoples simply reflect on the advantages of these principles of equality among peoples and see no reason to depart from them or to propose alternatives'.[91] This is a clear erosion of the nature of the hypothetical 'deliberation' leading to a social contract in *A Theory of Justice*. Rawls makes it even more explicit: 'The parties [to the social contract in *The Law of Peoples*] are not given a menu of alternative principles and ideals from which to select, as they are in *Political Liberalism*, or in *A Theory of Justice*'.[92]

What justifies such a change? Social contract stands *for something*, and the impoverishment thereof reflects a change in the mode of reasoning. In *Political Liberalism*, Rawls insisted that the social contract is a device to represent our moral reasoning on justice. It models 'restrictions on reasons in such a way that

[88] Ibid. 62–63.
[89] See a similar observation by Amartya Sen, *The Idea of Justice* (Harvard University Press 2009) 26.
[90] It appears only twice in *The Law of Peoples*: once explicitly but with a marginal role in the reasoning process, in a footnote, Rawls, *The Law of Peoples* (n. 60) 86 n. 35; and once implicitly, with hardly any operative function attached to it, ibid. 58.
[91] Ibid. 41.
[92] Ibid. 41.

it becomes perfectly evident which agreement would be made by the parties as citizens' representatives'.[93] In *The Law of Peoples*, he declares, accordingly: 'Since the original position includes the veil of ignorance, it also models what we regard as appropriate *restrictions on reasons* for adopting a political conception of justice ...'[94] Viewed in this way, the realism–utopianism dilemma returns. By disallowing the parties to the original position a choice from a reasonably broad menu of possible principles, and by confining their choice to those principles that can be culled only 'from the history and usages of international law and practice',[95] Rawls clearly identifies very rigorous restrictions upon the reasons available to those parties when the rules of international justice are decided. These reasons are largely confined to the already existing (although properly laundered) principles of customary law and good international practice.

This is in stark contrast to *A Theory of Justice*-style social contract, in which the parties had a reasonably broad 'menu of alternative principles and ideals from which to select' available to them. By discarding some of these 'alternative principles and ideals' (in particular, utilitarianism and intuitionism) in *A Theory of Justice*, Rawls was able to discharge the burden of showing why some reasons for adopting a conception of justice are better than others. It should be recalled that, in the deduction of a plausible conception of justice from the original position (the position, it should be emphasized, that merely modelled the right reasons to be taken into account, namely disinterestedness, reciprocity, universalizability, etc.), a particularly important role was played by the strategy of maximin. Maximin was supposed to be the most reasonable strategy adopted by rational individuals acting under conditions of uncertainty as to the actual scenario of events that will actually occur. It seems, however, that there is no maximin strategy at work in *The Law of Peoples*. If it were, it would be implausible for the maximin *not* to dictate something like a principle of global distributive justice and a robust international human rights regime (much more robust than what Rawls envisages). It may still be a controversial proposition: it could be argued that the parties would reject these two principles. However, the point is that, in *The Law of Peoples*, Rawls does not even allow the parties to the original position to *contemplate* these conceptions as potentially available options. Indeed, these conceptions do not even make it into the 'menu of alternative principles and ideals from which to select'.[96]

From the foregoing analysis, we can see how the complex model of moral reasoning on justice employed in *A Theory of Justice* has undergone a truly fundamental transformation in *The Law of Peoples*. *A Theory of Justice* model consisted,

[93] John Rawls, *Political Liberalism* (Columbia University Press 1993) 26.

[94] Rawls, *The Law of Peoples* (n. 60) 30, emphasis added. Here Rawls echoes his own identical formula from *Political Liberalism* (n. 93) 26.

[95] Rawls, *The Law of Peoples* (n. 60) 41.

[96] Ibid. 41.

to put it schematically, of three ingredients. First, it used the device of reflective equilibrium as a coherence-aimed framework oriented towards mutual adjustment and readjustment between our pre-reflective intuitive specific convictions of justice and general, abstract principles of justice. Second, the original position modelled the types of reasons that are acceptable when proposing principles of justice (or, put negatively, when discarding reasons that may be used self-servingly by individuals attempting to tailor the general principles of justice to serve their own individual needs). Third, and most substantively, the strategy of maximin was posited as the most rational strategy of decision-making under conditions of relative uncertainty. This involved extrapolating decision-making strategy into the field of moral reasoning. None of these three essential ingredients are present in *The Law of Peoples*, or, if they are, they each play a much less important role in representing a model of moral reasoning compared with *A Theory of Justice*. Reflective equilibrium is only present, if at all, in the palest of forms, and plays effectively no role in shaping the description of the original position. The original position has been eroded by restrictions on the types of reasoning about justice available to the parties. And the principle of maximin is absent, or at least is not detectable in the deliberative process leading to the eight principles of international justice. With the disappearance of these three devices, the features of the attractiveness and effectiveness of the social contract *qua* model of representation for moral reasoning on justice have almost completely vanished. In this manner, the second puzzle that presents itself in *The Law of Peoples* is: what explains the vanishing act of social contract methodology once Rawls turns his eyes to the supranational sphere?

These two puzzles—the status of illiberal peoples and the erosion of social contract methodology—point to the overarching value that is responsible for these features of the theory in *The Law of Peoples*. That overarching value is the ideal of toleration. There can be very little doubt in the minds of readers of *The Law of Peoples* that, whenever the troubling questions appear concerning the bias in favour of realism in the 'realistic utopia', it is the importance of toleration for other non-liberal societies that is provided as the response.[97] When explaining why liberals should not attempt to force their ideals of good society upon the non-liberal peoples, Rawls says: 'If all societies were required to be liberal, the idea of political liberalism would fail to express *due toleration* for other acceptable ways (if such there are, as I assume) of ordering society.'[98] In the same context, Rawls clarifies that his meaning of toleration goes beyond the precept of non-interference: 'to tolerate means not only to refrain from exercising political sanctions—military, economic, or diplomatic—to make a people change its ways. To tolerate also means to recognize these nonliberal societies as equal

[97] See Samuel Freeman, 'Introduction: John Rawls—An Overview', in Samuel Freeman (ed.), *The Cambridge Companion to Rawls* (Cambridge University Press 2003) 1, 46.

[98] *The Law of Peoples* (n. 60) 59, emphasis added.

participating members in good standing of the Society of Peoples, with certain rights and obligations . . . .'[99] Much later in the book, when he elucidates the reasons why he accepts that non-liberal but decent societies 'deserv[e] respect', he provides the following telling analogy: 'Liberal societies may differ widely in many ways: for example, some are far more egalitarian than others, yet these differences are *tolerated* in the society of liberal peoples. Might not the institutions of some kinds of hierarchical societies also be similarly *tolerable*? I believe this to be so.'[100] One can supply many more citations from Rawls's book that, whenever the puzzles as earlier identified arise, appeal to the ideal of toleration as the answer.

But if toleration is the answer, what exactly was the question? Before we inquire into whether the ideal of toleration can perform the onerous job it is assigned in Rawls's theory, it is important to clarify the *function* that the ideal of toleration may perform (if we share the assessment of its worth) in a conception of international justice such as Rawls's. To put it in negative terms, it is important to clarify what the ideal of toleration is *not* about in this context. It is not about the permissibility and the potential scope of governmental interference by one state (say, a liberal one) in the institutional and legal arrangements of another state (say, a non-liberal one).[101] This is consistent with what we have observed earlier. That is, an ideal theory of international justice does not directly provide any prescriptions for governmental policy vis-à-vis other states. Rather, it is about what good theoretical reasons we, as individual citizens, have to criticize and interfere, through the means available to us, in societies whose domestic institutions, distribution patterns, human rights record, etc. we dislike. The forms of interference available to us, as individuals, are usually related to the *advocacy* of change in another society: we as individuals do not have the means of coercive intervention. This sounds banal, but it needs to be clearly stated because Rawls himself, at times, seems to be oscillating between two orders: first, the order of an ideal theory containing prescriptions for individual liberal citizens, and second, the order of pragmatic policy proposals with prescriptions for governmental action. He says, for example: 'A decent hierarchical society meets moral and legal requirements sufficient to override the political reasons we might have for *imposing sanctions* on, or *forcibly interfering* with, its people and their institutions and culture.'[102] The principle of toleration relevant to the context of international justice has been assigned the role of explaining why we should embrace some non-liberal societies within the Law of Peoples. It does not, however, address the question of the acceptability of governmental sanctions or coercive interference.

[99] Ibid. 59.
[100] Ibid. 84, emphases added, footnote omitted.
[101] For a similar interpretation of Rawls, see Charles R. Beitz, *The Idea of Human Rights* (Oxford University Press 2009) 154.
[102] Rawls, *The Law of Peoples* (n. 60) 83, emphases added.

One important prior question, preceding questions of sanctions and interference, is whether we, as individuals, have good reasons for trying to effect change in societies that we dislike: the principle of toleration may pre-empt, and render improper, such an aspiration *at this stage*.[103] Therefore, the principle of toleration should be treated in the context of international justice as an ethical norm rather than a pragmatic policy recommendation. In this perspective, is this ethical norm capable of supporting the inclusion of hierarchical, non-liberal but decent peoples into the Society of Peoples with the consequences described by Rawls? Or, going backwards in the chain of reasoning, is it capable of persuading us to modify the rules of the social contract, with constraints on the options available, the abandonment of the maximin strategy, and—most importantly—the replacement of individuals by 'peoples' in the original position? I do not think so.

Toleration is an important ethical value. There are good moral reasons why we should often abstain from interference with other people's sincerely held values (and, consequently, with their behaviour based on these values), even if we reject them. Toleration is not (and, in a weaker version of the argument, need not be) based on some form of moral agnosticism. It can be (and, in a stronger version of the argument, must be) based on thick substantive moral reasons that deny us the moral right of imposing our moral values on those who do not share them. Liberals who believe in the value of toleration must, within limits, abstain from trying to impose liberal conceptions of life, such as the conception of an autonomous life shaped by the individual herself, subjected only or predominantly to one's own choices, upon other people. Liberal toleration requires, consequently, that we do not interfere with non-liberal forms of social life, insofar as they are necessary to support genuinely espoused preferences for non-autonomous conceptions of life.

Such a morally meaningful principle of toleration is, of course, a controversial ideal. It raises all sorts of different problems that have absorbed, and divided, liberals for decades. The most important and difficult of these problems is encapsulated in the question: should non-autonomous ways of life *adopted in a non-autonomous manner* also be respected, or is respect for non-autonomous ways of life due only when there has been an autonomous choice to live a non-autonomous life? We all know how difficult and fraught with dangers each option is. If we choose the former answer (extending respect for non-autonomy also to non-autonomous processes of deciding about non-autonomous life), our 'toleration' turns into an insensitivity to oppression, exploitation, discrimination, and coercion. Non-autonomous ways of life are often imposed upon people or are adopted (or accepted) by those people as a last resort to reduce suffering related to their lack of freedom. Insensitivity to this fact erodes the moral worth

[103] See Wojciech Sadurski, '"It All Depends": The Universal and the Contingent in Human Rights', in Claudio Corradetti (ed.), *Philosophical Dimensions of Human Rights* (Springer 2012) 125.

toleration has in the first place. But if we choose the latter answer (respect for non-autonomous ways of life but only if adopted freely, autonomously), then we run immediately into the seemingly insurmountable problem of distinguishing between second-order decisions *about* the choice of a way of life, and the first-order decisions that *constitute* a way of life. Human life does not divide so neatly into first-order and second-order decisions, or into our initial choices and their consequences.

Fortunately, in the context of discussing *The Law of Peoples*, we do not have to choose between the former and the latter answer. Rather, we are concerned with more integral liberalism: one that is more deferential to non-autonomous ways of lives (and is prepared to ignore the defects in terms of autonomous choices about such lives), and one that considers individual autonomy to be the paramount value dictating the parameters of, rather than being constrained by, the principle of toleration. We need not enter into this controversy because even if we adopted the broadest conception of toleration, one that is non-critical of the non-autonomous processes of choosing a way of life, we would nonetheless be doing it for the (alleged) good of the individual concerned. The moral worth of the principle of toleration would stem from the (alleged) benefit to the individual to whom toleration is due. Otherwise, toleration itself would be left in a moral vacuum. It would be perverse to demand toleration for someone's choices if we thought these choices to be at least partly non-autonomous, *and* there was no particular benefit (of moral significance) that such toleration conferred upon the individual concerned. Ultimately, toleration in terms of either conception is based upon normative individualism; it is the good of the individual that endows the ideal of toleration with moral worth.

The Law of Peoples, however, fails to identify any convincing connection between the principle of toleration and the good of the individuals who are to be tolerated. It is peoples, rather than individuals themselves, who are the avowed beneficiaries of the principle of toleration as announced in his book. If, however, a 'people', through its institutional design and practices, is intolerant towards some of its members, then the benefits of liberal toleration are due to those individuals rather than to the 'people' itself: *their* good is the ultimate source of the moral worth of toleration.[104] Rawls never tries to convince us, and we have no reason to believe, that the individual members of the illiberal but decent peoples are, on balance, the net beneficiaries of the principle of toleration as demanded in *The Law of Peoples*. The central question that would have to be asked is, what is the balance of benefits and costs for the individual members of decent hierarchical societies that results from adopting the principle of toleration of such societies? If Rawls had followed the line of reasoning suggested by this question, he

[104] See, similarly, Michael Blake, 'Toleration and Reciprocity: Commentary on Martha Nussbaum and Henry Shue', (2002) 1 *Politics, Philosophy & Economics* 325, 326.

would no doubt have had to give a rather complex and differentiated answer: he would have had to admit that the benefits and costs divide unequally *within* hierarchical societies, and that some are the beneficiaries while others (perhaps, a majority) are net losers. For example, adopting the principle of 'toleration' and applying it to gender inequality in a hierarchical society will make some people worse off (compared to adoption of the principle of interference), even though it will also make some people satisfied in sustaining their ways of life based, as they are, on societal discrimination against women. Now both parts of this proposition require a more subtle and nuanced exposition, rather than merely stating that men will benefit from such 'toleration' while women will be its victims. Certainly, there may be many men who would rather see the end of open discrimination, but who are unwilling to take steps towards resolving complex collective-action problems on their own. Likewise, there may be some women who feel such a strong attachment to their local culture that they will genuinely abhor any departure from traditional gender-defined roles, even if these mean deep inequality. The latter case will call for an investigation into the degree to which such commitments are genuine, as opposed to being a form of 'adaptive preferences', or having been adopted under pressure or fear of coercion, etc. I will not follow through on this line of argument because one thing is clear: this is *not* the type of question that Rawls entertains.[105] The connection between the principle of toleration and the unequal distribution of benefits and costs produced by the adoption of this principle for its alleged beneficiaries is not elucidated anywhere in *The Law of Peoples*. This consideration is simply precluded by identifying 'peoples' as the beneficiaries of the principle of toleration.

Moreover, an advocate of the principle of toleration *à la* Rawls would have to go a step further, and test not only whether different members of decent hierarchical societies *benefit* from non-interference by liberal societies: one would, in addition, have to affirm that they *supported* it. 'Toleration' towards someone who does not want it loses its moral bearings: it becomes indifference to someone else's misfortune. If *A* desires *B*'s interference aimed at changing *A*'s situation, then *B*'s abstention cannot be presented as 'toleration' in any meaningful sense of the word. Now, whether all (or even many) members of 'hierarchical but decent' societies in fact favour the policy of non-interference in their domestic arrangements is a very difficult thing to verify, even if only because, by the very description of those societies provided by Rawls, a reliable account of views, values, and public opinion in those societies is not easily available. By the same token, however, we can rarely say with any degree of certainty that all members of such societies *reject* the idea of interference from the outside. Some do and some do not, and it matters a great deal who actually does and who does not. It is a very plausible hypothesis that those who do support outside interference find

[105] But more in Sadurski, 'It All Depends' (n. 103).

themselves on the lowest rung of the social ladder and would thus be representative of the 'worst-off' people who, from *A Theory of Justice* perspective, would need to be taken into account *first* in designing the right system of justice. Unless we adopt the deeply implausible (and alien to the overall philosophical system of Rawls as developed in *A Theory of Justice* and *Political Liberalism*) collectivist ontology of a 'people', under which it constitutes a single entity with its own undifferentiated subjectivity, we have absolutely no reason to accept at face value the declarations of the *leaders* of decent hierarchical peoples (and of their ideologues) concerning the true 'values' of those peoples. Neither have we any reason to accept at face value the declarations of those leaders as to whether their people accept or reject the idea of interference from the outside (even though we know that internal dissent towards the leaders' declared ideology does not necessarily translate into support for external interference—but this is something we do not need to go into here). We know—on the basis of our empirical experience (and the debate about so-called 'Asian values' is helpful in this regard)[106]—that often, and probably more often than not, declarations by leaders of societies fitting Rawls's description of decent hierarchical peoples are nothing but ideological rationalizations of oppression, privilege, and authoritarianism.[107] We know that, when we are told that 'their' societies dislike the idea of democracy, of individual rights, of freedom of the press etc., these leaders of authoritarian societies are developing a self-serving, deceitful rationalization in order to exempt themselves from political accountability and critique. We must not take these ideological rationalizations at face value, nor believe that the citizens of societies subjected to this rule actually share them.

In conclusion: Rawls's 'public reason of the Society of Peoples' concerns the relationship between states, as designed by the states themselves, and the shape of international law as traditionally understood (with states being its only subjects). In its aspiration, rationales, and effects, it is fundamentally different from supranational public reason, as understood in this chapter.

5. Two Regional Human Rights Bodies and a Note on Autonomization

One of the striking features of several supranational adjudicatory bodies is their 'autonomization'. This concept refers to the growing irrelevance of states' consent as the main legitimating factor for those bodies. Used in this sense, the growing 'autonomy' of the ECtHR is the main case in point and will be discussed at some

[106] See Mark R. Thompson, 'Whatever Happened to "Asian Values"?', (2001) 12 *Journal of Democracy* 154.

[107] See, similarly, Henry Shue, 'Rawls and the Outlaws', (2002) 1 *Politics, Philosophy & Economics* 307, 312.

length in the next chapter. But the ECtHR is not the only instance of the way supranational courts have consolidated in this way, or which otherwise illustrates the growing disconnect between those courts and aspects of state consent. One other example is that of the Inter-American Court of Human Rights (IACtHR), which has assumed increased supervision over the execution of its own judgments in recent years. Under the Inter-American system, in the absence of an intergovernmental body equivalent to the Committee of Ministers of the Council of Europe, supervision was traditionally carried out once a year by the Organization of American States (OAS) General Assembly in a rather perfunctory way. The Court grew impatient with the thinness of this supervision and, in a landmark case of 2001,[108] announced that '[m]onitoring compliance with judgment is one of the elements that comprises jurisdiction'.[109] Accordingly, the Court went on to say that the sanction envisaged in the American Convention on Human Rights (ACHR) (reports by IACtHR to the OAS General Assembly on non-compliance with its decisions)[110] *assumes* that the IACtHR would exercise its inherent powers of supervision over the execution of its judgments in the domestic law of the respondent states. The Court also announced that the conduct of the respondent state in this particular case (Panama) showed beyond doubt that the state in the past had recognized the Court's powers of supervision of compliance. Consequently, the Court dismissed Panama's challenge to supervision in this case, and Panama proceeded to comply with the judgment. In this way, something that had initially been a typical intergovernmental sanction (the Art. 65 power of report by the IACtHR to the General Assembly of the OAS) came to serve, at least for a certain period,[111] as an instrument allowing the Inter-American Court to exercise an autonomous, *par excellence*, supranational authority to supervise compliance with the Convention, thus liberating it even further from the umbilical cord of state consent.

One may also add that, as has been the case with the European Convention on Human Rights (ECHR), the ACHR, while having no formal direct effect upon national systems, has largely penetrated those systems through individual states' incorporation of the Convention, either at the level of constitutional norms,[112] or in a sub-constitutional but supra-statutory form,[113] or statutory form. In

[108] *Baena-Ricardo et al. (270 workers) v. Panama* (judgment of 28 November 2003), discussed by Antônio Augusto Conçado Trindade, 'Compliance with judgments and decisions—The experience of the Inter-American Court of Human Rights: a reassessment', in *Dialogue between judges*, European Court of Human Rights, Council of Europe, 2014, 10–17 at 13 (available at http://www.echr.coe.int/Documents/Dialogue_2014_ENG.pdf (last accessed 17 June 2020).

[109] Quoted by Conçado, 'Compliance with judgments and decisions' (n. 108) 13.

[110] Article 65 of ACHR provides, inter alia, that in its reports, the Court 'shall specify, in particular, the cases in which a state has not complied with its judgments, making any pertinent recommendations'.

[111] Former President of the IACtHR, Antônio Trindade deplored the departure from this practice from the end of 2004, Conçado, 'Compliance with judgments and decisions' (n. 108) 15.

[112] e.g. Argentina, Venezuela.

[113] e.g. Costa Rica, Paraguay.

addition, the Convention itself (in Art. 2) requires member states to adopt such legislative or other measures as may be necessary to give effect to the Convention's rights, thus mandating legal effects of the Convention in ways similar to those that have been, de facto, affected by the ECHR upon the legislation of European states. A case where the Convention and the IACtHR case law were incorporated in Mexico is an interesting example. When the Inter-American Court issued a decision holding Mexico liable for human rights violations, it recommended a series of legislative reforms in addition to budgetary provisions, mainly concerning military criminal jurisdiction.[114] Following the ruling, the Supreme Court of Mexico issued a resolution in which, first, it conceded that it cannot review or assess the Inter-American Court's judgments for their correctness but must always comply with the judgment,[115] and then reminded the government that judgments of the IACtHR are binding on the state, that the decisions of the IACtHR to which Mexico is not a party should guide the decisions of all Mexican courts, and that the Constitution mandates 'conventionality review', that is, the review of law in light of the American Convention.[116] While a caveat is needed that, formally speaking, the resolution is not legally binding but only establishes 'criteria' to be used in deciding a case, its overall significance is manifold.[117] In particular, it established the power of all Mexican judges to review a domestic law for consistency with the American Convention, even if they cannot review it under the Mexican Constitution (which sets up a 'concentrated' system of judicial review that only federal judges may perform). From our point of view, of even greater significance is the assertion of the guiding character of the IACtHR guidelines on national judges even where Mexico was not a party to a case. The judicially driven recognition of the authority of the Inter-American Court vis-à-vis both national executives and the judiciary (a path, as one commentator called it, from 'ignoring the [Inter-American] Court's judgments to considering them legally binding')[118] is one example of the phenomenon of the 'autonomization' of the supranational bodies and their growing independence of state consent.

Just like the ECtHR (as will be shown at length in the next chapter), the IACHR is equipped with two sets of instruments which, theoretically, provide it with the means to conduct scrutiny of legitimate goals of national legislation, thus lending itself to a discussion in terms of 'public reason'. There is a list of legitimate grounds for limitations upon some of the rights of the American Convention of Human Rights (ACHR), and the canonical proportionality analysis in which the

[114] *Radilla Pacheco v. Mexico*, judgment by the IACtHR of 23 November 2009.

[115] Miscellaneous Case 912/2010, issued 14 July 2011; English translation available in https://law.utexas.edu/colloquia/archive/papers-public/2011-2012/03-19-12_The%20Rosendo%20Radilla%20Case%20(2010).pdf (last accessed 17 June 2020), paras. 16–17.

[116] Paras 19, 20, 28–29.

[117] See Christina M. Cerna, Note, 'American Convention on Human Rights—state responsibility—compliance with international decisions—military jurisdiction', (2013) 107 *American Journal of International Law* 199 .

[118] Ibid. 204.

detection of 'legitimate aims' is explicitly mentioned as an analytical step of the scrutiny.

As far as the first instrument is concerned, Articles 13 (freedom of thought and expression), 15 (right of assembly), 16 (freedom of association), and 22 (freedom of movement and residence) are examples of ACHR rights that can be restricted when it is necessary for goals such as rights of others, national security, public order, morals, or public safety. The catalogues of these aims only marginally differ from each other: for instance, the 'reputation of others' is only mentioned as a limitation ground for freedom of thought and expression, but this right is not accompanied by a limitation on the basis of 'public safety', which is listed in the other three articles. All four articles contain a requirement of 'necessity' (though Art. 13 omits to add 'in a democratic society') and they all require that the limitations are established 'by law'. In these respects, the structures of those non-absolute rights fully resemble the structures adopted in the European Convention.

In relation to the second instrument, namely proportionality analysis including scrutiny of legislative aims, the IACHR has adopted this approach since 2000,[119] and has expressly recognized the ECtHR's proportionality analysis as a model to follow. Prior to 2000, it used what was known as a 'subsumption model' under which the Court subsumed an alleged human right violation under the text of an appropriate article of the Convention. No balancing or proportionality scrutiny was engaged in under this traditional pattern.[120] Since 2000, however, the Court has started to use proportionality analysis, very much along the lines of the ECtHR pattern, though with one change which is of interest to our discussion—the analysis of legitimate aims is connected to a suitability test within a single stage, thus watering down the significance of scrutiny of legislative aims.

For example, in the well-known case of *Kimel v. Argentina*,[121] concerning the punishment of a famous investigative journalist for criminal libel on the basis of his accounts of massacres committed by the armed forces, the Court explained its use of proportionality analysis in this case in the following way:

[119] The Court had already foreshadowed the use of proportionality in its Advisory Opinion OC-5/85 of 13 November 1985. The Opinion concerned a request by Costa Rica concerning the interpretation of the compulsory membership of journalists in a professional association for consistency with the Convention. The Court explicitly referred to the ECtHR as a model followed, see para. 46, although it carefully identified certain differences between the wordings of the European and American Conventions, see para. 45. In its conclusions, the Court determined that, while the aim of public order (as included among the limiting grounds for Art. 13 of the American Convention) may justify compulsory licensing in other professions, in the case of journalism, restricting a right on that basis would violate the Article 13 rights of non-members of the association, and would not be consistent with the basic principles of democracy, para. 76.

[120] Laura Clérico, 'Limitaciones a los derechos constitucionales y control de razonabilidad (control de proporcionalidad)', in Julio César Rivera et al. (eds.), *Tratado de Derechos Constitucionales. vol I.* (Abeledo Perrot 2014) 507.

[121] Judgment of 2 May 2008.

> [I]n order to render judgment in the instant case the Court will (i) verify whether the legal definition of the crime of defamation affected the strict legality which is to be observed when restricting the freedom of thought and expression by means of criminal proceedings; (ii) examine whether the protection of the reputation of judges serves a legitimate purpose, in accordance with the provisions of the Convention and determine, if appropriate, the suitability of a criminal penalty in order to achieve the purpose sought; (iii) assess whether such measure is necessary; and (iv) examine the strict proportionality of such measure, that is, whether the penalty imposed on Mr. Kimel has fully guaranteed the right of the public official mentioned by the author of the book to have his honor respected, without rendering nugatory the latter's right to express his opinion.[122]

In this case, the Court established that 'protecting honor and reputation is a legitimate end' and immediately added, in the same paragraph, that criminal sanctions are suitable to achieve this purpose. However, based on the subsequent tests, namely necessity and proportionality *sensu stricto*, the Court concluded that the state had violated Mr Kimel's rights under Article 13 of the Convention.

Perhaps as a result of merging legitimate aim scrutiny with a suitability test, and the resultant thinning of the distinctiveness of legitimacy testing, no law has been ever judged by the Court as inconsistent with the Convention because of its illegitimate purposes. Just like its European counterpart, the Court is usually satisfied by the government merely reciting one of the limitation grounds in the Convention. At times, express scrutiny of legislative aims can be discerned in the judgments of the Court. However, these cases may be seen as feeble reflections of the ideal of PR. An example may be provided by *Palamara Iribarne v. Chile*,[123] a case considering the confiscation of a book written by a former military official, as well as punishment for criminal contempt. Announcing its understanding of proportionality analysis, the Court said that 'the restriction must be proportionate to the underlying interest and in direct furtherance of such legitimate purpose, interfering as little as possible with the effective exercise of the right to freedom of thought and expression'.[124] While the Court has not determined that the aim pursued by the restrictive measures was not legitimate, it nevertheless quoted extensively from statements made by the President of Chile to the effect that the crime of contempt must be reformed because, as was in practice at the time in Chile, it led to censorship and thus violated freedom of speech rights:

> the President of Chile stated that 'the offense of contempt ... does not seem to be a legitimate restriction on the freedoms of thought, opinion and information,'

[122] Para. 58.
[123] Judgment of 22 November 2005.
[124] Para. 85.

> and that 'that the existence of these provisions ... has degraded into an unjustified privilege ... for the benefit of certain [public officials ... which], through the intimidating power of the punishment that may be imposed ... prevents free debate from developing fully ... [and inhibits] citizens' control of decision-makers and political leaders'.[125]

As one can see, the Court wisely chose to 'merely' echo the political statements of the President, which clearly imply that the true aim of the law may have been to confer the privilege of immunity against public criticism upon some public officials. Here, the Court had an easy task because it could substitute its own judgement of illegitimate aim with a judgement already made by the highest state official—thus avoiding directly making such a judgement itself. In the end, the Court found that the criminal prosecution of Mr Palamara was effected in a disproportionate and unnecessary manner.[126]

Another case in which the legitimacy of an aim justifying a restriction of a Convention's right was questioned was *Usón Ramírez v. Venezuela*.[127] Mr Usón was a retired military officer convicted of the crime of 'slander against the National Armed Forces' after he appeared on a TV programme and expressed some critical opinions regarding the army's conduct towards several soldiers beaten in military prison cells. The IACtHR found that the criminal law was ambiguous (thus violating the principle of legality), and that it breached the Convention. It also found that the application of the law was not appropriate, necessary, and proportional. In announcing its method of scrutiny, the Court said that it would 'study whether the protection of the reputation of the Armed Forces is a legitimate end under the Convention and determine ... the applicability of a criminal sanction to achieve such end'.[128] The Court further announced that:

> when analyzing the legitimacy of the purpose in this case (the protection of the right to honor of the Armed Forces) the idea is not to determine whether the Armed Forces have an effective 'right' to honor or reputation; the analysis is to determine *if such purpose would be legitimate for the purpose of restricting the right* to freedom of expression of Mr. Usón Ramírez.[129]

Consequently, the Court felt compelled to engage in an analysis of the 'legitimate purpose' under the Convention, as instantiated by this particular case. More particularly, it would analyse whether the protection of the honour of an institution is a legitimate purpose for the restriction of a right to expression. The Court,

[125] Para. 86.
[126] Para. 88.
[127] Judgment of 20 November 2009.
[128] Para. 49 and similarly, para. 62.
[129] Para. 63, emphasis added.

however, avoided giving a clear answer to this question (saying that determining whether the Armed Forces have a 'right' to honour or reputation is not within the scope of its judgment),[130] though it opened the door to an affirmative answer when saying that:

> the Convention does not establish that the only restrictions to individual rights that may be legitimate are the restrictions to protect other individual rights. On the contrary, the Convention also establishes that any restrictions whose purpose is another reason not related to the exercise of individual rights recognized in the Convention are lawful.[131]

In the end, however, the Court recalled that 'the legitimacy of the purpose is only one of the elements in this analysis of proportionality',[132] and found the law violated the Convention on the grounds that the legislation under scrutiny was vague and ambiguous, and was used in a disproportionate manner.[133]

Palamara Iribarne and *Usón Ramírez* were unusual in that the putatively questionable legitimacy of the *aims* pursued by the state law were explicitly ascertained by the Court in its judgment. Usually, however, no weight is attached to this stage of argument. One technique through which legislative aims are downplayed is, as we have seen, through merging their scrutiny with the issue of their suitability. Another technique is by downgrading the status of aims, namely, by recharacterizing the 'legitimate' as 'allowed', and thus 'not forbidden' by the Convention. This is how the Court described the concept of 'legitimate aims' in the case of *Claude Reyes v. Chile*[134] concerning the complainants' access to information about a forestry company. Even though the Court described the aims for the restrictions of this right as merely 'not forbidden' by the Convention,[135] it found the state's refusal to provide the complainants with certain information to be in violation of Article 13, because the state failed to provide any written reasons for its refusal.[136] To conclude, by following the example of the ECtHR, the Inter-American Court adopted the attitude of downplaying the significance of the legitimate aims analysis. The Court further weakened it by merging this analysis with that of the 'suitability' of restrictions (representing these two tests as a single step in its proportionality analysis), and by lowering the threshold for 'legitimacy' as equivalent to 'not forbidden' by the text of the Convention. But, as the two cases mentioned above show, the issue of the legitimacy of aims has not been always invisible to the Court. As it has the same instruments at its disposal

[130] Para. 82.
[131] Para. 64.
[132] Para. 66.
[133] Para. 88.
[134] Judgment of 19 September 2006.
[135] Para. 90.
[136] Para. 95.

as those held by the ECtHR (an express list of legitimate derogations from rights and the proportionality analysis tool) it may, one day, choose to attach more weight to this stage of the scrutiny of states' measures.

Another example of largely self-induced autonomization by a supranational human rights adjudicator, effectively accepted by member states even though the enlargement of the competence cannot be traced directly to their consent, is ECOWAS (The Economic Community of West African States) Court, 'a new international human rights court for West Africa'.[137] Strictly speaking, in its original design, it was not primarily a human rights body, and was initially meant to help build a common market. The foundational document of the Court did not even mention human rights as part of its competence, and only vaguely provided that the Court 'shall ensure observance of law and the principles of equity in the interpretation and the application of the [ECOWAS] Treaty'.[138] But in fact, a vast majority of its decisions have concerned human rights.

Regarding its human rights jurisdiction, an unusual characteristic of the Court is that there is no specific ECOWAS legal instrument that prescribes the human rights that the Court would adjudicate. In contrast to the European and American regional systems, which interpret and apply their respective human rights conventions, ECOWAS has no human rights convention, charter, or declaration to apply. While this created a risk that the Court's human rights adjudication would be challenged as an 'overbroad delegation to interpret expansively this rapidly evolving area of international law',[139] the judges imaginatively grasped this opportunity to use their legal sources broadly. ECOWAS judges have applied not just those instruments that all ECOWAS member states have ratified (such as the African Charter, the Universal Declaration of Human Rights, and UN human rights covenants), but also a broad range of other sources. In doing so, the Court drew inspiration from the 1991 Protocol which included a directive for the Court to 'apply, as necessary, the body of laws as contained in Article 38 of the Statute of the International Court of Justice'.[140] Article 38 specifies that international conventions, custom, general principles of law, as well as judicial decisions and teachings of 'the most highly qualified publicists of the various nations', are all sources of international law, and shall be applied by the International Court of Justice (ICJ).[141]

The ECOWAS Court combined this method of extending its mandate over its consent-based competences with two other devices strengthening its

[137] Karen J. Alter, Laurence R. Helfer, and Jacqueline R. McAllister, 'A New International Human Rights Court for West Africa: The ECOWAS Community Court of Justice', (2013) 107 *American Journal of International Law* 737.

[138] Protocol (A/P.I/7/91) of 6 July 1991 on the Community Court of Justice, Art. 9(1).

[139] Alter, Helfer, and McAllister, 'A New International Human Rights Court for West Africa' (n. 137) 754.

[140] 1991 Protocol, Art. 19(1).

[141] Statute of the ICJ, Art. 38.

role: providing direct access for private litigants and abandoning a requirement to first exhaust domestic remedies. Regarding the first issue, in contrast to the African (under the African Charter on Human and Peoples' Rights), American, and pre-1998 European regional human rights systems, which provided for a tiered system of access (with commissions to vet complaints) and optional jurisdiction, the ECOWAS judges have repeatedly declared that private litigants 'have direct access to ... the Court when their human rights are violated'.[142] They have also extended access not only to individuals (expressly mentioned in the 2005 Protocol),[143] but also to NGOs, resisting challenges by governments that claim that direct access for NGOs should be denied because these litigants have no standing to challenge human rights violations before national courts. Insofar as the second device of extending the competences of the Court is concerned, the Court has not applied any requirement to first exhaust domestic remedies, again in contrast to other regional human rights systems, and despite the West African governments' repeated assertions that such a condition should be met before individuals can petition the Court. The judges of the Court have successfully rebuffed these assertions arguing that the lack of an explicit exhaustion rule in the instruments setting up the system was not an accidental omission, but a deliberate element of the system. This line of reasoning went as far as to facilitate situations where the ECOWAS Court has decided cases pending before domestic courts. In sum, by imaginatively applying a constellation of three interrelated devices: expanding the available legal sources for its human rights jurisdiction, providing and consolidating direct access for private litigants, and non-insisting on a requirement to exhaust domestic remedies before petitioning the Court, the ECOWAS Court has established itself as a supranational adjudicatory body of human rights that possesses a high degree of autonomy from its member states' consent.

The examples of IACtHR and ECOWAS tend to suggest that the idea of the 'autonomization' of initially traditional international organizations is a broader matter than the authority of those institutions over the implementation of their decisions. It is a concept which concerns a broad set of relationships between the organization and its member states, and describes a situation in which the states have lost control over the organization to a large degree. This may mean, among other things, the conferral of broad competences upon the organization, combined with the judicial *Kompetenz-Kompetenz* at the level of the organization itself, majority voting, difficult exit options for the member states, the secondary pedigree of an organization (i.e. that it was established by another international organization rather than by states), and complicated procedures for the revision

[142] *Tidjani v. Nigeria*, Case No. ECW/CCJ/APP/01/06, Judgment, para. 22 (28 July 2007), quoted by Alter, Helfer, and McAllister, 'A New International Human Rights Court for West Africa' (n. 137) 753–54.

[143] Supplementary Protocol A/SP.1/01/05 of 19 January 2005, Art. 4(d).

of an organization's founding treaty.[144] Other aspects of autonomization for supranational bodies include: the independence of the supranational authority's adjudicators from national governments (displayed through selection and tenure procedures, and de facto independence, revealed in the absence of political, financial and other pressures); a high degree of interpretive discretion in giving effect to legal sources underwriting the authority; broad rules of access which give standing not only to governments but also to individuals and NGOs; the construction of certain key legal terms and concepts by the international tribunal, independent of their meaning in municipal legal systems;[145] and the 'embeddedness' of supranational rules in domestic law, consisting of domestic legal enforcement (by courts) of supranational rulings,[146] etc.

In each of these cases, or their combination, it is no longer realistic to assert, as the traditional idiom goes, that the states are 'masters of the treaties'. Likewise, it is unrealistic to say that an organization's will expresses the sum, or a consensus, or a common denominator, of its member states' positions. In the case of the two courts discussed so far in this chapter, in addition to their arrogation of the power of oversight over the execution of their judgment (something not initially foreshadowed in their state-based design), the most striking aspect of 'autonomization' consists of the expansive nature of the interpretation of legal sources which leads to consequences unforeseen, and often viewed as undesirable, by the participating states. Whatever reasons the states have for compliance—a sense of international obligation based on a formal duty to comply with the judgments of the courts established by treaties to which they are a party, a sense of *noblesse oblige*, the fear of reputational losses resulting from 'naming and shaming', a rational calculus that compliance will impose upon other member states a duty to comply with judgments which will be unfavourable to them, but favoured by a state in any given case, and, yes, a perception that the court 'did the right thing' and conducted its reasoning in a convincing, rational, impartial, and well-argued manner, thus meeting the requirements of public reason—the connection between the states' original consent to a treaty setting up a system in which a supranational court forms part, and the state's current duty to comply, has been partly or completely broken.

[144] For a good discussion of different meanings of 'autonomy' of international organizations, see Peters, 'Constitutionalisation' (n. 37) 257–61.

[145] On the 'autonomous meanings' doctrine of the ECtHR, see Chapter 10, section 1.

[146] These are some of the criteria distinguishing 'transnational' from 'interstate' dispute resolution discussed and used by Keohane, Moravcsik, and Slaughter, 'Legalized Dispute Resolution' (n. 59) who do not actually use the words 'autonomy' and 'autonomization'—but for all practical purposes, it is the theme of their article. Using a template of political science rather than law, they nicely describe the 'transnational' approach as helping 'insulate dispute resolution to some extent from the day-to-day political demands of states' and 'impos[ing] real constraints on state behavior', ibid. at 488.

6. The WTO and 'Political Obiter Dicta'

Another example of legitimation through public reason at the supranational level is the dispute settlement system (DSS) within the WTO. Just like in the case of the ECtHR, to be discussed in the next chapter, there has been a growing tendency to characterize the WTO as (quasi-)constitutional.[147] The constitutional conceptualization discernible in WTO scholarship encompasses, in particular, the restructuring of the institutional architecture of the WTO so as to make it less provisional and less vulnerable to veto by losing parties, and less fragmented than its predecessor, the GATT. Changes have also produced the entrenchment of strong values, in particular of individual human rights, and the absorption of typically constitutional processes into dispute resolution. One aspect of this constitutional turn has been the way dispute settlement bodies have shifted from a traditionally political-diplomatic function to an adjudicatory, or court-like, form.[148] For our purposes, that is, the discussion of public reason-based legitimacy, the dimension of the *justification* of rulings is of particular importance. The evidence shows that WTO adjudicators are increasingly engaged in a deliberate quest for legitimacy amongst diverse audiences—especially in so-called 'trade and ...' cases. This refers to cases where adjudicators have to resolve tensions between trade liberalization and other values, such as consumer protection, public morals, labour rights, public health, environmental concerns, etc.[149]

In such cases, it is natural that there are intensified legitimacy concerns because WTO adjudicators exercise scrutiny over national choices on matters going beyond the original brief of the Organization. That is, these matters go beyond narrow trade considerations, and so intrude upon the sphere traditionally thought to be the domain of national democratic choices. In addition, there has been a general understanding that, in a sort of international division of labour between different systems of protection of trade, human rights, the environment etc., WTO panels should only be concerned with trade liberalization, the result of which means that 'the panels' lack of sensitivity to non-trade preferences follows less from any malevolent bias in the panelists than from the function of the dispute settlement system ...'[150] Hence, when the WTO DSS concerns non-trade interests, its legitimacy is at its weakest—reflected by the extra care that

[147] The literature is voluminous; perhaps the main book-length monograph by Deborah Cass, *The Constitutionalization of the World Trade Organization: Legitimacy, Democracy and Community in the International Trading System* (Oxford University Press 2005) is the most significant. For a critical discussion of recent WTO constitutionalization literature along these three doctrinal lines, see Jeffrey L. Dunoff, 'The Politics of International Constitutions: The Curious Case of the World Trade Organization', in Jeffrey L. Dunoff and Joel P. Trachtman, (eds.), *Ruling the World? Constitutionalism, International Law, and Global Governance* (Cambridge University Press 2009) 178, 184–92.

[148] See Jessica C. Lawrence, 'Contesting Constitutionalism: Constitutional Discourse at the WTO', (2013) 2 *Global Constitutionalism* 63, 82.

[149] Here I rely on an important work by Sivan Shlomo-Agon, 'Clearing the Smoke: The Legitimation of Judicial Power at the WTO', (2015) 49 *Journal of World Trade* 539.

[150] Kleinlein, 'Judicial Lawmaking by Judicial Restraint?' (n. 38) 1165.

the Appellate Body (AB) takes to explain its reasons, and also to justify its authority when reaching beyond the traditional goal of trade liberalization. The evidence shows that various legitimacy-enhancing rhetorical and argumentative strategies are pursued by the WTO AB, especially when the AB finds *against* the states in its rulings in the 'trade and ...' category. When one reads the AB's reports in such cases, for instance in the *US-Clove Cigarettes* case of 2012, one is struck by the careful explanatory, justificatory, and defensive tone of the Report, even though the AB overturned an important national regulatory choice (an anti-tobacco regulation prohibiting certain flavoured cigarettes).[151]

As WTO scholars and experts observe, there has been a steady move away from strict textual interpretation to more purposeful and contextual methods, which provide adjudicators with more discretion to place the argument in a broader set of societal values.[152] In the context of AB rulings this is expressed, for instance, in the appearance of separate explanatory paragraphs which aim to show sensitivity to national values and choices regarding non-trade values—and to emphasize the limited political implications of its rulings. Some scholars have even dubbed these explanatory paragraphs 'political obiter dicta'.[153] Even in the pre-WTO era, the GATT panels had been using a form of proportionality analysis (*sans le nom*) for some time, by demanding that exceptions to the GATT meet the requirements of the least restrictive means and necessity. For instance, in a case concerning Thailand's treatment of imported cigarettes, a panel stated that Thailand could prevail under the exception clauses of GATT only 'if there were no alternative measure ... which Thailand could reasonably be expected to employ to achieve its health policy objectives'.[154] The panel fleshed out the proportionality standards and carefully justified its decision, going so far as to identify possible alternative ways of protecting health values without infringing on trade to the same degree. It has also been noted that WTO arbitrators refer to other segments of international law more often, which produces a kind of horizontal cross-fertilization with the effect of enhancing the legitimacy of its rulings: 'Reference to interpretative norms of general public international law enhances the legitimacy of the dispute-settlement organs in adjudicating competing values, as they are not specific to a regime that has traditionally privileged a single value—that of free trade.'[155]

C.A. Thomas constructs the helpful notion of a 'community of legitimation' (or 'a legitimating community') and includes, in addition to 'the trade policy

[151] For a subtle analysis, see Shlomo-Agon, 'Clearing the Smoke' (n. 149) 563–87.

[152] Ibid. 568–70.

[153] See ibid. 581.

[154] GATT Panel Report: Thailand—Restrictions on Importation of and Internal Taxes on Cigarettes, 7 November 1990, quoted in Alec Stone Sweet and Jud Mathews, 'Proportionality Balancing and Global Constitutionalism' (2008) 47 *Columbia Journal of Transnational Law* 74, 158.

[155] Robert Howse and Kalypso Nicolaidis, 'Enhancing WTO Legitimacy: Constitutionalization or Global Subsidiarity?', (2003) 16 *Governance* 73, 87, endnote omitted.

insiders', 'human rights activists, officials from developing countries, other intergovernmental organisations, anti-globalisation protestors and environmental groups', etc. amongst this WTO legitimating community. He adds that '[t]he proliferation of these legitimating communities requires a careful rethinking of the grounds for the WTO's moral legitimacy to accommodate its new realities'.[156] There have been important external pressures upon the WTO to adopt a broad context-sensitive approach in these types of cases. In the 2006 *EC-Biotech* case, where considerations intersected with biological diversity and biosafety, the EU argued that '[t]he issues faced by the Panel have to be taken in their broader context.... [A] failure by the Panel to have regard to this broader context will risk *undermining the legitimacy of the WTO system*'.[157]

Proportionality has become an important pattern of WTO case law,[158] growing in significance and based on textual grounds in WTO agreements where the 'least trade restrictive' (or 'not more trade restrictive than required') or where 'necessary' measures are required. Much of what will be said in the next chapter about proportionality in the ECHR law applies, *mutatis mutandis*, to the WTO. Just as in the context of the ECtHR, the teleological and context-oriented reasoning characteristic of the proportionality analysis 'favors a debate among alternative normative preferences in the interpretation of a rule, [while] a simple appeal to text would hide those alternatives and preclude a debate'.[159] When WTO adjudicators engage in such a fully fledged proportionality analysis, they necessarily interfere with what has been traditionally considered as member states' regulatory autonomy. Here, special care on the part of the AB and panels in such cases is required. It has been suggested, for instance, that even when they do conduct a proportionality analysis, they should abstain from evaluating the importance of the *goal* (that the state cites to defend the measures it has taken) and only consider the costs of the alternative *means*, which are not less suited to pursue these goals.[160] This may be sensible advice. It does not detract from the fact, however, that WTO adjudication is contributing greatly to the development

[156] C.A. Thomas, 'The Concept of Legitimacy and International Law', LSE Law, Society and Economy Working Papers 12/2013, http://ssrn.com/abstract=2265503 24, footnote omitted (last accessed 23 August 2022).

[157] European Communities, *Second Written Submission in EC-Measures Affecting the Approval and Marketing of Biotech Products* (19 July 2004) para. 8, quoted in Lawrence, 'Contesting Constitutionalism' (n. 148) 78, emphasis added.

[158] But for a sceptical view about the importance of proportionality in WTO law, see Axel Desmedt, 'Proportionality in WTO Law', (2001) 4 *Journal of international Economic Law* 441. In contrast, for a view that proportionality 'underpins and inspires many of the specific rules laid down in the WTO Agreements', see Mads Andenas and Stefan Zleptnig, 'Proportionality: WTO Law in Comparative Perspective', (2007) 42 *Texas International Law Journal* 371, 426.

[159] See Miguel Poiares Maduro, 'Courts and Pluralism: Essay on a Theory of Judicial Adjudication in the Context of Legal and Constitutional Pluralism', in Jeffrey L. Dunoff and Joel P. Trachtman (eds.), *Ruling the World? Constitutionalism, International Law, and Global Governance* (Cambridge University Press 2009) 356, 369.

[160] See Ingo Venzke, 'Making General Exceptions: The Spell of Precedents in Developing Article XX GATT into Standards for Domestic Regulatory Policy', (2011) 12 *German Law Journal* 1111, 1138.

of international trade law. Further, such development has been largely independent of the states' own will, and instead due to the quality of the reasoning.

7. Between Statehood and the Supranational Sphere

What do the examples produced in the preceding sections of the chapter tell us about legitimacy in the new constitutional architecture of the world? And in particular, what can supranational legitimacy based on justification ('supranational public reason') tell us about the relationship between legitimacy and democracy at the state level? It would be unfortunate if the conclusion to draw from the preceding remarks were that supranationalism renders democracy redundant because legitimacy can be supported by justificatory discipline, without democracy. Rather than justification-based legitimacy eclipsing democracy, there is a potential for important synergy between them: national democracy supports supranational reason-giving (justificatory discipline) because in multi-level governance, states retain their meaningful constitutional status as important, though no longer exclusive, sites of legitimacy.

At the level of statehood, democracy supports supranational justificatory legitimacy because, at the end of the day, it is often the state that ensures compliance with supranational norms. Whether (as the rationalist strand of international relations theory suggests) state compliance in circumstances of thin or no supranational enforcement can be best explained by the rational self-interest of states (based on reputational values as a capital for future cooperation, and mutual expectations in the long-term, iterated collaboration) or (as the 'normative' strand would have it) on the persuasive pull of norms affecting states' incentives for compliance, states are often the best guardians of efficiency and legitimacy of supranational norm-producers.

And vice versa, supranational public reason may support and help improve national democracy. This is perhaps best seen in the field of international human rights at the state level. As Joshua Cohen and Charles Sabel note: 'human rights claims can be presented as elements of a global standard—*a global public reason*, itself part of global politics—that sets out conditions of acceptable treatment, requiring in particular that political societies assure conditions of membership for those who live in their territory.'[161] (The idea of 'global public reason' was also extensively used by Joshua Cohen in a separate article where he treated it as an essential element of the concept of global justice in a world marked by pluralism and embracing tolerance.)[162] In engaging with international human rights, legal and constitutional actors at state level commit themselves to transposing

[161] Cohen and Sabel,'Global Democracy?' (n. 20) 788, emphasis added.

[162] Joshua Cohen, 'Minimalism about Human Rights: The Most We Can Hope For?', (2004) 12 *Journal of Political Philosophy* 190.

'global standard[s]'—dubbed by Cohen and Sabel as 'global public reason'—to their state constitutional structures. For instance, an argument can be and has been made,[163] that when national constitutions make reference to international law and international standards, and in particular to international human rights law,[164] they tacitly empower—confer legitimacy upon—transnational adjudicatory bodies to scrutinize national laws and decisions, because those bodies are better positioned to ascertain and interpret transnational standards. For instance, by virtue of its position and expertise, the ECtHR is better placed to say what European standards are, and whether they are sufficiently close to being consensual. Having done so, the ECtHR can restrict or exclude a state's margin of appreciation on the matter, and in this way engage directly with domestic constitutional process. National constitutional references to international human rights law therefore 'invite' supranational human rights bodies to assume authority on particular matters, which can have an effect on the municipal system. This often occurs when there is a constitutional directive to interpret constitutional rights in accordance with international treaties, as is the case, for instance, in the Constitutions of Spain, Portugal, Colombia, Romania, and South Africa.[165] This kind of 'coordinated interpretation' restricts the interpretive freedom of the national constitutional court which, at the least, must give strong reasons why it does not intend to follow the international tribunal's interpretation.[166] Through a sort of 'boomerang effect', the wider epistemic basis available to supranational bodies can subsequently enhance the range of information (e.g. 'best practices') and normativity (foreign and supranational standards) available to national judges and politicians, and thus improve the quality of democratic decision-making at the national level.

Rather than a rivalry between the legitimacy of supranational versus state authorities, a superficially paradoxical situation instead arises: that is, the rise of legitimate supranational authorities does not detract from, but often enhances democratic statehood, and hence, the democratic legitimacy of states. This occurs, *first*, in consolidated democracies, when supranational adjudicatory authorities provide guidance about democratic practices to 'established' but

[163] Kumm, 'An Integrative Theory' (n. 36) 51–52.

[164] Among many, consider these two examples of constitutions referring to international human rights: the South African Constitution provides that 'When referring to the Bill of Rights, a court, tribunal or forum ... must consider international law' (Art. 39(1); and the Spanish Constitution requires that rights and liberties must be interpreted in conformity with the Universal Declaration of Human Rights (UDHR) and the 'international treaties and agreements thereon ratified by Spain' (Art. 10(2)).

[165] Constitution of Spain, Art. 10(2), quoted above; Constitution of Portugal, Art. 16(2); Constitution of Colombia, Art. 93(2); Constitution of Romania, Art. 20(1); Constitution of South Africa, Art. 39(1).

[166] Gerald L. Neuman, 'Human Rights and Constitutional Rights: Harmony and Dissonance', (2003) 55 *Stanford Law Review* 863, 895–97. See, similarly, Vicki C. Jackson, *Constitutional Engagement in a Transnational Era* (Oxford University Press 2010) 48.

inevitably defective democracies.[167] Even if a well-established national democracy gives proper effect to the opinions of the majority, it may be insensitive to minorities. Likewise, such states have built-in incentives to amend democratic procedures in ways that privilege the current political majority, in order to entrench it and obstruct the peaceful transfer of power. These dysfunctions of national democracy may be, to some extent at least, corrected by international human rights norms and by the intervention of supranational institutions. In other words, transnational intervention may do to national democracy what John Hart Ely famously proclaimed as the main function of judicial review within the United States' system of government: facilitate the representation of minorities and clear the channels of political change.[168] It can therefore protect national democracy against democratically adopted restrictions on democracy. *Second*, the transnationally driven enhancement of democracy occurs even more clearly in 'transitional' democracies, when bodies such as the Venice Commission supply recommendations about democratic constitutionalism, or bodies such as the European Commission issue reports about the progress of candidate states within the so-called framework of political conditionality. Supranational human rights norms are of particular importance in transitional regimes. While they do not establish the already-reached common denominator of rights already recognized and protected at a national level (as was the tacit understanding behind the initial setting-up of the ECHR system), rather they identify an aspiration, serving as a critical measure of law reform within the newly democratized state. Such human rights standards, backed by supranational institutions, resonate with the incentives of the new leadership (often recruited from former dissidents and democratic opposition) to align themselves with supranational bodies, and counter possible reversals to the bad old days of neglect of human rights. And *third*, perhaps most obviously, it occurs in the cases of so-called 'fragile' or 'failed states', when a number of supranational entities of different character, but often with great clout, assist with democratic capacity-building. In the latter category, 'constitutional intervention'[169] may be seen (when it works well) as a happy case of introducing constitutional essentials to a troubled state, in accordance with transnational standards, whether foreign, international, or supranational (as was the case for Bosnia or East Timor). When analysing what he called 'the Internationally Grounded Model' of constitution-making, Michel Rosenfeld noted that in such cases, the incorporation of certain external norms and

[167] See, for instance, a series of admonitions by the ECtHR to the United Kingdom that it should amend its law which disenfranchises all convicted prisoners, *Hirst v. United Kingdom (No. 2)*, Judgment of 6 October 2005, Appl. No. 74025/01) and *Greens and MT v. United Kingdom*, Judgment of 23 November 2010, Appl. nos. 60041/08 and 60054/08.

[168] John Hart Ely, *Democracy and Distrust* (Harvard University Press 1980).

[169] For the first use of this term, as far as I know, see Ulrich K. Preuss, 'Perspectives on Post-Conflict Constitutionalism: Reflections on Regime Change Through External Constitutionalization', (2006–07) 51 *New York Law School Law Review* 467, 493.

standards is accompanied by the fact that 'substantial decision making power over the substantive particulars of the constitution-in-the-making must be left in the hands of relevant political actors within the nation-state affected'.[170] Subject to respect for conditions of disinterestedness and non-bias of foreign interveners, and to the on-the-ground awareness that successful constitution-making would not have occurred in the absence of intervention, through this type of intervention, the national constitution-making process and its product acquires domestic legitimacy not *despite* but largely *thanks to* its alignment with supranational standards. Such internationally sponsored, or initiated, constitution-making in troubled states connects domestic state-consolidation (including through constitution-making or reform) with the global space of continuously revised and updated standards and norms of governance.

More generally, international and supranational standards often provide a back-up for democracy at the state level. It is the case not only in the instances of repairing specific national dysfunctionalities, as indicated in the paragraph above, but also by supplying an extra dimension that limits domestic powers and contributes to checks and balances. As Mattias Kumm noted, 'international legality ... has the tendency to limit the options of the executive branch to claim foreign affairs prerogatives and hereby shift the power of the executive branch in a way that endangers and potentially destabilizes democracy on the national level'.[171] This is a hypothesis that may need to be tested by specific examples. In some cases, intervention by multilateral institutions operating under supranational norms may actually strengthen the executive. However, this strengthening may have positive outcomes from the point of view of democracy and broadens the impact of stakeholders on a decision. In addition, international structures of norms and institutions provide an extra factor of visibility, accountability, and responsibility for state actions. Even if international law often leaves the specific procedures of ratification or implementation of international agreements to the national constitutional arrangements, those actions are necessarily catapulted into an international sphere with the effect of enhancing national separation of powers, federalism, checks and balances, and other constitutional guarantees. Abuses of power by domestic actors become more visible and lose much of their impunity when they become a matter of participation in an international process, and when other domestic actors and supranational entities become partners in the process. This is what may be called the 'straitjacket effect' of supranationalism, which ordinarily corrects national processes in the direction of liberal and democratic values.

[170] Michel Rosenfeld, *The Identity of the Constitutional Subject* (Routledge 2010) 207, reference omitted.

[171] Mattias Kumm, 'The Legitimacy of International Law: A Constitutionalist Framework of Analysis', (2004) 15 *European Journal of International Law* 907, 919.

We should therefore resist the temptation to perceive the supranational/national dynamic as a zero-sum game: nation-states are not necessarily displaced or sidelined by a new supranational authority, and their democratic qualities are not compromised.[172] There is often mutual enhancement, and the challenge for constitutional legal scholarship is to reconceptualize this coexistence. The reports of the death of the state are premature: national states are still key political actors in their territory, and that may not necessarily be a bad thing. In many contexts and for many purposes, states constitute an optimal unit within which people solve their collective problems, produce public goods, and generate commitments for accepting sacrifices related to those public goods. States often constitute frameworks for an optimal equilibrium between the capacity of individuals to feel an emotional sense of togetherness and solidarity on the one hand and requirements of political institutions to solve problems at a sufficiently high level, on the other. Changes in the international political architecture which we witness today, usually described as 'globalization', and in particular the emergence of new sites of non-state authority, described at the beginning of this chapter, go hand-in-hand with the persistence, and often the entrenchment of state powers. Indeed, when major human rights, economic, public health, environmental, etc. crises occur, the usual (and justified) aim of international intervention is addressed towards creating and improving the *state's* capacity to deal with it, rather than towards replacing state powers with those of international institutions. Since it is a *state* failure which is, more often than not, responsible for such crises, the solution is often seen to lie in state reform rather than replacement by non-state institutions. For instance, a general model of assistance by international bodies such as the World Bank or FAO is to make the states capable of assuming their responsibilities towards their citizens, rather than to bypass or subvert those states. This shows that states remain the primary form of territorial organization that can provide resources and satisfy the needs of the people.

It may not necessarily last very long. Indeed, it may well be that in the medium to long term, states will gradually continue to give way to supranational authorities. These authorities may dominate the global landscape, without any serious challenge to this status from competitors. In his ground-breaking history of international relations, published nearly thirty years ago, Hendrik Spruyt gestured to an intriguing hypothesis when he recalled 'that the fullest articulation of feudal organization and the church, both in a theoretical and practical

[172] For such a zero-sum-game approach to constitutionalism rather than legitimacy, see Anne Peters' theory of 'compensatory constitutionalism' where '[t]he constitutionalist reconstruction of international law' is viewed as 'a reasonable strategy to compensate for the deconstitutionalization on the domestic level, which is caused by globalization and global governance', Anne Peters, 'The Merits of Global Constitutionalism', (2009) 16 *Indiana Journal of Global Legal Studies* 397, 404–05, footnote omitted. In situations where '[n]ational constitutions are, so to speak, hollowed out and traditional constitutional principles become dysfunctional or empty ... we must ask for compensatory constitutionalisation on the international plane', ibid. 405.

sense, occurred shortly before their demise'. Spruyt went on to add: 'Such articulation seems to occur exactly when institutional challenges arise. Changes in communications, economics, and the environment challenge the scope of state authority and thus create incentives for actors to alter the existing institutional arrangements.'[173]

Whether these alterations will mean the demise of the powers of states is something that cannot be predicted (Spruyt notes, philosophically: 'In the long run, history sides with no one').[174] But at least in the predictable future, states as we know them will remain the privileged fora within which the preconditions for democracy (especially, electoral democracy) arise. They will not vanish even if, admittedly, they have to 'reinvent themselves in an increasingly overcrowded international scene ...'[175] For the time being, states are thought by many to be important and often indispensable instruments for achieving 'the psychological and material conditions that ensure the survival of their inhabitants'.[176] Often framed in national, religious, or ethnic terms, their symbolic appeal retains an attractive power, with the effect of ensuring the persistence of territorially organized entities. The existence of borders is reassuring to many people and resonates with the need for individual and group security. States also resonate with peoples' sense of identity, often informed by historically determined national borders and sovereignty-based pride. As long as a large number of people feel reasonably secure in their reliance on states as the best guarantors of their needs, including material and bodily safety, and those same people are much less inclined to trust that supra-state institutions can effectively provide such protection, the survival of states in their current form is assured. But this does not mean that legitimacy in the new world constitutional architecture remains at the mercy of democracy, often questionable and defective, in nation-states.

8. The Relationship between International and Constitutional Law

Focusing on legitimacy in the supranational sphere, and uncoupling legitimacy from its preoccupation with democracy of an electoral kind, helps us liberate ourselves from two problems that haunt international law. International law scholarship has been obsessed, over the decades, with twin problems: the 'existential' problem ('Does international law *exist*? Is it *real* law');[177] and the related problem

[173] Hendrik Spruyt, *The Sovereign State and Its Competitors* (Princeton University Press 1994) 193.
[174] Ibid.
[175] Vlad Perju, 'International Constitutionalism and the State: A Reply to Aoife O'Donoghue', (2013) 11 *International Journal of Constitutional Law* 1045, 1046.
[176] Michael Reisman, 'Designing and Managing the Future of the State', (1997) 3 *European Journal of International Law* 409, 415.
[177] See H.L.A. Hart, *The Concept of Law* (Oxford University Press 1961) 3, 77, 208–11.

of the relationship between international law (insofar as it *is* real law) and municipal law (monism versus dualism/pluralism, etc.). Both these problems boil down to the allegedly derivative, secondary, parasitic nature of international law (resting, as it has been predominantly believed, upon states' voluntary commitments) and the allegedly primary status of constitutional law (understood as the law concerning the institutions and the norms of nation-states). This image is based upon the Westphalian idea of a system of independent and sovereign states, with international law deriving its validity and binding force from states' consent, supplemented by international custom (often itself derived from state consent),[178] as detected in actual state practices. The irony of the matter is that, of course, at the outset of the Westphalian era, the states making up the overall international system were *anything but* electoral democracies. But with time, the separation of international and constitutional law, with the privileging of the latter, acquired added force by its appeal to democratic arguments. Since there are so few traces of democracy in the international system or in supranational governance—so the argument goes—constitutional law must be primary, in the way just outlined, in order to assure the primacy of democratic self-government at any level of authority.

But the idea of the primacy of constitutional over international law (an idea, I suggest, favoured by an insistence on democratic pedigree as the privileged source of the legitimacy of authorities in a multi-level system of governance) is a deeply flawed conception, for at least four reasons. *First*, it presupposes that there is a clear cleavage between constitutional and international law, which is plainly wrong: rather than a hiatus, there is continuity and multiple intersections. For one thing, there is a significant, and growing, overlap between the subject matter of international law and constitutional law. The former has taken up much of the agenda traditionally thought to be reserved for the laws of states (human rights, criminal matters, food safety and agriculture, environment, banking, labour relations, etc.). In fact, the expansion of the scope of international law has been so significant that it is hard to think of exclusive domains of municipal constitutional law which would, under all circumstances, be invisible to international law. Most strikingly, democracy itself—traditionally seen as an ideal whose locus is firmly based in state practice—is increasingly seen as a requirement of international law, through the 'emerging [international-law based] right to democratic governance'.[179] Manfred Nowak, a leading commentator on the International Covenant on Civil and Political Rights, observed not long ago that

[178] For an extended argument by a leading international law scholar that international custom is derivable from state consent, see Pierre-Marie Dupuy, *L'unité de l'ordre juridique international: Cours général de droit international public* (Martinus Nijhoff 2003) 168–79. As Dupuy concludes: '*Il faut … constater que l'on retrouve ainsi toujours le consentement des Etats à l'origine de la coutume, quelle que soient les interprétations de ses causes et de sa signification …*', ibid. 178–79.

[179] Thomas M. Franck, 'The Emerging Right to Democratic Governance', (1992) 86 *American Journal of International Law* 46.

'the main components of democracy, i.e., the right of the people to sovereignty, internal self-determination and equal participation in political decision-making processes together with the protection of minorities against the "tyranny of the majority", are already part of the international law of human rights'.[180] This mooring of democracy in supranational norms is even clearer at the level of regional supranational systems, in particular in the ECHR. Both the text of the Convention,[181] and the expansive interpretation by the European Court of the 'right to free elections',[182] indicate that democracy has become a binding norm of the European supranational order, with bodies such as the ECtHR and the European Commission for Democracy Through Law (Venice Commission) providing (respectively, binding and advisory) interpretations of this norm, regardless of individual governments' intentions and national constitutional systems' attempts to deviate from the norm.

Second, the idea of the primacy of constitutional law is based on the idea that the validity of international law is essentially founded on state consent or state practice. This idea is contradicted by the proliferation of supranational authorities, discussed earlier in this chapter, and where their norm-making, norm-interpretation, and norm-enforcement activities are *not* embedded in state consent. The phenomenon of the 'autonomization' of various international organizations, which produces norms binding on states that are not underwritten by prior state consent, is the most iconic indication of this fact. An increased number of treaties delegate legislative powers to treaty-based bodies, meaning that the link between state consent and the norms produced is attenuated, at best. Various international organizations arrogate to themselves, with no or very little effective protest by member states, powers that had not been originally conferred upon them—and effectively enforce their authority over member states, as illustrated by the example of the ECOWAS Court. The consent-centred basis of international law is hard to reconcile with the idea of *jus cogens*—of peremptory, non-derogable rules that apply to all actors regardless of their consent to them. Likewise, it is difficult to square it with the idea of the international law of human rights, which is premised on an idea of universality, regardless and, if necessary, despite a state's will (for instance, as expressed in the non-ratification

[180] Manfred Nowak, *UN Covenant on Civil and Political Rights: CCPR: Commentary* (2nd rev. edn., Engel 2005) 565, footnotes omitted.

[181] The Preamble to the ECHR states emphatically: 'Reaffirming their profound belief in those fundamental freedoms which are the foundation of justice and peace in the world and are best maintained on the one hand *by an effective political democracy* and on the other by a common understanding and observance of the human rights upon which they depend.' Convention for the Protection of Human Rights and Fundamental Freedoms, Rome, 1950, emphasis added. Art. 3 of Protocol 1 states: 'The High Contracting Parties undertake to hold free elections at reasonable intervals by secret ballot, under conditions which will ensure the free expression of the opinion of the people in the choice of the legislature.' Protocol 1 Art. 3. 1952.

[182] See, in particular, *Mathieu-Mohin and Clerfayt v. Belgium*. 9267/81. The Court made it clear that the reach of Art. 3, Protocol 1 is not limited to the very act of elections but extends also to the nature of the political system within which those elections take place.

of a universal human rights instrument) and conduct towards their own citizens. Traditional international law scholarship attempts to reconcile the existence of *jus cogens* with the consent- or custom-based sources of international law by postulating that the rules of *jus cogens* must be accepted 'by an *overwhelming majority* of states, crossing ideological and political divides'.[183] But this just shows that there are some rules of international law that will be binding towards some states that had not consented to them or had not practiced them. Once such inroads into consent or custom as sources of validity are made, it is hard to see what can be gained by insisting upon an 'overwhelming' majority of consenting states.

Third, as a matter of logic, the very idea that international law may be binding merely by virtue of state consent (as expressed in the way prescribed by the constitutional law of the states) simply sounds odd. The proposition that state consent is binding on the consenting state must in itself be based upon the prior normative proposition that expressions of consent produce binding effects on consenters, and if *its* source is in state consent (for instance, in the states' endorsement of the *pacta sunt servanda* rule), we encounter an infinite regression problem. There is no easy step from the *is* to the *ought*. In other words, there is a non sequitur from the historical fact that a state has expressed its consent to the directive that it should comply with it, absent some additional normative premises which themselves are not encompassed by the consent itself. In a classical work, Thomas Franck had argued precisely that 'the obligation of *pacta sunt servanda* itself cannot be derived from state consent' and that we should therefore search for 'another basis of common obligation, another "source" of legitimate authority'.[184] And this 'another source' must be other than the state's consent because we normally hold a state obligated under an international legal norm, regardless of whether it had adhered to a treaty stating that commitments must be honoured, such as the Vienna Convention on Treaties.[185] In a posthumously published article by Ronald Dworkin, the same point is expressed in opposition to a positivist conception of law: it will simply not do to say that the states should 'follow the principle that what they regard as law is law' (which is, we may add, equivalent to consent theory) because they 'need some other standard to decide what they should regard as law'. If we try to solve the dilemma by saying that states 'accept the principle that what other nations accept as law is law' (as is, we may add, equivalent to custom-based theory), then 'the other nations that each nation treats as making law for it need a test of what to treat as

[183] Malcolm Shaw, *International Law* (4th edn., Cambridge University Press 1997) 97, emphasis added, footnote omitted.

[184] Thomas M. Franck, *Fairness in International Law and Institutions* (Oxford University Press 1998) 29. See, similarly, Eduardo Moisés Peñalver, 'The Persistent Problem of Obligation in International Law', (2000) 36 *Stanford Journal of International Law* 271, 283–84.

[185] Vienna Convention on the Law of the Treaties, UN Doc. A/CONF. 39/27 (1969), Art. 26.

law for themselves'.[186] An appeal to the legitimacy of the international level as a starting point in the chain of legitimation helps us avoid this conundrum: a way of breaking out of the circle of 'law is what is regarded by the states as law'. The circularity necessarily involved in a consent-based theory of international law (what are the grounds for consent-based obligations, other than an unhelpful construction of second-order consent?) can be only overcome by an appeal to non-consent-based principles.

Fourth, and most importantly from the point of view of this chapter, *if we adopt a legitimacy perspective*, there is absolutely no reason to begin our journey of legitimation from the level of the nation-state, and only once we validate its norms as legitimate, 'move up' to the level of supranational authorities in order to confirm, derivatively, their legitimacy, rather than proceeding the other way round. When we pursue a *normative* argument about legitimacy in multi-level governance, we might as well begin from the international level, and derive normative sources of state legitimacy from international legal norms. After all, a great number of norms regarding the legitimacy of states are all norms *of international law*. For instance, consider the legal criteria of statehood, including criteria of self-determination, permanence, and sovereignty, which are the standards for eligibility for membership in the United Nations (UN). These days, membership in the UN is ultimate 'validation' of a state *qua* state—as a card-carrying member of international community. Consider also the norms applicable to the continuity of states and state succession, as well as the standards of recognition of states by other states.[187] In this way, the constitutional laws of states are engulfed and embedded in international law; they may be seen, so to speak, as the 'pensioner[s] of international law'.[188] There has been a lot of academic discourse lately about international law (including the UN Charter) being a sort of constitutional law for the international community.[189] This is the case in a literal, rather than metaphorical, sense for precisely this reason: international law may be seen to *constitute* the legal bases for national statehood, including by supplying a rule of recognition about what should count as a validly legal source of international law, such as the state's consent. To the extent that the state's consent is a source of international law obligations (as discussed just above), in itself

[186] Ronald Dworkin, 'A New Philosophy of International Law', (2013) 41 *Philosophy & Public Affairs* 2, 9. For a thoughtful discussion, see Gianluigi Palombella, 'The Principles of International Law: Interpretivism and its Judicial Consequences', EUI Working Paper, RSCAS 2014/70 (Robert Schuman Centre for Advanced Studies: Florence 2014).

[187] For legal criteria of statehood, see Montevideo Convention on the Rights and Duties of States, Art. I (signed 26 December 1933); for criteria of membership of the UN, see UN Charter Arts. 3–6; for a general discussion, see Ian Brownlie, *Principles of Public International Law* (2nd edn., Oxford University Press 1973) 80–108.

[188] Ibid. 34. It should be stressed that it is not necessarily Brownlie's own view, but rather a view which he attributes, with a slightly discernible sarcasm, to exponents of monistic theory, such as Hersch Lauterpacht.

[189] See, in particular, Bardo Fassbender, 'The United Nations Charter as Constitution of the International Community', (1998) 36 *Columbia Journal of Transnational Law* 529.

it derives force from a secondary rule of international law. And it is an established norm of international law that domestic legal rules (including domestic *constitutional* rules) cannot serve as an excuse for non-compliance with international law.[190] It is also recognized, as one of the principles of international law, that states have a general duty to bring their internal law into conformity with obligations under international law. This is so even if it is a partially 'imperfect' obligation; that is, where the mere fact of non-conformity is not yet seen as a breach of international law, but acquires such status when the state fails to perform the international obligation on a specific occasion.[191] There is a general presumption that national constitutions should be interpreted in a manner consistent with international law, or at least, in a manner which does not put the country in breach of international law.[192] So if we think that constitutional law makes a strong claim on our compliance, we had better think again: international law does as well. It is no wonder that Thomas Franck noted, over thirty years ago, that 'obedience to national authority is currently most often challenged in connection with the dissenting citizen's sense of an *international* or supranational obligation, and in connection with some sense of an "ought" which has its roots in a perceived *international* order'.[193] On the basis of this normative inference, we may therefore proceed top-down rather than bottom-up: we may see the legitimacy of states (their institutions, norms, and practices) as often dependent on legitimate norms of international law, rather than vice versa.

The fixed point from which we start in the chain of the normative argument about legitimacy, and the resulting movement of the argument—either top-down or bottom-up—is a matter of normative *choice*. It does not reflect an empirically knowable reality. And in fact, the 'choice' does not really exist, no more than in the chicken-or-egg dilemma. An interlevel normative discourse about legitimacy is reflexive rather than a one-way street. We go to and fro between different levels of governance in which we identify different traces of legitimacy: electoral, deliberative (public reason-related), and other. No single direction or particular starting point in this 'reflective equilibrium' of worldwide legitimacy discourse should be *a priori* privileged. Particular instances will be context-dependent, as a function of the nature of the specific issue we face, and the primacy as between international and national law will need to be settled depending on what sort of concerns are at stake.[194] The temptation to adopt democratic legitimacy in and of national statehood as a strong fixed point, one which informs all other legitimations of authority at any level of governance, is understandable. The value of

[190] See the Vienna Convention on the Law of Treaties, 1969, Art. 27.

[191] Brownlie, *Principles of Public International Law* (n. 187) 38.

[192] Jackson, *Constitutional Engagement* (n. 166) 55.

[193] Thomas M. Franck, *The Power of Legitimacy Among Nations* (Oxford University Press 1990) 12, emphases in original.

[194] See Jeremy Waldron, 'Response: The Perils of Exaggeration', (2011) 22 *European Journal of International Law* 389, 390.

democracy is great, and rightly so. In addition, many still see the international law-based 'right to democratic governance' as only embryonic. But the temptation should be resisted because it drives us into anachronistic, unhelpful, and sometimes incoherent conclusions about relationships between different levels of authority, such as the four problems arising from the alleged primacy of constitutional over international law, just depicted.

* * *

At the opening of this chapter, I argued that in the triangle of concepts—legitimacy, democracy, national statehood—we should resist the temptation to uncouple the link between national statehood and democracy. Such uncoupling is often a non-starter, due to the apparent weakness of democracy at a supranational level. Rather, we should follow a different strategy, and uncouple legitimacy and democracy (at least, of an electoral or participatory kind). We should further hypothesize that the legitimacy of supranational authorities is often grounded on the *type of arguments* provided by supranational entities, and in particular, their appeal to public reason—a legitimacy-conferring device well-suited to supranational authorities. And particularly good instances of such 'supranational public reason' (to be distinguished from Rawls's 'public reason of the Society of Peoples') are provided by adjudicatory or quasi-adjudicatory supranational bodies, such as the two regional human rights courts and the WTO dispute settlement branch mentioned in this chapter, and the ECtHR, to be discussed in the next chapter.

This is not to say that public reason-based legitimacy (especially when identified at the supranational level, as discussed in this chapter) must be always and necessarily privileged. After all, at the local, regional, municipal, or state level, legitimacy based exclusively on public reason is insufficient, because public reason is never disembodied. Rather, it is always articulated by some persons or institution, and the question of their democratic accountability is never inappropriate. But neither is democracy a sufficient 'fixed point' in the chain of legitimation, because purely 'choice sensitive' standards of fairness of collective decisions are rare or trivial. In this way, the proliferation of supranational authorities in our post-Westphalian world helps us to appreciate the richness of the concept of legitimacy, and the corresponding shallowness, both empirically and normatively, of an exclusive focus on democratic legitimacy in national statehood.

Both types of legitimating devices (the electoral pedigree of the institutions and the type of reasons with which they imbue their decisions) are required at *all* levels of norm-making—though they appear and are required in different proportions at different levels. My aspiration in this chapter has been to show that some supranational authorities open up space to legitimate their non-state-based authority by appeals to public reason, thus effectively filling the gap created by the comparative thinness of democratic legitimacy. To be sure, the requirements of public reason are not specific to the supranational sphere. But at a supranational level, they acquire a special urgency, due to the weakness of the form of democratic decision-making as the default legitimating factor.

I do not make a strong claim that public reason is the *only* legitimating device available to supranational authorities, just as I do not make a strong claim about the contrast between the public reason-based legitimacy of supranational authorities and the exclusively democratic legitimacy of national authorities. But I do not wish to protest too much: differences of degree matter. And once we take account of these important differences of degree, we are able to make better sense of the legitimacy of supranational authorities, often taken for granted, but rarely grounded in theory in a satisfactory way. More importantly, we will then be able to see the relationship between statehood legitimacy (mainly based, optimally, on electoral democracy) and supranational legitimacy (mainly based on public reason), not as mutually antagonistic and engaged in zero-sum competition, but rather as allowing scope for synergy.

10

European Court of Human Rights in Pursuit of Public Reason?

The foremost example of supranational public reason (PR) in action is the European Court of Human Rights (ECtHR). The ECtHR was initially set up as an extraordinary, super-appellate judicial body, but has become in recent decades (or at least, has become described as) a quasi-constitutional court.[1] From this point of view, its fundamental purpose is to scrutinize the *reasons* provided by states to justify laws and decisions that putatively infringe the Convention's rights. While an inquiry into the reasons proffered for individual decisions of lower courts is a typical approach for any appellate court, the scrutiny of reasons provided for *laws* is a constitutional function *par excellence*. This is most visible in ECtHR decisions that deem national laws (and not merely individual judgments) 'un-conventional', that is, inconsistent with the European Convention on Human Rights (ECHR). Invented by the Court, the procedure of so-called 'pilot judgments'[2] involves the identification of systemic defects in a state's legal system going beyond breaches of the Convention in an individual case. Such a procedure reaches the limits of the Court's legitimacy, traditionally understood, because it collides in the most obvious way with the right of national authorities to adopt legislation in conformity with local values.

By and large, the Court has been successful in establishing and defending its legitimacy in the eyes of national decision-makers, courts, and the European public, largely by virtue of a number of argumentative strategies it has used in its judgments. In particular, as I will show in section 1 of this chapter, its use of a proportionality analysis that is in alignment with equivalent proportionality analyses conducted by courts in member states,# has created a general background for the acceptance of the legitimacy of its judgments, even if they clash with the legislative choices of member states. Some aspects of its arguments clearly presuppose the adoption of a public reason ideal as a yardstick for evaluating the consistency of laws with the Convention. The Court's task in this

[1] See, e.g. A. Stone Sweet and H. Keller, 'The Reception of the ECHR in National Legal Orders' in Helen Keller and Alec Stone Sweet (eds.), *A Europe of Rights: The Impact of the ECHR on National Legal Systems* (Oxford University Press 2008) 3, 7.

[2] For my detailed discussion of pilot judgments, see Wojciech Sadurski, 'Partnering with Strasbourg: Constitutionalisation of the European Court of Human Rights, the Accession of Central and East European States to the Council of Europe, and the Idea of Pilot Judgments', (2009) 9 *Human Rights Law Review* 397.

Constitutional Public Reason. Wojciech Sadurski, Oxford University Press. © Wojciech Sadurski 2023.
DOI: 10.1093/oso/9780192869678.003.0010

respect, as I will show in section 2, has been greatly facilitated by a combination of, first, explicit catalogues of permissible legitimate aims that may justify restrictions on some rights, and second, a canonical proportionality analysis that assigns the assessment of legislative aims to a separate stage in argument, cited by member states of the Council of Europe in defence of the laws impugned. The Court has, however, almost always eschewed its authority to evaluate aims in this way. On the very few occasions in which it did express its doubts about the plausibility of the aims cited by the governments concerned, it either refused to attach any weight to these doubts and moved on to the next stage in the analysis (the necessity scrutiny), or identified another aim which it found legitimate, and for this reason moved on to the necessity scrutiny stage, which will be discussed in section 3. But as I will show, there are some problems with the use of the necessity criterion (when articulated in the Court's parlance terms in of 'pressing social need') as a device for aims detection. These problems arise in particular when the Court accords a wide 'margin of appreciation' (to use another Court's idiom) to a state under scrutiny, which corresponds to the lowering of the Court's standard of scrutiny. Finally, in section 4, I will discuss the puzzling case of the 'protection of morals' as a legitimate ground for the restriction of rights, which has been interpreted by the Court in different ways, and occasionally in a way incompatible with the ideal of public reason.

1. Proportionality Analysis and Alliances with Constitutional Courts

When the Court engages in scrutiny of the laws of a state, it walks on very thin ice because the process goes against the fundamental consensus that emerged from the way the Convention system was set up in 1950—that all the member states of the Council of Europe (CoE) have laws fundamentally consistent with the Convention (divergences being attributable to legitimate diversity, later to be permitted under the margin of appreciation). The role of the Court as an adjudicatory body was only to undo aberrational decisions when all domestic remedies had been exhausted, rather than to reform the law itself. This post-1950 consensus was always based on a kind of white lie and, as one of the greatest judges of the Court observed, in a dissenting opinion:

> Although, speaking generally, it is not part of the Court's legitimate function to incriminate the laws of member States merely because they are difficult to reconcile with the Convention ... yet I accept that where it is the law itself ... that produces ... the breach ... it (the law) may be impugned even though there has been no specific act or neglect on the part of the authorities ...[3]

[3] *Marckx v. Belgium* A 31 (1979); 2 EHHR 330, dissenting opinion of Sir Gerald Fitzmaurice J., para. 28.

The idea that such cases are the exception, and that scrutiny of individual decisions is the norm, was capable of being maintained in a group of like-minded, mainly West European countries that formed the Council until the breakdown of Communism. With the enlargement of the CoE upon the Central and Eastern part of the continent, with very lax membership conditions allowing for the admission of less-than-perfectly human rights observant states (often under a 'therapeutic theory', namely that it is better to have them in rather than out), this fiction could no longer be maintained with a straight face. As a result, the Court was called upon to issue rulings in cases which were triggered by a law's systemic defects rather than individual aberrational decisions of appellate courts.[4] Hence, the idea of pilot judgments followed, as the most evident symptom of the constitutionalization of the Court.

But these judgments run the Court into a fundamental legitimacy problem. Subsequently, the Court has sought to enhance its legitimacy to issue such 'pilot judgments' by: (a) relying upon the *political* branches of the CoE in which state consent is most operative (the formal green light for 'pilot judgments' came initially from a resolution and a recommendation by the intergovernmental branch of the CoE, the Committee of Ministers); (b) paying at least lip-service to the 'margin of appreciation' (a doctrine aimed at supporting a high degree of deference by the Court to a member state summoned before it, when there is no consensus in Europe on a given issue), (c) careful and explicit argumentation consistent with proportionality analysis, with its qualities of transparency and reviewability; and (d) allying itself with national constitutional courts whenever possible, by forming a sort of coalition against a recalcitrant legislature. I will only discuss the last two points below, as they are the issues most directly relevant to the theme of this chapter.

Of particular importance for supranational public reason is point (c). Mattias Kumm observed: 'The proportionality test ... provides a structure for the justification of an act in terms of public reason'.[5] As argued in Chapter 4 of this book, proportionality serves to discern the *aim* of restrictions on a constitutional right. By scrutinizing the relationship between the legislative means and the aims (in terms of suitability and necessity), it will check whether an asserted aim is likely to have been the real one. Kumm adds:

> Since comparatively little is decided [under a proportionality analysis] by acknowledging that a measure infringes a right, the focus of rights adjudication is

[4] I describe the impact of the enlargement of the ECHR system on the constitutionalization of the Court at some length in Wojciech Sadurski, *Constitutionalism and the Enlargement of Europe* (Oxford University Press 2012) Ch. 1.

[5] Mattias Kumm, 'Institutionalising Socratic Contestation: The Rationalist Human Rights Paradigm, Legitimate Authority and the Point of Judicial Review', (2007) 1(2) *European Journal of Legal Studies* 1, https://cadmus.eui.eu/bitstream/handle/1814/7708/EJLS_2007_1_2_9_KUM_EN.pdf?sequence=1&isAllowed=y (last accessed 23 June 2020) 12, italics removed.

> generally on the reasons which justify the infringement.... Assessing the justification for rights infringements is ... largely an exercise of structured practical reasoning without many of the constraining features that otherwise characterises legal reasoning.[6]

An important legitimating virtue of the proportionality analysis is that it has become a quasi-universal idiom for the contextual and purposeful analysis of legal rights. Judgments handed down as a result of a well-conducted proportionality analysis can be well recognized and understood by their addressees even in the absence of agreement on the results: the template of proportionality creates a common epistemic ground for different layers of authority. In turn, supranational courts have instructed national courts 'to deploy [the proportionality analysis], and announced that they would supervise how national judges actually do so'.[7] This diffusion acquires, naturally, a normative character, and the use of the proportionality analysis is seen as best practice.

As Michel Rosenfeld noted when writing about proportionality analysis and judicial balancing forming part of the constitutional ordering of different constitutional levels:

> using the same test within different layers and segments is likely to create parallels and greater congruity ... Proportionality and balancing ... can cement both vertical and horizontal congruences without relying on a hierarchy or any imposed conciliation across constitutional units.[8]

After all, it is not necessary that supranational decisions identify substantive *consensus* to be legitimate. This is often impossible, and in any event may not be useful for legitimacy. But there must be a degree of commonality in language, idiom, approach, and method of analysis; beyond that, divergences of values and choices need not undermine supranational legitimacy.[9] Judgments of a supranational court, such as the ECtHR, will be read and often applied by courts belonging to very different legal systems, and this awareness must be built into the reasoning provided by the ECtHR.

The broad, teleological dimension of proportionality analysis (mainly due to the inevitable scrutiny of the legislative goals, even with the proviso that this aspect of scrutiny is usually lenient, and where it is rather unusual for laws to be judicially voided at the stage of goal scrutiny—a point which will be discussed

[6] Ibid. 11–12.
[7] Alec Stone Sweet and Jud Mathews, 'Proportionality Balancing and Global Constitutionalism', (2008) 47 *Columbia Journal of Transnational Law* 72, 162.
[8] Michel Rosenfeld, 'Rethinking Constitutional Ordering in an Era of Legal and Constitutional Pluralism', (2008) 6 *International Journal of Constitutional Law* 415, 451–52.
[9] See Antje Wiener, 'Contested Meanings of Norms: A Research Framework', (2007) 5 *Comparative European Politics* 1, 7.

at greater length later in the chapter) provides an example of such a pattern. This pattern may be well understood and adopted across a broad range of legal cultures, while 'more formal types of arguments (e.g. textual interpretation) tend to be more dependent on the legal culture and language of a particular legal order, [and therefore] they travel less easily among different legal orders'.[10] In this way, proportionality analysis may be seen as the language and methodology by which judges of different legal systems can recognize their reasoning as familiar, and as conducted in a single, common register. There is a legitimating force to it in the same way that when doctors, priests, musicians, or computer experts from different countries meet, they can immediately recognize and validate each other's competence and authority—even if this only extends to their 'theoretical' authority, to use Raz's concept.[11] The universal, legitimating power of proportionality analysis may be seen as a password that provides an entry into the supranational conversation of judges; it 'gives the legal system an entry card into the global community of judges'.[12] Proportionality 'has become a *lingua franca* in [the] community [of judges], allowing its members to communicate and compare decisions and solutions to constitutional issues. A system that adopts proportionality can, therefore, more easily participate in this community and contribute to it'.[13]

It is not difficult to understand why this has happened. Proportionality may create a legitimacy-enhancing effect that conveys an illusion of strict, quasi-mathematical reasoning viewed as leading, in a value-free way, to a determinate outcome. The judge's task may be seen as merely filling out a checklist, adducing particular weight to various steps of the calculus. The illusion is, of course, deceptive.[14] However, at the level of the rhetoric of weighing and balancing allegedly quantifiable and mutually commensurate values, it may strengthen the appearance of a decision being purely legal, strictly constrained, untainted by policy choices and controversial value judgements. At the same time, its formulaic and canonical character adds to its transportability from one legal culture to another, and increases its transparency, a little bit like a 'step-by-step' cookbook, where the sequence of steps is patiently exposed to the reader.[15] The judgments, following a canonical pattern and observing the required sequence of steps and

[10] Miguel Poiares Maduro, 'Courts and Pluralism: Essay on a Theory of Judicial Adjudication in the Context of Legal and Constitutional Pluralism', in Jeffrey L. Dunoff and Joel P. Trachtman (eds.), *Ruling the World? Constitutionalism, International Law, and Global Governance* (Cambridge University Press 2009) 356, 370, footnote omitted.

[11] Joseph Raz, *Ethics in the Public Domain* (Oxford University Press 1994) 211.

[12] Moshe Cohen-Eliya and Iddo Porat, *Proportionality and Constitutional Culture* (Cambridge University Press 2013) 134.

[13] Ibid. 135.

[14] David Robertson, *The Judge as Political Theorist* (Princeton University Press 2010) 368.

[15] For more on this aspect of proportionality, but also on the weaknesses of this approach, see Wojciech Sadurski, 'Reasonableness and Value Pluralism in Law and Politics', in Giorgio Bongiovanni, Giovanni Sartor, and Chiara Valentini (eds.), *Reasonableness and Law* (Springer 2009) 129, 137–40.

tiers, will produce recognizable outcomes that lend themselves to relatively easy scrutiny in different legal cultures, even if legal and cultural diversity will lead to different weight being applied at different stages of the weighing and balancing.

At the same time, proportionality analysis, with its in-built context sensitivity, has the edge over a categorical approach to rights adjudication, in that it moderates the losing party's sense of loss.[16] Especially in the supranational context, the factor of moderating losses, where 'losers' may be the states whose laws have been found to breach of the Convention, is an important legitimacy-enhancing asset. But, going beyond this aspect of the consolation prize, the use of proportionality analysis provides the Court with an opportunity to recognize competing values, to articulate the complex weighing and balancing of the interests at stake, and to acknowledge the arguments for and against a given position. When skilfully employed, this may project an image of restraint, modesty, and respect for value pluralism, which is useful in a large supranational setting.

The quasi-universal acceptance of proportionality analysis as a common matrix for evaluating rights restrictions has also prevented the ECtHR's jurisprudence from collapsing into a 'lowest common denominator' approach. The internal workings of proportionality analysis, with its in-built presumption against rights restrictions displayed in the 'necessity' test (a test of the least restrictive alternatives), favours a strongly rights-protective approach and the ratcheting up of understandings of the Convention's rights.[17] And because proportionality analysis is underwritten by a highly rights-protective aspiration and a high degree of distrust in governmental intrusions into constitutional rights, the use of proportionality analysis in an inter- and supranational communication among judges is likely to produce a 'race to the top', where different courts pride themselves on being in a rights-protective league.[18] Since being rights-protective is the natural aspiration of any court, proportionality analysis provides a matrix for comparison, and for making such claims credible.

The argumentative authority of proportionality analysis by the ECtHR is not only revealed in cases where it *aligns itself* with proportionality analysis at the national level, but even more starkly when it occasionally *prevails over* the structure of rights adjudication on the national level, precisely because of the perceived absence of proper proportionality concerns at that level. This was the case, for instance, in the judgment by the Federal Supreme Court (FSC) of Switzerland in 2012, which found the Swiss treatment of legal aliens guilty of severe crimes to

[16] See Mary Ann Glendon, *Rights Talk* (The Free Press 1991) 155. See, similarly (though without specifically mentioning proportionality analysis), Laurence R. Helfer and Anne-Marie Slaughter, 'Towards a Theory of Effective Supranational Adjudication', (1997) 107 *Yale Law Journal* 273, 318–23.

[17] See, similarly, Alec Stone Sweet, 'A Cosmopolitan Legal Order: Constitutional Pluralism and Rights Adjudication in Europe', (2012) 1 *Global Constitutionalism* 53, 73–74. See also Alec Stone Sweet and Clare Ryan, *A Cosmopolitan Legal Order: Kant, Constitutional Justice, and the European Convention on Human Rights* (Oxford University Press 2018).

[18] Cohen-Eliya and Porat, *Proportionality and Constitutional Culture* (n. 12) 134–36.

be defective, as it provided for categorical expulsion without any resort to a test of proportionality.[19] The case concerned *X*, a Macedonian national who entered Switzerland legally, obtained a residency permit, and was later found guilty of violations of the Narcotics Act. Under the provisions of the Constitution passed in 2010 by popular vote, he was subject to an expulsion order, with the authorities having no discretion to take into account matters such as the severity of the crime or the risk of committing further offences. In its judgment, the FSC considered the conflict between these provisions of the Swiss Constitution and Article 8 of the ECHR (a right to private and family life). In particular, the FSC considered the case law of the ECtHR on the impact of state decisions upon one's residency when the person concerned has sufficiently strong personal or family ties in the state of residency. In particular, and most interestingly for our purposes, the FSC considered the requirement, under Article 8(2) of the ECHR, of balancing the private interests of the affected person remaining in the country, on the one hand, and the public interest in his or her removal, on the other. Since the Swiss law in question did not allow for such balancing and established a categorical rule that excluded any proportionality considerations, the FSC quashed the decision to expel *X*, thus basically setting aside the Swiss law for its insensitivity to proportionality as propounded by the ECtHR.

I turn now to point (d) in the list of argumentative strategies employed by the Court to enhance its legitimacy, namely, allying itself with national constitutional courts. When the ECtHR, as a supranational court, manages to 'enlist' a *national* court in its campaign against a particular national law that allegedly breaches the Convention, and can supply a convincing argument regarding a *specific* case that is parallel to a national constitutional court's *abstract* argument about the law, concerns about legitimacy are allayed, and may be put to rest. It is an illustration of a broader phenomenon: international adjudicative bodies sometimes form alliances with national courts, often against recalcitrant national executives and legislatures. The relatively greater legitimacy of national courts contributes to the legitimacy of an international tribunal and strengthens its review capacity, because it can find support in a national court's activism. National courts, in turn, also benefit from stronger international tribunals. International tribunals can bring resources to the table that may prove valuable to national courts, and can enhance their legitimacy, for instance, through the 'domestication' of the European Court by the national tribunal, when it is referred to favourably in judgments, or is praised in extra-judicial pronouncements by municipal judges and academic lawyers, etc.

[19] *X. v. the Migration Authority of Thurgovia*, Federal Supreme Court of Switzerland, 2C_828/2011 (2012), for a summary of the decision see a report by Council of Europe, Codices, SUI-2013-1-002, http://www.codices.coe.int/NXT/gateway.dll?f=templates&fn=default.htm (last accessed 28 August 2022).

Such synergy creates a win-win result for the legitimacy of both a national and supranational tribunal. From the point of view of the ECtHR, the gain is in terms of reducing the legitimacy difficulty (the Court is not seen to displace national choices if an important national actor is aligned with its reasoning), and also in terms of increasing the chances for national support for and compliance with the supranational court's ruling. Shai Dothan gives the example of the ECtHR's ruling against the UK concerning the detention of foreign nationals suspected of terrorist activities who could not be deported because they might be tortured in their states of origin. Dothan observed: 'The ECtHR could issue such a controversial judgment without damaging its legitimacy because it followed all the legal decisions made by the House of Lords in a judgment issued on the same case.'[20] On the other hand, national courts also stand to gain, in terms of legitimacy, from an alliance with the European Court. Apart from enjoying reputational gains as a by-product of its alignment with a highly prestigious international tribunal, a national court may find that its own clash with the national executive or legislature is reduced when the executive's standing is undermined in the international forum.[21] This is, of course, only a *possibility*. In some cases, the outcome may be just the reverse and backlash against the supranational authority could occur: when there is strong national support for the legislation questioned by the European and national courts alike, the legislature or the executive may successfully exploit the public's xenophobia and hostility towards 'external interference'.

An important aspect of the growing 'supranationalization' of the ECtHR and its increasing autonomy vis-à-vis member states of the CoE is the evolution of its role concerning the execution of its own judgments. The mechanism for the execution of the judgments is set out in Article 46 of the Convention, which provides that judgments are binding on the respondent states (para. 1), and that their execution is subject to the supervision of the Committee of Ministers (CoM) of the CoE. Originally, the Convention did not envisage any role for the Court in the execution phase, but Protocol 14 (which entered into force in 2010) modified the process by allowing the CoM to seek interpretative assistance from the Court to clarify obligations arising from a judgment and to institute proceedings before the Court to determine whether the respondent state has complied with a judgment. Hence, the traditional division of tasks between the Court and the CoM, in which the exclusive responsibility for monitoring the execution of judgments rested with the CoM, has been abandoned. Consequently, the Court has acquired significant powers in the process of the execution of its judgments. This is particularly pronounced with regard to 'pilot judgments', already mentioned above, where the Court has assumed a responsibility hitherto exercised by the CoM and has started specifically pronouncing on remedial measures to be

[20] Shai Dothan, 'How International Courts Enhance Their Legitimacy', (2013) 14 *Theoretical Inquiries in Law* 455, 463.

[21] See, for a more detailed analysis, Sadurski, *Constitutionalism* (n. 2) 21–24.

undertaken by the respondent state. This practice was consolidated and formalized in the Rules of the Court. New Rule 61 (adopted by the Court in February 2011) provides that the Court is to identify the type of remedial measure that the state is required to take at the domestic level, including that the Court may indicate a specific timeframe for the adoption of remedial measures. As has been observed, 'the Court might be said to be straying further into the territory of the Committee of Ministers, since it not only indicates the type of remedial measure required but also engages in a form of supervision of the process'.[22] The increasingly active role of the Court in the execution process is one of the indicia of its growing autonomous authority and its emancipation from the states as guardians of the implementation and execution of judgments, which was traditionally viewed as only declaratory in character, where the execution stage was left to the political will of the member states of the CoE.

The ECtHR may be seen to be an example of supranational public reason at work inasmuch as the Court's authority relies, primarily, upon the strength of its arguments about the reasons that can be provided for laws which putatively breach the Convention's rights. While the member states endowed the Court, by mutual consent, with legal grounds for its rulings (the Convention, including its successive Protocols), through its interpretation of the Convention, the Court has imposed more specific obligations upon states than they had necessarily anticipated and to which they would not have necessarily consented: they had tied their own hands in ways going beyond their control. The Court has established and consolidated this authority by a number of argumentative moves, and in particular through its inventive use of proportionality analysis (as discussed above), and aligning itself, argumentatively, with national courts, often against governments (also discussed above). In addition, one should mention the doctrine of effectiveness (*effet utile*). This is an important device in the Court's array of argumentative strategies, which requires that the provisions of the Convention be interpreted so as to safeguard rights that are 'practical and effective', rather than 'theoretical and illusory'.[23] This justified an expansive interpretation of Convention rights, including the recognition of broad positive obligations on states, which are not necessarily immediately detectable in the abstract articulation of a right itself.[24] Another argumentative device serving the expansion of rights protection is the doctrine of the 'autonomous meaning' of terms used in the Convention. This doctrine provides that the meaning of terms

[22] European Court of Human Rights, 'Seminar Background Paper: Implementation of the Judgments of the European Court of Human Rights: A Shared Judicial Responsibility?' (2014), http://www.echr.coe.int/Documents/Seminar_background_paper_2014_ENG.pdf 5 (last accessed 23 June 2020), footnote omitted.

[23] *Cossey v. United Kingdom*, 184 ECHR ser. A (1990).

[24] On the link between the doctrine of effectiveness and the finding of positive obligations, see P. van Dijk and G.J.H. van Hoof, *Theory and Practice of the European Convention on Human Rights* (3rd edn., Kluwer Law International 1998) 75.

contained in the Convention is independent of the meaning of those terms used in the domestic law of the member states. Thus, for instance, the Article 6 guarantee of a fair trial (applying to the 'determination of ... civil rights and obligations or of any criminal charge') has been applied by the Court, despite the fact that a municipal law may characterize a given dispute as falling under the category of 'administrative law' or describe an offence as 'disciplinary'.[25] This means, in practice, that the Court will protect European citizens' rights, despite what their member states have actually committed themselves to. The 'concepts' serve as shells for the 'conceptions' developed by the Court, regardless of and often against 'conceptions' recognized at the state level.[26]

Between them (and with the addition of the doctrine of 'evolutive' rather than static interpretation, where the Convention is seen as 'a living instrument which must be interpreted in the light of present-day conditions'),[27] these doctrines have served as the platform for expanding, or even 'inventing' new rights, well beyond what could have been anticipated by the contracting states. Tom Zwart lists the following 'new rights' found by the Court in the Convention: due process in administrative law; the right not to be exposed to pollutants; and the right of aliens to reside with their spouses, to receive financial support, and not to be removed if they are at risk of being exposed to inhuman treatment.[28]

The Court has, strictly speaking, no power to invalidate national laws, and the *erga omnes* force of its rulings is questionable. These effects depend largely upon decision-making by national officials. But it has established itself as a quasi-constitutional supranational court because it has become recognized as such by its audience. National constitutional courts, legislatures, and executives, as well as other actors such as NGOs, the legal community, journalists, and public opinion in general, view it as an authoritative interpreter and adjudicator of rights. As a consequence, the Court's rulings have affected the shape of the domestic laws of member states beyond the determination of a specific remedy to a particular victim for a breach and have often paved the way towards effecting legislative change, changing governmental practice, and influencing judicial decisions. The actual level of state compliance with the Court's rulings has been very high overall, to the extent that the judgments have been described as being 'as effective as those of any domestic court'.[29] By adopting a common template for analysing rights infringements, mainly along the lines of proportionality analysis, it has succeeded in identifying a shared platform for enforcing European

[25] See, e.g., *Engel & Others v. the Netherlands*, Judgment of 8 June 1976, ser. A no 22, 1 EHRR 647.

[26] For a subtle discussion of this point, see George Letsas, *A Theory of Interpretation of the European Convention on Human Rights* (Oxford University Press 2007) 37–57.

[27] See, e.g., *Matthews v. United Kingdom*, Judgment of 18 February 1999, Reports 1999-I, para. 39.

[28] Tom Zwart, 'More Human Rights than Court: Why the Legitimacy of the European Court of Human Rights is in Need of Repair and How it Can Be Done', in Spyridon Flogaitis, Tom Zwart, and Julie Fraser (eds.), *The European Court of Human Rights and Its Discontents* (Edward Elgar 2013) 71, 87–88.

[29] Barry E. Carter and Phillip R. Trimble, *International Law* (2nd edn., Little, Brown 1995) 309.

citizens' individual rights, jointly with national courts and often with the willing cooperation of executives and legislatures. As a result, there is now an effective 'overarching normative structure' of rights in Europe, with the ECtHR at its epicentre.[30]

Naturally, this was made possible by constitutional and judicial actions in member states, which established or recognized the European Convention as having—depending on the country—a supra-constitutional,[31] constitutional,[32] sub-constitutional but super-statutory,[33] or statutory rank,[34] in municipal legal systems. This formal incorporation, paving the way for the standing of individuals to invoke the ECHR (and ECtHR case law) in national courts, has been supplemented by the resolve of national courts to interpret national constitutional rights in accordance with the ECHR, whenever possible, and also by abiding with the ECtHR's case law. This does not mean that municipal courts will always agree with the Strasbourg Court's jurisprudence, particularly when a delicate balancing of competing values is at stake. As noted by Nico Krisch in his study of the position of the highest courts in Austria, Spain, and France towards Strasbourg case law, these courts 'assert a power to decide on the limits of the authority of the ECtHR'.[35] But at the very least, the ECtHR will always be taken into account and considered as an important factor in the national court's decision.[36]

At the end of the day, the legitimacy of the ECtHR in the national orders of member states of the CoE is not primarily due to its formal embeddedness in those national orders. The only *formal* obligation that member states have undertaken to abide by is contained in Article 53(1) of the European Convention, that is, to abide by the judgments of the Court to which they are parties. Even then, the effect is not immediate but depends on the political will of a state, with 'naming and shaming' being the main sanction available against a recalcitrant state. The Court does not enjoy the same position vis-à-vis CoE member states as the Court of Justice of the EU does vis-à-vis EU states. Specifically, there is no equivalent of supremacy/direct effect or preliminary reference procedure, which would give national courts direct access to the European human rights tribunal. Hence, whatever compliance effect it has acquired—which is, as already

30 Stone Sweet, 'Cosmopolitan' (n. 17) 62.

31 In the Netherlands.

32 e.g. in Albania, Austria, and Slovenia.

33 e.g. in Spain.

34 e.g. in Germany.

35 Nico Krisch, 'The Open Architecture of European Human Rights Law,' (2008) 71 *Modern Law Review* 183, 196.

36 See the *Görgülü* decision of the German Federal Constitutional Court (Decision of 14 October 2004, 2BvR 1481/04), which established that there is a strong *presumption* in favour of national courts applying ECtHR case law, except in exceptional circumstances and subject to the primacy of the German Constitution in case of conflict. As observed by a commentator, this judgment 'keeps the door open for a respectful dissent', Frank Hoffmeister, 'Germany: Status of European Convention on Human Rights in Domestic Law', (2006) 4 *International Journal of Constitutional Law* 722, 729.

said, high—must be largely due to its argumentative resources, combined with the strategic alliance with national municipal actors (especially, constitutional courts) who have incentives to form a coalition with the European Court.

These incentives, however, are limited, and do not translate to a strong obligation. Municipal courts can and do occasionally depart from the case law and interpretation of the ECtHR and, having 'taken into account' the ECtHR's approach, go their own way. Paradoxically, this latitude *increases* rather than diminishes the legitimacy of the ECtHR because in the numerically dominant cases when it does prevail, the acceptance of its supremacy is voluntary. National courts act as willing and autonomous gatekeepers, helping to align the law of their state with European legal standards of human rights. As a prerequisite for a successful coalition, there must be sufficient argumentative resources in the judgments of the European Court that help synergy to emerge, and to facilitate the effective influence of the ECtHR's judgments on the conduct of national decision-makers.

2. The Scrutiny of the Legitimacy of Legislative Aims

In the previous section of this chapter, I have sketched the ways in which, through various doctrinal and argumentative strategies, the ECtHR has succeeded in establishing itself as a truly supranational adjudicative body. I have looked at the role of the ECtHR from, so to speak, an external perspective, observing how its reasoning (and in particular, of the use of proportionality analysis) strengthens and consolidates the legitimacy of the Court. My argument was that the Court may be seen as an exemplar of supranational public reason, at least in its aspirations.

There is, however, a degree of artificiality to this exercise because 'public reason' is a *philosophical* conception. The ECtHR is not a philosophical institute but a legal body, reluctant to adopt broad and necessarily contested ideals such as public reason. And yet, public reason as understood in this book, both at a national and supranational level, is a philosophical concept meant to be applied to legal acts and decisions. Just as was the case in Part 2 of this book, which looked at public reason at the level of domestic constitutional law, we may try to use it both as an interpretive device (to help us understand legitimacy-promoting arguments used by legal actors) and as a critical tool (to criticize judgments and legislation that violate the principle of public reason) with respect to particular legal actors. In the case of the ECtHR, such an approach appears to be particularly appropriate because the way the Court implements the ideal of public reason in scrutinizing national laws at first glance seems straightforward, at least as far as non-absolute rights are concerned. Some Convention rights are formulated in an absolute way and do not permit any derogations or restrictions, such as the right to life (Art. 2), the right against torture (Art. 3), or the right not to be punished without a prior law proscribing a punishable action (Art. 7). However, some other rights, namely the rights to private life, freedom of religion, freedom of expression, freedom of assembly and association, and freedom of movement (Arts. 8, 9, 10, 11, and Art. 2 of Protocol 4, respectively) come with clauses establishing legitimate grounds for restrictions of those rights.

In fact, a distinction between 'absolute' Convention rights and those subject to proportionality analysis is not so clear-cut. One could argue, for instance, that section 2 of Article 1 introduces grounds for derogation, subject to the necessity proviso.[37] However, the technique of describing those derogations differs from those in Articles 8–11. For example, the right to life is not balanced against some other competing individual or social values. Rather, it is the case that some actions resulting in the killing of a person (such as defending a person from unlawful violence or effecting a lawful arrest) are not considered to contravene the right to life, subject to the necessity proviso. While leading ECHR scholar Steven Greer claims that proportionality features in the Court's judgments concerning these 'formally unqualified' rights, he goes on to observe: 'although in this context it effectively becomes an implicit strict or absolute necessity test . . .'[38] That is why, in order to trace the pursuit of public reason in the most representative instances of proportionality analysis by the Court, I only focus on cases where the Court has had to consider whether a state law has properly observed the limits on interfering with Convention rights, as provided for in the grounds for limiting the rights articulated in Articles 8–11 and Article 2 of Protocol 4.

The catalogues of these grounds read like a list of 'public reasons', including national security, public safety, prevention of crime, protection of public order, protection of health or morals, protection of the rights and freedoms of others, and maintaining the authority and impartiality of the judiciary. This recital is culled from all these Articles, though some Articles have different catalogues of derogation grounds than others. For instance, 'territorial integrity' figures in Article 10 (freedom of expression), but not in Articles 8, 9, and 11; 'the economic well-being of the country' figures in Article 8 (respect for private and family life), but not in the other Articles.

When the Court scrutinizes a national law (or a decision) of which an applicant complains, and the breach of any of these non-absolute rights is alleged, it proceeds in a standardized, canonical way, using the following steps: (1) it first

[37] Section 2 of Art. 1 reads: 'Deprivation of life shall not be regarded as inflicting in contravention of this article when it results from the use of force which is no more than absolutely necessary: (a) in defence of any person from unlawful violence; (b) in order to effect a lawful arrest or to prevent the escape of a person lawfully detained; (c) in action lawfully taken for the purpose of quelling a riot or insurrection.'

[38] Steven Greer, *The European Convention on Human Rights: Achievements, Problems and Prospects* (Cambridge University Press 2006) 217.

determines whether there was an 'interference' by the state with the Convention-protected right in the first place, and only if the answer is positive (as it almost always is, because the scope of a right is generally construed in a very broad way, and a determination of an 'interference' is in no way conclusive to the determination of breach); it then controls (2) whether the interference was prescribed by law (as opposed to being based on an individual, arbitrary decision), (3) whether it served a legitimate aim, and (4) whether it was 'necessary in a democratic society'. This last step has been interpreted by the Court as consisting of (4a) establishing a 'pressing social need' for the interference, and also (4b) checking whether it was 'proportionate to the legitimate aim pursued'. As is clear to anyone with an even cursory knowledge of the Court's case law, wherever breach is eventually established, it is usually ascertained in step (4).

From the point of view of public reason, the key step is step 3—or so one may think at first blush. An inquiry into the aim of legal interference with an individual right seems to be precisely what the conception of public reason is about. If the goal of legislation is legitimate in the Convention's terms and, at the same time, if the Convention's approved aims resonate with the ideal of public reason, then step 3 seems to ideally match the requirements of public reason. In practice, however, it is not exactly so, and the reality is more complicated. Complications are due to three issues that undermine the simple view that a public reason enquiry is consummated satisfactorily in step (3). *First*, the Court has almost always been willing to accept the government's recitals of 'legitimate goals' at face value, and almost never probes behind the declarations by governments about the goals pursued by the impugned legislation—even if those declarations were, to a reasonable observer, disingenuous. *Second*, the way the Court allocates the burden of its reasoning between steps (3) and (4) suggests that the argument about the real nature of the aim (something assumedly belonging to step (3)) is executed in step (4), which concerns necessity/proportionality, with its conclusions radiating back upon the understanding of the goal. *Third*, there is a puzzling case of the 'protection of morals' as a legitimate ground for restrictions of rights, which has been occasionally interpreted by the Court in a way incompatible with the general rationale behind the ideal of public reason. In the remainder of this section of the chapter, I will discuss the first point, and in the next two sections, points two and three, respectively.

The Court's determination of the goals pursued by the legislation at issue—either the legislation on its face, as creating an infringement of the applicant's rights, or a specific administrative or judicial decision which allegedly infringes his/her rights, with no further domestic remedies available—is usually laconic, formulaic, and totally non-critical of the legislator or other national decision-makers.[39] If the government is capable of identifying one (or more) of the

[39] There are exceptions, though, especially more recently. See, e.g., *OOO Flavus v. Russia*, Judgment of 23 June 2020, Appl. No. 12468/15, paras. 38 and 44 (Court finding lack of any legitimate aim for

grounds for rights restrictions listed in the relevant Article of the Convention, the Court normally accepts this explanation without probing into whether legislative intentions were in fact oriented towards that goal. All the intellectual work aimed at questioning the sincerity or rationality of citing this particular aim is relegated to the 'necessity' stage of the Court's inquiry.

Occasionally, but exceedingly rarely, the Court expresses some mild doubts about the aim cited by the government. Even then, however, the Court will refuse to finish its reasoning at this stage but proceeds as if these doubts should be bracketed and disregarded. In *Smith and Grady v. United Kingdom*,[40] a case concerned with the practice of investigating the sexual orientation of members of the armed forces and discharging those found to be homosexual, the government cited the goals of maintaining morale of service personnel, and of the fighting power and operational effectiveness of the armed forces (paras. 29, 66, and 74), as the grounds for its policy. The government asserted that these goals were subsumed under the legitimate aims of 'the interests of national security' and 'prevention of disorder', which by the terms of Article 8(2) can serve as grounds for restriction of the right to respect for private and family life. In a single, short paragraph, the Court commented that 'it finds no reason to doubt' that the exclusion of homosexual people was designed with a view to ensuring the operational effectiveness of the armed forces (para. 74).

This is a remarkable instance of the Court expressing unconditional confidence in the government's assurances. After all, the judgment of the Court contains strong evidence (largely relying on the government itself) that the applicants' conduct gave no grounds for complaint. Indeed, several facts indicated that each of the applicants were exemplary in the execution of their duties and were even considered for promotion. Moreover, the government did not contend that homosexual people were any 'less physically capable, brave, dependable or skilled than heterosexuals' (para. 76). The judgment also contains significant evidence, produced or confirmed by the government, that much of the risk to the cohesion and effectiveness of army units may not come from the fact that some members are homosexual or from their behaviour, but rather from actions, attitudes, and utterances by heterosexuals giving expression to their prejudice and hatred. The governmental report (the Homosexual Policy Assessment Team (HPAT) 1996) on which the government heavily relied in its submission to the ECtHR stated, inter alia, that the 'anticipated problems' arising from the integration of homosexual people into the armed forces included 'heterosexual

blocking an opposition website and on this basis finding a breach of Art. 10 of the Convention); *Kövesi v. Romania*, Judgment of 5 May 2020, Appl. No. 3594/19, paras. 196–99 (finding no legitimate aim in terminating of chief prosecutor's mandate following public criticism of legislative reforms); *Kamoy Radyo Televizyon v. Turkey*, Judgment of 16 April 2019, Appl. No. 19965/06, paras. 50–51 (violation of Art. 1 Protocol 1 to the Convention found on the basis of lack of any legitimate aim for the interference under challenge).

[40] Judgment of 27 September 1999, Appl. Nos. 33985/96 and 33986/96.

animosity, assaults on homosexuals, bullying and harassment of homosexuals, ostracism and avoidance … and resentment over imposed change especially if controls on heterosexual expression also had to be tightened …' (para. 54). As the Court concluded, quite plausibly, 'the perceived problems which were identified in the HPAT report as a threat to fighting power and operational effectiveness were founded *solely* upon the negative attitudes of heterosexual personnel towards those of homosexual orientation' (para. 96, emphasis added). Yet none of those facts or observations caused the Court to express doubt ('The Court finds no reason to doubt …') about the sincerity of the goals recited by the government.

There was just one minor doubt expressed by the Court at the goal scrutiny stage, and it concerned the *investigations* conducted by the army into the sexual orientation of its members. Those investigations, as well as their ultimate discharge, were part of the complaints by Smith and Grady to the ECtHR. Having accepted, at face value, the government's assurances as to the legitimate goal served by the discharges, the Court went on to say, 'The Court has more doubt as to whether the investigations continued to serve any such legitimate aim once the applicants had admitted their homosexuality' (para. 74). This is one of those rare instances where the Court offered any critical scrutiny of the government's assertions about its goals. And yet, this 'doubt' was immediately bracketed by the sentence that follows: 'However, given the Court's conclusion at paragraph 111 below, it does not find it necessary to decide whether this element of the investigations pursued a legitimate aim …' (para. 74). The paragraph to which this sentence refers (para. 111) is a short statement in which the Court confirms its conclusion that the conduct of investigations and discharge from service on grounds of sexual orientation were not justified under Article 8(2)—a conclusion reached as a result of the necessity scrutiny (step 4 in the list of steps enumerated at the beginning of this section of the chapter).

But this is putting the cart before the horse. If the doubts felt by the Court about the goals served by the post-admission investigations were serious, no further inquiry into *this* aspect of the complaint was warranted. The matter should have ended there and, at least as far as those investigations were concerned, the breach should have been found at step (3)—in the scrutiny of the legislative aim. By expressing a doubt, and then immediately bracketing it and proceeding as if the doubt did not matter, the Court disclosed that it did not take the goal stage of its scrutiny seriously. It is seen as a purely perfunctory stage of its reasoning, to be quickly disposed of so that the Court can get on with the truly serious task of necessity scrutiny. But the 'necessity' of a measure to the achievement of a goal is a moot point if the goal itself is illegitimate in the first place.

That the Court's analysis of legislative goals is purely perfunctory and lacking in seriousness is evidenced by some other important cases in which a rational person might reasonably develop doubts about the sincerity of the legislative aims cited by the governments concerned. (I am putting to one side those—admittedly rare—strange cases where the Court manufactures legitimate aims on behalf of the government, thus assisting the government failing to produce proper justification of a restriction under challenge.)[41] In *D.H. & Others v. Czech Republic*,[42] the Grand Chamber accepted the government's stated aim for the placement of Roma schoolchildren in special schools. That aim was expressed in terms of 'the desire to find a solution for children with special educational needs' (para. 198), or, as the government put it (as paraphrased by the Court), 'the adaptation of the education process to the capacity of children with specific educational needs' (para. 149). The Court found that the law only breached Article 14 (prohibition of discrimination) in conjunction with Article 2 of Protocol 1 (the right to education) because there was no 'reasonable relationship of proportionality between the means used and the aim pursued' (para. 208). In *Vojnity v. Hungary*,[43] the total removal of a father's access rights to his child after a divorce on the grounds that his religious convictions were detrimental to his son, was found to breach Article 14 in conjunction with Article 8. The Court accepted that the protection of the child was a legitimate aim of the measure (para. 33), and only found a breach under the necessity analysis (para. 36). But finding no evidence of harm to the child arising from the religious beliefs of a parent (para. 38), the Court should have paused to reflect on the *real* aim behind the measure. It would be not implausible to detect a strong element of animus towards the religion espoused by the applicant. However, the Court made no gesture towards second-guessing the government's true aims.

Occasionally, second-guessing is offered, albeit cautiously, *in dissenting opinions*. In the case of *Dubská and Krejzová v. Czech Republic*,[44] a challenge was made to a law that prevented some qualified health professionals from assisting in home births. The government asserted—and the Court agreed—that the reasons for the prohibition were protection of health and the rights and freedoms of others, namely the safety and health of mother and child (paras. 84 and 86). The Court accepted these assertions despite its own observation that not allowing medical professionals to assist mothers who wished to give birth at home 'may be said to increase rather than reduce the risk to life and health of the mother and the newborn' (para. 96). In his dissenting opinion, Judge Lemmens picked up on this inconsistency, and suggested that a different motive may have been at work: 'As in other countries, the issue of home births seems to be the object of a form of power struggle between doctors and midwives.'[45] After citing some facts about the arrogant approach of the Czech doctors' association in the negotiations around the matter, Judge Lemmens gently suggested 'that the

[41] See, e.g., *Surikov v. Ukraine*, Judgment of 26 January 2017, Appl. No. 42788/06, para. 82.

[42] Grand Chamber Judgment of 13 November 2007, Appl. No. 57325/00. The Second Section Judgment was handed down on 7 February 2006, with a no-violation conclusion.

[43] Judgment of 12 February 2013, Appl. No. 29617/07.

[44] Judgment of 11 December 2014, Appl. Nos. 28859/11 and 28473/12.

[45] Part 3 of the dissenting opinion of Lemmens J.

public-health argument put forward by the Government should not be overestimated'.[46] The applicants had put it more bluntly, asserting that the aim of the regulation was 'to protect the financial and power monopoly of the incumbent providers of institutional health care' (para. 85).

In each of the cases just noted, it could have been reasonably argued that the goals cited by the government were merely an *ex post facto* rationalization. Those goals could have been seen by the Court as a proxy for other goals that were much less wholesome, and certainly less compatible with the Convention's litany of legitimate objectives that are capable of justifying rights restrictions. However, there have also been some cases where the Court was somewhat less gullible, and less accepting of governments' declarations about the goals they pursued by questionable laws. Even then, however, greater scrutiny did not matter to the outcome. Whenever doubt about the goals was raised, it was quickly set aside by the Court, which then turned to the next step of its analysis. I will provide three examples of such an approach.

In *Bayatyan v. Armenia*,[47] the Grand Chamber found the absence of an alternative civilian service for conscientious objectors to military service to constitute a breach of Article 9. This time, the Court did not find the government's purported aim of the protection of public order (para. 117) to be convincing. The Court based its scepticism on the fact that, at the time of the applicant's conviction for his refusal to appear for military service, Armenia had already announced that it would introduce an alternative civilian service (paras. 117 and 127). However, rather than disposing of the matter at this stage, the Court declared that there was no need to inquire into whether the objectives underpinning the absence of such alternative service were legitimate because, 'even assuming that they were' (para. 117), the interference was incompatible with Article 9 because it failed the test of necessity (paras. 124 and 127). Hence, 'not convincing' turned out to be much less than 'not legitimate'. This approach suggests that the Court applied an extremely weak standard of legitimacy to its inquiry into legislative aims and placed all the burden of its argument upon the scrutiny of the necessity of the law. However, this scrutiny would have been unnecessary and redundant if the Court clearly established illegitimacy of the aim in the first place. The Court never explained why it did not do so, despite finding that the purported aim was 'not convincing'; indeed, nothing in the judgment suggests that the Court even felt the need to elucidate. And yet, as it gathered significant argumentative resources elsewhere in the judgment, the Court came close to suggesting that the non-exemption for religious minorities may have been motivated by a form of hostility towards minoritarian or even unpopular religions. That point is discernible in the Court's reiteration of its mantra that

[46] Ibid.

[47] Grand Chamber Judgment of 7 July 2011, Appl. No. 23459/03. The Third Section Judgment of 27 October 2009 ended with a no-violation verdict.

'pluralism, tolerance and broadmindedness are hallmarks of a "democratic society"'. The Court also engaged in a short civics lecture when it said, 'democracy does not simply mean that the views of a majority must always prevail', and that the state should show respect 'towards the beliefs of a minority religious group like the applicant's' (para. 126). The Court, however, refused to dot the i's and cross the t's, and stopped short of spelling out the true goal of the legislation.

In *Perinçek v. Switzerland*,[48] the Court agreed that the punishment of a public speaker for denying the fact of the Armenian genocide was aimed at 'protection of the rights of others', namely, the honour of the relatives of genocide victims (para. 75). However, it then found a breach of Article 10 on the basis of the absence of 'pressing social need' (para. 126). Remarkably, in this case the Court did engage in a critical (if laconic) scrutiny of *another* aim cited by the government—the prevention of disorder (para. 73). The Court responded to that argument by noting briefly that insufficient proof was produced about the suggestion that the applicant's comments posed a risk to public order (para. 75). This case shows that the Court is occasionally able to dismiss a stated goal on the basis of its implausibility, although in this case the force of the move was diluted by *another legitimate goal* being accepted at face value.

Finally, I turn to one of the most famous and momentous judgments in the entire history of the ECtHR: *Sejdić & Finci v. Bosnia and Herzegovina*.[49] It has been the only decision so far in which the Court found a *constitutional* provision of a member state incompatible with the Convention. The Court determined that the ineligibility of the applicants to stand for election to the House of Peoples and the Presidency on the grounds of their Roma and Jewish origins respectively was a breach of Article 14 (prohibition of discrimination) in conjunction with Article 3 of Protocol 1 (right to free elections). The decision generated a huge critical response and probably caused more outcry than almost any other judgment of the Court[50]—but for our purposes only one aspect is relevant. Under review was a constitutional arrangement under which only three 'constituent peoples'—Croats, Serbs, and Bosniacs—could be represented in top state political institutions. When responding to the government's submission that the goal of this constitutional structure was 'the establishment of peace and dialogue between the three main ethnic groups' (para. 34), the Court said that the rule excluding members of other nationalities from various offices may have served the legitimate purpose of restoration of peace *at the time of its enactment* (para. 45). Whether it still served a legitimate aim later on—specifically during the period after Bosnia and Herzegovina had ratified the European Convention—did not

[48] Judgment of 17 December 2013, Appl. No. 27510/08.
[49] Grand Chamber Judgment of 22 December 2009, Appl. Nos. 27996/06 and 34836/06.
[50] See, in particular, Christopher McCrudden and Brendan O'Leary, *Courts and Consociations: Human Rights versus Power-Sharing* (Oxford University Press 2013).

need to be decided, because the rule still violated the proportionality principle (para. 46).

What is wrong with this paraphrased statement—in which the Court declined to engage in any scrutiny of the legitimacy of the aim behind the impugned constitutional provisions—is clear. The proportionality principle, logically, enters the picture only *after* a legitimate aim is established. The ordering of the analysis in this way is necessary, because proportionality and necessity are relational concepts—they refer to the link between a given measure and the *legitimate* aim in pursuit of which it is enacted. If, for the sake of argument, the aim was not legitimate, the proportionality/necessity analysis is a moot issue. The Court *did* provide a strong argument about the violation of the principle of proportionality by the exclusion rule (paras. 47–50). Critical to this point was the Court's recognition that there were mechanisms of power-sharing that would not automatically lead to the total exclusion of representatives of communities other than the three main groups (para. 48). However, this only shows that the Court's doubts about the legitimacy of the goal in the post-ratification period did not carry any argumentative weight. While on the one hand, it has applied strict scrutiny, and thus a highly interventionist and activist approach to the analysis of proportionality, it has been surprisingly meek when evaluating (indeed, failing to evaluate) the legitimacy of the goal of the exclusionary rule.

It is time for interim conclusions. The ECtHR has at its disposal a handy scheme for evaluating legislative goals, and in particular, for testing them for consistency with public reason. The Court's case law shows, however, that the scrutiny of legislative aims in the context of the Court's broader scheme is usually purely perfunctory and formulaic. The Court has tended towards uncritically accepting governments' declarations about the goals pursued by the legislation impugned. Governments usually articulate those declarations in terms identical to, or fully compatible with, the textual catalogues of legitimate grounds for rights restrictions in the Convention. They are then simply repeated with minimal if any rewording in the Court's judgments, and summarily accepted. In the exceptional cases where the Court did express 'doubts' or 'hesitations' as to the goals declared by the government, the Court's scepticism did not result in a determination of breach on that basis. Rather, the Court either announced at this stage that the legislation would not survive necessity scrutiny anyway (and so considered itself under no duty to elaborate about the legitimacy of the goal, as in *Sejdić & Finci*) or found another operative goal that it accepted, rescuing the law from other objections (as in *Perinçek*).

The stage of the inquiry ostensibly concerned with the scrutiny of the underlying aim of an impugned law is therefore nearly redundant and almost never seriously used. In practice, it serves only as a stepping-stone to the real thing—the necessity analysis. It is at *that* stage that the goal reappears, in the context of scrutinizing how well tailored the legislative measures are to the achievement of this goal. It may well be that the illegitimacy of the goal will become an operative factor at this last, crucial stage of the Court's analysis. If so, while this approach may upset the elegant architecture of proportionality analysis, the practical outcome may be the same. Whether and in what way goal analysis is embedded in necessity scrutiny will be discussed in the next section of the chapter.

3. 'Necessity' Scrutiny and the Ascertainment of Legislative Goals

In a number of its decisions, the ECtHR has established an interpretation of the word 'necessary' that is neither synonymous with the 'indispensable' nor is it equivalent to the 'desirable' (or 'useful', or 'admissible').[51] The rejection of 'indispensability' as synonymous with necessity suggests that the Court has not adopted strict necessity in the *sine qua non* sense, but something weaker. Some measures will be found 'necessary' even though we can envision other ways of achieving the same constitutionally required or permitted goals. At the other extreme of the continuum, it is clear that if 'necessity' were to be equated with (or even came close to) 'desirability', then the textual requirement of 'necessity in a democratic society' (articulated in the Convention) would all but lose its critical meaning. The supervision of the observance of human rights by the European Court would be severely eroded.

In defining its standards of necessity, the Court has not been precise in its articulation of a middle ground between indispensability and desirability. In the most oft-repeated formulation, the Court has settled on a conception that 'necessary in a democratic society' means that any interference with a right must serve 'a pressing social need' and be 'proportionate to the legitimate aim pursued'.[52] Both these concepts have their problems, which will be discussed in turn.

The element of the formula requiring a 'pressing social need' is immediately attractive due to the pragmatic and elastic character of those words: what constitutes a 'pressing need' is a matter of a reasonable political judgement, rather than the type of quasi-logical analysis that the term 'necessity' might otherwise demand. The danger of using this concept, however, is its unfortunate disconnection from the *goals* to be pursued. The concept of 'necessity' is explicitly relational. Hence, any statement of necessity is incomplete without a determination of the goals to which a given law is related. By contrast, the concept of a 'pressing social need' may well appear without such a complement. In other words, the

[51] *Handyside v. United Kingdom*, Judgment of 7 December 1976, Appl. No. 5493/72, para. 48; *Dudgeon v. United Kingdom*, Judgment of 22 October 1981, Appl. No. 7525/76, para. 51.

[52] See, e.g., *Goodwin v. United Kingdom*, 22 ECHR 123, 143–44 (1996). For discussion, see Alastair Mowbray, *Cases and Materials on the European Convention of Human Rights* (Butterworths 2001) 411–12, 48.

notion of a 'pressing social need' is self-standing. It can be used independently of, or indeed disconnected from, the description of a goal in a way that the concept of 'necessity' cannot.

From the point of view of the theme of this chapter, this disconnect is of course unfortunate, because the use of the concept of a 'pressing social need' as a proxy for necessity may release the Court from investigating the legitimacy of the legislative goal. It is also unfortunate from the point of view of the integrity of the Convention system because, as Roberto Perrone rightly notes: 'Not every measure that is "necessary in a democratic society" is acceptable, but only those directed at safeguarding the specific interests mentioned in the Convention.'[53] In any event, I am not making the stronger point that the Court *has* actually used the concept of a 'pressing social need' in order to ignore the question of the legitimacy of legislative aims, but only the weaker one, that the temptation is there.

A reading of some cases suggests that the Court has been occasionally unwilling or unable to resist this temptation. In *Norris v. Ireland* (a case to which I will return in the next section of this chapter),[54] the Court considered Irish laws that interfered with Convention rights by criminalizing certain homosexual activities. While finding the law in breach of Article 8 of the Convention, it stated, inter alia: 'Applying the same tests [of injury to moral standards, as established in *Dudgeon v. UK*] to the present case, the Court considers that, as regards Ireland, it cannot be maintained that there is a "pressing social need" to make such acts criminal offences' (para. 46). While the conclusion is to be applauded, there is nothing in this statement that would suggest that the Court *relates* the pressing social need criterion to any specific goals identified in Article 8(2). Indeed, the above-quoted sentence is immediately followed by the Court turning to the issue of proportionality, as separate from the 'pressing social need' criterion. It is therefore clear that 'pressing social need' is used as a self-standing concept rather than a relational one.

The second criterion that must be met in order for an interference with a Convention right to be 'necessary in a democratic society' is that it must be 'proportionate to the legitimate goal pursued'[55] (note that both criteria must be fulfilled jointly rather than alternatively in order to meet the proper standard of necessity). But the interface between the standard of 'necessity' and 'proportionality' (*qua* a proxy for necessity) is not self-evident. Offhand, one may think that proportionality is neither a necessary nor a sufficient condition of necessity; in

[53] Roberto Perrone, 'Public Morals and the ECHR' (20 January 2014). University of Leicester School of Law Research Paper No. 14–02, available at SSRN: http://ssrn.com/abstract=2382086 8 (last accessed 23 June 2020).

[54] Judgment of 26 October 1988, Appl. No. 10581/83.

[55] See, e.g., *Smith & Grady* para. 87. Note that yet another idiom in which 'necessity' has been re-articulated by the Court is the formula of 'relevance and sufficiency', but I will not focus on it as it does not seem to add anything to the 'proportionality' requirement, with which it is often used interchangeably.

other words, that there may be (1) measures which are proportionate but not necessary, and (2) measures which are not proportionate and yet necessary. Both these non-correlations between proportionality and necessity are significant for our theme here, namely for goal detection. I will discuss them now in turn.

Regarding scenario (1), for each legitimate goal we may think of a measure that is proportionate, *in a sufficiently weak sense of proportionality*, and yet not necessary. The italicized words are crucial to my argument: it is important to note that the formula 'proportionate to the goal pursued' does not dictate any particular degree of connection between the measure and the goal per se. So if we understand this connection in a relatively weak fashion (i.e. as being remote from the notion of 'necessity' as 'indispensability'), we may well characterize a measure as 'proportionate' even if it is not the only one imaginable that would lead to the relevant goal—that is, one that is not 'necessary' for its achievement. The European Court *has* been willing to lower the standard of proportionality; after all, this is the whole point of distinguishing it from necessity as indispensability. Whenever the Court has applied a wide margin of appreciation at the stage of necessity scrutiny, by definition it has moved the point on the scale between indispensability and desirability in the direction of the latter. (This will be illustrated, below, by the case of *Mouvement Raëlien Suisse v. Switzerland*). By relaxing the standard of proportionality in this way, it becomes less helpful in enabling the Court to discern the *true* goal of the legislation impugned. This is because, as argued in Chapter 4, section 3 of this book, strict scrutiny (with the standard of means–goal relationship coming close to necessity as indispensability) is a device that screens out insincere declarations about legislative goals and identifies true goals—but only if it is truly 'strict'. This has often been observed in US constitutional scholarship: strict scrutiny may be justified by a suspicion that improper motives are at work and requires a close connection between the asserted aim and the legislative means adopted. Cass Sunstein put it this way: 'If a sufficiently close connection [between the asserted justification and the means adopted] cannot be shown, there is reason for skepticism that the asserted value in fact accounted for the legislation'.[56]

As for proposition (2), namely that there may be measures deemed necessary and yet not proportionate, this may initially seem odd. After all, one may have an intuitive sense that if a measure is necessary then *a fortiori* it is proportionate. But this is not so, and it all depends on the notion of proportionality we adopt. In particular, it is not so if we consider proportionality as proportionality *sensu stricto*, as distinguished from proportionality *sensu largo*. To summarize a well-known standard, proportionality in the strict sense of the word requires comparing the costs of rights restrictions with the benefits of achieving a constitutionally legitimate objective that may be fulfilled only by interfering with

[56] Cass R. Sunstein, *The Partial Constitution* (Harvard University Press 1994) 30.

a constitutional right.[57] The proportionality analysis *sensu stricto* demands that the latter benefits outweigh the former costs: if they do not, the rights restriction is impermissible under this test. Proportionality *sensu largo*, in turn, encompasses an analysis in terms of the suitability of means to a legislative end, of the least restrictive means possible, and of proportionality *sensu stricto*.

Now proportionality *sensu stricto* does not fully correlate with necessity. There may be legislative measures that will be found necessary and yet not proportionate *sensu stricto* because the balance of benefits and burdens turns out to be negative: the costs (of rights restrictions) prevail over the benefits (of accomplishing a goal). From the point of view of our theme in this section of the chapter, namely that of goal ascertainment, it is important to observe that when the Court applies *this* notion of proportionality, it uses a necessity proxy (proportionality) that is incapable of discerning the aim of the legislation with precision. If the standard of proportionality is not strictly correlated with necessity, the potential of proportionality in goal detection is lost.

While the Court has never clearly articulated its understanding of the standards of proportionality, it has occasionally used proportionality in precisely this sense. Consider *Dudgeon v. UK*,[58] a case concerning the prohibition of homosexuality in Northern Ireland. Having quickly disposed of the issue of a 'pressing social need' for making homosexual acts criminal offences, the Court moved on to the next step in its necessity scrutiny: 'On the issue of proportionality, the Court considers that such justifications as there are for retaining the law in force unamended are outweighed by the detrimental effects which the very existence of the legislative provisions in question can have on the life of a person of homosexual orientation like the applicant' (para. 60). The balancing of costs and benefits, on both sides of the equation, is unmistakeable. When considering the arguments for prohibition, the Court refers to a number of factors, including the fact of the strong and morally grounded opposition in Northern Ireland to legalizing homosexuality (para. 57) and the need to provide safeguards against the exploitation and corruption of those who are especially vulnerable by reason, inter alia, of their youth (paras. 49 and 62). On the other side of the equation, the Court notes the costs of interfering with 'an essentially private manifestation of the human personality' (para. 60), and that the 'nature of the activities involved' is such that they 'concern a most intimate aspect of private life' (para. 52). Comparing these costs and benefits, the Court concluded that the legal restrictions on the applicant were disproportionate 'to the aims sought to be achieved' (para. 61).

But there are, of course, other uses of proportionality in ECtHR case law, where proportionality is better calibrated to serve as a necessity standard, and that do

[57] Aharon Barak, *Proportionality: Constitutional Rights and their Limitations* (Cambridge University Press 2012) 340.

[58] Judgment of 22 October 1981, Appl. No. 7525/76.

not involve the balancing of benefits of the goal attainment and costs of rights infringement. It is in *those* cases that we can observe the Court's implicit use of that standard for goal detection. Consider the case of *Vajnai v. Hungary*,[59] in which the Court found that the punishment of a leader of a left-wing party for wearing a red star emblem at a demonstration in Budapest was a violation of Article 10. The punishment was meted out under a newly added provision of the Criminal Code, entitled 'The use of totalitarian symbols', which prohibited public uses and exhibits 'of a swastika, an SS-badge, an arrow-cross, a symbol of the sickle and hammer or a red star' (para. 16). According to the government the law was aimed at—using the terms of the Convention—the prevention of disorder and the protection of the rights of others (para. 33), something that the Court immediately agreed with (para. 34). The necessity scrutiny that followed the certification of the legitimacy of the goal is an example of the Court remorselessly demolishing the relevance of the prohibition to the goals asserted. The Court first demonstrated that the red star can be viewed not only as a symbol of totalitarian oppression under Communism, but also as a symbol of the international workers movement and the struggle for a more just society (para. 52). Second, the Court noted that Mr. Vajnai did nothing to show that his participation in the public life of Hungary would be in defiance of the rule of law (para. 53). And third, there was no evidence that the wearing of the red star would bring about public disorder in Hungary (para. 55).

These are all eminently plausible arguments. What the Court did *not* say, but what any reasonable reader may be excused for suspecting at this stage, is that the true goals of the restrictive law were different from those asserted. If the law is so clearly disproportionate to the aims of prevention of disorder and protection of the rights of other people, then the only credible conclusion is that the law was in fact triggered by some other motive—that it was meant to serve different goals for which it was better calibrated, such as hostility to certain political or philosophical ideals considered 'off limits'. But since *these* goals were clearly not suitable for governments to assert publicly as grounds for restrictions on speech, the government had to cite aims that were seriously incommensurate with the prohibition.

In this case, the Court's tacit goal ascertainment was argumentatively made possible by the very narrow 'margin of appreciation' granted to the government by the Court. In other words, the Court adopted a relatively low level of deference to the national authorities. However, this approach has not always been taken. When the Court chooses to grant a respondent state a wider margin of appreciation, that is, to manifest a greater deference to national institutions, the role of necessity scrutiny as a way of smoking out improper legislative goals is appropriately lower. Consider the already mentioned case of *Mouvement Raëlien*

[59] Judgment of 8 July 2008, Appl. No. 33629/06.

Suisse v. Switzerland.[60] The decision found that the Swiss authorities' ban on posters distributed by a small religious group dedicated to promoting contact with extra-terrestrials did not violate Article 10. In defending the ban under Article 10(2), the government cited the grounds of protection of health and morals, protection of the rights of others, and the prevention of crime. As emerged from the facts of the case, the three objectionable aspects of the posters were that they allegedly advocated for human cloning (which is prohibited in Switzerland), that they advocated for so-called 'geniocracy' (i.e. the rule by the wisest), and also that the movement's ideas might lead to the sexual abuse of children (para. 71). Now, everything about each of the three arguments seemed to be wrong, as clearly evidenced by the Court itself in its necessity scrutiny. While cloning itself was prohibited in Switzerland, advocacy of cloning was not. In any event, the only trace of cloning advocacy discernible in the posters was that they referred to the website of Clonaid, an organization set up by the movement that allegedly offered paid services in the area of cloning (para. 43). As to 'geniocracy', as allegedly offensive to democracy, it was never represented by the movement as a real political project with a tangible anti-democratic potential, but rather as a utopia to be fulfilled voluntarily (para. 44). Finally, the only link between the posters and the potential for sexual abuse of the children was that some former members of the movement had been convicted, outside the context of the organization's activities, of the sexual abuse of children. The movement's official position, on its website, strongly condemned paedophilia (para. 42). From the Court's description of the circumstances of the case, it is clear beyond any doubt: the idea that the posters of an admittedly bizarre but certainly marginal cult organization could pose any threat to 'health and morals' or the rights of citizens of Switzerland, or contribute to crime, seems preposterous.

And yet, the necessity scrutiny of the Court *failed* to discern any defects in the means–aims relationship, which was rhetorically made possible by the broad margin of appreciation granted to the state. It is here that we find the usual deference mantra (missing from *Vajnai*), encapsulated in particular in the declaration: 'The Court cannot interfere with the choices of the national and local authorities, which are closer to the realities of their country, for it would thereby lose sight of the subsidiary nature of the Convention system ...' (para. 64). No wonder that, under an approach so charitable to local authorities, the Court did not venture to speculate that the extraordinary prohibition on such innocuous posters might have been triggered by hostility to an unpopular minority religion.

There is one other important aspect of the sort of proportionality approach that the Court conducted in *Mouvement Raëlien*—the bundling of government objectives. In order to be credible, proportionality must be an attribute of a relation between a *particular* action (an act of state interference with a right) and

[60] Grand Chamber Judgment of 13 July 2012, Appl. No. 16354/06.

a *particular* aim. Yet, what the Court had on the table were the objections by the government to three different aspects of the impugned posters, and on the other hand, a motley assortment of the Convention's legitimate aims for restrictions. The Court bundled together all the objectionable aspects of posters on the one hand, and a long catalogue of legitimate aims for restriction on the other, in the following way: 'the Court takes the view that the national authorities were reasonably entitled to consider, having regard to all the circumstances of the case, that it was indispensable to ban the campaign in question in order to protect health and morals, protect the rights of others and to prevent crime' (para. 72). But this begs the question—does the alleged advocacy of cloning pose a threat to health, or morals, or the rights of others, or crime control? This impression is strengthened by the Court's (Grand Chamber's) extraordinary admission of its own gullibility in the opening paragraph from which these quotations are taken: 'Even though some of these reasons, taken separately, might not be capable of justifying the impugned refusal, the Court takes the view that the national authorities were reasonably entitled to consider ...' (para. 73). This is a sort of 'several bad arguments make one good argument' theory, and it explains (and at the same time, discredits) the strategy of bundling. Since connecting an interference based on particular objectionable aspects of the posters (say, 'geniocracy') to a particular legitimate aim (say, morals) would show how weak the argument is, the Court simply bundled the arguments together, thus making it impossible to trace the actual basis of the interference to a particular goal. All in all, the *Mouvement Raëlien* decision illustrates, in multiple ways, the pitfalls of an excessively low standard of proportionality. Note also that it is a relatively recent decision (2012)—so the Court cannot be defended on the basis that these were still early days in the development of its proportionality analysis.

There is one other ingredient of the necessity scrutiny that is textually present in the Convention and yet has played virtually no (or very little) role in the necessity scrutiny. It concerns the clause in all of the Convention's articles regarding restrictable rights: restrictions are only allowed if they are necessary '*in a democratic society*' for certain enumerated purposes. The 'democratic society' proviso adds a condition that has been rarely reflected upon. Without it, the architecture of derogation is elegant and simple: a restriction of a right must be 'necessary' in order to attain certain specified goals; the condition of a 'democratic society' adds an additional requirement, upsetting the structure. Literally considered, a right-restricting measure that is necessary in order to attain certain goals but is not consistent with the ideal of a democratic society, is not permissible under the Convention. What might that mean?

Offhand, the condition seems to be redundant and cosmetic only. For one thing, 'democracy' seems to be an attribute of a *state* rather than a *society*: it identifies an institutional political structure rather than societal relationships or phenomena. This is, of course, as a point about general democratic theory (going well beyond the bounds the Convention analysis) an immensely controversial proposition. However, for a *legal* document par excellence, such as the Convention, to refer to eminently vague notions about what is required by a democratic *society* (as opposed to the state) seems odd and impracticable, to say the least. (It is also very unlikely that the Strasbourg judges are well equipped to ascertain factors of a democratic *society*.)[61] Second, it is unclear how the 'democratic society' requirement adds value to the already existing conditions in the Convention. If, arguendo, a state properly implements the Convention rights, and all the restrictions of the rights are legitimate under the derogation rules, it is hard to see how the state can nevertheless be impeached on the basis that its otherwise legitimate restrictions of rights are inconsistent with the ideal of a 'democratic society', whatever it may mean. Put differently: the entire corpus of the Convention rights and the Court's case law constitutes a model of democracy, and the proviso of 'necessity in democratic society' does not seem to add any extra conditions. This triggers a counterfactual question: suppose that the government has successfully defended its right-restricting regulation as 'necessary' for the interests of national security, protection of the rights of others, etc. What would it take to say that they have upheld the burden of the necessity requirement, and yet they still fail to convince us that the restrictions are necessary 'in a democratic society'?

The Court's case law is of little help in answering this question. In the few cases where the Court explicitly takes up the 'democratic society' requirement (in the context of the limiting clauses of Arts. 8–11), it is formulaic and laconic. But it is not entirely meaningless. In *Smith & Grady*, the case concerning the discharge of homosexuals from military service, where, as we have already discussed, the Court found there was a breach of Article 8 at the necessity stage of scrutiny, it 'underline[d] the link between the notion of "necessity" and that of a "democratic society", the hallmarks of the latter including pluralism, tolerance and broadmindedness ...' (para. 87). Almost exactly the same formula was earlier adopted in *Dudgeon*, the case concerning the penalization of homosexual acts, where it was articulated in the following way: 'According to the Court's case-law, a restriction on a Convention right cannot be regarded as "necessary in a democratic society"—two hallmarks of which are tolerance and broadmindedness—unless, among other things, it is proportionate to the legitimate aim pursued ...' (para. 53).

In the eighteen years between *Dudgeon* and *Smith & Grady*, the 'hallmarks' of a democratic society have proliferated from two to three. But this does not

[61] In her thoughtful and critical reconstruction of the Convention's meaning of democracy, Susan Marks attributes to the Convention and the Court the view that '[d]emocracy is seen as primarily about government', Susan Marks, 'The European Convention on Human Rights and Its 'Democratic Society'', (1995) 66 *British Yearbook of International Law* 209, 232. Writing more specifically about democracy in the 'necessary in a democratic society' clauses, Marks says: 'Democracy is taken to be about institutions and procedures of public decision-making', ibid. 232.

matter. The *Dudgeon* formula seems to render the 'democratic society' proviso redundant. Read literally, it says that proportionality to the legitimate aim supersedes any objection based on necessity in a democratic society. It is hard to see how the 'democratic society' proviso can play any independent role under the *Dudgeon* formula. But the *Smith & Grady* formula is subtly different. It posits the 'democratic society' condition as independent, not bracketed by eventual determination of proportionality to the legitimate aim as it is in *Dudgeon*.

Perhaps there is only so much that can be read into the textual detail of judgments. In my view, the 'democratic society' clause acts as a rhetorical device—in the noble rather than pejorative sense of rhetoric as public argumentation meant to persuade the audience ('[w]herever there is a process of public argumentation, there is rhetoric').[62] The 'democratic society' clause is used to 'soften' the audience, as it were, and to prepare it for the conclusion on the issue of breach. No matter what level of margin of appreciation is eventually taken, the values of 'broadmindedness, tolerance and pluralism' attributed to the Convention-mandated 'democratic society' incline the Court—and its audience—to err on the side of the applicant's rights, as opposed to the public goals that may warrant restriction on the rights contained in the Convention.

It is now time to draw provisional conclusions for this section of the chapter. We have seen that goal detection, when it happens, occurs during the course of necessity scrutiny, rather than at the earlier assessment of government-declared goals stage. There is an immediate problem with the tacit rather than explicit determination of goals—a point to which I will return at the end of this chapter. For the moment, it is important to note that some aspects of necessity scrutiny, as conducted by the Court, are better suited to goal detection than others, and that they carry potential for some negative side effects, regardless of the goal detection effort. When the Court uses 'pressing social need' as a proxy for 'necessity', it may be quite effective in goal detection, but there is a risk that the social need will be understood in a self-standing rather than relational way. This decreases the effectiveness of goal detection because it is precisely thanks to the relational aspect of necessity that the true goal may be ascertained. This approach, in particular, may be facilitated (in an unfortunate way) in the 'bundling' of goals, where the Court avoids comparing a specific restriction to a particular individual goal, and instead vaguely considers the need for a restriction in the context of a broad package of objectives.

When the Court uses the proportionality test as a proxy for necessity, it oscillates between two interpretations of the test that it does not care to distinguish. The 'balancing *sensu stricto*' interpretation—involving a comparison of the costs of rights restrictions with the benefits of goal attainment in a particular

62 Neil MacCormick, *Rhetoric and the Rule of Law* (Oxford University Press 2010) 17.

context—has no potential for successful goal detection, because it cannot serve as a reliable proxy for necessity. There may be some measures that are necessary and yet fail the proportionality *sensu stricto* test. When, in turn, the Court applies the relevance-oriented interpretation of the proportionality test, everything depends on the level of scrutiny of proportionality of the measure to the goal: the stricter the scrutiny, the higher the potential for successful goal detection. However, when the Court accords a generous margin of appreciation to the state and, accordingly, lowers the level of scrutiny, the potential for goal detection is all but lost.

4. 'Protection of Morals' and Public Reason

One ground for state interference with citizens' rights raises special issues when considering whether the Court has been pursuing an ideal of public reason. When the Court uses the standard of protection of public morals as one of the legitimate aims of rights restrictions listed by the Convention, its task is qualitatively different from the task of judging the necessity of restrictions from the point of view of public health, safety, national security, or even 'rights and freedoms of others'. Naturally each of these standards lends itself to multiple interpretations, and there is, prima facie, nothing that renders them problematic as 'public reasons'. Furthermore, each of these goals may be interpreted disingenuously. They may be used by a defender of a law in order to cover up some other, 'non-public' reasons—but this is the whole point of necessity scrutiny. It may serve as a means to flush out improper motivations cloaked in the recitation of reasons that are public, but which serve only as a pretext. This is something that was discussed at length in previous sections of this chapter.

The 'protection of morals' ground is different. *Some* moral positions are inconsistent with public reason—but not because they are improperly interpreted, or because they have been misused to cover up some other, improper motivations. They may be antithetical to 'public reason' at their very core, when its interpretation is reasonable, conducted in good faith, and not disingenuous. Some moral positions, under the best interpretation that can be given to them, may strike at the very heart of the ideal of public reason, the point of which is that the motivations of legislation—and, correspondingly, the legislative aims—should be endorsable by all to whom they apply. When a legislator enforces moral positions that, by their very nature, cannot be endorsed by some citizens who must comply with the law, this violates the fundamental rationale of the ideal of public reason: the ideas of liberty, equal citizenship, and respect to all as free and equal citizens, as urged in Chapter 1 of this book. The simple question is, how can this general idea be reconciled with the European Convention's mandate that 'public morals' may serve as a legitimate ground for rights restrictions, since we know (or at least, may suspect) that some moral positions, at least under some interpretations, may be incompatible with public reason?

Some introductory conceptual observations are needed in order to place the European Court's approach to the 'protection of morals' in a broader framework, which will allow us to characterize and assess the Court's jurisprudence in this regard. In particular, two dichotomies are relevant. The first dichotomy contrasts the morally informed legal status of a practice with a moral assessment of the practice itself. Michael Perry, an American constitutional scholar exploring the various intersections of law and morality, has long argued that courts should take into account public morals (in the sense of 'conventional morality', as he occasionally called it).[63] He has, however, provided a strong caveat that in ascertaining conventional morality, the courts should look *not* at social values regarding what is right and wrong, but rather at moral judgements about what immoral behaviour should be legally prohibited. Only those 'commands to which [conventional moral culture] not only subscribes but believes should have the force of law and thus be legally binding on all, subscribers and nonsubscribers alike'[64] should be visible and relevant to courts. Without this distinction, Perry argued, we cannot draw a line between 'private morals' and 'public morals', and only the latter are relevant to the exercise of the judicial function.

There is a temptation, consistent with Perry's usage just described, to reserve the notion of '*public* morals' to moral judgements about the legal status of a particular practice, while all other morality (including private morals) would be about right or wrong per se. However, it would be somewhat counter-intuitive as a terminological fiat—is it really absurd to talk about public morals in a context other than legal prohibitions? For the purpose of our theme in this chapter, it is worth noting that the European Convention does not use the concept of 'public morals', but rather 'morals' *simpliciter*. Not much can be read into this legal drafting, especially since the Court has used both concepts interchangeably, and on occasion has talked about '*public* morals' somewhat contrary to the Convention's text, but it does so seemingly without attaching any significance to this qualifier.[65] But the distinction raised by Perry is very important. Rather than presenting it as an issue of 'public' versus 'private' morals (with predictable

[63] Michael J. Perry, 'Substantive Due Process Revisited: Reflections on (and beyond) Recent Cases', (1976) 71 *Northwestern University Law Review* 417, 446–47, n. 189.

[64] Ibid. 442, footnote omitted. In his more recent writings, Perry came to define 'public morals' as contrasted to 'sectarian morals', the latter being characterized by the fact that it is 'widely contested' (which is also the case of sectarian non-religious beliefs), see Michael J. Perry, *Human Rights in the Constitutional Law of the United States* (Cambridge University Press 2013) 125–26.

[65] See *Müller & Others v. Switzerland*, Judgment of 24 May 1988, Appl. No. 10737/84, paras. 39 (public morals), 43 (public morals), 43 *in fine* (morals), 36 (morals).

objections to the very idea of 'private morals'),[66] it is more prudent to characterize the dichotomy as that of 'first-order' and 'second-order' morals. First-order morals are about judgements concerning the rightness or wrongness of a given practice, while second-order morals are about moral judgements regarding whether and how the practice should be regulated by law. This is an easily recognizable distinction: there is nothing inconsistent about morally condemning abortion and, at the same time, believing that it should be legally available. Indeed, the discontinuity between condemnation and legal tolerance seems to be the test for a genuinely liberal approach to individual rights.

The second dichotomy is between morals in a descriptive sense, understood as conventional moral standards, and morals in a normative sense, consisting of judgements espoused by a speaker. The latter may serve as a standard to criticize the former—but not the other way around. H.L.A. Hart dubbed this distinction (picking up the late nineteenth-century utilitarian terminology) as between 'positive' and 'critical' morality, the former being 'the morality actually accepted and shared by a given social group', while the latter consists of 'the general moral principles used in the criticism of actual social institutions including positive morality'.[67] The target of Hart's criticism was Lord Devlin and his 'legal enforcement of morality' thesis. Hart, at the time, criticized Devlin for using, in a question-begging manner, 'positive morality' in his thesis: 'it would plainly be no sufficient answer [to the question about whether the enforcement of morality is justified] to show that in fact in some societies—our own or others—it was widely regarded as morally quite right and proper to enforce, by legal punishment, compliance with the accepted morality'.[68]

In one of his early essays, Ronald Dworkin used a very similar distinction to criticize Devlin, not for 'his idea that the community's morality counts, but [for] his idea of what counts as the community's morality'.[69] Dworkin's terminology of the antinomy was a moral position in the 'anthropological' rather than 'discriminatory' sense (using, of course, a now anachronistic, non-pejorative meaning of the word). In response to Devlin's use of a moral position in the former sense, Dworkin constructed an elaborate system of criteria for what constitutes a 'moral position'. In order to have one's views registered in the process of lawmaking and to qualify as a holder of a 'moral position', one's views must pass an analytical test that will remove prejudice, irrational emotions, rationalizations, and 'parroting', and also ensure sincerity and consistency within a moral position.[70]

[66] 'I do not think that one can talk sensibly of a public and private morality any more than one can of a public and private highway', Patrick Devlin, *The Enforcement of Morals* (Oxford University Press 1965) 16.

[67] H.L.A. Hart, *Law, Liberty, and Morality* (Stanford University Press 1963) 20.

[68] Ibid. 17–18.

[69] Ronald Dworkin, *Taking Rights Seriously* (Duckworth 1978) 255. Chapter 10, from which this quote is taken, had been initially published as an article in the *Yale Law Journal* in 1964.

[70] Ibid. 248–53.

Table 10.1 Meanings of 'Morals' in Judicial Usage

	Descriptive	Normative
First-order	(1)	(3)
Second-order	(2)	(4)

In my discussion of the ECtHR's approach to the 'protection of morals', I describe this dichotomy as 'descriptive' versus 'normative' senses of morals. It was captured well by Eyal Benvenisti: 'The adjudicating organ must either adopt a moral standard or defer to a relativistic approach based on comparative analysis.'[71]

These two dichotomies (first-order versus second-order morals, and morals in a descriptive versus normative sense) when combined produce four possibilities, as shown in Table 10.1 below.

In (1), a judge makes his or her view dependent on the dominant views about the wrongness (or otherwise) of certain practices, in (2), on the dominant views about what should be prohibited or legally tolerated, regardless of condemnation, in (3), on his or her *own* moral view about the rightness or wrongness of a given practice, and in (4), on his or her own moral view about the limits of prohibition, regardless of condemnation. For the lack of better words, position (1) may be called 'radically moralistic', and position (4), 'radically civil-libertarian' (or rights-protective). Positions (2) and (3) are intermediate, although a moment's reflection suggests that (2) comes much closer to (1) than to (3), and if one were to economize on the evaluative assessment of the ECtHR in this regard, (1) and (2) would be located on one side of the divide, and (3) and (4) on the other. Still, position (2) is a milder form of 'moralism' than (1).

Where does the 'protection of morals' jurisprudence of the ECtHR stand when viewed through this taxonomy? It is not easy to assign the Court's positions to any of the four categories just identified, which is not surprising: judicial opinions are not exercises in legal or moral theory. If, however, one reads the reasoning in those cases where 'protection of morals' was either the only or main factor in the decision, one gets the impression that all four positions are present, with different positions acquiring crucial argumentative value depending on the context. In the *Handyside* case[72]—a foundational decision for the Court's Article 10 jurisprudence, and the one where protection of morals was the *only* legitimate aim claimed by the government and considered by the Court—the Court commenced its 'margin of appreciation' argument with a statement (to be often repeated in the subsequent decisions) that 'it is not possible to find in the domestic

[71] Eyal Benvenisti, 'Margin of Appreciation, Consensus, and Universal Standards', (1999) 31 *NYU Journal of International Law & Politics* 843, 851.

[72] *Handyside v. United Kingdom*, Judgment of 7 December 1976, Appl. No. 5493/72, para. 48.

law of the various Contracting States a uniform conception of morals' (para. 48). It immediately continued: 'The view taken by their representative laws of the requirements of morals varies from time to time as well as from place to place ...' (para. 48). It seems that 'the conception of morals' and the 'requirements of morals' must belong to categories (1) or (2): it is certainly not the judges' 'normative' conception, but a descriptive moral position that appears in these statements. It may apply either to first-order or second-order conceptions. However, the reference inserted later to 'that pluralism, tolerance and broadmindedness without which there is no "democratic society" '(para. 49) suggests that second-order moral positions may figure in the Court's understanding of 'morals', at least alongside first-order positions, since these three values are typically second-order ideals.

The proposition that there is 'no uniform European conception of morals' was repeated in another important Article 10 case, *Müller v. Switzerland*[73] (para. 34), with similar effect. The difference was that in this case, the government cited two grounds for conviction and confiscation of allegedly obscene paintings—the protection of morals and the rights of others (para. 30). The Court effectively bundled these together, by announcing (without any argument) that there is 'a natural link between protection of morals and protection of the right of others' (para. 30). The Court echoed the Swiss courts in saying that 'conceptions of sexual morality have changed in recent years', but immediately followed this proposition by quoting, with approval, the Swiss court's view that the paintings in question were 'liable grossly to offend the sense of sexual propriety of *persons of ordinary sensitivity*' (para. 36, emphasis added). The italicized words, in connection with the fact that the Swiss government's interference in the painter's rights was upheld, suggest that it was category (1) in our taxonomy of moral positions which was taken into account by the Court.

In *Dudgeon*,[74] a decision which preceded *Müller* by seven years, the Court considered the 'protection of morals' jointly with the 'rights of others' as grounds for interference in Article 8—just as in *Müller*. Several statements suggest that, again, it falls under category (1) of the taxonomy of moral positions. Specifically, when scrutinizing the prohibition on homosexuality in Northern Ireland, the Court referred to the 'prevailing conception of sexual morality' at the time of the law's enactment and agreed that the general aim pursued by the legislation 'remains the protection of morals in the sense of *moral standards obtaining in Northern Ireland*' (para. 46 *in fine*, emphasis added). This, in connection with such concepts (used approvingly) as 'the moral ethos or moral standards of a society as a whole' (para. 47, see also para. 49), as well as 'the moral climate in Northern Ireland in sexual matters' and 'the moral fabric of society' (para. 57,

[73] *Müller & Others v. Switzerland*, Judgment of 24 May 1988, Appl. No. 10737/84.
[74] *Dudgeon v. United Kingdom*, Judgment of 22 October 1981, Appl. No. 7525/76.

referring approvingly to the government's submissions), tends to suggest that it is category (1) which dominates—just as in *Handyside* and *Müller*. But there is an important difference. Referring to the fact that 'a substantial body of opinion in Northern Ireland [is] opposed to a change in law [in a liberal direction]', the Court immediately asserts: 'Nevertheless, this cannot of itself be decisive as to the necessity for the interference with the applicant's private life . . .' (para. 59). This is amplified a little further: 'Although members of the public who regard homosexuality as immoral may be shocked . . . this cannot on its own warrant the application of penal sanctions when it is consenting adults alone who are involved' (para. 60). And further: 'the moral attitudes towards male homosexuality in Northern Ireland and the concern that any relaxation in the law would tend to erode existing moral standards cannot, without more, warrant interfering with the applicant's private life to such an extent' (para. 61). No equivalent assertions were made in *Handyside* or *Müller*, and they clearly belong to categories (3) and/or (4): that is, where the Court assumes a normative, critical position towards the conventional moral standards in the country of interference.

Let us note, parenthetically, that in both *Dudgeon* and *Müller* the Court explicitly connected the 'protection of morals' goal with that of protection of 'the rights and freedoms of others', even though these are two *separate* grounds for derogation in the Convention. In *Dudgeon*, where the breach of Article 8 was found in the operation of anti-homosexual laws, the Court said that it was 'somewhat artificial' to draw a rigid distinction between the two grounds because protection of 'moral interests and welfare' may come under both these labels. This is especially so in cases where the legislation in question aims to safeguard vulnerable members of society such as young people, who in this instance, it was argued, were in need of 'special protection' from the 'consequences of homosexual practices' by reason of their dependence or lack of maturity (para. 47). In *Müller*, where no breach of Article 10 was found in anti-obscenity regulations, the Court agreed that 'there is a natural link between protection of morals and the protection for the rights of others' (para. 30). By joining these grounds, the Court implicitly suggested that the 'morals' it has in mind must be equivalent to the conventional rather than critical moral position. If the protection of morals protects the rights of others at the same time, those 'rights of others' must consist of rights against being offended in one's own moral sensitivities, for instance when confronted with obscene paintings, as in *Müller*. This is a moralistic viewpoint *par excellence*, where moralism is understood as a position which mandates prohibition based on one's moral disapproval, without more. When the 'rights of others' are allegedly breached by what is considered to be immoral behaviour, morality is seen as equivalent to conventional moral standards, under which people have a right to be protected against offence to their sensitivities. The matter is slightly different in *Dudgeon* where the Court explicitly interpreted 'the rights of others' as belonging to the youth who must be 'protected' from homosexuality. In contrast to *Müller*, where the moralism discernible in the merging of 'public morals' and 'the rights of others' places it unmistakably in category (1) in our taxonomy, the *Dudgeon* merger of these two categories is softened by an aspect of protecting the youth against the 'harm' of homosexuality, as the Court saw it in 1981.

Norris,[75] a 1988 case concerning an anti-homosexuality law in Ireland, was very similar to *Dudgeon* in all relevant respects. For example, it was also based on the 'protection of morals' as the sole goal cited by the government and recognized by the Court, and also ended by finding that Article 8 was breached. Significantly, the Court rests its conclusion on the issue of breach on the dictum, quoted from *Dudgeon*, that the very fact that some members of the public may be shocked in itself cannot warrant penal sanctions (para. 46 *in fine*, quoting *Dudgeon* para. 60). So again, the Court applied a normative, or critical, notion of 'morals' in the key part of its argument.

Fast forward to 2012, and to the *Mouvement Raëlien*.[76] Here, as we have seen earlier in this chapter, 'public morals' was one of a large number of the 'goals' cited by the government, and uncritically recognized as legitimate by the Court, alongside the goals of prevention of crime, protection of health, and protection of the rights of others (para. 54). As we have also seen, the 'bundling' of these aims together into a single aggregate set renders it virtually impossible to trace the understanding, and the role, of any particular aim by the Court. But when one reads the judgment, and especially the First Section's judgment on which the Grand Chamber fully and unreservedly relies, one gets the impression that the 'protection of morals' plays, at best, a cosmetic role in the bundle. There is not a single passage, in either of the two judgments, where 'protection of morals' appears as an independent factor in the argument, and so it is impossible to analyse the Court's own understanding of those 'morals'. But of more importance than what the Court says is what the Court does *not* say. Having at its disposal a large inventory of maxims and dicta on public morals, including those on the irrelevance of the mere fact of societal disapproval of a practice (e.g. in *Dudgeon* or *Norris*, as just noted), the Court never relied on any such proposition. In other words, it never crosses the line dividing positions (1) and (2) on the one hand and (3) and (4) on the other. This was depicted and criticized, with great eloquence, in one of the dissenting opinions. Having recognized that the *Mouvement Raëlien* is 'undeniably in a minority position precisely because of its unpopular views', Judges Sajó et al. assert that the interference was based on 'the authorities' fear of being seen to be associated with an unpopular, even offensive, view', and go on to declare: 'Freedom of expression cannot be left to strive under the dictates of governmental fear of public sensitivities'.[77] It is hard to find a better statement of a position belonging to category (4) in our taxonomy.

[75] *Norris v. Ireland*, Judgment of 26 October 1988, Appl. No. 10581/83.

[76] *Mouvement Raëlien Suisse v. Switzerland*, Grand Chamber Judgment of 13 July 2012, Appl. No. 16354/06.

[77] Joint dissenting opinion of Sajó, Lazarova Trajkovska, and Vučinić, JJ., Part V *in fine*.

To conclude this section of the chapter: there is no single, coherent notion of 'morals' in the Court's jurisprudence of the 'protection of morals'. The Court does not make it clear whether it uses 'morals' in the first-order or the second-order sense, and whether it applies moral standards in a descriptive or normative/critical sense.[78] In fact, the Court oscillates between all these meanings, depending on the context and on the rhetorical use necessitated by the conclusions to its reasoning. Since the use of the 'protection of morals' as an aim justifying rights restrictions lends itself to excessive restrictions of rights (based, for instance, on the mere fact of moral reprobation for a particular practice),[79] and because it lends itself to usages which are antithetical to public reason (because some moral positions, in a descriptive sense, may be damaging to the value of public reason), this oscillation is unfortunate. The Court, if it were faithful to the fundamental principle of the effective protection of Convention rights, should only use 'public morals' as a ground for restriction of rights sparingly. It should be careful not to allow the interpretation of rights to degenerate into a form of legal moralism, under which the very fact of a particular moral reprobation for otherwise harmless acts translates into legal restrictions. It should also renounce forms of moral perfectionism under which some conceptions of the good life (including conceptions of sexual morality, or of artistic expression, or of associating with the 'right' people) are recognized by the authorities as superior to others, and enjoy legal protection for this superiority, especially through restrictions upon the practices considered morally inferior. It is all too easy to proudly proclaim a right as a norm, but then undermine it by restrictions alleged to serve '[public] morals'. If 'public morals' is understood in a first-order, descriptive way, as the conventional morality of a given society, and (for the sake of argument) this conventional morality is intolerant and oppressive, the 'morals' exception will swallow that right. Similarly, if the 'rights of others' are understood as the rights not to be offended or upset by someone else's behaviour that produces moral offence, the value of a Convention right will become negligible.

More fundamentally though, the questions regarding the meaning of 'morals', in the 'protection of morals' cases, should have been elaborated by the Court at the scrutiny of the legitimacy of legislative goals stage. This is because this kind of analytical positioning might have compelled the Court to establish that some asserted aspects of 'protection of morals' do not belong to protected morals at all, and so cannot form part of a 'legitimate aim' in the first place.[80] The Court would have to openly tackle the issue of whether morals, used in the sense of a legitimate legislative aim in the Convention, include those moral standards

[78] See, similarly, though using a different conceptual framework, Christopher Nowlin, 'The Protection of Morals under the European Convention for the Protection of Human Rights and Fundamental Freedoms', (2002) 24 *Human Rights Quarterly* 264.

[79] See Letsas, *A Theory of Interpretation* (n. 26) 120–23.

[80] See, similarly, Kai Möller, *The Global Model of Constitutional Rights* (Oxford University Press 2012) 183.

that are based merely on moral reprobation for someone's harmless action. The Court would also have to openly wrestle with the relationship between the protection of morals and the rights of others, including the question of whether we have a right not to be morally offended by someone's harmless conduct or lifestyle. On the rare occasions when it was conducted, discussion of the 'protection of morals' was relegated by the Court to the necessity stage, and this helped the Court to avoid articulating its understanding of morals. The Court could have behaved as if the notion of 'morals' was clear, and all that was required was to check the necessity of the measure to protect this goal. As the discussion above shows, 'morals'—in the 'protection of morals' ground—are anything but self-explanatory.

* * *

As it was shown in this chapter, the main burden of aim scrutiny (a place where we can try to discern expressions of the public reason approach) has been shifted to the necessity stage, where the Court considers whether restrictions were necessary (in a democratic society) to attain this aim. In purely practical terms, the transfer of goal analysis from the aim scrutiny stage to the necessity scrutiny stage may not have mattered: the outcome may have been the same. In all these cases, it may therefore be the case that breaches of the Convention *would have* been established at the aim scrutiny stage even if the breaches were actually found on the basis of the defective necessity link. So what does it matter?

If the only downside of the Court's puzzling gullibility at the aim scrutiny stage were the undermining of an elegant architecture of canonical reasoning, and of clarity in the Court's argument, then the Court can probably be excused for its strategy of evaluating the goals in a roundabout, surreptitious manner, rather than candidly and explicitly, at the stage of the argument when it was supposed to do so. However, clarity of argument is only one among the ideals that the Court pursues in its public reason-giving; another is that of legitimacy. It may be argued, and it is my primary hypothesis for explaining the reasons underlying the Court's adoption of this strategy, that questioning the state at the aim ascertainment stage—in practice, accusing the state of being disingenuous in providing aims which act as mere pretexts, while the true aims were of a much less wholesome character—brings the Court into a head-on collision course with the state, and risks weakening the Court's legitimacy, which is tenuous at the best of times anyway. It *may* be argued that postponing the exercise of aim ascertainment to a later stage and hiding it within the much more technical and complex necessity scrutiny stage, helps the Court to reduce reputational losses for the state found eventually to be in breach of the Convention, and thereby to maintain its legitimacy capital through a shrewd exercise in judicial diplomacy. After all, if the legislative restrictions are found 'unnecessary' to achieve a stated aim, it sounds more like an *error* on the part of the state. If, in contrast, the state is found to publicly provide an aim that is not credible under the circumstances, it sounds much more like *deceit*. If you are a state, you would rather be found to be mistaken rather than dishonest.

The force of this explanation (and consequent justification) is, nevertheless, limited. For one thing, the condemnation of a state may be also quite harsh and damaging when it is made at the necessity scrutiny stage. If necessity is blatantly missing, the only implication is that the government provided disingenuous aims concealing the true motives for a restriction. More importantly, however, the necessity scrutiny, at least as it is conceptualized and adopted as canonical by the Court, is an imperfect device for discerning the true goals of legislation—as shown in section 3 of this chapter. When necessity is translated into 'a pressing social need', the temptation for the Court is to consider it as a self-standing rather than a relational concept, in which case its capacity to ascertain goals is lost. When necessity is viewed through the prism of proportionality, the Court's capacity for goal ascertainment decreases with the lowered standard of proportionality (based on the broadening of the 'margin of appreciation'). The less strict a scrutiny of proportionality, the less capable the proportionality analysis is to serve as a proxy for necessity, in turn reducing latter standard's potential as a tool for credible goal ascertainment.

Appeals to the 'protection of morals' as one of the Convention-mandated legitimate grounds for rights restrictions raise partly similar and partly different issues from those just mentioned. One similarity rests on the fact that ambivalence about the meaning of 'morals' has allowed the Court to avoid assessing the credibility of citing this particular aim: if assessment of the aim were undertaken right at the 'legitimate goals' scrutiny stage, the Court would have had to explicate its own understanding of 'morals' for the purposes of Convention analysis. It has never done so because in the 'protection of morals' cases, the Court has also used (or under-used) the 'legitimate goal' stage in the manner described above—in a cursory, perfunctory, and non-critical way. The Court has never explained to the European public, therefore, whether the aim of protecting some sections of the public from the offence caused by certain practices held immoral by the majority can constitute part of the legitimate aim of 'protecting morals'. Rather, as shown in section 4 of this chapter, it has oscillated between a moralistic approach, whereby the fact of majoritarian condemnation counts as an argument for prohibition, and a liberal position, whereby moral standards held in the community do not warrant, per se, restrictive measures. Also, in failing to recognize the difference between moral positions regarding rightness or wrongness, and moral positions regarding legal tolerance or prohibition, the Court has failed to establish clear standards for the 'protection of morals' exception and helped to maintain (in an unfortunate way) its rights-restrictive potential.

Afterword

There is a temptation for the author of a book to use the 'Afterword' as a place to rehearse and reaffirm, briefly and in a triumphantly declaratory way, all the main lessons to be drawn from the individual chapters. I shall resist this temptation, and instead will only affirm what I take to be the most important point of the book; and secondly, issue a caveat about the modest ambitions behind the book.

The main point is this: a plausible conception of the common good, in a diverse and democratically governed society, is one which refers to legitimate motives for proposing and enacting collective, authoritative decisions, which can be applied to, and complied with, by those who do not necessarily agree with the substantive merits of those decisions. Concretization of such a conception can be found in the idea of public reason (PR), elaborated upon with some sophistication by political liberals, and most influentially by John Rawls. This idea resonates with a popular constitutional doctrine which calls for the invalidation of laws tainted by wrong (i.e. unconstitutional) motives: PR may be a useful tool in identifying which motives should be found unconstitutional. Any scrutiny that relies upon the second-guessing of actual legislative motives is prima facie unworkable; hence, what is needed is an objectified approach to motives, which can be detected through the reasonableness analysis based upon arguing from the effects back to (the most likely) motives. This is especially necessary when we do not have reliable evidence of the legislator's actual motives (though sometimes we *do have* this). But there are limits to the arbitrary manufacturing of reasons, and the test of PR is of value not only in the scrutiny (*à la* constitutional court) of laws already enacted, but also as an appeal to lawmakers (including the citizens acting as 'popular legislators') that only some *types* of arguments should be used in public discourse: namely arguments that can be endorsed by those who do not necessarily agree with the specific merits of the proposal. While at first blush it may be seen as a prescription for hypocrisy and 'political correctness', in fact the test of PR may play an important therapeutic and reflexive role: it may teach us to only use arguments in public discourse which are respectful of other fellow-citizens who may disagree along the dimensions of differing ideologies, religions, and philosophical outlooks.

PR as defended throughout this book is therefore a characteristically *liberal* ideal, and so the book may be seen as an interpretation of liberal constitutionalism. In Will Kymlicka's words: 'Liberal citizens must justify their political demands in terms that fellow citizens can understand and accept as consistent with their status as free and equal citizens. It requires a conscientious effort to distinguish those beliefs that are matters of private faith from those that are capable of public defence . . .'[1] But not all conceptions that posit restrictions on the *reasons* for laws are liberal. Consider a famous idea by Jean-Jacques Rousseau, that only those votes in the assembly that are aimed at identifying the public good (*volonté générale*) lead to legitimate outcomes, and that those parliamentarians who vote in accordance with their or their constituency's self-interest simply answer the wrong question.[2] It is surely a limit upon the sort of *reasons* which may render the law legitimate, and yet in the context of the broader political philosophy of Rousseau, it is not a liberal idea. Everything depends upon what *sort* of reasons are excluded by a given principle. If, for example, the reasons that are excluded are those that are inconsistent with the 'reason of state', understood in an anti-individualistic way (which, of course, is only one among many ways of understanding '*raison d'état*'), then it *is* a reasons-constraining idea, but it is certainly not liberal. Hence: only some reason-constraining conceptions are liberal. And vice versa, not all liberals are committed to PR as a reasons-restricting device. The idea of PR is only a subset of a broader liberal theory; for instance, one may adopt a typically liberal 'harm principle', or any of its equivalents, as a basis for restricting a state's interference with individual liberty and then justify it on non-public grounds. In a recent article, Jason Tyndal observes, correctly: 'It is the endorsement of a requirement of public justification that most clearly demarcates public reason liberalism from other versions of liberalism.'[3]

Further, the idea of PR is narrower than the general idea of justifiability because, in addition to the duty to justify, it provides standards for *what* reasons can be produced in the justification of the rules (i.e. that they should be such that they are not reasonably rejectable by any reasonable people). This move from *justifiability* to *acceptability*, which underlies the idea of PR, has been outlined by Bernard Williams (though not in the context of specifically discussing PR) in the following stylized steps:[4] every use of coercion by one group towards another requires legitimation (Williams dubbed it the Basic Legitimation Demand); the claim of a state to authority requires a legitimation to be given to every subject; some rationalizations of disadvantage, for instance in terms of race or gender, are invalid; hierarchical (or authoritative) structures are not self-legitimating; the absence of legitimation increases their coerciveness, and so the Basic Legitimation Demand yields 'a constraint of roughly equal acceptability (acceptability to each subject)'.[5] This is an eloquent, if somewhat roundabout, way of reaching the same destination as that leading to PR.

[1] Will Kymlicka, *Politics in the Vernacular* (Oxford University Press 2001) 296–97.

[2] See the discussion in Chapter 1, section 1, above.

[3] Jason Tyndal, 'Public Reason, Non-Public Reasons, and the Accessibility Requirement', (2019) 49 *Canadian Journal of Philosophy* 1062, 1064.

[4] Bernard Williams, *In the Beginning Was the Deed* (Princeton University Press 2005) 3–7.

[5] Ibid. 7.

So much for the main point of this book, as far as its normative message is concerned. Now for the caveat which I have anticipated at the beginning of these concluding remarks. As a reader would have noticed, the argument in the book has oscillated between the descriptive and the normative, between the Is and the Ought of constitutional argument. At the descriptive level, I attempted to show that many constitutional courts (but also politicians, academic lawyers, public commentators, etc.) often use arguments that resonate strongly with the ideal of PR. Like Monsieur Jourdain of Molière's play who spoke prose without knowing it, many judges (and other lawyers) often use PR-like patterns of argument without realizing it, or at least without acknowledging it openly. This is no wonder because PR is a par excellence philosophical notion, and the dominant 'modalities' of legal arguments are such that they do not lend themselves to an outright importation of moral-philosophical arguments.[6] If anything (and to borrow a recent rich and intriguing conceptual framework suggested recently by David Pozen and Adam Samaha), it may seem to be a constitutional 'anti-modality': it introduces the type of philosophical normative argument directly into constitutional reasoning that traditional canons of constitutional interpretation abhor (even though the whole function of Rawlsian public reason is to abstain from shaping constitutional law to match a particular, sectarian, comprehensive moral-religious position). But this fact should not prevent us, the commentators, from making sense of such real-life constitutional arguments in terms of a philosophical template that goes unacknowledged by judges and legislators, rather like adherents to the Economic Analysis of Law believe that some of the most plausible (to them) legal rules or decisions can be best articulated in terms of the pursuit of wealth maximization, even if the authors of those rules or decisions abstained from such a conceptualization. In this sense, PR may be seen as a heuristic device used to best understand, explain, and justify many laws and regulations, both in their national and supranational dimensions.

At the normative level, the argument of the book proposes that PR is an attractive standard for constitutional reasoning. Not only is it warranted by the grand ideals of respect for persons, equality. and freedom, but moreover, when actually discernible in real-life acts and judgements, it matches many of our strong moral intuitions about, for instance, freedom of speech, freedom of religion, or anti-discrimination laws. In each of these, and in many other legal areas, PR may serve as a convincing ideal that may help answer questions about the legitimacy of laws in controversial cases. It may provide that badly needed tie-breaker when we are in two minds about a given issue. And, to carry on for a moment the analogy with the Economic Analysis of Law drawn in the preceding

[6] See David E. Pozen and Adam M. Samaha, 'Anti-Modalities', (2021) 119 *Michigan Law Review* 729.

paragraph, when a given law or decision fails to implement its normative ideal, it may serve as the basis for a critique.

At both these levels, constitutional PR as proposed in this book has relatively modest ambitions. At the descriptive level, it does not argue that *all*, or the majority of the compelling legal rules and decisions in democratic-liberal states (because this is the proper habitat for PR) give effect to the ideal of PR. At the normative level, it does not urge that whenever a law on a controversial or difficult matter is needed, it should follow the ideal of PR. As a heuristic device and as a normative ideal, PR does not have the imperialist aspiration of occupying the entire constitutional field. But I do not want, in these last words, to protest too much. PR explains a lot, and it warrants a lot: not everything, but much. To prove more—that PR is *the only* plausible heuristic and normative device—would take another book, and another author.

Bibliography

Ackerman B.A., 'Beyond *Carolene Products*', (1985) 98 *Harvard Law Review* 713.

Ackerman Bruce, *We The People: Foundations* (Harvard University Press 1991).

Alexander Lawrence A., 'Introduction: Motivation and Constitutionality', (1978) 15 *San Diego Law Review* 925.

Alter Karen J., Laurence R. Helfer, and Jacqueline R. McAllister, 'A New International Human Rights Court for West Africa: The ECOWAS Community Court of Justice', (2013) 107 *American Journal of International Law* 737.

Alvarez Maria, 'Reasons for Action: Justification, Motivation, Explanation' in Edward N. Zalta (ed.), *The Stanford Encyclopedia of Philosophy* (Winter 2017 edn.), https://plato.stanford.edu/entries/reasons-just-vs-expl/ (last accessed 2 August 2022).

Amyot G. Grant, '"A Matter of Philosophical Preference?" Political Philosophy and Judicial Reasoning in the *Sauvé* case', (2011) 29 *National Journal of Constitutional Law* 1.

Anderson Elizabeth, 'What is the Point of Equality?', (1991) 109 *Ethics* 287.

Arneson Richard J., 'Neutrality and Utility', (1990) 20 *Canadian Journal of Philosophy* 215

Audi Robert, 'The Separation of Church and State and the Obligations of Citizenship', (1989) 18 *Philosophy & Public Affairs* 259.

Baer Judith A., *Equality Under the Constitution* (Cornell University Press 1983) 139.

Barak Aharon, 'Proportionality and Principled Balancing', (2010) 4 *Law & Ethics of Human Rights* 1.

Barak Aharon, *Proportionality: Constitutional Rights and their Limitations* (Cambridge University Press 2012).

Barron Jerome A. and C. Thomas Dienes, *First Amendment Law in a Nutshell* (West Publishing 1993).

Barry Brian, *Political Argument* (Routledge & Kegan Paul 1965).

Barry Brian, *Culture and Equality* (Polity Press 2001).

Baur Michael, 'On Actualizing Public Reason', (2003–04) 72 *Fordham Law Review* 2153.

Beck Ulrich, *Cosmopolitan Vision* trans. Ciaran Cronin (Polity Press 2006).

Beitz Charles R., *The Idea of Human Rights* (Oxford University Press 2009).

Benhabib Seyla, 'Is There a Human Right to Democracy? Beyond Interventionism and Indifference' in Claudio Corradetti (ed.), *Philosophical Dimensions of Human Rights* (Springer 2012).

Benvenisti Eyal, 'Margin of Appreciation, Consensus, and Universal Standards', (1999) 31 *NYU Journal of International Law & Politics* 843.

Berlin Isaiah, *Four Essays on Liberty* (Oxford University Press 1969).

Berman Paul Schiff, *Global Legal Pluralism* (Cambridge University Press 2012).

Beshle Donald L., 'God Bless the Child? The Use of Religion as a Factor in Child Custody and Adoption Proceedings', (1989) 58 *Fordham Law Review* 383.

Besson Samantha, 'The Authority of International Law—Lifting the State Veil', (2009) 31 *Sydney Law Review* 343.

Bice Scott H., 'Motivational Analysis as a Complete Explanation of the Justification Process', (1978) 15 *San Diego Law Review* 1131.

Bickel Alexander M., *The Least Dangerous Branch* (Bobbs-Merrill 1962).

Blake Michael, 'Toleration and Reciprocity: Commentary on Martha Nussbaum and Henry Shue', (2002) 1 *Politics, Philosophy & Economics* 325.

Bohman James, 'From *Demos* to *Demoi*: Democracy across Borders', (2005) 18 *Ratio Juris* 293.

Brest Paul, 'Palmer v. Thompson: An Approach to the Problem of Unconstitutional Legislative Motive', (1971) *Supreme Court Review* 95.

Brownlie Ian, *Principles of Public International Law* (2nd edn., Oxford University Press 1973).

Buchanan Allen, 'Rawls's Law of Peoples: Rules for a Vanished Westphalian World', (2000) 110 *Ethics* 697.

Buchanan Allen, 'Human Rights and the Legitimacy of the International Order', (2008) 14 *Legal Theory* 39.

Buchanan Allen and Robert O. Keohane, 'The Legitimacy of Global Governance Institutions', (2006) 20 *Ethics & International Affairs* 405.

Campbell Tom, 'Unlawful Discrimination' in Wojciech Sadurski (ed.), *Ethical Dimensions of Legal Theory* (Rodopi 1991) 153.

Carter Barry E. and Phillip R. Trimble, *International Law* (2nd edn., Little, Brown 1995).

Carter Stephen L., 'The Resurrection of Religious Freedom?', (1993) 107 *Harvard Law Review* 118.

Cass Deborah, *The Constitutionalization of the World Trade Organization: Legitimacy, Democracy and Community in the International Trading System* (Oxford University Press 2005).

Chandrachud Chintan (2016), 'Proportionality, Judicial Reasoning, and the Supreme Court', University of Cambridge Legal Studies Research Paper No. 12/2016, available on SSRN: https://papers.ssrn.com/sol3/papers.cfm?abstract_id=2720080.

Choudhry Sujit, 'So What is the Real Legacy of *Oakes*? Two Decades of Proportionality Analysis under the Canadian *Charter*'s Section 1', (2006) 34 *Supreme Court Law Review* 501.

Christie George C., *The Notion of an Ideal Audience in Legal Argument* (Kluwer 2000).

Clark J. Morris, 'Legislative Motivation and Fundamental Rights in Constitutional Law', (1978) 15 *San Diego Law Review* 953.

Clérico Laura, 'Limitaciones a los derechos constitucionales y control de razonabilidad (control de proporcionalidad)' in Julio César Rivera et al. (eds.), *Tratado de Derechos Constitucionales. vol I.* (Abeledo Perrot 2014) 507.

Cohen G.A., 'Where the Action is: On the Site of Distributive Justice', (1997) 26 *Philosophy & Public Affairs* 3.

Cohen Joshua, 'Deliberation and Democratic Legitimacy' in David Estlund (ed.), *Democracy* (Blackwell 2002) 87.

Cohen Joshua, 'Minimalism about Human Rights: The Most we Can Hope For?', (2004) 12 *Journal of Political Philosophy* 190.

Cohen Joshua and Charles F. Sabel, 'Global Democracy?', (2004-5) 37 *NYU Journal of International Law & Politics* 763.

Cohen-Eliya Moshe and Iddo Porat, *Proportionality and Constitutional Culture* (Cambridge University Press 2013).

Conçado Trindade Antônio Augusto, 'Compliance with judgments and decisions – The experience of the Inter-American Court of Human Rights: a reassessment', in *Dialogue between judges*, European Court of Human Rights, Council of Europe, 2014, 10-17 at 13 (available at http://www.echr.coe.int/Documents/Dialogue_2014_ENG.pdf (last accessed 17 June 2020).

Cunningham Frank, *Theories of Democracy* (Routledge 2002).

Curtis Kelsey, 'The Partiality of Neutrality', (2018) 41 *Harvard Journal of Law & Public Policy* 935.

Darwall Stephen, 'Two Kinds of Respect', (1977) 88 *Ethics* 88.

Darwall Stephen, 'Authority and Reasons: Exclusionary and Second-Personal', (2010) 120 *Ethics* 257De Búrca Gráinne, 'Developing Democracy Beyond the State', (2008) 46 *Columbia Journal of Transnational Law* 221.

Den Otter Ronald C., *Judicial Review in an Age of Moral Pluralism* (Cambridge University Press 2009).

Den Otter Ronald C., 'The Importance of Constitutional Public Reason' in Silje Langvatn, Mattias Kumm, and Wojciech Sadurski (eds.), *Public Reason and Courts* (Cambridge University Press 2020) 66.

Dershowitz Alan M., *Why Terrorism Works* (Yale University Press 2002).

Desmedt Axel, 'Proportionality in WTO Law', (2001) 4 *Journal of International Economic Law* 441.

Diggs B.J., 'The Common Good as Reason for Political Action', (1973) 83 *Ethics* 283.

Dixon Rosalind and Tom Ginsburg, 'Deciding Not to Decide: Deferral in Constitutional Design', (2011) 9 *International Journal of Constitutional Law* 636.

Doheny Shannon L., 'Free Exercise Does Not Protect Animal Sacrifice: The Misconception of *Church of Lukumi Babalu Aye v. City of Hialeah* and Constitutional Solutions for Stopping Animal Sacrifice', (2006) 2 *Journal of Animal Law* 121.

Dothan Shai, 'How International Courts Enhance Their Legitimacy', (2013) 14 *Theoretical Inquiries in Law* 455.

Downs Anthony, *An Economic Theory of Democracy* (Harper and Row 1957).

Dryzek John S., *Deliberative Democracy and Beyond* (Oxford University Press 2000).

Dunoff Jeffrey L., 'The Politics of International Constitutions: The Curious Case of the World Trade Organization' in Jeffrey L. Dunoff and Joel P. Trachtman (eds.), *Ruling the World? Constitutionalism, International Law, and Global Governance* (Cambridge University Press 2009) 178.

Dupuy Pierre-Marie, *L'unité de l'ordre juridique international: Cours général de droit international public* (Martinus Nijhoff 2003).

Dworkin Gerald, 'Paternalism' in Ralf Sartorius (ed.), *Paternalism* (University of Minnesota Press 1983) 19.

Dworkin Ronald, *Taking Rights Seriously* (Duckworth 1978).

Dworkin Ronald, *A Matter of Principle* (Harvard University Press, 1985).

Dworkin Ronald, *Law's Empire* (Fontana 1986).

Dworkin Ronald, *Sovereign Virtue* (Harvard University Press 2000).

Dworkin Ronald, 'Hart's Postscript and the Character of Political Philosophy', (2004) 34 *Oxford Journal of Legal Studies* 1.

Dworkin Ronald, *Justice in Robes* (Harvard University Press 2005).

Dworkin Ronald, *Is Democracy Possible Here?* (Princeton University Press 2006).

Dworkin Ronald, *Justice for Hedgehogs* (Harvard University Press 2011).

Dworkin Ronald, 'A New Philosophy of International Law', (2013) 41 *Philosophy & Public Affairs* 2.

Eberle Christopher J., *Religious Conviction in Liberal Politics* (Cambridge University Press 2013).

Eisenberg Theodore 'Reflections on a Unified Theory of Motive', (1978) 15 *San Diego Law Review* 1147.

Elefthariadis Pavlos, *Legal Rights* (Oxford University Press 2008).

Elster Jon, 'The Market and the Forum: Three Varieties of Political Theory' in Jon Elster and Aanund Hylland (eds.), *Foundations of Social Choice Theory* (Cambridge University Press 1986) 103.

Elster Jon, 'Deliberation and Constitution Making' in Jon Elster (ed.), *Deliberative Democracy* (Cambridge University Press 1998) 97.

Ely John Hart, 'The Constitutionality of Reverse Racial Discrimination', (1974) 41 *University of Chicago Law Review* 723.

Ely John Hart, *Democracy and Distrust* (Harvard University Press 1980).

Enoch David, 'The Disorder of Public Reason', (2013) 124 *Ethics* 141.

Enoch David, 'Political Philosophy and Epistemology: The Case of Public Reason' in David Sobel, Peter Vallentyne, and Steven Wall (eds.), *Oxford Studies in Political Philosophy*, vol. 3 (Oxford University Press 2017), Oxford Scholarship Online, doi 10.1093/oso/9780198801221.001.0001.

Eriksen Erik O., *The Unfinished Democratization of Europe* (Oxford University Press: Oxford 2009).

European Court of Human Rights, 'Seminar Background Paper: Implementation of the Judgments of the European Court of Human Rights: A Shared Judicial Responsibility?' (2014), http://www.echr.coe.int/Documents/Seminar_background_paper_2014_ENG.pdf. (accessed 7 September 2022)

Falk Richard and Andrew Strauss, 'On the Creation of a Global Peoples Assembly: Legitimacy and the Power of Popular Sovereignty', (2000) 36 *Stanford Journal of International Law* 191.

Fallon Jr., Richard H., 'The Supreme Court, 1996 Term—Foreword: Implementing the Constitution', (1997) 111 *Harvard Law Review* 54.

Fallon, Jr.,Richard H., 'Constitutionally Forbidden Legislative Intent', (2016) 130 *Harvard Law Review* 523.

Fassbender Bardo, 'The United Nations Charter as Constitution of the International Community', (1998) 36 *Columbia Journal of Transnational Law* 529

Finnis John, *Natural Law and Natural Rights* (Oxford University Press 1980).

Fitzgerald P.J., Acting and Refraining', (1967) 27 *Analysis* 133.

Flanders Chad, 'The Mutability of Public Reason', (2012) 25 *Ratio Juris* 180

Foisneau Luc, 'Gouverner selon la volonté générale: la souveraineté selon Rousseau et les théories de la raison d'État', (2007) 3 *Les Études philosophiques* 463.

Follesdal Andreas, 'When Common Interests Are Not Common: Why the Global Basic Structure Should be Democratic', (2009) 16 *Indiana Journal of Global Legal Studies* 585.

Forst Rainer, 'The Justification of Human Rights and the Basic Right to Justification: A Reflexive Approach', (2010) 120 *Ethics* 711.

Forst Rainer, 'Justice, Democracy and the Right for Justification: Reflections on Jürgen Neyer's Normative Theory of the European Union' in Dimitry Kochenov, Gráinne de Búrca, and Andrew Williams (eds.), *Europe's Justice Deficit?* (Hart 2015) 227.

Franck Thomas M., *The Power of Legitimacy Among Nations* (Oxford University Press 1990).

Franck Thomas M., 'The Emerging Right to Democratic Governance', (1992) 86 *American Journal of International Law* 46.

Franck Thomas M., *Fairness in International Law and Institutions* (Oxford University Press 1998).

Frankfurt Harry G., 'Freedom of Will and the Concept of a Person', (1971) 68 *Journal of Philosophy* 5.

Freeman Samuel, 'Political Liberalism and the Possibility of a Just Democratic Constitution', (1994) 69 *Chicago-Kent Law Review* 619.

Freeman Samuel (ed.), *The Cambridge Companion to Rawls* (Cambridge University Press 2003).

Freeman Samuel, 'Introduction: John Rawls—An Overview' in Samuel Freeman (ed.), *The Cambridge Companion to Rawls* (Cambridge University Press 2003) 1.

Freeman Samuel, 'Public Reason and Political Justifications', (2004) 72 *Fordham Law Review* 2021, 2055.

Freeman Samuel, *Justice and the Social Contract* (Oxford University Press 2007).

Freeman Samuel, 'Democracy, Religion & Public Reason', (2020) 149(3) *Daedalus* 37.

Fried Charles, 'Types', (1997) 14 *Constitutional Commentary* 55.

Friedrich C.J., *Constitutional Reason of State* (Brown University Press 1957).

Galston William A., *Liberal Purposes* (Cambridge University Press 2002).

Galston William A., 'Symposium Response', (2007) 1 *Journal of Law, Philosophy and Culture* 191.

Gardbaum Stephen, 'Limiting Constitutional Rights', (2007) 54 *UCLA Law Review* 789.

Garrett Brandon L., 'Unconstitutionally Illegitimate Discrimination', (2018) 104 *Virginia Law Review* 1741.

Gaus Gerald, *The Order of Public Reason* (Cambridge University Press 2011).

Giudice Michael, 'Global Legal Pluralism: What's Law Got to Do with it?' (Book review of Paul Shiff Berman, *Global Legal Pluralism* (Cambridge University Press 2012)), (2014) 34 *Oxford Journal of Legal Studies* 589.

Glendon Mary Ann, *Rights Talk* (The Free Press 1991).

Goodin Robert E., 'Laundering Preferences' in Jon Elster and Aanund Hylland (eds.), *Foundations of Social Choice Theory* (Cambridge University Press 1986) 75.

Goodin Robert E., 'Institutionalizing the Public Interest: The Defense of Deadlock and Beyond', (1996) 90 *American Political Science Review* 331.

Goodin Robert E., *Reflective Democracy* (Oxford University Press 2003).

Green Leslie, 'Two Worries about Respect for Persons', (2010) 120 *Ethics* 212.

Greenawalt Kent, *Private Consciences and Public Reasons* (Oxford University Press 1995).

Greer Steven, *The European Convention on Human Rights: Achievements, Problems and Prospects* (Cambridge University Press 2006).

Grimm Dieter, 'Proportionality in Canadian and German Constitutional Jurisprudence', (2007) 57 *University of Toronto Law Review* 383.

Grossman Nienke, 'Legitimacy and International Adjudicative Bodies', (2009) 41 *The George Washington International Law Review* 107.

Gunther Gerald, 'The Supreme Court, 1971 Term—Foreword: In Search of Evolving Doctrine on a Changing Court: A Model for a Newer Equal Protection', (1978) 86 *Harvard Law Review* 1.

Gutmann Amy and Dennis Thompson, *Democracy and Disagreement* (Harvard University Press 1996).

Habermas Jürgen, *The Inclusion of the Other: Studies in Political Theory* (MIT Press 1998).

Hardin Russell, 'Public Choice Versus Democracy' in John W. Chapman and Alan Wertheimer (eds.), *Majorities and Minorities: Nomos XXXII* (New York University Press 1990) 184.

Harsanyi John C., 'On Preferences, Promises, and the Coordination Problem: Reply to Regan', (1985) 96 *Ethics* 68.

Hart H.L.A., *The Concept of Law* (Oxford University Press 1961).

Hart H.L.A., *Law, Liberty, and Morality* (Stanford University Press 1962).

Hart H.L.A., *Law, Liberty, and Morality* (Stanford University Press 1963).

Hartley Christie and Lori Watson, *Equal Citizenship and Public Reason: A Feminist Political Liberalism* (Oxford University Press 2018).

Held David, *Democracy and the Global Order* (Stanford University Press 1995).

Helfer Laurence R., 'Constitutional Analogies in the International Legal System', (2003) 37 *Loyola of Los Angeles Law Review* 193.

Helfer Laurence R. and Anne-Marie Slaughter, 'Towards a Theory of Effective Supranational Adjudication', (1997) 107 *Yale Law Journal* 273.

Hogg Peter, *Constitutional Law of Canada* (Thomson/Carswell 2014).

Holmes Stephen, 'Gag Rules or the Politics of Omission' in Jon Elster and Rune Slagstad (eds.), *Constitutionalism and Democracy* (Cambridge University Press 1988) 19.

Howse Robert and Kalypso Nicolaidis, 'Enhancing WTO Legitimacy: Constitutionalization or Global Subsidiarity?', (2003) 16 *Governance* 73.

Huq Aziz Z., 'What is Discriminatory Intent?', (2018) 103 *Cornell Law Review* 1211.

Idleman Scott C., 'The Role of Religious Values in Judicial Decision Making', (1993) 68 *Indiana Law Journal* 433.

Idleman Scott C., 'The Concealment of Religious Values in Judicial Decisionmaking', (2005) 91 *Virginia Law Review* 515.

Isiksel Turkuler, 'Global Legal Pluralism as Fact and Norm', (2013) 2 *Global Constitutionalism* 160.

Issacharoff Samuel, Pamela S. Karlan, and Richard H. Pildes, *The Law of Democracy: Legal Structure of the Political Process* (4th edn., Foundation Press 2012).

Jackson Vicki C., *Constitutional Engagement in a Transnational Era* (Oxford University Press 2010).

Karst Kenneth L., 'The Costs of Motive-Centered Inquiry', (1978) 15 *San Diego Law Review* 1163.

Keohane Robert O., Andrew Moravcsik, and Anne-Marie Slaughter, 'Legalized Dispute Resolution: Interstate and Transnational', (2000) 54 *International Organization* 457.

Khaitan Tarunabh, 'Reading *Swaraj* into Article 15: A New Deal for All Minorities', (2009) 2 *NUJS Law Review* 419.

Khaitan Tarunabh, '*Koushal* v *Naz*: Judges Vote to Recriminalise Homosexuality', (2015) 78 *Modern Law Review* 672.

Khaitan Tarunabh, 'Legislative Review Under Article 14' in Sujit Choudry, Madhav Khosla, and Pratap Bhanu Mahta (eds.), *The Oxford Handbook of the Indian Constitution* (Oxford University Press 2016) 699.

Kleinlein Thomas, 'Judicial Lawmaking by Judicial Restraint? The Potential of Balancing in International Economic Law', (2011) 12 *German Law Journal* 1141.

Kogelmann Brian, 'The Supreme Court as the Fountain of Public Reason', (2018) 24 *Legal Theory* 345.

Krisch Nico, 'The Open Architecture of European Human Rights Law', (2008) 71 *Modern Law Review* 183.

Kugelberg Henrik D., 'Civic Equality as a Democratic Basis for Public Reason', (2021) *Critical Review of International Social and Political Philosophy*, https://doi.org/10.1080/13698230.2021.1905468, (accessed 7 September 2022).

Kukathas Chandran and Philip Pettit, *Rawls:* A Theory of Justice *and its Critics* (Polity Press 1990).

Kumm Mattias, 'The Legitimacy of International Law: A Constitutionalist Framework of Analysis', (2004) 15 *European Journal of International Law* 907.

Kumm Mattias, 'Institutionalising Socratic Contestation: The Rationalist Human Rights Paradigm, Legitimate Authority and the Point of Judicial Review', (2007) 1(2) *European Journal of Legal Studies* 1, https://cadmus.eui.eu/bitstream/handle/1814/7708/EJLS_2007_1_2_9_KUM_EN.pdf?sequence=1&isAllowed=y (last accessed 23 June 2020).

Kumm Mattias, 'The Cosmopolitan Turn in Constitutionalism: An Integrated Conception of Public Law', (2013) 20 *Indiana Journal of Global Legal Studies* 605.

Kumm Mattias, '"We Hold These Truths to be Self-Evident": Constitutionalism, Public Reason, and Legitimate Authority' in Silje Langvatn, Mattias Kumm, and Wojciech Sadurski (eds.), *Public Reason and Courts* (Cambridge University Press 2020) 143.

Kumm Mattias, 'An Integrative Theory of Global Public Law: Cosmopolitan, Pluralist, Public Reason Oriented' (unpublished draft, no date).

Kymlicka Will, *Politics in the Vernacular* (Oxford University Press 2001).

Landau Joseph, 'Process Scrutiny: Motivational Inquiry and Constitutional Rights', (2019) 119 *Columbia Law Review* 2147.

Langvatn, Silje, Mattias Kumm, and Wojciech Sadurski (eds.), *Public Reason and Courts* (Cambridge University Press 2020).

Larmore Charles, 'Public Reason' in Samuel Freeman (ed.), *The Cambridge Companion to Rawls* (Cambridge University Press 2003) 368.

Larmore Charles, *The Autonomy of Morality* (Cambridge University Press 2008).

Lasswell Harold, *Politics: Who Gets What, When, How?* (P. Smith 1950).

Lawrence Jessica C., 'Contesting Constitutionalism: Constitutional Discourse at the WTO', (2013) 2 *Global Constitutionalism* 63.

Letsas George, *A Theory of Interpretation of the European Convention on Human Rights* (Oxford University Press 2007).

Lister Andrew, 'Public Justification and the Limits of State Action', (2010) 9 *Politics, Philosophy, and Economics* 151.

Loewy Arnold H., 'Morals Legislation and the Establishment Clause', (2003) 55 *Alabama Law Review* 159.

MacCormick Neil, *Rhetoric and the Rule of Law* (Oxford University Press 2010).

MacDonald Euan, *International Law and Ethics After the Critical Change* (Martinus Nijhoff 2011).

Maduro Miguel Poiares, 'Courts and Pluralism: Essay on a Theory of Judicial Adjudication in the Context of Legal and Constitutional Pluralism' in Jeffrey L. Dunoff and Joel P. Trachtman (eds.), *Ruling the World? Constitutionalism, International Law, and Global Governance* (Cambridge University Press 2009) 356.

Majone Giandomenico, 'Europe's 'Democratic Deficit': The Question of Standards', (1998) 14 *European Law Journal* 5.

Mansfield Andrew S., 'Religious Arguments and the United States Supreme Court: A Review of Amicus Curiae Briefs Filed by Religious Organizations' (2008), available at http://works.bepress.com/andrew_mansfield/5 (last accessed 1 June 2020).

Marks Susan, 'The European Convention on Human Rights and Its "Democratic Society"', (1995) 66 *British Yearbook of International Law* 209.

Marmor Andrei, 'Authority, Equality and Democracy', (2005) 18 *Ratio Juris* 315.

Massey Calvin, 'The Role of Governmental Purpose in Constitutional Judicial Review', (2007) 59 *South Carolina Law Review* 1.

Mayo Henry B., *An Introduction to Democratic Theory* (Oxford University Press 1960).

McCrudden Christopher and Brendan O'Leary, *Courts and Consociations: Human Rights versus Power-Sharing* (Oxford University Press 2013).

Merton R.K., 'Insiders and Outsiders: A Chapter in the Sociology of Knowledge', (1972) 78 *American Journal of Sociology* 9.

Meydani Assaf, The *Anatomy of Human Rights in Israel* (Cambridge University Press 2014).

Meyerson Denise, *Rights Limited: Freedom of Expression, Religion and the South African Constitution* (Juta 1997).

Michelman Frank I., 'The Supreme Court, 1968 Term—Foreword: On Protecting the Poor Through the Fourteenth Amendment', (1969) 83 *Harvard Law Review* 7.

Mill John Stuart, 'On Liberty' (1859) in John Stuart Mill, *On Liberty and Other Writings*, ed. Stefan Collini (Cambridge University Press 1989).
Moon J. Donald, 'Rawls and Habermas on Public Reason: Human Rights and Global Justice', (2003) 6 *Annual Review of Political Science* 257.
Möller Kai, *The Global Model of Constitutional Rights* (Oxford University Press 2012).
Murphy Liam, *What Makes Law* (Cambridge University Press 2014).
Nagel Thomas, 'Moral Conflict and Political Legitimacy', (1987) 16 *Philosophy & Public Affairs* 215.
Nagel Thomas, *Equality and Partiality* (Oxford University Press 1991).
Nelson Caleb, 'Judicial Review of Legislative Purpose', (2008) 83 *New York University Law Review* 1784.
Neuman Gerald L., 'Human Rights and Constitutional Rights: Harmony and Dissonance', (2003) 55 *Stanford Law Review* 863.
Neyer Jürgen, 'Justice, Not Democracy: Legitimacy in the European Union', (2010) 48 *Journal of Common Market Studies* 903.
Neyer Jürgen, 'Justice and the Right to Justification: Conceptual Reflections' in Dimitry Kochenov, Gráinne de Búrca, and Andrew Williams (eds.), *Europe's Justice Deficit?* (Hart 2015) 211.
Nowak Manfred, *UN Covenant on Civil and Political Rights: CCPR: Commentary* (2nd rev. edn, .Engel 2005).
Nowlin Christopher, 'The Protection of Morals under the European Convention for the Protection of Human Rights and Fundamental Freedoms', (2002) 24 *Human Rights Quarterly* 264.
Offe Claus, '"Homogeneity" and Constitutional Democracy: Coping with Identity Conflicts through Group Rights', (1988) 6 *Journal of Political Philosophy* 113.
O'Neill Onora, *Toward Justice and Virtue* (Cambridge University Press 1996).
Note, 'Legislative Purpose and Federal Constitutional Adjudication', (1970) 83 *Harvard Law Review* 1887.
Note, 'Developments in the Law—Chapter Four: Animus and Sexual Regulation', (2014) 127 *Harvard Law Review* 1767.
Note, 'The Supreme Court—Leading Cases', (2018) 132 *Harvard Law Review* 132.
Nussbaum Martha C., *Frontiers of Justice* (Harvard University Press 2006).
Nussbaum Martha C., *Liberty of Conscience* (Basic Books 2008).
Pariente Rubén Marciel, 'Why not Extend Rawls' Public Reason Beyond Fundamental Issues?', (2020) 39 *Teorema* 105.
Patten Alan, 'Liberal Neutrality: A Reinterpretation and Defense', (2012) 20 *Journal of Political Philosophy* 249.
Paulus Andreas L., 'The International Legal System as a Constitution' in Jeffrey L. Dunoff and Joel P. Trachtman (eds.), *Ruling the World? Constitutionalism, International Law, and Global Governance* (Cambridge University Press 2009) 69.
Peñalver Eduardo Moisés, 'The Persistent Problem of Obligation in International Law', (2000) 36 *Stanford Journal of International Law* 271.
Perju Vlad, 'International Constitutionalism and the State: A Reply to Aoife O'Donoghue', (2013) 11 *International Journal of Constitutional Law* 1045.
Perrone Roberto, 'Public Morals and the ECHR' (20 January 2014). University of Leicester School of Law Research Paper No. 14-02, available at SSRN: http://ssrn.com/abstract=2382086 (last accessed 23 June 2020).
Perry Michael J., 'Substantive Due Process Revisited: Reflections on (and beyond) Recent Cases', (1976) 71 *Northwestern University Law Review* 417.
Perry Michael J., *Human Rights in the Constitutional Law of the United States* (Cambridge University Press 2013).

Peters Anne, 'The Merits of Global Constitutionalism', (2009) 16 *Indiana Journal of Global Legal Studies* 397.

Peters Anne, 'The Constitutionalisation of International Organisations' in Neil Walker, Jo Shaw, and Stephen Tierney (eds.), *Europe's Constitutional Mosaic* (Hart 2011) 253.

Peters Michael A., 'Information, Globalization and Democracy: The Utopian Moment?' *Global-e: A Global Studies Journal* (2 May 2008), https://www.21global.ucsb.edu/global-e/may-2008/information-globalization-and-democracy-utopian-moment (accessed 7 September 2022).

Petersen Niels, 'Legislative Inconsistency and the 'Smoking Out' of Illicit Motives', (2016) 64 *American Journal of Comparative Law* 121.

Petersen Niels, *Proportionality and Judicial Activism* (Cambridge University Press 2017).

Pettit Philip, 'The Common Good' in Keith Dowding, Robert E. Goodin, and Carole Pateman (eds.), *Justice and Democracy: Essays for Brian Barry* (Cambridge University Press 2004) 150.

Pettit Philip, *On the People's Terms* (Cambridge University Press 2012).

Pettit Philip, *Just Freedom* (Norton 2014).

Pildes Richard H., 'Avoiding Balancing: The Role of Exclusionary Reasons in Constitutional Law', (1994) 45 *Hastings Law Journal* 711.

Poggi Gianfranco, *The State: Its Nature, Development and Prospects* (Stanford University Press 1990).

Post Robert C., 'Cultural Heterogeneity and Law: Pornography, Blasphemy, and the First Amendment', (1988) 76 *California Law Review* 297.

Powell Jr., Lewis F., '*Carolene Products* Revisited', (1982) 82 *Columbia Law Review* 1087.

Pozen David E. and Adam M. Samaha, 'Anti-Modalities', (2021) 119 *Michigan Law Review* 729.

Preuss Ulrich K., 'Perspectives on Post-Conflict Constitutionalism: Reflections on Regime Change Through External Constitutionalization', (2006–07) 51 *New York Law School Law Review* 467.

Pringle Helen, 'Regulating Offence to the Godly: Blasphemy and the Future of Religious Vilification Laws', (2011) 34 *UNSW Law Journal* 316.

Quong Jonathan, *Liberalism without Perfection* (Oxford University Press 2011).

Raveson Louis S., 'Unmasking the Motives of Government Decisionmakers: A Subpoena for Your Thoughts?', (1985) 63 *North Carolina Law Review* 879.

Rawls John, *A Theory of Justice* (Harvard University Press 1971).

Rawls John, 'Justice as Fairness: Political not Metaphysical', (1985) 14 *Philosophy & Public Affairs* 225.

Rawls John, 'The Idea of an Overlapping Consensus', (1987) 7 *Oxford Journal of Legal Studies* 1.

Rawls John, *Political Liberalism* (Columbia University Press 1993).

Rawls John, 'The Idea of Public Reason Revisited' in *The Law of Peoples* (Harvard University Press 1999).

Rawls John, *The Law of Peoples* (Harvard University Press 1999).

Raz Joseph, *The Morality of Freedom* (Oxford University Press 1986).

Raz Joseph, 'Facing Diversity: The Case of Epistemic Abstinence', (1990) 19 *Philosophy & Public Affairs* 3.

Raz Joseph, *Ethics in the Public Domain* (Oxford University Press 1994).

Raz Joseph, 'Disagreement in Politics', (1998) 43 *American Journal of Jurisprudence* 25.

Raz Joseph, *Practical Reason and Norms* (2nd edn., Oxford University Press 1999).

Raz Joseph, *Value, Respect, and Attachment* (Cambridge University Press 2001).

Raz Joseph, 'On Respect, Authority, and Neutrality: A Response', (2010) 120 *Ethics* 120.

Regan Donald, 'On Preferences and Promises: A Response to Harsanyi', (1985) 96 *Ethics* 56.

Reisman Michael, 'Designing and Managing the Future of the State', (1997) 3 *European Journal of International Law* 409.

Ripstein Arthur, *Equality, Responsibility, and the Law* (Cambridge University Press 1999).

Rivers Julian, 'Proportionality and Variable Intensity of Review', (2006) 65 *The Cambridge Law Journal* 174.

Robertson David, *The Judge as Political Theorist* (Princeton University Press 2010).

Rosenfeld Michel, 'Rethinking Constitutional Ordering in an Era of Legal and Constitutional Pluralism', (2008) 6 *International Journal of Constitutional Law* 415.

Rosenfeld Michel, *The Identity of the Constitutional Subject* (Routledge 2010).

Rousseau Jean-Jacques, 'The Social Contract' 274 (trans. Gerard Hopkins) in *Social Contract: Essays by Locke, Hume and Rousseau*, with an Introduction by Sir Ernest Barker (Oxford University Press 1948).

Sadurski Wojciech, *Giving Desert its Due* (D. Reidel 1985).

Sadurski Wojciech, *Moral Pluralism and Legal Neutrality* (Kluwer 1990).

Sadurski Wojciech, *Equality and Legitimacy* (Oxford University Press 2009).

Sadurski Wojciech, 'Partnering with Strasbourg: Constitutionalisation of the European Court of Human Rights, the Accession of Central and East European States to the Council of Europe, and the Idea of Pilot Judgments', (2009) 9 *Human Rights Law Review* 397.

Sadurski Wojciech, 'Reasonableness and Value Pluralism in Law and Politics' in Giorgio Bongiovanni, Giovanni Sartor, and Chiara Valentini (eds.), *Reasonableness and Law* (Springer 2009) 129.

Sadurski Wojciech, *Constitutionalism and the Enlargement of Europe* (Oxford University Press 2012).

Sadurski Wojciech, 'Democratic Legitimacy of the European Union: A Diagnosis and Some Modest Proposals', (2012) 32 *Polish Yearbook of International Law* 9.

Sadurski Wojciech, ''It All Depends': The Universal and the Contingent in Human Rights' in Claudio Corradetti (ed.), *Philosophical Dimensions of Human Rights* (Springer 2012).

Sandel Michael J., Book Review (John Rawls, *Political Liberalism*), (1994) 107 *Harvard Law Review* 1765.

Scanlon T.M., 'Rawls's Theory of Justice' in Norman Daniels (ed.), *Reading Rawls: Critical Studies of A Theory of Justice* (Basil Blackwell 1975) 169.

Scanlon T.M., *What We Owe To Each Other* (Harvard University Press 1998).

Scanlon T.M., 'Rawls on Justification' in Samuel Freeman (ed.), *The Cambridge Companion to Rawls* (Cambridge University Press 2003) 139.

Scharpf Fritz W., *Governing in Europe: Effective and Democratic?* (Oxford University Press 1999).

Schauer Frederick, *Playing by the Rules* (Oxford University Press 1991).

Scheffler Samuel, 'Choice, Circumstance, and the Value of Equality', (2005) 4 *Politics, Philosophy and Economics* 5.

Scheuerman William E., 'Cosmopolitanism and the World State', (2014) 40 *Review of International Studies* 419.

Schwartzman Micah, 'The Completeness of Public Reason', (2004) 3 *Politics, Philosophy & Economics* 191.

Schwartzman Micah, 'The Sincerity of Public Reason', (2011) 19 *Journal of Political Philosophy* 375.

Schwartzman Micah, 'Must Laws Be Motivated by Public Reason?' in Silje Langvatn, Mattias Kumm and Wojciech Sadurski (eds.), *Public Reason and Courts* (Cambridge University Press 2020) 45.

Sen Amartya, *The Idea of Justice* (Harvard University Press 2009).
Shaw Malcolm, *International Law* (4th edn., Cambridge University Press 1997).
Shlomo-Agon Sivan, 'Clearing the Smoke: The Legitimation of Judicial Power at the WTO', (2015) 49 *Journal of World Trade* 539.
Shue Henry, 'Rawls and the Outlaws', (2002) 1 *Politics, Philosophy & Economics* 307.
Smith Nicholas, 'Freedom of Religion in the Constitutional Court', (2001) 118 *South African Law Journal* 1.
Solum Lawrence B., 'Constructing an Ideal of Public Reason', (1993) 30 *San Diego Law Review* 729.
Solum Lawrence B., 'Public Legal Reason', (2006) 92 *Virginia Law Review* 1449.
Spruyt Hendrik, *The Sovereign State and Its Competitors* (Princeton University Press 1994).
Stellios James, *Zines's the High Court and the Constitution* (The Federation Press 2015).
Stone Julius, *Social Dimensions of Law and Justice* (Maitland 1966).
Stone Sweet Alec, 'A Cosmopolitan Legal Order: Constitutional Pluralism and Rights Adjudication in Europe', (2012) 1 *Global Constitutionalism* 53.
Stone Sweet A. and H. Keller, 'The Reception of the ECHR in National Legal Orders' in Helen Keller and Alec Stone Sweet (eds.), *A Europe of Rights: The Impact of the ECHR on National Legal Systems* (Oxford University Press 2008) 3.
Stone Sweet Alec and Jud Mathews, 'Proportionality Balancing and Global Constitutionalism', (2008) 47 *Columbia Journal of Transnational Law* 74.
Stone Sweet Alec and Clare Ryan, *A Cosmopolitan Legal Order: Kant, Constitutional Justice, and the European Convention on Human Rights* (Oxford University Press 2018).
Straut Charles B., 'Due Process Disestablishment: Why *Lawrence v. Texas* Is a First Amendment Case', (2016) 91 *New York University Law Review* 1794.
Sunstein Cass R., 'Disrupting Voluntary Transactions' in J.W. Chapman and J.R. Pennock (eds.), *Markets and Justice: Nomos XXXI* (New York University Press 1989) 279.
Sunstein Cass R., *The Partial Constitution* (Harvard University Press 1994).
Tasioulas John, 'The Legitimacy of International Law' in Samantha Besson and John Tasioulas (eds.), *The Philosophy of International Law* (Oxford University Press 2010) 97.
Thomas C.A., 'Of Facts and Phantoms: Economics, Epistemic Legitimacy, and WTO Dispute Settlement', (2011) 14 *Journal of International Economic Law* 295.
Thomas C.A., 'The Concept of Legitimacy and International Law', LSE Law, Society and Economy Working Papers 12/2013, http://ssrn.com/abstract=2265503(accessed 23 August 2022).
Thompson Dennis F., 'Public Reason and Precluded Reasons', (2004) 72 *Fordham Law Review* 2073.
Thompson Mark R., 'Whatever Happened to 'Asian Values'?', (2001) 12 *Journal of Democracy* 154.
Tondini Matteo, 'Beyond the Law of the Enemy: Recovering from the Failures of the Global War on Terrorism Through Law', (2007) 3 *Jura Gentium: Rivista di filosofia del diritto internazionale e della politica globale* 1.
Trachtman Joel P., 'Constitutional Economics of the World Trade Organization' in Jeffrey L. Dunoff and Joel P. Trachtman (eds.), *Ruling the World? Constitutionalism, International Law, and Global Governance* (Cambridge University Press 2009) 206.
Trakman Leon E, William Cole-Hamilton, and Sean Gatien, '*R v Oakes* 1986-1977: Back to the Drawing Board', (1998) 36 *Osgoode Hall Law Journal* 83.
Tribe Laurence H., *American Constitutional Law* (2nd edn., Foundation Press 1988).
Tribe Laurence H., 'The Mystery of Motive, Private and Public: Some Thoughts Inspired by the Problems of Hate Crime and Animal Sacrifice', (1994) *Supreme Court Review* 1.

Tushnet Mark, *Taking the Constitution Away from the Courts* (Princeton University Press 1999).

Tussman Joseph and Jacobus tenBroek, 'The Equal Protection of the Laws', (1949) 37 *California Law Review* 341.

Tyndal Jason, 'Public Reason, Non-Public Reasons, and the Accessibility Requirement', (2019) 49 *Canadian Journal of Philosophy* 1062.

Vallier Kevin, 'In Defense of Idealization in Public Reason', (2020) 85 *Erkenntnis* 1109.

van Dijk P. and G.J.H. van Hoof, *Theory and Practice of the European Convention on Human Rights* (3rd edn., .Kluwer Law International 1998).

Vatter Miguel, 'The Idea of Public Reason and the Reason of State: Schmitt and Rawls on the Vauchez Political', (2008) 36 *Political Theory* 239.

Vauchez Antoine, *Démocratiser l'Europe* (Seuil 2014).

Venzke Ingo, 'Making General Exceptions: The Spell of Precedents in Developing Article XX GATT into Standards for Domestic Regulatory Policy', (2011) 12 *German Law Journal* 1111.

Villa Dana, 'Political Violence and Terror: Arendtian Reflections', (2008) 1 *Ethics & Global Politics* 97.

von Bogdandy Armin, 'Globalization and Europe: How to Square Democracy, Globalization, and International Law', (2000) 15 *European Journal of International Law* 885.

von Bogdandy Armin and Ingo Venzke, 'On the Democratic Legitimation of International Judicial Lawmaking', (2011) 12 *German Law Journal* 1341.

Waldron Jeremy, 'Rights and Majorities: Rousseau Revisited' in John W. Chapman and Alan Wertheimer (eds.), *Majorities and Minorities: Nomos XXXII* (New York University Press 1990) 44.

Waldron Jeremy, *Liberal Rights* (Cambridge University Press 1993).

Waldron Jeremy, *Law and Disagreement* (Oxford University Press 1999).

Waldron Jeremy, 'What Can Christian Teaching Add to the Debate about Torture?', (2006) 63 *Theology Today* 330.

Waldron Jeremy, 'Public Reason and "Justification" in the Courtroom', (2007) 1 *Journal of Law, Philosophy and Culture* 107.

Waldron Jeremy, *Torture, Terror, and Trade-offs: Philosophy for the White House* (Oxford University Press 2010).

Waldron Jeremy, 'Response: The Perils of Exaggeration', (2011) 22 *European Journal of International Law* 389.

Waldron Jeremy, 'Isolating Public Reasons' in Thom Brooks and Martha C. Nussbaum (eds.), *Rawls's Political Liberalism* (Columbia University Press 2015) 113.

Walker Neil, 'Beyond Boundary Disputes and Basic Grids: Mapping the Global Disorder of Normative Orders', (2008) 6 *International Journal of Constitutional Law* 373.

Walker Neil, 'Justice in and of the European Union' in Dimitry Kochenov, Gráinne de Búrca, and Andrew Williams (eds.), *Europe's Justice Deficit?* (Hart 2015) 247.

Walzer Michael, *Spheres of Justice* (Basil Blackwell 1983).

Wiener Antje, 'Contested Meanings of Norms: A Research Framework', (2007) 5 *Comparative European Politics* 1.

Wiener Antje et al., 'Global Constitutionalism: Human Rights, Democracy and the Rule of Law', (2012) 1 *Global Constitutionalism* 1.

Williams Bernard, 'Internal and External Reasons' in *Moral Luck* (Cambridge University Press 1981) 101.

Williams Bernard, 'Internal Reasons and the Obscurity of Blame' in *Making Sense of Humanity* (Cambridge University Press 1995) 35.

Williams Bernard, *In the Beginning Was the Deed*, ed., Geoffrey Hawthorn (Princeton University Press 2005).

Wolgast Elizabeth H., 'The Demands of Public Reason', (1994) 94 *Columbia Law Review* 1936.

Woolman Stu and H. Botha, 'Limitations' in Stu Woolman and Michael Bishop (eds.), *Constitutional Law of South Africa*, (2nd. edn., Juta 2014).

Worden Blair, 'Two Letters on Treason' *The New York Review of Books*, 9 January 2014, 20.

Wright J. Skelly, 'Color-Blind Theories and Color Conscious Remedies', (1980) 47 *University of Chicago Law Review* 213.

Zurn Christopher F., *Deliberative Democracy and the Institutions of Judicial Review* (Cambridge University Press 2007).

Zurn Christopher F., 'Constitutional Interpretation and Public Reason: Seductive Disanalogies' in Silje Langvatn, Mattias Kumm, and Wojciech Sadurski (eds.), *Public Reason and Courts* (Cambridge University Press 2020) 323.

Zürn Michael, 'Democratic Governance Beyond the Nation-State: The EU and Other International Institutions', (2000) 6 *European Journal of International Relations* 183.

Zwart Tom, 'More Human Rights than Court: Why the Legitimacy of the European Court of Human Rights is in Need of Repair and How it Can Be Done' in Spyridon Flogaitis, Tom Zwart, and Julie Fraser (eds.), *The European Court of Human Rights and Its Discontents* (Edward Elgar 2013) 71.

Index

For the benefit of digital users, indexed terms that span two pages (e.g., 52–53) may, on occasion, appear on only one of those pages.

Tables are indicated by *t* following the page number